AF674465

SOCIAL AND ECONOMIC SECURITY IN INDIA

SOCIAL AND ECONOMIC SECURITY IN INDIA

Edited by

S. Mahendra Dev

Piush Antony

V. Gayathri

R.P. Mamgain

INSTITUTE FOR HUMAN DEVELOPMENT

NEW DELHI

Published by

INSTITUTE FOR HUMAN DEVELOPMENT
IAMR Building, 3rd Floor, I.P. Estate,
Mahatma Gandhi Marg, New Delhi-110 002
Phone : 3358166, 3321610; Fax : 3319909
e-mail : ihd@vsnl.com; website: www.ihdindia.com

Distributed by

MANOHAR PUBLISHERS AND DISTRIBUTORS
4753/23, Ansari Road, Daryaganj, New Delhi
Phones: 3262796, 3289100 Fax : (011) 3265126
e-mail : manbooks@vsnl.com
website : manbooks.com

First Published, 2001

ISBN 81-900948-4-x

A part of the publication cost of this book has been met by the Friedrich Ebert Stiftung

Laser Typesetting :

S.P. PRINTECH
Laxmi Nagar. Delhi-92, Phone : 2214076

Printed at :

D.K. Fine Arts Press, Delhi-52

Contents

Part IV : EMPLOYMENT AND INCOME SECURITY

Part V : VULNERABLE GROUPS

Part VI : STATE AND MICRO-LEVEL EXPERIENCES

Preface

The concept of social security has for long been associated with developed countries marked by high growth rates and an organised sector whereby the package of the benefits depends on the level of growth attained. The validity of this traditional approach to social security centered around growth-oriented measures, however, has been questioned in the context of developing countries, characterized by low growth rates and high growth rates of population combined with rampant poverty and illiteracy. Moreover, majority of their population lives outside the mainstream of development and has little or no access to any form of social security. Such a dismal scenario underscores the need for a broader interpretation of social security, which accounts for a high degree of deprivation and vulnerability in the developing countries. Given this broad perception of social and economic security, state and social institutions do have a pivotal role to play in providing social security to the weaker and the marginalised sections.

This volume, drawing from the contributions of a seminar organised by the Institute for Human Development in April 1999, focusses on social security measures undertaken by the state and civil society in a comprehensive manner with a particular emphasis on vulnerable groups, falling mostly within the unorganised sector. Beginning with an overview of the social security system in the country, providing a macro-perspective to the policies and programmes, it comprises of six sections: basic needs—food, nutrition, health and housing; education; employment and income security; vulnerable groups; and state and micro-level experiences. Essentially, the book highlights the importance of adopting a multi-faceted approach in revamping our social security system so as to ensure that the basic needs of the poor and marginalised sections of the population are fully met. More importantly, it sets out the limitations of social policies towards the target groups and analyses aspects of vulnerability and deprivation faced by people in the non-targeted sectors. It emphasises the need for and importance of comprehensive social security policies designed to benefit specific vulnerable groups such as women, the aged, tribal communities and the scheduled castes especially in a liberalised economic environment. The papers in this volume provide useful guidelines and alternative frameworks to address the social security needs of targeted groups of people.

During the short period of its existence, the Institute for Human Development has contributed significantly in promoting study and research in the issues relating to diverse areas of human development through research projects, seminar/workshops and publications. This volume is an important contribution to the existing literature on social policies besides being a useful addendum to social activists and other voluntary workers engaged in promoting the welfare and rehabilitation of the disadvantaged groups in the country.

The four editors of the volume deserve all acclaim for bringing out this outstanding publication.

Alakh N. Sharma
Director, Institute for Human Development
New Delhi

October 15, 2000

Acknowledgements

This volume would not have been possible without the assistance and support of several individuals and institutions. It merits mention at the outset that the seminar on which this volume is based was sponsored by the International Labour Organisation and Indian Council of Social Sciences Research. Thanks are also due to Friedrich Ebert Stiftung for providing financial support in meeting part of the publication expenses of this volume.

We owe an immense debt of gratitude to Professor Alakh N. Sharma, who gave his unstinted support and advice at various stages of this project, right from coordinating the seminar to the publication of this volume. We are also grateful to Professor T.S. Papola and Professor K.P. Kannan for providing their valuable advice in planing the book.

We are thankful to S.P. Sharma and Madhavi Chauhan for preparing the manuscript. Thanks are also due to A.K. Karan, Rajesh Shankar, Smita Sahai and Alok Anand, colleagues at the Institute for Human Development, for contributing to the publication of the book in various ways. Finally, we owe special thanks to AJC Bose for his valuable help in bringing out the volume. We are grateful to all the contributors for patiently adhering to the time schedule.

New Delhi *Editors*

September 5, 2000

1

Introduction: Towards a Holistic Perspective of Social Security

S. Mahendra Dev, Piush Antony, V. Gayathri and R.P. Mamgain

I. CONTEXTUALISING SOCIAL SECURITY

For most of its history, social security theories have focused on developed countries, with an emphasis on growth-mediated social policies. And for a long period of time, it was thought that there is a linear relationship between social security measures and economic growth. These measures consisted of varying levels of complex and expensive programmes of social insurance, income maintenance, etc. Thus, depending on the level of a country's economic development, different packages of social security measures were advocated. Although the western approaches have been dominant, in the recent decades the universality of growth-oriented measures and formal workforce centric models has been questioned. An influential contribution to this has been the growing awareness of the successful experience of countries that followed support-led security measures under conditions of lower growth rates. For example, the experiences of countries like Chile, Costa Rica, Cuba, China and Jamaica show that the basis of their success vis-a-vis social security measures was direct public support rather than rapid income growth (Dreze and Sen, 1989). There is considerable evidence from these countries to show that economic growth has followed rather than preceded wide-ranging measures of public support. Moreover, the impressive performances of Sri Lanka and the state of Kerala prove that their successes do not lie in the size of financial allocations to particular public provisions but in creating the political, social, and economic conditions for ensuring the efficiency and spread effect of social security programmes to the deprived sections of the population. These experiences further emphasise the need for developing countries to adopt need-based mechanisms to reduce the vulnerability of the large majority of the population which is out of the formal workforce.

An analysis of both the strategies—growth-mediated and support-led—undoubtedly brings out the symbiotic relationship between economic growth and social security. Both the strategies, in varying degrees, absorb a considerable proportion of the public resources. To reiterate, the significance of economic growth cannot be overlooked since the public resource-base needs to be enhanced for supporting security measures. At the same time, equitable growth cannot be ensured unless vulnerability of large sections of the populace is reduced through social security mechanisms. This indicates that economic growth is a necessary but not a sufficient condition for providing social security. For most of the developing countries, the social security policies are caught in this conundrum. In the absence of steady economic growth, these countries find it difficult to increase the share of public expenditure. Coupled with this is the low level of efficacy of the existing programmes in terms of their targeting, coverage, and implementation strategies. The problem is further compounded by the structural constraints of traditional societies that prevent the even percolation of security gains. It is now being recognised that in traditional societies like India, social institutions play a significant role in providing social security in terms of minimum levels of living. The state thus faces the dilemma of whether to recognise and co-opt these institutions or to create newer institutions that can overcome the structural constraints perpetuated by traditional institutions. For instance, the family is being questioned for its altruism as there is inequitable intra-household distribution and allocation of resources (Agarwal, 1994). Similarly, the strong caste-class nexus in rural areas prevents community institutions from reaching out to lower social groups.

Understanding the significance of diverse agencies and various forms of inequality in framing social policies thus forms a driving force in widening the concept of social security in developing countries. The genesis of such an understanding can also be traced to the conflict between the traditional notions of social security and the newer approaches to the analysis of insecurity and vulnerability brought out by the contemporary development theory. The traditionalist approach to social security has been criticised, as it is unable to appreciate the differences in the historical growth patterns of employment between the developed and developing countries and thus, is too narrow. The counter-criticism of the newer approaches, ranging from social protection to human security is that it is plagued by relativism.

The significance of differences in vulnerability and diversities in deprivation has also led to disillusionment with the traditional social theories. Instead of traditional-structuralist explanations, there is now the alternate complex interrelationship between factors of deprivation. However, it is not necessary to discard the causal explanations in order to understand the interrelationships between different forms of insecurity, vulnerability and deprivations. Instead, to design a comprehensive social security regime, concepts that can capture and account for the major systems and different patterns of insecurity need to be evolved.

II. THE CHANGING CONTOURS OF THE DISCOURSE

Until the mid-1980s, the ILO's understanding of social security formed the dominant discourse. It refers mainly to specific public programmes involving social assistance and social insurance largely by the state. This definition presumes that the members of society have already reached an acceptable standard of living and the main aim of social security is to protect the members of society from a fall in their standard of living. Implicit in this is the understanding of social security as a concept whereby the core of income and welfare is assured through regular participation in work and production, leaving only specific contingencies to be tackled through public policy.

The need for a broader concept of social security began to be articulated by communities living in the developing countries as it was gradually established that the reigning western notion of social security does not take into account the high degree of deprivation and vulnerability of the majority of the population. Further, the search for a more comprehensive notion of social security arose simultaneously with the increasing economic globalisation of the world. This was followed by the increased interest evinced by other development organisations, mainly, the UNDP and the World Bank, resulting in the emergence of newer concepts and approaches in the discourse on social security. It is being observed that the discussion on social security is increasingly polarised into social risk management and human security.

Social risk management consists of public measures intended to assist individuals, households and communities in managing income risks in order to reduce vulnerability, improve consumption, smoothen and enhance equity while contributing to economic development. While this emphasis on income security and human security is conceptualised as a system of social structures and practices which ensures the safety of all people, it is defined in terms of safety from chronic threats such as hunger, disease and protection from sudden and hurtful disruptions in the patterns of daily life, be it in homes, jobs or in communities (UNDP, 1994). It can be discerned from the definition that it provides a generic notion of security that runs very closely to the concept of human development. Taking cognisance of the fact that social security is defined in terms of protection against human deprivations, any attempt towards human development may be conceived as a social security measure. Though social security mechanisms aim at human development, at the operational level, a clear distinction has to be made between human development measures and social security mechanisms. Social security measures primarily aim at removing vulnerability by preventing a decline in the living standards in general, and promoting basic living standards in particular, during economic contingencies

Such an understanding of social security is clearly articulated by Ahmed et al. (1990) as follows: "Social security is viewed neither exclusively in terms of means nor exclusively in terms of objectives. Broadly speaking, our concern is with the direct role that public action can play in reducing human deprivation and eliminating vulnerability in a developing country. The focus is on the use of a class of means (broadly, public action) to pursue a category of objectives (broadly reduction of deprivation and vulnerability).' The appropriateness of incorporating deprivation and vulnerability is justified by the fact that many of the developing countries have large shares of employment in unorganised / informal sectors. And, the workers in the informal sector do not have access to the benefits of traditional social security measures."

Human development is a prerequisite for the effective implementation of social security measures for it builds the capabilities of individuals so that they are entitled to security gains. And, social security mechanisms provide a safeguard against the risk of individuals relapsing to a below minimum standard of living during economic crises and contingencies. This complementarity in objectives cannot be mistaken for isotopic similarity. Similarly, social security cannot be reduced to social risk management though it forms an essential component of it. In the context of developing countries, social security can neither be limited to social risk management nor equated with human development. Therefore, in an analysis of the existing social security scenario in India, the pivotal role of state emerges as a crucial factor.

III. SOCIAL SECURITY IN INDIA

Social security reached its pinnacle in the provisions that have been enshrined in the Constitution of India and subsequently in the legislation that the central government as well as various state governments have enacted. The achievement of social security is measured in terms of a series of legislative enactments, starting with the protective measures enshrined in the Constitution. The social security programmes in India consist of two autonomous parts: (i) protective social security measures, largely for the organised sector such as medical care, and benefits relating to sickness, maternity, old age, etc.; and (ii) promotional security for the unorganised sector in terms of self-employment, wage employment, and provision of basic needs (food, health and education). The fact that these initiatives and measures, due to inherent problems, reach a very small section of the populace is seen as a minor problem that can be remedied given time, by extending the ambit of social security to various vulnerable groups within the unorganised sector.

Until recently the contemporary debate on social security in India overlooked some of the issues raised by the poverty and vulnerability statistics. For instance, in spite of the well-established linkage between employment and social protection, the proportion of workers in the organised sector declined from 13 per cent to 10 per cent in the past decade (Ginneken, 1998). Clearly, the much debated structural adjustment policies of the government have played a more important role than what the government is willing to concede in contributing to the increased volume of insecurity amongst workers. Similarly, extending the same logic, individual schemes such as old-age pensions for agricultural labourers and redeeming measures by the states such as Tamil Nadu and Kerala have been especially neglected. On promotional issues, again, in spite of a plethora of public measures like public distribution system and employment guarantee schemes, the question of efficacy is raised about the legislative enactments as well as the enforcement and implementation agencies. The ineffectiveness of these promotional security measures often portrays the state as an agency with merely a progressive face bereft of any real intention of providing a secure present or future for its citizenry.

Concerns such as these are repeatedly being discussed with an aim to provide a more wholesome and comprehensive social policy. The present volume is a contribution to this collective endeavour towards framing an appropriate social policy— a policy that encompasses a diverse range of issues and caters to the needs of various social groups, especially the vulnerable sections, by analysing situations and instances wherein the state has attempted through its diverse arms to provide social security to its people. Further, it attempts to expand the range of issues addressed while focusing on some of the sectors that have been studied in depth (such as health, education, and food security). The basic objective is to provide a synoptic account of social security in India.

The need for a comprehensive analysis of the existing social security regime forms the immediate context of this volume. It is hoped that such an analysis would help formulate plausible strategies for sector-specific interventions and gap-filling initiatives to reach out to the disadvantaged groups and finally, to the necessary adjustments needed in the public expenditure pattern. From the spectrum of social security policies, certain themes have been selected based on their relative significance and coverage. These are organised into six sections, consisting of an overview section, followed by social security issues pertaining to basic needs (food, health, and housing), education, employment, vulnerable groups, and state and micro-level experiences. In presenting an overview of the social security scenario, the volume provides a macro perspective to relate to the essays on specific sectors and state experiences. And, finally an exclusive chapter on financial aspects of social security provides the backdrop for assessing the feasibility and the social costs involved in specific programmes.

IV. MACRO PERSPECTIVE

Social security policies are always analysed within the framework of welfare state theories. The extent of welfarism undertaken by the nation-states consequently, became the benchmark in understanding different social security mechanisms. This approach evaluated social security policies in terms of the quantum of the programmes and aggregates of expenditures. It, obviously, showed developing countries in a poor light because of the relative paucity of resources allocated for social security in these countries. Though the expenditure set aside for social security is important, it does not necessarily reflect the fiscal status of a country. It is thus imperative to understand the evolution of political development of nation-states in the context of its political priorities and the embryonic development of social security measures. In a democratic country like India, this assumes significance since the potential beneficiaries of social security measures, especially of basic needs, often belong to less articulate and less powerful groups.

Given this situation, unless the state prioritises social security as an integral part of governance, lack of public demand and resource constraints will remain as convenient justifications for abysmal performance of social security measures. The experience of states like Kerala and Tamil Nadu reiterates state sponsored public participation as an effective strategy in carrying out both promotional and protective social security measures with comparatively low levels of economic growth and public expenditure. The overview chapter (Mahendra Dev, chapter 2), while providing a macro perspective to the social security policies in the country, evaluates the performance of different types (components) of social security, with special emphasis on the provisions for the unorganised sector. The chapter concentrates on analysing the impact of the myriad promotional strategies on the unorganised sector, both with respect to individual components such as health, employment, food, and education and in relation to vulnerable groups like women, and the aged. The thrust, therefore, is on assessing the impact of the state strategies on the resource-poor who cannot enter the free market.

Chapter 3 (Thakur and Venkata Ratnam) is an exhaustive treatment of social security within the organised sector. Against the background of constitutional and legal provisions related to social security for workers, it analyses the emerging trends in the organised sector. This is further posited against an analysis of 200 agreements between workers and management. These analyses vividly bring out the shift from welfarism in the organised sector. With the removal of ceilings and reduction of direct tax rates, the private sector has been moving away from the elaborate cafeteria approach to the provision of employee benefits and social security for its managers to a more simple approach to administering employee benefits and social security benefits. Employee stock options and asset building programmes have been two major elements of recent strategies to reward and retain people. While older workers have been pressing for greater provision of retirement benefits, younger workers are reflecting a credit-card mentality and seek up-front cash payment while showing least interest in long-term social security benefits.

The chapter on financing social security (Prabhu and Iyer, chapter 4) presents facts, which further corroborate the disturbing trends. By analyzing the protective and promotional security expenditures of the union government and 15 major state governments, it is observed that the state governments emphasise one or two promotional social security programmes to the neglect of protective measures, indicating the lack of an integrated perspective regarding social security. Hence, possible interventions in the fiscal sphere for ensuring adequate financing of social security schemes in Indian states are advocated.

V. FOOD, NUTRITION, HEALTH AND HOUSING

If social security measures have to target essentially those vulnerable groups who are historically disadvantaged, basic needs obviously assume priority. Accordingly, individual capabilities have to be essentially built up vis-a-vis basic needs for ensuring an effective participation of these groups in the workforce, market and in political processes. The chapters comprising this part of the book deal with food, health, and shelter. Education as a basic need and security is yet to be recognised even at the policy levels despite the fact that India houses the largest illiterate population. Recognising its intrinsic relationship to social security, a separate section is devoted to education.

There has been a paradigmatic shift in the concept of food security from food availability and stability to household food insecurity, and from assessment of input measures like energy intake to output indicators such as anthropometric measures and clinical signs of malnutrition. This shift demands focused research with innovative methods to understand the nature and extent of food insecurity and nutrition deprivation at the household level (Radhakrishna, chapter 5). Therefore, one of the emerging concerns with regard to food security in India is to provide safety mechanisms for the poorer households, especially for vulnerable groups.

While recognising the need for further government investments in nutrition security, an analysis of the nutrition status of children in Tamil Nadu, brings out various management and operational issues related to nutrition interventions (Rajivan, chapter 6). Prevention of malnutrition, role of non-financial factors and reorientation of the existing programmes promise a substantial improvement in the nutrition status of the population.

Taking stock of India's achievements and shortcomings in the health sector, chapter 7 (Shivkumar) points to the neglect of equity considerations and argues for a strong equity-orientation that makes health policy focus more sharply on the poor and neglected communities. It also argues that there is an urgent need for greater public debate and dialogue on health matters. It advocates increased community involvement in the management of health care and emphasises that health issues need to be accorded political priority for rapid promotion of health care and human development.

Rapid urbanisation demands the provision of basic amenities, especially housing within urban agglomerations. In rural areas too, housing becomes an important basic need for millions of the poor. An analysis of the housing situation in India brings out stark disparities across different states, regions within states, and across different social segments (Kundu, chapter 8). While public policy and investments can contribute greatly towards meeting the housing need, the equity considerations become important. Basic infrastructure development in urban slums and in rural areas and housing pose enormous challenges in meeting the needs of the poor in the coming years.

VI. EDUCATION

It is now well established that building of educational capabilities has the maximum multiplier effect compared to all other basic needs. Education is important not only for ensuring higher growth but also for its intrinsic value. The experience of many developed countries and the extraordinary performance of the state of Kerala in the development indicators clearly emphasise the importance of promotion of primary education to achieve larger social goals. Despite large scale advocacy efforts from educationists, policy makers and intelligentsia, in general towards this, India needs to make substantial efforts in meeting the goal of education for all. Therefore, the social security measures needed in the education sector have to gain priority, and this is being highlighted in three chapters dealing with the issues of inequality, financial requirements and community perception.

The structural factors—caste, class and gender inequalities—that perpetuate social inequalities ostensibly form the basis of unequal access to education (Srivastava, chapter 10). It is, therefore, argued that in order to provide educational security for its populace, the state should not only focus on issues of poverty but also address these issues effectively. Though the recent policy initiatives show an apparent concern for improving educational security, it fails to do so, largely because these are still constrained by macro-economic and political imperatives.

This is further substantiated through an analysis of the nature and pattern of household expenditure on education (Tilak, chapter 9). The irony of free elementary education in India is exposed as the available evidences suggest that across income categories, all the households have to spend a considerable portion of their earnings on education. Children from the poorer strata, thus, are in a disadvantageous position due to the high cost of education. This observation is valid in the context of the almost total absence of security measures that can be accessed by the poor households. In addition, they are deprived of the opportunity of educating children, due to escalating cost of primary education, which worsens their vulnerability. Hence, education security is not yet the privilege of a large number of children in India. The problem is particularly acute in certain states, namely, Bihar, Rajasthan, Madhya Pradesh and Uttar Pradesh (De, Noronha and Samson, chapter 11). The PROBE survey reveals the absence of education security for children in the rural areas of these states, despite the increased awareness. Though several provisions have been made by the state, major hurdles like access, particularly at upper primary stage, high cost of schooling, poor quality of schooling, failure of support system like *anganwadis* for motivating children for schooling, still remain. Hence, all the papers of the section bring out the failure of the state to ensure education security and the lack of commitment towards education. Unfortunately this most repeated assertion still remains a recommendation.

VII. EMPLOYMENT

The social security measures in most of the countries are conceived in terms of workplace benefit and not as a civil right, essentially protecting the income disparities of those with low wage earnings and those who fall out of the workforce. Rather than the affordability argument extended to non-replication of successful western models, the major problem for countries like India lies in the fact that 92 per cent of the workforce fall under the category of unorganised workers. Given the insecurities inherent in the unorganised sector, these workers should ideally be the targets of any social security measures. Hence, one of the major hurdles that impede the progress of social security measures in India has been that of identification and coverage of these workers. One of the strategies often practiced and advocated is that of organising these workers. Provisioning of employment security is another state-driven strategy in this regard. The Employment Guarantee Scheme (EGS) of Maharashtra, created through legislation, aims to provide employment on public works projects on demand. Such labour market intervention has an impact on employment security of the rural poor (Mahendra Dev and Ranade, chapter 13). A programme such as the EGS acts as proxy unemployment insurance, and indeed, is financed by a payroll tax at the state level in Maharashtra. The direct benefit of this lies in generating employment and income to the participating workers. The indirect benefits are asset creation, participation of women, upward pressure on agricultural wages, seasonal and stabilisation benefits, slowing rural-urban migration enabling the poor to participate in the political processes.

A more detailed discussion on the various issues related to employment security is provided in chapter 12 (Sharma and Mamgain). The western models of employment security, which are geared towards cyclical and open unemployment, are irrelevant for India. For, though most people are employed, open employment is merely 2 per cent and underemployment is about 8 per cent. The income levels of a large proportion of those employed are extremely low as reflected in the high incidence of poverty. Moreover, there is wide labour market discrimination and prevalence of some socially unacceptable forms of employment such as child labour. An employment security system in India, therefore, ought to pay attention to these features of the labour market. In this context, it is suggested that extending the coverage of minimum wages and its strict enforcement are crucial measures to ensure a minimum income. This, in turn, calls for guaranteeing a minimum number of days of employment for casual labour and improving the productivity of the self-employed in the informal sector through appropriate support system and fiscal measures. Further, it is imperative to provide livelihood security to a large number of vulnerable workers—mostly independent producers like marginal farmers, tribals etc.—who are not integrated with the labour market and whose livelihood is invariably threatened by market forces.

This chapter also reviews the various employment generating programmes and policies of income protection. It is observed that though their impacts have not been satisfactory, they need to be strengthened through effective institutional structures and better targetting. Nevertheless, the system of employment security can be effective only when employment is growing fast and hence, employment intensive-growth strategy directed towards agriculture, small scale sector and the emerging service sector has to be recognised as an essential booster.

VIII. VULNERABLE GROUPS

Social security, in its simplest sense, means measures that a society collectively takes to protect its weakest members. The vulnerable members of any society tend to be those who are deprived of social, economic, political and civic rights due to pre-existing ideologies that determine social arrangements. Thus, lower caste groups, because of the caste system; women, because of gender ideology; widows, due partly to social stigmatisation and lack of access to and control over economic resources; and the elderly, being economically unproductive, obviously constitute the vulnerable section of the population. This section takes up each of these cases to analyse the existing programmes or the lack of it in dealing with the special needs of these groups.

The Scheduled Castes (SC) , implying those castes scheduled by the state as socially and economically deprived, are placed in the spectrum of social security measures ranging from those that provide capital and other productive assets to education and facilities for skill development (Thorat, chapter 17). An examination of the current status of the SCs with respect to occupational pattern, unemployment and poverty in India vividly exposes the inability of social security measures in making any dent in their status.

By analysing the existing social security measures that are made available to women workers, chapter 14 (Gayathri) brings out the benign as well as visible ways by which the policies reinforce the prevailing gender ideologies. Based on the major trends in the employment pattern of women in the formal workforce in India, it argues that if employment generation is an important macro condition for providing security, it is necessary that economic growth is not only more broad-based but also more employment-intensive. Further, it discusses women as full-time workers in the care economy and highlights the point that the involvement of women in the market economy as full-time or part-time workers or to be completely excluded from it mainly depends on the options they can make vis-a-vis the care economy. Finally, it urges that the state social security policies cannot be oblivious to the intrinsic relationship of women's lives to the care economy and the need to intervene in this as a necessary step towards enhancing women's participation in the labor force.

A similar situation is predicted for the aged as well (Alam and Antony, chapter 16). The twin forces of a changing demographic profile of the population and the steady erosion of traditional family norms in India have resulted in a situation, where its elderly population would require a well-conceived and publicly supported social security system. The age structure of the population, the consequences of the growing old-age dependency burden on the labour force, the morbidity pattern and the psychological pressures that the aged have to face amply substantiates this argument. Based on the analysis of the health status of the elderly population vis-a-vis morbidity, this chapter stresses the need to evolve an insurance mechanism, which is perhaps the only way to meet the health care requirements of the aged.

Tribal groups, the most vulnerable population, as in the case of other state programmes, are distanced from the mainstream in the area of social security as well. Given the market incursions coupled with the erosion of traditional modes of livelihood their vulnerability is ever increasing amidst a number of government initiatives. Legislations and welfare programmes in this regard exist more as minuscule relief measures (Dayal and Karan, chapter 18). Moreover, since the development programmes being run in the tribal regions have been of a non-participative nature, most of the tribal groups feel alienated from these programmes. The case of tribal groups in the Jharkhand region exemplifies this and points out to the daunting task of the state towards developing a social security programme for the tribals.

Enriching the discussion on vulnerable groups, Dreze and Khera (chapter 15) deal with the 'blind spot' in the social security system. Identifying freedom from violence or physical security as one of the capabilities that contribute to the quality of life, it analyses the crime data at the district level. Further, it explores the links between murder rates at the district level and various socio-economic variables such as poverty, urbanisation, literacy and the demographic and social composition of the population. Interestingly, the analysis shows that among the development-related variables 'poverty' and 'urbanisation' bear no significant association with murder rates, while female-male ratio has strong negative correlation with the murder rates. The finding that districts with high female-male ratios have lower murder rates implies a strong link between gender relations and criminal violence. It further, provokes one to consider social security for women and other vulnerable sections of the population from a much wider social angle.

IX. STATE AND MICRO-LEVEL EXPERIENCES

The quasi-welfare status along with low levels of growth and lack of political will in consolidating public support towards social policies have resulted in India's poor performance in providing social security. However, there have been a few successful states such as Kerala and Tamil Nadu that have achieved impressive gains in their social security efforts. As mentioned above, there are a few initiatives undertaken by particular states, which demonstrate the potential for replicability in dealing with specific issues of social security. An analysis of the varying experiences of states brings out lessons as well as deeper insights for the much-needed revamping of the social security system in India. It also points out drawbacks of particular mechanisms that failed to cater to the specific needs of the population. This section is devoted to such state and micro-level learnings that can contribute to macro-level suggestions.

The case of Kerala, obviously highlights its impressive performance in social sectors achieved mainly through state-sponsored social security measures with public support (Kannan and Francis, chapter 19). It also demonstrates the possibility of extending the provisioning of social security to a larger proportion of the population who are outside the formal sector of employment. Compared to other states, the state spends a larger share of its budgetary resources on state-assisted social security programmes like food security and employment security, which need to be further strengthened rather than expanded. Nevertheless, along with the lessons, suggestions to focus on employment generation and strengthening social security arrangements for women, SCs and STs, (though not discriminated in their basic entitlements and capabilities, but face discrimination in other domains like employment and labour markets) apply to other states as well.

An analysis of the employment and food security situation in Uttar Pradesh raises the issue of the right to a secure life as the most elemental of all social security concerns (Nisha Srivastava, chapter 20). In this regard, it considers the modifications to the erstwhile JRY in the revised JGSY scheme as a blow for employment security. The main argument is that while there are many ways in which the design of social security schemes can be faulted and the dearth of finances in a resource-starved economy can cause constraints, it is essentially the crises in governance that has made social security cover for the poor a dream.

The two chapters on the experience of Andhra Pradesh together provide an exhaustive analysis of the state policies (chapters 21 and 22). Among the many efforts to protect the entitlements of the vulnerable, the most popular—rice subsidy scheme—has substantially reduced the poverty level (to 30 per cent) in the state(Indrakant and Swaminathan). However, the scheme covers 70 per cent of the population indicating the large number of non-poor enjoying the benefits of the scheme. At the same time, micro-level studies indicate that a good number of households, for various reasons, are excluded from the scheme. The targetting errors are relatively large in backward areas, especially the errors of excluding the poor. Though better results could be achieved with proper targeting, a more rational policy is suggested in order to supply a large quantity of foodgrains through PDS at a price higher than the present rate, instead of the existing policy of issuing a small quantity of foodgrains at a highly subsidised price. The recent efforts of the government through a statutorily backed employment programme along with modified rice subsidy scheme and ICDS programme are predicted to take the state a long way towards fulfilling the vision of *Swarna* Andhra Pradesh (Golden Andhra Pradesh). However, the crucial factor still relates to the political priorities and populist measures that the changing state governments adopt.

The post-liberalisation period is analysed, again, with reference to the state of Andhra Pradesh (Vijay, chapter 22). The opening up of markets has resulted in the growth of new industries. The most obvious impact of this has been an increase in the process of flexibilisation and, therefore, informalisation in the new industries, resulting in the conditions of labour supply becoming highly vulnerable. Examining the social security benefits of labour in the organised sector in the context of its informalisation, the Mehboob Nagar case reveals that besides the well-recognised insecurities like lack of job security and absence of a minimum level of wages, inadequate housing and health facilities, old-age and retirement benefits, several other insecurities are faced by the contract and casual labourers. These are access to food, shelter and credibility for getting new job. At the same time, it is interesting to note that several of these insecurities are being overcome in the new townships by resorting to different mechanisms through different institutions. And, the factors that determine access to such social security institutions include caste, gender, and dependency ratios. A similar experience, though more organised, is shared by the study of the Mathady workers (Datta, chapter 23). When the state fails to provide security mechanisms to underprivileged unorganised sector workers, many innovative experiments of alternate security arrangements can be predicted.

X. WAY AHEAD

Any attempt to revamp our social security system ought to be a multi-faceted approach wherein the basic needs for a decent living of the poor and marginal sections are met. Ostensibly, the present policy framework addresses largely the issues related to the organised sector. The purpose of this volume has been to vividly bring out the policy limitations vis-a-vis its target sector as well as to extend the discourse into various aspects of vulnerability and deprivation faced by those in the non-targeted sector, which not only exceeds 90 per cent but also shows signs of an increase in magnitude. The agenda of liberalisation and globalisation adopted by the country over the last one decade further underscored the need for comprehensive social security policies for a large section of the society including specific vulnerable groups like the aged, women, tribals and the scheduled castes.

The volume is, thus, an attempt to bring out an agenda for future, through an analysis of the specificities of various segments of the society in terms of the social security status and needs. Within the organised sector employment, there are areas of concern like increasing casualisation, retrenchment, moving away from welfare measures etc., which need further exploration in order to address the emerging security issues.

An absolute majority of the workforce in the unorganised sector implies that by and large, the population is insecure and lacks basic needs like education, health, housing, food and nutrition. And, lack of employment security for this segment invariably indicates insecurity in basic needs. This vicious cycle further points to the imperative need for a comprehensive policy. All the essays clearly provide policy directions and alternative frameworks in specific sectors to address the social security needs of the concerned group. But the irony is that social security is yet to gain a sound footing in the development policies of the country. Moreover, the stakeholders of varied interests and identities are yet to build up any kind of pressure group among the political circles. Researchers and others concerned have to continue their efforts to further substantiate their concern for social security as well as to voice it in the corridors of policy making.

References

Agarwal, B. (1994), *A Field of One's Own: Gender and Land Rights in South Asia*, Cambridge University Press, Cambridge.

Ahmed, E., Jean Dreze, J. Hills and A. Sen (1991), *Social Security in Developing Countries*, Oxford University Press, Oxford.

Dreze, J. and A. Sen (1989), *Hunger and Public Action*, Clarendon Press, Oxford.

Ginneken, W.V. (1998), *Social Security for All Indians*, Oxford University Press, New Delhi.

UNDP (1994), *Human Development Report*, Oxford University Press, New York.

PART I

SOCIAL SECURITY IN INDIA: AN OVERVIEW

2

Social Security in India: Performance, Issues and Policies

S. Mahendra Dev

I. INTRODUCTION

By now it is well known that the definition of social security in developing countries is much broader as compared to that for developed countries.[1] Social security arrangements have long history in India. Since Independence, India has extended formal social protection measures such as old-age benefits, insurance, health benefits, etc., to workers in the organised sector, which was less than 10 per cent of the total workforce in India. For workers in the unorganised sector and the other poorer sections of the population the emphasis has been on promotional measures. Social security is a relatively neglected area in terms of both research and policy in India. There has been very little discussion on this subject in Indian Plan documents. There is thus a need to document and analyse the concepts, problems, policies and effectiveness of the programmes relating to social security for the Indian population.

The most recent justification for formulative viable social security programme is the initiation of economic reforms in 1991. This led people to advocate the need for strengthening social security programmes in order to face the negative consequences of reforms. One important factor contributing to the increase in the number of workers in need of social welfare is the likely labour retrenchment in the public sector. This sector is currently protected by employment legislation, and its privatisation will lead to retrenchment. In the unorganised sector, the increased need for social security is due to dismantling of subsidised and targeted credit programmes, which previously benefitted small scale industry and agriculture (Harriss-White, 1995). Decline in public investment in agriculture, reduction in input subsidies and liberalisation of trade may lead to an increase in the agricultural prices. The increase in food prices combined with a reduction in food subsidies will raise the real cost of living for the vast majority of the population. It may be noted, however, that the problem of social insecurity had been severe even before the economic reforms were introduced. Indeed, many of the social security programmes are important irrespective of whether we have economic reforms or not. At the same time, it is true that reforms may create some new problems relating to social security and may necessitate some modifications in the existing programmes and introduction of new programmes.

II. COMPONENTS OF SOCIAL SECURITY: PERFORMANCE AND ISSUES

To assess the performance of social security programmes in terms of their impact on the poor and vulnerable groups, it is useful to divide social security into different components. According to National Commission on Rural Labour (GOI, 1991), there are strong linkages between the three types of security, namely food, employment and health (Parthasarathy, 1996). To these three types of social security, we may add education security and security for women as they are very important for improving the well-being of the population in general and poor and vulnerable sections in particular. It may be noted that though security measures for women form part of the four types of securities (food, employment, health and education) it is taken up separately to bring out certain specific issues related to women and their work.

We examine here the changes over time in five types of securities viz., food, employment, health, education and women with emphasis on pre and post-reform comparisons. The evaluation is undertaken mostly at national level and important issues relevant to each of the components are discussed separately.

1. Food and Nutritional Security

(i) Concept

Food and nutritional security implies the availability of food at all times, that all persons can have access to it, that it is nutritionally adequate in terms of quantity, quality and variety, and that is acceptable within the given culture. Only when all these pre-conditions are in place, can a population be considered to be 'food and nutritionally secure'.

(a) Per capita availability of foodgrains

Table 1 provides quinquennial averages of per capita net availability of foodgrains and pulses. It shows that till 1981-85 the per capita availability of foodgrains has been stagnant and increased in 1986-90, 1991-95 and 1996-98. Over the last 50 years it witnessed an increase of only about 10 per cent. During the same period the per capita availability of pulses declined significantly.

(b) Access to food

The expenditure on food (calorie intake) with some allowance for non-food expenditure is mostly used as a basis for determining the poverty line. Thus, the incidence of poverty in a region may give some indication of the extent to which food is accessible to households.

Till 1973-74, National Sample Survey (NSS) data were available annually. Between 1972-73 and 1992-94, five quinquennial surveys have been carried out with a large sample village. The 'thin' samples are good enough to provide reliable estimates at the all-India level and the variance may be high at state level.

The trends during the first 24 years of pre-reform period (1951 to 1973-74) shows that (a) rural poverty varied between 44 per cent to 64 per cent and

Table 1
Per Capita Net Availability of Foodgrains and Pulses: Quinquennial Averages

Five year average	Foodgrains (grams per day)	Pulses (grams per day)
1954-58	437.7	68.3
1961-65	461.1	60.7
1966-70	434.0	48.6
1971-75	442.6	44.0
1976-80	441.8	43.0
1981-85	456.1	39.3
1986-90	473.9	40.0
1991-95	484.4	37.5
1996-98*	492.2*	34.8*

Note: * Triennial average.
Source: Calculated by the author based on data available in *Economic Survey, 1998-99*.

(b) urban poverty varied between 36 per cent without any significant trends. However, both rural and urban poverty ratios showed a decline in the late 1970s and in the 1980s.

Has poverty worsened after the reforms? Since the introduction of economic reform in 1991, there has been a debate whether the reform measures have adverse effects on the social sector and the poor. First, we look at the estimates based on both large and thin samples. The estimates for the period 1973-74 to 1998 are given in Table 2. Datt's estimates presented in Table 2 show that rural poverty declined in the 1980s and it has not declined in the 1990s as compared to 1990-91. In fact it increased to above 40 per cent in 1992 and 1994-95. On the other hand, urban poverty declined significantly in the 1990s. Gupta's estimates also show similar trends on rural poverty. However, in 1998

Table 2
Trends in Poverty: 1973-74 to 1998, All-India

	Datt's estiamtes		S.P. Gupta's estimates		
	Rural	Urban	Rural	Urban	Total
19973-74	55.72	47.96	–	–	–
1977-78	50.60	40.50	–	–	–
1983	45.31	35.65	45.65	40.79	44.48
1986-87	38.81	34.29	–	–	–
1987-88	39.23	36.20	39.09	38.20	38.86
1988-89	39.06	36.60	–	–	–
1989-90	34.30	33.40	33.70	36.00	34.28
1990-91	36.43	32.76	32.04	35.29	35.11
1991	37.42	33.23	–	–	–
1992	43.47	33.73	41.70	37.80	40.70
1993-94	36.66	30.51	37.27	32.36	35.07
1994-95	41.02	33.50	38.03	34.24	36.98
1995-96	37.15	28.04	38.29	30.05	36.08
1997	35.78	29.99	38.46	33.97	37.23
1998 (Six months)	–	–	45.25	34.58	43.01

Source: Estimates based on NSS data on consumer expenditure.

the rural poverty increased to around 45 per cent. His study also indicates that probably growth was not trickling down in the 1990s.

Next, we look at the estimates based on quinquennial surveys for the pre- and post-reform period. The estimates based on Expert Group (GOI, 1993) method are presented in Table 3. It shows that the eighties recorded faster decline in rural poverty and the decline slowed down considerably after the introduction of reforms. On the other hand, urban poverty showed faster decline in the post-reform period.

Table 3
Percentage of Population below Poverty Line: All-India

Year	Rural		Urban		Total	
	Poverty ratio	Annual decline	Poverty ratio	Annual decline	Poverty ratio	Annual decline
1977-78	53.0	–	45.2	–	51.3	–
1983	45.7	-3.24	40.8	-2.25	44.5	-3.11
1987-88	39.1	-3.41	38.2	-1.45	38.9	-2.95
1993-94	37.3	-0.78	32.4	-2.71	36.0	-1.29

Source: Economic Survey, 1997-98, Government of India, Ministry of Finance.

To sum up, the impact of economic reforms on poor in India so far has not been as bad as in the Latin American countries. On the other hand, it has not been as favourable as in some of the East Asian countries.

There are significant regional disparities in the incidence of poverty. These are presented in Table 4. It shows that almost all the states have experienced a decline in the proportion of population falling below the poverty line since 1973-74 in rural and urban areas. In spite of the decline in poverty over the last two decades, the regional disparities are high even in 1993-94 poverty levels. Thus, while there were states like Punjab, Jammu & Kashmir, Gujarat and Andhra Pradesh, where the incidence of rural poverty was below 25 per cent, there were states like Bihar, Orissa, Assam, Uttar Pradesh where over 40 per cent of the respective rural population continued to remain poverty stricken. Similar disparities can be seen in urban poverty.

Access to foodgrains under PDS: There are several studies on regional variations in PDS based on data from *Bulletin on Food Statistics* for different years and the NSS 42nd round data relating to the year 1986-87.[2] A study by Radhakrishna et al. (1997) uses two sources to examine regional allocations and the access of the poor to food under PDS. These are first, household level data on utilisation of PDS collected by the NSSO during July 1986-June 1987 (42nd round of NSSO) and second, the results of four selected village studies on PDS in 1995. Some of the conclusions of their study are:

(i) There is a regional mistargeting in the distribution of foodgrains through PDS. While the off-take by states like Kerala and Andhra Pradesh, which are implementing subsidised food scheme, is high, the off-take by the poorer states like Bihar, Orissa and Madhya Pradesh is low.

(ii) Targeting and access to PDS by the poor has been unsatisfactory.

Table 4
Poverty Across States: Head Count Ratio (Based on Modified Expert Group Methodology), 1973-74 to 1993-94

State	1973-74	1977-78	1983	1987-88	1993 -94	Annual % decline between 1977-78 and 1993-94
			Rural			
Andhra Pradesh	48.41	38.11	26.53	20.92	15.92	5.31
Assam	52.67	59.82	42.60	39.35	45.01	1.76
Bihar	62.99	63.25	64.37	52.63	58.21	0.52
Gujarat	46.35	41.76	29.80	28.67	22.18	3.88
Haryana	34.23	27.73	20.56	16.22	28.02	-0.07
Himachal Pradesh	27.42	33.49	17.00	16.28	30.34	0.62
Jammu & Kashmir	45.51	42.86	26.04	25.70	22.72	3.89
Karnataka	55.14	48.18	36.33	32.82	29.88	2.94
Kerala	59.19	51.48	39.03	29.10	25.76	4.24
Madhya Pradesh	62.66	62.52	48.90	41.92	40.64	2.66
Maharashtra	57.71	63.97	45.23	40.78	37.93	3.22
Orissa	67.28	72.38	42.60	57.64	49.72	2.32
Punjab	28.21	16.37	13.20	12.60	11.95	1.95
Rajasthan	44.76	35.89	33.50	33.21	26.46	1.89
Tamil Nadu	57.43	57.68	53.99	45.80	32.48	3.53
Uttar Pradesh	56.53	47.60	46.45	41.10	42.28	0.74
West Bengal	73.16	68.34	63.05	48.30	40.80	3.17
All-India	56.44	53.07	45.65	39.09	37.27	2.18
			Urban			
Andhra Pradesh	50.61	43.55	36.30	40.11	38.33	0.79
Assam	36.92	32.71	21.73	09.94	7.73	8.62
Bihar	52.96	48.76	47.33	48.73	34.50	2.14
Gujarat	52.57	40.02	39.14	37.26	27.89	2.23
Haryana	40.18	36.57	24.15	17.99	16.38	4.90
Himachal Pradesh	13.17	19.44	09.43	06.29	9.18	4.58
Jammu & Kashmir	21.32	23.71	17.76	17.47	14.20	3.15
Karnataka	52.53	50.36	42.82	48.42	40.14	1.41
Kerala	62.74	55.62	45.68	40.33	24.55	4.98
Madhya Pradesh	57.65	58.66	53.06	47.09	48.38	1.20
Maharashtra	43.87	40.09	40.26	39.78	35.15	0.82
Orissa	55.62	50.92	49.15	41.63	41.64	1.25
Punjab	27.96	27.32	23.79	14.67	11.35	5.34
Rajasthan	52.13	43.53	37.94	41.92	30.49	2.20
Tamil Nadu	49.40	48.69	46.96	38.64	39.77	1.26
Uttar Pradesh	60.09	56.23	49.82	42.96	35.39	2.85
West Bengal	34.67	38.20	32.32	35.08	22.41	3.28
All-India	49.01	45.24	40.79	38.20	32.36	2.07

Note: 1. Poverty estimates in the table have been accepted as official estimates;
2. In the last Col., - refers to increase in poverty ratios.

Source: Cols. 2 to 6 from Malhotra (1997).

(iii) Empirical evidence of urban bias seems to be weak— bias was severe only in two states, viz., Jammu and Kashmir and West Bengal.

(iv) In states like Andhra Pradesh and Kerala, the access of the poor to PDS is much better, though even in these states, per capita monthly PDS cereal purchases tended to be regressive.

NCAER data on PDS for 1993-94 show that there are considerable regional disparities in the use of PDS by the rural population. As compared to the all-India figure of 39 per cent, less than 10 per cent of the population were using PDS in poor states like Bihar, Orissa and Uttar Pradesh.

After the introduction of economic reforms, the PDS is perceived to be the biggest safety net to protect the poor from the effects of reforms (Mooij, 1994). How effective is PDS as a safety net for reducing poverty in India? Parikh (1994) says that "the cost effectiveness of reaching the poorest 20 per cent of households through PDS cereals is very small. For every rupee spent less than 22 paise reach the poor in all states, excepting in Goa, Daman and Diu where 28 paise reach the poor. This is not to suggest that PDS does not benefit the poor at all, but only to emphasise that this support is provided at high cost".

Using NSS 1986-87 household level data, Radhakrishna et al. (1997) estimate the extent of income transfer through PDS to the poor, and the consequent reduction in poverty in terms of percentage and of its severity. According to their study, the overall transfer gains were very meager although there were differences in income transfers between the commodities and across states.

Calorie intake and malnutrition: For the bottom 30 per cent of the population, there has hardly been any perceptible improvement in calorie intake in the rural and urban areas. As shown in Table 5, the per capita calorie intake for the lowest 30 per cent of the population was 1678 cal per day in the rural areas and 1682 cal per day in the urban areas. This is a matter of concern because the bottom 30 per cent of the population is deprived of the minimum food intake that is adequate for providing them with the required energy.

Table 5
Average Per Capita Calories (Cal/day): All-India

Expenditure groups	Rural				Urban			
	1972-73	1977-78	1983	1993-94	1972-73	1977-78	1983	1993-94
Lowest 30 per cent	1504	1630	1620	1678	1579	1701	1627	1682
Middle 40 per cent	2170	2296	2144	2119	2154	2438	2148	2111
Top 30 per cent	3161	3190	2929	2672	2572	2979	2506	2405
All	2268	2364	2222	2152	2107	2379	2099	2071

Source: Radhakrishna et al. (1997).

In spite of self-sufficiency in foodgrains, the problem of malnutrition is acute and widespread. It is extremely serious among women and children. The proportion of pregnant women with anemia is as high as 88 per cent. At the all-

India level in 1993-94 (National Family Health Survey) around 53 per cent of the children under five are underweight. The percentage of child malnutrition is higher in Bihar (63), Uttar Pradesh (59), West Bengal (57), Madhya Pradesh (57) and Maharashtra (54).

(ii) Key Issues

(a) Trends in investment in agriculture

Higher investment in agriculture and rural infrastructure is a necessary condition for increasing agricultural growth. Government's role is important not only for raising public investment but also for inducing private investment. The worrying aspect is that growth rate in agricultural investment rose only for a decade following the Green Revolution and later it declined significantly for both public and private sectors. Public investment in real terms at 1980-81 prices was Rs.1796 crore in 1980-81 but declined to Rs. 1154 crore in 1990-91. After a modest increase to Rs. 1316 crore in 1994-95, public investment declined to Rs. 1132 crore in 1996-97. The decelerating trends in public investment is a matter of concern, though private investment in agriculture has grown substantially in the nineties. Even after shifting the base year to 1993-94, the declining trend in public investment is clearly visible. As shown in Table 6, the increase in public investment has not been satisfactory during the Eighth Plan. Clearly, efforts need to be made to increase public investment and encourage private investment in agriculture.

Table 6
Gross Capital Formation in Agriculture

(Rs. crore)

Year	Total	Public	Private
	(at 1980-81 prices)		
1960-61	1668	589	1079
1970-71	2758	789	1969
1980-81	4636	1796	2840
1990-91	4594	1154	3440
1991-92	4729	1002	3727
1992-93	5372	1061	4311
1993-94	5031	1153	3878
1994-95	6256	1316	4940
1995-96	6961	1268	5693
1996-97	6999	1132	5867
	(at 1993-94 prices)		
1993-94	13523	4467	9056
1994-95	15021	4971	10050
1995-96	15876	4928	10948
1996-97	16610	4689	11921
1997-98	16344	4220	12140
1998-99	16457	3876	12581

Source:Economic Survey, 1999-2000, Government of India.

(b) Implications of shifts in consumption patterns

The consumption patterns have been shifting over time from (i) coarse cereals to fine cereals and (ii) from cereals to non-cereals like milk, eggs, etc. What are the implications of the shifts in consumption patterns away from coarse cereals to fine cereals and from cereals to non-cereals for poverty? These are discussed below:

The poverty line is computed based on a fixed basket of 1973-74 which satisfied the minimum calorie requirement of 2400 kcal for rural areas and 2100 kcal for urban areas. Hence all the poverty estimates since the early 1970's are critically linked with that of the base year (1973-74). The poverty line per person per month in 1973-74 was Rs. 49.09 in rural areas and Rs. 56.64 in urban areas. The estimation of poverty in 1993-94 is based on the consumption basket of 1973-74 evaluated at 1993-94 prices. The updated rural poverty line for 1993-94 was Rs. 206 for rural and Rs. 281 for urban areas, according to which rural and urban poverty ratios were 37.3 per cent and 32.4 per cent, respectively.

These estimates of poverty assume that the consumption basket of the base year does not change, and the head count ratio correctly identifies the calorie deficient group. But in fact, since the consumption basket has been changing, the calorie deficient group is larger than the head count ratio defined poor. The report of the Expert Group on Poverty (GOI, 1993) indicated that around 66.6 per cent of the total population were below calorie norm in 1983, while the usual head count ratio was 45 per cent in the same year (Table 7). The gap between the poor as defined by the Expert Group poverty line and the number of persons below the calorie norm has been widening over the last ten years. By 1993-94, the gap was almost 30 per cent, since almost 66 per cent of the rural population were below the calorie norm in 1993-94. Similar disparities in official poverty estimates and those based on calorie deficiency can be seen for both rural and urban areas (Table 7). Hence the updated poverty line for 1993-94, which ignores changes in the consumption basket, might be an incorrect description of adequate purchasing power that buys 2400 calories.

Table 7
Persons below Poverty Line and below Calorie Norm (%)

	Rural		Urban		Total	
	1983	1993-94	1983	1993-94	1983	1993-94
Below official poverty line (Expert Group Methodology)	45.7	37.3	40.8	32.4	44.5	36.0
Below the calorie norm (2400 kcal for rural and 2100 kcal for urban)	70.5	70.0	54.3	56.0	66.6	66.0
Gap between the two norms	24.8	32.7	13.5	23.6	22.1	30.0

Source: GOI (1993) for 1983; Planning Commission, personal communication for 1993-94.

Base year poverty lines updated to 1993-94 price level in rural and urban areas are Rs. 205.84 and Rs. 281.35, respectively. In fact, the true cost of providing adequate calories in 1993-94 is Rs. 320 per capita per month and

Rs. 398 per capita per month in rural and urban areas, respectively for the poor.[3] This increase in cost of calories has adverse implications for the poor. The Report of the Expert Group also says, "where these shifts in consumption pattern are predominant, the cost of requisite calories is becoming higher. There is thus, a decline in the average intake of calories across expenditure classes even though, the real per capita expenditure has been rising."

(c) Targeting of PDS

Following the recommendations of the Chief Ministers' Conference in July 1996, the government decided to streamline the public distribution system in the form of Targeted PDS (TPDS). The TPDS virtually retains all other earlier characteristics of the system with increased scope for abuse at the retail outlet level. The government's approach to TPDS relates to income-based means test. This is a known fact that it is difficult to identify the poor based on incomes.

There is some consensus among experts that the present form of PDS is not helping the poor (except in a few states) and that it is not a cost-effective anti-poverty programme. The reaction to this consensus are of two kinds: the first centres on the removal of PDS and introduction of Employment Guarantee Scheme and, the second, relates to the issue of targeting. Since universal PDS has not been working properly, many argued that targeting of PDS to the poor would benefit the poor. Both views are an overreaction to the problem. One need not bother too much about leakages to non-poor particularly in the case of food subsidies. The objective should be to reach the poor by having a wide coverage (even with some leakages to non-poor) with innovative linkages with employment and nutrition programmes. There is also a need for decentralisation in procurement. This may reduce the costs of transportation, etc. Further, involvement of Panchayati Raj Institutions are expected to improve the performance of PDS in a significant way.

(d) Increase in issue price alone may not reduce food subsidy

The government has recently increased the issue prices for PDS to contain food subsidy. It may be noted that an increase in the issue price may not be the right way to reduce food subsidies. Because of political economy considerations, the government has been increasing procurement prices. Again, because of political compulsions, the government has been procuring whatever the farmers sell them. This leads to higher buffer stocks of foodgrains than what is required for PDS and other purposes.[4] As a result the storage costs have increased significantly. Unless this problem is tackled, one can not reduce subsidies by merely increasing issue prices.

(e) Nutrition programmes

As mentioned earlier, malnutrition among children and women is severe in India. Integrated Child Development Services Programme (ICDS) is one of the main programmes for providing nutrition. It integrates supplementary nutrition with primary health care and informal education. Some of the findings of the study by Radhakrishna et al. (1998), on the impact of ICDS on malnutrition reveal that (a) ICDS has been successful in reducing malnourishment among pre-school children; (b) there has been a decline in the percentage of rural children afflicted by moderate and severe malnutrition from 62.5 in 1975-79 to 52.5 in 1988-90 and further to 50.9 in 1994, and severe malnutrition from 15.0 to 8.7 and further to 7.5; and (c) the contribution of ICDS to the decline in the percentage of severely malnourished children was low (about 8 per cent). According to the study, the limited impact of ICDS on malnutrition could be due to meager allocation of budgetary resources to ICDS, and extremely poor coverage in states with higher needs and programme inefficiency.

2. Employment Security

For increasing the purchasing power of and achieving food security for the poor, they have to be provided employment. The workers in the organised sector who have regular employment and an assured source of income need measures to protect their income in the event of contingencies which tend to deprive them of or reduce thier income. In the case of the workers in the unorganised sector who have neither regular jobs nor an assured income, their primary need is employment and food security.

(i) Employment Trends

We provide here a summary of the recent trends in employment and unemployment.

(a) Trends in work participation rates at the all-India level show: (i) stability in crude worker population ratios; (ii) decline in WPR standardised for age distribution; and (iii) rise in WPR for male and female if we consider daily status.
(b) Growth rate of employment during the period, 1972-73 to 1987-88 showed a deceleration. It increased during 1988-94 but was still lower than that of the 70s. The elasticity of employment also showed similar trends—the growth of employment over the past two and half decades has, on an average, been lower than the rate of growth in the labour force.
(c) There has been a slow change in the structure of the workforce. The share of agriculture in the total workforce started declining only in the early 70s—it declined by 9 percentage points during the period, 1972-73 and 1993-94. During the same period, there has been a significant increase in the share of rural non-agricultural employment.
(d) The proportion of the self-employed has shown a steady decline over the years, while a corresponding increase has mostly been observed in the number of casual labourers.
(e) Though the shares of the organised and unorganised sectors in aggregate employment have remained constant at 10 and 90 per cent respectively, the share of the unorganised sector in manufacturing, construction and transport sectors, has increased significantly.
(f) The unemployment rates for the period, 1973-88 show that open unemployment increased while daily status rate declined. During the period, 1987-94, there was no sign of any increase in open unemployment as well as CDS unemployment rate at the level of all-India except in the case of rural males under daily status. The share of educated in total unemployment has been increasing.

The unemployment rates show that, contrary to expectations, there has not been much increase in unemployment during the reform period. However, these aggregate numbers hide regional and local level variations on the impact of reforms on employment and unemployment. According to Parthasarathy (1996): "structural adjustment by encouraging multinational business using sophisticated technology in agricultural sector could displace people engaged in traditional sectors. Workers occupied in the traditional processing sector suffer from competition in the input and product markets. Those displaced are not absorbed because of lack of skills and training in new occupations generated". Access in point is that of artisanal fishermen who can not compete with mechanised boat owners. An increase in employment insecurity due to casualisation of labour and generation of employment mainly in low-paid unrecognised sector are some of the other problems in the labour market. It may also be noted that the concept of time rate of unemployment has not been able to capture the dimensions of underemployment, particularly in the case of self-employed. The unemployment rates in India are low because the poor are too poor to be unemployed.

However, some trends like slowing rate of growth in rural non-farm employment, the rising share of casualisation, especially the sharp rise in the proportion of casual labour among the educated workforce, the stagnant (jobless growth) or declining share of organised sector in total employment and the higher unemployment levels in urban areas, particularly among females and slow growth in rural real wages call for closer examination for initiating appropriate corrective steps.

(ii) Key Issues

High labour intensive pattern of economic growth is important for creation of productive employment. The key question hereby is, how to make employment productive apart from creating more jobs. The approaches which require treating employment as a mere by-product of growth, or seeking solution of the unemployment problem in special employment programmes as such, are inadequate. Therefore, it is considered necessary that a relatively rapid growth of employment is built into the growth strategy itself. Of course, market forces alone can not be relied upon to provide gainful work for all due to distortions in the labour and other markets. Public intervention is necessary to ensure adequate employment opportunities and also enable the labour force to access these opportunities.

Although the Draft Ninth Plan shows that the elasticity of employment to GDP in agriculture is around 0.5, studies using cost of cultivation data have shown that the elasticity of employment in agriculture has declined from around 0.7 in the 1960s to around 0.3 in the early 1980s. However, the additions to workforce given in Table 8, show that agriculture is still the dominant labour absorber if we ignore the drought year 1987-88. Looking at different regions, the potential for labour absorption in agriculture seem to be high in eastern region and dry land areas. However, in the case of agriculture, the potential for *indirect employment* in the form of agro industries like *food processing* seem to be higher than for direct employment. Allied activities like dairy sector has also a high potential for employment.

Table 8
Industrial Distribution of Additions to the Number of Workers: 1972-73 to 1993-94 (%)

Sector	1972-73 to 1977-78	1977-78 to 1983	1983 to 1987-88	1987-88 to 1993-94
Agri. & allied	49.85	51.09	16.17	62.74
Mining and quarrying	0.40	2.06	2.06	0.70
Manufacturing (incl. repair)	20.41	14.35	16.53	6.59
Electricity, gas, water	1.03	0.30	0.30	1.05
Construction	0.24	5.85	25.50	0.71
Trade, hotel & restaurants	13.39	6.93	20.76	8.70
Transport, storage & communications	4.29	5.42	3.96	4.10
Other services	9.56	14.74	14.73	16.82
Total	100.00	100.00	100.00	100.0

Source: Visaria (1998) as quoted in Anant and Sundaram (1998).

The key issues concerning employment security are discussed below:

(a) Employment in industrial sector

The employment elasticity for aggregate manufacturing sector has declined over time from around 1.198 during 1973-78 to 0.231 during 1988-94. How is the employment elasticity going to be effected by the economic reforms? According to one view, the liberal economic environment may encourage the growth of labour intensive productions and this in turn would increase employment elasticity. In other words, the composition of industry may shift in favour of labour intensive industries. Reforms are also expected to lead greater flexibility in the labour market. Some others view the price of input is the one which is responsible for choice of technique by the manufacturers. The reforms may lead to an increase in the cost of labour which would encourage capital intensive industrialisation.

(b) The puzzle of jobless growth in factory sector

There has been a debate on the factors responsible for jobless growth in the factory sector in the 1980s. According to one view, higher real wages and job security regulations were responsible for the stagnation in employment (World Bank, 1989). The employment security regulations provide strong incentives for large employers to minimise labour hiring on a regular basis. On the other hand, labour market flexibility would encourage more labour intensity. Bhalotra (1998) says that wages per man-hour has not increased over time and there is an upward trend in the wage elasticity estimated by the World Bank.

However, employment growth in factories during the period, 1986-93, was significantly positive at 2.1 per cent per annum. The rate of man-hours growth at 0.62 per cent per annum was smaller than the earlier period. "Employment growth is expected to have been encouraged both by greater capital utilisation (implied by hours growth) and by the increase in product market competition in the 1980s."

(c) Educated unemployment

Incidence of open unemployment among the educated has always been high and continues to be high, though there has been a sharp long-term decline in the rates. The decline has been the sharpest among females, especially in urban areas, though the incidence of unemployment among educated females continue to be far higher than among educated males. The sharpest long-term decline in the incidence of unemployment among graduates has been in the case of graduate females in urban areas while the rate of decline has been the lowest in the case of graduate females in rural areas.

With the exception of educated males in rural and urban areas and graduate males in urban areas, other groups of the educated, especially graduates, suffer from very high levels of unemployment. The benefits of the growth process and of the efforts to promote self-employment among the educated do not seem to have been adequate to absorb the educated, especially educated females at a rate necessary to liquidate unemployment among these groups. Restructuring of the educational and skill development systems and removal of gender bias and other factors responsible for labour market rigidities need to be carried out urgently besides initiating steps to diversify the rural economy.

(d) Problem of 'working poor'

In India, unemployment *per se* is not the main problem. Many people are working in the unorganised sector which is characterised by low earnings, poor working conditions and lack of social security protection. Our estimates reveal that the incidence of poverty is the highest for casual labour in both rural and urban areas. The incidence of poverty declined for all the categories of workers over the last decade. However, the rate of decline in poverty ratios was the lowest for casual workers while it was highest for regular workers. These results can be interpreted to mean that casualisation may be associated with immiserisation in the sense of low incomes. Also they showed that the incidence of poverty for casual labourers and self-employed was higher than that for the unemployed.

(iii) Special Employment Programmes

We need, however, government interventions in the form of wage and self-employment programmes till economic growth takes care of the employment security of the people. These programmes are discussed below:

(a) Wage employment programmes

Given the magnitude of the problem of large incidence of unemployment in the unorganised sector primarily in rural areas, the problem of unemployment in the country cannot be tackled via the provision of unemployment compensation (Nayyar, 1996). However, alternative means of providing employment like labour intensive public works can play a helpful role in addressing the problem of employment security. They are easy to administer as they are based on self-targeting mechanism. There are many direct and indirect benefits due to public works programmes. An evaluation of Employment Guarantee Scheme in Maharashtra shows that the programme has reduced unemployment in Maharashtra; increased the incomes of many participating households; acted as an insurance mechanism; impacted on agricultural growth and agricultural wages; organised the rural poor into a political force and has had a considerable impact on women (Mahendra Dev, 1996, 1996a). These large scale employment programmes have also played an important role in the prevention of famine in India. The experience of Maharashtra illustrates the feasibility of certain kinds of social security arrangements, even in a poor country, when the government has adequate incentives to take appropriate action. There has been a suggestion to use employment programmes only during drought years, purely as an insurance against the effects of bad crop. It has been argued that employment schemes are useful in these years as was the case during the drought of 1987-88—but are only of limited value in a normal year.

Presently, the Jawahar Rozgar Yojana (JRY) and Employment Assurance Scheme (EAS) are the major rural public works programmes in India. But these programmes have not been as successful as the EGS in Maharashtra. The Ninth Plan document recognises some of the deficiencies of the government programmes.

Regarding asset creation, a large number of public works have been taken up at the village level. The assets created under JRY include social forestry, soil conservation works, minor irrigation and flood control works, construction of village tanks, land development, construction of rural roads, etc. The concurrent evaluation of JRY (1992) shows that 73 per cent of the funds were spent by village *panchayats* on community assets. The productivity improvement due to these assets is expected to create more sustained employment. However, it was noticed that considerable attention was given to the construction of link roads in several states and about 45 per cent of the expenditure was incurred on the creation of rural roads. In some states, the expenditure on roads was far in excess of the national average. It is true that the roads are important but they have to be 'all weather roads' and not the type of the roads which get washed away in the next monsoon.

An interesting dimension of the PDS and rural works programmes is that they seem to work remarkably well during drought years as relief programmes. There is evidence to the effect that the poor have better access to food during periods of scarcity as compared to normal years. It is worth examining why the bureaucracy which works efficiently during drought years fails to deliver in the normal years. Thus, there is lot of scope for improvement in the functioning of safety net programmes.

(b) Self-employment programmes

There has been a debate in the literature on the impact of self-employment vs. wage employment programmes in reducing poverty. Dreze (1990) and some others advocate wage employment programmes because they have a self-targeting nature and other secondary benefits. On the other hand, Dantwala (1985) favours self-employment programmes like IRDP because they increase the skills of the workers. Dantwala's recent views on the subject are: "In an earlier debate on wage vs. self-employment, I had expressed my preference for the latter. I should now like to slightly modify the alternative as skilled vs. unskilled unemployment. I would like to submit that an employment programme/policy which does not enhance the skill of the participant is, at best, a relief measure.... It is argued that the poor need work immediately and cannot afford to wait for skill acquisition. This situation can not be ignored. Hence the need is for Employment Guarantee Scheme type of programmes which are not skill demanding. But equally they are not skill promoting. My worry is that this type of employment of the poor and their self-reliance leaves the country unprepared to face the challenge of the technological revolution which we cannot arrest at our frontiers. Is there a way through which the needs of today can be reconciled with the challenge of the future?" (Dantwala, 1996, p. 563). This shows that employment security schemes should include the programmes that improve the skills of the workers. This is important because, in future, skill based workers are going to get much higher wages and the wage employed people continue to get lower wages particularly in the post-reform period.

(c) Minimum wages

In many areas, the market wages are lower than minimum wages and the minimum wages fixed in many states, in turn, are lower than minimum subsistence wage. Although different state governments have revised the minimum wages, the wages fixed still remain very low for the unorganised workers. In most cases the statutory minimum wages fixed and their revisions do not seem to have taken into consideration the minimum requirements of a worker's family to rise above the poverty line. In many states, the actual wages are 50 per cent of the minimum subsistence wage. According to some calculations, a fair wage works out to Rs. 125 per day providing minimum wages, which forms part of employment security.

3. Health Security

(i) Performance

The performance of India in terms of health and other human development indicators has not been satisfactory as compared to many other developing countries. According to the UNDP's Human Development Report 1997, India ranks 138 among the 170 countries of the world. A comparison of India and China would perhaps reveal the slower development of health security in India. Life expectancy in India is 59 years compared to 69 years in China. India has an infant mortality rate (79 per thousand live births) which is two and a half times that of China, 31) and three and a half times the proportion of low birth weight babies (33 per cent in India compared with China's 9).[5] Sanitation and drinking water facilities are also very poor in India as compared not only to China but many other developing countries.

The states of Kerala, Tamil Nadu and Himachal Pradesh have done well in terms of demographic and health indicators as compared to the rest of the states. It is well known that health insecurity is very high in states like Bihar, Madhya Pradesh, Orissa, Rajasthan and Uttar Pradesh. Kerala's experience shows that female literacy was one of the most important factors behind fertility decline. However, the recent experience of Andhra Pradesh reveals that fertility decline can occur even at relatively lower levels of female literacy.

Health security and food security are interlinked. It is known that even if food is accessible, malnutrition can occur if proper hygienic conditions are not available. The NSS 43rd round data shows that poor people spend less on their health in absolute and relative terms as compared to the non-poor. The cost of health maintenance for the poor is expected to increase as the cost of medicines is likely to increase if patent rights are given to patent holders. Privatisation of health services is also likely to adversely affect the maintenance cost of health for the poor.

An analysis of the cost of treatment shows that the costs are high precisely in those states where health care facilities are least widespread. The relative burden of treatment in government hospitals for the bottom 10 per cent of the population is below 30 per cent in Kerala, Tamil Nadu and West Bengal whereas it varies between 100 and 230 per cent in Assam, Bihar, Haryana, Punjab, Rajasthan and Uttar Pradesh. According to Krishnan (1996), "the present health care system in India is highly regressive with regard to the distribution of the burden of treatment and that it contributes to the perpetuation of poverty in the country".

(ii) Key Issues

The government's national health programme focusses on strengthening of the primary health care infrastructure, expanding secondary health care facilities, optimising tertiary care, and building-up of the referral and linkage system. But the performance of rural health care system has not been satisfactory.

The most important form of intervention that would increase social security relates to development of health care systems. It is well known that there are limitations of private enterprise in the domain of health care. This is the one field where there is an overwhelming need for bold initiatives and comprehensive reform, an area that has been neglected for long. There has been deterioration in the basic framework of public health care programmes. For example, many health care activities are displaced by family planning programmes. In many states, priority has been given to family planning programmes as compared to rural health care systems.

A viable health support programme is needed for (a) the improvement of the health policy environment; (b) the development of community based health financing schemes focussing on health needs of the poor; (c) introducing institutional reforms for health insurance; (d) capacity development in the planning and design of public sector health programmes; (e) development of regulatory mechanisms to ensure quality of public/private sector health care services; (f) establishing linkages with NGO initiatives; and (g) implementing special schemes for people with disabilities.

(a) General health insurance

This is one of the components of health security. India does not have a comprehensive health insurance programme as a result of which only a small group of people belonging to the organised sector enjoy some measure of health security. Krishnan (1996) advocates hospitalisation insurance for the poor and suggests some institutional arrangements for its effective implementation. Self Employed Women's Association (SEWA) in association with the United Insurance Company started a health insurance scheme in 1992. It provides health security for women.

Another approach to the provision of health security is embodied in a community based cooperative financing scheme for health care provision known as the Sewagram health care system. It is egalitarian, accessible, affordable, participatory and accountable. It is based on the principle whereby members contribute according to their financial capacity but services are provided according to the needs of the members, thereby ensuring that the selection of beneficiaries is just equitable.

(b) Comprehensive policy for elderly

With the expected breakthrough in reducing fertility and mortality, the proportion of the elderly in India is likely to rise in the coming years. According to the population projections prepared for the Ninth Plan, the number of persons aged 60 and above will rise from 54.5 million in 1991 to 70.6 million in 2001 and to 113 million in 2016;[6] by when the share of aged in the total population is likely to increase to 8.9 per cent.

There is, therefore, a need for a comprehensive policy for taking care of the problems of the elderly. Informal methods for obtaining income security, such as India's joint family, are increasingly unable to cope with the enhanced life span and medical costs in old age. Hence, these need to be supplemented by formal arrangements. The security benefits for the aged can be in two forms: pension funds and health insurance.

(i) *Social insurance*: Social security for the elderly, or more appropriately, social insurance against poverty (income security) and ill health (health security) is a contractual arrangement that the elderly sign with the government, which in turn finances it by taxing the working young. Thus, the contract is 'paid for' by the elderly during their working lives, and is expected to be honoured when they are old. This is why a social insurance provision needs government intervention, since a private provider cannot guarantee that the contract will be honoured as he runs the risk of bankruptcy.

(ii) *Health insurance intervention*: Any provision of health insurance to the elderly will necessarily require government intervention because of the possibility of market failure. There is practically none or very little provision for health insurance for the elderly in India. Based on the surveys of the NSSO, NCAER and the National Family Health Survey it has been noted that the elderly population suffer from severe physical and mental disabilities. Furthermore, increasing diagnostic and drug prices have also contributed to their vulnerability. The elderly also suffer from growing disease burden. There are basically three schemes for health insurance to which the elderly can have access in the Indian market. They are: Mediclaim, Senior Citizens Unit Plan and Bhavishya Arogya Yojana. The Mediclaim statistics show that the total number of people covered is a modest 1.3 million, of which the elderly probably constitute a small fraction. This shows that total coverage for health services for the elderly is minuscule, in that only a tiny fraction of the nation's 54 million elderly have the benefit of assured medical services. Therefore, it becomes imperative to design comprehensive health insurance scheme for the elderly with the support of the government.

4. Education Security

(i) Performance

Education is important for achieving employment, food and health security. India has the largest concentration of illiterates in the world. Latest data for the year 1997 show the literacy rate to be around 62 per cent. There are significant disparities in literacy rate between rural and urban areas. In 1991, the literacy rates for urban males and rural males were 81.0 per cent and 57.8 per cent, respectively and for urban females and rural females they were 63.9 per cent and 30.3 per cent, respectively. India is well behind China in basic education. In 1990-91, adult literacy rates in India were as low as 39 per cent for women and 64 per cent for men, compared with 68 per cent for women and 87 per cent for men in China. As shown by Dreze and Sen (1995), in contrast to India's massive problem of illiteracy among boys and girls, China is now quite close to universal literacy in the younger age-groups. In India, 26 per cent of adolescent boys (age 15-19) and 48 per cent of adolescent girls, were found to be illiterate. In China, on the other hand, only 3 per cent of boys and 8 per cent of girls were illiterate in 1990.

There are also significant regional disparities (Table 9). While states like Kerala, Himachal Pradesh, Maharashtra, Tamil Nadu and West Bengal have shown impressive gains in education, Bihar, Madhya Pradesh, Uttar Pradesh, Rajasthan and Andhra Pradesh continue to lag behind the rest of the country.

Table 9
Total Literacy Rate

(per cent)

State	1981	1991	1997
Andhra Pradesh	29.84	44.09	54
Bihar	26.20	38.48	49
Gujarat	43.70	61.29	68
Haryana	36.14	55.85	65
Karnataka	38.46	56.04	58
Kerala	70.42	89.81	93
Madhya Pradesh	27.87	44.20	54
Maharashtra	47.18	64.87	74
Orissa	34.23	49.09	51
Punjab	40.86	58.81	67
Rajasthan	24.38	38.55	55
Tamil Nadu	46.76	62.66	70
Uttar Pradesh	27.16	41.60	56
West Bengal	40.94	57.70	72
All-India	36.23	52.21	62

Source : 1. Census for 1981 and 1991; 2. NSSO for 1997.

(ii) Key Issues

(a) Basic education and child labour

The neglect of primary education is one of the biggest failures of Indian development policies. Child labour is the most vulnerable group among the workers and does not have education security. India has probably the largest number of child labour in the world. Conventionally, a working child is defined as a child in the age-group of 5 to 14 who is doing labour, either paid or unpaid. We should, however, define a working child as a child who is deprived of the right to education and childhood. The child population can be grouped into three categories: 'school-going children', 'child labour', 'non-labour and non-school goers'. According to NSS data, the last category forms about 50 per cent of the child population and they are potential child labourers. Therefore, the child labour problem should address not only the category of child labour but also the category of non-labour and non-school goers.

(b) Determinants of child labour

The classic defence offered by apologists for child labour is that it is caused by poverty. It is true that poverty is one of the main determinants of supply of child labour. The policy prescriptions for preventing this trend is income generating programmes for parents of the working children to ensure payment of minimum wages to the poor etc. However, the economic dependence of the families is only a part of the explanation for the persistence of child labour. Indeed, across states, there is no correlation between incidence of poverty and incidence of child labour. Some time utilisation studies for the children suggest that most of the children who are not attending school are not doing much work either. Also, the direction of causation does not necessarily run from child labour to non-attendance. This can be other way round in the sense that drop-out children take up productive work of their own choice or through parental pressure as a 'default occupation'(Dreze, 1999). A case study of worker's children in Calcutta shows that two-thirds of working children 'work as they have nothing else to do as the schools are not very attractive and teaching conditions are poor'.[7] Thus, the schooling system is partly responsible for the persistence of child labour.

(c) Need for compulsory education

The introduction of compulsory education for children is a necessary condition for the reduction and abolition of child labour. In a narrow sense this mean that it is mandatory for parents to send their children to school and their failure to do so will make them liable to penal action. In a broad sense compulsory education may be interpreted as "(i) a compulsion on the state to provide adequate schooling facilities to all children, and (ii) subject to that, an obligation of the parental community to send all children to school. Thus understood compulsory education is a broad notion."[8] The most important thing is that the introductions of compulsory education would put much needed pressure on the state to expand schooling facilities. The argument against compulsory education is that it leads to official harassment of parents and poor families who send their children to school lose earnings from child labour. It may be noted that non-coercive means can be used for promoting compulsory education. The girl child is going to be particularly benefitted from the implementation of compulsory education.

The 83rd Constitutional amendment speaks of "the right to compulsory education". The compulsory education and right to education become meaningful on the fulfilment of two conditions: (a) provisions of adequate facilities at a convenient distance, and (b) provision of free education. Introducing compulsory education before these conditions are met would be putting the cart before the horse (Dreze, 1999).[9]

(d) Education guarantee scheme

In 1997, the government of Madhya Pradesh introduced the Education Guarantee Scheme, a community centred, rights-based initiative to universalise primary education. Under the scheme the government guaranteed: (a) the provision of a teacher and the payment of his or her salary, training of teachers, and (b) the teaching of learning material. Also, in contingencies it undertook the responsibility of starting a school within 90 days wherever there was a demand from community without a primary schooling facility within one km provided this demand came from at least 25 learners in case of tribal areas and 40 learners in case of non-tribal areas. In the budget 1999-2000, the Government of India proposes to implement Education Guarantee Scheme (EGS) at the national level. It envisages the provision of an elementary school in every habitation, which does not have such a school within a radius of one km. At least 1.8 lakh such schools will become operational during the next three years of the Ninth Plan. However, there seems to be some flaw on the EGS. While the logic behind the scheme is sound, it is too much to expect the local communities in poor areas to demand a school and manage it afterwards. The resources available under the existing centrally sponsored education schemes will be mobilised to support this initiative. In other words, the budget has not provided any additional resources for this scheme.

(e) Education and skill improvement for workers

The illiteracy among rural workers ranges from 43.7 per cent for males to 78.5 per cent for females in 1993-94. The corresponding numbers for urban workers are 18.4 per cent for males and 48.9 per cent for females (Table 10). As the numbers show, the problem is much more severe among rural labourers as compared to urban labourers. Again, within rural areas female workers suffer much more due to illiteracy. With this incidence of illiteracy, the economic reforms may widen the gap between skilled and unskilled workers at least in the short run. Education security should thus include programmes for skill improvements among the workers.

5. Security for Women

(i) Performance

Although women are not a minority group (like child labourers and disabled persons), they constitute a disadvantaged and vulnerable group in the Indian society. They have been victims of unabated gender violence, both societal as well as domestic. Women comprise the largest section of population living in absolute poverty and they represent the poorest of the poor. Gender discrimination against women is one of the all pervading forms of deprivation. A most telling demographic symptom of such deprivation is the presence of an adverse sex ratio which declined from 934 females per 1000 males in 1981 to 927 females per 1000 males in 1991. Table 11 shows that seven out of the 10

Table 10
Distribution of Indian Workers (15+) by Education Category, 1993-94

Education category	Illiterate	Literate upto primary	Middle and above	Total	% share in workforce
Agriculture					56.6
Rural male	49.3	28.4	22.3	100.0	32.4
Rural female	81.2	13.2	5.6	100.0	20.0
Urban male	39.6	30.4	30.0	100.0	2.5
Urban female	70.7	19.1	10.2	100.0	1.7
Non-agriculture					43.4
Rural male	28.0	31.0	41.0	100.0	12.1
Rural female	61.7	20.5	17.8	100.0	3.1
Urban male	16.3	25.4	58.3	100.0	23.1
Urban female	41.8	199.9	38.3	100.0	5.1
Total (agri+non-agri)					100.0
Rural male	43.5	29.1	27.4	100.0	44.5
Rural female	78.6	14.2	7.2	100.0	23.1
Urban male	18.6	25.9	55.5	100.0	25.6
Urban female	49.0	19.7	31.3	100.0	6.8

Source: NSS 50th round on Employment and Unemployment.

Table 11
Ten Districts with Lowest Child Sex Ratio

Sl. no.	District	State	Girls per 1000 boys (0-6 age-group)
1.	Salem	Tamil Nadu	849
2.	Bhind	Madhya Pradesh	850
3.	Jaisalmer	Rajasthan	851
4.	Kaithal	Haryana	854
5.	Jind	Haryana	858
6.	Amritsar	Punjab	861
7.	Faridkot	Punjab	863
8.	Bathinda	Punjab	865
9.	Kurukshetra	Haryana	867
10.	Hissar	Haryana	867

Source: UNICEF (1995), *The Progress of Indian States.*

districts with the lowest child sex ratio are in two of the richest states (in terms of per capita income) namely, Punjab and Haryana. India's adverse sex ratio reflects the increasing neglect of women's health and social subordination (UNDP, 1999).

Women's marginalisation is also reflected in their lack of control over assets and resources. Regarding literacy, district level figures show enormous disparities: rural female literacy ranges from a little over 4 per cent (96 per cent illiterate) in Barmer district in Rajasthan to 94 per cent in Kottayam district. The thirteen most backward districts in terms of female literacy are located in Bihar, Madhya Pradesh, Rajasthan, Orissa and Uttar Pradesh. A study of variations in mortality rates of children under 5, across 296 districts of India shows that higher levels of female literacy have been associated with higher levels of child survival. By contrast, variables relating to the general level of development and modernisation are not associated with child mortality rates (Dreze and Sen, 1995).

(ii) Key Issues

(a) Empowerment of women

The prevention of women from participation in social, political, and economic life affects not just the women but the whole population. This underscores the need for empowering women. One important way of empowering them is by ensuring them a share in decision making at the local level. This is what the 73rd Amendment of the Constitution seeks to achieve by reserving not less than one-third of the total seats of the Panchayati Raj Institution and one-third of the posts of chairpersons for women at various levels. Women's empowerment is not an easy task in areas where women have been subjected to multiple deprivation and discrimination. Participation of women in local participatory politics has been greatly slowed down by illiteracy.

The following are the critical areas that require immediate attention regarding women:[10]

- Inadequacy of institutional mechanisms for the advancement of women
- Persistent and institutionalised discrimination against the girl child
- Feminisation of poverty
- Gender blindness in macro-economic policies
- Invisibility of women's contribution to the economy and environmental sustenance
- Poor participation by women in decision making structures and processes
- Gender gaps in literacy, education and health
- Growing trend of violence against women
- Barriers encountered by women in accessing legal entitlements (e.g., land rights)
- Gender biased societal norms
- Negative portrayals and perpetuation of gender stereotypes by mass media.

(b) Neglect of widows

In 1991, there were about 33 million widows in India and the condition of widows is one of the most neglected social issues in the country. Widowhood is responsible for the poor quality of life of many Indian women. Only 3 per cent of all Indian men are widowed, as compared to 8 per cent of women. This large gap primarily reflects the high incidence of remarriage among widowers. In many places, the widows cannot participate in most of the social functions. According to some estimates, the mortality rates are, on an average, 86 per cent higher among elderly widows than among married women of the same age.[11] The basic factors behind the disadvantages and insecurity faced by many Indian widows are brought out in a study of North Indian villages (Dreze and Sen, 1995)). These are:

(i) Their legal rights are violated and large majority of widows have very limited and insecure property rights. Widows lose not only a potential source of independent income but also the bargaining power with in-laws, sons and other supporters.

(ii) They expected to stay in the husband's village and face the social isolation.

(iii) They have limited freedom to remarry.

(iv) The segmentation of labour market by gender severely restricts their employment opportunities. Also, they tend to be concentrated in the older age-groups and their labour force participation rate is lower than that for married women.

(v) Most of them get little economic support from their family or at community level—there is no evidence of a joint family providing support to widows and majority of them live on their own with unmarried children or stay with their adult son as dependents.

How do we provide income and social security to widows? Some of these problems faced by Indian widows can be seen as an integral part of the gender inequalities in India. One way is to provide property rights, particularly land rights to women. So far, the strategy of land reforms has not given much importance to the existing gender inequalities in land inheritance laws and ceiling laws. Women are more dependent on agriculture for a livelihood than men, as men shift to non-farm employment. It is estimated that 20 per cent of the rural households are defacto female-headed. Yet, very few women have titles of land and even fewer control it. Therefore, ensuring women's effective command over land in the form of land rights will be one of the measures needed for providing income security for widows.[12]

6. Protective Social Security Schemes

The protective social security measures introduced by the government are aimed at helping the poor in removing/reducing contingent poverty. These are discussed below:

(i) Organised Sector

The organised sector which consists of the government sector, the public sector and the private organised sector has access to the conventional types of social security schemes. In the nineties only 26 million workers were organised out of 262.3 million workers (around 10 per cent) in the country. Social security schemes in the organised sector can be divided into three types: (a) Employers' Liability Schemes; (b) Social Insurance Scheme and; and (c) Provident Funds.

We will not go into the details of the working of these schemes, while some of which do not seem to be working well. For example, a report on Maharashtra's Employment State Insurance Scheme (ESIS) documents that the ESIS is not helping the beneficiaries. Besides corruption, the facilities in the hospitals are very poor and ESIS is plagued by callousness.

(ii) Unorganised Sector

As mentioned above, around 90 per cent of Indian workers are in the unorganised sector. We already discussed in detail various forms of social insecurity faced by the poor. Several state governments have attempted to provide various protective social security measures for the unorganised poor and vulnerable sections of the society. Prasad (1995) presents a review of social security schemes and programmes carried out by various states in India. The main issues emerging from the review are quoted as: "(a) Almost all states and union territories have old-age pension schemes. A few states such as Andhra Pradesh, Gujarat, Kerala and Tamil Nadu also have special pension schemes for agricultural labour; (b) Tamil Nadu, Kerala, Gujarat and Orissa have pension schemes for destitute widows and the physically handicapped; (c) While Maharashtra has introduced an employment guarantee scheme, other states like Tamil Nadu, Kerala and Gujarat has unemployment relief schemes; (d) Maternity benefits for landless agricultural labour have been introduced in Gujarat, Karnataka and Kerala to compensate loss of wage due to absence at work, allowance however are payable for the first and second issues only; (e) Health care as a part of social security does not seem to exist in any state; (f) Gujarat, Tamil Nadu and Maharashtra have certain welfare schemes exclusively for women and children while a number of other states offer welfare benefits for various categories of population below the poverty line" (p. 794).

In most of the states, old-age pension schemes cover a large number of beneficiaries whereas in Kerala and Tamil Nadu the coverage extends to even other schemes. Prasad's study (1995), however, indicates large inter-district variations in the coverage of the social security schemes.

In the 1995-96 budget, the then Finance Minister announced the following schemes to help the unorganised and vulnerable sections. (a) National Bank for Agriculture and Rural Development (NABARD) will open an exclusive line of credit cooperatives and Regional Rural Banks for meeting the credit needs of Scheduled Tribes; (b) Scheme for loans to Khadi and Village Industries through banking sector; (c) NABARD will extend refinancing to commercial banks also for extending credit to cooperative handloom institutions; (d) Special programmes mainly for targets at the rural areas: (a) One million houses to be built in 1995-96, (b) Introduction of National Social Assistance Scheme which consists of three components: (i) Minimum old-age pension of Rs. 75 per month to people above 65 years of age who are below the poverty line, (ii) Lumpsum survivor benefits to poor households, on the death of primary bread earner, or Rs. 5,000, (iii) Pre-natal and post-natal maternity care to poor women, (c) Group Life Insurance Scheme.

The above measures are the first-ever attempts to introduce protective measures at the all-India level.

III. FINANCING OF SOCIAL SECURITY PROGRAMMES

Some issues relating to the financing of social security schemes are discussed below:

1. Reforms and Financing of Social Sector

Here we look at the changes in public expenditure on social sector in the post-reform period. Guhan (1996) examines the pattern of social expenditure during the reform period (1990-91 to 1995-96). He looks at the trends in social expenditure (rural development + social services) excluding food subsidy in the central budget and the total expenditure incurred by all the states for the above period. He concludes that "in the final outcome, what is of concern is that the GDP ratio of outlays at both levels taken together has declined in the first four years of adjustment". "Given the magnitudes of poverty and deprivation in India, their absolute level at less than 7 per cent of GDP is also grossly inadequate for rural development and the entire gamut of social services". (Guhan, op. cit. pp. 1096-97). He also observes that the outlays on rural development and social services as ratio of total expenditures at the state level declined marginally. It may be noted that, the study does not look at the trends in interstate variations and different components in the plan and non-plan expenditure.

Many studies have shown that social sector expenditure declined considerably during the first few years of the reforms and this could affect human development indicators. The per capita expenditure on social services for all states together was lower in the post-reform period as compared to 1990-91(Table 12). In the poorer states the per capita expenditure on education and all social services declined considerably in the post-1991 period, while the rich states have not shown any decline in expenditure in this area during this period. The expenditure patterns show that the reforms have had an adverse effect on human development, particularly in the poorer states. They also suggest that there is a need for an increase in the expenditure on social sector in poorer states like Bihar, Madhya Pradesh, Orissa, Rajasthan and Uttar Pradesh. If public policy concentrates on stepping up social expenditure in these states, India's human development would get a boost.

Table 12

Index of Per Capita Public Expenditure on Social Services (1981-82 Prices)

Group of states	1990-91	1991-92	1992-93	1993-94	1994-95
Health*					
Poor states	100	96	95	102	97
Middle income states	100	94	93	99	98
Rich states	100	96	97	97	96
All states	100	95	94	100	97
Education					
Poor states	100	90	92	87	91
Middle income states	100	95	94	99	99
Rich states	100	101	100	104	104
All states	100	95	95	95	97
All social services**					
Poor states	100	94	93	92	93
Middle income states	100	96	93	97	97
Rich states	100	99	98	100	101
All states	100	96	95	96	97

Note : Poor states include Bihar, Madhya Pradesh, Orissa, Rajasthan and Uttar Pradesh. Middle income states include Andhra Pradesh, Assam, Karnataka, Kerala, Tamil Nadu and West Bengal. Rich states include Gujarat, Haryana, Maharashtra and Punjab; *includes medical and public health; **includes, *inter alia*, education, health, housing & urban development, and social welfare.

Source: Tulasidhar (1997).

2. Source of Financing Social Security and Available Options

It may be noted that social security is not the responsibility of the state only. Local communities and non-governmental organisations also have an important role to play in providing social security for the poor. It is true that there has been a decline in the extended family and community participation even in rural areas. But there is still scope for voluntary organisations and private sector to help the poor.

The state, however, continues to play a major role in providing social security for the poor. There are various options available for mobilising the resources for financing social security. The Human Development Report (1990) mentions the following options for financing human development:

(a) *Taxes Revenue:* Extra resources can be raised by reducing tax avoidance and tax evasion;

(b) *Discriminating user fees:* The structure of user fees could be such that a better-off pay for services and the poorer sections pay nothing more than nominal fees, particularly for primary education and primary health care;

(c) *Voluntary organisations contributions;*

(d) *Reallocating budgetary resources within sectors:* Shifting expenditure from low priority to high priority uses say, from curative to preventive health or from tertiary to primary education;

(e) *Reordering budgetary priorities across sectors :* Shifting expenditures from military to social sectors.

A mix of the options including utilisation of funds allocated for defence expenditure contribute towards financing social sectors in India. For example, Guhan (1994) advocates mobilising additional resources in the form of direct taxes for social assistance in India. According to his calculations, a moderate surcharge on the incomes of the top 12 per cent of households (about 20 million households) can be expected to yield about Rs. 14,000 millions per annum utilisation of which would meet the likely cost of the package.

According to one estimate, if the government imposes a 2 per cent tax on gross assets of the top 500 companies, the corporation tax collection will rise by Rs. 11, 300 million. If such a tax is imposed on the entire corporate tax the revenue generated will be even higher. The total revenue thus realised can be used for different purposes including expenditure on social sectors. Also it needs to be noted that the bulk of the expenditure on education and health is incurred by the states—for example, in 1994, states accounted for around 90 per cent of the total expenditure on medical and public health. Therefore, the states play a more important role than the centre in building capabilities.

Lastly, options like the SEWA (Self Employed Women's Association) insurance schemes and other innovative programmes which can increase financial viability of the programmes on social security have to be explored.

3. Experiences of Some States

(i) Kerala and Tamil Nadu

Some of the states have taken important measures towards the implementation of social security schemes. These measures and lessons that can be learnt from them are discussed below:

The states of Kerala and Tamil Nadu have been relatively successful in implementing both promotional and protective social security measures. In terms of economic growth, Kerala's performance can be considered to be poor; but her achievements in terms of basic needs and standard of living have been spectacular. For example, the infant mortality rate in Kerala was 13 per thousand whereas it was 110 in Orissa and 74 per thousand at the all-India level in 1993. Direct public action on health and education are responsible for Kerala's success in levels of living. The differences in the progress achieved in the areas of health and education between Kerala and other states seem to lie more in the efficiency with which the facilities are effectively used rather than in just the allocation of resources. Some people attribute Kerala's success partly to historical reasons. It may however be noted that the Malabar region was far behind Travancore and Cochin regions in social development at the time when the Kerala State was formed (Ramachandran, 1997). But, state action helped the Malabar region to catch up with the other regions in social development by the 1980s. Apart from this, the role of public participation and local leadership is also important for Kerala's success. Kerala has also been successful in implementing the protective social security measures effectively. The Kerala model, however, is not useful for increasing growth in commodity production (agriculture, industry, etc.)

Turning to Tamil Nadu, the economic performance in the state has been lower but the quality of human development indicators have been higher than those for India as a whole. Tamil Nadu is a pioneer in the implementation of the nutrition schemes and protective social security measures. It may be noted here that there are two important state-sponsored special nutrition programmes in Tamil Nadu, namely, Chief Minister's Nutrition Meal Programme (CMNMP) and Tamil Nadu Integration Nutrition Project (TNIP). The first programme which is considered as the largest feeding programmes in the world, has improved the nutrition of many school-going children. The TNIP showed that a limited package of health-linked nutrition interventions is operationally feasible in rural India in a cost-effective manner. As regards protective social security measures in Tamil Nadu, it is true that some shortcomings were found in one scheme in a district, but an overall evaluation of all the schemes in the state are yet to be done. Other states in India and other developing countries can learn many lessons from the experiences of Kerala and Tamil Nadu about how much can be done in the area of protective social security measures at reasonable cost to help the chronically poor, who cannot afford loss of earnings. Lessons can also be learnt from the drawbacks of the schemes in these two states.

(ii) Other States

Apart from Kerala and Tamil Nadu, some other states have also taken important initiatives in recent years. Employment Gurantee Scheme in Maharashtra, primary education in Himachal Pradesh and Madhya Pradesh, public distribution in Andhra Pradesh, and land reform in West Bengal are some notable examples that merit mention. In contrast, in less developed states like Bihar, Uttar Pradesh, Rajasthan, there seems to be apathy towards the need to develop social security programmes.

(iii) Effectiveness of Schemes

While India has introduced many promotional and protective social security programmes, the main problem is inefficient utilisation of funds provided under government programmes as well as by some of the NGOs. It is true that in a poor country like India, we need more social expenditure as compared to the relatively rich, developing countries in Asia. This is particularly the case in the poorer states where per capita expenditure on health, education and other social priority sectors is very low. It may be noted, however, that due importance should be given to the effective utilisation of the funds provided under various programmes. In other words, we have to examine how efficiently funds allocated to food subsidy, rural development and social services are utilised. In most of the promotional and protective social security programmes, there is scope for a lot of improvement in this area through better administration.

Dantwala (1993) discusses the paradox of 'adequate expenditure' on the social sector and low performance. He raised this question several times since 1959. In the 1980s, he wrote that "the typical response of policy makers to the inadequate achievement is to allot larger public funds for these (social) programmes and urge credit institutions to deploy more funds for their implementation. But the more important desiderata lie elsewhere ... Apart from misutilisation and quite often non-utilisation of the funds, the administrative machinery and the organisations, arrangements needed for their optimum use are ill-conceived, weak, inefficient and often non-existing" (Dantwala, 1983).[13] This clearly suggests that mere provision of funds is not enough and that the organisation of government social security programmes is equally or more important in order to impact on the poor more effectively. Decentralised delivery systems assume importance in this context (Guhan, 1994).

In order to ensure that the government's promotional and protective programmes have the maximum impact on the poor, decentralisation, easy access to information, and social mobilisation are important. These are discussed below:

(a) Decentralisation

Many attempts have been made to evaluate government programmes in India. Basically, the effectiveness of these programmes is limited because of 'top down' approach, lack of people's participation and poor delivery systems. However, an important landmark in the 1990s is the 73rd and 74th amendments to the Constitution which for the first time after three decades provide for a system of local government based on mandatory elections. The amendments require that Panchayats and Nagarpalikas should be involved in all the social security programmes including identification of the poor for targeted programmes like new revamped PDS, self- and wage employment programmes, health and education and, protective social security schemes. There are reservations for women in panchayats as a step towards their empowerment. However, as shown above, many women are illiterate and the power may still vest in the hands of the elite. Mere involvement of panchayats may not provide social security to the poor. The accountability of panchayats should be improved. Several conflicts involving the transfer of financial resources and powers to local authorities remain to be resolved. Consequent to these amendments Kerala and West Bengal decided to devolve 40 per cent of the plan funds to panchayats.

(b) Access to information

One way of increasing the accountability of panchayats and other local bodies is to have access to information on the use of panchayat funds for implementing all the promotional and protective schemes in villages. The people of Rajasthan have pioneered the recent struggle for acquiring the right to information. The initiative for this struggle came out of a process begun by the *Mazdoor Kisan Shakti Sangathan*, a people's organisation working in central Rajasthan. The struggle which began to gain focus in 1994 through the organisation of four public hearings in that region has now spread to other parts of Rajasthan with the involvement of a cross section of citizens, organisations and the media. The public hearings articulated the need for transparency and social audit of development expenditure. The demand for transparency in development expenditure of the state is one of the ways by which the people can realise their rights.

(c) Social mobilisation

NGOs and CBOs can play an important role in creating an environment conducive for social mobilisation and sustainable human development. The main objective of social mobilisation is to induce the poor to create participatory organisations based on the direct and full participation of all members of the community from varied socio-cultural backgrounds, irrespective of income, caste, gender or other discriminating characteristics. The eradication of poverty or reducing it to manageable limits in India would require a major political initiative and strategic thrust in which social mobilisation of the poor to contribute to growth plays a critical note. Even for the success of government programmes the of social mobilisation or empowerment of people is important. Accordingly government should engage in strategic planning which includes creating an enabling framework, setting of objectives, committing resources, acting as catalyst—especially for capacity building—and above all engaging in a process of social mobilisation which involves, *inter alia*, above all making people's organisations and people themselves responsible for the management of certain activities. It is noteworthy in this context that NGOs and CBOs (community based organisations) play vital role in strengthening the hands of the government. However, there is also a need for accountability of these voluntary organisations.

(d) Complementary strategies

Some problems of poor and vulnerable groups need to be tackled by having complementary strategies. For example, child labour is a complex issue and therefore requires complementary strategies and the involvement of all sections of civil society, i.e., NGOs, human right activists, lawyers, media, trade unions, employer's organisations, academics and so on. Some of the strategies that need to be implemented are income-generating programmes for parents of working children, payment of minimum wages to the poor, empowerment of the poor, especially women, better law enforcement, the convergence of social services in areas more prone to child labour, and providing shelter to street children.

Apart from this, there are anti-poor biases built into a host of existing policies, regulations and laws which cut across all sectors and vitiate any benefit that accrues to deprived communities.

IV. CONCLUDING OBSERVATIONS

This paper provides an overview of the performance of social security programmes and the issues relating to the policies, financing and effectiveness of these programmes. The framework needed for an analysis of social security schemes for the Indian poor in particular and the population in general is given in Table 13. It shows that the performance can be analysed in terms of five types of securities: food, employment, health, education and women. Although there is overlapping of the beneficiaries in all other types, it is better to categorise these separately because of their importance.

Table 13
A Framework for Social Security in India

Components	Indicators	Data collection	Public action	Effectiveness of public action
Food security Employment security	Income and several non-income indicators	Large scale surveys; Micro surveys; Surveys based on participatory approach.	Government (promotional: land reforms, PDS, JRY, health, education;	Decentralisation (Panchayats, Nagar Palikas); Access to information;
Health security			Protective: old age pensions, maternity	Social mobilisation Infrastructure; Freedom of press;
Education security			benefits etc. NGOs; CBOs; Self-help groups	Political pressure groups
Women's security				

Source: Mahendra Dev (1996).

We need to have both income and non-income indicators for analysing the performance of social security schemes and data collection should include date collected through surveys based on participatory approach also along with large-scale and micro surveys. The role of NGOs, CBOs and self-help groups should increase in a significant way in order to supplement the government efforts. The effective implementation of the programmes necessitates decentralisation of decision making, access to information, social mobilisation, etc.

Finally, a few words about the economic reforms initiated in the country since 1991 would be in order. As argued by Dreze and Sen (1995), economic reforms would lead to greater economic opportunities for the population. However, in the context of marketisation, there is a substantial section of society which does not have the resource power to enter into market operations. In order to ensure that these people survive, the government and those who are already in the market have the responsibility of providing social security (food, employment, health and education) to the large sections of unorganised workers and other vulnerable groups who are out of the market. Regional disparities in human development seem to be increasing after liberalisation. As such public action in terms of public investment in physical and human infrastructure is necessary in order to reduce these disparities.

Notes

1. For example, see Ahmed et al. (1991), Dreze and Sen (1989), Guhan (1988; 1992).
2. Among others see Parikh (1994), Suryanarayana (1995). The NSS published data do not give enough information to look at the access of poor to PDS. Therefore, some researchers have used household level information for the year 1986-87 to examine access of poor to the PDS.
3. Personal communication from Planning Commission.
4. See Patnaik (1997) on the problem of high food stocks and fiscal deficit.
5. For more details see Dreze and Sen (1995).
6. According to some alternative projections, number of persons aged 60 and above will rise even more rapidly to 124 million forming 10.2 per cent of the total population by 2016.
7. See Dreze (1999).
8. Dreze (1999).
9. On basic education, see PROBE (1999).
10. For more details, see GOI (1995).
11. For some other details on widows in India, see Dreze (1990).
12. On the general issue of women's land rights in India, see Agarwal (1994).
13. This was quoted by Dantwala (1993). On the effectiveness, Dreze and Sen (1989) say "the distinction of China and Kerala or Sri Lanka does not lie in the size of financial allocation to particular provisions". According to them the real success lies in creating political, social and economic conditions for implementing the public programmes effectively with determination.

References

Agarwal, Bina (1994), *A Field of Ones Own: Gender and Land Rights in South Asia*, Cambridge University Press, Cambridge.

Ahmed, Ehtisham, J. Dreze, J. Hills and A. Sen (1991), *Social Security in Developing Countries*, Clarendon Press.

Anant, T.C.A. and K. Sundaram (1998), "Wage Policy in India: A Review", *The Indian Journal of Labour Economics*, Vol. 41, No. 4.

Bhalla, Sheila (1998), "Trends in Poverty, Wages and Employment in Rural India", in Radhakrishna, R. and Alakh N. Sharma (eds.), *Empowering Rural Labour in India: Market State and Mobilisation*, Institute for Human Development, New Delhi.

Bhalotra, S. (1998), "The Puzzle of Jobless Growth in Indian Manufacturing", *Oxford Bulletin of Economics and Statistics*, Vol. 60, No. 1.

Chatterjee, Mira and J. Vyas (1998), "Organising Insurance for Women Workers: The SEWA Experience", SEWA, Ahmedabad, (mimeo).

Dantwala, M.L. (1983), "Rural Development: Investment without Organisation", *Economic and Political Weekly*, Vol. 18, No. 18.

—— (1985), "Garibi Hatao: Strategy Options", *Economic and Political Weekly*, Vol. 23, Nos. 6 & 7.

—— (1993), "The Vision and the Reality: Comments on the Report of the Economic Programme Committee, 1948", *IASSI Quarterly*, Vol.12, Nos. 1 & 2.

—— (1996), "Employment Guarantee Scheme", *Economic and Political Weekly*, Vol. 31, No. 9.

Dreze, Jean (1990), *Widows in Rural India*, Development Economics Research Programme, Division Paper Series, No. 2, London School of Economics, London.

——(1999), "Right to Education, Creating an Enabling Environment", *The Times of India*, March 31.

—— and A. Sen (1989), *Hunger and Public Action*, Clarendon Press.

—— (1995), *India: Economic Development and Social Opportunity*, Oxford University Press, Delhi and Oxford.

ESCAP (1992), *Social Development Newsletter*, No. 27.

GOI (1991), *Report of the National Commision on Rural Labour*, Study Group Report on Economic and Social Security, Government of India, Ministry of Labour, New Delhi.

—— (1993), *Report of the Expert Group on the Estimation of Proportion and Number of Poor*, Perspective Planning Division, Planning Commission, Government of India.

—— (1995), *Annual Report*, Dept. of Women and Child Welfare, Govt. of India, New Delhi.

Guhan, S. (1988), "Social Security in India: Looking One Step Ahead", *Bulletin of the Madras Institute of Development Studies*, August.

—— (1992), "Social Security Initiatives in Tamil Nadu 1989," in Subramanian, S. (ed.), *Themes in Development Economics, Essays in Honour of Malcolm Adiseshaiah*, Oxford University Press, Delhi.

—— (1994), "Social Security Options for Developing Countries", *International Labour Review*, Vol. 133, No. 1.

—— (1996), "Social Expenditures in the Union Budget", *Economic and Political Weekly*, Vol.30, Nos. 18-19.

Harriss-White, Barbara (1995), "Economic Restructuring: State, Market, Collective and Household Action in India's Social Sector", *The European Journal of Development Research*, Vol. 7, No. 1.

Krishnan, T.N. (1996), "Health, Poverty and Labour", *The Indian Journal of Labour Economics*, Vol. 38, No. 1.

Mahendra Dev, S. (1995), "Government Interventions and Social Security for Rural Labour", *The Indian Journal of Labour Economics*, Vol. 38, No. 3.

—— (1996), "Employment Gurantee Scheme", *Economic and Political Weekly*, March 2.

—— (1996a), "Experience of India's (Maharashtra) Employment Guarantee Scheme: Lessons for Development Policy", *Development Policy Review*, Vol. 14, No. 3.

Malhotra, Rajeev (1997), "Incidence of Poverty in India: Towards a Concensus on Estimating the Poor", *The Indian Journal of Labour Economics*, Vol. 40, No. 1.

Mooij, E. Jos (1994), "Public Distribution System as a Safety Net: Who is Saved?", *Economic and Political Weekly*, Vol. 29, No. 3.

Nayyar, Rohini (1996), "Unemployment Compensation and Employment Services in India", *The Indian Journal of Labour Economics*, Vol. 39, No. 2.

Parikh, K.S. (1994), "Who Gets How Much from PDS: How Effectively Does It Reach the Poor?", *Sarvekshana*, Vol. 17, No. 3.

Parthasarathy, G. (1996), "Social Security and Structural Adjustment", *The Indian Journal of Labour Economics*, Vol. 39, No. 1.

Patnaik, Prabhat (1997), "Some Reflections on Employment and Unemployment", *The Indian Journal of Labour Economics*, Vol. 40, No. 4.

Prasad, Eswara, K.V. (1995), "Social Security for Destitute Widows in Tamil Nadu", *Economic and Political Weekly*, Vol. 30, No. 15.

PROBE (1999), *Public Report on Basic Education in India*, Oxford University Press, New Delhi.

Ramachandran, V.K. (1997), "On Kerala's Development Achievements", in Dreze, Jean and A. Sen (eds.), *Indian Development: Selected Regional Perspectives*, Oxford University Press, Delhi.

Radhakrishna, R., K. Subbarao, S. Indrakant and C. Ravi (1997), *India's Public Distribution System: A National and International Perspective*, World Bank Discussion Paper No. 380, The World Bank, Washington D.C.

Radhakrishna, R., S. Indrakant and C. Ravi (1998), *India's Integrated Child Development Services Programme Assessment and Options for Reform*, Centre for Economic and Social Studies, Hyderabad.

Suryanarayanan, M.H. (1995), "PDS Reforms and Scope for Community-based Targeting", *Economic and Political Weekly*, Vol. 30, No. 13.

Tulasidhar, V.B. (1997), "Resources for Human Development: Notes on Selected Topics", Background paper for UNDP Report, *India: The Road to Human Development*, UNDP.

World Bank (1989), *India: Poverty, Employment and Social Services*, A World Bank Country Study, Washington.

3

Social Security for Organised Labour

C.P. Thakur and C.S. Venkata Ratnam

I. INTRODUCTION

Social security manifests the "natural desire of communities for protection from life's problems, from uncertainty, from disease and deprivation... (It is) the protection which society provides for its members—through a series of public measures—against the economic and social distress that otherwise would be caused by the stoppage, or substantial reduction of earnings resulting from sickness, maternity, employment injury, unemployment, invalidity, old age and death; the provision of medical care; and the provision of subsidies for families with children" (ILO, 1998). The 'cradle-to-grave' philosophy envisages social protection to the needy from the pre-natal (pre-birth and maternity benefits) to posthumous (death benefits) care.

A worker/employee has two components of his life: social life and worklife. Invariably, there is a reciprocal influence between the two. Social life enriches worklife while good social life reinforces the productive capacity of the workforce. Any civilised society expects to blend decent work (ILO, 1998a) with decent social and family life. In this context the economic and social component of social security measures needs to be carefully integrated. Broad trends in this direction exist but their management has left certain areas where there is an imbalance of one or the other kind causing major stress and strain for the stakeholders. The combination of a welfare state, democratic polity and the established social security system pioneered by government or the employer, has influenced the current picture with its strengths as well as its weaknesses.

In the Indian context, the entire social security system for the organised sector is influenced by the following four factors:

(i) The British policy to raise labour cost in the established industries to offset the cost-disadvantage of mother-country industries (textiles in Manchester, for instance).

(ii) In the early phase of industrialisation, there was a need to promote the commitment of the workforce to industrial and urban life.

(iii) A policy of corporate paternalism envisaged the provision of a variety of benefits, both to promote loyalty of employees and as a part of non-union strategy (Thakur, 1985).

(iv) The welfare state concept emerged in the post-independence era which encouraged a series of welfare and protective legislations based on relevant International Labour Organisation conventions. Several of the social security and welfare measures have become statutory obligations of employers. The pressure by the trade unions further enhanced and reinforced the governmental measures for social security.

The provision for social security encompasses assistance: a) for maintenance (of self and family)/livelihood; b) in the event of loss or reduction of income due to involuntary unemployment; c) for covering the cost incurred due to sickness, accident, invalidity, or old age; and d) by way of redistribution of cash, goods and social services education, health, subsidised housing, etc. to the more needy sections of the community

ILO Convention No. 102, Social Security (Minimum Standards), 1952, covers nine branches of social security: medical care and benefits addressed to sickness, unemployment, old age, employment injury, family size, maternity, invalidity and widowhood (see Annexure I for select list of ILO conventions on the subject).

India has not ratified ILO Convention No. 102 on social security. However, social security in its broad sense, is envisaged by the Constitution of India in terms of the Directive Principles of State Policy. India also enacted several legislations that provide for certain mandatory benefits in respect of certain kinds of employment. Such benefits include medical care, sickness, employment injury, maternity, invalidity and survivor's benefits, and welfare funds/schemes. They cover mostly organised sector employment.

In the year 2000, India's population exceeded a billion with a labour force of around 376 million. For the past two decades, the size of the organised labour force stagnated at around 28 million. This paper deals with the social security provisions for this 28 million strong labour force. The structure of employment in the organised sector is given in Table 1.

Table 1
Structure of Employment in Organised Sector in India, 1998

(in millions)

Government sector	19.418
Central	3.253*
State	7.458
Quasi-government	6.461
Local bodies	2.246
Private sector	8.478

Note: * Including 1.927 million employed in 246 central public sector companies.

II. MAJOR SOCIAL SECURITY PROVISIONS IN INDIA

The following provisions of the Directive Principles of State Policy refer to the state's obligation for social security:

— *Article 38:* The state should strive to promote the welfare of the people by securing and protecting as effectively as it may a social order in which justice - social, economic and political—shall inform all the institutions of the national life.
— *Article 39:* The state should in particular direct its policy towards securing inter alia, that the health and strength of workers, men and women, and the tender age of children are not abused and that citizens are not forced by economic necessity to enter avocations unsuited to their age or strength.
— *Article 41:* The state shall make provision for securing just and humane conditions of work and for maternity relief.
— *Article 43:* The state should endeavour to secure work to all workers, a living wage conditions of work ensuring a decent standard of life and full enjoyment of leisure and social and cultural opportunities, etc.
— *Article 47:* The state should regard the raising of the level of nutrition and the standard of living of its people and the improvement of public health as among its primary duties.

The Directive Principles of State Policy are, however, not justiceable, and even today, more than 50 years since we became a Republic, all of these still remain cherished, but elusive ideals. As a ratio to GDP at current market prices, the central government expenditure on the following social services decreased from 2.4 per cent during 1947-57 to 1.7 per cent in 1999-2000: education, health and family welfare, water supply, sanitation, housing, rural development, social welfare, nutrition and minimum basic services. There is a need to raise it substantially.

India has enacted several legislations to provide social security to the industrial workers. The most important legislations are :

— Workmen's Compensation Act, 1923
— Employees' State Insurance Act, 1948
— Employees' Provident Fund and Miscellaneous Provisions Act, 1952.
— Sèparate laws to cover coal mines and tea plantations.
— Maternity Benefit Act, 1961
— Payment of Gratuity Act, 1972
— The Pension Ordinance, 1995 (amended in 1996)
— Separate legislations for workers employed in *beedi,* cine and mining industries, which provide for housing, medical, educational and recreational facilities. There is a separate legislation for ports and docks, which deals with their employment conditions and safety, and health aspects.

The Workmen's Compensation Act, 1923, provides for compensation to workmen or their survivors in cases of industrial accidents and occupational diseases, resulting in disablement or death. The compensation in case of death ranges from Rs. 50,000 to Rs. 2.28 lakh and for permanent total disablement, from Rs. 60,000 to Rs. 2.74 lakh.

The Employees' State Insurance Act, 1948, provides for health care and cash benefits in cases of sickness, maternity and employment injury. The ESI scheme is operational in 642 centres in 22 states/union territories. In 1998-99, the number of insured persons was 8.82 million and the number of beneficiaries, 34.20 million. Health and medical-care facilities are provided to workers through a network of 134 hospitals, 43 annexes and 1452 dispensaries throughout the country. The ESI scheme is jointly administered by the central and state governments. While the central government formulates the scheme, recovers the contributions from employers of covered establishments with the help of its recovery officers, builds the infrastructure (hospitals, dispensaries, etc.), and provides 7/8th of the total expenses, state governments contribute one-eighth of the costs, post medical officers, specialists and paramedical staff, procure and install equipment, dispense medicines and have the overall responsibility for the management of the hospitals/dispensaries. The Director General (DG), ESIC, is the chief executive officer of the corporation and functions under the overall supervision and control of the board and committees/councils formed thereunder.

The Employees' Provident Fund & Miscellaneous Provisions Act, 1952, is applicable to 177 industries/classes of establishments employing 20 or more workers. The wage ceiling for coverage is Rs. 5,000 per month. About 22 million workers are presently covered under the Act. The benefits available to the workers include the provident fund, employees' deposit-linked insurance and a pension to the workers and their families.

The Provident Fund, Pension Fund and Deposit-Linked Insurance Fund are administered by the Employees Provident Fund Organisation under the overall supervision and direction of the Central Board of Trustees and Committees there under.

The Maternity Benefit Act, 1961, regulates the employment of women before and after childbirth and provides for 12 weeks of maternity leave, medical bonus and certain other benefits. The Act is not applicable to the employees covered under the ESI Act, 1948. The Payment of Gratuity Act, 1972, provides for payment of gratuity at half month's wages for every completed year of service or part thereof, in excess of seven months. The maximum amount of gratuity payable under the Act was raised from Rs. one lakh to Rs. 3.5 lakh with effect from September 24, 1997. There is no wage ceiling fixed under the Act.

The Industrial Disputes Act has provisions for job and income security for the workmen covered under the Act. The Minimum Wages Act guarantees minimum wages and the Payment of Wages Act guarantees that wages are paid as stipulated and in accordance with certain norms on time limits for payment, payment for extra work, permissible deductions, etc. The Act also provides for the payment of compensation in the event of retrenchment. Any retrenchment, closure or lay-off requires notice, consultation, compensation and prior administrative clearance by a competent authority. Also, way back in 1957, the resolution on 'automation without tears' of the tripartite Indian Labour Conference provided that there will not be any retrenchment as a result of automation.

All these legislations are the results of the intense struggles and lobbying of trade unions. Over a period, benefits under various legislations have been improved, particularly in terms of coverage, income ceilings for eligibility and quantum of contributions by employers and benefits to workmen. Over and above these legislative provisions, collective agreements at the enterprise/ industry level have provided for further improvements in many of the benefits covered by the legislations referred to above. Also, in many instances, certain non-statutory welfare and social security benefits have been introduced and improved.

Basically, the government has adopted a dual strategy in the matter of social security. For the 8 per cent workforce engaged in the organised sector, the government introduced a variety of social security schemes through a series of legislations. Though the government has adopted multiple strategies for the provision of social security for organised labour, all of them are funded by employers and some by employees too: employers liability for accident relief and maternity benefits; social insurance for health benefits through contributions from employers and employees; social assistance through welfare fund legislations funded through taxes on employers; retiral benefits like provident fund, pension and gratuity, which are savings schemes with joint contributions from employees and employers.

Excepting gratuity, all these schemes are largely funded by employers and administered by the government. For instance, 12 per cent of the wages on provident fund, 4.81 per cent by way of gratuity, 4 per cent by way of ESI contribution, and 8.33 per cent (in the case of loss-making units) up to a maximum of 20 per cent (in the case of profit-earning companies, according to a formula) by way of bonus. There are also many instances of mutual-benefit thrift societies, consumer cooperatives, etc., to encourage savings, to make loans available at concessional terms and to provide essential commodities and daily necessities at cheaper rates. These are largely run by employees and their unions through cooperatives, usually with support from the employers. This apart, employers provide a variety of non-statutory benefits to provide for children's education, medical care, accident insurance, housing assistance, employment on compassionate grounds, etc. The total cost to companies on account of these social security and welfare benefits would amount to at least 40 per cent of the wage bill.

The government schemes of social assistance are the only means of social assistance for about 92 per cent of the workforce in the unorganised sector and the non-working population. While the initiative to introduce social assistance schemes largely came from the central government, certain state governments – for instance, Kerala, Tamil Nadu, West Bengal and Maharashtra – have brought out schemes for the poor, the vulnerable and special occupational groups in the unorganised sector located in a geographical area.

Employers' liability schemes for the organised sector are notoriously subjective in their approach and social assistance schemes for the unorganised sector are usually subject to tremendous budgetary constraints (Subrahmanya, 1995; 1999). Employers, workers and their unions are unhappy with the way provident fund and employees state insurance schemes are administered. The staff costs and leakages in social assistance programmes are scandalous in some cases. It is for these reasons, that the government came out with a proposal to introduce a skill-development fund with a levy on the wage bill, which employers' organisations resisted, fearing that the extra burden of the levy may be spent mostly on staff costs and other administrative overheads with scant provision, if any, for skills for the target group.

III. MEDICAL CARE, SAFETY, OCCUPATIONAL HEALTH AND WELFARE FUNDS

1. Medical Care and Health Benefits

Medical care and health benefits for employees should provide for cases of sickness, maternity, employment injury and occupational health/diseases. Medical care and health benefits are not statutory except in the case of maternity, employment injury and occupational health/diseases. However, over the years, collective bargaining provided for a measure of relief through a variety of allowances and reimbursements. Most employers today concede amounts ranging from Rs. 30 per month to one month's basic salary (plus dearness allowances in some cases) to workmen either as medical allowance or medical reimbursement, either for domiciliary treatment alone or for both domiciliary treatment and hospitalisation. Employers in most large-scale private sector firms typically provide a mediclaim insurance facility to those workers who are not covered by the Employees' State Insurance Act, 1948. Alongside, insurance cover is also provided for accident relief, etc. And most of such benefits form part of collective agreements rather than being given solely at the discretion of the employer. Collective agreements provide for a variety of benefits and safeguards. For instance, in several companies, of late, collective bargaining provisions provide for milk or cash allowance in cases where exposure to certain industrial processes results in vitamin deficiency. The second computerisation agreement in the banking industry (1987) provides that pregnant women can refuse to work before computer terminals if they feel that it is unsafe for themselves and the baby to be born.

As mentioned earlier, the ESI Act provides for health care and cash benefits to employees covered by it in cases of sickness, maternity and employment injury. The Workmen's Compensation Act (WCA), 1923, provides for compensation in cases of accidents arising out of or in the course of employment but does not provide for medical care. The WCA introduced the concept of strict liability of the employer in all cases regardless of the negligence of the worker, except in cases of drunkenness, drug abuse at the workplace and willful disobedience of an order to use a safety device (Gonsalves et al., 1993). In any accident arising "out of or in the course of employment", minimum compensation was payable to the dependent or the employee as set out in the schedules. The Factories Act (FA), 1948; is the basic legislation on health and safety at the workplace and provides clauses on various measures the employer should take to ensure the health and safety of workers. Section 89 of the FA lists 29 chronic diseases which arise out of and in the course of employment and which can be called 'occupational diseases'. The employer is responsible for providing remedies for them though the burden of proof of the employee having contracted the disease out of or in the course of employment, falls on the employee himself/herself. The 1987 amendments to FA make it mandatory for the employers to disclose information regarding dangerous chemicals and processes. In the wake of the

Bhopal tragedy, the 1987 amendments to the FA listed several steps that the employer should take in industries using hazardous processes. A hazardous process is defined as any process or activity in relation to an industry specified in the first schedule of the FA, where, unless special care is taken, raw materials used therein, or the finished product, by-product wastes or affluents would (a) cause material impairment to the health of persons engaged in or connected therewith; or (2) result in pollution of the general environment. Such precautionary measures include (ibid.):

— Special approval by a site approval committee.
— Compulsory disclosure of information by management regarding hazards of chemicals to workers, local public and factory inspectors.
— Preparation of an emergency plan by employers.
— Periodic health examination of workers.
— Work environment standards which indicate the maximum permissible concentration of chemicals in the work environment.
— A complete list of threshold limit values and short-term exposure limits for 123 hazardous chemicals mentioned in Schedule 11 of the FA.

(i) Patterns of Health Care Provision

In the public sector, particularly in banks, and core sector industries like steel, coal, petroleum, etc., the medical benefits provided to all full-time permanent employees are virtually unlimited. Reimbursement of expenses for major ailments is at least 75 per cent of the total expenditure incurred, if not 100 per cent. But in the private sector, with the possible exception of certain organisations like the Tata Iron and Steel Company, medical benefits for non-executive employees is usually limited to a maximum of a few thousand rupees, including both domiciliary and hospitalisation expenses. The entitlements rarely exceed Rs. 20,000 and only in exceptional cases go upto Rs. 1,00,000 or more. In a few public sector companies, the life-time limit per insured employee was raised to Rs. 2,50,000 (Hindustan Petroleum Corporation Limited, for instance) and in rare cases an annual limit of Rs. 3,00,000 per insured person was fixed subject to a ceiling of Rs. 1,50,000 per illness (Industrial Credit and Insurance Corporation of India, for instance). In contrast, it is rare to find private sector companies providing insurance cover at such liberal terms. Also, it must be stressed that, in small private sector firms which are not covered in this paper, the maximum a company would spend on an employee and his/her family in a year for health care is usually one month's basic pay. There limits do not apply to the statutory liability of employers concerning injuries/accidents arising out of or in the course of employment.

(ii) Health Care Insurance in India

The Life Insurance Corporation (LIC) in 1993 introduced a scheme to provide insurance cover for four major ailments, viz., cancer, tuberculosis, kidney problems and heart diseases and discontinued the scheme after a few months, as announced by it at the time of launching the scheme itself.

The mediclaim insurance policy offered by the four subsidiaries of the General Insurance Corporation provides only one standard plan that fails to meet the varied requirements of different groups of individuals. The health care insurance benefits neither fully cover costs nor provide for the escalation in costs of chronic ailments. The ceilings are woefully inadequate and the schemes exclude (a) people over 75 years of age, (b) post-hospitalisation expense even in major illnesses, and (c) caesarian delivery, AIDS, etc. Due largely to the monopoly of the insurance business and partly to the ignorance, negligence and other difficulties of the insured persons and the beneficiaries, the services of insurance companies are far from satisfactory. The delays in settlement of claims are vexatious. In the 1990s, however, some public sector companies, particularly in the oil sector, have been able to negotiate better terms with the health insurance companies. As a result, for instance, in Hindustan Petroleum Corporation, the health insurance benefits of its non-executive employees have considerably improved. Not only have the limits for various items been raised substantially, but insurance cover is also provided for life without age restrictions. Of course, the quantum and range of benefits is a function of the choice of the scheme and affordability in terms of premium payable, with or without contributions from the employees concerned. On matters concerning wages and benefits for non-executive employees in India, it is usually the public sector which sets the pace. With regard to executives, particularly at the higher echelons, however, it is the other way round the private sector rather than the public sector. Being the trendsetter, therefore, it can be reasonably expected that, in the large-scale private sector firms, too, such improvements will become the order than the exception.

Under Section 80-D of the Income Tax Act, the medical insurance premium is deductible upto Rs. 6,000 which does not cover the premium for a family of four. The limit for tax-sheltered medical assistance for non-salaried people is Rs. 10,000. If one includes the medical allowances and reimbursements, the tax exemption for salaried people also works out to be similar, if not more.

Employed or unemployed, an overwhelming majority of the population in India have little chance of survival if they suffer from any major illnesses, because the costs of health care are so prohibitively high that even the life-time savings of most salaried persons would be grossly inadequate. While the situation is not bad for employees in cash-rich profitable public sector firms and the government, most private sector employers fail to provide any relief beyond the agreed monetary ceilings as they often lack the will and/or wherewithal and because of the fear of setting a precedent that could turn into a prerogative later.

The Government of India has made provident fund portable in mid-1990s. There was a demand for the introduction of pension schemes and also for making them portable. Already, within government service, pensions are portable, if given on the consent of the employer. It is most likely that employees and trade unions will soon demand making health insurance also portable. Making health insurance portable may not add to the cost of employers though it may deter job mobility, while it would help the employees immensely and, of course, hurt the interests of the health insurance business. In these changing times, employers are arguing for increasing rather than decreasing labour mobility, greater flexibility in labour adjustment and even providing extensions of healthcare to early retirees. Also, the resistance of employers to any proposal for making health insurance portable is unlikely to be stiff.

Health insurance provided by employers is being extensively used in very large organisations, in both the public and the private sectores, and will certainly become much more extensive in the years to come as an integral, if not a major element of health care delivery system in India. Insurance companies will be under increased pressure from their clients, existing and potential, to drastically improve the coverage, simplify procedures and improve administration of health delivery. The liberalisation of insurance is likely to accelerate such a development.

Health care problems increase with the passage of time due to the neglect of basic requirements such as potable drinking water, clean air and sanitary living conditions. Low level of literacy (with 48 per cent still illiterate) and poverty (even relatively better paid workers live in abject poverty due to imposed circumstances, inherited liabilities and acquired habits) tend to worsen the problem. Together, they make it difficult to distinguish between general health and occupational health-related problems and often makes it easy for employers to evade the responsibility of occupational health/diseases, if they wish so. Contrarily, the unsanitary conditions in the community and the absence of public health facilities may also place additional responsibilities on the employers. Some employers, in both the private and the public sectors, extend their medical care facilities to the community in which they operate. In the small-scale private sector firms medical care is usually limited at best to cash disbursement equal to one month's basic pay (and does not include dearness or any other allowances) in a year. In the organised sector, the provision of medical care to employees by employers, if at all, is usually at the sole discretion of the latter.

Pressure for employer-provided medical care increases in view of the inadequacy of public health care programmes on the one hand, and the mounting health care costs, on the other. Where an annual ceiling exists for domiciliary treatment and/or hospitalisation, collective agreements may provide for allowing the unspent amounts to be accumulated. Even encashment at the time of retirement after a minimum period of service may also be encouraged to avoid the abuse of medical benefits while in service.

Medical care and health benefits, other than those provided under the ESI Act, are applicable only to full-time permanent employees. This excludes over 90 per cent of the workforce in the country from the provision of meaningful health care. There will be pressure to provide medical care for casual, contract and part-time workers, but the 1989 agreement in the Indian Iron and Steel Company, Burnpur, extended several benefits, including the voluntary retirement scheme, to contract workers.

There is a tendency to convert some health-related benefits into cash due to the pressure of workers' demands as well as to overcome some of the administrative problems. This defeats the very purpose for which such benefits were created. Examples of this include converting the practice of providing milk to those who work in certain industrial processes for compensating them against energy loss and vitamin deficiency, into cash payments.

Post-retirement medical-care benefits will be an important item on the agenda of collective bargaining. The problem has acquired a new dimension with early retirements and soaring medical costs.

The inadequacies of the ESI scheme and health insurance plans call for their drastic overhaul. Health insurance and accident insurance covers need to be made more comprehensive, with higher and varied monetary limits and portable mediclaim schemes with no age limits.

There is a need for innovative schemes to provide full cover for the treatment of chronic diseases like TB, cancer, heart and kidney failure as well as drug-abuse, AIDS, etc.

Employers need to evolve new approaches to communicate customised healthcare information to suit the varied employee groups, introduce novel plans to reward healthy lifestyle behaviours such as variable deductions for smokers and non-smokers. They should insist on the inclusion of performance standards and guarantees in contracts with healthcare providers to ensure quality services at comparable cost, and use report cards to rate health care providers and help employees to be informed of Health care choices. Employers may, as in developed countries, also establish networks comprising medical professionals with a proven track record of containing costs and delivering high quality services.

2. Safety

Safety has entered the agenda of collective bargaining in a big way since the Bhopal tragedy in 1985 when several thousand employees and others were killed in an accident in the Union Carbide plant. The Factories Act was amended by incorporating several tough provisions in Chapter IV-A relating to hazardous processes. A safety committee consisting of equal representation of both workers and management is made statutory and the members and the committee are vested with rights. Even workers' right to information, etc., are explicitly mentioned in the amended Act. Nearly a decade later, some of the central trade union federations also formed an umbrella organisation called the Trade Union Programme for Environmental Protection (TUPEP). Convention No. 155 of the International Labour Organisation gives employees the right to refuse to work if the workplace is considered potentially unsafe. The 1987 Bank Computerisation Agreement concedes to pregnant women employees in banks the right to refuse to work before computer terminals. In quite a few cases, safety and health issues were also negotiated in return for a cash compensation or allowance. To the extent it gave employees and their unions a say in matters concerning their own safety it is a welcome development. But the extent that this led to safety being negotiated at a price, it is an unwelcome development.

In the sphere of safety and environment, particularly the latter, the non-governmental organisations and public interest litigation by environmental lawyers like M.C. Mehta played a major role. Both High Courts and the Supreme

Court ordered the closure of several thousand units in Delhi, Tamil Nadu, Kanpur, West Bengal and Gujarat, among other places. Given the perceived short-term trade off between the environment and jobs, a section of employers argues that environmental control should be more strictly enforced prospectively than retrospectively. In fact, during the short term also, environmental control should be given greater attention prospectively than retrospectively. Actually, in the short term measures to protect the environment may create job-displacement rather than net job-loss. It is true, however, that some may lose their jobs, while others may find new opportunities.

In 1991, new legislation on public liability insurance was brought to deal with the problem arising out of a settlement of claims of the victims in industrial and other disasters. Though some of these measures became possible through means other than collective bargaining, the role and contribution of tripartite consultations among government, unions and employers cannot be undermined.

Employers in India, by and large, consider their responsibility limited to initiating formal measures aimed at meeting legal obligations including the provision of protective equipment, etc. They generally seem to have a condescending view of the attitudes and ability of workers to participate in environmental issues. Consultations in participative fora are usually confined to matters relating to safe work practices, training in safety, safety awards, good housekeeping practices, etc., rather than on subjects like pollution control and prevention. In recent years, the pressure of competition is inducing employers to take the initiative to involve workers in finding ways and means to reduce costs through reduction of waste, better utilisation of inputs (including energy), etc., which directly or otherwise manifest concern for a better environment.

Though collective bargaining is beginning to address itself to issues concerning occupational safety, health, the workplace and community environment, there is a need for restraint in treating health, safety and environmental issues as bargaining points. In developing countries such as India, the trade-off between the environment and jobs, occupational health and safeguarding employment, which is a source of livelihood, may in the short run, apply brakes to the efforts towards making the workplace and working and community environment, clean and safe. Alongside, greater employee-participation, citizens initiatives, community-interest groups and consumer rights fora can and should put greater pressure for ensuring environmental conservation in a preventive rather than merely a curative spirit.

3. Occupational Health

The three important legislations in the area of occupational safety and health are:

(a) Factories Act, 1948; (b) Mines Act, 1972; and (c) Dock Workers (Safety, Health & Welfare) Act, 1986.

The Factories Act, 1948, regulates health, safety, welfare and other working conditions of workers in factories. It is enforced by state governments through their factory inspectorates. The Directorate General Factory Advice Service & Labour Institutes (DGFASLI) functions as a technical arm of the ministry for coordinating matters concerning the safety, health and welfare of workers in factories with the state governments while being directly responsible for administering the provisions of Dock Workers (Safety, Health & Welfare) Act, 1986. DGFASLI conducts training programmes, studies and surveys on various aspects relating to the safety and health of workers through the Central Labour Institute in Mumbai and three Regional Labour Institutes at Calcutta, Chennai and Kanpur, and another being set up at Faridabad.

The Mines Act, 1952, provides for measures for the health, safety and welfare of workers in the coal, metalliferous and oil mines. For giving effect to various provisions in the Mines Act and the rules and regulations framed thereunder, the Directorate General of Mines Safety (DGMS) conducts inspections and inquiries, issues competency tests for appointments to various posts in the mines, and organises seminars/conferences on various aspects of safety for workers. The overall emphasis of the DGMS is to reduce the number of accidents in mines. The Dock Workers (Safety, Health & Welfare) Act, 1986, contains provisions for the health, safety and welfare of workers in ports/docks and is administered by the DGFASLI. There are inspectorates of dock safety at the major ports in India. The overall emphasis in the activities of the inspectorates is to contain the accident rates and the number of accidents at the ports.

Though the government has set up 16 laboratories throughout the country to study the link between work and health, documentation on occupational health/diseases is weak and the steps to deal with the problem of occupational health/diseases are far from satisfactory in most instances. Bhat (1994) reports that every year, 1.8 lakh workers die and 110 million get injured in occupational accidents. "According to these (government) officials, he reports there has not been a single case of occupational disease in Gujarat, though 34.12 per cent of its 41.3 million population are industrial workers ....(and).... random surveys carried out by the National Institute of Occupational Health (NIOH) show, for instance, that the prevalence of byssinosis among the textile workers of Ahmedabad is 9.2 per cent." Bhat also quotes S. H. Clerk, Professor of Occupational Health, Gandhi Labour Institute, Ahmedabad, and a former Deputy Director of the Industrial Toxicology Research Centre, Lucknow, as follows: "Neither the management, nor the workers nor the government is interested in reporting the cases. To the management, it means higher 'costs', for the workers so afflicted have to be paid compensation; the workers themselves tend to hide the ailment, fearing loss of the job and the authorities concerned are just indifferent."

4. Welfare Funds

Statutory welfare funds have been set up in coal, mica, iron ore, manganese ore, limestone and dolomite mines and in the *beedi* and cine industries to supplement the efforts of employers and government. Large companies in the public and the private sectors in coal and iron ore mines such as Coal India Ltd. and Tata Colliers, provide a variety of welfare facilities like water supply, medical care, education, housing, canteen, etc., to their employees.

IV. SOCIAL SECURITY REFORM DURING THE PERIOD OF STRUCTURAL ADJUSTMENT

During the 1990s, though the policies of liberalisation, privatisation and globalisation have, as discussed later, increased job insecurity, amendments to the Companies Act and recommendations of Justice Mohan Committee on revision of pay and benefits for officers in the central public sector have resulted in improvements in employee benefits. But such improvements are based on the employers' capacity, not employees' needs.

In 1996, the government introduced a pension scheme for employees in the organised sector from the employers' contribution to the provident fund and the accumulated contributions to the family benefit scheme. The government has also proposed allowing provident fund/pension funds to be invested in debentures and shares. National centres of trade unions have reacted to it adversely on the ground that assumed higher returns are associated with higher risks and in view of the recent trends in stock markets and the failure of several non-banking financial institutions they are not confident of putting their retirement benefits at risk.

In the context of globalisation, the mobility of labour is expected to increase. There is a need for coordination to extend social security benefits to mobile/migrant labour—both inter-state migrant labour and cross-border migrants.

The younger workforce in the new economy (information, communication and entertainment) are known to be developing a credit- card mentality and seeking immediate cash returns in lieu of long-term and post-employment retiral benefits. Some multinationals and software companies have approached the government authorities with the plea that their employees do not want superannuation schemes.

1. Privatisation

There are two kinds of issues relating to privatisation and social security for organised labour in India. One relates to the consequences of privatisation and the resulting implications, if any, for social security. Employers are seeking to replace job security with income security. Structural adjustments at the enterprise level and privatisation have generally resulted in a significant downsizing of workforce in many companies.

Since retrenchment is difficult and where more than 100 persons are employed, it requires the prior permission of the appropriate authority, which is usually difficult to obtain in a large number of cases, voluntary retirement schemes provide for the extension of the benefits of housing for a limited period (upto two to five years), house building advance at the time of voluntary retirement, children's education facility in company schools, medical and hospitalisation benefits, and leave-travel concession till the date of normal age of superannuation. For example, in the Tata Iron and Steel Company (TISCO), the VRS scheme provides, among other things, for the following: i) voluntary retirees and their families are entitled to medical benefits till the age of superannuation and, after attaining the age of 60, as per benefits available to retiring employees. b) voluntary retirees who stay outside

Jamshedpur and do not wish to avail of the company's hospital facilities are entitled to a group mediclaim policy of the New India Insurance Company for a total coverage of Rs. 95,000 per annum, each, for self and spouse subject to a deduction of Rs.100 per annum per head; and c) employees separating from the company and desirous of starting business or vocation are also eligible for a loan of Rs. 2 lakh or 50 per cent of the pension benefits, whichever is less.

When the Department of Telecom is corporatised and the Delhi Vidyut Board privatisation is negotiated with unions, unions have insisted and obtained guarantees from the central and state governments, respectively that their retirement benefits would continue to be under the administrative control of the appropriate government which will be responsible for further accumulation during the period of their service, even after corporatisation/privatisation, as the case may be, and paid for by the government.

2. Job Security

Job security is, unfortunately, not being given as much importance as in past. Earlier, sick units in the private sector were nationalised. In recent years, sick public sector units have been privatised. In the former, job-security was a prime consideration while, in the latter, job security for at least one or two years is a prime condition in some countries, including India (Modern Bakeries, for instance).

It was once believed that companies promoted excellence by focusing on life-long employment and job-security guarantees. Now life-long employability, based on the need for continuous learning and updating/ upgrading of skills, etc., is considered a viable alternative to life-long employment. Income security is being considered an alternative to job security. As seen in Table 1, in the context of the Asian financial crises, several South-east and East Asian countries have adopted social accords to deal with the jobs' crises mainly through skill-development. This should form an integral part of any strategy of social protection.

Several countries believed till recently that redundancy can be fought by retraining and redeployment. True, skill's obsolescence can be prevented or minimised by retraining. But, when the new jobs created are less than the job-losses plus the fresh additions to the labour force, redeployment will solve the problem of the redundant workers, not the unemployment of the fresh entrants into the job market. With older workers' taking away new jobs, fresh entrants into the job market remain unemployed.

Enterprises and employees should take as much interest and responsibility as the government in establishing social safety nets. Safety nets should be created by them too, because these would help them in the event of a job/income-loss due to any business downturn or failure or both.

The best guarantee against possible job-loss is to prevent skills obsolescence through continuous training and retraining. Updating and upgrading skills is the ideal insurance for life-long employability. Multi-skilling can provide the required flexibility and resilience.

India has some special schemes to provide relief and livelihood opportunities for the unemployed. Some states like Maharashtra have implemented employment-guarantee schemes. Such schemes cover a very small percentage of the target population and the relief provided does not usually lift the so-called beneficiaries out of poverty. The administrative costs of dispensing such benefits is considered to be disproportionally high. There are leakages and abuses in administration. There is as yet no unemployment insurance scheme for the workers affected by market risks and/or restructuring. In the mid-1980s the Government of India established the Textile Workers' Rehabilitation Fund through a levy on textile mills to pay compensation to workers affected by the closure of sick textile mills. It envisages the payment of 75 per cent of the pay last drawn in the first year of losing the job, 50 per cent in the second year, and 25 per cent in the third year. The Government of India also established a National Renewal Fund (NRF) in 1992 with the following objectives: providing compensation to workers rendered surplus, providing retraining and redeployment, striving for area-regeneration, and setting up of an insurance mechanism for income guarantee. As seen from Table 2, between 1992-1999, over 90 per cent of the NRF money was spent on funding voluntary retirements, mainly in central public sector undertakings. The record of counseling, retraining and redeployment is rather poor, and overall disappointment with the scheme may eventually lead to withdrawl of the scheme.

Table 2
Performance of National Renewal Fund, 1992-99

Aspect	Total from 3.2.1992 to date (as on 31.3.99)
Financial allocation	Rs.22,620 million
Expenditure incurred	Rs.12,223 million
Expenditure on voluntary separations	Over Rs.18,000 million (90 per cent of total expenditure of NRF)
No. of workers who took voluntary retirement with NRF funds	1,28,384 workers (the number of people who took voluntary retirement with company's own funds would be at least twice this number).
No. of employee assistance centres (EAC)/employee resource centres (ERC)	557 EACs in 16 states and 47 ERCs in 47 central public sector undertakings
No. of workers surveyed by EACs	97,768
No. of workers counselled	52,177
No. of workers retrained	35,899
No. of workers redeployed	11,360

Source: Ministry of Industry and Department of Public Enterprises, Government of India.

The existing legal provisions for payment of retrenchment compensation to the workers (15 days' pay for every year of completed service) is considered grossly inadequate. Several companies have introduced schemes which provide for higher compensation than mandated by law, to those who they want to retire early, voluntarily. Profitable companies proactively restructuring their enterprises through downsizing may have the capacity and commitment to develop such schemes and make payments over and above the legally mandated amounts. Sick and closed units, however, often do not have the capacity and commitment to even settle legal dues. Social safety nets are needed to take care of the latter kinds of situations. Moreover, social safety nets should also be considered for providing subsidies to economically depressed industries facing financial difficulties so as to arrest any resort to retrenching of workers (to keep employment within the enterprises during the crisis period) and also minimise the effect of lay-offs and retrenchments.

The best time to plan and establish social safety nets is when the economy is doing well. Usually, however, most countries realise the need for a social safety net when they are in deep crises, which is the time when the need is the greatest but the capacity is the least.

V. TRENDS AND ISSUES

1. Job and Income Security

Indian legislation provides job and income-guarantees to permanent workmen covered by the Industrial Disputes Act. The 1957 Indian Labour Conference resolved that for automation to be introduced without tears, technological progress should not result in retrenchment. For more than three decades, this tripartite agreement provided the bulwark against retrenchment, though in a number of cases, agreements on voluntary separation schemes have resulted in payments which are several times higher than the compensation provided for retrenchment under the Industrial Disputes Act. A recent report of the South Asian Multi-disciplinary Team of the International Labour Organisation suggested that, if workforce adjustments become necessary, income-guarantee measures should be introduced before the current job protection is done away with. Thus, collective bargaining has, over the years, been responsible for maintaining job-guarantees and, where workforce reductions became inevitable, voluntary separations are introduced with lumpsum payments which provided a semblance of guarantee against income-loss resulting from job-loss. The problem, however, is that lumpsum payments usually result in immediate spending by way of redemption of loans or meeting family obligations like education, marriage, etc., and thus fail to provide adequate income cover over a longer period.

2. Zero to Full Cover

Collective bargaining has helped workers in the organised sector to improve the statutory welfare benefits significantly, particularly with regard to health care, housing, and dependants' care in case of untimely death. In recent years, there has been no progress towards the creation and/or improvement of retirement benefits. While, for workers in the unorganised sector, there is hardly any medical or health insurance cover, in the organised sector, the medical care provisions range from a paltry one month's basic to near-full medical cover for self and family members not merely up to retirement but till death. The children, however, do not get medical cover if they are not minors or if they are not dependents. For a large section of employees in the private sector who account for about one-third of about 28 million employees in the organised sector, the medical benefits are extremely limited and rarely cover chronic aliments, if they do not arise out of work-related injuries or occupational diseases.

3. Welfare to Moneyfare

One notices a trend towards converting most of the employee benefits into cash and seeking payments in cash. Employers find it expedient to concede such demands from trade unions because of the numerous problems they face in administering a variety of welfare benefits here are some examples:

— There is a problem in getting company buses to bring employees to the workplace on time. The tendency is to get rid of the system of running company buses by the company or a contractor and, instead, grant liberal loans to assist employees to own and commute on their own transport. A second option is to grant a liberal transport allowance or reimbursement.

— There are but few large enterprises which do not have one problem or other in running canteens. Therefore, the tendency is to close the canteen facility, except where it is statutory, and offer a canteen allowance to individual employees instead of providing the facility of a subsidised canteen.

— Milk is provided to employees working in hot and hazardous areas with a view to make up for the nutrition deficiencies. In the wake of complaints about the quality of milk and other malpractices, a defensive management offered a milk allowance in cash in lieu of milk itself. The unions agreed. The workers were happy that they got a little more money in their hands but the original purpose for which the particular benefit was conceived was lost sight of. For, not many would use that money for purchasing and consuming milk.

Such examples abound. Gradually, conversion of many such benefits into cash have become dysfunctional in as much as the purpose for which the benefits were originally conceived began to be defeated.

Painfully, in several cases, even workers' safety and welfare can be and has been bargained for. Coal miners, who are engaged in underground mining activities, were insisting at one time on an allowance to induce them to carry a small piece of equipment which sends signals to outsiders about their whereabouts in the unfortunate event of their having been trapped in a mine collapse or water deluge. Quite a few collective agreements provided for special allowances, presumably as compensation for the harmful consequences of their work and working conditions on their health and safety. Many groups of workers, who were exposed to dust, gases, fumes, radiations, etc., fought and succeeded in getting some cash allowances as a token of reparation or compensation.

There are some other instances where such conversion into cash did not have a negative impact on the workmen though, from the organisation's point of view, once again, the purpose was defeated. One such example that can readily be thought of concerns the conversion of the uniform allowance into cash and putting that money, along with the money similarly accumulated through conversion of other benefits, into an annuity type insurance scheme to provide succour by way of annuity payments in the post-retirement period. In the absence of a pension scheme and other social security benefits, such attempts proved attractive to workers as something on which they can depend in their old age.

4. Ceilings Raised and/or Removed

During the 1990s, the ceiling on gratuity has been raised from Rs. one lakh to over Rs. two lakhs. The wage limit has also been raised to Rs. 2,500 or Rs. 3,500 for certain purposes. The slab system of dearness allowance and removal of house rent allowance have been some other developments in the 1990s resulting from legislative amendments and collective agreements. There is also a proposal to remove the salary limit's eligibility and quantum of bonus under the Bonus Act.

5. Portable Benefits

In the past, pension schemes were designed to reward people for long and loyal service. Now, people want to take away their cash-balance pension money with them when they shift jobs so that they do not lose their pension contributions, whether they are in the late 20s or late 50s. Employees who call it a day midway through their careers can still expect to receive a substantial benefit by way of a cash-balance plan—more than they would under the most traditionaly defined benefit pension plans.

The workforce in a high-turnover environment considers pension benefits much before retirement as irrelevant because, today, the prospect of life-time employment is much dimmer than in the past. Companies must also realise that they cannot be make workers tied to them by giving them a pension. As pensions become portable, employers are introducing age-weighted profit-sharing plans.

Besides pensions, provident fund and health benefits, can also be portable. Already, in India, provident fund is portable. Health plans also need to be made portable. For the existing health insurance schemes benefit the insurance companies more than the companies and the individuals who give business to the insurance companies. Since health insurance premium increases with age at the time of insurance and also based on past medical history, the workforce in an environment which is conducive to a high turnover feel that they are at a tremendous disadvantage if their insurance requests are considered afresh when they shift from one company/group insurance to another company/group insurance.

6. Administration

There have been several reviews of ESI and provident fund schemes. In recent years, with the use of information technology, more information is also available. While the objectives of the schemes and the benefits under them are laudable, there is a growing concern and dissatisfaction with the high costs of administration, low quality of service manifesting in poor quality drugs, discourteous behaviour, delays, inefficiencies and even allegations about rampant corruption in dispensing benefits.

The government has taken initiatives to reduce the number of returns and registers to be maintained, computerise the system of accounting and set up a

National Institute for Training and Research in Social Security. While these are steps in the right direction, their effect on the quality of service and administration of relevant social security benefits is still not palpable. The Employees Provident Fund Organisation is found wanting in the timely issue of statements of accounts and settlement of claims. There is also a feeling among the members that the organisation is not doing enough to maintain the intrinsic value of their savings, which is otherwise eroded by the effect of inflation. Members expect better returns on their savings and hassle-free transactions through passbooks and a more convenient mode of delivery such as a bank branch or even a post office. Significantly, the Employees' Pension Scheme was amended recently making it obligatory to settle claims within 30 days, or pay 12 per cent interest to the claimant for the period of delay, which would be recoverable from the salary of the provident fund commissioner concerned.

7. Financing

As discussed earlier, social security and employees' welfare funds should have been established when the firms and the national economy were doing well. Unfortunately, this was not done adequately.

In the context of structural changes in the economy, with the increasing unemployment among the educated and with larger number of the employed in the formal sector either swelling the ranks of the unemployed or forced to enter the unorganised sector, the problem of providing income security to the workers affected by restructuring at the enterprise and economy levels is tremendous. The NRF could not measure up to the task. Except for a handful of cash-rich companies, others have difficulty in making workforce adjustments through early/voluntary separations. In many sick companies, workers have been without pay and/or benefit revision since 1992. In many other units in limbo, workers have jobs but no incomes. In several other chronic cases, the workers lost their jobs but did not get even their statutory dues.

Even the Government of India is expected to face a serious problem in sustaining the commitments it has made to its employees with regard to pension and other retirement benefits. Already, with the improvements recommended by the Fifth Pay Commission and accepted by the government (see Annex II), the commitment to give pensions accounts for 10 per cent of the budget. Due to increasing longevity and inflation and the prospect of a few income earners having to support more pensioners, the commitment on pension is likely to account for one-third of the government budget.

There is a need for a more realistic way of generating funds to augment social security provisions. Firstly, there is a case for increasing the budgetary provision from the present less than two per cent to at least six per cent over the next few years. Secondly, a strategic approach is called for which seeks a better balance between risk and return while investing social security funds so that the yield from a given size of fund rises appreciably without undue risk. Thirdly, there is a need for a dual approach to deal with the accumulated problem of the past in making arrangements for providing income security to the large numbers who would become redundant in the process of integration with the global economy. Additional sources of funds for this should come from contributions from the World Bank and IMF, special budgetary allocations, part of the sale proceeds of surplus land in sick/closed units, part of the disinvestment proceeds, etc. For the future, companies must be encouraged to subscribe to insurance policies to cover the market-risks of unemployment with a view to providing income security with defined contributions and benefits. Such insurance schemes would cover the problem of frictional unemployment but not that of the general unemployment of fresh entrants into the labour market. For the latter category and for the unorganised sector the government has inherent responsibilities.

8. Integration

Though the social security schemes and benefits for the workforce in the organised sector differ in scope, there is a significant overlap in their coverage of clients. This provides the rationale for integrating various social security schemes and extending the coverage to even larger sections of the workforce. This would lay the foundations for a comprehensive social security scheme, reduce the overhead costs of the administration of individual schemes and make it easy for employers to comply with statutory and non-statutory returns and save themselves from avoidable harassment from a battery of inspectors separately under each scheme. Several committees and commissions, the Indian Labour Conference and even the committees of Parliament have been debating the case for integration and the tangible benefits that accrue from it, since the mid-1950s. The first National Commission on Labour (1969) endorsed the proposal with a recommendation to extend the scope of an integrated social security scheme to cover retirement/family pension and unemployment insurance. The Commission observed: "Our view is that an ideal arrangement would be to gradually work towards a comprehensive social security plan by pooling all the social security collections in a single fund which different agencies can draw upon for disbursing various benefits according to needs. A budget can be drawn up on this basis every year on a notional contribution, which could be determined taking into account the possible disbursements during the year. ... a large fund would be available with government. In lieu of the use of such funds by government, it should be possible for it to cover some extra contingencies to which the beneficiaries are likely to be exposed. We recognise that the details of this idea will have to be worked out by experts and the goal envisaged in this proposal reached in stages." Surely, the Second National Commission is likely to echo similar views as did the National Labour Law Association whose Draft Labour Code (1994) recommended the setting up of a National Social Security Authority of India with central and state boards of social security as autonomous corporate bodies, merging all existing schemes to administer a modified version of the benefits that provide a comprehensive coverage of social security benefits.

VI. CONCLUSION

The sustainability of social security measures in terms of financial viability arises when accrual to the fund is not proportionate to the demands on it. This is likely to grow further due to the changing workforce demography and structural adjustment dislocations. Second, the financial management of the fund is such that the costs are rising while the returns are yet to generate a surplus. The dilemma concerns balancing of risk with return. Third, the government largely controls the administration of the programme. Fourth, possible mismangement and corruption in the administration of the programmes have to be kept in view.

The government continues to have a welfare-orientation but is both reluctant and unable to raise contributions commensurate with the needs from its budgetary resources. Its prime concern seems mainly to encourage savings in the economy. Social security contributions form the bulwark of household savings. The government finds such contributions as cheap, yet substantial, for financing its own activities.

As far as employers are concerned, they want income and other sources of security for their employees, which is efficiency-enhancing. This also encourages the latter's commitment and loyalty. At the same time, they want to reduce the incidence of the cost of social security. An unfortunate symptom occurs where employers default on their social security contributions and, worse, when they even use them as working capital. Despite pressure from the government, the token penalties fail to serve as a deterrent. Workers' interest continues to lie in seeking further improvement of existing benefits and obtaining a pension as a third retirement benefit. Recent collective bargaining agreements in the traditional manufacturing sector concentrate on higher demands on non-wage benefits, including post-retirement and deferred-payment benefits. Certain tax provisions and deferred-payment arrangements as well as flexibility of borrowings, have encouraged this trend. The younger workforce in the new-economy industries, however, is more keen to have everything in terms of current and cash payments.

Employee-shareholding and profit-sharing are becoming universal particularly in the new-economy industries like information, communication and entertainment. This is gradually spreading to other sectors as well. Its impact remains to be seen.

We have covered only the organised sector. If we bring in the unorganised sector, we run into a public policy dilemma of (a) combining internal social responsibility of business vis-à-vis its employees, and (b) the larger social responsibility of business across the entire spectrum of the economy. The obvious macro-inequity is entering the domain of national debate. In order to sustain these benefits for the organised sector it would be imperative to promote the rate of growth of the economy with increasingly more decent employment and employment opportunities. The disturbing aspect is that the gap has been widening over the past several decades. Under conditions of slow growth or stagnation, there is the risk of the growing inequity emerging as an explosive issue. The redeeming feature is that recent initiatives for social security are directed towards the unorganised sector and the hitherto socially excluded vulnerable sections of the population. If this trend is sustained, it holds promise for a better future for the disadvantaged sections. Hopefully, the second National Commission on Labour, which is specifically vested with the task of providing an umbrella framework for the unorganised sector, will provide some innovative and workable ideas.

Annexure I

Select Social Security Conventions of the ILO

Comprehensive Standards

Recommendation No.67: Income Security, 1944
Convention No.102: Social Security (Minimum Standards), 1952
Convention No.118: Equality of Treatment (Social Security), 1962
Convention No.157: Maintenance of Social Security Rights, 1982
Recommendation No.168: Maintenance of Social Security Rights, 1982

Protection in the various Social Security Branches

1. *Medical Care and Sickness Benefit*
   Convention No.24: Sickness Insurance (Industry), 1927
   Convention No.25: Sickness Insurance (Agriculture), 1927
   Recommendation No.69: Medical Care, 1944
   Convention No.130: Medical Care and Sickness Benefits, 1969
2. *Old Age, Invalidity and Survivors' Benefit*
   Convention No.35: Old-Age Insurance (Industry), 1933
   Convention No. 36:Old-Age Insurance (Agriculture), 1933
   Convention No.37: Invalidity Insurance (Industry, etc.), 1933
   Convention No.38: Invalidity Insurance (Agriculture), 1933
   Convention No.39: Survivors' Insurance (Industry, etc.), 1993
   Convention No.40: Survivors' Insurance (Agriculture), 1933
   Convention No.48: Maintenance of Migrants' Pension Rights, 1935
   Convention No.128: Invalidity, Old-Age and Survivors' Benefits, 1967
   Recommendation No. 131: Invalidity, Old-Age and Survivors' Benefits, 1967
   Convention No. 71
3. *Employment Injury Benefit*
   Convention No. 12L Workmen's Compensation (Agriculture), 1921
   Convention No. 17: Workmen's Compensation (Accidents), 1925
   Convention No. 23: Workmen's Compensation (Jurisdiction), 1925
   Convention No. 18: Workmen's Compensation (Occupational Diseases), 1925
   Convention No. 19: Equality of Treatment (Accident Compensation), 1925
   Recommendation No. 25: Equality of Treatment (Accident Compensation), 1925
   Convention No. 42: Workmen's Compensation (Occupational Diseases) (Revised), 1934
   Convention No. 121: Employment Injury Benefits, 1964
   Recommendation No. 121: Employment Injury Benefits, 1964
4. *Unemployment Benefit*
   Convention No. 44: Unemployment Provision, 1934
   Recommendation No. 44: Unemployment Provision, 1934
   Convention No. 168: Employment Promotion and Protection against Unemployment, 1988
   Recommendation No. 176: Employment Promotion and Protection against Unemployment, 1988
   Convention No. 8, Recommendation No. 10
5. *Maternity Benefit – Maternity Protection*
   Convention No. 3: Maternity Protection, 1919
   Convention No. 103: Maternity Protection (Revised), 1952
   Recommendation No. 95: Maternity Protection, 1952

Annexure II

Social Security for Government Employees: Fifth Pay Commission

Government employees, specially those employed by the central government, enjoy maximum security in accordance with rules framed under Article 309 of the Constitution of India.

Their medical facilities include medical reimbursement, outpatient, domiciliary, specialist referral and in-patient treatment. Several government departments like the railways, defence, police and ordnance factories have excellent facilities of their own for medical care. The Fifth Central Pay Commission has recommended compulsory medical check-ups for all central government employees beyond the age of 40 years, once in three years at government's cost, the introduction of health credit cards and formulation of a medical insurance scheme as an alternative to the existing medical reimbursement scheme. They are eligible for 10 day's sick leave in a year, compensation for death or disability, and 90 day's maternity leave twice in the entire careers of women employees with less than two children. The Fifth Pay Commission has recommended increasing maternity leave to 135 days and an additional paternity leave of 15 days. The government has also opened central schools, referred to as *Kendriya Vidyalayas,* at various places throughout the country to provide quality education at affordable rates to the children of central government employees.

The central government employees are also entitled to pension with an option to commute up to one-third of it, gratuity and encashment of earned leave. These are benefits to which employees are not required to contribute. The Fifth Pay Commission also recommended raising the retirement age of central government employees from 58 to 60 years. The central government employees can opt to retire voluntarily, under a special scheme, after completing 20 years of service.

In the past, the amount of pension was determined on the basis of a uniform formula of 50 per cent of the average emoluments for a qualifying service of 33 years or more, and proportionately less for a lesser period of service. The average emoluments were to be worked out on the basis of emoluments drawn during the period of 10 months preceding the date of retirement. The Fifth Pay Commission has recommended the existing pensionary benefits up to 67 per cent, the extra 17 per cent over and above 50 per cent, being made up by contributions from the employees to a pension fund. It also suggested that pension benefits be computed based on average emoluments drawn during the last six months of service. The Commission has also recommended an additional pension of one per cent for each year of service beyond 33 years and the indexing of pensions to provide for full neutralisation of the cost of living. It has also recommended the removal of ceilings on gratuity and 100 per cent neutralisation even in the case of family pension. Family pension is payable at 30 per cent of pay subject to some ceiling, to the family of a government employee in case of the latter's death while in service or after.

The total cost of social security on the above benefits is being met from the budgetary sources on a pay-as-you-go basis. The sustainability of these benefits over the long run remains to be seen, particularly with the increase in the number of pensioners and rise in benefits and indexisation of pensions.

References

Bhat, A.K. (1994), "Dangerous Work", *The Hindu Survey of the Environment*, Chennai.

Gonsalves, C. et al. (1993), *Leading Cases on Occupational Health and Safety*, Friedrich Ebert Stiftung, New Delhi.

International Labour Organisation (1998), *World Employment Report, 1997-98,* Geneva.

—— (1998a), *Decent Work,* Geneva.

Subrahmanya, R. K. A.(1995), *Evolution and Status of Social Security Systems in India*, Social Security Association of India and Friedrich Ebert Stiftung, New Delhi.

—— (1999), *Social Security: A Critical Survey*, B.R. Publishing Corporation, Delhi.

Thakur, C.P. (1985), *Corporate Strategy on Fringe Benefits,* Spectrum Publishing House, New Delhi.

4

Financing Social Security: A Human Development Perspective

K. Seeta Prabhu and Sandhya V. Iyer

I. INTRODUCTION

Social security is a term that has traditionally been used by the International Labour Organisation (ILO) to denote protection against economic and social distress caused by the stoppage or fall in income resulting from death, old age, sickness, employment injury, maternity and temporary unemployment (ILO, 1984). The connotation of the term has been broadened by Dreze and Sen (1989), who regard social security as "an *objective* to be pursued through *public means* rather than narrowly defined set of particular strategies". The difference between the two connotations is that the ILO concept is aimed at providing relief in the event of specific contingencies, whereas Dreze and Sen's concept views social security as comprising, in addition, promotional and preventive components such as measures that aim at improving endowments, exchange entitlements, real incomes and social consumption.

The conventional model of social security comprising only protective social security measures is inappropriate for India as less than 8 per cent of the workforce is engaged in regular employment in the organised sector (IAMR, 1999). The informal sector provides the bulk of employment, though the incomes accruing to people from such employment is inadequate, as reflected in the fact that 35.97 per cent of total population or 312 million people were below the poverty line in 1993-94 (Planning Commission, 1997). Income deprivation is an important cause of deprivation in basic education, health and nutrition. The poor also suffer from fluctuating incomes and lack of protection from unexpected contingencies. Thus, if social security is to be meaningful for the poor, the provision of such security has to include promotional as well as protective measures. Moreover, provision of social security cannot be treated in isolation from the goal of attaining higher levels of human development in the country. Social security, in fact, provides the necessary conditions for human development to take place.

While the need for providing social security to India's poor in the above context is immediate, the implementation of requisite measures poses problems on account of enormous resources required to cover the large number of poor on the one hand, and conflicting demands on scarce government resources on the other.[1] The issue can be resolved only if government policy is committed to providing sustained support and is cohesive enough to reap the synergies involved in designing and implementing an integrated package of measures that minimises costs. When compared to these requirements, public policy in India has been sporadic, fragmented across departments and ministries and utterly lacking in focus. Moreover, many of the components of social security are the responsibility of state governments whose political commitment to the cause of the poor varies substantially. It is not surprising, therefore, to find that the situation with respect to social security is quite dismal in India despite some attention being paid to it over the past decades.

In view of the above, this paper makes a preliminary attempt at examining the level and pattern of financing of social security in Indian states from a human development perspective. In the next section we provide the conceptual framework within which the subsequent analysis is set. In section III, the main characteristics of government financing of social security in India are outlined. Section IV is devoted to an examination of the levels and patterns of government financing of social security across 15 major Indian states as well as the centre. In section V, we examine the rank correlation between select variables. In the last section we bring together the main conclusions of the paper and discuss their implications for social security provision in the country.

II. CONCEPTUAL FRAMEWORK

The conceptual framework governing our analysis is set out in the enclosed chart. Financing of social security is considered in the light of the linkages between economic growth and human development. We focus on social security provision by the government alone and do not include in this paper the contribution of households and firms to such provision. Social security is considered a means to achieve human development.

Government policy has two main strands, economic policy and social policy. Economic policy comprises monetary, fiscal and such other policies, though our attention here is only on fiscal policy. A separate social policy is necessitated by the fact that links between economic growth and human development are weak. This is due to structural factors such as unequal distribution of income, asset and employment. Social policy influences fiscal policy through its impact on the level and pattern of social sector expenditure. Additionally, social policy includes in its ambit the creation and nurturing of institutions that facilitate provision of social security. Thus, the government's own social security expenditure as well as the institutional framework in existence together influence public provisioning of social security. Social security measures comprise promotional and protective measures. Promotional social security includes the provision of (a) education, health and nutrition, and (b) assets and employment. Protective social security comprises mainly provision of social insurance and social assistance.

The social security components identified above correspond to "the gradation of measures that proceed, like a set of three concentric circles from wider to narrower domains of specificity while recognising that all three sets of measures are called for" (Guhan, 1994). In Guhan's terms, the outer circle of promotional measures would include macroeconomic and institutional measures of major importance for poverty alleviation that operate at the macro and micro levels. These measures are general in nature and though they are oriented towards the poor, they may not be confined to them. Primary education, primary health and nutrition are cited as examples of this set of measures. The middle circle would comprise measures more directly targeted at the poor. Examples include poverty alleviation programmes such as asset redistribution, employment creation and food security. The impact of these measures is also more direct on the incomes of the poor through which they affect human development levels. The inner circle would contain specific measures aimed at providing relief from or protection against deprivation. These measures are necessary to the extent that at the current juncture deprivation is not or cannot be averted through promotional measures. The benefits accrue to the vulnerable sections after means-testing and are aimed at providing immediate relief of a limited nature.

We have named these three sets of measures as Level I, II and III, respectively. The three sets of measures differ in the time frame that is required by each to have an impact on social security. Level I measures take a fairly long

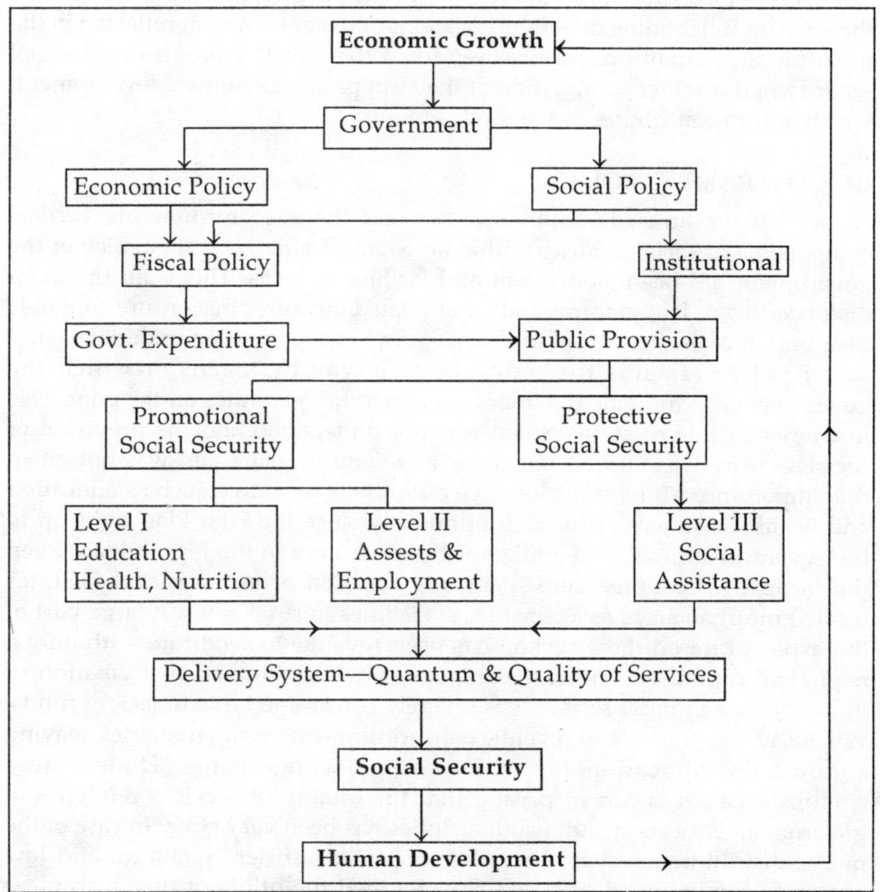

time, stretching over at least a decade or two, to make an impact on economic growth via increased levels of human development. In the case of Level II measures, the time frame within which they affect social security for the poor would be less than that required for the first set of measures. A period of 3-5 years seems reasonable in view of the empirical evidence available with respect to asset and employment programmes implemented in the country. The time frame within which Level III measures make an impact on the livelihoods of the poor is immediate.

It is also obvious that the various measures referred to above cater to different age-groups of the population. Education and nutrition measures target mainly children; employment and asset provision are mainly for those in the working-age-group, and the last set of measures are for the old and destitute who lack alternative means of support. It is also necessary to note that since level I, II and III measures address varying needs of distinct segments of the population over different time periods, they are not mutually exclusive. In fact, it may be argued that they complement each other and ought to, in the first instance, be initiated simultaneously though the number of years over which each set of measures needs to be implemented may vary. The impact of the three sets of measures on social security for the poor depends considerably on the efficient functioning of delivery systems of the government reflected in the quantum and quality of services rendered therein. The provision of social security in this wider connotation of the term promotes human development, which in turn contributes to economic growth.

III. GOVERNMENT POLICY

As against the linkages outlined above and the need to integrate various components of social security within an overall framework, the policy of the government has been ambivalent and lacking in focus. This is all the more disconcerting as land reforms and other related measures that ensure equitable distribution of the benefits of economic growth have not been undertaken and social policy remains the only effective way by means of which the government can mitigate the impact of structural inequities on the poor. This instrumental role of social policy was not understood and the provision of social security was viewed merely as a welfare measure and was not given due importance till recently. Relative allocations to sectors such as education and health have been reduced continuously since the First Plan right up to the Seventh Plan with some hike forthcoming only in the Eighth Plan. Even the meagre allocations were spent on provision of tertiary level facilities located in urban areas as against basic facilities in rural areas. A large part of the expenditure on these sectors has been revenue expenditure with only a negligible capital expenditure component, which implied that creation of infrastructure in these sectors was severely constrained due to lack of funds. What is worse, the bulk of revenue expenditure was spent on salaries, leaving a miniscule allocation for materials and components. Under these circumstances, it is not surprising that the quality of services rendered in government education and health facilities has been very poor.[2] In case of the public distribution system, irregular supply, insufficient quantum and low quality of foodgrains distributed have blunted the utility of this instrument as a measure of ensuring food security. These factors together have led to the phenomenon of chronic underutilisation of social infrastructure created by the government at considerable public cost, perpetuating further the conditions of illiteracy, ill-health and under-nutrition among the poor. Various asset distribution programmes implemented since the Fourth Plan period have also had limited success on account of large amount of leakages and poor implementation. Government's employment programmes have had a greater degree of success though the quantum of employment provided falls far short of the magnitude required for alleviating poverty.

With respect to protective social security, the Directive Principles of State Policy refer to the state's responsibility in ensuring social security, social insurance, and welfare of labour, invalidity and old-age pensions as well as maternity benefits. The provision of social security is a joint responsibility of the Union and state governments as the subject falls under the Concurrent List. Various laws have been passed since Independence to provide a number of protective measures that benefit mainly the organised sector workers. These include legislations governing the payment of provident fund, gratuity, maternity benefits, employment injury, survivor benefits and retirement pensions. The provision of protective social security for the bulk of workers in the unorganised sector and for the self-employed has been negligible and consists mainly of old-age pensions. The first state to introduce legislation for this purpose was Uttar Pradesh in 1957. This was followed by other states during the 1960s and 1970s. Some states such as Kerala and Tamil Nadu have, in addition, various provisions for providing pensions to destitute widows and physically handicapped as well as survivor benefits to families in the event of the death of an earning member due to occupational hazards and the like.

The policy towards social security is marked by a singular lack of appreciation of its broader connotation and its importance for human development. In the absence of a cohesive policy on social security, there is lack of an overall perspective within which various measures may be located. Consequently, the responsibility for implementation of various schemes introduced during the Five Year Plans is scattered across departments and ministries with a plethora of schemes and programmes intending to address the target population divided on the basis of residence, gender and sector.

The problem is particularly acute in the case of programmes for poverty alleviation, health and nutrition, and social security and welfare. Table 1 highlights the problem with respect to these programmes. It is evident that programmes for income security are scattered over as many as six departments belonging to four diverse ministries, viz., Ministry of Rural Areas and Employment, Ministry of Human Resource Development, Ministry of Urban Areas and Employment, and Ministry of Industry. Similarly, programmes for health and nutrition are spread across three departments in two ministries, viz., Ministry of Health and Family Welfare and Ministry of Human Resource Development. Though health and nutrition are complementary to each other, nutrition programmes are the responsibility of the Department of Women and Child Development in the Ministry of Human Resource Development whereas disease control programmes are under the purview of the Department of Public

Health in the Ministry of Health and Family Welfare. Social security provision is again undertaken by three departments spread across three ministries of Finance, Coal and Labour. Given the notorious lack of inter-departmental and inter-ministerial coordination, it is not surprising that the provision of social security in India is piece-meal and haphazard.

An additional factor that compounds this unsatisfactory situation in the Indian context is that several components of social security are the responsibility of state governments.[3] Since the political commitment of governments towards provision of promotional and protective components varies across states, the degree of security available to the poor differs sharply. The state of Kerala, which has been acclaimed for its concern towards human development, has managed to provide an array of promotional as well as protective social security measures despite relatively modest levels of income. The state of Maharashtra has been at the forefront in implementing the Employment Guarantee Scheme, which provides unskilled work in rural areas as a measure of income security, though its efforts in providing protective social security measures has been unsatisfactory. With respect to protective social security, states such as Kerala and Tamil Nadu provide in addition to old-age pensions, various pensions to destitute widows and physically handicapped as well as survivor benefits to families in the event of the death of an earning member due to occupational hazards and the like. However, despite relatively high levels of unemployment, there is a lack of a concerted thrust towards employment generation in these states. Thus, individual states concentrate on specific components of social security and fail to reap the synergies inherent in the integrated provision of promotional and protective measures.

IV. FINANCING OF SOCIAL SECURITY: LEVELS AND PATTERNS

It is surprising that despite the implementation of various schemes by state governments over a fairly long period, discussion on the level and pattern of social security expenditure taken as a whole is conspicuous by its absence. Analysis is confined to specific aspects such as rural development, education, health, protective social security schemes and the like, but rarely do analysts examine state government expenditure within the overall framework of promotional and protective social security. This could partly be due to the non-availability of requisite data on social security in its broader connotation. Most of the items that are of interest are minor heads in budget documents and are not readily accessible across states. The Reserve Bank of India publishes data compiled from state budget documents in its annual article on state finances. However, this data concentrates on the heads reported in the Annual Financial Statement which contains mainly major heads of expenditure and does not cover many of the minor heads that are required for our purposes. The analysis in this paper has been possible on account of being provided access to the data compiled by the National Institute of Public Finance and Policy (NIPFP), New Delhi, from state budget documents.

In what follows, we examine the levels and patterns of promotional and protective social security provision at the level of the central government as well as 15 major Indian states for the period covering the early 1990s. In keeping

Table 1
Distribution of Social Security Programmes Across Departments and Ministries: Union Government, 1998

Sl. no.	Social security programme	Sub-department/ department	Ministry
	Income Security: Assets & Employment		
1.	Jawahar Rojgar Yojana	Rural Employment/Dept. of Rural Employment and Poverty Alleviation	Ministry of Rural Areas and Employment
	(a) Indira Awas Yojana	Housing/Dept. of Rural Employment and Poverty Alleviation	... do ...
	(b) Million Wells Scheme	Other Rural Development Programme/Dept. of Rural Development	... do ...
2.	Integrated Rural Development Programme	Special Programmes for Rural Development/Dept. of Rural Employment and Poverty Alleviation	... do ...
3.	Employment Assurance Scheme	Rural Employment/Dept. of Rural Employment and Poverty Alleviation	... do ...
4.	Training of Rural Youth for Self-employment	Special Programmes for Rural Development/Dept. of Rural Employment and Poverty Alleviation	... do ...
5.	Development of Women and Children in Rural Areas	Other Rural Development Programmes/Dept. of Rural Employment and Poverty Alleviation	... do ...
6.	Mahila Samridhi Yojana	Women's Welfare/Dept. of Women and Child Development	Ministry of Human Resource Development
	(a) Support to Training & Employment Programme	Women's Welfare/Dept. of Women and Child Development	
7.	Nehru Rojgar Yojana	Urban Development/Dept. of Urban Development	Ministry of Urban Affairs & Employment
8.	Prime Minister's Integrated Urban Poverty Eradication Programme for Small Towns	Urban Development/Dept. of Urban Employment and Poverty Alleviation	... do ...
9.	Swarna Jayanti Rojgar Yojana	Urban Development/Dept. of Urban Employment and Poverty Alleviation	... do ...
10.	Prime Minister's Rojgar Yojana	Khadi and Village Industries/Dept. of Small Scale Industries and Agro and Rural Industries	Ministry of Industry
	Health and Nutrition		
1.	Disease Control Programmes like TB, Leprosy, AIDS, etc.	Public Health/Dept. of Health	Ministry of Health and Family Welfare
2.	Reproductive and Child Health Programme- Maternal and Child Health	Family Welfare Services/Dept. of Health and Family welfare	... do ...
3.	Integrated Child Development Services	Social Security & Welfare-Child Welfare/Dept. of Women and Child Development	Ministry of Human Resource Development

with the conceptual framework outlined in Section II, we classify social security expenditure into three categories, viz. Level I, II and III. It may be recalled that Level I includes all those expenditures that contribute to human development in the long run but may not necessarily be directed towards the poor. Included in this category are expenditures on budget heads of elementary education, rural and public health, family welfare and nutrition programmes. Level II includes expenditure on programmes more properly focused on the poor, i.e., asset and income security programmes. Thus, expenditure on budget heads under rural development and rural employment are included in this category. Though Guhan (1993) had identified expenditure on food security as belonging to this category, we were unable to include it owing to non-availability of data for some states like Andhra Pradesh in the NIPFP data set. Expenditure on Level I and II together constitute expenditure on promotional social security. Level III comprises expenditure on protective social security. In the Indian context, expenditure under the budget head of social security and welfare captures this dimension[4].

In Tables 2-4 we set out the data pertaining to social security expenditures on Level I, II and III for the Centre as well as 15 major Indian states. Averages for the years 1991-92 to 1994-95 are presented in terms of share in Net State Domestic Product (Table 2), share in total revenue expenditure (Table 3), and share of individual components in total social security expenditure which is defined by us to constitute the combined expenditure on Level I, II and III (Table 4). The following significant features that emerge from a perusal of the tables may be highlighted:

1. Total expenditure on social security at the level of 15 major states constituted only 2.63 per cent of SDP and 16.63 per cent of total revenue expenditure. There was however, considerable variation across states. Bihar recorded the highest level of expenditure, 4.15 per cent of NSDP and 22.04 per cent of total revenue expenditure, whereas Punjab reported the lowest levels at 1.33 per cent of NSDP and 9.63 per cent of revenue expenditure. Kerala's level (3.55 per cent of NSDP and 18.82 per cent of revenue expenditure) was equalled or exceeded only by the states of Assam and Bihar. Significantly, the high income states of Punjab, Maharashtra and Haryana recorded levels of expenditure that were lower than the 15 states' average whereas the low income states of Assam, Bihar, Madhya Pradesh, Orissa, Rajasthan and Uttar Pradesh recorded levels substantially higher than the mean. Middle income states that recorded relatively high levels of expenditure were Kerala, Tamil Nadu and Karnataka in that order.

2. Within overall social security expenditures, the emphasis on various components differed across states. Level I measures (comprising elementary education, rural and public health, family welfare and nutrition) were given greater importance by the three southern states of Kerala, Karnataka and Tamil Nadu; Gujarat among high income states and Assam, Bihar, Madhya Pradesh, Rajasthan and Uttar Pradesh among low income states. In all these states, the expenditure on Level I items was higher than the average for the 15 states both in terms of proportion of NSDP and revenue expenditure. However, Kerala's level of 2.77 per cent

Table 2
State-wise Proportion of Government Expenditure on Social Security in NSDP, 1991-95

(per cent)

Sl. no.	State	Level I					Level II			Level I+II	Level III	Level I+II+III
		Ele. Edn.	Rl. & Ph.	F.W.	Nutrition	Total	Assets	Emplt.	Total	Promo-tional	Protec-tive	Total
[1]	[2]	[3]	[4]	[5]	[6]	[7=3+4+5+6]	[8]	[9]	[10=8+9]	[11]	[12]	[13=11+12]
1.	Andhra Pradesh	1.19	0.15	0.18	0.04	1.56	0.29	0.29	0.58	2.14	0.19	2.33
2.	Assam	2.92	0.22	0.20	0.04	3.38	0.23	0.07	0.30	3.68	0.20	3.88
3.	Bihar	2.16	0.18	0.23	0.03	2.60	0.22	0.81	1.04	3.64	0.51	4.15
4.	Gujarat	1.60	0.14	0.13	0.25	2.13	0.18	0.21	0.39	2.52	0.10	2.62
5.	Haryana	0.99	0.11	0.11	0.08	1.29	0.07	0.10	0.17	1.46	0.63	2.09
6.	Karnataka	1.59	0.04	0.17	0.16	1.95	0.22	0.21	0.43	2.39	0.44	2.83
7.	Kerala	2.37	0.16	0.21	0.04	2.77	0.12	0.27	0.39	3.16	0.39	3.55
8.	Maharashtra	0.73	0.10	0.09	0.04	0.95	0.04	0.29	0.33	1.28	0.15	1.44
9.	Madhya Pradesh	1.81	0.18	0.17	0.06	2.22	0.12	0.49	0.61	2.83	0.21	3.04
10.	Orissa	1.53	0.16	0.24	0.12	2.05	0.15	0.55	0.70	2.75	0.48	3.24
11.	Punjab	0.72	0.16	0.10	0.00	0.98	0.02	0.07	0.09	1.07	0.26	1.33
12.	Rajasthan	2.09	0.24	0.24	0.08	2.65	0.28	0.33	0.62	3.27	0.14	3.41
13.	Tamil Nadu	1.71	0.12	0.19	0.62	2.64	0.11	0.31	0.42	3.06	0.38	3.45
14.	Uttar Pradesh	1.67	0.22	0.25	0.02	2.16	0.22	0.43	0.65	2.82	0.23	3.04
15.	West Bengal	1.16	0.14	0.13	0.02	1.45	0.10	0.31	0.41	1.86	0.21	2.07
16.	Mean	1.46	0.15	0.17	0.11	1.89	0.15	0.33	0.48	2.37	0.26	2.63
17.	Centre	0.02	0.00	0.01	0.00	0.03	0.02	0.04	0.07	0.10	0.05	0.15

Source: Computed from NIPFP Data Bank & Reserve Bank of India (1998), *Report on Currency and Finance: 1997-98*, Vol. II. Statistical Statements, p. 6.

of NSDP and 14.71 per cent of revenue expenditure, was exceeded only by Assam. Interestingly, the high-income states of Punjab, Maharashtra and Haryana incurred expenditure levels that were substantially lower than the mean.

3. Within Level I expenditures, overwhelming emphasis was placed on only one component, viz., elementary education, with other components of rural and public health, family welfare and nutrition receiving negligible allocations (Table 4). Elementary education alone accounted for 50 to 75 per cent of total revenue expenditure on social security in most states. The allocations to rural and public health were negligible and hovered around 0.2 per cent of NSDP, with Karnataka recording the lowest level of 0.04 per cent of NSDP on this head. In terms of the proportion of revenue expenditure, most of the states reported spending less than 1 per cent of total revenue expenditure on rural and public health with the level being marginally above 1 per cent in the states of Assam, Madhya Pradesh, Punjab, Rajasthan, Uttar Pradesh and West Bengal. The situation with respect to nutrition was pathetic with the level of expenditure being less than 0.1 per cent of NSDP and less than 0.5 per cent of revenue expenditure in most states. The level of expenditure was higher in Tamil Nadu (0.62 per cent of NSDP and 3.26 per cent of revenue expenditure) followed by Gujarat (0.25 per cent of NSDP and 1.68 per cent of revenue expenditure) and Orissa (0.12 per cent of NSDP and 0.63 per cent of revenue expenditure). Among these states, the low level of expenditure in Andhra Pradesh may be due to the fact that the state implements a food subsidy programme that benefits a majority of population and therefore the emphasis on direct nutrition support programmes may be minimal. In Punjab and Haryana, rural prosperity may render such schemes redundant.

4. Expenditure on Level II measures (asset and employment programmes) was relatively high (i.e. higher than the 15 states average) in the states of Andhra Pradesh, Bihar, Madhya Pradesh, Orissa, Rajasthan and Uttar Pradesh. Among these, four states, viz., Bihar, Madhya Pradesh, Rajasthan and Uttar Pradesh incurred relatively high expenditure on Level I measures as well. Andhra Pradesh, which incurred relatively low expenditure on Level I measures, spent relatively high amounts on asset and employment programmes. Within Level II measures, employment programmes were much more important than asset programmes in all states except Assam and Karnataka. In Andhra Pradesh, both components received more or less similar allocations.

5. Expenditure on Level III measures was very low accounting for less than 1 per cent of NSDP in all states under consideration. Haryana recorded the highest levels of expenditure in this category (0.63 per cent of NSDP and 4.46 per cent of total revenue expenditure). These measures were relatively important in Kerala, Karnataka and Tamil Nadu among middle income states, and Bihar and Orissa among low-income states. The lowest level of spending was in Gujarat (0.10 per cent of NSDP and 0.64 per cent of revenue expenditure).

Table 3

State-wise Proportion of Government Expenditure on Social Security in Total Revenue Expenditure, 1991-95

(per cent)

Sl. no.	State	Level I					Level II		Level I+II	Level III		Level I+II+III
		Ele. Edn.	Rl. & Ph.	F.W.	Nutrition	Total	Assets	Emplt.	Total	Promotional	Protective	Total
[1]	[2]	[3]	[4]	[5]	[6]	[7=3+4+5+6]	[8]	[9]	[10=8+9]	[11]	[12]	[13=11+12]
1.	Andhra Pradesh	7.84	0.97	1.20	0.25	10.26	1.91	1.94	3.84	14.11	1.25	15.36
2.	Assam	15.47	1.18	1.05	0.23	17.93	1.21	0.37	1.58	19.51	1.08	20.59
3.	Bihar	11.48	0.98	1.20	0.15	13.81	1.18	4.32	5.50	19.31	2.73	22.04
4.	Gujarat	10.55	0.95	0.86	1.68	14.04	1.19	1.35	2.54	16.58	0.64	17.22
5.	Haryana	6.98	0.76	0.75	0.55	9.05	0.51	0.70	1.22	10.26	4.46	14.73
6.	Karnataka	9.88	0.25	1.03	0.98	12.14	1.36	1.32	2.69	14.82	2.75	17.57
7.	Kerala	12.57	0.84	1.09	0.20	14.71	0.64	1.43	2.07	16.77	2.05	18.82
8.	Maharashtra	5.99	0.80	0.73	0.30	7.81	0.36	2.40	2.75	10.57	1.25	11.82
9.	Madhya Pradesh	10.56	1.08	0.99	0.33	12.96	0.71	2.85	3.56	16.52	1.25	17.77
10.	Orissa	8.04	0.85	1.26	0.63	10.77	0.79	2.88	3.67	14.44	2.54	16.98
11.	Punjab	5.20	1.18	0.70	0.02	7.10	0.13	0.49	0.63	7.73	1.90	9.63
12.	Rajasthan	11.20	1.26	1.30	0.44	14.21	1.52	1.79	3.32	17.52	0.76	18.28
13.	Tamil Nadu	9.05	0.64	1.03	3.26	13.99	0.60	1.63	2.23	16.22	2.03	18.25
14.	Uttar Pradesh	9.75	1.28	1.48	0.11	12.62	1.29	2.53	3.82	16.44	1.33	17.77
15.	West Bengal	8.71	1.06	1.02	0.12	10.90	0.78	2.33	3.11	14.01	1.55	15.57
16.	Mean	9.23	0.94	1.06	0.67	11.91	0.97	2.08	3.05	14.96	1.67	16.63
17.	Centre	0.10	0.03	0.07	0.01	0.21	0.13	0.28	0.40	0.62	0.30	0.91

Source: Computed from NIPFP Data Bank.

Table 4

State-wise Share of Government Expenditure on Components of Social Security in Total Social Security Expenditure, 1991-95

(per cent)

Sl.	States	Level I					Level II		Level I+II	Level III	
no.		Ele. Edn.	Rl. & Ph.	F.W.	Nutrition	Total	Assets	Emplt.	Total	Promot-ional	Protec-tive
[1]	[2]	[3]	[4]	[5]	[6]	[7=3+4+5+6]	[8]	[9]	[10=8+9]	[11]	[12]
1.	Andhra Pradesh	51.06	6.29	7.80	1.63	66.79	12.42	12.61	25.03	91.81	8.19
2.	Assam	75.11	5.74	5.10	1.14	87.09	5.87	1.79	7.67	94.75	5.25
3.	Bihar	52.09	4.44	5.43	0.70	62.65	5.37	19.58	24.95	87.60	12.40
4.	Gujarat	61.28	5.53	4.97	9.75	81.53	6.91	7.86	14.76	96.29	3.71
5.	Haryana	47.42	5.13	5.12	3.77	61.44	3.48	4.77	8.25	69.69	30.31
6.	Karnataka	56.23	1.42	5.85	5.58	69.08	7.76	7.54	15.29	84.37	15.63
7.	Kerala	66.78	4.47	5.82	1.08	78.14	3.39	7.58	10.97	89.12	10.88
8.	Maharashtra	50.67	6.74	6.15	2.54	66.10	3.03	20.27	23.30	89.40	10.60
9.	Madhya Pradesh	59.43	6.06	5.55	1.88	72.92	4.02	16.03	20.05	92.97	7.03
10.	Orissa	47.31	4.99	7.43	3.70	63.43	4.66	16.95	21.61	85.04	14.96
11.	Punjab	54.02	12.23	7.32	0.16	73.73	1.36	5.14	6.49	80.22	19.78
12.	Rajasthan	61.28	6.89	7.11	2.42	77.71	8.34	9.79	18.13	95.84	4.16
13.	Tamil Nadu	49.60	3.53	5.62	17.88	76.63	3.30	8.94	12.24	88.87	11.13
14.	Uttar Pradesh	54.87	7.22	8.30	0.63	71.03	7.26	14.23	21.49	92.52	7.48
15.	West Bengal	55.99	6.78	6.53	0.77	70.06	4.98	14.98	19.96	90.02	9.98
16.	Mean	55.52	5.66	6.40	4.05	71.63	5.81	12.51	18.32	89.94	10.06
17.	Centre	11.44	3.14	7.46	1.26	23.30	14.07	30.17	44.24	67.54	32.46

Source: Social Security Expenditure from NIPFP Data Bank.

6. When the shares were considered in terms of promotional and protective measures, with Level I and II constituting the former category and Level III constituting the latter, it is evident that promotional measures accounted for a share of 70 per cent (Haryana) to 96 per cent (Gujarat) across states (Table 4) with the 15 states average being 90 per cent. Protective measures, which provide immediate relief to the destitute, were paid greater attention only in Haryana where the relative share in total social security expenditure exceeded 30 per cent. Other states reporting a relatively high share exceeding the mean for 15 states were Karnataka (16 per cent) and Orissa (15 per cent) while Bihar, Kerala and Tamil Nadu recorded a share of 11 to 13 per cent.
7. The centre's allocations to social security constituted only 0.15 per cent of Gross Domestic Product and less than 1 per cent of total revenue expenditure. Over 44 per cent of the centre's expenditure was spent on asset and employment programmes (Level II measures), 32 per cent on social assistance programmes (Level III measures) and 23 per cent on Level I measures. Within Level I, elementary education constituted a major share followed by family welfare, and rural and public health in that order.

V. SOCIAL SECURITY EXPENDITURE, POVERTY AND TAX REVENUE

We computed rank correlations between some of the variables considered above in order to understand better the links between social security expenditure, income and human poverty and tax revenue. We used the computation of Prabhu and Kamdar (1998) on the extent of human poverty across 15 major Indian states for the purpose. Since income and human poverty are negative indicators, the ordering of the states was done in an inverse manner with the state recording the lowest level of poverty being ranked 1 and the state with the highest level of poverty being ranked 15. The data for income and human poverty are reported in Table 5 and rank correlations in Table 6.

It is interesting to note from Table 5 that states with relatively high incomes do not necessarily have low levels of poverty. In fact, the relatively rich state of Maharashtra had over 36 per cent of its population below the poverty line in 1993-94 placing it at the 10th rank (below states such as Tamil Nadu and West Bengal) when 15 major states were ranked in inverse order of incidence of poverty. The state's position with respect to human poverty[5], calculated as average deprivation with respect to three outcome indicators—percentage of population illiterate, percentage of population not expected to live up to 40 years of age and percentage of children undernourished—was even worse. In 1989-93, Maharashtra had nearly 41 per cent of population under human poverty (Prabhu and Kamdar, 1998). Despite these unfavourable factors, government expenditure on social security was among the lowest among 15 states. Also interesting was the fact that even among the two high income states with similar economic conditions, viz., Haryana and Punjab, the former chose to allocate higher amounts to protective social security measures (Level III expenditures) as compared to the latter.

Rank correlations of expenditure on various levels of social security as proportion of NSDP with income and human poverty (Table 6) also provided interesting insights. Among the three levels of expenditure, ranks of states on

Table 5
Selected State-wise Indicators of HPIM, IPOV and TASDP

Sl. no.	State	HPIM 1989-93	IPOV 1993-94	TASDP 1991-95
1.	Andhra Pradesh	46.23	22.19	10.38
2.	Assam	43.26	40.86	0.39
3.	Bihar	54.50	54.96	16.24
4.	Gujarat	39.75	24.21	13.07
5.	Haryana	36.35	25.05	10.30
6.	Karnataka	43.62	33.16	14.85
7.	Kerala	20.09	25.43	17.13
8.	Maharashtra	40.84	36.86	9.45
9.	Madhya Pradesh	50.18	42.52	12.09
10.	Orissa	46.13	48.56	11.32
11.	Punjab	38.35	11.77	8.72
13.	Rajathan	47.02	27.41	12.50
14.	Tamil Nadu	38.11	35.03	15.54
15.	Uttar Pradesh	51.74	40.85	11.86
16.	West Bengal	44.38	35.66	10.65

Note: (a) HPIM—Human Poverty Index Modified; (b) IPOV—Income Poverty Index (head count ratio); (c) TASDP—Tax to SDP Ratio.

Sources: (a) HPIM from Prabhu and Kamdar, 1998; (b) IPOV from Malhotra, R., 1997. (c) TASDP computed from RBI Bulletin and Report on Currency and Finance.

Table 6
Rank Correlation

Sl. no.	Indicator	Value
1.	HPIM & SSES I	–0.14
2.	IPOV & SSES II	–0.44
3.	IPOV & SSES III	–0.28
4.	TASDP & SSES T	0.71
5.	TASDP & SSES I	0.70
6.	TASDP & SSES II	0.44
7.	TASDP & SSES III	0.26

Note: (a) Rank correlations computed for 15 major Indian states; (b) HPIM—Human Poverty Index Modified; (c) IPOV—Income Poverty Index (head count ratio); (d) TASDP—Tax to SDP Ratio; (e) SSES T, SSES I, SSES II, SSES III, indicate respectively share in NSDP of Total, Level I, Level II, Level III Social Security Expenditure.

Sources: (a) HPIM from Prabhu and Kamdar, 1998; (b) IPOV from Malhotra, R., 1997; (c) TASDP computed from RBI Bulletin and Report on Currency and Finance; (d) Social Security Expenditure from NIPFP Data Bank.

Level II expenditures were better related to ranks on incidence of income poverty.[6] The rank correlation between income poverty and Level III expenditures followed next in order of importance with the lowest value being reported for Level I expenditure and human poverty. The results are not very surprising in view of the fact that unlike programmes for improving education and health, asset and wage employment programmes were designed specifically to augment the incomes of those below the poverty line.

Tax Effort and Social Security Expenditure

Another important question is whether social security provision is related to the tax revenue available to states. This question assumes importance in view of the trend observed internationally where countries providing a high level of social security have relatively high tax-GDP ratio often around 30 per cent or more. The data for Indian states could be considered from two points of view, viz., ratio of total tax revenue including states' share in central taxes to NSDP and states' own-tax revenue to NSDP. We have opted for the broader definition that includes states' share in central taxes. It is evident from Table 5 that even when the broad concept is used, the extent of tax revenue raised falls considerably short of the norms observed internationally. More importantly, the rank correlation between tax ratio and social security expenditure as percentage of NSDP is positive and fairly high for total and Level I social security expenditure pointing to the fact that availability of higher tax revenues could translate into higher social security expenditures.

VI. CONCLUDING REMARKS

The above empirical analysis indicates that, overall the level of expenditures incurred by the centre and the states on concerns of social security seem exceedingly paltry in relation to the magnitude of deprivation in the country. There is an overwhelming emphasis on promotional social security measures, which by their very nature, would yield benefits to households as well as the economy only in the long run. Even within promotional measures, there is a difference in emphasis, with some states emphasising education and others giving greater importance to asset and employment programmes. There does seem to exist a trade-off between these two sets of measures as evident from the experience of Assam and Kerala which have placed overwhelming emphasis on elementary education to the neglect of direct poverty alleviation programmes. There is not much evidence of a balanced package of promotional and protective measures being implemented in any of the states. The utter negligence of rural and public health in all states is a serious cause of concern. Given this fragmented and inadequate provision of social security by the government on the one hand and the large number of poor who depend on public provisioning for minimal social security on the other, the chances of attaining better levels of social security and human development in the foreseeable future seem remote.

An important constraint that further aggravates the dismal situation is the fiscal crunch being faced by the state governments since the mid-1980s. The situation has deteriorated in the 1990s with the initiation of economic reforms. This has also resulted in a deceleration in real per capita expenditure incurred by the state governments on social services in all states except Kerala and Tamil Nadu (Prabhu and Sarker, 1998). Under the circumstances, the states may find it increasingly difficult to implement a more comprehensive scheme of social security that would demand higher allocations from budgetary resources. It was observed that there existed a positive and fairly high correlation between ranking of states on the basis of tax-NSDP ratio and proportion of NSDP spent on social security. Thus, the question of social security provision is inextricably liked with fiscal reforms. The scope of fiscal reform should encompass not only taxation of hitherto untapped sectors such as agriculture but also cover the gamut of issues comprising restructuring of state government expenditure to reduce the burden of non-merit subsidies, imposition of reasonable user charges for social services, insurance schemes where feasible as in the case of curative health care and coverage of some contingencies for the poor households. Needless to add, reforms are also required for improving the pattern of expenditure within education and health sectors. These measures should be aimed at making the delivery systems for social security function more efficiently as they play a pivotal role in translating increased allocations into better social security outcomes for the poor.

Notes

1. An estimate by the World Bank (1995) for the health sector indicated the magnitude of resources required in just four Indian states for bringing the quantum and quality of services to acceptable levels. The resource requirements indicated were of the order of Rs. 1,51,839 million for filling up the gap in infrastructure facilities and an annual recurring cost of Rs. 46,588 million to maintain the infrastructure. This implied that governments of the concerned states had to spend additionally 57 to 163 per cent of their annual total government expenditure on health and family welfare. In the case of education, Ramachandran et al. (1997) have estimated that the low attainment states of Bihar, Madhya Pradesh, Rajasthan and Uttar Pradesh would have to spend 5 per cent of their State Domestic Product every year for a period of five years in order to achieve the target of universal primary education.
2. For further details on these issues, see Prabhu, 1999.
3. Though education is in the Concurrent List implying that both the union and the state governments have an equal responsibility towards the development of this sector, in effect, it is the state governments that bear the bulk of expenditure on this head. In 1990-91, the share of the union government was confined to only 12 per cent of total government expenditure on the sector whereas the state governments had to incur 88 per cent of the expenditure (Tilak, 1995). Ironically, though health is a state subject, the union government plays an important role on account of expenditure on family welfare and had a share of 25 per cent in total government expenditure on the subject in 1990-91 (World Bank, 1995).
4. We considered including expenditure under the budget head of welfare of Scheduled Castes and Scheduled Tribes in this category but refrained from doing so as the expenditure incurred is on a variety of schemes affecting various age-groups and is a mixture of both direct and indirect payments. Since our focus was on direct payments to the destitute, we confined our analysis to expenditure on social security and welfare alone.
5. The methodology for calculation of human poverty in Prabhu and Kamdar (1998) is different from that of the UNDP (1997). The UNDP included indicators representing three dimensions, viz. deprivation in knowledge, deprivation in longevity and deprivation in decent living standard in terms of economic provisioning to calculate the Human Poverty Index (HPI). The indicators represent both outcomes as well as inputs that determine these outcomes. Considering this procedure unsatisfactory, Prabhu and Kamdar used only outcome indicators representing deprivation in education, health and nutrition for calculating the human poverty index, giving equal weights to the three dimensions.
6. The value of the rank correlation is negative on account of poverty being a negative indicator.

References

Dreze, J. and A. K. Sen (1989), *Hunger and Public Action*, Clarendon Press, Oxford.

Guhan, S. (1993), "Social Security for the Poor in the Unorganised Sector: A Feasible Blueprint for India", in Parikh, K. and R. Sudarshan (eds.), *Human Development and Structural Adjustment*, Macmillan, Madras, pp.203-37

—— (1994), "Social Security Options for Developing Countries", *International Labour Review*, Vol. 133, No. 1, pp. 35-53.

Institute of Applied Manpower Research (IAMR) (1999), *Human Resource Profile—India: Some Selected Statistics*, Manak Publications Pvt. Ltd., Delhi.

International Labour Organisation (ILO) (1984), *Introduction of Social Security*, 3rd Edition, Geneva.

Malhotra, Rajiv (1997), "Incidence of Poverty in India: Towards a Concensus on Estimating the Poor", *The Indian Journal of Labour Economics*, Vol. 40, No. 1.

Planning Commission (1997), *Estimate of Poverty*, Government of India, Press Information Bureau, New Delhi.

Prabhu, K. Seeta (1998), "Social Sectors in Economic Development", *Journal of Social and Economic Development*, Vol. 1, No. 2, pp. 268-287.

—— (1999), "Social Sectors during Economic Reforms: The Indian Experience", *Oxford Development Studies*, Vol. 27, No. 2, pp. 187-200

—— and Sangita Kamdar (1998), "Human Poverty and Income Poverty: Linkages and Implications", Paper presented at the Symposium on *Reforming India's Social Sectors: Strategies and Prospects*, Department of Economics, Mumbai (*mimeo*).

—— and P.C. Sarker (1998), *Trends in Social Sector Expenditure in Indian States: 1974-75 to 1995-96*, Department of Economics, University of Mumbai (mimeo).

Ramachandran, V.K., V. Rawal and M. Swaminathan (1997), "Investment Gaps in Primary Education: A State-wise Study", *Economic and Political Weekly*, Vol. 32, pp. 39-52.

Tilak, J.B.G. (1995), *Costs and Financing of Education in India: A Review of Issues, Problems and Prospects*, Research Projects on Strategies and Financing of Human Development, Centre for Development Studies, Thiruvananthapuram.

UNDP (1997), *Human Development Report*, United Nations Development Programme, Oxford University Press, New York.

World Bank (1995), *India: Policy and Finance Options for Strengthening Primary Health Care Services*, Report No. 13042, IN.

PART II

Food, Nutrition, Health and Housing

5

Food Security : Emerging Concerns

R. Radhakrishna

I. INTRODUCTION

The concept of food security has undergone considerable modifications in recent years. Food availability and stability were considered good measures of food security till the seventies and the achievement of self-sufficiency was accorded high priority in the food policies of developing countries. However, though some countries were successful in achieving self-sufficiency by increasing their food production and could also improve their capacity to cope with year-to-year fluctuations in production, they could not solve the problem of chronic household food insecurity.

This necessitated a change in approach and as a result food energy intake of the vulnerable groups is now given prominence in assessing food security. It has become common practice to estimate the number of food insecure households by comparing their calorie intake with required norms. However, the widely accepted norms of the level of calorie intake required for overcoming under-nutrition have been questioned. Nutritionists argue that the energy intake is a poor measure of nutritional status, which depends not only on the nutrient intake but also on non-nutrient food attributes, privately and publicly provided inputs and health status (Martorell and Ho, 1984). The non-food factors which influence biological absorption are also considered as important for food security as food factors.

It is suggested that the assessment of malnutrition should be based on output measures rather than input measures (ibid). The suggested output measures include anthropometric measures, clinical signs of malnutrition, biochemical indicators and physical activity. Output indicators are more closely related to health and functional capacity. Among the output measures, anthropometric measures are considered to have an advantage over other indicators since body measurements are sensitive to even minor levels of malnutrition whereas biochemical and clinical indicators, on the other hand, are useful only when the level of malnutrition is extreme.

In policy design, a distinction is made between the hardcore of chronically food insecure households and the transitory, which temporarily are subject to hunger during the off-season, drought and inflationary years and so forth.

Transitory food insecurity is associated with the risks related to either access or the availability of food. Policies such as those relating to price stabilisation, credit, crop-insurance and temporary employment creation are initiated for stabilising the consumption of the vulnerable groups. In contrast, the problem of chronic food insecurity is primarily associated with poverty. The strategy to overcome this problem includes short-term intervention to raise the purchasing power of the poor through the endowments of land and non-land assets and by generating employment opportunities, as well as long-term growth-mediated interventions to improve food availability and raise incomes (agricultural production programmes, infrastructure, human resource development, etc.).

India is one of the few countries which have experimented with a broad spectrum of programmes for improving food security. It has already made substantial progress in terms of overcoming transient food insecurity by giving priority to self-sufficiency in foodgrains and through public procurement and distribution of foodgrains, employment programmes, etc. However, despite a significant reduction in the incidence of poverty (from 55 per cent in 1973-74 to 36 per cent in 1993-94), chronic food insecurity persists as a large proportion of India's population (a) is still below the poverty line, (b) has no access to safe drinking water and primary health care, and (c) has been exposed to adverse environment hygienic conditions.

This paper reviews the trends in food and nutrition deprivation in India using a wide range of input and output measures, including per capita consumption of food, per capita food energy intake, and malnutrition based on anthropometric measures. The focus of the paper is on household food and nutrition deprivation rather than food security at the national level based on conventional criteria such as self-sufficiency and stability in food availability.

II. TRENDS IN FOOD PRODUCTION

Over the years, India has made rapid progress in the production of food (Table 1). The annual growth rate of food production including non-cereal food increased from 2.1 per cent during the 1960s to 3.0 per cent in the subsequent decade and further to 3.8 per cent during the 1980s.[1] Between 1960 and 1980, food production barely kept pace with the population but in the 1980s per capita food production increased at a satisfactory rate of 1.6 per cent per annum. There seems to have been some diversification in food production in the 1980s on account of the impressive growth of output of oilseeds and livestock products. The diversification of food production more or less conforms to the growth pattern of domestic demand.

India achieved near self-sufficiency in the availability of foodgrains by the mid-seventies. The trend rate of foodgrain production improved from 2.3 per cent during the 1970s to 2.8 per cent in the eighties (Sawant and Achuthan, 1995). It is particularly noteworthy that India could build enough buffer stocks to cope with year-to-year variations in foodgrain production. Field studies reveal that during the 1987 drought, foodgrain price stability, PDS supplies and the availability of consumption credit enabled drought affected villages to maintain their consumption at the same level as in normal years (Acharya, 1989; Bidinger, et al., 1990). The annual fluctuations in the per capita availability of

Table 1
Annualised Compound Growth Rates of Food and Agricultural Production

(Per cent per annum)

Year	Food production		Agricultural production	
	Aggregate	Per capita	Aggregate	Per capita
1961-62 – 1971-73	2.11	-0.10	2.03	0.81
1971-73 – 1981-83	3.00	0.84	3.20	0.94
1981-83 – 1991-93	3.77	1.62	3.82	1.67
1989-91 – 1995-97	2.66	2.21	0.18	0.36

Sources: FAO, *State of Food and Agriculture*; CSO, *Statistical Pocket Book, India*.

foodgrains declined in the eighties and nineties when compared to the previous period (Rao and Radhakrishna, 1997) and there was a decline in the seasonal as well as regional variations in the prices of foodgrains (Bhalla, 1994).

The growth of foodgrain production slowed down in the nineties. The trend growth rate during the decade has been lower than the historical growth rate. What is particularly noteworthy is that the up-trend in foodgrain production has barely kept pace with population growth. Ironically, even at the slow growth rate of foodgrain production, the supply has outstripped the effective market demand and the nineties has seen a rapid increase in the stock of foodgrains held by the government. Disposal of stocks has become a cause of concern.

The relative cereal price which showed a decline in the seventies and eighties, registered a rise in the nineties. An increase in cereal price significantly reduced the calorie intake of the poor as is brought out by available food price elasticity estimates which show that for the poor, the food (calorie) price elasticity is numerically large. The upward trend in the real price of cereal in the nineties had coincided with a slowdown in the decline of poverty. Moreover, in high inflation years cereal price rose even higher (Ravi, 2000).

III. FOOD AND NUTRIENT INTAKE

1. Cereal Consumption

NSS consumption data reveal that the per capita consumption of cereals has been declining since the early seventies (Rao and Radhakrishna, 1997). Between 1970-71 and 1993-94, the per capita cereal consumption declined by 0.52 per cent per annum in the rural areas and by 0.27 per cent per annum in urban areas. The all-India rural per capita consumption fell from 15.25 kg per capita/ month in 1977-78 to 13.40 kg in 1993-94 while the urban consumption fell from 11.62 kg to 10.60 kg during the same period.

The declining trend is visible across all the states with the exception of Kerala, West Bengal and Orissa. It is very prominent in Punjab and Haryana. The absolute fall of about 4 kg per capita per month in the rural areas of Punjab and Haryana and about 2 kg in urban areas occurred mainly due to a reduced consumption of coarse cereals. What is striking is the low per capita intake of cereals in Punjab, the most prosperous state (11 kg in rural areas and 9 kg in the urban areas in 1993-94) and high intake in the backward state of Orissa (16 kg in rural areas and 13.40 kg in urban areas). This is partly due to the diversification of the food basket in Punjab in favour of non-cereal food, particularly milk and milk products, egg and fish, vegetables and fruits, etc. It merits mention that cereal price induced inflation would hurt the poor of the backward regions most.

2. Food Consumption

The NSS estimates of consumption of food items and nutrients for India for the years 1972-73 and 1993-94 indicate that the per capita cereal intake declined although the per capita total expenditure in real terms increased by 1.17 and 1.31 per cent per annum in rural and urban areas, respectively (Table 2). However, the fall in cereal consumption was offset by an increase in the consumption of non-cereal food. In fact, the per capita food expenditure increased at 0.49 per cent per annum in rural areas and 0.51 per cent per annum in urban areas of India. However, these increases were not commensurate with the increase in the per capita total expenditure. In the recent period, the per capita food expenditure tended to stagnate or decline (Ravi, 2000).

Despite this moderate increase in food expenditure, the nutrient intake did not improve between 1972-73 and 1993-94: the per capita calorie intake declined at 0.25 per cent per annum in rural areas and 0.08 per cent in urban areas. The

Table 2
Growth Rates of Per Capita Cereal, Food and Total Expenditure at 1990-91 Prices and Per Capita Calorie Intake

(Per cent per annum)

	Bottom 30%	Middle 40%	Top 30%	All classess
Rural				
Per capita food expenditure				
1970-89	0.09	-0.58	-1.28	-0.69
1990-98	-1.38	-2.34	-2.43	-2.14
Per capita calorie expenditure				
1970-89	1.34	0.87	0.74	0.89
1990-98	-0.48	-0.78	-1.12	-0.88
Per capita total expenditure				
1970-89	0.16	0.15	0.40	1.18
1990-98	-0.96	-0.63	-1.76	-1.53
Per capita cereal expenditure				
1970-89	1.71	1.40	1.45	1.54
1990-98	1.19	1.11	1.23	1.18
Per capita food expenditure				
1970-89	0.07	-0.33	-0.18	-0.18
1990-98	-0.67	-0.55	0.30	-0.28
Per capita calorie expenditure				
1970-89	1.29	1.19	0.69	0.97
1990-98	-0.08	-0.03	-0.23	-0.08
Per capita total expenditure				
1970-89	0.31	0.05	0.32	0.21
1990-98	-0.58	-0.74	-0.05	-0.44
Per capita cereal expenditure				
1970-89	1.44	1.50	1.40	1.45
1990-98	1.70	2.27	3.31	2.77

Source: Ravi (2000).

stagnancy or marginal decrease in the food energy intake despite improvement in incomes was due to the decline in the consumption of cereals, which is the cheapest source of calories.

For the lowest 30 per cent of the population, there has hardly been any increase in the per capita cereal expenditure at constant prices in the rural as well as urban areas. It seems, the improvement in economic access to food made possible by income growth did not result in a higher consumption of cereals.[2] The saturation in cereal consumption would not be a major cause of concern if the food energy intake levels of the poor were nutritionally adequate. The per capita calorie intake in 1993-94 was 1,678 kcal per day in rural areas and 1,682 kcal per day in urban areas (Table 3). This section of the population was deprived of an adequate diet that would provide the required food energy.[3] Their low nutrient intake would have an adverse effect on the health and nutritional status of both adults and children.

Table 3
Average Per Capita Calorie Intake in India

Expenditure classes	Rural				Urban			
	1972 -73	1977 -78	1993 -94	1972 -94	1972 -73	1977 -78	1993 -94	1972 -94
	K.Cal./day			Annual growth rate (%)	K.Cal./day			Annual growth rate (%)
Lower 30%	1504	1630	1678	0.4	1579	1701	1682	0.2
Middle 40%	2170	2296	2119	-0.1	2154	2438	2111	0.0
Top 30%	3161	3190	2672	-0.6	2572	2979	2405	-0.1
All classes	2268	2364	2152	-0.2	2107	2379	2071	0.0

Source: Rao and Radhakrishna (1997).

There has also been a substantial diversification of the consumption basket of the poor in favour of non-cereal items, particularly non-food items.[4] The changes in the composition of diet have increased the cost of calories (Radhakrishna and Ravi, 1992). The non-food expenditure at constant prices has been expanding among all income groups of rural and urban areas throughout but its rate of expansion was higher in the nineties, even among the poor (Ravi, 2000). A question of topical interest is: are the poor households not buying food items from a nutritional perspective? Studies suggest that the poor suffer from micro-nutrient (vitamin 'A', riboflavin and naichin) deficiencies due to lack of variety in their diet (NNMB reports). It is therefore important to analyse the implications of the changes in dietary preferences on the nutritional and health status of the poor. So long as the diversification of the consumption basket improves nutritional status, even though it may not add calories, it should not be a cause of concern. Another important issue that evokes interest is: what would be the impact of economic reforms and liberalisation on food habits? There is hardly any study which throws light on these issues.

Presently, the picture that emerges is that there is a decline in the per capita consumption of cereals particularly in the nineties which saw the begining of the decline for the poorest 30 per cent (Table 2). The apparent cause of national self-sufficiency in cereals is the slow growth of aggregate cereal demand (about 2 per cent per annum in aggregate terms and negative in per capita terms), which is due to changes in consumer preferences, so that there has been no noticeable improvement in the per capita intake of calories and protein. Clearly, despite the decline in income poverty, the food poverty (i.e. proportion of households consuming less than the caloric norm) might not have declined.

It needs to be observed that there has been substantial inter-state variation in the per capita food energy intake (Table 4). While the average intake of calories was very low in Kerala and Tamil Nadu, it was high in Madhya Pradesh and Karnataka. There does not seem to be a strong positive correlation between the calorie intake and the per capita SDP of the states.

Table 4
Per Capita Calorie Intake in Selected States

(Kcal/day)

State	Rural			Urban		
	1972-73	1983	1993-94	1972-73	1983	1993-94
Andhra Pradesh	2103	2204	2052	2143	2009	1992
Assam	2074	2056	1983	2135	2043	2108
Bihar	2225	2189	2115	2167	2131	2188
Gujarat	2142	2113	1994	2172	2000	2027
Haryana	3215	2554	2491	2404	2242	2140
Karnataka	2202	2260	2073	1925	2124	2026
Kerala	1559	1884	1965	1723	2049	1966
Madhya Pradesh	2423	2323	2164	2229	2137	2082
Maharashtra	1895	2144	1939	1971	2028	1989
Orissa	1995	2103	2199	2276	2219	2261
Punjab	3493	2677	2418	2783	2100	2089
Rajasthan	2730	2433	2470	1841	2140	1922
Tamil Nadu	1955	1861	1884	1841	2140	1922
Uttar Pradesh	2575	2399	2307	2161	2043	2114
West Bengal	1921	2027	2211	2080	2048	2131
All -India	2266	2221	2153	2089	2089	2071

Source: NSS Report No. 405.

IV. NUTRITIONAL STATUS OF RURAL HOUSEHOLDS

The National Nutrition Monitoring Bureau (NNMB) provides the nutritional status of rural households in seven sample states for the periods, 1975-80, 1988-90 and 1994. NNMB classified rural children aged 1-5 years into different nutritional grades based on weight for age (Gomez classification). The results show that the percentage of children suffering from severe malnutrition declined from 15 in 1975-79 to 8.7 in 1988-90 and further to 7.5 in 1994 (Table 5). If those classified in moderate and severe malnutrition ranges are considered together, the percentage of children afflicted by malnutrition declined from 62.5 in 1975-79 to 52.5 in 1988-90 and further to 50.9 in 1994. It is thus evident that in spite of some improvement in nutritional status, nearly half of the rural children suffer from malnutrition.[5] State-wise, the decline in the percentage of severely malnourished children is very visible across all NNMB sample states except Orissa, and is very striking in Kerala and Tamil Nadu.

Table 5
Per cent Distribution of Children (Aged 1-5 Years) by Nutritional Grade in Rural Areas of Selected States

State	Period	Normal	Mild	Moderate	Severe
Kerala	1975-79	7.5	35.7	46.5	10.3
	1988-90	17.7	47.4	32.9	2.0
	1996-97	22.4	50.3	25.3	2.0
Tamil Nadu	1975-79	6.2	34.2	47.0	12.6
	1988-90	8.0	42.0	45.8	4.2
	1996-97	14.2	48.9	33.9	3.0
Karnataka	1975-79	4.6	31.1	50.0	14.3
	1988-90	4.8	38.1	48.8	8.3
	1996-97	9.5	38.6	45.5	6.4
Andhra Pradesh	1975-79	6.1	32.4	46.1	15.4
	1988-90	8.7	39.5	44.3	7.5
	1996-97	7.3	38.0	47.5	7.2
Maharashtra	1975-79	3.2	25.4	49.5	21.9
	1988-90	6.7	38.0	47.5	7.8
	1996-97	7.4	35.0	49.8	7.8
Gujarat	1975-79	3.8	28.1	54.3	13.8
	1988-90	7.3	33.9	45.8	13.0
	1996-97	4.6	31.7	46.8	17.0
Madhya Pradesh	1975-79	8.4	30.3	45.1	16.2
	1988-90	17.7	27.4	38.9	16.0
	1996-97	–	–	–	–
Orissa	1975-79	7.5	35.9	41.7	14.9
	1988-90	8.1	34.6	46.6	10.7
	1996-97	3.2	42.3	50.3	4.1
All states*	1975-79	5.9	31.6	47.5	15.0
	1988-90	9.9	37.6	43.8	8.7
	1996-97	9.0	40.4	44.3	6.3

Notes: Based on National Centre for Health Statistics (NCHS), standards;* Pooled estimates for Kerala, Tamil Nadu, Karnataka, Andhra Pradesh, Maharashtra, Gujarat, Madhya Pradesh and Orissa.

Source: National Nutritional Monitoring Bureau, *Report of the Repeat Surveys – Rural, 1999*, National Institute of Nutrition, Hyderabad.

There are substantial inter-state variations in the malnutrition levels of children below five.[6] In 1994 the percentage of moderately/severely malnourished children varied between 34 in Kerala and 57 in Gujarat. In terms of nutritional status of children, middle income states such as Kerala, Tamil Nadu and Andhra Pradesh performed better than higher income states like Gujarat and Maharashtra. Not surprisingly, poorer states such as Madhya Pradesh and Orissa showed the worst performance. It is noteworthy that despite the low food energy intake of children in Kerala and Tamil Nadu, these states could perform better. National Family Health Survey (NFHS) data also reveal more or less similar patterns except for Gujarat[7] (Table 6).

NNMB data indicate that 49 per cent of the rural adult population in the seven sample states suffer from chronic energy deficiency (CED) in 1994 (Table 7), and that the extent of malnutrition among the adults was closer to that of children (51 per cent). The regional patterns are similar to those of malnutrition among the children (NNMB). CED was found to be lower in Kerala (33 per cent)

Table 6
NFHS Etimates of Malnutrition among Children under Age Four in 1993

State	Weight-for-age % below2 S.D. (underweight)			Height-for-age % below2 S.D. (stunted)			Weight-for-height % below2 S.D. (wasted)		
	Rural	Urban	Total	Rural	Urban	Total	Rural	Urban	Total
Andhra Pradesh	52.1	40.2	49.1	na	na	na	na	na	na
Assam	51.8	37.3	50.4	53.5	39.6	52.2	11.4	5.6	10.8
Bihar	64.1	53.8	62.6	61.8	55.2	60.9	22.7	16.3	21.8
Gujarat	45.8	40.5	44.1	44.6	41.6	43.6	20.3	16.1	18.9
Haryana	39.4	33.0	37.9	48.0	42.4	46.7	5.7	6.4	5.9
Himachal Pradesh	48.3	30.2	47.0	na	na	na	na	na	na
J & K	na	na	44.5	na	na	40.8	na	na	14.8
Karnataka	na	na	54.3	na	na	47.6	na	na	17.4
Kerala	30.6	22.9	28.5	29.6	21.5	27.4	11.5	12.0	11.6
Madhya Pradesh	59.4	50.1	57.4	na	na	na	na	na	na
Maharashtra	57.5	45.5	52.6	50.8	39.1	46.0	21.5	18.3	20.2
Orissa	na	na	55.3	na	na	48.2	na	na	21.3
Punjab	47.4	40.0	45.9	40.4	38.4	40.0	21.4	14.3	19.9
Rajasthan	41.1	43.9	41.6	43.0	43.5	43.1	17.7	29.1	19.5
Tamil Nadu	52.1	37.3	46.6	na	na	na	na	na	na
Uttar Pradesh	na	na	49.8	na	na	49.2	na	na	16.2
West Bengal	na	na	56.8	na	na	43.2	na	na	11.9
North East									
Arunachal Pradesh	40.3	36.2*	39.7	52.7	61.7*	53.9	10.6	14.9*	11.2
Manipur	31.6	25.9	30.1	34.9	29.6	33.6	8.3	10.2	8.8
Nagaland	30.5	19.7	28.7	32.7	31.0	32.4	14.1	5.6	12.7
Tripura	53.0	31.6	48.8	49.1	33.3	46.0	19.7	8.8	17.5
Meghalaya	47.2	37.5	45.5	55.5	29.7	50.8	20.1	14.1	18.9
Mizoram	34.5	22.0	28.1	54.0	29.1	41.3	2.3	2.2	2.2
All-India	59.9	45.2	53.4	54.1	44.8	52.0	2.3	2.2	2.2

Notes: Children below 2 S.D. from the international reference population median are treated as suffering from malnutrition; * Based on 25-49 cases.
Source: National Family Health Survey (NFHS), 1993.

and Tamil Nadu (37 per cent) and higher in Gujarat, Maharashtra and Madhya Pradesh (about 50 per cent).

Inter-state comparisons reveal a weak correlation between nutritional status and per capita SDP as well as between nutritional status and per capita calorie consumption. The state level mismatch between the food intake and nutritional status could be attributed to the differences in education, health, availability of safe drinking water, and environmental sanitation which intervene between food and nutritional status. A better environment would reduce food wastage caused by infections and diseases. The improved nutritional status at a comparatively lower level of consumption of food energy as observed in Kerala and Tamil Nadu could be due to better health care and nutritional intervention.

Does all this imply that the calorie intake matters little? While empirical evidence tends to suggest a positive association between the calorie intake and nutritional status, the responsiveness is likely to be affected by the factors relating to health and environment. What is a desirable diet from a nutritional

Table 7
Estimates of Distribution of Percentage of Adults by BMI Grade in Rural Areas of Selected States

State	BMI Grade		
	CED	Normal	Obesity
Kerala	33.2	56.5	10.3
Tamil Nadu	37.3	53.1	9.6
Karnataka	53.8	41.9	4.3
Andhra Pradesh	49.4	46.4	4.2
Maharashtra	51.0	44.6	4.4
Gujarat	53.1	42.1	4.8
Madhya Pradesh	53.3	46.0	0.7
Orissa	57.3	41.1	1.6
Pooled	48.5	46.5	5.0

Note : CED – Chronically Energy Deficient.
Source: NNMB Report, 1996.

perspective thus remains unsettled in view of the controversies. It is also unclear as to how much of the malnutrition is due to an inadequate diet and how much due to the environment.[8]

V. PUBLIC DISTRIBUTION SYSTEM (PDS)

The PDS in its present form—a producer price-support-cum-consumer subsidy programme—has evolved in the wake of foodgrain shortages of the sixties. It was then mainly confined to urban areas and food deficit areas with its emphasis primarily on price stabilisation till the late seventies. The welfare dimension of the PDS has gained importance since the early eighties and its coverage has been extended to rural areas in some states as well as to areas with a high incidence of poverty. The food subsidy cost accounted for 0.5 per cent of GDP in 1998-99. In the wake of economic reforms, the PDS is perceived to be the main safety net to protect the poor from potential short-run, price-induced adverse effects of economic reforms.

1. Trends in PDS Supplies

PDS supplies have increased rapidly since the mid-sixties: the annual average supply increased from 6.5 million tonnes during 1961-65 to 18.4 million tonnes during 1990-92, declined to 12.86 million tonnes in 1994-95 and then increased to 18.69 million tonnes in 1998-99. A noteworthy feature of these trends is the response of government supply to fluctuations in production; it is higher in drought years than in normal ones. For instance, in 1979-80 and 1987-88—the years associated with low foodgrain production—the government supplies were substantially higher than in normal years. In both the years, the government increased the supplies through both PDS and employment generation programmes to prevent famine, though the procurement levels were lower than in normal years. It is noteworthy in this context that there were only a few instances of deaths due to starvation.

Studies suggest that PDS operations are not very sensitive to inflationary situations (Parikh, 1992). The foodgrain price stabilisation measures were ineffective in combating the foodgrain price hikes engineered in part by the speculative trade practices. Large increases in foodgrain prices brought the poor people close to the poverty line at great nutritional risk. Generally, high inflation rates are associated with food inflation which in turn hurts the poor most (Ravi, 2000).

2. Pricing and Subsidies

The recent large increases in procurement prices and the consequent upward revisions in the central issue prices have had an adverse impact on the efficacy of the PDS. The price advantage to the farmers has resulted in the Food Corporation of India (FCI), a parastatal agency established in 1965, buying up more wheat and rice than it can manage for the simple reason that the FCI had no option but to buy whatever is offered to it at the minimum support price. On the other hand, due to large increases in the issue prices, the off-take of cereals from the PDS had declined from 19 million tonnes in 1991-92 to 12.86 million tonnes in 1994-95. Consequently, buffer stocks have reached uneconomic levels, far exceeding the norms suggested by the technical group constituted by the government.[9] Studies suggest that the economic costs of withholding foodgrains from the market would be high. The withholding of foodgrains would increase the open market price which would hurt the poor more, and the very poor the most since all the poor are not covered by the PDS. Even those who are covered by the PDS depend on the open market for a major portion of their foodgrain requirements.

The sharp increases in the minimum support and central issue prices explain the abnormal increase in the carrying cost of buffer stocks in 1993-94 and 1994-95. In 1994-95, out of the central food subsidy amount of Rs. 51 billion the carrying costs of buffer stocks amounted to 36 per cent (Radhakrishna, et al., 1997). The excess stock over the minimum norm is estimated to have involved an additional central government expenditure amounting to about half of the carrying cost.

Despite the increasing trend of the central food subsidy, consumer cereal subsidy (FCI economic cost minus its sales realisation) has declined from Rs. 32 billion in 1992-93 to Rs. 23.5 billion in 1994-95. What is more disquieting is the decline in the subsidy amount that has gone to the poverty alleviation programmes (PDS, RPDS/ITDP, JRY and EAS) which received Rs. 16 billion in 1994-95, i.e. about 30 per cent of the central food subsidy (Radhakrishna et al.,1997). The share of the poor in the food subsidy would be much less than 30 per cent since a significant portion of the PDS supplies had gone to the non-poor.

3. Access to PDS Food

It is important to ask whether the poor have benefited from the increased tempo of the PDS operations and what is the efficacy of the PDS in distributing food to the poor. Many empirical studies have shown severe biases in the inter-regional distributions of the PDS supplies—states with the high incidence of poverty such as Bihar, Orissa and Madhya Pradesh received a lower share. Further, with few exceptions, the PDS remained an untargeted programme (Jha, 1991; Mahendra Dev and Suryanarayana, 1991; Radhakrishna, et al., 1997).

The PDS seems to suffer from an urban bias in some of the states in which its network has spread. In Jammu & Kashmir, Karnataka, Maharashtra and

West Bengal, the per capita purchases from the PDS as well as their share in the market purchases of cereals were higher in the urban areas. Among these states, the urban bias was extreme in Jammu & Kashmir and West Bengal. It should be understood that on the whole the major issues are associated with the universal character of PDS entitlement and the regional mistargeting rather than the urban bias (Radhakrishna et al., 1997).

The PDS is not functioning at all in the states with high concentration of the poor, due to the lack of the desired initiative on the part of the state governments (ibid). The prospect of these states providing safety nets to the poor on the basis of spending from their own resources would seem to be bleak since they are facing a severe fiscal crunch. The scheme of providing 10 kg/ month to a poor household at half the economic cost involving 7.2 million tonnes per annuam benefiting 60 million households, introduced in 1997, has not made a significant impact on the access of food since the delivery systems in the poorer states are weak. However, after the introduction of the new scheme, the share of cereal subsidy in food subsidy increased to 90 per cent in 1998-99 from 27 per cent in 1994-95 because of the increased quantity lifted by the states with a better PDS network.

In comparison with other anti-poverty programmes, PDS has been found to be the costliest (ibid). PDS has been found to deliver 100 kcal of nutrients at three times the cost under the direct nutrition programmes of ICDS. In terms of cost of per rupee income transferred, PDS has also been found to be inferior to employment programmes.

4. Reforming PDS

Any proposal for a reformed and restructured food transfer programme for India needs to be made against the backdrop of the changing agricultural and institutional scenario in India.[10] In particular, three aspects of change need to be highlighted (Radhakrishna et al., 1997): First, India's agricultural economy has vastly changed since the early sixties. Overall, national-level shortages have abated and the country's cereal production is growing faster than the effective demand. The relatively poor eastern region—West Bengal in particular—has seen a significant improvement in foodgrain production. Incidence of poverty has steadily fallen since the 1950s. Second, except in tribal and a few dry land areas, agricultural marketing infrastructure is well-developed and integrated. Third, the Panchayat Raj Institutions (PRIs) will now be entrusted with the responsibility of implementing all major poverty alleviation programmes.

Given these changes, and the weaknesses and constraints under which the FCI currently operates, the study by Radhakrishna et al. (1999), has recommended a reduced role for FCI, by phasing out government controls over foodgrain markets as well as procurement operations. FCI could be allowed to compete in the market, free from controls, but with the added advantage of scale economies. FCI may, over time, become an effective player in the market. Its new role could be to stabilise price of foodgrains within a band, and to maintain strategic buffer stocks or equivalent foreign exchange reserves; it could intervene in the market by offloading stocks.

The subsidy cost saved as FCI goes out of procurement operations could be distributed to PRIs in the form of food stamps or vouchers. The poor—identified by PRIs—may be given these vouchers, to be exchanged for food either at PDS outlets or at regular private grain stores. Where such a voucher programme is difficult to administer, these outlets may still supply grain, but introduce PRI-administered identification of the poor. One sub-option is to link food voucher programme with other programmes depending upon availability, such as employment programmes (JRY/EAS), or nutrition programmes (ICDS). These measures are most likely to ensure targeting without incurring additional costs. At the same time, the poor may be offered some choice in the type of grains as well as retail outlets. The existing PDS shops could still continue to function, but only as normal grain retail outlets (like any other private dealer) rather than as outlets supplying "subsidised" commodities as in the past.

The above structural change would ensure that the income transfer effected through the PDS would go to the intended beneficiary without incurring a huge cost on administration as is the case at present. It would also strengthen other programmes that confer large benefits to the poor such as JRY and ICDS, as well as democratic institutions such as the Panchayat Raj.

VI. GROWTH, POVERTY AND FOOD DEMAND: CHANGING SCENARIO

The proportion of people below the poverty line remained above 50 per cent with no evidence of a downtrend till the mid-seventies, which continued to decline during the remaining part of the decade and during the eighties (Table 8). In the rural areas, the decline has slowed in the nineties. The decline in the rate of growth of per capita total expenditure and somewhat worsening inequalities have contributed to the slow down (Ravi, 2000) (Table 2). In contrast, in urban areas the decline in poverty accelerated in the nineties. Despite worsening inequalities, the significant improvement in the rate of growth of per capita expenditure has hastened the process of decline in poverty in urban areas (Ravi, 2000). The consumption data also revealed a widening of rural-urban disparities during the decade, 1990s (ibid), which also contributed to the slow down in the decline in poverty in the rural areas.

The incidence of poverty still remains high notwithstanding the introduction of several poverty alleviation programmes (PAPs) by the government. Public spending (by the centre and state governments) on the PAPs, including the PDS, was 1.36 per cent of the GDP in 1993-94 and presently accounts for about 8-10 per cent of the budgetary expenditure (both at centre and state levels). Most of the schemes suffer from loose targeting and leakages and are cost ineffective. Consequently, the income transfer costs are high. However, employment programmes, particularly the Maharashtra Employment Guarantee Scheme and nutrition programmes seem to be better targeted because of the provision for self-selection.

1. Poverty Projections

A growth rate of 6-7 per cent during the Ninth Plan is considered to be attainable with the possibility of sustaining it beyond the plan period. In the long-term perspective, if macro-economic stability is maintained and if expenditure inequalities are sustained at historical trends without further worsening, the high growth will hasten the process of decline in poverty.

Table 8
Trends in Head Count Ratio, Poverty Gap and FGT Measures in Rural and Urban India

Year	Rural				Urban			
	Poverty line	HCR	PG	F.G.T.	Poverty line	HCR	PG	F.G.T.
1970-71	33.30	57.45	18.10	7.34	43.33	52.63	17.03	6.95
1972-73	40.24	56.45	18.18	7.52	50.74	50.19	16.12	6.55
1973-74	48.10	53.14	16.29	6.44	59.06	50.76	15.51	6.03
1977-78	59.10	57.73	17.60	6.83	81.75	54.99	18.35	7.79
1983	91.00	46.88	13.36	4.92	125.05	45.85	13.56	5.09
1986-87	107.60	42.33	11.29	3.90	152.54	38.52	10.99	3.87
1987-88	117.60	40.66	10.09	3.22	167.57	40.04	11.24	3.89
1988-89	126.70	37.65	9.00	2.75	178.13	37.50	10.34	3.51
1989-90	133.00	33.40	7.51	2.16	190.57	36.37	9.65	3.16
1990-91	148.98	36.66	8.72	2.67	212.36	35.35	9.47	3.16
1991	173.20	38.83	8.75	2.50	240.07	36.42	9.74	3.24
1992	183.00	40.25	9.70	2.99	248.88	35.06	9.34	3.03
1993	184.70	40.77	9.27	2.71	257.92	37.68	10.08	3.37
1993-94	200.20	34.88	7.82	2.25	280.81	32.52	8.36	2.60
1994-95	225.80	40.04	8.93	2.54	308.21	35.44	9.39	3.00
1995-96	254.70	38.68	8.60	2.44	344.07	31.00	7.56	2.17
1997	265.40	33.27	7.48	2.10	361.75	28.92	7.09	2.04
1998	280.80	39.01	8.92	2.59	389.94	30.40	7.61	2.26
	Annualised growth rates							
1970-90	–	-2.50	-4.14	-5.78	–	1.96	-2.90	-4.01
	–	(-7.10)	(-8.62)	(-9.00)	-	(-6.88)	(-7.05)	(-6.92)
1990-98	–	-0.73	-1.30	-2.09	–	-3.05	-4.39	-6.59
	–	(1.59)	(1.88)	(1.82)	_	(-1.22)	(-1.14)	(-1.42)

Notes: 1. Poverty lines (Rs. per month per capita) for 1973-74 are those of Planning Commission. For other years, they have been adjusted for prices; 2. Figures in the parenthesis are t-values; 3. HCR–Head Count Ratio; PG–Poverty Gap.

Source: Ravi (2000).

The projections (Table 9) are made assuming that private consumption will grow at 5 per cent between 1994 and 2000 and 6 per cent between 2000 and 2020; that the rural-urban distribution of population and rural-urban differences in the per capita expenditure distribution will follow the past trends, and that the inequality of expenditure distribution will remain constant at the 1993-94 levels in rural and urban areas. The projections show that in rural areas, 28 per cent will remain poor in 2000, 11 per cent in 2010 and 3 per cent in 2020 and in urban areas, 21 per cent will be poor in 2000, 4 per cent in 2010 and 1 per cent in 2020. In absolute terms, the number of poor persons in India will decline from 377 million in 1994 to 266 million in 2000, 115 million in 2010, and further to 35 million in 2020. This decline in absolute numbers despite a projected increase of population from 909 million in 1994 to 1,344 million in 2020 would be due to high growth without much worsening of inequalities. Of the projected 256 million poor in 2000, 130 million, i.e. about half will continue to be very poor.

Table 9
Projected Expenditure Distribution

Expenditure groups	Rural				Urban			
	Estimated distribution		Projected distribution		Estimated distribution		Projected distribution	
	1994	2000	2010	2020	1994	2000	2010	2020
Very poor	20	14	6	2	19	11	2	0
Moderately poor	18	15	9	5	14	10	4	1
Poor	38	29	15	7	33	21	6	1
Non-poor lower	29	28	23	16	25	22	12	4
Non-poor higher	33	43	62	77	42	57	82	95
Non-poor	52	51	85	93	67	79	94	99
All	100	100	100	100	100	100	100	100

Note: Persons below 75 per cent of the poverty line (PL) are defined as very poor; persons between 75 per cent of PL and PL as moderately poor; persons between PL and 150 per cent of PL as non-poor lower; and above PL non-poor high. Poverty lines are those of the Planning Commission given at 1993-94 period. Using the log-normal distribution fitted to the 1993-94 NSS data, projections of expenditure distribution in the year 2000, 2010 and 2020 are made on the following assumptions: (a) Aggregate private expenditure will grow at 5 per cent during 1994-2000 and at 6 per cent during 2000-2020; (b) The ratio of urban to rural per capita expenditure will increase at the historical rate; (c) The inequality in expenditure within rural and urban areas will remain the same as in 1993-94; (d) Population figures are based on recent estimates released by the Registrar General of India.

Source: CESS Project on Food Demand.

The need to focus the food security programme more on the very poor to prevent food distress on account of less than adequate access to foodgrains will remain in the coming years. In the case of the poor near the poverty line, policies promoting broad-based growth would help in improving their lot. Notably, if the poverty-reducing effect of high growth is supplemented by well-targeted cost effective food distribution and/or employment programmes, the problem of chronic cereal deficiency can be overcome to a large extent in the next decade. Based on the previous discussion on malnutrition, it can, however, be argued that even if cereal needs of the poor are met, malnutrition may persist due to other deprivations.

2. Projections for Food Demand

Based on the above assumptions, the household food demand is projected to increase by 4.44 per cent between the years 2000 and 2010, which is closer to the targeted agricultural growth rate in the Ninth Plan (Table 10). The projected annual rate of increase in the household demand varies among the food items: it is more than 5 per cent for milk and milk products, 4-5 per cent for meat, egg and fish, sugar and gur and edible oils and 2.5 per cent for cereal items. These differential growth rates imply substantial diversification of the food basket in favour of non-cereal food, particularly miik, meat, etc. The contribution of population growth to growth in the cereal demand is very significant as it accounts for more than three-fourths of the increase. Clearly, the shifts in tastes observed in the historical data have dampened the growth of cereal demand. The household demand for the cereals in future will slow down and will eventually level off at about the rate of growth of population which itself is likely to decline.

Table 10
Projected Annual Growth Rate in Total Household Demand by Commodity Group during 1994-2020

	1994-2000	2000-2010	2010-2020
Rice	2.66	2.58	2.23
Wheat	2.98	3.06	2.69
Other cereals	0.93	0.76	1.01
All cereals	2.49	2.49	2.24
Milk and milk products	5.34	5.80	5.21
Edible oil	3.96	4.40	4.26
Meat, egg and fish	4.61	5.05	4.74
Sugar and gur	4.11	4.55	4.15
Other food	4.58	5.26	5.21
All food	4.41	4.41	4.32
Non-food	6.55	7.81	7.37
Total	5.00	6.00	6.00

Note: Projections are based on an integrated demand model and on NSS rounds from 1977-78 to 1993-94 which include the latest round. The projections are made at the relative prices of 1993-94 and the assumptions about the variables are those given in Table 5.
Source: CESS Project on Food Demand.

The other sources of demand for cereals are seed, feed, and processing by industry; these together accounted for about 12.5 per cent of the cereal production in 1993. The feed demand which accounted for about 6 per cent of the cereal production in 1993, is likely to be influenced by the growth rate of consumption of milk and milk products as well as meat, egg and fish (i.e. 4-5 per cent per annum). Since, cereals may replace other types of feed, the demand for cereals for feed may grow at a higher rate than that of the total feed demand. Taking into consideration all aspects, a maximum growth rate of 4.5 per cent can be assumed for the non-household cereals demand while the growth rate of the national demand (household and non-household) can be assumed at 2.8 per cent during 2000-2010 and 2.5 per cent during 2010-2020. Even if the growth is successful in reducing poverty, the growth of the cereal demand may not exceed the above rates to any significant extent. It is pertinent to note that the household cereal demand has been projected assuming that the historical downward trend in the per capita consumption of cereals due to a change in tastes will be arrested and food demand will depend only on population, the per capita income, the level of urbanisation, and income inequalities. Hence, the estimated growth rate of 2.8 per cent is likely to be on a higher side.

Coming to the supply side, the above pattern of domestic demand requires a substantial diversification of agriculture and allied sectors. For matching the growing food demand, food production would have to grow at a rate of 4.4 per cent up from the growth rate of 3.4 per cent achieved during the seventies and the eighties. The objective of national food security requires that not only the deceleration in the growth rate of foodgrain/agricultural production experienced in the 1990s as well as the weaknesses of the PDS should be overcome, but also that the long-term problem of sustaining a growth rate of about 2.8 per cent in the cereal production during 2000-2010 and 2.5 per cent during 2010-2050 should be solved. It could be appreciated that these are not out of reach since India could achieve higher rate in the 1980s.

VII. WTO AND FOOD SECURITY

The Indian agricultural scene has witnessed changes following the economic reforms in the nineties as well as with the establishment of World Trade Organisation (WTO) in the mid-nineties. While the world trading environment has become more liberal, transparent and rule bound than before, it would have become even more favourable had the developed countries adhered strictly to the Uruguay Round agreement and permitted better access to imports from developing countries.

India seems to be a victim of thirty years of agricultural policy with a focus on a production strategy of spreading HYV-seed-fertilizer technology in a few potential regions mainly aimed at achieving self sufficiency. Consequent to the adoption of this stategy India achieved self-sufficiency in foodgrains by the mid-sixties and was faced with the problem of disposing off huge foodgrains stocks. It needs to be observed that the self-sufficiency in foodgrains is partly due to the weak purchasing power of the poor classes. As a remedial measure, it is suggested that India should diversify its agriculture and get a foothold in the world market. The accelerated and diversified agricultural growth would enhance the food security by improving the purchasing power of the poor.

However, even after the establishment of WTO in 1995, the agricultural trade of developing countries including India has not improved much in the transition period since agricultural prices have sharply declined in the world market and also because there has been no reduction in the degree of protection by the developed countries. The protectionist measures are coming in the form of non-tariff measures and preventing the entry of goods from developing countries by resorting to anti-dumping restrictions in one form or another. Some concessions under the Green Box do not favour developed countries. Some of these concerns should figure in the next round of negotiations.

The deceleration in the agricultural growth which India experienced during the nineties is more due to internal factors such as decline in public investment in agriculture, slow down in the growth in fertilizer consumption, slow rise in the expenditure on agricultural research and so on. It is argued that if India is to benefit from the emerging opportunities opened up by liberalised agricultural trade, major reforms have to be undertaken on the domestic front. It is recognised that cereal prices in the world market which have declined during the nineties are unlikely to rise on account of reforms in the developed countries. India should depend on cost-reducing technology through domestic reforms, promote agricultural diversification and put pressure on the developed countries to open up their markets for our agro-processed production.[11]

While formulating an appropriate agricultural strategy some key issues of concern that need to be addressed are: How to utilise the emerging opportunities from liberalised trade for the diversification of economic activities in rural areas? What reforms are needed to improve the purchasing power of the poor? What type of safety nets are needed to protect the food security from the fluctuations on international agricultural prices which are more volatile than domestic prices?

VIII. CONCLUDING OBSERVATIONS

While India could achieve some success in combating transitory food insecurity caused by droughts or floods, it has failed to make much dent in chronic food insecurity reflected in the low energy intake and high incidences of malnutrition.[12] The improvement in nutritional status has also been very slow.

While high growth sustained for more than a decade would significantly reduce income poverty by 2010, the chronic food insecurity is likely to persist. Moreover, with the recent shift to a more market-oriented and outward-looking macro-policy, the poor are likely to be exposed to the risk of market uncertainties. As a result several types of programmes need to be targeted to the poor aimed at (i) preventing distress on account of inadequate access to food in periods of crises through the PDS and employment programmes; (ii) helping the poor to get access to food in normal periods by raising their purchasing power through the endowment of land and non-land assets and better access to credit facilities; increasing employment generated both through normal growth process and income transfers through the PDS, and more directly through employment programmes; (iii) introducing programmes associated with human resources development to enable the poor to achieve larger income increases from participating in the growth process; (iv) reducing malnutrition among children and women through the ICDS, MDM, etc.; and (v) improving the basic services to the poor through provision of safe drinking water. The portfolio of PAPs should be contextual and suit the specific needs of the poor communities. Socially excluded groups are highly heterogeneous and, therefore, poverty reducing effects of any intervention based on a uniform package of programmes would be weak.

In view of the emerging trends in foodgrain production, India's entry into the WTO, and the weaknesses of PDS, the existing highly centralised PDS may be replaced with a two-tier system consisting of (i) a national tier to stabilise the food prices within a band conforming to WTO regulations and (ii) a local tier focussed on the task of providing a safety net to the poor. The national tier may be operated by the FCI and the local tier by the local governments.

Improvement in food consumption is a necessary but not a sufficient condition for overcoming the problem of malnutrition in India. Apart from inadequate food consumption, the other important causes of malnutrition are high incidence of gastrointestinal and respiratory infections and behavioural factors such as faulty breastfeeding and weaning practices, all of which contribute to the low absorption of nutrients from the food consumed. Economic growth, left to itself, may not have a dramatic impact on nutritional status in the near future, although it provides greater opportunities for public intervention. Effective and efficient food and environmental interventions are needed until the poor are freed from food and nutritional insecurity.

(This paper is drawn from Rao and Radhakrishna 1977; and Radhakrishna 2000).

Notes

1. The growth rates of food and agricultural production in various sub-periods are similar since food accounts for a major portion of the agricultural output (Table 1).
2. The per capita cereal consumption of the poor remained the same despite a significant improvement in their real per capita expenditure and a decline in the relative cereal price. This counter-intuitive result could be attributed to the changes in the consumer preferences (Radhakrishna, 1991; Radhakrishna and Ravi, 1992; Suryanarayana, 1995; Meenakshi, 1996).
3. There is considerable disagreement about the minimum calorie consumption per consumer unit per diem. Sukhatme (1982) and Minhas (1991) have questioned the sanctity of the calorie norms widely used by nutritionists and considered them to be exaggerated. However, the calorie intake of the poorest 30 per cent was lower than the norms suggested by Sukhatme.
4. The share of cereals in the marginal budgets of the very poor in rural areas was found to decline from 53 per cent in 1964-77 to 39 per cent in 1977-86 and from 39 to 29 per cent in urban areas (Radhakrishna and Ravi, 1990).
5. Children of the poor communities suffering from malnutrition not only do not achieve full genetic growth potential and end up as adults with small body size but are also exposed to a greater risk of child mortality. Pelletier et. al,. (1996) identify malnutrition as a major cause of death in developing countries. Their results reveal that malnutrition, by virtue of its synergistic relationship with infectious disease ha[illegible] a powerful impact on child mortality in India.
6. The inter-state variations in malnutrition of under-fives are more or less similar to those in infant mortality rate (Radhakrishna and Narayana, 1993). While all the NNMB repeat surveys reveal poor record of rural Gujarat in terms of the nutritional status. NFHS reveals better performance. This needs further examination.
7. Kerala and Tamil Nadu have better health care and educational facilities and coverage of the PDS. The per child public expenditure on nutrition as well as per capita public expenditure on social sector have been high in these two states for the past few decades.
8. Sekler (1982) observes that severe malnutrition is caused by nutrient intake deficiency and the 'moderate' and 'mild' malnutrition is due to environmental factors. He argues that the former problem calls for nutritional intervention and the latter environmental intervention. There is as yet, not much empirical basis for his position.
9. While foodgrain stocks reached uneconomic levels during 1993-96, they have fallen below the required stocks in the late 1996 and early 1977. The decline could be partly attributed to the shortcomings of food management. Without perceiving the expected decline in foodgrain production, foodgrains were exported when the international prices were low and domestic prices were on an upward trend.
10. For more details, see Radkahrishna et al. (1997).
11. C.H. Hanumantha Rao has suggested an agricultural strategy for accelerating agricultural growth in the changed context. See his presidential remarks in Krishna Rao (2000).
12. India has made impressive progress in reducing the problem of hunger. Estimates of hunger based on self-perception as well as behaviour provided by Minhas (1991) show that about 15 per cent of the rural and 17 per cent of the urban households might be classified as hungry in 1983. The hunger estimates might be much lower now. Gopalan (1995) observes that overcoming the problem of hunger is not the same as elimination of malnutrition. The former can be achieved through the intake of cereals, while the latter will deamed other non-cereal food as well as access to safe, better sanitary conditions, quality of care, etc.

References

Acharya, S.S.(1989), *Socio-economic Impact of 1987 Drought in Rajasthan*, Department of Agricultural Economics, Rajasthan Agricultural University, Jaipur.

Bhalla, G.S.(1994), "Policies for Food Security in India", in Bhalla, G.S. (ed.) *Economic Liberalisation and Indian Agriculture*, Institute for Studies in Industrial Development, New Delhi.

Bidinger, P.D. et al. (1990), *Economic, Health and Nutritional Consequences of the Mid-1980s Drought on a Tank Irrigated, Deccan Village in South India*, Resource Management Programme, Economics Group, Progress Report 98, ICRISAT, Hyderabad.

Gopalan, C. (1995), "Towards Food and Nutritional Security", *Economic and Political Weekly*, Vol. 30, No. 52, December 1995, pp. A-134-141.

Jha, S. (1991), *Consumer Subsides in India: Is Targetting Effective?*, Indira Gandhi Institute of Developement Studies, Bombay.

Krishna Rao, Y.V. (ed.) (2000), *New Challenges Facing Indian Agriculture*, Visalaandhra Publishing House, Hyderabad.

Mahendra Dev, S and M.H. Suryanarayana (1991), "Is PDS Urban Biased and Pro-rich: An Evaluation", *Economic and Political Weekly*, Vol. 26, No. 41.

Mortorell, R. and T.J.Ho (1984), "Malnutrition, Morbidity and Mortality", *Population and Development Review*, A Supplement to Vol. 10, pp. 49-68.

Meenakshi, J.V. (1996), "How Important are Changes in Taste? A State Level Analysis of Food Demand", *Economic and Political Weekly*, Vol. 31, No .50, December 14, pp. 3265-69.

Minhas, B.S. (1991), "On Estimating the Inadequacy of Energy Intakes: Revealed Food Consumption Behaviour Versus Nutritional Norms (Nutritional Status of Indian People in 1983)", *The Journal of Development Studies*, Vol. 28, No. 1, pp. 1-38.

Parikh, K.S. (1992), "Importance of Food and Agriculture Policies in the Success of Structural Reforms in India", Invited paper, *29th European Association of Agricultural Economists*, Hohentreim, Germany.

Pelletier, D.L., E.A. Frongillo, Jr., D.G. Schroeder and J.P. Habicht (1995), "The Effects of Malnutrition on Child Mortality in Developing Countries", *Bulletin of the World Health Organisation*, Vol. 73, No. 4, pp. 443-448.

Radhakrishna , R. (1991) , "Food and Nutrition: Challenges for Policy", *Journal of the Indian Society of Agricultural Statistics*, Vol. 43, No. 3, pp. 211-227.

—— (2000), "Food Security, Nutrition and Poverty", in R.V. Chandrasekhera Rao, A. Prasanna Kumar and K. C. Reddy (eds.), *Indian Development: Economy, Polity and Society*, Sterling, New Delhi.

—— and C. Ravi (1990), *Food Demand Projections for India*, Centre for Economic and Social Studies, Hyderabad.

—— (1992), "Effects of Growth, Relative Price and Preferences on Food and Nutrition", *Indian Economic Review*, Vol. 27, Special Number, pp. 303-323.

——and K.V. Narayana (1993), *Nutrition Programmes in India: Review and Assessment*, Centre for Economic and Social Studies, Hyderabad.

—— K. Subba Rao, S.Indrakant and C. Ravi (1997), *India's Public Distribution System: A National and International Perspective*, World Bank Discussion Paper No. 380.

Rao, C.H. Hanumantha and R.Radhakrishna (1997), "National Food Security: A Policy Perspective for India", Plenary paper, 27th *International Conference of Agricultural Economists*, August 10-16, Sacramento, California.

Ravi, C. (2000), *Complete Demand Systems, Welfare and Nutrition: An Analysis of Index Consumption Data*, Centre for Economic and Social Studies, Hyderabad.

Sawant, S.D. and C.V. Achuthan (1995), "Agricultural Growth Across Crops and Regions", *Economic and Political Weekly*, Vol. 30, No. 12, March 25, pp. A-2-A13.

Sekler, D. (1982), "Small but Healthy", in Sukhatme, P.V. (ed.).

Sukhatme, P.V. (1982), "Poverty and Malnutrition", in Sukhatme, P.V. (ed.), *Newer Concepts in Nutrition and Their Implications for Policy*, Maharashtra Association for the Cultivation of Science, Pune, pp. 11-64.

Suryanarayna, M.H. (1995), "Growth, Poverty and Levels of Living: Hypotheses, Methods and Policies", *Journal of Indian School of Political Economy*, Vol. 7, No. 2, pp. 203-55.

6

Nutrition Security in Tamil Nadu

Anuradha Khati Rajivan

I. INTRODUCTION

Adequate nutrition security for individuals is, both an end valuable in itself and a means to promote the productive potential of the population. This paper aims to (a) document the unprecedented growth and sustained investments in the nutrition sector through a direct provision of food, food supplements and health inputs by the state in Tamil Nadu (T.N.), and (b) to explore the nutrition situation prevailing in the state.

Given the importance placed by the government of T.N. in promoting programmes and providing nutrition, section II contains a description of the background and growth of direct nutrition services under the state government. An analysis of levels and clear trend improvements in outcome indicators used to represent nutrition status is contained in section III. Weights-for-age, birth weights, secular changes in body sizes and male-female differences are examined. Section IV presents a brief discussion on the difficulty of attributing the outcomes primarily to the state's direct nutrition investments. Section V contains suggestions on future directions—a focus on *prevention* rather than *management* of malnutrition, putting in place independent nutrition surveillance, recognition of the importance of non-nutrition factors, and emphasis on moving towards a child-rights approach to nutrition. The paper ends with a caveat in section VI explicitly bringing out an implicit assumption made while using anthropometric data.

II. STATE INVESTMENTS IN DIRECT NUTRITION

1. Focus

While it is recognised that protected drinking water, environmental sanitation, general health services, the public distribution system which provides food grain access to households through controlled prices, all contribute to the overall nutritional status, this paper focuses on the direct provision of food, nutrients and related health services for the nutritionally vulnerable sections of the population in T.N.. This is important because of the massive size of the operations which have grown and stabilised over the last two decades, operations which have had the first call on the state budget and have not been allowed to be affected by financial constraints.

2. Moving from Hunger to Nutrition

Providing food is not equivalent to providing nutrition. In fact, it is debatable whether nutrition can be 'provided'. Food can be provided. Nutrition, on the other hand, is the outcome of interactions between a variety of factors and processes, including health care, environmental hygiene, etc.

Providing food for children outside the home is not a new idea in T.N. In some form or other this has been in operation since as farback as 1956. Starting with schemes meant primarily to combat hunger, nutrition consciousness has been built in since the early 1980s. Various models were tried for school-going children starting with the provision of meals in elementary schools, combining public and state contributions, and later by starting central kitchens, through the cooperation of school headmasters, etc.

While initially feeding programmes may have been started to combat hunger in a visible centre-based fashion, the state being seen as the provider, over the years the governments in T.N. have made serious attempts to combine provision of food under the Noon-Meal Programme (NMP) with other services like health care, immunization, growth monitoring, pre and post-natal care for women, communication and nutrition education. This has been done through programmes like the Integrated Child Development Services Scheme (ICDS) and the T.N. Integrated Nutrition Project (TINP), which have been integrated with the Noon-Meal Programme infrastructure for pre-schoolers. The state's nutrition effort, however, does have a strong 'food bias'. Resource constraints have not reduced the coverage or calorific content of food over the decades.

While the state has been spending significantly on the NMP and has brought about an integration of all major health and nutrition interventions for children, it is only in 1994 that a State Policy on Nutrition has been explicitly documented with technical support from the UNICEF. Tamil Nadu is probably the first state to have such a policy, following the National Nutrition Policy of 1993.

The State Policy for the first time provided explicit recognition that food alone cannot eradicate malnutrition. Unlike the NMP, under which feeding starts after two years of age, ICDS and TINP have been well aware of the limitations of feeding *per se*, especially after the age of two years by which time considerable damage could already have taken place, much of it irreversible, and the synergistic relationship between health and nutrition is explicitly recognised. The policy document, in fact, goes a step further by starting, "Feeding programmes, which seek to improve the nutritional status among the already malnourished children are less likely to be effective, and are expensive and therefore non-sustainable" (Government of Tamil Nadu, undated).

3. Noon-Meal Programme

Starting on July 1, 1982, T.N. saw the beginning of one of the largest phased expansions of mid-day feeding through the Noon-Meal Programme (NMP). This is the major hunger programme. For the first time the state focused on the difficult to reach pre-school age-group, 2+ to 5 years, who cannot be covered unless physically brought there by an adult. Successive governments have continued to commit very significant portions of the state's budget to this programme. This has resulted in the establishment and staffing of one of the most expensive network of centres for providing noon-meal in the state. The programme has a clear 'food bias'. Recently, in 1997, it has also caught the imagination of the Government of India, which is now supporting similar efforts in all states.

Given the present size and scale of its operations the state's NMP, integrated with the health and nutrition schemes for pre-school children, pregnant and lactating women, the TINP and ICDS schemes, is the first of its kind to have been attempted before. The scheme feeds a population of over 8.3 millions nearly every day, not through dry rations or pre-cooked items like biscuits, but by serving hot rice meals cooked on the spot for all. Indeed the sheer logistics can be mind-boggling. Nevertheless, these schemes have grown and stabilised over the last 20 years. Debate and discussion on such massive direct action by the state can benefit the programmes and shape future policy.

4. Who are Covered?

The 1982 NMP started by covering that section of the vulnerable population which until then had been considered hard to reach—those below 5 years. Operationally, this is the hardest age-group to cover, though in terms of nutritional efficiency, perhaps the better age-group than older children to tackle before irreversible damage has set in. Rural children in the age-group 2+ to 4+ were first covered through a network of NMP centres. During the same year the programme was expanded in stages to cover first urban pre-school children, then rural and urban primary school children and finally older school children in rural areas up to 15 years of age (i.e. class X). In 1983 old-age pensioners were covered under this programme and in 1984 it was further expanded to cover older urban school children, up to 15 years of age. In the mid-nineties, as the programme operations became streamlined, it was understood that the scheme had come to stay; that pregnant women could also benefit and that the marginal cost of adding them to the already large list of eligible persons would be within acceptable limits. So, from December 1995 women also enjoy the benefit of noon-meal for a four months period during pregnancy. The scheme is now a combination of a hunger-health-nutrition effort with social security for the old, destitute and widows.

School children eat their noon meal at school. The other categories, i.e. pre-school children, pensioners, pregnant and lactating women eat at the pre-school centres. Data on numbers of NMP centres and individuals covered vary at different counts as they are based on attendance figures recorded in the numerous centres and the administration has been trying to streamline programme operations. Latest data show that taking all pre-school as well as school centres together, in all there are nearly 71,138 noon-meal programme centers feeding over 7.78 million children and over 0.53 million adults, adding up to 8.31 million meals per day (Table 1).

It may be seen from Table 1 that the pre-school NMP centres have now been merged with those of two other child development programmes—the TINP and ICDS, a merger that is discussed in the following section.

Table 1
Direct Nutrition Coverage in T.N., 1999-2000

	Scheme	No. of centres	No. of children covered	No. of adults covered	Total covered
A.	Pre-school centres				
	ICDS (Standard)	10,482	4,63,122	1,40,782	6,03,904
	TINP (WB-ICDS-III)	19,500	9,05,633	3,91,040	12,96,673
	Other urban pre-school	720	29,309	3,680	32,989
	Total (All pre-school)	30,701	13,98,064	5,35,502	19,33,566
B.	School centres				
	Rural	38,378	59,16,829	Nil	59,16,829
	Urban	2,059	4,72,760	Nil	4,72,760
	Total (All school centres)	40,437	63,89,589	Nil	63,98,589
	Total (A + B) All centres	71,138	77,87,653	5,35,502	83,23,155

Source: Government of Tamil Nadu (1999-2000), *Policy Note*, Social Welfare and Nutritious Meal Programme Department, Chennai.

Virtually any child between the ages of two and 15 years is eligible for a noon meal at the cost of the state. Though there was an income criteria, in practice any willing child in the eligible age -group is permitted to participate. In fact it is the relatively poorer sections of the population who participate. One estimate indicates that at present around 33 per cent of the pre-school age-group actually avails of the benefits under the programme (Shantha, 1997). It appears that over the years the percentage of participating pre-schoolers may have come down due to the mushrooming of nursery schools in urban and rural areas and rationalising attendance figures at the centres. The percentage is likely to be significantly higher for the school-age population. Around 30 per cent is a high percentage if it is recognised that those in poverty situations are more likely to avail of the noon meal (the percentage of population below the poverty line ranging around 25-30, depending on which figures are accepted).

5. Integration with Other Child Development Schemes

The centrally-sponsored ICDS was introduced in T.N. in 1975, starting with just three projects: two rural and one urban. At present, there are 113 standard ICDS projects (69 in rural areas and 44 in urban slums). An integrated package of health, supplementary nutrition, together with cognitive and psycho-social services was contemplated for children under six. Their services are provided through a network of *anganwadis*—one for around 1000 population. The norm is higher for population in urban areas and lower in tribal. Pregnant and lactating women are also covered. Specifically, five services are available: health check-ups, immunisation, referral, education on health and nutrition, and supplementary nutrition. This last service is actually the noon meal under the NMP. The cost of nutrition supplements alone is borne by the state government while the central government bears all other costs; actually more than half the costs are on account of the food component alone. In four districts the Swedish International Development Agency (SIDA) provided additional resources from 1989 to 1999. During the last four years an additional evening snack of nutritious *sundal* was provided for children who stayed up to 4 p.m. under SIDA funding.

In 1980 the pilot T.N. Integrated Nutrition Project (TINP) was introduced with funding from the World Bank. This was far more focused, with the under-36 months old being targeted. This was a scheme with a much smaller 'food bias'. TINP focused on educating the women and others in the household (e.g. mothers-in-law) regarding breast feeding, weaning, immunisation, growth monitoring, and so on. Growth monitoring was an innovative feature, which attempted to make invisible malnutrition visible through plotting each child's weights against his/her age every month on chart which compared the actual growth to a norm. Mothers were taught how to interpret the chart which was suitably designed. Very selective supplementation, that too for a fixed period based on recorded growth, was undertaken. This helped control food costs and also ensured near universal growth monitoring. But soon after TINP's introduction, the state announced the massive NMP, which did not have such targeting with the intention of economising on food costs. The NMP had multiple objectives. This led to a problem of policy clarity.

By 1989 TINP operated in 173 rural blocks. Its successor, TINP-II expanded coverage to 316 blocks, eventually with 18,352 centers. This time-round decision making had to take into account the reality of the massive NMP which had come to stay and which covered children up to 5+ years among pre-school children. So TINP-II took up non-ICDS areas, and put in place its integrated package of services, adding to it pre-school education for children over three years. As it began operations through the already established network of NMP centers it was possible to operationalise TINP-II in a very short period. From 1998 the TINP was renamed as the WB-ICDS-III in keeping with the standard nomenclature for the country for child development services, while retaining its distinct identity, indicating that it is supported under World Bank funding. Very recently, from August 2000, as per the comprehensive policy of the state government, a decision has been taken to adopt selective feeding based on growth monitoring on the TINP/WB-ICDS pattern in the standard ICDS areas also, eliminating internal inconsistencies.

Thus, as seen in Table 1, for the below six years old, between the standard ICDS and TINP (now the WB-ICDS), all rural blocks in the state have in place integrated services for child development and most urban areas are also covered under ICDS. In all, this accounted for 30,701 pre-school noon-meal centers, 1,398,064 children and 535,502 adults. The 'pure' NMP centers (non TINP, non-ICDS) operate in a few urban pockets (720 centers with around 29,309 children) for children 24 months of age and above. Thus the NMP for the under six is integrated with either standard ICDS or TINP converted WB-ICDS, providing the supplementary nutrition component. The noon meal is perhaps better described as a *substitute* rather than a supplementary nutrition input, as it is in lieu of a home meal, rather than in addition. There are also 40,437 school NMP centres in rural and urban areas covering around 6,389,589 school children.

For the pre-school population, while the process of integration has contributed to streamlining policy and implementation as well as clarity in expectations among the population, it has led to considerable variation in staffing at the centre level. While the need for rationalisation of staffing based on workload is well understood, governments have found it hard to take up the sensitive issues of relocation and retrenchment. Moreover, the numbers are large—over thirty thousand centers have a staff of nearly one lakh women, who themselves are now an effective pressure group, for long perceived as overworked and underpaid.[1]

Integration was not an issue for the school centres and the 714 urban pre-school centres outside ICDS and TINP. Here there is a separate noon-meal organiser, a cook and a helper in each centre, taking the staff strength to nearly 180,000.

As part of the process of integration, NMP centres became available for TINP and ICDS, and vice versa. It was not always easy to find suitable buildings for children to assemble, store food commodities and records, cook and have adequate water supply facilities. Most centres are in *panchayat* union buildings, other public buildings, specially constructed government centres, or rent-free private buildings. Where no such building is available, a small rent of Rs. 50 per month is provided. School centres are run in the school buildings.

While full integration has taken place at the village level, with no overlap or wastage, this has not taken place at the district and state level. A district can have both standard ICDS and WB-ICDS offices and staff, which function independently. At the state headquarters there are two independent programme heads. This leads to different guidelines, variations in service delivery based not on variations in local needs, but due to the different programmes, for similar population groups. "If these projects can be administered by one single set of functionaries, enough humanpower can be saved for innovations in community capacity building and training... . At the state level, merger of these two projects can solve several issues in worker management as well as problems of trained staff moving in and out of two companion projects" (Shantha, 1997).

III. LEVELS AND TRENDS IN NUTRITION INDICATORS

1. Human Development, Economic Development and Incidence of Underweight Children

A look at comparative international data in *Human Development Reports* show that countries high on the human development scale show a lower percentage of underweight children under five years of age as compared to the medium, low human development countries. During the period 1990-97, on an average, 30 per cent of children in this age-group in the world were underweight—12 per cent in high human development countries, 19 per cent in medium (excluding China the figure increases to 23 per cent), and as high as 45 per cent in low human development countries (excluding India the figure decreases to 37 per cent). The figure for India was as high as 53 per cent. Even Pakistan (38 per cent) and Nepal (47 per cent) had lower percentages of underweight children than India (UNDP, 1998).

A direct correlation between levels of economic development and percentage of children underweight is also seen. Among all developing countries the figure for the under five years old children stood at 30 per cent for the least developed countries it was 39 per cent as compared with the world figure of 30 per cent.

2. Prevalence of Low Body Sizes and Persistence of Undernutrition

Even the most favourable data show that on the basis of weight-for-age, around half the children under five continue to be underweight, showing the widespread and persistent prevalence of current malnutrition.

Depending upon the classification system used (Gomez, IAP or the SD)[2] and the reference population weight standards adopted (US-NCHS or Harvard) for defining the various degrees of undernutrition, the actual percentages of children classified as 'normal', 'mild undernutrition', 'moderate undernutrition' and 'severe undernutrition' vary. Also, the programmes are expected to select the worst-off cases and focus largely in rural areas. Hence direct comparisons of results across different studies and monitoring data of programme participants in T.N. is not possible. However, changes over time can be assessed with comparable data. Whichever classification is used, the conclusion is that around half or more of children in the 1-5 years age-group are underweight in India.

This in itself is a cause for serious concern from the human development point of view. If this persists, batch after batch of children will display eventual stunting (low height-for-age), ending up with lower completed adult heights.

Data in Table 2 shows that in T.N. around 46.6 per cent of children below five years are underweight.[3] The percentages are higher in rural areas (52.1 per cent) as compared with urban (37.3 per cent) as per 1992-93 data. While this is better than the all-India situation of 53 per cent overall, Kerala, Haryana and even Rajasthan seem to be doing better than T.N.

Child development programme data (from the Tamil Nadu Integrated Nutrition Project, TINP) also tends to show high percentages of underweight[4] children among participants during the 1980s and 1990s (Table 3). Less than 50 per cent are classified as 'normal' in various years except for the baseline for 1995.

Table 4 brings out the contrast in respect of levels in percentages of children classified as normal on the one hand, and those suffering from malnutrition of various grades on the other, depending upon the classification system (Gomez or IAP) based on the same NCHS standards. With the same data the Gomez classification shows a sharply decreased percentage as normal; grade III under Gomez is equivalent to Grades III plus IV under IAP. In any case, whatever be the exact percentages, clearly, less than half the children below five years of age are normal, whatever the classification system used. This indicates the widespread prevalence of current malnutrition even in the late 1990s.

One problem with widespread malnutrition, and in particular undernutrition, is that smaller than normal children start to appear as the norm in the eyes of parents since most children are like that. This hampers alert signals, which could otherwise goad caregivers to intervene and parents to seek out treatment. This is where strategic inputs like growth monitoring through

Table 2
Prevalence of Malnutrition among Children Aged 1-4 Years in India and Selected States, 1992-93

(Per cent)

Country/ State	Underweight (weight-for-age below 2SD of median)			Stunted (height-for-age below 2SD of median)			Wasted (weight-for-Height below 2SD of median)		
	Rural	Urban	Total	Rural	Urban	Total	Rural	Urban	Total
India	59.9	45.20	53.10	54.10	44.80	52.00	18.00	15.80	17.50
Andhra Pradesh	52.1	40.00	49.10	-	-	-	-	-	-
Assam	51.8	37.30	50.40	53.50	39.60	52.50	11.40	5.60	10.80
Bihar	64.1	53.80	62.60	61.80	55.20	60.90	22.70	16.30	21.80
Gujarat	45.8	40.50	44.10	44.60	41.60	43.60	20.30	16.10	18.90
Haryana	39.4	33.00	37.90	48.00	42.40	46.70	5.70	6.40	5.90
Himachal Pradesh	48.3	30.20	47.00	-	-	-	-	-	-
Jammu & Kashmir	-	-	44.50	-	-	40.80	-	-	14.80
Karnataka	-	-	54.30	-	-	47.60	-	-	17.40
Kerala	30.6	22.90	28.50	29.60	21.50	27.40	11.50	12.00	11.60
Madhya Pradesh	59.4	50.10	57.40	-	-	-	-	-	-
Maharashtra	57.5	45.50	52.60	50.80	39.10	46.00	21.50	18.30	20.20
Orissa	-	-	53.30	-	-	48.20	-	-	21.30
Punjab	47.4	40.00	45.90	40.40	38.40	40.00	21.40	14.30	19.90
Rajasthan	41.1	43.00	41.60	43.00	43.50	43.10	17.70	29.10	19.50
Tamil Nadu	52.1	37.30	46.60	-	-	-	-	-	-
Uttar Pradesh	-	-	49.80		-	49.20	-	-	16.20
West Bengal	-	-	56.80		-	43.20	-	-	11.90

Note: - Not available. Children below two standard deviation of the international reference population median are considered malnourised.

Source: International Institute for Population Sciences (1995), *National Family Health Survey: India, 1992-93*, Bombay.

the use of growth charts based on external norms like the US NCHS standards can be useful. But their effectiveness depends on community education rather than their primary use being restricted to internal use by programme staff for screening to select the cases of growth faltering for nutrition supplements and referral.

3. Positive Trends

While levels of malnutrition may be high, the trend shows a clear improvement in the nutrition status of the pre-school children in T.N. over the last two decades. Independent data as well as project data (though not directly comparable) clearly demonstrate this common trend. Table 5 captures the trend observed in the project data while Tables 6 to 8 present the situation for T.N. as compared with India as a whole based on independent data.

Looking at the independent data in Table 6 from the National Institute of Nutrition, we see that weight-for-age showed improvements between the two decades 1975 to 1996. At the all-India level the distribution of children by weight-for-age[5] showed an increase in the percentage of normal (>90 per cent

Table 3
Percentage Distribution by Nutritional Status of 0-36 Month Old Children in Tamil Nadu Integrated Nutrition Project, 1992-93 to 1997

		Normal	Grade I	Grade II	Grades III & IV
1.	Baseline (phase I-III) survey (1992-93^)	41.4	34.9	18.8	4.9
2.	National family health survey (1992-93)	43.8	33.0	19.1	4.1
3.	Baseline (phase-IV& V) survey (1995)	54.6	29.6	13.1	2.8
4.	Monitoring data (December 1995)	40.0	39.4	16.8	3.8
5.	Mid-term survey (April/May 1996)	44.7	26.5	19.0	9.8
6.	Monitoring data April 1996	43.8	40.7	14.3	1.2
7.	Monitoring data December 1996	45.4	40.0	13.5	1.1
8.	Endline survey (October 1997)	48.4	35.2	13.4	3.0

Note: ^The age group for the 1992-93 baseline and 1997 endline surveys was 6-36 months which would be expected to give slightly higher figures than the 0-36 months aggregate. The Terminal Evaluation figures referred to nine districts for which data were availale at the time of preparation of the implementation completion report.

Source: World Bank (1998), *Implementation Completion Report India, Second Tamil Nadu Integrated Nutrition Project*, Report No. 17755.

of reference weight) and mildly malnourished (75-90 per cent of reference weight) children in the 1-5 years age-group; correspondingly, the percentage of severe malnutrition fell over the two decades (NIN, 1999). Starting from a low 5.9 per cent, the incidence of normal children increased to 8.9 per cent, and the share of children mildly malnourished rose from 31.6 to 40.6 per cent. Correspondingly, the share of children severely malnourished more than halved from 15 to 6.2 per cent. The rest of the children were mildly or moderately undernourished. The same trend is observed in the corresponding T.N. figures, with the percentages of normal and mild malnutrition higher than the all-India figures and the percentages of severely malnourished lower. It is also seen that the extent of increase in normal and reduction in severe malnutrition is much sharper in T.N. as compared with the pooled India figures.

Data for eight states including T.N. is captured in Table 7 for the years 1975-79, 1988-90 and 1994. Here again the trends are confirmed for T.N. and the eight states combined. But disaggregated data are interesting. Two states actually show a decline in the percentage of children in the normal category—Andhra Pradesh and Orissa. Gujarat does not show a steady upward trend. Karnataka and Madhya Pradesh show an improvement of a little less than 2 percentage points. In contrast, Kerala's normal percentage doubles even though the base itself is highest at the start in 1975-79. Maharashtra and T.N. also show more than doubling in the normal percentages. Thus, T.N. does better than most other states studied.

Table 4
Distribution of 0-60 Months Children in Tamil Nadu by Weight-for-Age

(Per cent)

Age-group (months)	Sex	No.	IAP classification Nutritional grade: Normal	Grade I	Grade II	Grade III	Grade IV
0 - 36	Boys	16921	45.7	36.4	14.5	2.9	0.5
	Girls	15551	51.2	33.9	12.3	2.3	0.3
	Pooled	32472	48.4	35.2	13.4	2.6	0.4
36 - 60	Boys	7747	34.9	45.5	16.7	2.6	0.3
	Girls	6817	44.8	39.5	13.6	2.0	0.1
	Pooled	14564	39.5	42.7	15.3	2.3	0.2
0 - 60	Boys	24668	42.3	39.3	15.2	2.8	0.5
	Girls	22368	49.3	35.5	12.7	2.2	0.3
	Pooled	47036	45.6	37.5	14.0	2.5	0.4

Age-group (months)	Sex	No.	Gomez classification Nutritional grade: Normal	Grade I	Grade II	Grade III
0-36	Boys	16921	17.3	48.5	30.8	3.4
	Girls	15551	20.2	50.5	26.6	2.6
	Pooled	32472	18.7	49.5	28.8	3.0
36 - 60	Boys	7747	6.3	54.2	36.6	2.9
	Girls	6817	10.3	56.4	31.1	2.2
	Pooled	14564	8.2	55.2	34.0	2.6
0 - 60	Boys	24668	13.9	50.3	32.6	3.2
	Girls	22368	17.2	52.3	28.0	2.5
	Pooled	47036	15.4	51.3	30.4	2.9

Note: *NCHS Standards are used.
Source: NIN (1998).

Table 5
Trend in Nutritional Status of Rural Tamil Nadu 0-36 Months Children

Year	Normal	Grade 1	Grade II	Grades III & IV
1983	18.6	33.7	35.4	12.3
1984	18.0	32.5	35.7	13.8
1985	20.0	34.1	35.5	10.4
1986	20.5	33.6	35.1	8.4
1987	18.8	38.6	35.4	7.2
1988	19.3	39.9	34.6	6.2
1989	21.3	41.5	32.3	4.9
1990	24.0	42.2	29.6	4.2
1991	25.6	43.2	27.4	3.8
1992	27.1	44.3	25.7	2.9
1993	30.6	46.4	20.3	2.7
1994	36.3	41.4	19.1	3.2
1995	14.5	39.9	16.5	2.1
1996	43.8	40.0	14.9	1.3
1997	47.3	39.6	12.3	0.8
1998	50.1	38.5	10.7	0.7
1999	52.1	37.6	9.8	0.5
2000	55.1	36.2	8.3	0.3

Note: TINP Programme Data 1983-1999 IAP Classification using Harvard standards.
Source: Internal Programme Data, Office of the Project Coordinator, WB, ICDS III, Chennai.

Table 6
Distribution of 1-5 Year Old Children by Weight-for-Age* 1975-1996

Extent of undernutrition	India (Pooled)		Tamil Nadu	
	1975	1996	1975	1996
Normal >90 per cent	5.9	8.9	6.2	14.4
Mild 75-90 per cent	31.6	40.6	34.2	49.2
Moderate 60-75 per cent	47.5	44.3	47.0	33.5
Severe <60 per cent	15.0	6.2	12.0	2.9

Note: * Gomez, using US-NCHS reference weights.
Source: NIN (1999b).

Table 7
Percentage Distribution of Children Aged 1-5 Years by Nutritional Status in Rural Areas of Selected Indian States, 1975-79, 1988-90 and 1994

State	Period	Normal	Mild	Moderate	Severe
Andhra Pradesh	1975-79	6.10	32.40	46.10	15.40
	1988-90	8.70	39.50	44.30	7.50
	1994	4.80	46.10	41.70	7.40
Gujarat	1975-79	3.80	28.10	54.30	13.80
	1988-90	7.30	33.90	45.80	13.00
	1994	4.80	28.00	55.10	12.10
Karnataka	1975-79	4.60	31.10	50.00	14.30
	1988-90	4.80	38.10	48.80	8.30
	1994	6.20	40.60	46.00	7.20
Kerala	1975-79	7.50	35.70	46.50	10.30
	1988-90	17.70	47.40	32.90	2.00
	1994	15.10	50.60	32.60	1.70
Madhya Pradesh	1975-79	8.40	30.30	45.10	16.20
	1988-90	17.70	27.40	38.90	16.00
	1994	10.20	36.10	42.10	11.60
Maharashtra	1975-79	3.20	25.40	49.50	21.90
	1988-90	6.70	38.00	47.50	7.80
	1994	8.60	37.20	43.70	10.50
Orissa	1975-79	7.50	35.90	41.70	14.90
	1988-90	8.10	34.60	46.60	10.70
	1994	6.30	40.40	47.90	5.40
Tamil Nadu	1975-79	6.20	34.20	47.00	12.60
	1988-90	8.00	42.00	45.80	4.20
	1994	13.20	46.70	36.80	3.30
All eight states	1975-79	5.90	31.60	47.50	15.00
	1988-90	9.90	37.60	43.80	8.90
	1994	8.50	40.40	47.90	5.40

Note: Nutritional grades are based on Gomez Classification using NCHS standards.
Source: NIN (1999a).

At the bottom end the percentages of children in the severely malnourished category decreased in all states. The declines were sharpest for Kerala, T.N. and Orissa. Karnataka, Maharashtra and Andhra Pradesh were able to halve the percentage of children in the severely malnourished category. The decline was the lowest from 13.8 to 12.1 per cent in Gujarat. The decline was the most remarkable in Kerala because its original level itself was the lowest at 10.3 per cent and yet its final 1994 level was also the lowest at 1.7 per cent. T.N. is clearly among the top three performers in child nutrition outcomes.

As per the programme data (TINP) for 17 years on participants (Table 5), the percentage of children in the nutritionally most vulnerable 6-36 months age-group with normal weight-for-age[6] increased steadily from just 18.6 per cent in 1983 to over 52 per cent in 1999. The levels are higher than the NIN results. This may be due to differences in classification system, characteristics and age of the population studied and hence are not directly comparable. Simultaneously, the percentage of children showing moderate malnutrition (grade II) as well as severe malnutrition (grades III and IV) showed a systematic decline, the former from over 35.4 to 9.8 per cent and the latter from 12.3 to just 0.5 per cent. Again, the levels are not comparable with NIN figures. The percentage of children mildly malnourished (grade I) was around 33 to 43 per cent with a mild upward trend. This indicated that children in grade III and IV climbed up to grades II, I and normal, and those in grade II climbed to I and normal.

To what extent these improvements are directly attributable to state policy as against a trend effect associated with general improvements in the socio-economic conditions is, however, less clear. To the extent the improvements in nutritional grades are keeping with a similar positive trend in the all-India figures, they may be the result of overall development. However, it is also true that the extent of improvements observed in T.N. are greater than those observed in many other states in India. It is likely that programme effects, to the extent that they exist, are positive.

4. Low Birth Weight

Low birth weight (LBW) is defined as weight at birth less than 2500 grams. Birth weights are significant in as much as they set the pattern for future growth of a person. They are also positively associated with infant mortality, and prevalence of diseases like diarrhea. Table 8 shows that among developing countries 19 per cent of children born recorded low birth weights in 1990, with the corresponding figure for Asia being higher at 21 per cent. Even African countries had a lower percentage of low birth weight cases at 15 per cent. The figure for developed countries was as low as 7 per cent while the global figure stood at 17 per cent. Data from various states in India in 1990 showed that the Kerala (Thiruvananthapuram) figures were the lowest at 15.3 per cent and Gujarat (Baroda) the highest at 46.4 per cent. T.N. (Madras) stood somewhere in between at 23 per cent—a little higher than the corresponding Asia figure. The overall incidence of LBW has been around 30 per cent. Mean birth weights were clearly higher than 2500 grams in all states except Gujarat (Table 8).

For T.N., district-wise average and low birth weight figures are given in Table 9. While the average birth weight for the state stood at 2.63 in 1995, it increased to 2.75 in 1999 suggesting that there may be a decline in the percentage of low birth weight cases over time. The percentage of low birth weight cases stood at 15.34 per cent in 1999, well below the Asia figure of 21 per cent, but over double the figure for developed countries. Among the districts only Virudhanagar had an average birth weight which was less than

Table 8
Birth Weights of Infants in Different Regions of India (per cent with LBW) with International Comparisons of LBW, 1990

Study centre/ country	Mean birth weight grams	Birth weight below 2,500 gms. (per cent)
India	2764+545	25.1
Varanasi	2628 + 504	30.6
Madras	2710+ 536	23.0
Trivandrum	2881+ 533	15.3
Calcutta	2673+394	20.1
Jamshedpur	2693+437	19.0
Baroda	2449+520	46.4
Bombay	2597+441	34.9
Asia (1990)		21.0
Africa (1990)		15.0
Developing countries (1990)		19.0
Developed countries (1990)		7.0
Global (1990)		17.0

Source: Ramachandran (1993); UNDP (1998).

2.50 kgs in 1995, but which went up to 2.76 in 1999. Overall, an improvement in average birth weight is taking place in T.N..

TINP programme data on recording of low birth weight cases shows a far lower percentage of low birth weight incidence, ranging between a low of 3.6 per cent in phase I districts to a high of just 5.3 per cent in phase IV, averaging to 4.5 per cent overall (pooled) among the weights recorded. According to National Institute of Nutrition (NIN), this does not seem reconcilable with other data and may be unrealistic. Earlier baseline and mid-term evaluations of TINP have yielded LBW of 22 per cent and 23 per cent, respectively (NIN, 1998).

If this last programme data is excluded, the T.N. situation on birth weights is somewhere in between the ranges prevailing in other states, with the trend being clearly positive. Kerala shows the highest mean birth weight and the lowest percentage of low birth weight cases even without a massive network of direct nutrition inputs, but in the background of higher human development indicators. Given this, the relative strength of programme and non-programme effects on birth weights cannot be established.

5. Weight-for-Age by Sex

A bias against females is found in the data on IMR and in the overall sex ratio. This apart, other non-health indicators like education, ownership of assets, participation in decision making, etc., also show a distinct bias against females. In the case of anthropometric outcomes, however, lower values for females have not been well established. Outside Asia, certainly, it appears that differences by sex are small and often insignificant.[7] When data are converted into standardised percentages of reference weight-for-age, and if there are systematic biases in the reference population but not in the sample being studied, then standardisation could also lead to spurious results.

In India, in the early 1980s data from West Bengal did show lower weight-for-age outcomes for females (Sen and Sengupta, 1983). Absolute weight values

Table 9
Average Birth Weights in 1995 and 1997 and Low Birth Weight Cases by District in Tamil Nadu

District	Average birth weight		Low birth weight
	1995 (Kgs)	1999 (Kgs)	(per cent)
Chennai		2.80	14.34
Kancheepuram	2.62	2.72	17.37
Tuticorin	2.68	2.74	14.97
Coimbatore	2.62	2.80	14.88
Dharmapuri	2.67	2.77	12.69
Dindigul	2.68	2.86	12.50
Virudhunagar	2.45	2.76	14.70
Kanyakumari	2.56	2.81	11.31
Madurai	2.63	2.83	15.92
Ooty	2.53	2.71	25.21
Vellore	2.62	2.76	16.62
Sivaganga	2.71	2.67	15.29
Erode	2.59	2.76	16.47
Pudukottai	2.70	2.82	12.45
Nagapattinam	2.58	2.76	12.96
Ramanathapuram	2.69	2.82	13.14
Salem	2.60	2.65	18.03
Thanjavur	2.56	2.72	20.82
Thiruvannamalai	2.65	2.77	13.69
Trichirapalli	2.64	2.77	15.03
Tirunelveli	2.67	2.78	16.73
Cuddalore	2.67	2.68	12.96
Villupuram	2.61	2.73	15.28
Tiruvarur		2.65	19.21
Perambalur		2.68	13.59
Karur		2.77	13.57
Theni		2.70	19.23
Tiruvellore		2.75	14.71
Namkkal		2.66	18.89
Tamil Nadu	2.63	2.75	15.34

Source: DPH CSSM Programme Data, 1997 and 1999.

among well-to-do Hyderabad boys and girls from 12-36 months of age and among a birth cohort of children of a high socio-economic group from birth to 36 months of age in Delhi (Ghosh, 1986) showed slightly higher levels for males, but their statistical significance is not known.

Routine monthly monitoring data in the TINP and ICDS programme areas do not present weights segregated by sex. Had that been done, it would have provided a valuable source to track not only differences by sex, but also changes over nearly two decades, from 1980 until 2000, and more.

However, an exploration of weight differences by sex in T.N. is available for the period 1980-1989 using CNC records. The districts of Madurai and Ramnathapuram show higher values for males. Further, (a) the condition of both males and females improves over the nine year period from 1980-1989; (b) both boys and girls from upper socio-economic classes do better than those from the worse off; (c) but the male-female gap is significantly less among SC households as compared with the others; and (d) the male-female gap itself decreases over this period (Rajivan, 1991).

As part of the endline evaluation of TINP done by NIN, male-female comparisons are made a decade later, for 1997 (Table 4). Here it is concluded that girls do no worse than boys so far as weight-for-age is concerned. In fact, the female percentages are slightly better than those of males. This is true, separately for the 0-36 months as well as for the 36-60 months age-groups. The normal and grade I percentages for females are higher than those for males, while simultaneously the grades III and IV percentages are lower, both under the IAP and Gomez classifications.

From this it is tempting to infer that it is the state's direct nutrition intervention efforts (like the TINP, ICDS and the noon-meal schemes) which are gender neutral, and thus independent of society's tendencies, selection of the worst-off cases may be a contributory factor in improving the relative position of females. Such a conclusion is certainly consistent with the data available. But much more careful analysis is needed before such a result can be conclusively established.

It would have been of interest to explore male-female differences over the 17–20 years for which TINP has been in operation based on monitoring data. Even if the levels are different (higher for normal and grade I, lower for grades III and IV), a comparison of male-female gaps based on comparable data from the same source over a long-time period would be of considerable interest. While programme monitoring has yet to take up sex as a significant analytical category, it could be taken up right away without much additional cost.

A look at recent data for 1-5 year olds, pooled from nine states (Andhra Pradesh, Gujarat, Karnataka, Kerala, Madhya Pradesh, Maharashtra, Uattar Pradesh, West Bengal, and Tamil Nadu) for 1996-97, show that male and female undernutrition is comparable (NIN, 1997). No bias against females is now observed in weight-for-age. Hence it is difficult to definitely claim that the state's direct nutrition interventions may be the primary factor responsible for the insignificant male-female differences in recent years.

6. Secular Changes in Average Body Sizes

An increase in average heights and weights over time, especially in a less developed country, indicates a sustained, general improvement in nutrition security and living standards. This phenomenon has been observed in developed countries. On an average, as compared with the early immigrants into the USA, the next generation has been taller. In Japan the average height of female basket ball players has risen. Children of Indian parents born and brought up in the US have been taller than their cousins growing up in India, reflecting better health and nutrition environment.

The NIN data showed that over the period 1975-79 to 1996-97 mean heights and weights for different ages and sexes did not increase significantly for T.N. The same was the case of Orissa, Gujarat (except school ages and adolescents), Andhra Pradesh, Maharashtra, and Karnataka. In respect of Kerala alone there was an overall increase in heights (1-2 cms) and weights (2-3 kgs) among males and females for all age-groups. In Gujarat both boys and girls of school ages and adolescents showed an increase. However, in all states the values were significantly lower than the NCHS norms (NIN, 1999). Thus, no secular increase in body size has been established in T.N.

7. Ranking by District

Ranks were determined on the basis of monitoring data on participating children in age-group 6-36 months in 19[8] districts from 1996 to 1999 where TINP (now WB-ICDS-III) is in operation. First, ranks were given for each of the four years based on percentage of children in the category *normal plus grade I* representing relatively better nutritional status based on programme monitoring data. Second, the overall rank for the four year period was calculated based on rank sums and a re-ranking. A similar exercise was repeated for the *'grades III plus IV'* in order to rank districts by relatively poor nutritional status. Tables 10 and 11 contain the ranking data. As grade II is an intermediate grade which is impacted by positive and negative changes in both *normal and grade I* as also by those in *grades III and IV,* ranking of grade II was not found meaningful.[9]

An examination of the ranking in respect of the categories *normal plus grade I* and *grades III plus IV* show that, by and large, there was remarkable stability over the period in respect of ranking by nutritional grades, of course, with some notable exceptions.

Of the top five districts overall in the *normal plus grade I* category (Kanyakumari, Coimbatore, Vellore, Tuticorin and Erode), as many as four are also at the top in respect of low percentages in *grades III plus IV* (Kanyakumari, Erode, Coimbatore and Vellore), showing remarkable congruence of the top ranks at the high and low ends of weight-for-age.

The congruence among the bottom ranks also exists but is less remarkable. In respect of the bottom five ranking districts in the *normal plus grade I* (Cuddalore, Nagapattinam, Villupuram, Ramnathapuram and Trichy), two (Nagapattinam and Ramnathapuram) are found among the bottom five in *grades III plus IV* also. The remaining three are at middle to low ranks of nine and eleven. None are at high ranks of five or less. Similarly, among the bottom five ranking districts in *grades III plus IV* (Virudhunagar, Nagapattinam, Ramnathapuram, Tirunelveli and Tiruvannamalai), two are among the bottom five of the categories *Normal plus grade I* (Nagapattinam and Ramanathapuram). The remaining three are at middle to low ranks of 8, 11 and 12. None are at a high rank.

Kanyakumari, which is more like Kerala, ranked first for the relatively high percentage of children in the *normal plus grade I* in each of the four years, thus being overall first during 1996-1999. It also ranked first for three out of four years and second for one year for having low percentage of children among the poorer *grades III plus IV*, thus gaining an overall first rank for 1996-1999 here also. It is of interest to note that female literacy is the highest in this district. This gives us a clue about the criticality of non-nutrition factors which affect nutrition status.

For *normal plus grade I* the worst overall district was Cuddalore with rank 19. Individual ranks were 19, 17, 18 and 19 for the four years, showing consistently relatively low percentages of children in the better nutritional categories of *normal plus grade I.* In respect of the nutritionally worst categories of *grades III plus IV*, however, Cuddalore does better, improving its overall rank to eight (4, 9, 9 and 6).

For *grades III plus IV* the worst district overall is Virudhunagar with rank 19 and individual ranks 17, 18, 19 and 19 for the four years. However, the district improves its overall rank in respect of percentages of children in the category *normal plus grade I* to 11. Though the overall rank is better, there is a decline from rank nine to rank 16 over the period 1996-1999.

By and large, ranking of a district did not change by more than five places over the period. While Tirunelveli showed a cumulative decline in the upper and lower grades, Salem showed a cumulative improvement.

8. Child Nutrition Status and Mortality

It seems possible for nations to control mortality without corresponding improvements in nutritional status as seen in Table 2. This is also borne out from studies on India on child mortality and infant mortality rate (IMR) in conjunction with diet surveys, clinical surveys and nutritional anthropometry by the NNMB which indicate that better child survival does not necessarily mean better health and nutrition (NIN, 1997). It appears that mortality control can be achieved even in poverty[10] and in the presence of malnutrition. But promotion of better nutrition status requires not only a more holistic approach, it also needs active and sustained behaviour changes among the population.

District level programme data from T.N. is also consistent with this (Tables 10 and 11). Ranking of districts by nutritional performance for the below 36 months children was not found correlated to IMR. It seems to be quite possible to have a high IMR but relatively better performance in child weights and vice versa. Dharmapuri district with the highest IMR among the 19 of 68.2 ranked 13 in the *normal plus grade I* category but two in the *grades III plus IV.* Cuddalore with the second lowest IMR of 30 (next to Kanyakumari's 15.9 which is an outlier) ranked the lowest at 19 among *normal plus grade I* and eight in the *grades III plus IV.*

Thus, it seems possible that even when mortality is controlled, nutritional status may or may not improve. Separate efforts in this respect are needed. To a large extent mortality control involves less cost, time and effort from the side of the household with the state taking the lead in respect of immunisation and provision of other health services. Malnutrition control, on the other hand, requires care-givers to spend time and effort in adopting nutrition conducive practices, even if the state provides free nutrition inputs. Children have to be fed frequently in small quantities during weaning, boiling water takes time and uses up valuable fuel, minimising conversion of supplementary feeding from government programmes into substitute feeding by withdrawing or reducing home food imposes a direct cost, physically taking the small child to nutrition centres takes parental time (unlike school children, pre-school children are more likely to depend on an adult to be taken to and from the centres) and so on. All this is not only time consuming, but also eats into household finances.

IV. TREND EFFECTS vs. EFFECTS OF DIRECT NUTRITION SERVICES

While massive and sustained investments in direct nutrition programmes have been taking place in T.N. under the state budget, one must also look elsewhere to analyse the causes behind the nutrition outcomes. While some of the improvements no doubt are attributable to the investments, other factors, no less important, are no doubt at work. These are part of the overall trend improvement in the human condition, particularly women's condition. Moreover, the daily noon-meal feeding largely operates as a *substitute* meal, rather than as a nutrition *supplement* in as much as parents withdraw home feeding when a child has eaten in the centre. Finally, the investments are focussed on those already malnourished. To an extent then, one should not expect very strong anthropometric effects.

Of course, the direct nutrition investments do have other benefits, no less important: control of hunger and providing minimum food security, promoting school attendance, providing crucial child care facilities not normally available to rural households, functioning as an income supplement to households to the extent home feeding is replaced by centre feeding, the public popularity of noon meals in a democratic society, promotion of social harmony in a society with caste divisions when all children sit down to eat together every day, etc.

V. DIRECTIONS FOR FUTURE

1. Prevention vs. Management of Malnutrition

T.N.'s nutrition policy document provides a clue for the future where it says, "Feeding programmes which seek to improve the nutritional status among the already malnourished children are less likely to be effective, and are expensive and therefore non-sustainable." (Government of Tamil Nadu, undated). This is an important recognition. With two decades of sustained direct interventions among the malnourished, no doubt useful in the short run, the future generations would be better served if priority is given to prevention of malnutrition rather than to its management, after a person is diagnosed as malnourished. This would imply a conscious multi-sectoral approach with multiple policy instruments, the NMP, standard ICDS and WB-ICDS-III being a part of a wider set.

Given that the state is committed to nutrition improvements, a clear distinction in actual operation (in addition to policy documents) between short-term and long-term approaches would be useful. Direct interventions like the existing schemes are useful short-term instruments for those children, pregnant and lactating women who are currently malnourished or are at nutritional risk already. Batch after batch of children are receiving inputs to combat their inadequate nutritional status after they become malnourished.

The long-term objective should be to eliminate malnutrition altogether. Hence, for the long run, reduced direct food provisions can be combined with an increasing emphasis on strategies for community education and participation to bring about widespread consciousness among men and women about the importance of good nutritional status and the ability to recognise poor growth cases to be able to trigger behaviour changes. Growth charts are an important educational tool already in use that can make invisible undernutrition visible. These charts should invariably be with the parents rather than in the centres, to be an effective tool. When a majority of the children are underweight, parents are likely to think that their child is normal—like everybody else—unless demonstrated otherwise based on an external norm.

Increasingly, the focus could shift to orienting all adolescents, boys and girls, who are to be the parents of the future, rather than women who are already pregnant and whose habits may be rather fixed.

Focused strategies to minimise the incidence of low birth weights are likely to pay rich dividends as the future growth pattern of the child would then be more likely to be nearer normal. The prevalence of low birth weights is a cause for concern. Children with weight less than 2.5 kgs at birth carry the handicap of being at additional nutritional risk. This has also contributed to the relatively higher prevalence of undernutrition among infants below six months of age as compared with older children. The aim should be to eliminate cases of low birth weight. For this one may have to take a look at not only maternal malnutrition, but also to step back to focus on the growth patterns of adolescent girls, the future mothers.

Instead of waiting for an undernourished and anemic woman to get pregnant and then intervene, if better growth is promoted among adolescent girls during their rapid growth spurt, they are likely to make healthier mothers in future. Adolescents of small weights and heights, combined with nutritional deficiencies like anemia, should be an area of concern. Given the heavy investments in direct nutrition, inclusion of nutrition supplements to adolescent girls who are the future mothers, preferably in forms not perceived as food substitutes which could result in withdrwal or reduction of home food, would be a step in the right direction. If resources are a constraint, and if the smallest section of the population is to be identified for food supplementation, it would be the adolescent girl.

Timing and adequacy of weaning foods is another critical area. Breast feeding is near universal and not a problem in T.N., especially among the poorer sections of the population. However, attention to the timing of introducing complementary weaning foods in addition to continuing human milk may be needed. There is a tendency to delay this in India. After four months of age mother's milk is not enough and needs to be supplemented through suitable weaning foods. While this is part of nutrition education in programme areas, most programmes of dissemination are passive. More effective interactive dissemination of correct information through trained humanpower combined with monitoring of adoption of complementary feeding and weaning practices may be more productive.

Community participation is a difficult area, easier to state than to bring about. But a beginning having been made by holding local body elections after a gap of decades, and with the one-third reservation for women, one might hope for greater push and pull factors to operate in the women and child sector. Similarly, the network of women's self-help groups operating in the districts could prove to be an effective medium for information dissemination in an interactive way through trained communicators.

Combining nutrition education with women's capacity building, empowerment and incomes in the hands of women through training, promoting regularity in savings and long-term credit access is also important. This achieves two things: one, women become aware and ambitious on behalf of themselves and their children; and two, they have the purchasing power combined with status within the household to take responsible decisions for their children. This can promote an increased effective demand for food and nutrition security, leading to improvements in overall health and nutrition status. Women's empowerment has been getting a very big boost with the extension of a major micro-finance scheme for poor women in T.N., the T.N. Women's Development Project, commonly called *Mahalir Thittam* (i.e. Women's Scheme). The scheme promotes social and economic empowerment among women through women's organisation into active self-help groups (SHGs), rotation of their collective savings to help satisfy emergency and consumption needs of households, reduce the dependence on moneylenders, institutional credit access and income generation in the hands of women. The project's pilot phase has[11] already demonstrated that poor rural women are credit worthy and can become numerate and financially savvy even when semi-literate. Over seven lakh women in T.N. are reported as participating in the programme by August 2000 with the numbers growing every month. Strengthening and integrating Women's Working Groups of TINP with SHGs on the tried and tested SHG pattern, thus institutionalising economic empowerment systems among women, rather than working in independent compartments given that they are in the same villages, would help in establishing inter-sectoral linkages across schemes.

2. Growth Monitoring and Nutrition Surveillance

Growth monitoring is prevalent on a regular basis in the former TINP and now WB-ICDS-III as well as standard ICDS programme areas. But growth charts can serve as a more effective educational tool if they are in the hands of the parents rather than programme staff. This can be encouraged.

At present weight-for-age and other detailed health and nutrition related monitoring data is available only for programme participants. These are from the relatively worse-off sections of society and do not reflect the overall nutrition condition prevailing. About two-thirds of the child population remains outside this system. Moreover, programme data is always open to questions of reliability, as it is generated by protagonists. It is suggested that an independent nutrition surveillance system be put in place on the basis of a suitable sample design and coverage to be able to make, at the very least, comparisons by location—rural versus urban; by district; by season—to pinpoint time of the year for greater attention; by sex—males vs. females; by economic status—better-off vs. worse-off; by birth order—earlier born vs. later born; by educational status of parents; time trends, etc.

Further, a suitable panel for monitoring a cohort from birth to adulthood may be set up. This will be able to aid policy as well as function as a communication tool. Currently, the NNMB is an agency monitoring the nutrition status at the state and national levels. But for states to be able to take targeted corrective action, below state level data is also required. The technical services of NNMB could be used in setting up such a system which might even fit in with the national monitoring on nutrition. Given that T.N. already has a massive structure for nutrition interventions (staff and centres), the additional costs (financial and organisational) of surveillance would not be prohibitive.

3. Recognition of Non-food Factors

Various studies have shown the importance of factors like improved water supply, reduction in infections, near universal immunisation providing herd immunity, etc., in improving nutritional status. In fact, as the NIN (1999b) report shows, during the 1975-97 period there was no significant improvement in nutrient intake, and yet, an improvement in nutritional status of pre-school children was observed.

Many of the non-food factors require very little effort on the part of individual households or child care-givers. Many of these are under the purview of the state, and hence comparatively easier to control as against activities that require child care-givers to put in special effort, acquire better knowledge and adopt nutritionally conducive practices. For example, it is easier to just provide a protected water supply point in a village than teach all the mothers the importance of diarrhea management with ORT combined with small and frequent feeds, and to ensure such practices within households.

Some states, including T.N., have tended to focus on the provision of food supplements or substitute meals under state budgets, a traditional role of the family. While the importance of food inputs cannot be denied, the comparative advantage of governments in providing non-nutritional inputs, including general education, nutrition education and poverty alleviation, needs to be re-emphasised not only in the interest of better nutrition security, but also because of their effects on the overall human condition.

Other non-food factors like female education, income generation in the hands of women and control over family size as higher order births are greater nutritional risk, are also crucial.

4. Child Rights to Nutrition

T.N.'s nutrition programmes can almost be thought of as entitlement programmes, akin to what might be called soft rights—something accepted by society and political leadership and which is unlikely to be questioned for reasons of resource constraints. As the NMP has the first call on the state's resources, like the food subsidies under the public distribution system (Rajivan, 1993), soft rights to nutrition can be said to have been established. However, these are not hard rights, in the sense of being ensured through legislation with legal recourse in case of non-compliance. To what extent child care can or should be made the responsibility of the state rather than of the parents is an area open to question. At what level should the state step in—the local government, the district administration, the state government, the central government?

This is a territory not yet debated within government, though there are individuals, groups and agencies, including UNICEF, who have in place some thinking on the subject. A rights approach, as hard rights, would imply legally enforceable rights—with laws on entitlement and institutional arrangements to make corrections when the right is not fulfilled, together with resource arrangements in cases of non-compliance (Kent, 1995). More work is needed in this area.

VI. CAVEAT: AN IMPLICIT ASSUMPTION IN SOCIAL USES OF ANTHROPOMETRY

The complication of obesity and the need for weight control may be applicable among the relatively better-off sections and some urban areas. Of course, this may be not a complication in rural areas, and among a majority of the population, not only in T.N. but in most less developed countries. At the same time it may be recognised that a tendency has been observed in some developed countries for the worse-off to display signs of poor nutrition with obesity due to the increased reliance on 'junk food'. This has been observed among the less educated sections of the population in the US, Canada, especially among new immigrant communities. One may look out for a beginning of this in metros in India also.

Apart from the complication of obesity, what could be the reason to assume that higher weights, heights and other signs of growth and acceleration in maturation are good in themselves? It is only because higher weight and other signs of growth are associated with improvements in the overall biological condition of children, and therefore of future adults, that anthropometric outcomes are valued. Data on older children from Belgium (Renson et al., 1983), on conscripts from Poland (Brajezewski, 1985), children from Czechoslovakia (Parizkova and Berdychova, 1977), and from Canada (Jequier et al., 1979) show that while larger body sizes were generally associated with better socio-economic backgrounds and urbanisation, they were also associated with inferior performance in certain functional traits like absolute grip strength, grip strength for weight, stroke volume, pulse rate after exercise, etc.

These findings should serve as a reminder that whatever makes children from better environments grow more steadily and faster, does not necessarily make them more fit physiologically or even more likely to achieve fuller expression of their physical, intellectual or cultural potential. However, unfortunately, in many societies including India, such associations still continue. And, in spite of important exceptions to which attention is drawn here as an alert signal, differences in childhood growth are in fact associated with morbidity, mortality and physiological functioning capacity.

Notes

1. From January 1996 the 'Worker' category has been brought under time scale of pay from the original consolidated wages paid as part timers. The scale itself has been revised upwards after the Fifth Pay Commission to Rs. 600-10-700-20-1100 per month. They are also eligible for DA at 41 per cent of pay. Thus, she gets to take home around Rs. 1200. The Helper and Cooks categories continue to be on consolidated pay, taking home Rs. 550 and Rs. 610 per month.

2. Gomez classification (4 grades): >=90 per cent of reference weight-for-age: Normal; 75-90 per cent of reference weight-for-age: Grade I or mild malnutrition; 60-75 per cent of reference weight-for-age: Grade II or moderate malnutrition; <60 per cent of reference weight: Grade III or severe malnutrition.

   Indian Academy of Pediatrics (5 grades); >80 per cent of reference weight-for-age: Normal; 71-80 per cent of reference weight-for-age: Grade I malnutrition; 61-70 per cent of reference weight-for-age: Grade II malnutrition; 51-60 per cent of reference weight-for-age: Grade III malnutrition; <=50 per cent of reference weight-for-age: Grade IV malnutrition.

Standard Deviation Classification: How many SDs away from the median weight-for-age class captures the extent of gap from the normal. Less than or equal to 3SD of weight-for-age or height-for-age indicates severe undernutrition or stunting, respectively. A gap of 3SD-2SD below median is relatively less severe indicating moderate malnutrition; 2SD-1SD is mild; and 1SD to median or above is taken as normal.

3. Weight-for-age below 2SD of median in 1992-93.
4. IAP classification based on the Harvard standards of weight for age.
5. Gomez classification using US NCHS standards.
6. IAP classification based on Harvard standards.
7. See for example, results from Africa (Strauss, 1990; Svedberg, 1987) and Latin America (Schofield, 1979; Thomas et al., 1988).
8. Comparable data is not available for other districts and hence, regretfully, those districts had to be excluded from the comparison.
9. An increase (or decrease) in grade II cannot be unambiguously categorized as an improvement since it could be the consequence of a decrease (increase) in the percentage in the normal plus grade I category or a decrease (increase) in the percentage of grades III plus IV.
10. Say, due to public health services like universal immunisation, environmental sanitation etc., which require only one time or little continuous effort by the general population.
11. Started a decade ago in a limited area with assistance from the International Fund for Agricultural Development (IFAD), Rome. It is now being expanded to cover all districts in T.N. under the state budget in phases.

References

Brajezewski, C. (1985), *Spoleczne Roznice w budowie fizycznej I wydolnosci mlodych mezczyzn,* (mimeo).

Ghosh, Shanti (1986), *A Longitudinal Study of the Outcome of a Birth Cohort*, Project No. 01-658-2, Delhi.

Government of Tamil Nadu (undated), *Tamil Nadu State Policy on Nutrition,* Department of Social Welfare and Noon Meal Programme.

Jequier, J.C. et al. (1979), *"Externe and interne Fehlerquelle einer Langschnittuntersuchung"*, in K. Willimezik and M. Grosser (eds.), *Die Motorische Entwicklung im Kindes-und Jugendalter.*

Kent, George, (1995), *Nutrition Rights in Tamil Nadu, India,* University of Hawaii, September.

NIN (1997), *25 Years of National Nutrition Monitoring Bureau,* National Institute of Nutrition, Indian Council of Medical Research, Hyderabad.

—— (1998), *Endline Evaluation of Tamil Nadu Integrated Nutrition Project – II* , Hyderabad.

—— (1999a), *Report of Repeat Survey, 1988-90,* Hyderabad.

—— (1999b), *Report of Second Repeat Survey – Rural (1996-97),* Hyderabad.

Parizkova, J. and J. Berdychova (1977), "The Impact of Ecological Factors on Somatic and Motor Development of Pre-school Children," in Eiben, O. (ed.), *Growth and Development and Physique*, Akademiai Kiado, Budapest.

Rajivan, A.K. (1991), *Weight Variations among Pre-schoolers: An Analysis of Evidence from Rural Tamil Nadu,* Unpublished Ph.D. dissertation, University of Southern California, Los Angeles.

—— (1993), *Tamil Nadu's Nutrition Programme as a Nutrition Entitlement* (mimeo).

—— (1996), "Measurement of Gender Differences Using Anthropometry," *Economic and Political Weekly*, Vol. 31, No. 43, October 26.

Ramachandran, P. (1993), "Low Birth Weights: The Indian Experience", *NFI Bulletin,* Vol. 14, No. 4.

Renson, G. Beunen, M.Ostyn, J. Simons, D.Van Gerven and R.Wellens (1983), *"Socio-geographic Variation of Physical Fitness of 12-19 Year Old Belgian Boys."*, Bull. Soc.Roy.Belge. Anthropol. Prehist, Vol. 94, pp. 177-192..

Schofield, S. (1979), *Development and the Problems of Village Nutrition*, Croom Helm, London.

Sen, A.K. and S. Sengupta (1983), "Malnutrition of Rural Children and the Sex Bias", *Economic and Political Weekly*, Annual Number, Vol. 18, Nos. 19-21.

Shantha, E.V. (1997), *Services That Matter: An Overview of Child Care Services in Tamil Nadu*, M.S. Swaminathan Research Foundation, Monograph 7, Chennai.

Strauss, J. (1990), "Households, Commodities and Preschool Children's Nutrition Outcomes: Evidence From Cote d' Ivoire", *Economic Development and Cultural Change*, pp. 231-261.

Svedberg, P. (1987), *Undernutrition in Sub-Saharan Africa: A Critical Assessment of the Evidence*, World Institute for Development Economics Research, Helsinki, (mimeo).

Thomas, D., J. Strauss and M. Henriques (1987), *Child Survival, Nutritional Status and Household Characteristics: Evidence from Brazil*, Economic Growth Centre Discussion Paper 542, Yale University.

—— (1988), *Child Survival, Height-for-Age and Household Characteristics in Brazil* (mimeo).

UNDP (1998), *Human Development Report, 1997*, Oxford University Press, New Delhi.

7

Health and Human Security: Some Considerations for Priority Setting

A.K. Shiva Kumar

I. TAKING STOCK[1]

Poor health remains one of the most dominant causes of human deprivations in India. More than 50 years after independence, ill health continues to devastate the lives of several millions—economically and emotionally. Nothing can be more unnerving than frequent illnesses; nothing can be more unsettling to a poor family than premature death. Ensuring health security therefore becomes essential for advancing human security and for promoting social justice.

There has been a noticeable expansion in the physical provisioning of health services in India. Between 1951-97, the number of hospitals increased from 2,694 to 16,000; and the number of hospital beds went up from 117,178 to over 870,000. During the same period, the number of doctors went up from 61,840 to 484,401; and the number of nurses grew from 16,550 to over 565,000. By 1997, there were 2,628 community health centres, 22,446 primary health care centres and 136,379 sub-centres spread throughout the country (Table 1). The country has also acquired a reputation for high quality research and medical teaching, as well as for its super speciality institutions.

According to the *Human Development Report 1998*, India's public expenditure on health was 1.8 per cent of GDP in 1990. This was less than the public expenditure incurred on health by China (2.1 per cent of GDP), the same as Sri Lanka, and more than Thailand (1.1 per cent of GDP) and Malaysia (1.3 per cent of GDP). If both public and private expenditures are considered, then India spends relatively more on health than many other developing countries.

The physical expansion of health services and public expenditures have led to gains in health status. Life expectancy at birth nearly doubled between 1951-96, and infant mortality rates were halved between 1975-95. Many of the major communicable diseases like small pox have been successfully controlled. Despite these achievements, India is far from realising the Health for All goals by the year 2000 (Table 2).

Table 1
Expansion of Health Services in India

	1951	1961	1971	1981	1991	1996-97
Medical colleges	28	60	98	111	128	NA
Hospitals	2,694	3,094	3,862	6,804	11,174	16,000
Dispensaries	6,515	9,406	12,180	6,751	27,431	NA
Community health centres				217	2,071	2,628
Primary health centres	725	2,565	5,112	5,740	20,450	22,446
Sub-centres			28,489	51,405	130,984	136,379
Hospital beds	117,178	230,000	348,655	569,495	810,548	870,000
Doctors	61,840	83,756	151,129	268,712	394,068	484,401
Dentists	3,290	3,582	5,512	8,648	10,751	23,953
Nurses	16,550	35,584	80,620	154,280	340,208	565,000

Source: Data are from Ministry of Health and Family Welfare, Government of India, quoted in Government of India (1997).

Table 2
Illustrative Goals for Health and Family Welfare by 2000

Indicator	Most recent estimate		Goal for the year 2000
1. Infant mortality rate	71.0	(1997)	Below 60
2. Perinatal mortality rate	44.3	(1993)	30-35
3. Crude death rate	8.9	(1996)	9
4. Maternal mortality rate	4.37	(1992-3)	Below 2
5. Life expectancy at birth (years)			
Male	59.0	(1989-93)	64
Female	59.7	(1989-93)	64
6. Babies with birth-weight below 2000 grams (per cent)	30 .0	(1992)	10
7. Crude birth rate	27.2	(1996)	21
8. Effective couple protection rate (per cent)	45.4	(1998)	60
9. Total fertility rate	3.5	(1995)	2.2
10. Pregnant mothers receiving antenatal care (per cent)	62.3	(1992-3)	100
11. Deliveries by trained birth attendants (per cent)	52.5	(1997)	100
12. Immunisation status (per cent)	35.4	(1992-3)	100

Source: Government of India (1999) and International Institute for Population Studies (1995).

The shortfalls in health and human development are huge.[2] Close to 2 million children die every year, almost the same number as in 1960; and most of these deaths are avoidable. Almost 55 per cent of children under five—some 75 million of them—are malnourished. Iodine deficiency affects the normal development of some 250 million Indians, and accounts for an estimated 90,000 stillbirths and neonatal deaths every year. It has led to 2.2 million Indian children being afflicted with cretinism and another 6.5 million becoming mildly retarded. Close to 85 per cent of Indian women are anaemic on account of iron deficiency. An estimated 110,000 women die every year from causes related to pregnancy and childbirth.

Yet another striking feature of health in India is the persistence of widespread inequalities. Health outcomes vary across states, between rural and urban areas, and within communities. Figure 1 shows mortality differentials at the national level.

Figure 1
Mortality Differentials in India, 1989-92

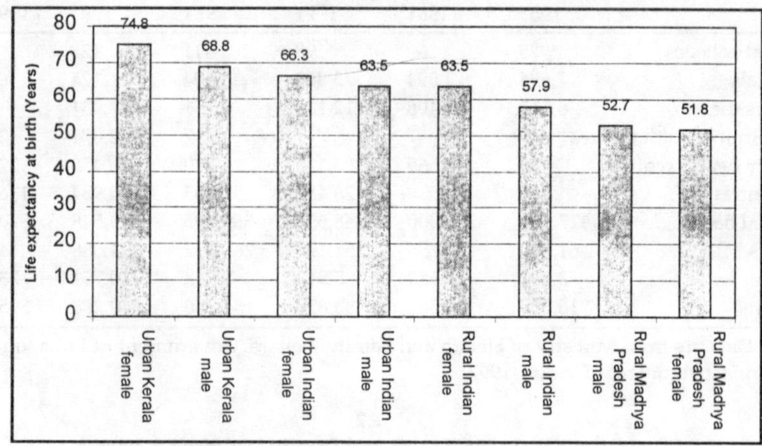

Source: Registrar General of India (1996).

Life expectancy at birth between 1989-93 was the highest in Kerala (72 years) and the lowest in Madhya Pradesh (54 years). The gap in life expectancy among rural women in the two states is even larger. Between 1989-93, life expectancy at birth among rural women in Kerala was 74.8 years, and it was 51.8 years in Madhya Pradesh—a gap of 23 years.

Table 3 presents data on socio-economic and demographic indicators for two sets of Indian states: two of India's richest states (Punjab and Maharashtra) and two of the poorest states (Bihar and Uttar Pradesh) in terms of per capita income. Corresponding data for Kerala—the state with the best record of social development in India, and for India are also presented.

Table 3
Socio-economic Indicators for Selected States

	Population in millions 1999	Per capita SDP (Rs.) 1994-95	% of pop. below poverty line 1993-94	IMR 1996	Life expectancy at birth (years) 1989-93		Literacy rate 1991		% children < 4 malnourished 1992-93
					Female	Male	Female	Male	
Two richest states									
Punjab	23	14,188	12	52	67.6	65.2	50	66	45.9
Maharashtra	90	13,112	37	48	65.4	63.0	52	77	54.2
Two poorest states									
Uttar Pradesh	166	5,331	41	85	55.1	56.5	25	56	59.0
Bihar	98	3,816	55	72	57.2	59.7	23	52	62.6
Kerala	32	6,983	25	13	74.7	68.8	86	94	28.5
India	981	8,281	36	72	59.7	59.0	39	64	53.4

Sources: Column 3 is from *Economic Survey 1996-97* (GOI, 1997); Column 4 is from Planning Commission; Columns 5, 6 and 7 are from SRS (Registrar General of India, 1996); Columns 8 and 9 are from Census of India; Column 10 is from NFHS 1992-93 (IIPS, 1995).

Over 260 million people live in Uttar Pradesh and Bihar, two of the poorest states in India. On the other hand, only 113 million live in the two richest states—Punjab and Maharashtra. Also, over a third of India's 350 million people below the poverty line live in the two states of Uttar Pradesh and Bihar. The two richest states, Punjab and Maharashtra, account for only 10 per cent of India's poor living below the poverty line. In general, higher levels of literacy and higher levels of income co-exist with better health outcomes. But a closer look at the data reveals that it is possible to have good health security (like in Kerala) even at low levels of income. Much has to do with the extent of public provisioning of basic social services by the state. At the same time, it is also apparent that high incomes do not necessarily translate into good health. Women in Punjab, for instance, live on average, seven years less than women in Kerala even though Punjab enjoys more than double the per capita income of Kerala.

The shortfalls in health and the failure to ensure universal access to good health reflect serious development failures. They represent a violation of human rights, a gross neglect of equity considerations and the perpetuation of social injustice. In the sections that follow, important dimensions of this neglect are discussed as a basis for signalling what the immediate health priorities ought to be.

II. CHILD SURVIVAL: UNFINISHED AGENDA

Children below 18 years of age account for almost 40 per cent of India's population.[3] The proportion of children however varies across states. Children in the age group 0-14 years account for 39 per cent of the population in Madhya Pradesh; they account for only 28 per cent of the population in Kerala. In 1996, India reported an infant mortality rate (IMR) of 72 infant deaths per 1,000 live births—down from 129 in 1976. Deaths under 15 years of age account for almost 45 per cent of all deaths in Madhya Pradesh; they account for only 7.3 per cent in Kerala. Infant mortality also varies between rural and urban areas, across communities, according to the level of female education, and by the place of delivery (Table 4).

According to the National Family Health Survey 1992-93, infant mortality rate (IMR) among children born to illiterate mothers was 101 infant deaths per 1,000 live births—more than two and a half times higher than the infant mortality among children born to mothers who had completed at least their high school education. Again, the IMR in rural areas was 94; it was 59 in urban areas. Infant mortality is highest (77.5) when delivery takes place at home and the lowest when it takes place at a private health facility.

Mortality differentials are also striking across communities. For instance, prevalent rates of infant mortality among Scheduled Caste (107) and Scheduled Tribe communities (91) are among the highest in the country. Progress among these communities has also not kept pace with the rest of society. What is disturbing is that the gaps are widening. A special study on child mortality carried out by the Sample Registration System in 1978 revealed that the IMR among Scheduled Caste communities was 12 per cent higher than the national average. In 1992-93, according to the National Family Health Survey, the IMR among Scheduled Caste communities was 24 per cent higher than the national

Table 4
Infant Mortality Differentials in India

Mother's education	
Illiterate	100.6
Literate < middle complete	62.5
Middle school complete	56.1
High school complete	37.2
Caste/Tribe	
Scheduled Caste	107.3
Scheduled Tribe	90.5
Others	82.2
Residence	
Urban	59.4
Rural	94.3
Place of delivery	
Public health facility	59.1
Private health facility	38.5
Home	77.5
Total	86.3

Source: International Institute for Population Sciences (1995).

average. Again, in 1978, the IMR among Scheduled Tribe communities was 120—almost 12 per cent lower than the national average. In 1992-93, the IMR among Scheduled Tribe communities was 91—almost 6 per cent higher than the national average.

Even today, child survival is a serious problem for the poor states. IMR in 1996 varied from a low of 13 in Kerala to a high of 97 in Madhya Pradesh. Communicable diseases remain responsible for a significantly high proportion of deaths among the least healthy populations. The prevalence of high levels of infant mortality in the poor states—and also in Punjab compared to Kerala, suggest that India has a long way to go in terms of assuring children their rights to survival and development. There is much that is needed to ensure universal health care for children. Despite the official claims that immunisation coverage among children is over 90 per cent, the 1992-93 National Family Health Survey (NFHS) revealed that only 35 per cent of children were fully immunised. There are also big differences between the mortality experience of poor and rich Indian states (Table 5). Compared to the 113 million residents of the two richest states (Punjab and Maharashtra), the 260 million residents of the two poorest states are[4] *much more likely to die young*—45 per cent of deaths in the poorest states occur among infants and children below 15 years of age, compared to the 23 per cent of deaths that occur in the richest states among infants and children below 15 years of age—and *much less likely to die old*—33 per cent of deaths in the poorest states occur to people of 60 years and older compared to 45 per cent of deaths that occur in the richest states among people of 60 years and older.

For health policy to have an equity orientation, it must be oriented towards the priorities of the poor. It is obvious that the poor will be best served with a

Table 5
Percentage Distribution of Population and Deaths in Selected States,1996

	Sex ratio (1991)	% of population in the age group		% distribution of deaths by broad age group			
		0-4 years	60+	0-4	5-14	15-59	60+
Two richest states							
Punjab	888	10	8	21	3	29	47
Maharashtra	936	11	7	22	4	29	45
Two poorest states							
Uttar Pradesh	882	12	7	39	6	23	33
Bihar	912	13	6	35	8	26	31
Kerala	1,040	9	9	5	2	25	68
India	929	11	7	30	5	27	38

Source: Sample Registration System, Office of the Registrar General of India.

renewed emphasis on reducing child mortality and focusing on the health and survival problems of children.[5]

III. ANTI-FEMALE DISCRIMINATION IN HEALTH

The prevalence of anti-female biases in Indian society and the systematic discrimination against girls and women are well known.[6] Such discrimination is striking in both education and health. For instance, according to the Census of India 1991, literacy rates among women (38 per cent) were much lower than among men (64 per cent). But less known is the fact that India has one of the highest female-male gaps in literacy rates in the world. The PROBE team (1999) notes, for instance, that only five countries have a higher female-male gap in literacy than India: Bhutan, Syria, Togo, Malawi and Mozambique. Rajasthan alone has as large a population as all these countries combined, and no country in the world has a higher female-male gap than Rajasthan.

In health too, it is common to observe large disparities in achievements between women and men. Several measures pick up this inequality and discrimination against girls and women. At a macro level, an important indicator is the female-to-male ratio in the country's population. In most countries where women and men receive equal care and treatment, women due to their biologically determined stronger constitution live longer than men and outnumber them. It is thus common to find 105 women for every 100 men in many of the industrialised countries. Even in Africa, the female-to-male ratio is 102. But in India, there were less than 93 women for every 100 men in 1991. Again, it is common to find life expectancy among women exceeding that of men by 4-5 years in the industrialised countries. In India, until the 1980s, men lived longer than women did. Even between 1989-93, life expectancy among men was more than among women in rural Bihar, rural Madhya Pradesh, rural Orissa, and rural Uttar Pradesh. At the national level, women between 1989-93 outlived men—but only marginally by less than a year. But despite the narrowing of gaps in life expectancy, however, discrimination against girls and women continues. Instances of female feticide and infanticide in specific regions and among specific communities, as well as pre-natal tests in order to abort female foetuses are widely reported in many parts of the country.

The preferential treatment given to males is most striking in the case of children. It is very common to see boys receiving better and more prompt care than girls. For instance, a study carried out by the Paediatrics Department of two teaching institutions in Ludhiana revealed that 65 per cent of children who came to the outpatient department were boys, and only 35 per cent were girls. Again, boys accounted for 84 per cent of all children admitted as in-patients. And a higher proportion of female children admitted as in-patients died compared to male children, suggesting that even the lower number of girl children who were admitted were brought later during their course of illness.[7]

More recent data on morbidity also reveal the persistence of anti-female biases. The 1992-93 National Family Health Survey asked respondents whether children under the age of four years had suffered from fever, or were ill with a cough accompanied by fast breathing during the two weeks before the survey. Such reported data on morbidity needs to be interpreted with caution. There are several problems that arise relating to the accuracy of the reporting when respondents are asked to recall morbidity status of their children over the preceding two weeks of the survey. Many respondents may not recall minor ailments. There could also be under-reporting of fevers especially since many rural families would not have taken the temperature of the child to ascertain whether she or he had fever. Their response, therefore may have overlooked the onset of mild fever. Subjectivity also plays a major role in self-reporting.[8] Similarly, limited knowledge and regular occurrence of respiratory problems may make parents respond incorrectly to the questions. Apart from levels of awareness, morbidity reporting will also be affected by the season during which the survey was conducted. Typically, higher levels of morbidity would be reported during the monsoons and during severe winter. It may have been difficult to ensure uniform weather conditions in all regions during the survey. Commenting on the levels of inter-state differentials in reported morbidity among children becomes difficult.

Statistical analysis does not reveal any systematic association of morbidity reporting across the states with levels of per capita income, the prevalence of poverty in the state, or for that matter, even with levels of literacy.[9] There is, however, an interesting pattern that is worth noting (Table 6). Close to 10 per cent of children in Kerala were reported to be suffering from cough accompanied by fast breathing whereas the proportion was only 4.3 per cent in Bihar. Similarly, 35.4 per cent of Kerala's children were reported to have had fever in the two weeks preceding the survey as against 21.1 per cent in Bihar and 10.7 per cent in Rajasthan. Why is it that morbidity levels among children in Kerala are higher than among the children of Bihar? Some of the differentials in reporting may be due to factors relating to seasonality or differences in the ability of respondents to recall morbidity status accurately. However, pending a more careful investigation, it seems premature to conclude hastily that Kerala's children are less healthy than the children of Bihar. On the contrary, given Kerala's far superior position with respect to the provisioning of basic social services and literacy, it seems difficult to believe that Kerala's children suffer from higher levels of morbidity than children of Bihar do. A logical

Table 6
Morbidity among Children

Zone/state	% of children under 4 years of age suffering in previous two weeks from: Cough accompanied by fast breathing	Fever
India	6.5	20.2
North		
Delhi	4.8	11.4
Haryana	5.4	18.6
Himachal Pradesh	6.4	19.9
Jammu region of J&K	4.4	21.6
Punjab	3.1	19.9
Rajasthan	4.9	10.7
Central		
Madhya Pradesh	4.7	15.8
Uttar Pradesh	7.2	19.1
East		
Bihar	4.3	21.1
Orissa	10.4	32.1
West Bengal	10.2	29.4
North-east		
Arunachal Pradesh	8.7	20.1
Assam	11.3	24.6
Manipur	14.5	25.3
Meghalaya	5.9	15.8
Mizoram	4.1	26.6
Nagaland	6.1	15.9
Tripura	22.8	35.5
West		
Goa	5.6	21.4
Gujarat	5.8	18.5
Maharashtra	5.9	21.7
South		
Andhra Pradesh	4.9	16.5
Karnataka	3.4	16.9
Kerala	9.7	35.4
Tamil Nadu	8.6	17.7

Source: International Institute for Population Sciences (1995).

explanation for the reporting of higher morbidity among children in Kerala could be the higher levels of health awareness and the better access to health care in Kerala than in Bihar. That the levels of education and access to health care influence health-seeking behaviour is borne out by data from the NFHS relating to treatment of children.

Whereas only two-thirds of children born to *illiterate* mothers were taken for treatment when they suffered from fever or cough accompanied by fast breathing, the proportion went up to 80 per cent or so where the mother had *completed high school*. Again, health-seeking for treatment tends to be higher in urban than in rural areas where public provisioning of health services, and hence access is relatively better (Table 7).

Table 7
Treatment of Morbidity among Children

	% of children under 4 years suffering from cough accompanied by fast breathing in previous 2 weeks who were taken to a health facility or provider*	% of children under 4 years suffering from fever in previous 2 weeks who were taken to a health facility or provider*
Residence		
Urban	77.1	79.4
Rural	63.9	63.4
Mother's education		
Illiterate	62.4	62.9
Literate < middle school	70.4	69.9
Middle school complete	72.0	78.8
High school and above	84.9	78.4
Caste/Tribe		
Scheduled Caste	64.0	67.7
Scheduled Tribe	59.1	55.0
Others	67.6	68.2
Total	66.3	66.8

Note: *Includes government/municipal hospital, private hospital/clinic, primary health care centre, sub-centre, doctor, or other health professional.
Source: International Institute for Population Sciences (1995).

However, what is striking about the reported morbidity data on children is the extremely strong gender differentials—nationally and across the states. Table 8 presents data on differentials in reporting on child morbidity across the states.

For India, we find that 7.1 per cent of boys were reported to be suffering from cough accompanied by fast breathing during the two weeks preceding the survey; the proportion was only 5.9 per cent for girls. Similarly, 19.4 per cent of boys were reported to be suffering from fever in the two weeks preceding the survey; the proportion was only 1.7 per cent for girls. A closer look at data across the states (Table 8) reveals that:

(i) In 20 out of 24 states, a *higher proportion of male than female children* suffered from cough accompanied by fast breathing during the two weeks preceding the survey in 20 out of 24 states. Even in the four states where more girls than boys were reported to be ill, the differential was extremely small (between 0.3-0.8 per cent).

(ii) In 21 out of 24 states, a *higher proportion of male than female children* suffered from fever. Again, in the four states where more girls than boys were reported to suffer from fever, the differential was extremely small (between 0.2-1.1 per cent).

The consistently higher reporting of morbidity among boys raises a question: Could it be that boys are generally more sick during childhood than girls when in fact girls are typically more neglected and less cared for than boys? A more likely explanation is that illnesses among boys are more remembered than among girls, and hence more frequently and accurately reported.

Table 8
Gender Differentials in Children's Morbidity

State	% of children under 4 years suffering from cough accompanied by fast breathing in previous 2 weeks			% of children under 4 years suffering from fever in previous 2 weeks		
	Male	Female	Excess of male over female reporting	Male	Female	Excess of male over female reporting
Haryana	7.0	3.4	3.6	20.3	16.6	3.7
Tripura	24.5	21.0	3.5	35.2	35.7	(0.5)
Assam	12.9	9.7	3.2	25.8	23.5	2.3
Manipur	16.1	12.9	3.2	29.1	21.8	7.3
Kerala	11.1	8.2	2.9	36.7	34.0	2.7
Mizoram	5.5	2.7	2.8	27.3	25.9	1.4
Nagaland	7.3	4.9	2.4	18.2	13.4	4.8
Punjab	4.1	1.9	2.2	20.9	18.8	2.1
Madhya Pradesh	5.7	3.8	1.9	17.2	14.2	3.0
Gujarat	6.7	4.9	1.8	13.5	11.7	1.8
Orissa	11.2	9.5	1.7	32.0	32.2	(0.2)
Andhra Pradesh	5.6	4.1	1.5	17.1	15.8	1.3
Uttar Pradesh	7.8	6.5	1.3	20.2	18.2	2.0
Bihar	4.9	3.7	1.2	23.0	19.1	3.9
Karnataka	3.9	2.8	1.1	17.2	16.5	0.7
Himachal Pradesh	6.8	6.0	0.8	19.3	20.4	(1.1)
Tamil Nadu	9.0	8.3	0.7	18.0	17.5	0.5
Rajasthan	5.2	4.6	0.6	10.8	10.6	0.2
Goa	5.8	5.4	0.4	22.7	20.1	2.6
Delhi	4.9	4.7	0.2	11.8	10.5	1.3
Maharashtra	5.7	6.0	(0.3)	22.6	20.7	1.9
West Bengal	10.0	10.3	(0.3)	29.2	29.6	(0.4)
Arunachal Pradesh	8.5	8.9	(0.4)	20.9	18.8	2.1
Meghalaya	5.5	6.3	(0.8)	16.5	14.9	1.6
India	7.1	5.9	1.2	21.1	19.4	1.7

Source: International Institute for Population Sciences (1995).

Data on treatment confirms such a gender bias and brings out the strong bias in favour of boys and against girls. The NFHS data reveal that 70.1 per cent of boys suffering from fever were taken to a health facility or provider. The corresponding proportion for girls was 63.1 per cent. Again, 70.8 per cent of boys suffering from cough accompanied by fast breathing were taken to a health facility or provider; the proportion among girls was only 60.8 per cent. Again, in 13 out of 18 states, more boys than girls who suffered from cough accompanied by fast breathing were taken to a health facility or provider. Again, in 17 out of 18 states, higher proportions of boys than girls suffering from fever were taken to a health facility or provider. The consistently higher proportion of boys who were taken to a health facility or provider almost throughout the country confirms the persistence of strong anti-female biases in Indian society (Table 9).

Table 9
Gender Differentials in Treatment for Children

State	% of children under 4 years suffering from cough accompanied by fast breathing in previous 2 weeks who were taken to a health facility or provider*			% of children under 4 years suffering from fever in previous 2 weeks who were taken to a health facility or provider*		
	Male	Female	Excess of male over female reporting	Male	Female	Excess of male over female reporting
Haryana	7.0	3.4	3.6	20.3	16.6	3.7
Maharashtra	84.5	61.0	23.5	78.1	72.4	5.7
Orissa	62.9	48.1	14.8	57.8	47.1	10.7
Rajasthan	59.7	47.4	12.3	69.5	53.1	16.4
Madhya Pradesh	66.6	54.4	12.2	70.7	57.3	13.4
West Bengal	67.6	55.7	11.9	64.4	54.1	10.3
Andhra Pradesh	73.5	61.8	11.7	73.2	65.9	7.3
Uttar Pradesh	73.0	62.4	10.6	72.8	68.2	4.6
Bihar	77.3	66.9	10.4	64.3	54.0	10.3
Kerala	84.9	76.6	8.3	75.4	72.7	2.7
Haryana	85.3	77.8	7.5	87.0	86.5	0.5
Gujarat	75.4	70.5	4.9	79.7	71.8	7.9
Himachal Pradesh	78.8	76.4	2.4	87.0	76.3	10.7
Assam	41.0	40.4	0.6	32.0	31.5	0.5
Tamil Nadu	67.2	67.6	-0.4	74.8	71.5	3.3
Karnataka	72.1	76.7	-4.6	75.1	78.3	-3.2
Delhi	84.4	92.1	-7.7	88.1	80.9	7.2
Goa	78.1	86.7	-8.6	88.9	83.9	5.0
India	70.8	60.8	10.0	70.1	63.1	7.0

Note: *Includes government/municipal hospital, private hospital/clinic, primary health care centre, sub-centre, doctor, or other health professional.
Source: International Institute for Population Sciences (1995).

IV. CRISIS IN REPRODUCTIVE AND WOMEN'S HEALTH

A glaring manifestation of the anti-female bias in health is the large-scale neglect of women's health and in particular, reproductive health.[10] Reliable and systematic information on women's health status including maternal mortality and morbidity are not readily available. However, as discussed earlier, part of the neglect in women's health is captured by the extremely low levels of life expectancy among women in India—around 63 years in 1997. This is much lower than the observed life expectancy among women in East Asia (72.2 years), or even Sri Lanka (75.4 years) and China (74.5 years). A major factor for the low life expectancy among women is the unacceptably high levels of maternal mortality. Estimates of maternal mortality vary from 555 deaths per 100,000 live births during 1982-86 (Mari Bhat et al., 1995) to 437 deaths per 100,000 live births (according to NFHS 1992-93). The WHO-UNICEF estimate places India's maternal mortality rate at 570 deaths per 100,000 live births. Besides high maternal mortality risks, women also suffer from a high risk of morbidity associated with reproduction. Unsafe abortions are also a major cause of maternal mortality and morbidity. The official figures suggest around 600,000 cases of Medical Termination of Pregnancy (MTP) every year in close to 9,500 government-approved clinics and hospitals throughout the country. But most estimates suggest that this is only a small fraction of the additional five to six million abortions that take place every year at unrecognised facilities by unqualified practitioners.[11] Table 10 presents some indicators of health care relating to women's reproductive health.

Access to proper reproductive health care is shockingly poor. At the national level, nearly two-thirds of deliveries take place without the assistance of a health professional. In the case of Uttar Pradesh and Bihar, it is over 80 per cent. In 1992-93, almost 76 per cent of pregnant women did not receive iron and folic acid tablets as part of their prenatal care. Access to safe contraception is again very limited. The couple protection rate was 20 per cent in Uttar Pradesh and 23 per cent in Bihar.

Some of the high incidence of mortality and morbidity related to reproduction can be attributed to the general neglect of adolescent health in India. In 1987, adolescents accounted for almost 45 per cent of maternal deaths in rural India. Data reveal that over a third of young women get married when they are between 15-19 years old when they are still in their adolescence. The proportion is as high as 50 per cent in Bihar. The median age at first birth was 19.3 years for India. And many of them have children born to them at a young age when the risks are greatest. The NFHS survey also revealed that 58 per cent of 13-19 year old girls were mothers or pregnant with their first child. Around 10 per cent of all pregnancies in married adolescents aged 15-19 years result in spontaneous abortion or still birth; and maternal mortality is around one-and-half to two times higher for adolescent girls than for older women. The NFHS data also suggest that induced abortion is more likely among adolescents aged 15-19 years than among older women aged 20-24 years.[12]

V. PROMOTING HUMAN SECURITY THROUGH HEALTH

Formulating health policy is not easy. It is complicated by the need for policy to address a number of inter-connected considerations: philosophical and ethical, cultural, social, environmental, nutritional, legal, educational (promotive), preventive and curative. Further, the context for policy formulation varies widely especially as the country is experiencing different phases of demographic transition, as well as simultaneously an epidemiological transition and a health transition.[13] Policy needs to address all three stages of the health transition simultaneously: typical health problems associated with low levels of development, the rapid emergence of diseases of affluence and changing life-styles, and new environmental and behavioural threats. The health sector is also affected by many unanticipated and unacknowledged threats including outbreaks of epidemics, AIDS, environmental health, violence, and accidents. Finally, priority setting in health poses a challenge as all age groups (and diseases) demand simultaneous attention and urgent action. Concerns of old age are as important as care of children; care of children is as important as doing something about women's health. Policymakers face a real problem of allocating limited and often shrinking resources for different purposes. However, recognising the difficulties of policy formulation in health does not offer a justification for doing little or doing things badly.

Table 10
Indicators Relating to Reproductive Health

	Maternal mortality rate per 100,000 births 1982-86	% of deliveries assisted by health profes-sionals	Couples effectively protected (%)	% of births during 4 years preceding the survey to women who received			Crude birth rate	Total fertility rate	Singulate mean age at marriage (years)	Females 15-19 years currently married (%)	% of 13-19 years who are mothers or pregnant with first child	% of 6-14 year old girls attending school	Median age at first birth (years)
				antenatal care	2 doses of tetanous toxoid	iron/folic tablets vaccine							
Two of the richest states													
Punjab	369*	48.3	58.7	87.9	82.7	24.8	25.0	2.92	21.1	14.4	64.4	77.8	21.4
Maharashtra	393	53.2	53.7	82.7	71.0	43.9	26.3	2.86	19.3	36.2	68.1	76.6	18.9
Two of the poorest states													
Uttar Pradesh	931	17.2	19.8	44.7	37.4	11.2	35.9	4.82	18.6	39.6	49.4	48.2	19.6
Bihar	813	19.0	23.1	36.8	30.7	12.1	32.1	4.00	18.0	50.3	48.2	38.3	18.8
Kerala	234	89.7	63.3	97.3	89.8	87.8	19.6	2.00	22.1	13.4	59.2	94.8	20.9
India	555	34.2	40.6	62.3	53.8	25.5	28.7	3.39	20.0	38.4	57.7	58.9	19.3

Sources: Estimates in Column 2 are from Mari Bhat et al. (1995) except for Punjab which is from UNICEF (1995). Rest of the data are from International Institute for Population Sciences (1995).

India's limited success in promoting good health points to basic flaws in policy formulation, in setting priorities and in implementing health programmes. Most assessments of India's health sector highlight the inadequacy of facilities, the poor quality of services, and the deteriorating state of physical infrastructure. People also have unequal access to health care in India. The poor, the landless and most marginalised communities find it extremely difficult to access good quality health care. Either public provisioning is grossly inadequate, or the services are far too expensive for people to afford. Equally pronounced is the urban bias in the location of health facilities that reflects an unfair appropriation of health care by the rich and the urban dwellers. High levels of inefficiency in the delivery of health services are reported throughout the country. It is common to hear of demotivated staff and an over-burdened system that is on the verge of a serious breakdown. Given this situation, how do we go about promoting human security through health?

First, policy has to be guided by a strong rights perspective, not by a traditional welfare orientation. The rights perspective views individuals as legitimate claimants to universal health care, not as passive recipients of doles from the state. The rights approach also emphasises non-discrimination. In other words, no one can be excluded on the grounds of caste, class, religion, or any other factor, from having universal access to quality care. The state has an obligation to ensure that these rights are assured and fulfilled. In the absence of such an orientation, it is not surprising that India has failed to meet its commitments, both national and global, for ensuring that the rights of all citizens are met.

Second, health policy has to be re-oriented by giving it a strong equity orientation. Concerns of efficiency have traditionally dominated discussions on priority setting and allocation of resources in health. Equity considerations have largely been neglected.[14] The efficiency arguments are becoming even stronger now with the rising costs of health care provisioning, the mismanagement of public health systems, the big push for state minimalism and the increasing faith in markets. There is frequent talk of the private sector playing a more important role in health, but the discussions do not even note the limitations of private provisioning of universal health care. In fact, the push for privatisation has become an excuse for abdication of responsibilities by the state. On the positive side, however, it is encouraging to see the development discourse being shaped by a strong rights perspective that assigns high priority to neglected groups in society, to the poor, and the unreached. Such a perspective further reinforces the need for equity considerations to determine priorities. From the perspective of the poor and the neglected, then, urgent interventions are needed to (a) rapidly promote child survival and development particularly among the socially backward communities (b) eliminate the discrimination against girls and women, and (c) invest significantly in advancing women's health, and more specifically their reproductive health.

Third, health policy needs to recognise the strong inter-connections that health has to other sectors of the economy. Health outcomes are influenced by investments not only in health, but also by actions taken in a number of closely related sectors such as education, water and sanitation, food security, environment, housing, employment and rural development. Policy must find ways of effectively linking health to vital aspects of development like clean water, sanitation, poverty alleviation, compulsory primary education, more effective demand for food and nutrition, greater public awareness and participation in health—all of which are critical components of a genuine health and development strategy. What we find instead is an adhoc approach to health that does not make the most of synergetic and convergent actions at the community level.

Fourth, there is a large mismatch between health spending and outcomes that reflects serious inefficiencies in the delivery of health care. Several factors have been identified for the poor record on implementation including low levels of public participation, poor functioning of the public health care system, displacement of public health priorities by family planning goals, low visibility of preventive health interventions, misplaced priorities, and poor local governance.[15] India has in place a gigantic health care system that is largely self-serving; it has bypassed a majority of people. It is critical to make the system more responsive and accountable to the people it is meant to serve. This is not a problem unique to health, but cuts across most development sectors. Often, the solutions are relatively simple and known. It is in the management of programmes that we observe serious shortcomings. There is need for more effective decentralisation, active people's participation, greater transparency in operations, better monitoring and reporting on progress, and accountability to the public.

Fifth, there is the issue of resources. Clearly the efficiency of public spending has to be improved. And more financial resources will be needed if all citizens, women, men and children, have to be assured access to quality care. It is often pointed out that India being a "poor" country cannot afford to spend so much on social development. This is not true. There are poorer countries that have been able to ensure universal schooling and health care. In India, it is not a matter of resources; it is much more a question of priorities. Much of the discussion during the period of reforms has concentrated on economic issues. There has been very little discussion on health financing (apart from a limited discussion on health insurance). It is true that even the poor will be willing to pay for good quality services. But before asking them to pay for services, the state must assure that reliable and appropriate facilities are in place. We need far more serious debate and discussion on health insurance and ensuring universal health coverage. There has to be a more rational allocation of resources for health that must be linked to efforts by the state to mobilise additional resources. However, it is important to recognise that interventions for promoting health security including universal access to basic education and good quality health care, better access to a wider mix of contraceptive choices, greater influence of women and control over decision making, wider participation of women in public decision making, and improved access to basic social services are also investments that will greatly enhance the quality of people's lives. Significantly, these very investments and interventions are also critical for accelerating India's growth and economic progress.

Sixth, health outcomes are determined by the technology choices that society makes, by the legislative framework that the state develops, by the priority that the political system assigns, and by the institutional arrangements that are put in place to ensure universal access to health care. But most significantly, health outcomes are determined by the actions of individuals and households, and by the influence that society has on such behaviour. People have to be informed and they have to be convinced to take health actions in their own interest. This is true when we are talking of reproductive health or changing diets to address the question of malnutrition, the treatment of diarrhoea, or even smoking. To a large extent, changes in behaviour and attitudes are brought about by the spread of education that influences both the desire and the ability of individuals to seek out appropriate health care. But it is equally important to change societal attitudes and mind-sets that dominate health-seeking behaviour and health care practices. New societal norms need to be established, and community pressures have to be built up for general compliance. For instance, ensuring that every child gets fully and properly immunised is as much the responsibility of the State as it is of the family and the community. Similarly, ensuring that every child goes to school requires not only appropriate physical provisioning of school facilities by the state, but more importantly, the inculcation of a societal norm whereby no child is denied the opportunity to learn. Many of the factors that contribute to health risks such as early marriages, or the denial of freedoms to women, or the attitude towards fertility decisions are deeply rooted in social customs. It is society's failure to recognise women's roles and contributions that contributes to their unequal treatment, and adversely affects the respect they command in society. If health policy has to succeed, it must be backed by strong public advocacy to change traditional beliefs and establish new norms for society.

Finally, there is need for collective action to promote health at all levels. It is often extremely difficult, almost a luxury, for the poor and disadvantaged in society to overcome their insecurity and fight for their rights. There are several examples of successful interventions by non-governmental organisations that have worked closely with the community to promote health.[16] Such interventions need to be analysed, replicated wherever possible, and scaled up nationally. Health is also an area where the state has a critical role to play in ensuring universal access to all citizens. There is however need for informed debate and public discussion on the role of the state in the present context of economic reforms and globalization. Public discussion is also vital as several questions of ethics need to be resolved with transparency and conviction that they will not harm the interests of people. Again, many health problems remain invisible and therefore tend to get neglected. It must become the responsibility of the press, the media, social activists and researchers to highlight such neglected concerns, and ensure that they get on to the public agenda for action. Active public monitoring and public scrutiny are critical for ensuring that the goal of universal access to good quality health care is fully realised. What India needs urgently is concerted public action of this kind to rapidly promote health security and human development.

Notes

1. Several reports in recent times have carried out a comprehensive review of the health sector. See, for instance, Voluntary Health Association of India (1997).
2. For a review, see Shiva Kumar (1997a; 1997b) and UNICEF (1995).
3. The population of children under 14 years of age is expected to go up from 347 million in 2001 to 350 million by the year 2016.
4. This is similar to the analysis done by Gwatkin (1993).
5. Child survival outcomes are directly affected by measures that include efforts to universalise basic education, promote employment and incomes, improve provisioning of basic social services including access to safe drinking water and proper sanitation, reduce levels of malnutrition, extend the efficacy of the health system, and empower women to take decisions—both within the household and at the community level.
6. For a comprehensive discussion, see Dreze and Sen (1995) and the references therein.
7. Cited in UNICEF (1995). There are several other studies that point to such gender biases. See, for instance, Kynch and Sen (1982), Sen and Sengupta (1983), and the discussion in Dreze and Sen (1995).
8. For a discussion on the role of subjectivity and self-reporting of illnesses, see Sen (1994).
9. Regressing the reported proportions of children who had fever during the last two weeks before the survey and per capita income for a sample of 24 states yields a R^2 value of around 0.13. We obtain a similar value of R^2 when we regress proportions of children who had fever during the last two weeks and literacy rates. The association of reported morbidity (fever) among children with the proportion of population below the poverty line yields a R^2 value of 0.03.
10. Several scholars have commented upon the neglect of women's health. Some of the more recent publications include articles contained in Das Gupta, Chen and Krishnan (1995); Mukhopadhyay (1998); and Pachauri (1999).
11. See the discussion in Khan et al. (1999).
12. See the discussion in Mamdani (1999).
13. The literature on health transition describes the different transitions as follows: The demographic theory postulates that, in response to socio-economic development, high birth and death rates in pre-modern societies shift to low levels of births and deaths through, initially, a more rapid decline of mortality, followed by a slower decline of fertility. The epidemiological theory postulates that, as mortality declines, a marked shift occurs in the distribution of major causes of death. Whereas high mortality populations suffer from the diseases of poverty and under-development (infectious, nutritious and reproductive health hazards), low mortality populations experience health problems of urbanisation and affluence (chronic cardiovascular disease and cancer).
14. For a more detailed discussion, see Shiva Kumar (1999) and the articles in Rao (1999).
15. For a useful overview and discussion, see Dreze and Sen (1999).
16. Pachauri (1994) describes a number of such successful initiatives by non-governmental organisations.

References

Das Gupta, Monica, Lincoln C. Chen, and T.N. Krishnan (eds.) (1995), *Women's Health in India*, Oxford University Press, New Delhi.

Dreze, Jean and Amartya Sen (1995), *India: Economic Development and Social Opportunity*, Oxford University Press, New Delhi.

—— (1999), "Public Action and Social Inequality", in Harris-White, Barbara and S. Subramanian (eds.), *Illfare in India*, Sage Publications, New Delhi.

Government of India (1997), *Economic Survey 1996-97*, Economic Division, Ministry of Finance, New Delhi.

—— (1999), *India's Progress Towards Reproductive Health Goals (ICPD + 5)*, Ministry of Health and Family Welfare, New Delhi.

Gwatkin, Davidson (1993), *Dealing with Distributional Considerations: The Search for a Progressive Strategic Response to the Health Transition*, Discussion Draft Paper prepared for the Harvard Health Transition Seminar, Harvard Center for Population and Development Studies, Cambridge.

International Institute for Population Sciences (1995), *National Family Health Survey 1992-93*, IIPS, Bombay.

Khan, M.E., Sandhya Barge, Nayan Kumar and Stina Almorth (1999), "Abortion in India: Current Situation and Future Challenges", in Pachauri (ed.).

Kynch, Jocelyn and Amartya Sen (1983), "Indian Women: Well-being and Survival," *Cambridge Journal of Economics*, Vol. 7.

Mari Bhat, P.N., K. Navaneetham and Rajan S. Irudaya (1995), "Maternal Mortality: Estimates from an Econometric Model, " in Das Gupta, Chen and Krishnan (eds.).

Mamdani, Masuma (1999), "Adolescent Reproductive Health: Experience of Community-based Programmes", in Pachauri (ed.).

Mukhopadhyay, Swapna (ed.) (1998), *Women's Health, Public Policy and Community Action*, Manohar Press, New Delhi.

Pachauri, Saroj (ed.) (1994), *Reaching India's Poor: Non-Governmental Approaches to Community Health*, Sage Publication, New Delhi.

—— (ed.) (1999), *Implementing a Reproductive Health Agenda in India: The Beginning*, Population Council, India.

Rao, Mohan (ed.) (1999), *Disinvesting in Health*, Sage Publication, New Delhi.

Registrar General of India (1996), "SRS Based Abridged Life Tables 1989-93", *SRS Analytical Studies Report No. 1 of 1996*, Government of India, New Delhi.

Sen, Amartya (1994), "Objectivity and Position: Assessment of Health and Well-being", in Lincoln C. Chen, Arthur Kleinman and Norma C. Ware (eds.), *Health and Social Change in International Perspective*, Harvard School of Public Health, Boston.

—— and Sunil Sengupta (1983), "Malnutrition of Rural Children and the Sex Bias", *Economic and Political Weekly*, Vol. 19 (Annual Number).

Shiva Kumar, A.K. (1997a), *Poverty and Human Development: Getting Priorities Right*, Human Development Report Office Occasional Paper No. 30, HDRO, New York.

—— (1997b), "Human Development in Crisis: Investment Failures in Health and Education", in C. Steve Larue (ed.), *The India Handbook*, Regional Handbooks of Economic Development, Fitzroy Dearborn Publishers, Chicago.

—— (1999), "The Formulation of India's Health Policy," in Rao (ed.).

The PROBE Team (1999), *Public Report on Basic Education*, Oxford University Press, New Delhi.

UNDP (1998), *Human Development Report 1998*, Oxford University Press, New York.

UNICEF (1995), *The Progress of Indian States*, UNICEF India Country Office Publication, New Delhi.

Voluntary Health Association of India (1997), *Report of the Independent Commission on Health in India*, VHAI, New Delhi.

8

Access of Urban Poor to Housing Amenities: Aspects Concerning Social Security

Amitabh Kundu

I. INTRODUCTION

Access of urban poor to housing and basic amenities has been one of the avowed concerns in the country since the inception of planning. With the launching of the programmes of liberalisation and structural adjustment, this issue has received special attention of researchers and policy makers (Kundu, 1993). The dominant view in recent years seems to be that the deficiencies in the availability of dwelling units and related amenities are because of planned interventions and not in spite of them. Administrators and researchers have argued that ensuring efficiency in the functioning of public agencies by making them accountable to market-based institutions and reactivating the private sector would go a long way in increasing the total production of these amenities. That alone, it is argued, can ensure their availability to all sections of the population, including the poor. The alternative viewpoint, confined to a small segment scholars and administrators, is that the present level of deprivation of the poor is a consequence of the failure of planning or the latter being hijacked by market forces. Within this perspective, many harbour the apprehension that increased privatisation of housing and basic services would reduce their availability to the poor, endangering their social security.

Unfortunately, the available data do not permit a rigorous analysis of the impact of the policy changes during the eighties and early nineties on the availability of housing and basic amenities to people in different income/consumption brackets in different states of the country. However, a limited investigation into these questions can be attempted using the data brought out by the last Population Census and National Sample Survey (NSS).

In section II, following the introductory section, the availability of housing and select basic amenities like water supply, toilets and electricity has been analysed at the national level. This has been done by building comparable indicators for the seventies, eighties and early nineties. A similar analysis has been attempted across the states and the size classes of urban centres in the subsequent section. An attempt has also been made here to identify the socio-economic factors that explain the spatial variation. Section IV analyses the problems and issues concerning vulnerability of the urban poor with regard to housing and other basic amenities using secondary and primary data. The programmes and schemes currently being implemented in the country have been overviewed in sectionV, highlighting the recent modifications/alterations. Here, the thrusts is on how these changes would affect the availability of these amenities to the urban poor. In the last section, an attempt has been made to understand the implications of the macro-strategy of globalisation and the changing policy perspective for the provision of basic services of the poor focussing on their access to basic amenities and their overall social security.

II. HOUSING CONDITIONS AND LEVEL OF BASIC AMENITIES: THE MACRO SCENARIO

Rapid growth of urban population and low investment in urban development in the past have created serious shelter problems and deficiencies in basic amenities in the towns and cities of the country. Although housing stock seems to have grown more or less at the same rate as population or households, the rate of capital formation in formal housing has been extremely low during the eighties. The same is true for investment in basic services (Kundu and Moitra, 1999). The shortages are more serious for urban poor due to inequality in the access to these amenities.

Table 1 presents the existing housing scenario, using the Population Census data. The figures for rural areas have been presented along with the corresponding urban figures for a comparative assessment. It may be noted that the number of houses constructed during 1961-71 was 13.7 million as against 14.9 million during 1951-61. This can be explained in terms of mass housing programmes launched during the fifties to rehabilitate the refugee population coming to India at the time of partition. The schemes for industrial workers and dock labourers also led to large-scale construction of row houses during this period. Subsequently, however, the outlays on public sector housing have declined. As a result, a smaller number of dwelling units were built during the sixties, compared to the previous decade.

The growth rate in total housing stock during the seventies works out to 25.5 per cent (absolute increase being 23.7 million), which is higher than that of the sixties or fifties, viz., 17.3 per cent and 23.1 per cent, respectively. This reduced the pressure on housing marginally, as may be inferred from the slight decline in the values of the indicators like persons per house, persons per room, households per house, etc., in Table 2. The growth in housing stock has been faster in urban as compared to rural areas, the two rates being about 50 per cent and 20 per cent during 1971-81. As a result, despite the rapid demographic growth in towns and cities and a decline in the size of (urban) households, implying a faster growth in the number of households than of population, the pressure on housing stock declined in urban areas.

The high level of housing activity during the seventies continued in the eighties as well, as revealed through the housing estimates (from the houselisting operation) of 1991 Census. The housing stock in 1991 has been placed at 108.5 million in rural and 38.7 million in urban areas. This gives the overall growth rate during the eighties as being slightly above 26 per cent, close

Table 1
Population, Households and Housing Stock

(in millions)

Sl. no.	Particulars	1961 R	1961 U	1961 T	1971 R	1971 U	1971 T	1981* R	1981* U	1981* T	1991* R	1991* U	1991* T
1.	Population	360.3	78.9	439.2	438.6	108.8	547.4	525.5	159.7	685.2	627.2	217.2	844.3
2.	No. of households	68.7	14.8	83.5	78.0	19.0	97.0	94.1	30.7*	124.8	111.6	39.5	151.1
3.	Total housing stock (in million)	65.2	14.1	79.3	74.5	18.5	93.0	88.7	28.0	116.7	111.5	38.7	146.6
	(a) *Pucca*	8.5	6.5	15.0	14.2	11.8	26.0	18.8	18.1	36.9	34.2	28.7	62.8
	(b) Semi-*pucca*	24.1	4.9	29.0	27.6	4.3	31.9	33.3	6.8	40.1	39.7	7.0	46.8
	(c) Serviceable *katcha*	24.8}			23.8}			25.7}			27.4	3.8	31.2
		}	2.8	35.3	}	2.4	35.1	}	3.1	39.7			
	(d) Unserviceable *katcha*	7.8}			8.9}			10.9}			10.3	1.1	11.4
4.	Usable housing stock (a+b+c of item 3 for rural and a+b for urban)	57.4	11.4	68.8	15.6	16.1	81.7	77.8	24.9	102.7	101.2	35.7	136.9

Note: Usable housing stock excludes all *katcha* houses in urban areas and unserviceable *katcha* houses in rural areas.

*The figures for population, households and housing stock include the estimated values for the states where Population Census could not be conducted. The number of households in urban areas (in these states) is obtained after adjusting for congestion factor.

Source: National Building Organisation, 1990; and Census of India, 1991.

Table 2
Select Indicators of Housing Situation in Urban India

(in millions)

Sl. no.	Particulars	1961 R	1961 U	1961 T	1971 R	1971 U	1971 T	1981 R	1981 U	1981 T	1991 R	1991 U	1991 T
1.	Persons per house												
	(a) Population per house	5.33	5.64	5.55	5.90	5.88	5.89	5.92	5.70	5.87	5.78	5.69	5.76
	(b) Population per usable house	6.31	7.04	6.43	6.61	6.76	6.64	6.75	6.74	6.75	6.19	6.08	6.17
2.	Persons per room	2.62	2.62	2.62	2.77	2.78	2.77	2.77	2.53	2.71	–	–	–
3.	Households (HH) per house	1.05	1.06	1.05	1.07	1.06	1.07	1.07	1.06	1.07	1.03	1.05	1.03
4.	Size of HH	5.24	5.33	5.26	5.62	5.73	5.64	5.58	5.20	5.55	5.62	5.49	5.59
5.	Per cent HH in one room unit	48.12	53.05	49.00	47.26	50.10	47.82	44.38	45.80	44.72	40.82	39.55	40.49
6.	Per cent *pucca* houses	13.0	46.1	18.9	19.1	63.8	28.0	21.2	64.6	31.6	30.6	72.8	41.6
7.	Per cent semi-*pucca* house	37.0	34.7	36.6	37.0	23.2	34.3	37.5	24.3	34.4	35.6	17.7	31.0
8.	Per cent vacant houses	5.50	7.23	5.80	6.02	7.47	6.31	4.99	6.41	5.33	–	–	–
9.	Per cent houseless population	0.27	0.37	0.29	0.35	0.43	0.36	0.33	0.39	0.34	0.09	0.05	0.06

Source: Census of India (1961, 1971, 1981 and 1991) and NBO (1990 and 1991).

to the corresponding figure for the seventies. The rural housing stock increased by 26 per cent as compared to the urban growth rate of over 38 per cent. Thus, there was a decline in the urban growth rate but a marginal increase in the rural growth rate, when compared to the seventies. Also, the growth rate of population in urban areas was about the same as for the housing stock during eighties while the former was less than the latter during the seventies. The housing stock, however, grew at a slightly faster rate than the population in rural areas during 1981-91. Interestingly, the growth rate in the number of *pucca* houses in urban areas has been 59 per cent only, compared to the rural growth figure of 82 per cent. One may, therefore, conclude that the improvement in housing conditions during the eighties has been low in urban areas when compared to the rural areas (Table 2).

It is important to note that the average size of urban household, which was 5.73 in 1971 came down to 5.20 in 1981. Subsequently, this has gone up to 5.49 in 1991 (Table 2). This can be explained in terms of the arrival of relatives and friends from rural areas and their absorption within the existing urban households. The decline in the number of households which are houseless and percentage of households residing in one room units would possibly suggest that some people have added rooms to their tenements. The rise in the percentage of *pucca* houses from about 64 per cent in 1971 to over 71 per cent in 1991 reflects an improvement in the quality of housing in urban areas.

The pattern emerging from an analysis of the information from the 38th, 44th and 49th rounds of National Sample Survey (NSS) broadly corresponds to that noted above. The percentage of urban households in *pucca* houses had gone up from 57.6 to 71.0 during 1983-88. The increase during 1988-94, however, was very low the figure going up only to 73.8 per cent. Correspondingly, the figure for *katcha* houses had come down substantially during 1983-88 from 16.9 per cent to 10.9 per cent the decline in the subsequent five year period was nominal 2.6 percentage point only. Similarly, the share of households in semi-*pucca* houses came down signficantly from 26 per cent to 18 per cent during the first period, the figure remained stuck at 18 per cent during the second period (Table 3).

It may be pointed out that as per the methodology recommended by the Expert Group (Planning cCmmission, 1993), marginally modified subsequently, poverty has gone down in urban areas from 40 per cent to 33 per cent, which is much higher than the decline in rural poverty from 39 per cent to 37 per cent. It should be possible to explain the phenomenon in terms of substantial reduction in the in-migration of the rural poor into urban areas. This has resulted in an overall decline in rural-urban (RU) migration as also the growth rate of urban population.

One would expect a rising trend in rental housing in urban areas with rapid urbanisation, increasing mobility and general improvement in the housing situation. Surprisingly, however, the percentage of households residing in rental premises has remained the same or gone down during the eighties. According to the NSS data, the figures have declined from 37.6 per cent in 1983 to 35.8 in 1993 (Table 4). The Population Census, however, suggests a sharper decline from 46.5 per cent to 34.1 per cent during 1981-91. But this is partly due to a change in the classification system. In the 1991 Census, a new category viz.

Table 3
Percentage Distribution of Urban Households by Structure of Building

State	*Katcha*			Semi-*pucca*			*Pucca*		
	1983	1988-89	1993	1983	1988-89	1993	1983	1988-89	1993
India	16.43	10.92	8.3	25.72	17.79	17.9	57.22	71.04	73.8
A.P.	26.47	21.85	16.6	22.84	16.42	15.3	50.06	61.67	68.1
Assam	44.74	33.49	20.5	25.02	27.03	30.8	30.22	35.18	48.7
Bihar	27.76	15.75	9.2	22.62	17.67	25.0	49.35	66.33	65.9
Gujarat	10.61	3.12	6.6	24.75	15.11	12.1	64.22	81.77	81.2
Haryana	5.56	2.38	5.6	13.50	4.15	7.4	80.82	93.47	87.0
H.P.	13.43	2.62	2.0	30.37	27.54	15.2	55.92	69.59	82.8
J & K	11.49	5.40	4.2	19.31	18.63	15.0	45.28	75.97	80.7
Karnataka	12.40	10.64	13.5	39.96	26.69	23.1	47.20	62.65	63.4
Kerala	17.20	13.77	10.8	27.93	17.52	16.2	54.64	65.54	73.0
M.P.	16.05	9.73	4.8	34.29	35.21	36.7	48.57	55.06	58.4
Maharashtra	13.78	5.64	3.1	33.11	19.66	15.2	52.89	74.69	81.7
Manipur	47.73	40.90	20.5	45.53	48.35	69.2	3.02	8.82	10.2
Nagaland	27.69	9.24	9.2	45.78	34.11	52.2	25.60	54.60	58.5
Orissa	31.10	29.43	16.8	28.77	17.37	27.8	39.21	53.09	55.4
Punjab	6.94	3.25	3.3	11.87	7.78	4.7	80.44	88.92	92.0
Rajasthan	11.94	5.95	4.4	11.14	6.93	8.3	75.16	87.11	87.3
Sikkim	2.82	6.77	8.7	46.88	11.26	8.5	49.70	81.97	82.9
Tamil Nadu	19.85	18.56	13.6	23.29	17.37	17.2	56.21	64.03	69.2
U.P.	13.80	9.95	7.3	22.96	15.11	15.7	62.88	74.91	77.0
West Bengal	12.49	6.73	6.8	26.87	20.00	22.4	60.25	73.27	70.8
UTs									
A. & N. Island	19.20	3.10	0.6	30.38	9.74	4.2	50.42	87.16	95.2
Chandigarh	4.87	0.00	1.9	4.97	4.96	7.8	90.16	95.04	90.3
Dadra & Nagar Haveli	0.00	0.00	17.2	0.00	17.42	20.6	0.00	82.58	62.2
Delhi	6.32	2.20	2.7	13.52	8.70	10.2	79.78	9.10	87.1
Mizoram	18.71	55.00	7.9	74.23	67.38	40.7	7.06	26.38	51.3
Pondicherry	34.55	50.97	10.7	18.83	8.95	20.1	46.62	40.08	69.1

Source: Based on data from National Sample Survey Organisation, 38th, 44th and 49th rounds.

"others", has been introduced to cover the households living in houses that are neither owned nor rented. A large number of them had possibly reported as living in rented premises in previous Censuses, contrary to the actual situation, to avoid eviction or other legal complications. This would depress the percentage of rental premises in recent years.

It is possible to analyse the trend in the availability of a limited number of basic amenities, using Population Census and NSS data. As per the Census, the percentage of households having safe drinking water facility[1] in urban areas (of India excluding Assam) has increased from 75.1 to 81.4 during 1981-91. The corresponding figures for electricity are 62.5 and 75.8, while those for toilets are 58.2 and 63.9 respectively (Table 5). The NSS reports an interesting pattern of improvement over time. The percentage of households having no latrine has declined significantly from 36.8 to 31.1 during the period from 1983 to 1988-89 (Table 6a). The figure has, however, gone down only marginally to 30.6 per cent

Table 4
Percentage Distribution of Urban Households by Rental Characteristics

State	Percentage of HHs living in rented houses			Average per capita monthly rent (Rs.)					
				Actual			Imputed		
	1983	1988-89	1993-94	1983	1988-89	1993-94	1983	1988-89	1993-94
India	37.56	36.96	35.8	17.28	32.7	55.5	23.90	67.75	100.4
A.P.	38.07	41.42	41.5	18.96	40.43	65.3	17.94	56.44	64.2
Assam	27.65	37.81	37.8	19.83	40.24	60.0	22.07	70.41	112.8
Bihar	30.70	39.60	41.8	12.20	24.41	49.8	13.09	44.96	74.1
Gujarat	41.70	36.51	32.3	14.74	32.38	51.6	29.94	73.03	115.5
Haryana	31.83	27.50	23.4	20.10	41.05	57.1	29.16	67.01	104.5
H.P.	47.32	46.29	49.3	22.40	31.07	–	26.46	97.04	–
J & K	14.21	12.17	27.5	21.00	28.30	–	34.86	61.44	–
Karnataka	41.21	40.08	39.2	19.45	37.77	64.8	24.79	61.11	97.3
Kerala	16.30	13.26	13.7	24.17	40.34	58.7	25.35	60.41	97.4
M.P.	33.61	29.62	32.4	13.50	56.07	58.8	15.90	618.84	74.8
Maharashtra	48.22	42.13	37.9	13.07	22.74	53.0	28.26	83.83	118.9
Manipur	4.10	6.91	8.4	16.60	43.27	–	2.88	122.29	–
Nagaland	51.09	39.85	58.9	20.22	51.91	–	10.49	59.01	–
Orissa	26.51	40.63	43.3	13.02	29.55	62.6	13.33	34.15	70.9
Punjab	32.29	27.60	27.3	20.83	34.89	50.9	32.90	79.76	139.8
Rajasthan	24.76	27.40	28.3	15.00	30.76	55.1	15.16	54.43	89.8
Sikkim	69.43	75.02	71.5	24.00	48.47	–	19.67	96.92	–
Tamil Nadu	43.41	45.50	49.2	20.22	33.07	62.2	19.10	32.09	74.7
Uttar Pradesh	29.84	29.52	23.0	13.84	26.74	41.9	18.04	53.46	86.1
West Bengal	45.83	42.94	40.3	18.51	22.17	35.8	29.01	59.81	118.6
UTs									
A. & N. Island	42.25	50.69	61.7	16.03	56.21	–	37.99	86.18	–
Chandigarh	77.30	73.46	55.4	33.82	47.89	–	145.85	210.18	–
Delhi	33.43	37.06	36.0	39.00	71.97	–	72.11	230.01	–
Goa	40.43	39.09	67.1	21.39	51.43	–	39.86	85.29	–
Mizoram	27.98	28.14	16.5	28.05	48.55	–	30.95	73.38	–
Pondicherry	25.74	25.55	23.1	16.84	62.52	–	28.69	50.91	–

Source: Based on data from National Sample Survey Organisation, 38th and 44th rounds.

in 1993. Correspondingly, the percentage of households with flush system has moved up from 20.1 to 26.9 during the first period. The increase during the second period, however, is very modest, going up to only 28.5 in 1993 (Table 6b). This pattern is also observed for households having access to septic tank (toilets).[2] Furthermore, as opposed to the increase in the coverage of safe drinking water by 6.3 percentage points during 1981-91 as per the Census, NSS reports the figure to have remained static at 88 per cent during the period from 1986-87 to 1993[3]. One would, therefore, argue that the progress in providing basic amenities has slowed down in the post-liberalisation phase. The same is true in the context of housing development as well, as discused above. Electricity, however, seems to be an exception since the increase in its coverage has also been sustained during the early nineties as well.

Table 5
Percentage of Households having Select Civic Amenities in Urban Areas in Different States of India

India/state and UT	Electricity		Toilet facility		Safe drinking water	
	1981	1991	1981	1991	1981	1991
India	62.5*	75.8*	58.2*	63.9**	75.1*	81.4**
	61.6	75.9	57.4	63.6	74.1	81.6
Andhra Pradesh	52.2	73.3	44.1	54.6	63.3	73.8
Arunachal Pradesh	64.3	81.0	64.6	75.1	87.9	88.2
Assam	0.0	63.2	0.0	86.1	0.0	64.1
Bihar	50.1	58.8	53.0	56.5	65.4	73.4
Goa	0.0	0.0	49.5	55.8	52.3	61.7
Gujarat	74.4	83.0	60.1	65.7	86.8	87.2
Haryana	82.2	89.1	58.1	64.3	90.7	93.2
Himachal Pradesh	89.4	96.2	55.1	60.0	89.6	91.9
Jammu & Kashmir	92.2	0.0	64.5	0.0	86.7	0.0
Karnataka	62.0	76.3	53.3	62.5	74.4	81.4
Kerala	54.6	67.7	59.1	72.7	39.7	38.7
Madhya Pradesh	56.4	72.5	52.7	53.0	66.6	79.4
Maharashtra	70.5	86.1	59.4	64.5	85.6	90.5
Manipur	48.3	75.5	62.7	70.2	38.7	52.1
Meghalaya	59.6	83.0	70.2	85.7	74.4	75.4
Mizoram	50.1	85.5	24.5	84.4	8.8	19.9
Nagaland	58.4	75.6	65.3	75.1	57.2	45.5
Orissa	51.7	62.1	41.9	49.3	51.3	62.8
Punjab	85.4	94.6	64.8	73.2	91.1	94.2
Rajasthan	63.7	76.7	56.5	62.3	78.6	86.5
Sikkim	71.8	92.4	53.2	77.7	71.9	92.9
Tamil Nadu	61.6	76.8	51.3	57.5	69.4	74.2
Tripura	92.1	80.4	95.7	96.3	67.9	71.1
Uttar Pradesh	54.6	67.8	62.1	66.5	73.3	85.8
West Bengal	57.9	70.2	77.7	78.8	79.8	86.2
Union Territories						
A. & N. Islands	78.2	90.6	70.9	65.7	91.9	90.9
Chandigarh	85.5	85.5	78.5	79.8	99.4	97.7
D. & N. Haveli	67.7	87.6	42.8	65.1	54.3	91.0
Daman and Diu	85.9	95.5	42.9	45.8	67.0	86.8
Delhi	74.9	81.4	68.0	66.6	94.9	96.2
Lakshadweep	96.4	99.1	31.6	64.7	3.6	18.8
Pondicherry	58.1	71.7	41.5	50.0	84.2	86.1

Note: *Excludes Assam; **Excludes Jammu & Kashmir. The all-India figures without any star include the estimated values of the states in which Census could not be conducted.

Source: Household Tables, Census of India, 1981 and 1991.

III. DEPRIVATION IN HOUSING AND BASIC AMENITIES: AN INTER-STATE AND INTER-URBAN ANALYSIS

The inter-state variation in housing conditions and availability of basic amenities in urban areas using the Census data reveals an interesting pattern (Tables 3 and 5). However, in view of the socio-cultural factors affecting the nature of demand for these amenities, the interpretation of the variation in these indicators, as reflecting the inter-state disparity in the level of basic amenities, would have to be done with caution (Kundu and Moitra, 1999). One may, nevertheless, observe that many of the poorer states, like Andhra Pradesh, Bihar, Orissa, Madhya Pradesh, Kerala, etc., report a low percentage of urban households living in *pucca* houses or covered under the amenities due to lack of affordability. There is, thus, a positive relationship, though not highly significant, between the level of economic development and the quality of housing or access to the related amenities, covered in the analysis. The exceptions to this are the less developed states of Himachal Pradesh (in case of water supply and electricity), Uttar Pradesh (in case of water and toilets), Rajasthan (in case of only water supply) and Assam and Kerala (in case of only toilets) that report relatively high values. Similarly, some of the developed states

Table 6a
Percentage of Urban Households having Access to Different Civic Amenities

State	No latrine			Service latrine		
	1983	1988-89	1993	1983	1988-89	1993
India	36.82	31.08	30.6	18.08	11.72	7.4
Andhra Pradesh	51.77	41.53	36.8	12.45	6.72	3.3
Assam	6.99	6.39	7.0	36.30	18.75	14.7
Bihar	45.21	38.97	35.1	13.39	5.95	7.2
Gujarat	34.12	26.09	27.2	8.15	3.10	0.8
Haryana	42.80	37.15	31.6	34.07	20.09	7.5
Himachal Pradesh	39.13	43.83	27.0	24.74	15.31	5.3
Jammu & Kashmir	20.66	21.74	32.1	65.36	49.79	26.7
Karnataka	44.20	36.05	35.2	5.55	1.82	2.1
Kerala	26.67	18.67	15.7	2.59	0.30	0.2
Madhya Pradesh	47.48	45.63	43.3	22.45	13.40	9.9
Maharashtra	26.61	23.20	23.1	13.97	6.80	2.9
Manipur	1.90	0.00	5.1	31.83	0.00	11.1
Nagaland	3.23	6.22	0.9	51.38	6.65	28.2
Orissa	56.13	49.80	55.4	12.91	5.93	5.8
Punjab	39.40	30.98	21.1	28.48	17.39	7.1
Rajasthan	49.07	38.56	37.2	18.89	13.09	7.3
Sikkim	28.40	9.76	8.5	10.20	10.44	28.4
Tamil Nadu	47.64	40.10	36.1	15.55	10.32	6.4
Uttar Pradesh	33.62	28.65	32.5	39.31	31.45	23.5
West Bengal	13.29	17.54	21.2	16.51	7.54	5.6
Union Territories						
A. & N. Islands	30.39	27.94	23.0	26.10	16.18	5 2
Chandigarh	14.31	17.87	11.3	3.70	1.31	0.0
D. & N. Haveli	0.00	18.10	30.7	0.00	0.00	4.2
Delhi	27.28	18.74	29.4	14.07	17.67	11.1
Mizoram	10.29	0.13	0.4	3.73	5.29	0.1
Pondicherry	66.54	60.53	19.3	4.47	3.51	3.6

Note: The shares of households haviing different types of amenities have been worked out as percentages of the total households having access to amenities.

Source: Based on data from National Sample Survey Organisation, 38th, 44th and 49th rounds.

Table 6b
Percentage of Urban Households having Access to Different Civic Amenities

State	Septic tank			Flush system			Others		
	1983	1988-89	1993	1983	1988-89	1993	1983	1988-89	1993
India	20.67	25.84	29.6	20.13	26.92	28.5	4.30	4.22	3.80
A.P.	24.56	32.93	36.0	9.24	13.4	20.4	1.98	5.20	3.5
Assam	32.18	39.6	55.1	2.20	6.4	3.2	22.33	28.42	19.8
Bihar	34.09	39.07	46.3	3.91	11.37	7.1	3.40	4.36	4.0
Gujarat	28.33	20.18	23.9	28.52	49.84	46.8	0.88	0.76	0.8
Haryana	3.18	14.49	12.2	19.01	27.02	47.9	0.94	0.00	0.9
H.P.	9.32	9.29	25.3	25.26	30.97	41.1	1.55	0.18	1.1
J & K	3.33	5.23	21.4	5.81	15.73	17.6	4.84	7.43	1.0
Karnataka	11.46	20.23	26.3	34.48	40.11	31.9	4.31	1.55	4.5
Kerala	38.87	37.60	44.2	4.78	8.93	6.4	27.09	34.44	33.2
M.P.	14.14	21.33	29.8	10.16	18.07	16.5	5.77	1.0	0.4
Maharashtra	22.37	30.87	26.0	35.57	37.40	47.3	1.48	1.66	0.5
Manipur	5.38	14.13	13.0	3.75	9.53	0.2	57.14	76.34	70.7
Nagaland	40.03	30.16	38.9	0.63	41.62	5.7	4.73	15.35	26.3
Orissa	25.65	33.97	30.5	3.45	4.93	6.4	2.46	5.38	1.9
Punjab	2.69	6.40	9.7	26.97	42.87	59.4	2.46	2.04	2.7
Rajasthan	12.82	26.64	31.0	15.63	19.97	19.5	3.59	3.7	4.6
Sikkim	60.22	36.09	47.0	0.54	41.78	4.4	0.64	1.93	11.7
Tamil Nadu	14.77	22.77	32.9	20.0	25.30	23.7	1.04	1.45	0.9
Uttar Pradesh	5.95	14.01	14.0	19.64	24.86	29.1	1.48	0.7	0.8
West Bengal	52.91	47.07	54.1	6.81	17.35	11.4	10.48	10.22	7.5
UTs									
A.& N.Islands	38.85	45.44	68.1	3.32	8.29	0.9	1.34	1.9	2.5
Chandigarh	0.99	0.50	0.2	71.00	80.34	88.2	0.00	0.00	0.3
D. & N.Haveli	0.00	68.55	27.1	0.00	13.35	38.0	0.00	0.00	0.00
Delhi	4.52	6.91	8.5	49.61	55.11	49.2	4.42	1.15	1.6
Mizoram	9.21	18.59	20.8	0.53	12.04	0.3	76.24	61.62	78.4
Pondicherry	20.46	28.76	43.8	8.53	4.05	31.0	0.0	3.15	2.4

Note: The share of households having different types of amenities have been worked out as percentages of the total households having access to amenities.

Source: Based on data from National Sample Survey Organisation, 38th, 44th and 49th rounds.

like Karnataka, Tamil Nadu and West Bengal have low values for *pucca* housing in urban areas. Further, Tamil Nadu reports low coverage of households with toilet facilities and drinking water, Karnataka with toilets only and West Bengal with electricity.

The percentage of households having flush toilets as per the NSS data (Table 6b), however, exhibits a strong positive relation with economic development, much more than any other indicator of amenities. Besides the Union Territories of Chandigarh and Delhi, the states that report high percentages of households having the flush system are Gujarat, Karnataka, Tamil Nadu and Punjab. West Bengal and Tamil Nadu are the only two developed states that report low values while Himachal Pradesh is the only backward state which reports a high value.

Improvement in housing conditions and availability of basic amenities during the eighties do not show any regular pattern (Tables 3, 4, 5 and 6). One may, nonetheless, observe that in many less developed states, the decline in the percentage of households in *katcha* houses is low as in Orissa, Kerala and Uttar Pradesh. Similarly, the decline in the percentage of households having no latrine is marginal in the case of Madhya Pradesh, as per the NSS data. Himachal Pradesh and Jammu & Kashmir are the two less developed states where the figures have actually gone up. However, even among the developed states, there are a few that report a nominal decrease in the value of this indicator. Pondicherry is a unique case where the percentage of *katcha* houses has gone up, possibly due to high growth in slum population. Similar is the case of West Bengal with regard to latrine facility.

The variation across size classes of urban centres shows regularity and a distinct pattern. The percentage of households covered by each of the three amenities increases systematically with the size class of urban centres, except for class VI towns (Tables 7a and 7b). Importantly, class VI towns have special character because many among these have been established or are managed by the government departments, public agencies, military establishments or private industries. These, therefore, enjoy a special status and high level of amenities. It is indeed very disturbing that in class V towns, having a population between 5,000 and 10,000, the percentage of households not covered by toilet, electricity and drinking water facilities are 61, 41 and 28, respectively in 1991 (Table 7b). The corresponding figures for cities with more than 5 lakh population are 22, 17 and 14 per cent only. Similarly, while 14 per cent of the people in class V towns have none of these three amenities, the corresponding figure for the 5 lakh plus cities is less than 3 per cent. On the other hand, the percentage of households having all the three amenities in class III, IV and V towns is about 30 per cent only while that for class I cities, is twice as large (Table 7b).

When we analyse the inter-state disparity for different size classes of urban centres, it works out to a low figure in case of larger cities. This is because in the latter, the differences in socio-cultural factors are less important as these would have high literacy levels, modern values etc. Also, most of the class I cities have a high per capita income, a high percentage of manufacturing activities and, correspondingly, a high level of investment in basic amenities, in all states. Small towns, on the other hand, are different both in terms of economic as well as cultural factors across states, and this affects their level of basic services resulting in disparity.

Understandably, the variations in the percentage of households having the amenities across size class of urban centres are not as high as those across states. The size class disparity is, however, relatively high in the less developed states like Bihar, Orissa, Kerala, Madhya Pradesh and Uttar Pradesh, with the important exception being Himachal Pradesh (Kundu et al., 1996). The developed states, on the other hand, report a low variation, with the small and medium towns reporting a reasonable level of coverage. The states of Punjab and Haryana, for example, report a very low percentage of households as not having any of the facilities in even smaller size class of towns, viz. less than 20,000 population. The figures for other developed states like Gujarat,

Table 7a
Percentage of Households Covered by Amenities in Different Size Class of Urban Centres in 1981

Class	Electricity	Drinking water	Toilet
Class I (1 lakh plus)	61.90	75.36	58.00
Class Ia (1 to 3 lakh)	52.48	71.34	46.98
Class Ib (3 to 5 lakhs)	49.29	61.46	44.87
Class Ic (5 lakh plus)	45.97	73.21	62.8 0
Class II	58.19	70.33	51.90
Class III	54.76	65.37	45.42
Class IV	48.95	61.75	40.23
Class V	45.74	56.43	37.93
Class VI	51.26	56.62	39.63
Urban India	61.90	75.36	58.00

Source: Household Tables, Part viii, A & B (i & ii) (for different states), Census of India, 1981.

Table 7b
Percentage of Households Covered by Amenities in Different Size Class of Urban Centres in 1991

Class	Electricity	Drinking water	Toilet	All amenities	No amenities
Class I	80.69	84.36	73.67	59.45	3.45
Class Ia	74.84	81.00	63.08	49.01	5.31
Class Ib	78.01	77.28	63.92	49.13	5.97
Class Ic	82.57	86.14	77.69	63.51	2.65
Class II	73.50	79.17	57.58	44.16	6.26
Class III	65.69	75.45	49.56	35.20	9.12
Class IV	62.19	73.84	43.08	30.38	11.47
Class V	59.19	72.18	38.75	27.82	13.91
Class VI	69.72	78.59	47.44	37.52	9.31
Urban India	76.51	81.84	66.43	52.46	5.17

Source: Unpublished Household Tables (available in computer floppies) from Population Census (1991).

Karnataka, Maharashtra, Tamil Nadu and West Bengal are also low, viz. less than 10 per cent. In case of toilet facilities, however, the developed states of Maharashtra and Tamil Nadu exhibit a low percentage of served households in towns with less than 20 thousand population in 1991. The figures are even lower than those for the backward states of Uttar Pradesh and Himachal Pradesh. One would, therefore, infer that the average level of amenities, except toilet facilities, are reasonably satisfactory in the developed states in all size class of towns, although the class I cities have an edge over the others. In the backward states, however, the level of amenities in larger towns is high (although less than satisfactory) while the smaller towns exhibit a very high level of deficiency and deprivation.

There has been a significant improvement in the availability of basic amenities across states and size classes of urban centres during 1981-91. The increase, however, is much more pronounced in the case of class I cities when compared to towns in the other size categories, as may be seen in Table 7a and 7b. The percentage of households having electricity, for example, has gone up from 62 to 81 in class I cities during 1981-91. Similarly, the figures have improved from 75 to 84 in case of drinking water and from 58 to 74 in case of toilet facilities. The corresponding increase for other size classes of urban centres is much less. The fact that in the less developed states of Kerala, Madhya Pradesh, Bihar and Orissa, the percentage of households covered by toilet facilities in towns with less than 50,000 population has remained stable or even registered a decline must be viewed with concern. In Orissa, a significant fall is noted even in the case of class II towns. In developed states like Maharashtra, West Bengal and Tamil Nadu also such a decline is perceived but only in one or two size categories. One would, therefore, argue that small and medium towns, particularly those located in less developed states, should be the major concern of government policy in the context of provision of basic amenities.

It can be argued that a larger incidence of secondary and high-valued tertiary activities in large cities gives the people residing there, a high level of income. In the small and medium towns, on the other hand, the earnings of the people are low, due to the poor economic base and lack of employment opportunities in the organised sector (Kundu, 1992). These towns have a weak base of manufacturing sector and a high percentage of workforce dependent on agriculture. Instability in their economy is reflected in high fluctuation/ variation in their demographic growth over time as also across regions within the states (Kundu, 1983). One would argue that many of the small and medium towns are not in a position to generate funds to provide civic services to all sections of the population and stabilise their economic base.

One general point emerging from the analysis in this section is that the identification of indicators of vulnerability and deprivation that would be meaningful in any inter-state comparison, is extremely difficult. This, as argued above, is due to significant variation in physiographic and socio-cultural factors within the country. As a consequence people in different regions perceive the need of having concrete houses, toilets or availability of water from certain sources, etc. very differently. The interpretation of the indicators built up by using the available secondary data on housing or basic amenities, therefore must be done with a lot of qualification. Capturing "non-food poverty" through a set of indicators is, thus, fraught with much greater risk and errors of subjectivity than calorie- linked poverty. Resolving the controversies with regard to desirable levels of different types of amenities and making their absence the basis for the identification of deprivation or vulnerability for policy purposes would be an extremely challenging task. In view of the limited success of the Expert Group, set up by the Planning Commission (1993), in sorting out such controversies and methodological issues involved in measuring food-linked poverty, one may not be very enthusiastic about working out indicators for capturing non-food poverty or social security in basic amenities. More importantly, these indicators are unlikely to get the support of policy makers at the centre and states as constituting the basis for resource allocation and planned intervention.

IV. ISSUES CONCERNING POVERTY, VULNERABILITY AND SOCIAL SECURITY

The information available from the NSS in its various rounds, pertaining to consumption expenditure as well as housing and other amenities, provides interesting insights into the interdependencies between poverty, availability of amenities and quality of life. This can be analysed to understand the dynamics of development of slums and the nature of vulnerability of the population. Importantly, however, many of the details pertaining to intra-city variation, qualitative dimensions of the facilities, etc., are not available from the NSS or for that matter any other official source. The data gathered for micro-level studies for different cities are extremely helpful in filling this gap. An attempt has been made in this section to understand the issues and problems regarding vulnerability and social security of the poor with regard to these amenities, using both secondary as well as primary data.

Importantly, the NSS, for the first time in 1993 in its 49th round provided information on the quality of housing and availability of basic amenities by canvassing a uniform definition of slums from 21 states and union territories. Although a few of the states and union territories have been left out in the sampling, the coverage was much better than that of the 31st round, which had covered only the slums in class I cities of 1971, along with only two class II cities, viz. Shillong and Pondicherry. Happily, the 49th round covered all the slums that have been so declared by respective local bodies, as also the undeclared slums identified by field officials, using the criteria of compactness of habitation, quality of the structure and inadequacy of basic amenities. Information has been gathered from knowledgeable persons in the area and subsequently verified physically by the officials of the NSS.

Notably, about 90 per cent of the slums are known to be located in residential areas while only 5 per cent are in industrial areas in the year 1993. The distance from motorable roads in case of 98 per cent of the slums is less than one km. The corresponding figure for primary schools is 90 per cent. The situation is similar to that obtaining in non-slum areas since exactly 90 per cent of the urban households in the total sample have a school within one km. A similar picture emerges for other amenities as well. One could, therefore, argue that the slum and non-slum areas are distributed more or less evenly within cities, and distance is not an important factor in determining the access of the slum dwellers to the various amenities. If a smaller percentage of households in the slums are covered by the facilities, it is because of other constraints and not the physical distance.

Further, it would be wrong to assume that most of the slums are on private premises and consequently face a serious threat of eviction, given the increasing land values and liberalisation of the land market in recent years. Indeed, about 62 per cent of the slums are located on public land. Indian Railways account for about 13 per cent of the total slums located on public land. Surprisingly, more than 53 per cent of these are on the land of municipal bodies. One would, thus, infer that despite pressure on the local bodies to mobilise resources internally, they have not been able to muster the political will to launch massive slum clearance programmes in an attempt to obtain land for commercial purposes. It may further be argued that in case the local bodies are supported administratively and financially to take up schemes for rehabilitation of the slum population, obtaining land titles would not be a major constraint. This is because the title, in case of more than half of the total slums on public land, already rests with these bodies. There are, however, evidences that the local bodies are succumbing to the pressure of resource mobilisation and entering into land deals with private agencies, mostly through leasing out plots, in lieu of certain infrastructural investments or provision of basic amenities. These have long-term implications for land use and the micro-environment of the city that unfortunately are not receiving adequate attention of planners.

An analysis of NSS data reveals that 15.3 per cent of urban households resided in slum areas in 1993. The slums, however, constituted an extremely heterogeneous category. The physical structure can be described as *katcha* in case of 35 per cent slums, while for another 34 per cent it would be semi-*pucca*. This implies that more than 30 per cent of the slums have predominantly *pucca* structures. Importantly, 87 per cent of the *pucca* slums have access to tap water. For semi-*pucca* slums, the figure is 73 per cent while for *kutcha* slums it works out to around 30 only. Tap water was available for 65 per cent of the slum population while for the average urban dwellers, the figure is marginally higher, viz. 70 per cent. The real difference between the slum and non-slum areas, however, emerges in terms of nature of access to the facility. About 64 per cent of the households in slums have taps only at the community level while for non-slum households, this problem exists only for 25 per cent.

It is a common but erroneous assumption among planners that the urban poor reside in non-*pucca* houses or slum colonies. Only 13 and 25 per cent of the poor households live in *katcha* and semi-*pucca* houses while as many as 60 per cent live in *pucca* houses.[4] Similarly, the percentage of poor living in slums would be around 22, the remaining living in non-slum areas. Taking the share of population residing in *katcha* houses or slum colonies as a proxy for urban poverty would, thus be grossly misleading.

An important point is that the share of *katcha* dwelling units to the total units, built during the last five years, would be around 15 per cent. The figure is much higher than the share of these houses in the total housing stock in urban areas, which is less than 10 per cent. It appears anomalous that despite this high share, the share of *katcha* houses should have gone down from 18 per cent to 8 per cent during 1987-93. One can possibly explain this by the fact that the rate of depreciation for *katcha* houses is much higher than for other categories and so is the risk of their destruction and demolition. Understandably, the poor have to run even faster to stay at the same place with regard to housing. The seriousness of the housing situation of the poor in urban areas can be assessed from the fact that 53 per cent of the *katcha* houses and 19 per cent of semi-*pucca* houses are in bad condition needing urgent repairs. These figures are very high when compared to the figure of 3 per cent only for *pucca* houses. Also, the share of *katcha* houses in the total repairs, alterations and improvement work is 26 per cent, which is much higher than their share in housing stock or new constructions. This implies that those living in temporary structures have to regularly undertake repair work to keep their units habitable. This is the reason why we observe that a larger proportion of the *katcha* houses above 40 years of age are in good condition than these among semi-*pucca* or *pucca* structures.

An analysis of the data from the 49th and earlier rounds, pertaining to access to housing and basic amenities, suggests that a substantial portion of the benefits provided by the public agencies are cornered by middle and upper income households. Field-based studies in various large cities further indicate that the poor mostly draw water from public stand posts (PSP), where it is available for short durations at a low pressure and the supply is erratic. Moreover, the number of persons dependent on one PSP or tubewell is high, resulting in long queues and hours of waiting. The per capita water consumption for these people works out to be extremely low and so would be the amount of subsidy, even when water is given free to them. The rich, on the other hand, get a smaller subsidy per unit of water (as they have to pay a higher rate), but since their total consumption is very high, their total subsidy works out as very high. Moreover, many among the poor do not get water through PSPs and have to depend on private or public tubewells and handpumps. The quality of water in such cases is generally unsatisfactory, often causing water-borne diseases and, sometimes, epidemics (Kundu, 1993).

The situation is far more serious with regard to sanitation. The percentage of urban households not having any toilet facility in 1993 works out to about 31, which is much higher than the figure for drinking water. Correspondingly, the percentage of slums without toilet facilities is as high as 54. This is much higher than that for the urban poor, which is less than 45 per cent.[5] Among the households that do have toilets, a large majority share the facility with their neighbours. Micro-level surveys further reveal that the most of the free community toilets built by state governments or local bodies are rendered unusable due to lack of maintenance. As a consequence, the poor are unable to use these and are often forced to defecate in the open. Defecation in open space, along with overflowing toilets and drains pose a major health problem, particularly during the rainy season. Even in large cities, which are reported to have been fully or partially covered by an underground system, most of the slum colonies remain unsewered.

The other major problem in the slums is that of drainage, since about 52 per cent of the households here report having either *katcha* open system or total absence of drainage facility. Water-logging in the rainy season occurs for as many as 60 per cent of the slums. This problem exists in non-slum areas as well, but the corresponding percentage figure is less.

The ward or locality level data available from Population Censuses as also from microstudies for a few large cities, indicate that intra-city variation in the level and quality of amenities is high and increasing over time. The growing importance of private entrepreneurship in urban areas has meant select localities having higher income and "affordability" opting for high quality amenities. Indeed, a few non-governmental and community-based organisations that emerged during the past few decades are trying to improve the quality of life in the slum areas by mobilising the community and government machinery at the state and local level. There is, however, no denying the fact that the well-to-do have a much larger capacity to organise themselves and better access to institutions at state levels providing these facilities. Even the local bodies would have a vested interest in serving the groups that are politically and economically powerful. Involvement of the private sector and voluntary agencies, therefore, may not necessarily reduce inequality in the access to civic amenities.

Several field-based studies have come out with the conclusion that the problem of the poor is not one of non-affordability of the current expenses but of capital expenditure involved in obtaining a new water connection or toilet facility. The user charges, in general, are very low and do not show significant progressivity. In fact, pricing of water and other basic services has not been applied as an instrument to rationalise their use which could help generate funds for the local bodies to cross-subsidise the provision of these facilities in slums and other low income colonies. The taxes collected by these bodies for providing sanitation and sewerage facilities from the handful of households that have access to these, are extremely low and do not cover even the cost of maintaining the system. The subsidies provided through the public agencies in basic services in urban areas, often justified in the name of the poor, are, thus, cornered by richer sections who can afford to pay.

In the old parts of several large cities, several households are often in need of replacement of their local pipelines providing domestic connections. There is a risk of epidemics breaking out due to seepage of sewer water through corroded pipes for potable water supply. This problem has been noted as serious even in a developed state like Gujarat. Many among the poor are not able to perceive the imminent danger of water pollution and would be unwilling to pay the necessary user charges. In several large and small towns, the risk of epidemics is high also due to shallow tube wells provided in slum areas.

Improvements in the case of water supply facilities have been reported in about 50 per cent slums, while the figure for roads is 42 per cent, as per the data from the 49th round of the NSS. For drainage and garbage disposal, improvements are noted in about 30 per cent slums. Unfortunately, only 18 per cent of slums reported improvement in latrine facilities while for sewage it was still less, viz. 10 per cent only. The improvement pattern, thus, does not correspond to the critical areas of deficiency, as identified above, using the data from the NSS. The major problems faced by the slum population were noted to be that of drainage and absence of toilet facilities—the areas where the improvements have been the least.

In case of slums reporting improvement work on roads, water supply, drainage and garbage disposal facilities during the last five years, more than 90 per cent are those where these activities have been undertaken by government agencies. This reflects the insignificant role played by the private sector and NGOs in slum improvement. The important role played by the local bodies is evident from the fact that while 35 per cent of the slums have no provision for garbage disposal, 80 per cent of the remaining depend on the municipal bodies for this crucial service. It is only for latrines and sewerage that the non-governmental agencies can claim a share of about 10 per cent. There are, however, states like Gujarat and Haryana where the NGOs claim a share of more that 50 per cent of the slums reporting improvements in water supply. For latrine facility, the figure is as high as 85 per cent in Haryana, while for Madhya Pradesh and Uttar Pradesh, it is above 35 per cent.

V. SHELTER AND BASIC AMENITIES TO URBAN POOR: CHANGING PROGRAMMES AND PERSPECTIVES

An analysis of the anti-poverty programmes undertaken by the central, state and local governments, particularly those for providing basic services to urban poor reveals that the major concerns and areas of emphasis have changed significantly during recent years probably due to the changing perspectives at the macro level. The origin of the urban poverty alleviation initiatives goes back to the early 1950s when the Community Development Programme (CDP) was introduced. It was basically for *in-situ* upgradation of shelter and improvement of neighbourhood through provision of basic facilities at the community level. Unfortunately, CDP was operated at a low key, receiving only a small allocation in the Central budget.

It was only in the seventies that a major scheme, namely, Environmental Improvement of Urban Slums (EIUS), was introduced (in the Fifth Plan) with the objective of improving the living conditions of the slum population. This was subsequently transferred to the state governments in 1974. The Seventh Plan, too, took explicit note of the growing incidence of slums and poverty in the urban areas and launched the Urban Basic Service (UBS) Programme, in collaboration with UNICEF. It was meant to improve the access of the poor to basic amenities such as education, health care, sanitation and safe drinking water through a participatory approach. In 1990, an attempt was made to sharply focus the activities on the poor and the programme was renamed as the programme of Urban Basic Services for the Poor (UBSP).

Another important programme launched during the Seventh Plan, basically for generation of employment for the poor, was the Nehru Rojgar Yojana (NRY). This had a significant component meant for the upgradation of dwelling units and was implemented within a participatory framework. Besides self-employment (SUME) and wage employment schemes (SUWE), it had a Scheme for Housing and Shelter Upgradation (SHASU). SHASU provided technical training to construction workers and financial assistance to the economically weaker sections for housing and shelter upgradation. The beneficiaries were entitled to government subsidy along with housing loan from Housing and Urban Development Corporation (HUDCO).

The Prime Minister's Integrated Urban Poverty Eradication Programme (PMIUPEP) was launched in 1995 with the aim of improving the quality of life of the urban poor, involving direct participation of the target groups. Another centrally sponsored programme meant for the slum dwellers was the National Slum Development Programme (NSDP), launched in 1996. This was later modified (in the Ninth Plan) into a special central assistance programme for the states. It relies on the creation of community structures for slum improvement and gives greater autonomy to the states, urban local bodies and community-based societies for designing and carrying out development works according to local needs.

The Ninth Plan has attempted to rationalise and integrate the existing anti-poverty programmes, following the recommendations of the Hashim Committee[6] (1994). It has launched a new programme, namely, Swarna Jayanti Sahari Rozgar Yojana (SJSRY), subsuming earlier programmes such as NRY, UBSP and PMIUPEP. It is a centrally-sponsored scheme, applicable to all urban areas with expenditure being shared in the ratio of 75 : 25 between the centre and states/UTs. The programme has both self-employment and wage-employment schemes reorganised from the respective components of NRY and PMIUPEP. The shelter upgradation components of both these programmes have, however, been merged with the NSDP.

Besides these, low-cost sanitation schemes have also been taken up from time to time by different state governments, mostly with 50 per cent of the cost coming to the beneficiary as a grant and the remaining as a loan at a low rate of interest. And yet, these have remained beyond the affordability of the people below the poverty line. This is understandable since about 80 per cent of their total consumption expenditure (NSS data for the year 1993-94) is on food and energy, leaving very little for the improvement of the basic services. In cities, where people have been provided with toilets under certain programmes, the recovery of the capital costs has been very low and consequently these could not be taken up on a long-term basis or replicated in other cities.

An overview of the strategy for poverty removal in the urban areas, including the schemes for provision of basic amenities, reveals that there has been a gradual but perceptible shift in the approach during the past few decades. Special anti-poverty programmes for income/employment generation in the late eighties and nineties supplementing programmes of shelter upgradation and for provision of amenities suggest that rather than treating poverty as a deficiency of basic needs of the poor such as health, education, water supply, sanitation and housing, employment and income generation are being viewed as important components.

The programmes pertaining to basic services were financed largely by the central government during and before the seventies. In the eighties and nineties, however, there has been a distinct shift of responsibility from the central to the state governments and local bodies. Importantly, the Eighth as well as the Ninth Plan have placed greater reliance on private capital, institutional finance and resource mobilisation by concerned public agencies. Understandably, it is far easier to mobilise funds through these sources for income-generating schemes than those linked to basic services. This, too, has altered the character of the anti-poverty programmes, with regard to both to their content as well as the stipulations for implementation. Currently, the subsidy coming from the central government, directly as a grant or indirectly through low interest rate, is marginal in most of the programmes, certainly much less than that provided in the earlier schemes.

The changes in the nature of the schemes and their pattern of financing have affected the availability of basic services, particularly with regard to the poor, adversely. This is because many of the state governments have closed down the programmes after the discontinuation of central assistance. A few others have opted for institutional funds for the projects at high rates of interest, instead of making budgetary provision. This has understandably diluted the pro-poor bias. The weak financial position of the state governments and local bodies has seriously hampered their implementation or altered the nature of the schemes. Furthermore, international funding agencies as well as national agencies like HUDCO, are insisting on cost recovery by increasing water rates, property taxes and so on. Many local bodies have found it difficult to comply with this requirement and consequently have not been able to avail of institutional finance, even at subsidised rates.

Most of the current anti-poverty programmes, including those focussing on shelter upgradation and basic amenities envisage involvement of local bodies, private agencies, non-governmental organisations and communities. The government fund constitutes only a part of the total resources, with the remaining expected to come from institutional sources, private entrepreneurs and the residents of the town or locality. This automatically creates a situation wherein the agencies or people providing substantial funds enjoy some authority in designing the details of the project, its exact location etc. The organisations providing loans, for example, would have an interest in recovering their money in a short time. For that, they can dictate the terms in such a manner that the original objectives of the programme get undermined. Within this framework of decentralisation, the urban poor who can contribute, at best, their labour and a small amount of money, would have very little say in working out the details of the projects or their implementation.

It would be important to analyse how the recent changes in the anti-poverty programmes, particularly in the Ninth Five Year Plan, have made an impact on the access of the poor to shelter and basic amenities. Besides the changes in the composition of the programmes and their financing pattern, as discussed above, there have also been modifications in the norms and stipulations that have altered the thrust, coverage and targeting of these programmes. The most significant point is that the allocation for anti-poverty programmes has gone down in recent years. The per capita figure for the nineties is about 24 per cent less than in the mid-eighties. Further, these have a higher loan component and smaller grant, as compared to earlier years.

Secondly, there is an attempt at better targeting towards people who are likely to succeed in their economic ventures and pay back the instalments. For this purpose, banks, other financial institutions and NGOs are involved in the designing and implementation of the programmes. Their involvement is sought to ensure that beneficiaries have affordability and would repay the loans. Finally, group-based activities are encouraged as these ensure better compliance of norms and lower default rates on loan repayment. Encouraging women groups to participate is also expected to ensure better cost recovery, fewer transfers of property rights and higher benefits to the women and children through familial bonds. All these would invariably lead to lower emphasis on provision of services and greater thrust on employment generation.

The above overview suggests that under the new perspective there is an attempt to make the anti-poverty programmes part and parcel of the general development plan. While this would increase economic viability and cost recovery, there is a serious risk of missing out the most vulnerable groups among the poor. Additionally, larger cities with a stronger economic base stand to benefit more by this restructuring. Small and medium towns, particularly those in backward states, are likely to be bypassed as a consequence of this changed perspective.

Importantly, there have been significant changes in the system of urban governance, particularly since the launching of the programme of structural adjustment in 1991, that are likely to have a far-reaching impact on the availability of the amenities to the poor and their vulnerability. The 74th Constitutional Amendment, for example, has the provision that the committees at the ward level could decide about the nature of amenities, based on the capability and willingness of the residents to pay. This is likely to further accentuate intra-urban inequality in terms of the level and quality of basic services. One would infer that the people residing in the low income pockets may not be willing to share the cost of improving the services, while the local body may try to escape from this responsibility under the pretext of decentralisation of functions. Consequently, the slum pockets in the heart of large cities or their peripheries may have a serious deficiency of civic amenities, causing health hazards for the entire city population.

In many states, construction of dwelling units in urban areas is permitted only when the individuals or their cooperatives undertake to build their own water supply and sewerage/sanitation system, placing no extra burden on the local body. Inability to meet this requirement as per the specifications of the civic authorities often puts the settlements of the urban poor into the unauthorised or illegal category. This results in the municipal bodies taking no formal responsibility for these outlying areas, further accentuating intra-urban disparity.

In some of the towns, the responsibility of constructing and maintaining latrines has been given to NGOs. One "successful" case here is that of Sulabh International, an NGO which runs on business principles. Sulabh builds and maintains toilets and bathing facilities and recovers the costs through user charges. However, in the localities where the residents are extremely poor or unruly, it has failed to recover even the running expenses. In many such cases, institutional arrangements have been such that the maintenance expenditure is borne by the local bodies or development authorities (on whose behalf it provides the service). This does not really solve the problem of cost recovery, but merely amounts to passing the buck to some other organisation.

Most of the schemes for the provision of basic services in low-income colonies have been taken up in the past by the concerned state government departments or para statal agencies that are meant for the general public and not specifically for the poor. The responsibility of maintaining these facilities in the slum areas, too, rests with the general administration of the municipalities that do not keep separate funds for the purpose. It is argued that the existing institutions for providing these amenities lack in sensitivity for the poor and the slum population. As a result of this kind of organisational arrangement, the elites at the state and local level dominate the decision-making in the selection of projects for providing amenities, their location, upkeep, etc., and corner most of the benefits.

It is indeed true that in a few states, special agencies have been created in recent years to meet the needs of the poor and the slum dwellers. There are Slum Clearance Boards that take up relocation as well as integrated housing projects for the poor, including provision of water and sanitation facilities. In some of the metropolitan cities, there are Slum and Squatter Wings within the Development Authorities or the Corporations. It is, however, unfortunate that none among these agencies have had much administrative power or financial support from the state governments. Consequently, they could not take up infrastructure development projects for the poor in any significant manner. This kind of anomaly can be noted even at the national level. Despite the creation of a separate department concerned with the problems of the poor in the Ministry of Urban Affairs and Employment (as also several other ministries in the central government), no attempt has made to strengthen it or the other related institutions entrusted with the task of meeting the needs of the poor.

VI. CONCLUSIONS AND RECOMMENDATIONS

The analysis in this paper based on secondary data brings out a significant disparity in the availability of basic amenities across states and size class of urban centres. Developed states generally report a high percentage of households living in *pucca* houses and having access to drinking water, electricity and toilet facilities. Similarly, class I towns, particularly the metropolises, enjoy a distinctly higher level of these amenities compared to other urban centres. In the developed states, the smaller towns, too, report a modest coverage of households under the amenities. The situation in less developed states is, however, quite different. Here, the class I cities have a reasonably high coverage but the situation in small towns is alarming. About a fifth of the population in these towns live in totally dehumanised conditions as they have to do without safe drinking water, electricity and toilet facilities. Most importantly, the progress in terms of coverage of urban population through the amenities has slowed down considerably in the post-liberalisation phase.

The larger incidence of secondary and high valued tertiary activities in large cities gives the people residing there a high level of income. In the small and medium towns, due to poor economic base and lack of employment opportunities in the organised sector, income level of the people is low. These towns have a weak base of manufacturing sector and a high percentage of the workforce is dependent on agriculture. Instability in their economy is reflected in high fluctuation/variation in their demographic growth over time as also across regions within the states. One could argue that most of the small and medium towns are not in a position to generate funds to provide civic services to all sections of population and stabilise their economic base.

Disparity in the levels of earning of the local bodies (as also the facilities provided by them) across size categories is noted as high—the smaller towns reporting a per capita tax revenue which is one third that of class I cities. The resource crunch is acute in case of the backward states, where the per capita grant given by the state governments to local bodies is low. It may further be noted that the small and medium towns in these states have experienced rapid growth in population that puts tremendous pressure on their infrastructure and basic services.

A few policy guidelines seem to be emerging from the analysis in the paper. One would stress on greater equity in the provision of basic services as inter-state and inter-urban disparities have acquired alarming proportions. The less developed states that are not in a position to allocate requisite funds for this purpose, should get central assistance through infrastructure development or basic service schemes. Small and medium towns, particularly in the backward states, must get special assistance from the central/state government, as their economic bases are not strong enough to generate adequate resources. This would imply increasing the resources allocated to urban development, as recommended in the report of the National Commission on Urbanisation. There must, however, be stipulations in the schemes to ensure that most of this fund is channeled for the provision of basic services for the urban poor and slum improvement.

Constitutional amendment for decentralisation of financial powers is not sufficient for generating resources at the town level. This must be backed up by actual devolution of powers and responsibilities and their use by the municipal bodies. The management capacities of these bodies need to be strengthened by providing for additional technical personnel and training the existing staff so that they can organise their affairs in a better manner, including mobilisation of tax and non-tax resources. It has been noted that manufacturing activities at the town level show a strong relationship with the availability of infrastructure and services. One may, therefore, argue that the provision of amenities in small urban settlements, besides being a goal in itself, would help in generating non-agricultural employment and diversifying their economic base.

The capacity of the government to generate employment directly through anti-poverty programmes is likely to remain limited. Past experiences suggest that there has been considerable leakage in these programmes. Banks and other financial institutions have shown extreme unwillingness to finance these as the risk of non-recovery is very high. Also, the assets created through such programmes have not contributed significantly to the development potential or long-term income-generating capacity of the towns. It is, therefore, recommended that the anti-poverty programmes should primarily be focussed on provision of basic amenities.

The schemes attempting to provide a standard package of infrastructural facilities and subsidised capital to entrepreneurs in all or a large number of towns for promoting industrial development is unlikely to succeed. Instead, a limited number of towns with development potential must be identified in each state and attempts should be made to link these with the national and international market. For this, only select infrastructure that are missing in these towns and are hampering their economic growth, need to be provided. Identification of the towns and their infrastructural needs must be done at the state level through a careful analysis of their socio-economic characteristics, past growth experiences, etc.

The capacity of the urban poor to pay for basic services would continue to remain low during the next few years of structural adjustment as the prospect of an increase in their real income does not seem very bright. Reduction in government grants, larger borrowing from institutional sources, increases in the rate of interest for public agencies involved in the provision of the amenities, etc. are likely to further affect the access of the poor adversely. It is nonetheless true that much of the subsidised amenities, provided through the governmental programmes during the seventies and eighties, have gone to high and middle income colonies. It would, therefore, be necessary to restructure these programmes and schemes and ensure that the subsidies are made explicit and, through strict stipulations, targeted to vulnerable sections of the population. Further, it would be important to create a formal structure for project implementation such that the private agencies, partially financing the projects of basic services, are obliged to function within the framework of development plan. Also, there should be proper monitoring of the project so that the vested interests at the local level do not corner a large part of the benefits on the basis of their financial contribution to the project or other machinations.

The role and functioning of the central/state government and public sector institutions sharing the responsibility of providing basic services in urban areas need to be altered to bring in a distinctly pro-poor bias. During the past three decades their investments in infrastructure development and basic services have not been spatially balanced. Also, they have not exhibited sensitivity in favour of the urban poor in their functioning. In view of this and also the resource crunch in the economy, privatisation, partnership and community-based projects have become necessary. Making the local bodies, development authorities and para statal agencies depend increasingly on their internal resources and institutional finance is also strongly recommended, which is supposed to bring in efficiency and accountability in their functioning. There is, however, an apprehension that this changed perspective and a consequent decline in public investment can create serious disparity between rich and poor localities. It can also increase disparity in the levels of amenities across towns. It would, therefore, be important that the minimum standards for the amenities are determined in realistic terms and the state and local governments take the overall responsibility of providing these to all sections of the population, irrespective of their income or affordability. They may fulfil the task by engaging or supporting private organisations, NGOs and CBOs.

Notes

1. Households having water supplied through a tap, hand pump or tube well, situated within or outside their premise, are considered as having access to safe drinking water facility.
2. Interestingly, the trend in the percentage of households residing in *pucca* houses is similar—going up by 20 percentage point from 51.21 during 1983-88 (38th and 44th round) but registering a nominal increase of 2.8 points only during 1988-93 (44th and 49th round). Furthermore, the percentage figures reported in the 49th and 50th rounds are about the same.
3. The figures from Census and NSS cannot be compared straightaway. One can nonetheless compare the trends observed from the two sources.
4. The percentage of households not having toilet facility among the bottom three deciles is around 38 per cent , while for the next upper decile it is 40 per cent. The percentage of poor housesholds to the total is likely to be between 30 to 40 per cent. It would, therefore, be reasonable to hold that the proportion of poor households living in *pucca* houses is around 38 per cent.
5. The percentagee of houseshold not having toilet facility among the bottom three deciles is arounds 45 per cent, while for the next upper decile it is 40 per cent. It would, therefore, be reasonable to hold that the share of poor households without toilets is less than 38 per cent.
6. The Hashim Committee, which was set up to review and rationalise the centrally-sponsored schemes for poverty alleviation and employment generation, has made recommendations for (i) combining the self-employment components of NRY and PMIUPEP into a single programme applicable for all urban areas of the country, (ii) merging of the urban wage employment components as well as the physical

infrastructure development component under and NRY and PMIUPEP to form a separate programme with a distinct identity to be applicable to all urban areas with a population of less than 5 lakhs, and (iii) shelter upgradation by housing components under NRY and PMIUPEP to be retained as a separate scheme or to be merged with slum development/basic services schemes operating at present.

References

Kundu, Amitabh (1983), "Theories of City Size Distribution and the Indian Urban Structure: A Reappraisal", *Economic and Political Weekly*, July.

——(1992), *Urban Development and Urban Research in India*, Khamma Publications, New Delhi.

——(1993), *In the Name of the Urban Poor: Access to Basic Amenities*, Sage Publications, New Delhi.

—— and S. Moitra (1999), "Access of Urban Poor to Basic Services: An Analysis in the Changing Perspective of Urban Government in India", in Mathur, O.P. (ed.), *India: The Challenge of Urban Government*, National Institute of Public Finance and Policy, New Delhi.

——and D. Kundu (1996), *Housing and Basic Amenities in Urban India: An Analysis of Regional Pattern and Accessibility in the Context of Changing Perspective of Government*, (Working Paper), Planning Commission, New Delhi.

Planning Commission (1993), *Report of the Expert Group on Estimation of Proportion and Number of Poor*, Government of India, New Delhi.

PART III

EDUCATION

9

Household Expenditure on Education: A Few Stylised Facts

Jandhyala B.G. Tilak

Social security and safety nets are part and parcel of social development, a process which serves to widen and deepen people's access to basic needs as precondition for sustainable human development over time.

ESCAP (2000, p. 129).

I. INTRODUCTION

Social security programmes are crucial in ensuring that various segments of the population have reasonable access to basic social services in all times. Education can be viewed as one of the best measures of ensuring social security. For the same reason, elementary education is also considered an important component of basic minimum needs. In fact, it is considered as a *basic human need*. Literature on human capital as well as human development has laid considerable emphasis on education—as an instrument and as a measure of human development. As per the Constitutional Directive of India, elementary education is to be provided free to all. However, this is not the case in reality. Families are found to be spending a lot on acquiring 'free' elementary education. This paper is concerned with the magnitude, nature and pattern of family expenditure on education. Earlier Minhas (1992) and Tilak (1996) have briefly analysed the then available national evidence on this aspect. They were based on the 42nd round of the National Sample Survey conducted in 1986-87. After the National Policy on Education 1986 was formulated, considerable emphasis was placed on education, especially free elementary education. But has there been any change? The available evidence based on small sample surveys (e.g. PROBE, 1999) confirms the continuation of the phenomenon of huge household expenditures on acquiring primary education. The present paper, based on the 52nd round of the National Sample Survey conducted in 1995-96, analyses the nature and pattern of household expenditures on education. These are described here as a set of stylised facts. No attempt has been made to compare these estimates with the earlier ones, as there are variations in concepts, definitions and measures. The paper is descriptive in nature and does not have any theoretical pretenses. The following section presents a brief description of public and household expenditures on education. Section III describes a large set of facts on family expenditures on education. Section IV draws a few major policy implications.

II. EXPENDITURE ON EDUCATION

Expenditures on education are of two types: those incurred in the individual domain, and those incurred in the institutional (or public) domain. These two are respectively familiar as household or family expenditures and public expenditures. Together they constitute the expenditures incurred on education in the social domain (Majumdar, 1983). Individual expenditures refer to expenditures incurred by the students and/or their parents for the education of the children. So it is also referred to as household or family investment in education. Institutional expenditures are referred to as public expenditures and if properly defined, they can be called government expenditures on education. Both public and household expenditures in education are of high significance not only because of their magnitudes, but also because of the nature and characteristics that are associated with those investments. While public expenditures can provide the educational facilities, only household expenditures will make it possible to take advantage of them. The two are so inter-related and inter-dependent that, in the absence of either of them, there is likely to be under-allocation of resources for education (Panchamukhi, 1989). "Unless the two kinds of investments match there can be only empty or over crowded classrooms" as Majumdar (ibid, p. 28) rightly observes.

Data on public expenditures on education in India are relatively easily available from the publications of the Department of Education, Ministry of Human Resource Development, Government of India and a few scholars have attempted detailed analyses of public expenditures based on such data.[1] But data on household expenditures are scarce. Accordingly, knowledge about the extent of household expenditures is rather limited. Serious efforts have not yet been made to collect data on household expenditures on a regular basis for a long time, as it was considered too trivial to bother about, and/or that such information is not necessary for planning of public resources.[2] The result is that research on household expenditures on education is very much limited. But the need for such a knowledge on household expenditures—the magnitude of household expenditures, the pattern of household expenditures on various levels of education and the determinants of household expenditures—is, of late, increasingly being felt by academics as well as educational planners and policy makers. It is being increasingly realised that to ignore household investment is too costly for educational planning in the long run. Lack of detailed knowledge on these aspects leads to formulation of inefficient and unsound policies on fees, scholarships, subsidies and even total public expenditure on education, as it seems to have happened in India.

The lack of empirical studies on household expenditures on education is being increasingly felt in a period when public budgets for education are dwindling, and household and private finances are being looked upon with hope. It has been argued that households have the ability to pay for education; and that they are also willing to pay for education. This is argued to be true not only in case of higher education, but also in case of elementary education; and that the potential willingness to pay for education can be tapped, so that government funds for education can even be reduced and reallocated in favour of other sectors. Counter-arguments are also being made in this context. Public policies are being formulated. But there is no systematic evidence on this and related aspects. There is indeed a major gap in research in India. The present study is a modest attempt in this direction and attempts to fill the gap to some extent.

What is the household investment in education and why is it made? Chart 1 presents a taxonomy of costs of education. Household costs include direct or visible and indirect or less visible costs. The less (or invisible indirect costs refer to opportunity costs, also known as foregone earnings. The direct costs include payments to the schools such as tuition, examinations fees, development fees, registration fees and several other types of fees and charges, and other costs, which are not necessarily paid to the school. The latter includes expenditures on textbooks and stationery, uniforms, travel, hostel, private tuition, etc. The present paper is confined to direct costs – the expenditures incurred by the families on education of their children. Indirect or opportunity costs of education are important and earlier research also found that they are sizeable (Tilak, 1988). But they are not considered here. Here we are primarily concerned with household expenditure on education.

Generally high levels of household investments in education are favoured on three main grounds: (a) Government does not have adequate resources to finance education and hence households have to necessarily finance their education , at least partly; (b) It is believed by some that household expenditures, specifically fees, would improve internal efficiency in the system, by making the children more serious about their studies, and, (c) Household

Chart 1
Taxonomy of Costs of Education

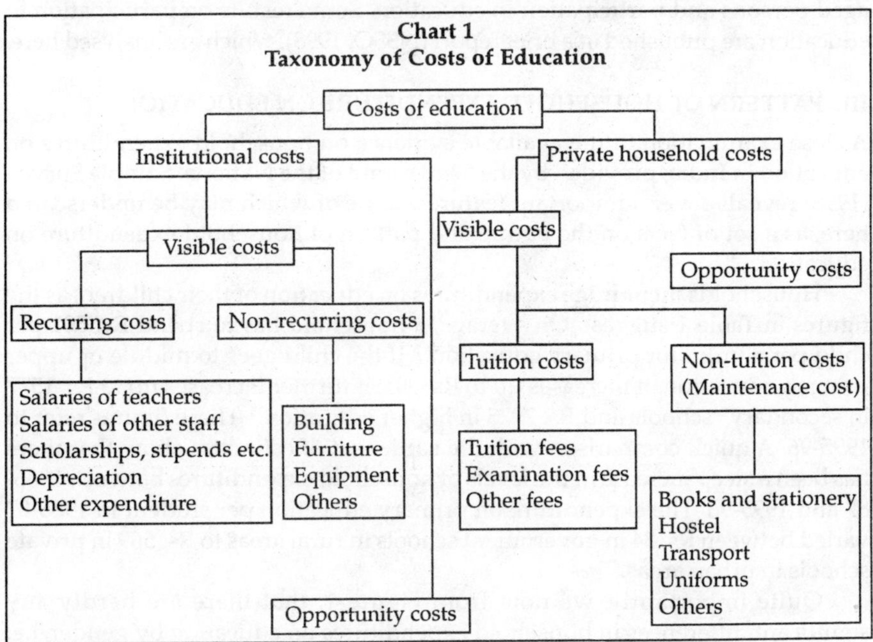

Source: Tilak (1988).

expenditures reflect both ability to pay and willingness to pay for education; it is argued that the ability and willingness to pay need to be fully exploited. At the same time, there are the following strong arguments against household expenditures: (a) The phenomenon of household expenditures, particularly on lower levels of education is against the letter and spirit of the free and compulsory education in many countries, as enshrined, for example, in the Constitution of India, and in several UN declarations, including Convention of the Rights of the Children and Universal Declaration of Human Rights. (b) Household expenditures interfere with demand for education; high levels of household expenditures may force the poor not to opt for schooling at all. (c) Household expenditures reflect and perpetuate inequities in the system, as rich households might spend more and poor households less. (d) It is also argued that high levels of household expenditure on education reflect high levels of inefficiency on the part of the government in providing it.

The phenomenon of household expenditures on education is also interpreted as transforming education into a commodity: households buy education, by paying for it. This is argued to be inconsistent with the very nature and philosophy of education.

Based on a preliminary examination of the 52nd round of the National Sample Survey, a few stylised facts on the nature and pattern of household expenditures on education are derived here. The survey was conducted during July 1995-June 1996. The survey covered, in all, 72,883 (43,000 rural and nearly 30,000 urban) households living in 7,663 rural villages and 4991 urban blocks in the country. The survey covered all the states and union territories geographically and covered four main areas: utilisation of maternity and child health-care services, morbidity and utilisation of medical services, problems of aged persons and participation in education. Some results on participation in education are published in a brief report (NSSO, 1998), which are analysed here.

III. PATTERN OF HOUSEHOLD EXPENDITURE ON EDUCATION

A close examination of the available evidence on household expenditures on education in India, provided by the 52nd round of the National Sample Survey (1998) reveals several important features, some of which may be underscored here, as a set of facts on the nature and pattern of household expenditure on education.

Households incur huge expenditures on education of their children, as the figures in Table 1 suggest. On average, a household has to spend Rs. 501 per child per annum for primary education.[3] If the child goes to middle or upper primary education, it increases up to Rs. 901; it further increases up to Rs. 1577 in secondary[4] schools and Rs. 2923 in higher education.[5] These figures refer to 1995-96. A quick comparison with the earlier set of estimates show that there has been a steep increase in the levels of household expenditures between 1986-87 and 1995-96. The expenditure on primary education per student in 1986-87 varied between Rs. 84 in government schools in rural areas to Rs. 569 in private schools in urban areas.[6]

Quite importantly, we note from Figure 1, that there are hardly any significant differences in household expenditures on education by gender, i.e. between girls and boys. The national level aggregates clearly show that there

Table 1
Average Annual Household Expenditure per Student (Aged 5-24), 1995-96

(Rs.)

	Rural			Urban			Total		
	Male	Female	Total	Male	Female	Total	Male	Female	Total
Primary	305	286	297	1197	1092	1149	507	494	501
Middle	640	641	640	1590	1456	1529	904	933	915
Secondary	1192	1156	1180	2288	2136	2219	1552	1619	1577
Higher	2283	2323	2294	3338	3260	3304	2879	2995	2923
All	605	516	570	1750	1609	1686	919	882	904

Source: See the text.

Figure 1
Gender-Equality in Household Expenditure on Education

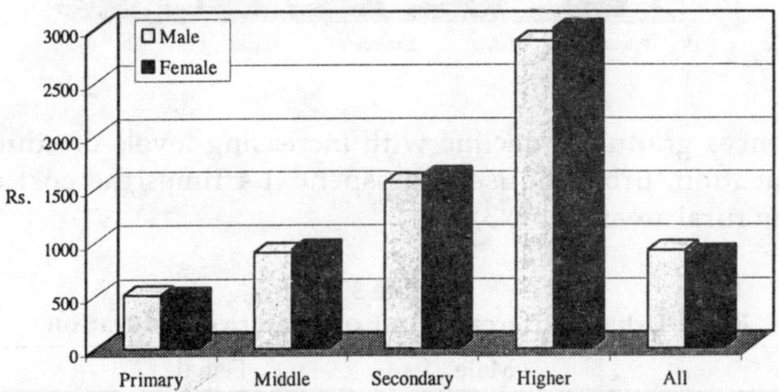

is not much gender discrimination in the households on spending on education, as the coefficients of discrimination[7] in Table 2 reveal. In fact, except for a small difference in primary schools, the differences favour girls in other levels of education. This is particularly true in rural areas and for the country as a whole. In urban areas, the differences are against girls in all levels of education; but the differences are only marginal.

Table 2
Coefficient of Gender Discrimination in Household Expenditure on Education

	Rural	Urban	All areas
Primary	0.0664	0.0962	0.0263
Middle	-0.0016	0.0920	-0.0311
Secondary	0.0311	0.0712	-0.0414
Higher	-0.0172	0.0239	-0.0387
All	0.1725	0.0876	0.0420

Source: See the text.

Perhaps the importance of girls' education is recognised by the families, and accordingly they do not discriminate against girls with regard to spending on their education, as compared to the boys.

But rural-urban differences in household expenditures are striking (Figure 2). A household in urban areas has to spend nearly four times the amount that a rural household spends on the primary education of its child.

Figure 2
Rural-Urban Differences in Household Expenditure on Education

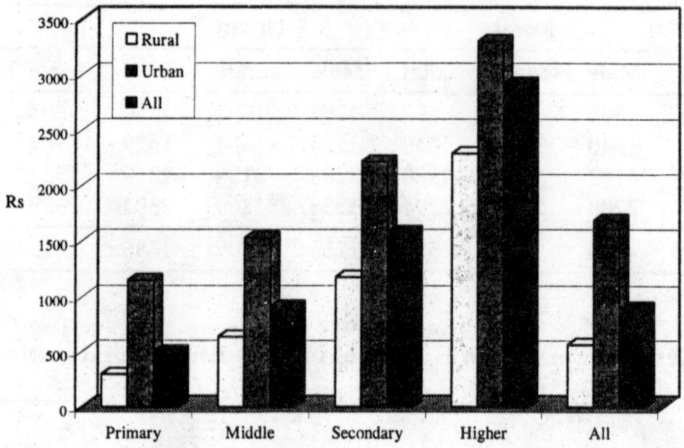

The differences gradually decline with increasing levels of education. In higher education, urban households spend 1.4 times the cost of higher education in rural areas (Table 3).[8]

Table 3
Rural-Urban Differences in Expenditure on Education

	Male	Female	All
Primary	0.255	0.262	0.258
Middle	0.403	0.440	0.419
Secondary	0.521	0.541	0.532
Higher	0.684	0.713	0.694
All	0.346	0.321	0.338

Source: See the text.

The above figures do not make a distinction between different types of schools—government, local body,[9] government aided,[10] and private schools.[11] Generally it is argued that primary and upper primary education in government, local body and even government aided schools is provided rather 'free' and that households do not have to spend any significant amounts when children attend such schools.

But the available evidence shows that this is not true. Even in government schools, children incur huge expenditures. However, the household expenditure on education in government schools is the lowest, followed by local body schools, which in turn was followed by government aided schools. The corresponding figures are the highest in case of private schools (Figure 3). What is interesting to note in Table 4 is that this is true for all levels of education, with no exception at all. The difference between the private schools and the government schools is as high as 5.5 times in primary schools, and the difference comes down gradually to 2.1 times in higher education. It is most generally felt that rich households spend more on education than low income households. This is found to be true at every level of education, and it also

Figure 3
Household Expenditure on Education per Student, 1995-96

(Rs.)

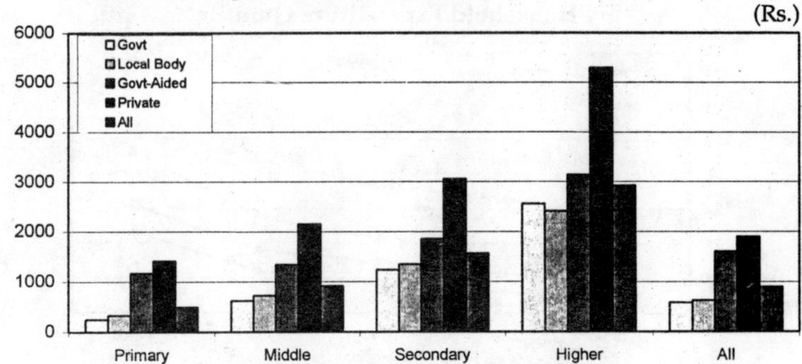

Table 4
Average Annual Expenditure per Student by Level of Education and Type of Institution

(Rs.)

	Type of institution					
	Govt.	Local body	Govt-aided	Private	All	Private/ Govt. ratio
Primary	257	338	1181	1424	501	5.54
Middle	622	726	1346	2156	915	3.47
Secondary	1236	1349	1861	3061	1577	2.48
Higher	2559	2415	3143	5296	2923	2.07
All	580	628	1615	1904	904	3.28

holds between every two successive income groups. Based on total household expenditures, households are classified into five expenditure quintiles: 0-20 (the bottom income group), 20-40, 40-60, 60-80 and 80-100 (the top income group). Average household expenditure of the top income group on education is 6.1 times the expenditure of the bottom income group. In fact, we notice a smooth upward rising expenditure curve of the different expenditure quintiles (Figure 4) .

There is also no intersection of curves between levels of education and the quintiles. The effect of wealth on household expenditure on education is clearly noticeable. The wealth effect[12] is quite pronounced in primary education, and declines with increasing levels of education, as the last column in Table 5 reveals.

The differences between several types of primary schools are vast, compared to differences in the higher levels of education. As a result, rich households can spend a much higher level of expenditure on primary education than poor households, but when it comes to higher education, since differences between colleges are marginal, and hence the differences in household expenditures are also marginal; even the rich households do not feel the need to spend significantly higher amounts on their children than what poor households do.

Of the several items of expenditure of the households on education, fees forms the singlemost important item at any level of education, as shown in

Figure 4
Household Expenditure on Education per Student by Household Expenditure Quintile (Rs.)

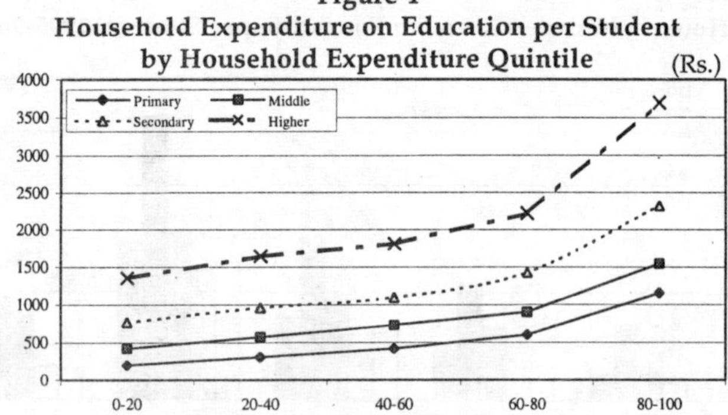

Table 5
Average Annual Expenditure per Student by Expenditure Quintile

(Rs.)

	Household expenditure quintiles						Wealth
	0-20	20-40	40-60	60-80	80-100	All	effect
Primary	197	306	419	598	1150	501	1.1652
Middle	426	575	726	900	1547	915	0.3969
Secondary	768	961	1096	1424	2322	1577	0.1917
Higher	1353	1645	1810	2220	3694	2923	0.0934
All	300	472	647	923	1836	904	0.6770

Note: See the text (end note no. 12) for the 'wealth effect.'

Table 6.[13] Fees includes tuition fee, examination fees and "'other' fees and 'other' payments". Though tuition fee is sizeable, other fees are not insignificant. Even in primary education, 20 per cent of the expenditure of the households on education goes in the form of tuition fees, and another 10 per cent in the form of other fees (Figure 5).

In case of higher education, the tuition fee forms 25 per cent and other fees 16 per cent. On the whole, all types of fees form 30 per cent of the household expenditure on education in primary education, 23 per cent in middle and secondary education and 41 per cent in higher education. So neither primary education nor any other level of education is fee-free (Table 6).

The second most important item, after fees, is books and stationery. About one-fourth to nearly 30 per cent of the total expenditure of the households on education is accounted for by books and stationery. This is important even in the case of primary education, where textbooks and stationery are said to have been provided free to a majority of the children. This may be due to the provision by the government being grossly inadequate. In elementary education the third important item is uniforms, which is also said to be provided by the government free to many, if not all children.

Private coaching is found to be important only in case of secondary education, and not necessarily at other levels of education, though the phenomenon does exist at all levels of education. On average, 14 per cent of children in rural areas and 18 per cent in urban areas in all levels of education together, take private coaching. High proportion of students going for private

Table 6
Average Annual Expenditure per Student on General Education by Item of Expenditure and by Level of Education

(Rs.)

Item of expenditure	Level of education							
	Primary		Middle		Secondary		Higher	
	Rs.	%	Rs.	%	Rs.	%	Rs.	%
Tuition fee	100	19.96	124	13.55	197	12.49	721	24.67
Exam fee	11	2.20	24	2.62	66	4.19	174	5.95
Other fees and payments	39	7.78	64	6.99	106	6.72	303	10.37
Total fees	150	29.94	212	23.17	369	23.40	1198	40.99
Books	67	13.37	153	16.72	272	17.25	506	17.31
Stationery	63	12.57	126	13.77	190	12.05	290	9.92
Uniform	118	23.55	212	23.17	248	15.73	84	2.87
Transport	31	6.19	42	4.59	98	6.21	351	12.01
Private coaching	48	9.58	125	13.66	326	20.67	307	10.50
Other expenses	25	4.99	45	4.92	74	4.69	187	6.40
Total	501	100.00	915	100.00	1577	100.00	2923	100.00

Figure 5
Items of Household Expenditure on Primary Education

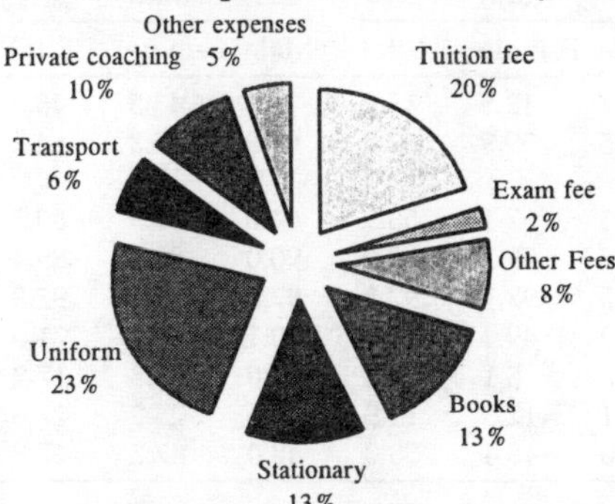

coaching obviously reflects the poor quality of education and instructional process offered in schools, whether they are government or private schools.

Unfortunately these data are not available by the type of school, i.e., the available information does not help us know the extent of expenditure on fees in government primary schools vis-a-vis other types of schools. Such information is available by the type of school and not at the same time by level of education. Considering all levels of education together, it can be noted that it is not only fees, but also expenditure on every item of education that is higher in government aided schools than in government and local body schools, and is the highest in the private schools (Table 7). The exceptions are very few. Expenditure on private coaching, and also books and stationery is higher in case of children attending government aided schools than the other schools. Further, except transport and to some extent private coaching in rural areas, a majority of the students have to spend on all other items, including fees, books, stationery, uniforms and 'other' expenses (Table 8) and they have to spend considerable amounts (Table 9).

Table 7
Average Annual Expenditure per Student in General Education by Item of Expenditure and by Type of Institution (Rs.)

Item of expenditure	Govt. & local body	Govt. aided	Private	All
Tuition fee	35	303	678	149
Exam fee	24	51	51	31
Other fees & payments	39	137	154	68
Books	114	228	216	145
Stationery	93	166	148	112
Uniform	130	238	274	164
Transport	30	137	134	59
Private coaching	84	284	186	130
Other expenses	37	71	63	45
Total	585	1615	1904	904

Table 8
Proportion of Students Incurring Expenditure on Different Items
(As per cent of corresponding estimated no. of students of sector and sex)

Item of expenditure	Rural			Urban			Total		
	Male	Female	Total	Male	Female	Total	Male	Female	Total
Tuition fee	16.7	12.5	15.0	48.8	43.5	46.3	25.5	22.8	24.4
Exam fee	64.5	59.9	62.7	64.9	63.3	64.2	64.6	61.1	63.2
Other fees & payments	60.1	57.1	58.9	61.0	59.9	60.5	60.4	58.0	59.4
Books	80.6	79.1	80.0	90.0	88.7	89.4	83.2	82.3	82.8
Stationery	97.5	97.1	97.3	97.8	97.8	97.8	97.6	97.3	97.5
Uniform	47.2	49.4	48.1	70.1	72.1	71.0	53.5	57.0	54.9
Transport	8.8	6.1	7.8	17.0	17.3	17.2	11.1	9.9	10.6
Private coaching	14.1	12.6	13.5	29.6	25.2	27.6	18.4	16.8	17.7
Other expenses	51.0	48.4	50.0	48.0	47.7	47.9	50.2	48.2	49.3

Education, particularly elementary education is expected to be provided free by the government. But the concept of 'free' is given a narrow interpretation so as to confine to fees, and that too tuition fees only.[14] NSSO also adopted a similar definition and those who are not required to pay tuition fees are considered to be receiving education 'free'. How many students get free education going even by this narrow definition? NSSO provides some valuable information. Only 76 per cent of the children in primary schools receive 'free' education; the proportion declines to 71 per cent in upper primary education, to 57 per cent in secondary and 14 per cent in higher education. Of course, these figures in Table 10 refer to all types of schools. It may be argued that primary and middle education is provided free in government and local body schools. But the available evidence given in the later half of Table 10 shows that 92 per cent of the children in government schools and 87 per cent of the children in local body schools receive free primary education. The remaining students pay tuition fees. In government aided schools which are also generally expected to provide free elementary education, 55 per cent of the children seem to be paying fees in primary schools. The general

Table 9
Average Annual Expenditure per Student on General Education by Item of Expenditure

Item of expenditure	Rural			Urban			Total		
	Male	Female	Total	Male	Female	Total	Male	Female	Total
Rs. per student									
Tuition fee	50	41	47	410	367	390	149	150	149
Exam fee	26	19	23	52	48	50	33	29	31
Other fees & payments	43	37	40	139	128	134	69	67	68
Total fees	119	97	110	601	543	574	251	246	248
Books	120	99	111	229	214	222	150	137	145
Stationery	95	84	91	160	162	161	113	110	112
Uniform	123	127	125	252	258	255	159	171	164
Transport	39	25	34	117	122	119	61	58	59
Private coaching	71	54	64	318	243	284	139	117	130
Other expenses	37	30	34	73	68	71	47	43	45
Total	605	516	570	1750	1609	1686	919	882	904
Per cent									
Tuition fee	8.26	7.95	8.25	23.43	22.81	23.13	16.21	17.01	16.48
Exam fee	4.30	3.68	4.04	2.97	2.98	2.97	3.59	3.29	3.43
Other fees & payments	7.11	7.17	7.02	7.94	7.96	7.95	7.51	7.60	7.52
Total fees	19.67	18.80	19.30	34.34	33.75	34.05	27.31	27.89	27.43
Books	19.83	19.19	19.47	13.09	13.30	13.17	16.32	15.53	16.04
Stationery	15.70	16.28	15.96	9.14	10.07	9.55	12.30	12.47	12.39
Uniform	20.33	24.61	21.93	14.40	16.03	15.12	17.30	19.39	18.14
Transport	6.45	4.84	5.96	6.69	7.58	7.06	6.64	6.58	6.53
Private coaching	11.74	10.47	11.23	18.17	15.10	16.84	15.13	13.27	14.38
Other expenses	6.12	5.81	5.96	4.17	4.23	4.21	5.11	4.88	4.98
Total	100.00	100.00	100.00	100.00	100.00	100.00	100.00	100.00	100.00

presumption that very few students in colleges pay fees is also not found to be true. Hardly 19 per cent of the students in government colleges receive free education. Others pay tuition fees, in addition to other fees.

When we look at the distribution of students who receive free education by household expenditure quintiles, one can notice a somewhat 'progressive' distribution, though at the same time it must be mentioned that 15 per cent of the children belonging to bottom income groups (bottom quintile) in primary schools and 85 per cent of the same bottom income group in higher education pay tuition fees. All children are of course expected to receive free education at primary and middle levels. In case of higher education, on the whole, 79 to 88 per cent of the children do not receive free education and they are more or less evenly distributed across different expenditure quintiles.

When we look at the proportion of students in elementary education getting free education in different states, we do not find any systematic pattern (Table 11). In Delhi only 34 per cent of the children receive free education. Many children in metropolitan cities may be enrolled in fee-paying private schools. Probably for the same reason, we find that in Chandigarh also, only 46 per cent of the children receive free education. In Assam, Orissa and Andaman and

Table 10
Proportion (per 1000) of Students in General Education Getting 'Free' Education by Level of Education, Expenditure Quintile, and Type of Institution

	Primary	Middle	Secondary	Higher
Quintile group				
00-20	845	792	715	145
20-40	811	770	664	214
40-60	774	740	631	162
60-80	725	711	572	159
80-100	604	621	486	123
Type of institution				
Government	919	859	679	188
Local body	866	786	644	156
Govt aided	445	526	493	74
Private	54	56	92	16
Not recorded	934	887	786	891
All	760	714	574	143

Nicobar Islands, more than 95 per cent of the children receive free primary education. Similar differences could be found in case of upper primary education (Table 11).

Inter-state variations in household expenditure on education are quite marked, as depicted in Figures 6 and 7. Figure 6 refers to all levels of education, and Figure 7 to primary education. There are enormous variations in the levels of household expenditure on education between different states. Expenditure per student varies between Rs. 287 in Lakshadweep and Rs. 2,878 in Delhi. Among the major states, the variation is between Rs. 592 in Madhya Pradesh and Rs. 1,853 in Punjab.

These figures refer to the average for all levels of education. The inter-state variations are higher in case of lower levels of education. For example, in primary education, it ranges between Rs. 248 in Lakshadweep (Rs. 251 in Assam) and Rs. 2335 in Delhi (Rs. 1162 in Punjab). The coefficient of variation is as high as 0.7 in primary education, 0.5 in middle education and 0.45 in secondary education. It declines to 0.3 in higher education (Table 12).

Further, rural-urban differences and gender differences also vary between several states as shown in Table 13. Except in Dadra & Nagar Haveli, in no state or union territory does expenditure in rural areas exceed that in urban areas. In fact, expenditure in rural areas forms 25 per cent (in Andhra Pradesh) to a maximum of 77 per cent (in some of the small states and union territories) of the expenditure in urban areas in various states. In several major states, the highest proportion is around 50 per cent only, except in Kerala where it is 65 per cent. Considering gender, rural-urban and inter-state variations, one can note the vast difference: while in Madhya Pradesh rural households spend Rs. 279 (in Lakshadweep Rs. 261) per female child on her education, in urban areas in Punjab and Delhi nearly or above Rs. 3000 is spent on the education of a male child (Table 13).

Anyway, inter-state variations, measured by the coefficient of variation is the least in the case of household expenditures on education of urban female children. The value of the coefficient is 0.35; and it is 0.36 in case of urban male

Table 11
Proportion of Students Getting 'Free' Elementary Education (1995-96)

(per cent)

State/UT	Primary	Middle
Andhra Pradesh	71.50	66.70
Arunachal Pradesh	76.10	77.40
Assam	95.10	93.30
Bihar	78.40	75.70
Goa	53.70	90.60
Gujarat	83.50	74.90
Haryana	54.10	61.10
Himachal Pradesh	84.80	80.80
Jammu & Kashmir	55.70	70.70
Karnataka	84.30	75.30
Kerala	80.50	84.00
Madhya Pradesh	85.20	79.50
Maharashtra	81.70	64.50
Manipur	56.40	57.30
Meghalaya	54.90	62.00
Mizoram	89.50	88.50
Nagaland	33.80	33.10
Orissa	94.90	87.80
Punjab	56.30	51.80
Rajasthan	69.50	52.90
Sikkim	87.10	93.40
Tamil Nadu	85.00	81.80
Tripura	90.70	90.60
Uttar Pradesh	60.70	57.10
West Bengal	91.80	91.30
Andaman & Nicobar Islands	96.30	96.80
Chandigarh	46.30	39.70
Dadar & Nagar Haveli	54.70	94.60
Daman & Diu	64.10	97.70
Delhi	34.30	35.60
Lakshadweep	65.30	96.50
Pondicherry	75.10	87.90
All India	76.00	71.40

children. But in rural areas the variations are high: 0.56 among male children and 0.55 among female children.

IV. SUMMARY AND CONCLUSIONS

Education can be viewed as one of the best measures of ensuring social security as it enhances the capabilities of individuals which in turn reduces the chances of vulnerability. While it can itself be regarded as a measure of social and human security, it also influences other measures of social security. It enables people and governments to realise the importance of provision of social security, on the one hand, and on the other and more important side, it might reduce the need for public expenditure on other measures of social security. On this ground, this paper has examined the extent, nature and pattern of household expenditures on education.

Research on household expenditures on education in India is very limited. But the importance of such research is increasingly being realised, particularly

Figure 6
Household Expenditure on Education per Student, by States

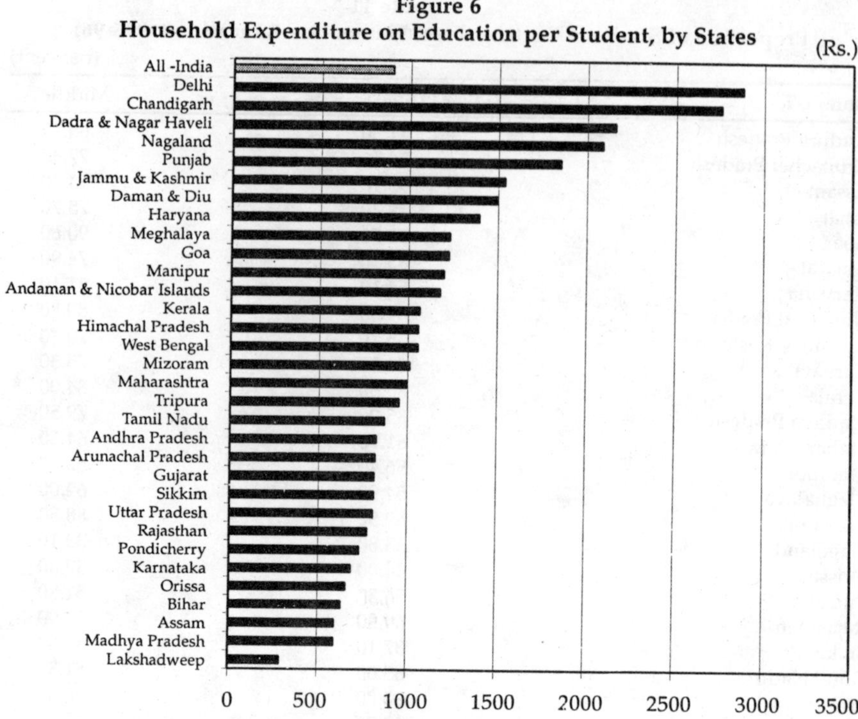

Figure 7
Household Expenditure on Primary Education per Student

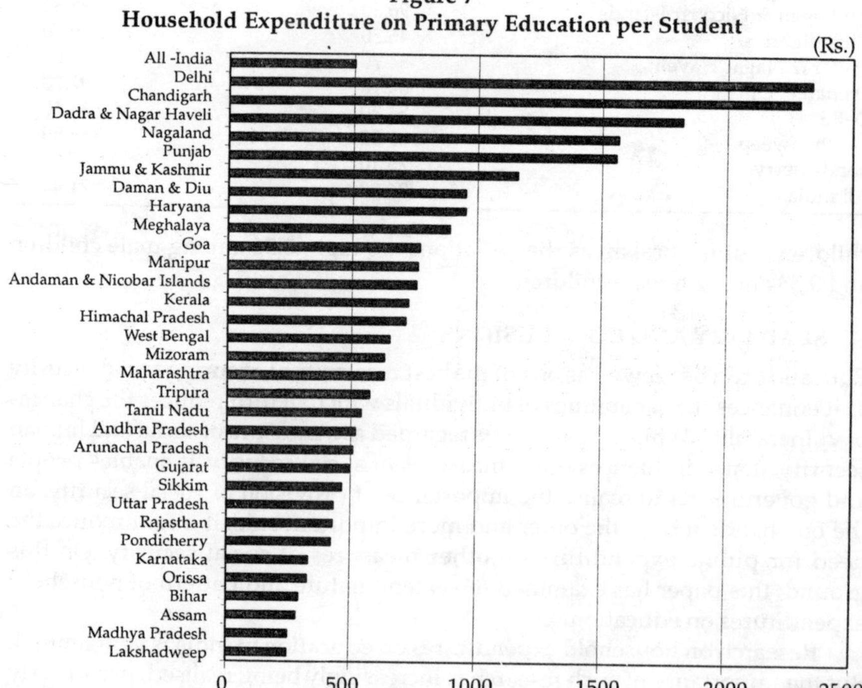

Table 12
Average Household Expenditure per Student in General Education (Rural plus Urban)

(Rs.)

State	Primary	Middle	Secy.	Higher	All
Andhra Pradesh	430	820	1541	3081	825
Arunachal Pradesh	631	977	1498	1455	821
Assam	251	498	998	2261	594
Bihar	330	579	1153	2327	631
Goa	631	968	1459	2899	1225
Gujarat	423	700	1498	2352	815
Haryana	953	1502	2391	3409	1395
Himachal Pradesh	573	1058	1777	2966	1058
Jammu & Kashmir	952	1305	2127	4874	1538
Karnataka	294	602	1130	2886	686
Kerala	725	849	1259	3102	1066
Madhya Pradesh	333	666	1274	2000	592
Maharashtra	540	819	1483	3518	996
Manipur	769	1161	1679	2517	1199
Meghalaya	890	1239	2233	2070	1232
Mizoram	756	1033	1402	1718	1011
Nagaland	1556	1932	2816	4480	208
Orissa	284	682	1233	2150	65
Punjab	1162	1780	3241	4307	1853
Rajasthan	518	831	1400	2016	778
Sikkim	762	697	1189	1998	814
Tamil Nadu	464	827	1502	3465	872
Tripura	494	1039	2234	2142	952
Uttar Pradesh	507	947	1535	2407	808
West Bengal	433	1298	2653	3914	1056
Andaman & Nicobar	715	1258	1907	1796	1179
Chandigarh	2287	2546	3228	3876	2757
Dadar & Nagar Haveli	1820	555	3413	1823	2158
Daman & Diu	1566	1041	1614	3503	1496
Delhi	2335	2710	3952	3298	2878
Lakshadweep	248	302	413	—	287
Pondicherry	652	609	761	2724	732
All-India	501	915	1577	2923	904
Coef. of variation	0.701	0.517	0.451	0.313	0.525

in the context of dwindling public budgets for education and in the context of formulation of alternative policies on financing education, more specifically on the scope for cost recovery in education. Public policies that are being formulated are at best, based on thin research evidence. The present study is a modest attempt to fill this major gap in research in the Economics of Education in India.

Using the published data of the 52nd round of the National Sample Survey on "Participation in Education", conducted in 1995-96, it is attempted in the present study to derive a few facts on: (a) the extent of household expenditure on education; and (b) the pattern of household expenditure on education. A close examination of the national and state level estimates highlights some important dimensions on the size and nature of household expenditures on education, some of which confirmed general hunches, some questioned our

Table 13
Average Household Expenditure per Student in Rural and Urban Areas

(Rs.)

State	Rural			Urban			All	rural/urban ratio (%)
	Male	Female	All	Male	Female	All		
Andhra Pradesh	399	417	406	1696	1591	1646	825	24.7
Arunachal Pradesh	593	671	628	1504	1631	1545	821	40.6
Assam	518	489	506	1411	1341	1380	594	36.7
Bihar	483	375	450	1444	1228	1357	631	33.2
Goa	923	1251	1090	1392	1473	1431	1225	76.2
Gujarat	466	366	423	1593	1290	1456	815	29.1
Haryana	1154	894	1050	2352	2326	2340	1395	44.9
Himachal Pradesh	984	864	930	2224	1897	2086	1058	44.6
Jammu & Kashmir	1275	992	1171	2750	2093	2397	1538	48.9
Karnataka	450	362	416	1392	1171	1285	686	32.4
Kerala	897	992	944	1490	1407	1449	1066	65.1
Madhya Pradesh	389	279	347	1181	1049	1126	592	30.8
Maharashtra	556	472	519	1725	1583	1658	996	31.3
Manipur	1249	899	1095	1464	1405	1439	1199	76.1
Meghalaya	1005	1141	1074	1833	1989	1897	1232	56.6
Mizoram	866	855	861	1216	1243	1229	1011	70.1
Nagaland	1818	1785	1802	2638	2825	2728	2087	66.1
Orissa	571	416	508	1499	1253	1385	657	36.7
Punjab	1468	1297	1394	2970	2568	2786	1853	50.0
Rajasthan	571	424	531	1389	1352	1374	778	38.6
Sikkim	637	731	684	2408	2166	2293	814	29.8
Tamil Nadu	619	479	559	1487	1363	1427	872	39.2
Tripura	922	742	847	1783	1639	1713	952	49.4
Uttar Pradesh	587	436	536	1860	1703	1789	808	30.0
West Bengal	709	570	648	2115	1979	2054	1056	31.5
Andaman & Nicobar	1054	953	1008	1435	1537	1487	1179	67.8
Chandigarh	1601	1324	1471	2843	2847	2845	2757	51.7
Dadar & Nagar Haveli	2311	2076	2204	980	1786	1322	2158	166.7
Daman & Diu	1368	994	1231	1986	1720	1873	1496	65.7
Delhi	2222	1036	1740	3103	2825	2962	2878	58.7
Lakshadweep	265	261	264	351	357	353	287	74.8
Pondicherry	659	529	602	763	818	786	732	76.6
All India	605	516	570	1750	1609	1686	904	33.8
Coef. of variation	0.562	0.546	0.537	0.364	0.345	0.349	0.525	

presumptions, some provided new insights, and a few were really startling. Among many, five important ones could be noted as follows:

Households spend considerable amounts on the education of their children. Contrary to general impressions, the level of expenditure on education is indeed quite high.

Quite interestingly, contrary to general presumptions, there are no significant gender differences in household expenditure on education. Households spend similar amounts on the education of their boy and girl children. The differences, which are marginal, mostly favour girls, except in primary education, where the difference is small and is in favour of boys.

But other types of inequalities are striking. They include rural-urban inequalities, inter-state variations, and also inequalities in expenditures by households with different income levels (expenditure quintiles). Inequalities—rural-urban, or by expenditure quintiles — in expenditures on education seem to be quite high in primary education, and they seem to be declining with increasing levels of education. This is true in case of inter-state variations in expenditure per student as well.

Substantial differences exist in household expenditures between expenditure on children attending government schools, local body schools, government aided private schools and private schools. Expenditure in the private schools is the highest, followed by government-aided schools, local body schools and government schools in the same order.

While households spend considerable amounts for every level of education, they also spend on acquiring even primary education that was expected to be provided free by the state. There is nothing like 'free' education in India. Household expenditures on education are sizeable: households from even low income groups spend a lot on acquiring education, including and specifically elementary education. Tuition and other fees account for the largest proportion of expenditure on education.

Before we finally conclude, a couple of major implications of the study may be noted:

(a) Provision of free primary and upper primary education is important; this reduces household expenditures considerably, and hence the demand for education might increase. Apart from providing tuition fee-free, government may abolish all kinds of fees in primary and upper primary levels of education. Further, it may be valuable if noon-meals, textbooks, uniforms, etc., are provided to most of the children in elementary education, as they would further reduce the need for household expenditures considerably. Efforts may be made to provide truly 'free' education.

(b) Secondly, and interestingly, it is found that all types of inequalities in household expenditure on education—by gender, rural-urban, household expenditure quintiles, and even by type of education—are the highest in primary education and the least in higher education. Apart from substantiating the need for free elementary education, it also raises the following question: Does this mean that primary education of the kind and form being offered by several types of schools in the country, tends to accentuate inequalities, and on the other hand, is it higher education that may provide cohesiveness, bridging gaps between different groups of population? While this may require more in-depth probing, this seems to be at least tentatively true.

(c) Lastly, from the research point of view, which would also considerably help sound policy making, it is important that household surveys on education are conducted at regular intervals to collect reliable and detailed data on household expenditure on education.

(This paper is partly drawn from a project report on 'Household Expenditure on Education,' completed recently at the National Institute of Educational Planning and Administration, New Delhi. The valuable research assistance of Geetha Rani is gratefully acknowledged.)

Appendix

Table A.1

Average Annual Expenditure per Reporting Student* in General Education, by Item of Expenditure and by Level of Education (Rs.)

Item of expenditure	Level of education: Primary	Middle	Secondary	Higher
Tuition fee	512	595	611	996
Exam fee	21	35	85	202
Other fees & payments	73	99	155	446
Books	89	173	290	536
Stationery	65	128	193	298
Uniform	245	305	388	552
Transport	743	526	441	636
Private coaching	409	601	1064	1714
Other expenses	53	86	137	344
Total**	507	921	1588	2964

Note: * Average for each item is based on the number of students reporting for that particular item; ** the components do not add up to the total average expenditure and each item is averaged over different numbers of students.

Table A.2

Average Annual Expenditure per Reporting Student* in General Education, by Item of Expenditure and by Type of Institution (Rs.)

Item of expenditure	Type of institution: Govt. & local body	Govt. aided	Private	All
Tuition fee	339	692	766	613
Exam fee	40	71	70	50
Other fees & payments	67	211	261	115
Books	146	241	221	175
Stationery	96	169	150	115
Uniform	265	347	371	298
Transport	461	610	691	561
Private coaching	583	973	860	732
Other expenses	74	138	140	92
Total**	589	1621	1911	912

Note: Same as in Table A.1.

Table A.3

Average Annual Expenditure per Reporting Student* in General Education, by Item of Expenditure, Sector and Gender (Rs.)

Item of expenditure	Rural			Urban			Total		
	Male	Female	Total	Male	Female	Total	Male	Female	Total
Tuition fee	301	332	311	841	844	842	584	658	613
Exam fee	40	32	37	80	76	78	51	47	50
Other fees & payments	71	64	69	227	214	221	115	116	115
Total fees	412	428	417	1148	1134	1141	750	821	778
Books	148	125	139	254	241	249	180	167	175
Stationery	97	86	93	164	166	165	116	113	115
Uniform	261	258	260	360	357	358	297	300	298
Transport	446	415	436	685	703	693	547	584	561
Private coaching	502	427	475	1076	963	1028	755	696	732
Other expenses	73	62	69	153	143	148	94	89	92
Total**	611	521	576	1766	1622	1700	928	890	912

Note: Same as in Table A.1.

Table A.4

Proportion (per 1000) of Students in General Education Getting 'Free' Education, by Level of Education, Household Expenditure Quintile Group and Type of Institution

	Primary	Middle	Secon-dary	Higher	Primary	Middle	Secon-dary	Higher	Primary	Middle	Secon-dary	Higher
Quintiles		Urban male				Urban female				Urban all		
0-20	864	817	772	25	907	822	721	304	881	819	761	75
20-40	858	802	685	231	888	879	788	421	871	829	709	260
40-60	845	809	647	171	895	853	799	25	865	825	692	149
60-80	831	817	604	150	857	820	761	157	843	818	651	152
80-100	707	718	553	171	731	775	620	240	717	739	578	195
Type of institution												
Government	922	873	682	177	937	894	785	307	929	880	713	213
Local body	895	815	672	183	910	853	690	371	901	830	676	224
Govt. aided	606	654	521	78	689	720	675	123	642	680	573	92
Private	51	56	172		75	107	126	5	60	72	154	2
Not recorded	986	907	829	969	974	848	998		980	876	865	929
All	826	786	615	166	860	823	703	219	840	799	643	181
Quintiles		Urban male				Urban female				Urban all		
00-20	732	738	639	217	771	763	678	131	751	749	657	180
20-40	610	622	582	209	652	710	636	169	629	664	606	192
40-60	454	562	494	420	508	581	618	225	179	571	551	168
60-80	309	378	398	115	326	467	511	220	317	433	449	164
80-100	161	229	246	59	179	302	326	97	169	261	283	75
Type of institution												
Government	851	767	575	145	866	795	633	209	858	780	601	172
Local body	742	683	506	36	793	727	693	138	766	704	598	89
Govt aided	277	313	342	39	328	438	479	97	300	370	404	65
Private	44	44	34	37	54	42	47	7	49	43	40	24
Not recorded	842	955	552	697	716	877	767	705	784	919	662	701
All	485	490	422	95	523	563	512	152	503	523	463	120

Table A.5
Average Expenditure per Student in General Education, by Level of Education, Expenditure Quintile, and Type of Institution

(Rs.)

	Primary	Middle	Secy.	Higher	All	Primary	Middle	Secy.	Higher	All	Primary	Middle	Secy.	Higher	All
Quintiles			Rural male					Rural female						Rural all	
00-20	145	346	697	1347	238	134	318	655	1272	185	140	337	687	1334	218
20-40	200	442	836	1549	349	192	421	765	1272	276	197	435	819	1508	321
40-60	255	540	864	1405	438	214	503	795	1705	352	239	526	843	1450	406
60-80	348	620	1077	1967	627	301	630	968	1762	494	327	624	1045	1915	573
80-100	656	978	1649	2744	1158	649	968	1507	2601	1047	653	974	1597	2696	1114
Type of institution															
Government	219	548	1087	2229	479	219	555	1038	1928	399	219	550	1072	2146	448
Local body	223	533	1045	1984	456	223	553	1001	2464	384	223	541	1034	2089	428
Govt. aided	693	893	1368	2437	1130	529	868	1257	2847	987	622	883	1331	2565	1076
Private	902	1240	1836	3831	1148	925	1267	1866	2454	1153	911	1249	1848	3292	1150
All	305	640	1192	2283	605	286	641	1156	2323	516	297	640	1180	2294	570
Quintiles			Urban male					Urban female						Urban all	
00-20	361	578	924	1366	500	332	552	804	1362	456	347	566	868	1364	480
20-40	649	856	1131	1623	831	614	792	1152	1836	799	633	826	1140	1711	816
40-60	1011	1190	1493	2011	1236	987	1039	1356	1905	1141	1000	1122	1430	1964	1192
60-80	1613	1701	2007	2423	1824	1454	1523	2010	2380	1715	1540	1619	2008	2403	1774
80-100	3218	3307	4124	4381	3762	2875	3270	3680	4356	3505	3060	3291	3919	4370	3647
Type of institution															
Government	509	923	1675	2691	1146	470	864	1529	2992	1066	490	896	1609	2820	1109
Local body	714	1148	1903	3137	1141	621	995	1712	2359	1016	671	1074	1809	2734	1081
Govt. aided	1652	1884	2530	3568	2181	1525	1734	2364	3261	2006	1594	1816	2455	3432	2102
Private	1975	2933	4200	6795	2664	1866	2908	3928	5957	2511	1926	2922	4073	6453	2596
All	1197	1590	2288	3338	1750	1092	1456	2136	3260	1609	1149	1529	2219	3304	1686

Table A.6

Average Expenditure per Student in General Education, by Various Items of Expenditure

(Rs.)

	Tuition fee	Exam fee	Other fee	Books	Stationery	Uniforms	Transport	Private coaching	Others	Total
						Rural male				
Primary	33	9	22	51	52	80	13	26	19	305
Middle	38	20	42	136	112	163	18	72	39	640
Secondary	71	64	81	254	176	201	90	188	66	1192
Higher	369	169	217	430	246	88	425	152	188	2283
Type of institution										
Govt. and local body	15	22	31	102	85	109	23	56	34	477
Govt. aided	103	48	91	212	149	181	119	171	56	1130
Private	344	40	93	164	118	185	84	73	48	1148
All	50	26	43	120	95	123	39	71	37	605
						Rural female				
Primary	28	8	20	49	51	84	9	20	18	286
Middle	34	20	38	131	112	183	18	70	36	641
Secondary	76	54	73	238	170	237	81	168	59	1156
Higher	392	146	343	425	264	133	318	158	143	2323
Type of institution										
Govt. and local body	10	15	24	82	74	111	14	41	26	398
Govt. aided	86	35	85	175	138	199	82	137	50	987
Private	347	45	104	167	115	201	64	65	45	1153
All	41	19	37	99	84	127	25	54	30	516
						Rural all				
Primary	31	8	21	50	52	82	11	23	19	297
Middle	36	20	41	134	112	170	18	71	38	640
Secondary	73	61	79	249	174	212	87	182	64	1180
Higher	375	162	252	429	251	101	395	154	175	2294
Type of institution										
Govt. and local body	13	19	28	94	81	110	20	50	31	446
Govt. aided	97	43	89	198	145	188	105	158	54	1076
Private	345	42	97	165	117	191	77	70	47	1150
All	47	23	40	111	91	125	34	64	34	570

(Table A.6 contd.)

					Urban male					
Primary	336	22	102	125	102	232	94	140	45	1197
Middle	337	33	123	199	158	307	103	268	62	1590
Secondary	411	76	145	312	214	302	106	632	89	2288
Higher	966	180	339	575	294	56	293	439	196	3338
Type of institution										
Govt. and local body	119	43	77	198	138	198	65	242	65	1146
Govt. aided	509	61	190	261	187	283	161	440	88	2181
Private	1030	60	215	261	176	347	182	322	72	2664
All	410	52	139	229	160	252	117	318	73	1750
					Urban female					
Primary	299	20	88	117	99	230	93	107	39	1092
Middle	292	30	106	191	157	305	91	218	55	1456
Secondary	380	70	155	307	219	313	124	474	93	2136
Higher	884	182	329	523	338	98	366	350	190	3260
Type of institution										
Govt. and local body	114	41	79	176	144	208	68	175	53	1058
Govt. aided	455	54	170	247	185	284	171	346	85	2006
Private	926	57	198	265	176	357	191	256	84	2511
All	364	48	128	214	1621	258	122	243	68	1609
					Urban all					
Primary	318	21	96	122	101	231	93	125	42	1149
Middle	316	32	116	195	157	306	67	245	59	1529
Secondary	397	73	150	310	217	307	114	560	91	2219
Higher	931	181	334	552	313	74	325	400	194	3304
Type of institution										
Govt. and local body	117	42	78	188	141	203	67	211	59	1105
Govt. aided	485	58	181	255	186	284	166	397	87	2102
Private	984	59	207	263	176	351	186	293	77	2596
All	389	50	134	222	161	255	119	284	71	1686
					All persons					
Primary	97	11	38	66	63	121	30	43	24	494
Middle	123	24	62	152	128	227	44	123	43	933
Secondary	220	62	112	271	193	273	101	313	75	1619
Higher	745	171	333	495	317	108	353	296	177	2995
Type of institution										
Govt. and local body	35	21	37	105	91	135	27	73	32	556
Govt. aided	301	46	134	216	165	248	133	247	70	1570
Private	678	52	158	223	150	290	136	174	67	1929
All	149	29	67	137	110	171	58	117	43	882

Note: Totals do not add up to 1000, as 'not recorded' category is not listed here.

Table A.7
Average Expenditure per Reporting Student in General Education, by Various Items of Expenditure

(Rs.)

	Tuition fee	Exam fee	Other fee	Books	Stationery	Uniforms	Transport	Private coaching	Others	Total
					Rural male					
Primary	264	16	41	70	54	204	622	288	41	308
Middle	289	29	64	155	114	270	297	420	73	645
Secondary	272	79	115	271	178	353	376	742	118	1199
Higher	553	193	293	463	255	576	640	1143	302	2370
Type of institution										
Govt. and local body	186	35	53	132	87	245	387	446	66	481
Govt. aided	342	62	133	226	150	318	508	663	108	1131
Private	396	50	165	169	120	304	540	545	101	1150
All	301	40	71	148	97	261	446	502	73	611
					Rural female					
Primary	284	15	40	66	53	210	549	251	41	290
Middle	304	29	59	152	114	271	314	423	70	645
Secondary	359	70	105	256	172	358	381	637	103	1162
Higher	612	162	486	440	268	497	503	1195	271	2338
Type of institution										
Govt. and local body	197	26	43	108	76	241	367	376	53	401
Govt. aided	364	49	137	188	139	306	458	576	97	992
Private	421	63	186	171	117	315	481	471	108	1157
All	332	32	64	125	86	258	415	427	62	521
					Rural all					
Primary	271	16	40	69	53	206	596	273	41	301
Middle	294	29	62	154	114	270	303	421	72	645
Secondary	296	76	112	266	176	355	377	708	113	1187
Higher	569	184	346	457	259	544	602	1158	294	2361
Type of intitution										
Govt. and local body	189	31	49	123	83	244	381	421	61	449
Govt. aided	349	57	134	212	146	313	492	632	104	1079
Private	405	55	173	170	119	309	521	518	103	1153
All	311	37	69	139	93	260	436	475	69	576

(Table A.7 contd.)

					Urban male					
Primary	720	39	181	147	105	311	868	611	101	1211
Middle	781	52	196	216	161	365	759	842	125	1601
Secondary	868	102	222	332	219	432	511	1528	175	2310
Higher	1226	213	522	600	300	573	636	1950	387	3352
Type of institution										
Govt. and local body	485	70	133	236	141	324	583	937	135	1155
Govt. aided	817	89	293	273	190	373	694	1248	172	2190
Private	1127	89	340	267	179	409	806	1057	167	2681
All	841	80	227	254	164	360	685	1076	153	1766
					Urban female					
Primary	688	37	159	140	102	307	773	542	86	1102
Middle	800	49	172	210	160	357	738	815	113	1465
Secondary	932	96	242	325	223	433	614	1332	186	2151
Higher	1214	214	503	564	349	550	695	1899	369	3283
Type of institution										
Govt. and local body	550	69	137	215	147	323	621	811	114	1064
Govt. aided	852	81	269	259	187	367	720	1151	168	2015
Private	1006	85	324	269	178	416	772	937	181	2519
All		838	76	214	166	357	703	963	143	1622
					Urban all					
Primary	706	38	171	144	103	309	821	581	94	1160
Middle	789	51	185	214	160	362	750	831	120	1539
Secondary	895	99	231	329	221	432	557	1446	180	2238
Higher	1221	214	514	584	321	559	664	1930	379	3322
Type of institution										
Govt. and local body	512	69	135	226	144	323	600	884	125	1113
Govt. aided	832	85	282	267	189	370	706	1208	170	2110
Private	1073	87	333	268	179	412	790	1007	174	2608
All	840	78	221	249	165	358	693	1028	148	1700
					All persons					
Primary	512	21	73	89	65	245	743	409	53	507
Middle	595	35	99	173	128	305	526	601	86	921
Secondary	611	85	155	290	193	388	441	1064	137	1588
Higher	996	202	446	536	298	552	636	1714	344	2964
Type of institution										
Govt. and local body	339	40	67	146	96	265	461	583	74	589
Govt. aided	692	71	211	241	169	347	610	973	138	1621
Private	766	70	261	221	150	371	691	860	140	1911
All	613	50	115	175	115	298	561	732	92	912

Note : Totals do not add up as, 'not recorded' category is not listed here.

Table A.8

Average Expenditure per Student in General Education in Rural Areas, by State

(Rs.)

State	Male					Female					Person				
	Primary	Middle	Secy	Higher	All	Primary	Middle	Secy	Higher	All	Primary	Middle	Secy	Higher	All
Andhra Pradesh	205	473	850	1734	399	270	656	893	1337	4174	234	546	863	1581	406
Arunachal Pradesh	437	771	1426	973	593	539	1050	410	—	671	483	893	1027	973	628
Assam	190	412	953	2403	518	211	420	839	1672	489	199	415	903	2087	506
Bihar	235	441	972	1905	483	222	442	904	3138	375	230	442	957	2044	450
Goa	485	833	915	2689	923	644	890	1349	2494	1251	550	858	1185	2574	1090
Gujarat	182	372	1169	2013	466	160	353	949	1626	366	172	364	1087	1849	423
Haryana	738	1260	2138	2819	1154	621	1076	1889	6450	894	687	1191	2058	3001	1050
Himachal Pradesh	514	1006	1682	3186	984	485	926	1523	3156	864	501	965	1620	3176	930
Jammu & Kashmir	703	1038	1897	4059	1275	742	932	1901	1918	992	721	1000	1898	3776	1171
Karnataka	132	360	921	2346	450	132	394	935	1401	362	132	372	926	2194	416
Kerala	709	737	1060	2951	897	603	662	1211	3671	992	658	701	1137	3414	944
Madhya Pradesh	196	485	960	1462	389	190	412	811	1854	279	193	459	940	1596	347
Maharashtra	266	479	992	1710	556	265	512	949	1754	472	266	493	976	1717	519
Manipur	691	1043	1961	3201	1249	562	997	1390	1451	899	625	1027	1719	2655	1095
Meghalaya	635	1090	2013	—	1005	853	1162	2686	953	1141	753	1126	2304	906	1074
Mizoram	618	1046	1125	4200	866	667	907	1351	—	855	639	988	1213	4200	861
Nagaland	1271	1686	2526	5116	1818	1155	1620	2960	9370	1785	1210	1659	2720	6092	1802
Orissa	187	625	1097	1839	571	213	561	969	1668	416	199	601	1058	1805	508
Punjab	916	1438	2758	4033	1468	856	1167	2693	3432	1297	890	1314	2733	3778	1394
Rajasthan	320	649	1151	1989	571	308	604	1226	1005	424	316	641	1161	1777	531
Sikkim	607	539	834	2290	637	762	515	928	1345	731	686	527	880	2021	684
Tamil Nadu	302	586	1120	3697	619	225	517	1260	3592	479	267	556	1172	3675	559
Tripura	499	851	2394	1875	922	399	1001	1671	1327	742	456	912	2109	1655	847
Uttar Pradesh	337	696	1210	2129	587	293	668	1075	2048	436	320	688	1184	2106	536
West Bengal	268	960	1969	2990	709	219	1026	1702	2940	570	245	988	1878	2978	648
Andaman & Nicobar Is.	655	1159	1591	—	1054	590	969	1788	2570	953	623	1075	1668	2570	1008
Chandigarh	526	1591	2452	5165	1601	819	1031	2066	2590	1324	635	1301	2210	4425	1471
D & N Haveli	1563	334	3638	1865	2311	2065	431	2964	1788	2076	1863	365	3453	1822	2204
Daman & Diu	1691	886	1281	—	1368	1188	650	1148	—	994	1523	792	1229	—	1231
Delhi	1056	1814	4264	1175	2222	467	1744	2288	—	1036	702	1792	3822	1175	1740
Lakshadweep	228	307	366	—	265	229	270	349	—	261	228	293	356	—	264
Pondicherry	445	918	774	—	659	806	278	596	1195	529	529	448	704	1195	602
All-India	305	640	1192	2283	605	286	641	1156	2323	516	297	640	1180	2294	570
Coef. of variation	0.703	0.483	0.548	0.421	0.562	0.719	0.469	0.494	0.717	0.805	0.707	0.473	0.523	0.471	0.537

Table A.9
Average Expenditure (Rs.) Per Student in General Education in Urban Areas, by State

(Rs.)

State	Male					Female					Person				
	Primary	Middle	Secy	Higher	All	Primary	Middle	Secy	Higher	All	Primary	Middle	Secy	Higher	All
Andhra Pradesh	1072	1384	2184	3842	1696	884	1256	2415	3481	1591	981	1328	2295	3684	1646
Arunachal Pradesh	1450	1183	1971	1628	1504	1586	1616	1678	1837	1631	1490	1305	1846	1662	1545
Assam	895	1169	1723	2762	1411	878	1256	1553	3595	1341	886	1207	1655	3066	1380
Bihar	910	1264	1741	2641	1444	863	1109	1546	2430	1228	890	1198	1657	2586	1357
Goa	689	1290	1823	5301	1392	832	1019	1813	3415	1473	740	1147	1818	4103	1431
Gujarat	1007	1312	2103	3081	1593	983	1198	1664	1992	1290	996	1260	1921	2621	1456
Haryana	1841	2447	3175	3438	2352	1809	2356	2890	3820	2326	1827	2410	3029	3625	2340
Himachal Pradesh	1204	2403	3101	2947	2224	1470	1508	2849	2398	1897	1316	1948	2996	2776	2086
Jammu & Kashmir	1656	1784	2755	8267	2750	1511	2263	2565	3470	2093	1567	2053	2687	5688	2397
Karnataka	827	1296	1506	3293	1392	727	911	1493	3263	1171	778	1096	1500	3281	1285
Kerala	1127	1446	1534	2741	1490	831	1259	1678	2547	1407	968	1369	1605	2632	1449
Madhya Pradesh	820	1137	1624	2164	1181	697	1017	1584	2072	1049	767	1087	1608	2131	1126
Maharashtra	1102	1336	2128	4441	1725	1004	1171	1901	4383	1583	1056	1262	2017	4414	1658
Manipur	1172	1548	1565	2513	1464	1132	1384	1636	1965	1405	1156	1478	1598	2330	1439
Meghalaya	1713	1677	2071	2232	1833	1730	2061	2186	2800	1989	1722	1817	2117	2364	1897
Mizoram	974	1070	1505	1644	1216	1003	1191	1528	1476	1243	988	1128	1515	1573	1229
Nagaland	2334	2748	2816	3105	2638	2441	2665	3139	5244	2825	2385	2710	2993	3665	2728
Orissa	863	1164	2108	2500	1499	830	1013	1651	2699	1253	848	1089	1890	2562	1385
Punjab	1903	3124	4408	5000	2970	1773	2307	3459	4608	2568	1846	2747	3973	4774	2786
Rajasthan	1172	1278	1807	1921	1389	1106	1232	1701	2808	1352	1146	1258	1766	2188	1374
Sikkim	2224	2324	2942	1524	2408	1645	2057	2984	—	2166	1983	2188	2964	1524	2293
Tamil Nadu	893	1290	2037	3780	1487	901	1359	1833	2852	1363	897	1322	1937	3368	1427
Tripura	864	2144	2674	3004	1783	831	1635	2953	3422	1639	847	1914	2804	3186	1713
Uttar Pradesh	1478	2004	2354	2487	1860	1311	1562	2385	2727	1703	1402	1801	2367	2604	1789
West Bengal	1058	1900	3874	3977	2115	1043	2142	3390	5012	1979	1050	2008	3678	4371	2054
Andaman & Nicobar Isles	846	1695	2216	1449	1435	933	1559	2525	2018	1537	891	1629	2368	1782	1487
Chandigarh	2529	2617	3126	3644	2843	2228	2816	3442	4107	2847	2380	2727	3279	3850	2845
D. & N. Haveli	516	1323	1282	2150	980	1847	1362	3001	1625	1786	879	1343	2074	1874	1322
Daman & Diu	1620	1912	2423	3072	1986	1641	1436	1717	5658	1720	1627	1611	2073	3503	1873
Delhi	2559	2964	4192	3747	3103	2329	2676	3739	3056	2825	2453	281	3961	3312	2962
Lakshadweep	327	235	490	—	351	277	424	430	—	357	309	333	476	—	353
Pondicherry	588	735	859	1772	763	809	503	727	7581	818	694	651	808	3139	786
All India	1197	1590	2288	3338	1750	1092	1456	2136	3260	1609	1149	1529	2219	3304	1686
Coef. of variation	0.462	0.396	0.393	0.442	0.364	0.422	0.394	0.373	0.413	0.345	0.435	0.405	0.370	0.329	0.349

Notes

1. For example, among many, Tilak (1995) made an extensive review of analysis of public expenditures on education, based on the literature as well available statistical information.
2. For example, household expenditures do not feature prominently in the massive report of the Education Commission (1966).
3. The estimates discussed in this section refer to average expenditure of the households per student. Expenditure on every item is obviously higher if we concentrate on 'reporting' students only. Some details are provided in Tables A.1 to A.3 and Table A.7 in the Appendix on the extent of expenditure per reporting student.
4. Secondary education/schools include senior/higher secondary level as well.
5. Higher education here refers to what is described as 'above higher secondary level' in the NSSO (1998).
6. These figures are based on the 42nd round of the National Sample Survey, conducted in 1986-87. The results of the survey were published in NSSO (1991; 1993). See also Tilak (1996).
7. The coefficient of discrimination, D, is defined as ($HHEX_m$ / $HHEX_f$) – 1. HHEX refers to household expenditures on education, and the subscripts m and f to males and females, respectively. This is similar to the coefficient of gender discrimination originally proposed by Becker (1957). Higher the value of the coefficient, higher is the degree of discrimination against girls and vice versa. If the coefficient is zero, it means no discrimination. A negative value of the coefficient means discrimination against boys, or discrimination in favour of girls.
8. Rural-urban differences are calculated in Table 3 simply as a ratio of expenditure in rural areas to the corresponding figures in urban areas.
9. Local body schools are those run by panchayats, *zilla parishads, mandal parishads*, municipalities, etc. They receive aid from the state.
10. They are generally referred to as private aided schools – privately managed schools and aided by government. Here they are referred to as government aided schools, as the aid is by the government, and it is felt that it is a more appropriate nomenclature.
11. Private schools in this paper refer to only those private schools that do not receive any aid from the government, unless otherwise mentioned. Specifically private schools that receive aid from the government are not included in the category of private schools.
12. A simple measure of wealth effect is estimated here as follows:

    $$W= (HHEXED_{q5}/HHEXED_{q1})\times 100/HHEXED_{q*}$$

    where W is the wealth, HHEXED refers to household expenditure on education, subscript q5 refers to the fifth (top) expenditure quintile, q1 to the bottom (first) expenditure quintile, and q* to the mean expenditure of all quintiles.

    This is a marginally modified version of Filmer and Pritchett (1999), which was also used by Tilak (2000).
13. See also Tables A.6 and A.7 in the Appendix for more details.
14. See Tilak (1996) for more details on this aspect.

References

Becker, Gary S. (1957), *Economics of Discrimination*, University of Chicago Press, Chicago (2nd edition, 1971).

Education Commission (1966), *Education and Development: Report of the Education Commission 1964-66*, Ministry of Education, New Delhi (Reprint: National Council of Educational Research and Training, New Delhi, 1971).

ESCAP (2000), *Economic and Social Survey for Asia and the Pacific 2000*, United Nations, New York.

Filmer, Deon and Lant Pritchett (1999), "The Effect of Household Wealth on Educational Attainment: Demographic and Healthy Survey Evidence", *Population and Development Reviews*, Vol. 25, No. 1.

Majumdar, Tapas (1983), *Investment in Education and Social Choice*, Cambridge University Press, Cambridge.

Minhas, B.S. (1992), "Educational Deprivation and its Role as a Spoiler of Access to Better Life in India", in Dutta, A. and M.M. Agrawal (eds.), *The Quality of Life*, Indian Institute of Advanced Study/B.R. Publishing Co., Shimla.

NSSO (1991), "Participation in Education", National Sample Survey Organisation (NSS 42nd Round, July 1986-June 1987), *Sarvekshana*, Vol. 14, No. 3, Issue No. 46.

—— (1993), "Participaton in Education", *Sarvekshana*, Vol. 16, No. 4, Issue no. 55; and Vol. 17, No. 3, No. 56.

—— (1998), *Attending an Educational Institution in India: Its Level, Nature and Cost*, NSS 52nd round (1995-96), Report No. 439, Government of India, New Delhi.

Panchamukhi, P.R. (1989), *Economics of Educational Finances*, Himalaya Publishers, Bombay.

PROBE (1999), *Public Report on Basic Education*, Oxford University Press, New Delhi.

Tilak, J.B.G. (1988), "Costs of Education in India", *International Journal of Educational Development*, Vol. 8, No. 1, pp. 25-42.

—— (1995), *Costs and Financing of Education in India: A Review of Issues, Trends, and Problems*, Discussion Paper 5, Studies on Human Development in India, UNDP Research Project on Strategies and Financing of Human Development, Centre for Development Studies, Thiruvananthapuram.

—— (1996), "How Free is 'Free' Primary Education in India?", *Economic and Political Weekly*, Vol. 31, Nos. 5 & 6 (February 3 & 10), pp. 275-82; and pp. 355-66.

—— (2000), *Education Poverty in India*, Occasional Paper No.29, National Institute of Educational Planning and Administration, New Delhi.

10

Inequality and Education Security

Ravi S. Srivastava

I. INTRODUCTION

It is widely believed that education has vital and important links with the achievement of income and health security. A number of recent studies provide ample evidence of the mutual analytical and empirical linkages between human resources and poverty in India (Tilak, 1989; Dreze and Sen, 1995; 1997; Krishnan, 1996; World Bank 1991, 1997). Improvement in educational performance, specially of women, is closely related to health and fertility behaviour. Female literacy and workforce participation are important determinants of variations in child mortality (Kishor, 1994). Better educated women are more likely to marry late, exercise greater control over the choice of the size of family and have fewer children and adopt family planning methods on a larger scale (IIPS, 1994). A smaller number of pregnancies alone, are likely to result in better maternal and child health and lower maternal and child mortality. Better education is more likely to be associated with greater utilisation of health services by women and children (Krishnan, 1996a) and improved health and hygiene practices again lowering maternal and child mortality and leading to improvement in health.

Improvement in health and education have important implications for the supply and demand of labour. Evidence in India shows that the offer price for labour improves with the health and educational attainments of the labour force (World Bank, 1997). On the other hand, the lack of education leads to greater vulnerability in labour markets. Large differentials in human resource endowments between social groups and gender have, by depressing the returns to labour of socially disadvantaged groups, women, and children, been an important cause of high relative inequalities and endemic poverty among these groups and women.

Apart from the instrumentalist (though important) role of education (along with good health) in raising incomes and growth, and biasing these towards the poor, good health and education are also intrinsically important in that, they improve people's capabilities. Women's education and health, for instance, go well beyond these aims and include improvement in gender equality and gender relations and women's empowerment. While the probability of sending a child to school improves with parent's education, and the probability of sending a girl child to school improves with mother's education, parental education also has an important bearing on both school retention and school performance of children (PROBE, 1999; Srivastava, 1997b; World Bank, 1997).

Answers as to why households value education confirm that respondents interviewed often have multiple objectives in mind and do not value education exclusively in narrow economic terms (Bhatty, 1998). For instance, questions relating as to why girls should be educated often leads to the answer that 'at least they will be able to write letters home'. This speaks volumes about the value which parents place on a girl's education in terms of reducing her potential vulnerability and isolation inside the four walls of her in-law's home. Again answers as to why boys should be sent to school very often placed 'will improve his/the household's social standing' almost at par with 'will improve his/her economic prospects'.

In India, where educational access has traditionally been confined to upper caste males, the spread of education among socially disadvantaged groups and women has extremely significant implications for the economic progress of these groups. The spread of education among the poorer groups and women has a significant influence on their participation in democratic processes and in influencing the priorities of development in accordance with the principles of sustainable development and local needs. With the move towards devolution, following the 73rd Amendment, the absence of widespread literacy is a serious obstacle in empowering women and socially disadvantaged groups who have acquired the possibility of taking responsibility of formal leadership in the various rungs of local self-government. To the extent that decentralisation and devolution can improve efficiency and design of development programmes, particularly those relating to the poor, the absence of literacy and education is likely to affect the performance of these programmes. Low educational levels of the population encourage lack of transparent functioning and information flows and reduce the accountability of government. Thus, better education can have important repercussions on the design and implementation of development strategies and their impact on the poor.

It is clear that access to education increases self-esteem and social dignity, reduces vulnerability and powerlessness. Thus, education has a direct impact on virtually all dimensions of deprivation (physical, social, economic, political and psychological) enumerated by Chambers (1995). According to Dreze and Sen (1995), education (and health) can be seen to be valuable to the freedom of a person in *at least* three distinct ways, viz. its *intrinsic importance;* its *instrumental roles (personal, and social process), and its empowerment and distributive roles.*

There is, however, another dimension of education. Unequal access to education which creates information asymmetries, provides unequal access to formal sector jobs and opportunities, and enhances the social status and prestige of one section of the society—can shape or reinforce power relations in the society, in much the same way as unequal access to land or physical assets can. Here access to education, on the one hand, and lack of access, on the other, are the two sides of the same coin, sustaining the exercise of power over.those who are rendered powerless and vulnerable. Beginning with Srinivas's pioneering work, a number of other studies demonstrate that as rural power relations have become partially delinked from ritual status and land ownership, access to education and formal sector jobs have played an important role in shaping the emerging configuration of forces in the countryside (Srinivas, 1959; Beteille, 1965; Lieten and Srivastava, 1999).

This could explain the reluctance of major political parties and successive governments to enforce universal elementary education for over fifty years despite the Constitutional mandate. The broad argument in this paper is therefore to suggest that the expansion of educational opportunity has to be understood in terms of (changes in) the social relations, constituted by a complex interplay of caste, class, gender and ethnic dimensions which naturally differ from region to region. Public action, if it has to achieve significant success, has to be contextualised taking into account these social relations and their specific impact on educational opportunity.

II. ACCESS TO EDUCATION: OVERALL DIMENSIONS

Several surveys in the 1990s show that, quality and learning issues apart, nearly one-third of rural children in the age group 6-13 continue to be out of school in rural India.[1]

Table 1 (from the NSSO 52nd round) gives the age specific attendance ratios for the age-groups 6-10 and 11-13 years. At the all-India level, 35 per cent of rural children in the age-group 6-10 years and 33 per cent of the children in the age-group 11 to 13 years were out of school in 1995-96. In urban India, 17 per cent of children in the younger age-group and 15 per cent in the older age-group were out of school.

Educational participation across the states shows the well-known pattern. The BIMARU states are at the bottom of the rankings in rural India, but Orissa, West Bengal, Jammu & Kashmir and Andhra Pradesh are also low down. On the other hand, apart from Kerala and Himachal, the participation of children in education is high in some of the other southern (Tamil Nadu, Karnataka), western (Maharashtra and Gujarat), northern (Jammu and Kashmir), and north-western states (Punjab and Haryana).

The problem of late entry in schools is reflected in several states where attendance ratios for 6-10 year olds are significantly lower than those for 11-13 year olds. Jammu & Kashmir, West Bengal, Orissa, Uttar Pradesh, Rajasthan and Bihar all reflect this pattern. In a recent survey of living conditions in Uttar Pradesh and Bihar carried out in 1997-98 (hereafter called the 'UP-Bihar Survey'), the average age of Class I students was estimated at 7.8 years.[2]

With the above pattern of children's participation in education, there is a large concentration of out-of-school children in a few states. Among the 6-14 year olds, nearly 40 per cent of the out-of-school children are in Uttar Pradesh and Bihar, while the BIMARU states together have about 55 per cent of such children. With the addition of three more states—Orissa, West Bengal and Andhra Pradesh, just seven states together have about 76 per cent of out-of-school children. Thus, the high level of educational deprivation in these states demands an explanation.

Table 1
Age Specific Attendance Ratios, 1995-96

State	6-10 years				11-13 years			
	Persons	Male	Female	F/M	Persons	Male	Female	F/M
				Rural				
Kerala	97	96	97	1.01	97	97	98	1.01
Himachal Pradesh	91	91	90	0.99	93	97	90	0.93
Tamil Nadu	90	94	85	0.90	71	77	64	0.83
Maharashtra	86	89	83	0.93	80	85	74	0.87
Punjab	84	87	80	0.92	84	87	81	0.93
Haryana	81	85	77	0.91	85	90	80	0.89
Gujarat	77	81	73	0.90	72	78	65	0.83
Assam	72	72	73	1.01	79	78	82	1.05
Karnataka	72	77	65	0.84	65	75	53	0.71
Andhra Pradesh	71	73	68	0.93	53	60	46	0.77
Jammu & Kashmir	65	76	53	0.70	78	83	73	0.88
West Bengal	65	69	61	0.88	71	74	67	0.91
Orissa	61	69	54	0.78	64	73	54	0.74
Madhya Pradesh	60	66	54	0.82	60	68	52	0.76
Uttar Pradesh	59	67	49	0.73	63	77	46	0.60
Rajasthan	53	67	37	0.55	58	74	36	0.49
Bihar	41	48	32	0.67	54	64	40	0.63
All-India	65	71	58	0.82	67	75	57	0.76
State				Urban				
Himachal Pradesh	98	96	100	1.04	95	95	96	1.01
Kerala	97	98	97	0.99	97	97	98	1.01
Tamil Nadu	93	92	93	1.01	82	82	81	0.99
Maharashtra	91	91	90	0.99	94	94	94	1.00
Haryana	89	92	86	0.93	92	95	88	0.93
Punjab	89	92	85	0.92	91	89	93	1.04
Andhra Pradesh	88	90	87	0.97	79	80	77	0.96
Gujarat	87	86	87	1.01	87	91	83	0.91
Karnataka	87	86	88	1.02	86	90	82	0.91
Assam	83	86	80	0.93	90	93	88	0.95
Jammu & Kashmir	83	76	87	1.14	94	94	93	0.99
Rajasthan	81	83	78	0.94	83	88	77	0.88
Orissa	80	80	79	0.99	80	81	79	0.98
Madhya Pradesh	79	82	76	0.93	87	88	84	0.95
West Bengal	77	79	75	0.95	83	83	83	1.00
Uttar Pradesh	72	73	69	0.95	76	80	72	0.90
Bihar	63	66	59	0.89	81	85	78	0.92
All-India	83	84	82	0.98	85	87	83	0.95

Source: NSS 52nd Round.

III. CLASS, CASTE AND EDUCATIONAL DEPRIVATION

The correlation of class and caste with educational access is to be expected but the wide variation across regions is still quite surprising.

Table 2 derived from the NCAER/HDI 1994 Survey shows that the average enrolment rate for 6-14 year olds in rural India, for household incomes above Rs. 62,000 was 84.4 per cent but the coefficient of variation for Indian states was as low as 8 per cent. There was a shortfall from this average in the case of a few states including a few high achievers such as Haryana and Karnataka and the BIMARU states. But the average achievement for this group of income earners is typically high and very close to the national average even in the case of the BIMARU states, with high income households in Uttar Pradesh and Bihar achieving 98 per cent and 99 per cent of the national average.

Table 2
Enrolment Rate of 6-14 Year Olds in Rural India by Household Income Group

Region/state	Household income groups: Up to 20,000	20,001-40,000	40,001-62,000	Above 62,000	All groups	Ratio to Indian av.: Up to 20,000	Above 62,000	Highest to lowest group
Kerala	96.9	96.5	96.6	98.9	96.9	1.60	1.17	1.02
Himachal Pradesh	88.0	94.4	94.7	90.1	90.8	1.45	1.07	1.02
Punjab	77.8	81.5	84.1	93.2	82.1	1.28	1.10	1.20
Maharashtra	75.9	79.5	85.3	87.8	79.2	1.25	1.04	1.16
North-eastern Rg.	75.6	76.5	89.6	79.8	78.6	1.25	0.95	1.06
Tamil Nadu	75.4	79.2	87.0	94.7	78.1	1.24	1.12	1.26
Haryana	65.0	76.1	83.2	83.0	74.8	1.07	0.98	1.28
Gujarat	67.6	83.0	78.7	88.1	74.4	1.11	1.04	1.30
Karnataka	68.8	73.9	77.8	78.0	71.7	1.13	0.92	1.13
Andhra Pradesh	68.2	72.1	80.0	96.1	71.6	1.13	1.14	1.41
Orissa	58.9	77.8	80.2	90.7	65.5	0.97	1.07	1.54
West Bengal	56.1	71.7	76.8	90.5	62.0	0.93	1.07	1.61
Uttar Pradesh	52.3	64.4	73.2	82.6	61.5	0.86	0.98	1.58
Rajasthan	51.6	57.8	73.3	78.5	58.7	0.85	0.93	1.52
Madhya Pradesh	49.2	62.8	68.0	76.2	57.6	0.81	0.90	1.55
Bihar	48.1	64.2	68.3	83.2	56.9	0.79	0.99	1.73
Rural India	60.6	70.8	77.4	84.4	67.1			
C.V.	21.0	14.0	10.4	8.0	16.2			

Source: NCAER/HDI Survey, 1994 (NCAER, 1999).

In comparison, the interstate differences in enrolment rates in the lowest income group are much higher, with a coefficient of variation of 21 per cent. The enrolment rate for this group in Kerala and Himachal was 60 per cent and 45 per cent higher than the national average. The shortfall from the average is also quite high in several states, especially in the BIMARU states. The enrolment rate of children from this income group is 21 per cent below the national average in Bihar, 19 per cent in Madhya Pradesh, 15 per cent in Rajasthan and 14 per cent in Uttar Pradesh.

The last column in the table gives the ratio of the enrolment rate in the highest income group to the enrolment rate in the lowest income group. Many of the high performers—Kerala, Himachal Pradesh and the north-eastern region—show a nearly flat curve indicating that enrolment rates in the highest and lowest income groups are very nearly equal. In contrast, in all six states with lowest rankings, enrolment rates in the highest income group are at least 50 per cent higher than those achieved by households in the lowest income group.

Thus, the poor enrolment rates of states like Bihar or Uttar Pradesh are not across the board. In fact, children from well-off households in these states have enrolment levels which are quite comparable to the high achieving states. The difference lies in the unequal access to education across the groups, reflected in the exceptionally low enrolment rates of children belonging to the poor households.

Filmer and Prichett (1998) reach a similar conclusion using the National Family Health Survey data for 1992-93. They use principal component analysis to group households by economic categories and show the disparate chances of enrolment facing children from different economic groups. At the all-India level, the 'wealth gap' representing the difference in enrolment rates of 6-14 year olds between the top 20 per cent households and the bottom 40 per cent households is 44.2 per cent. This is exceeded by all the educationally poor states with the highest wealth gap emerging in Bihar (56.2 per cent) and the lowest in Kerala (8.8 per cent) (World Bank, 1998, p. 13). The coefficient of variation in state-wise enrolment rates are low for the top economic group but high for the lowest group.

Occupational status and the mode of livelihood of households, another proxy for 'class' is strongly related to educational access. Among rural households, landless labourers generally have the lowest enrolment status, whereas salaried earners and households with sizeable businesses have the highest enrolment rates (NCAER, 1999; Srivastava 1997a; UP-Bihar Survey, 1997-98). Children of migrant casual or contract workers and other mobile groups such as nomadic people have very low enrolment rates (Vyasji, 1999).

The social background of individuals is a strong determinant of educational access in India, but this too shows significant variation across states. Table 3 gives enrolment rates for 6-14 year olds across social groups based on the NACER/HDI Survey. The interstate variation across the two social groups considered to be educationally deprived—Muslims and SC/ST—is striking.

Table 3
Enrolment Rate of 6-14 Years by Social Group

Region/ state	SC/ST	Hindus	Muslim	Other minority	All groups	SC & ST/ all groups
Kerala	92.1	96.0	96.8	98.9	96.9	0.95
Himachal Pradesh	84.7	91.2	77.9	94.4	90.8	0.93
Punjab	65.5	80.1	62.0	83.4	82.1	0.80
Maharashtra	69.8	79.3	89.2	75.8	79.2	0.88
North-eastern region	87.9	86.7	56.9	86.0	78.6	1.12
Tamil Nadu	73.9	77.6	81.4	84.1	78.1	0.95
Haryana	64.4	77.9	32.0	84.6	74.8	0.86
Gujarat	65.8	74.9	67.3	100.0	74.4	0.88
Karnataka	63.1	71.5	81.4	80.2	71.7	0.88
Andhra Pradesh	65.8	71.0	76.9	72.8	71.6	0.92
Orissa	47.5	65.3	54.2	83.4	65.5	0.73
West Bengal	60.1	65.9	53.6	59.9	62.0	0.97
Uttar Pradesh	51.1	63.9	46.2	90.0	61.5	0.83
Rajasthan	47.3	59.8	39.3	56.9	58.7	0.81
Madhya Pradesh	46.4	57.4	56.7	85.4	57.6	0.81
Bihar	43.9	55.5	51.6	50.1	56.9	0.77
Rural India	57.4	67.8	57.3	79.2	67.1	0.86
C.V.	23.34	16.17	28.83	17.84	16.25	

Source: NCAER/HDI Survey 1994 (NCAER, 1999).

The coefficient of variation for these groups is 28.8 per cent and 23.3 per cent, respectively. Enrolment among SC/ST is more than twice as high in Kerala (92.1 per cent) compared to Bihar (43.9 per cent). Similarly, enrolment among Muslims is more than twice as high in Tamil Nadu (81 per cent), Maharashtra (89.2 per cent) and Kerala (96.8 per cent) than it is in Rajasthan (39.3 per cent). Enrolment rates among Muslim children are higher than the corresponding rates among Hindu children in all the Southern states (Tamil Nadu, Kerala, Andhra Pradesh and Karnataka) as well as in Maharashtra.

A comparison of SC/ST enrolment rates with the overall enrolment rates is also very revealing. Apart from the North-eastern states, there is a shortfall in SC/ST enrolment rates in all states.[3] There are five states (Kerala, Himachal Pradesh, Andhra Pradesh, Tamil Nadu and West Bengal) where the deficit in SC/ST enrolment is less than 10 per cent compared to the overall enrolment rates. In four other states (Maharashtra, Haryana, Gujarat and Karnataka), the deficit is between 10 and 15 per cent. In the remaining states, the deficit is more than 15 per cent, rising to 23 per cent in the case of Bihar and 27 per cent in the case of Orissa. The UNDP-GOI studies carried out in seven states (Uttar Pradesh, Bihar, Rajasthan, Orissa, Kerala, Tamil Nadu and Andhra Pradesh) in 1996-97 showed a very similar picture: SC/ST and non-SC/ST differentials were very low in the three Southern states, but significant and high in the three Northern states and Orissa.[4]

Since there are a multitude of social groups, many of whom are recognised as being 'educationally backward', the limited distinction between Scheduled Castes and non-scheduled Castes probably obliterates some of the other differences. The Table 4, taken from the UP-Bihar Survey in four NSS regions of Uttar Pradesh and Bihar (Eastern Uttar Pradesh and Bundelkhand, central and northern Bihar), referred to earlier, shows the differences across caste/class in enrolment rates in Uttar Pradesh and Bihar.

Table 4
Enrolment Rates of 6-13 Year Olds by Social Group and Consumption Quintile in U.P. and Bihar

	Per capita consumption quintile					
Social group	1 (Low)	2	3	4	5 (High)	Total
Upper caste	83.48	92.73	85.15	92.70	93.26	91.59
Middle caste	54.32	76.37	47.61	73.29	91.42	69.15
Backward agricultural	50.65	59.73	75.97	64.95	87.05	69.52
Backward other	50.28	64.20	66.58	76.03	79.60	64.00
Muslim upper	54.61	45.96	76.72	56.02	100.00	60.01
Muslim backward	48.43	46.55	58.21	60.63	70.74	54.53
SC/ST	40.66	52.55	54.28	66.61	65.14	50.64
Total	47.14	59.27	66.86	71.92	86.38	64.96

Source: UP-Bihar Survey (1997-98).

Enrolment rates of upper caste children in Uttar Pradesh and Bihar are higher than enrolment rates among SC children by about 80 per cent. The enrolment rate of poor SC children (those in the lowest quintile) is less than half the enrolment rate of upper caste children in any quintile. While almost half of the total SC children are out of school, 60 per cent of the poorest SC children are not in school but in Bihar, two-thirds of the poorest SC children are not in school. On the other hand, over 90 per cent of the upper caste children are in school in UP and Bihar. *For these elite social groups in the educationally poor states, educational participation is, therefore, a non-issue.*

No doubt enrolment rates increase in the higher consumption classes but the large variation in enrolment within each quintile suggests that there are other factors—social, cultural or institutional which account for these differences in schooling. These factors have been discussed in detail in a number of studies (PROBE Report, 1999; Nambissan, 1996). Studies from Uttar Pradesh and Bihar show that social exclusion is a strong deterrent to educational participation (Vyasji, 1999).

The clear conclusion emerging from the evidence shows caste (social identity) and class relations as strong determinants of access to schooling in the educationally poor regions/states.

IV. GENDER AND SCHOOLING

Gender differentials in the access to education increase the vulnerability and lack of security faced by women, and become important constraints in accessing health and other securities. Gender disparities compound the existing large class and social disparities in vast areas of the country. In fact, gender disparities often tend to persist even when class and social disparities in access to elementary schooling have virtually disappeared. Logit and Probit models when applied state-wise to UNDP-GOI field data show that gender and parental education status were the most important determinants of the enrolment status of children (Srivastava, 1997).

The UNDP-GOI field researches throw up striking contrasts between the three southern states and the four northern and eastern states studied with regard to gender and social disparities in access to education. Gender and social group (caste group as well as community-wise) disparities in enrolments are quite small in Kerala which has achieved near universal enrolments, and in a few of the study villages female enrolment rates are actually higher than male enrolment rates. Enrolment rates vary between the Tamil Nadu study villages but are quite high, and gender and social group differences are again quite small. Discontinuation in these regions became a major problem at the high school stage. In Andhra Pradesh, where both study districts have low enrolment rates, gender disparities were found to be quite high, but social group disparities were unexpectedly low. In the four northern and eastern states, which also have low educational performances, gender and social group disparities were remarkably high. *Except in Kerala, the girl child emerged as the major deprived group in each of the study areas* (Vaidyanathan, 1997; Srivastava, 1997a, 1997b). Another striking conclusion emerged with respect to the Scheduled Castes and Scheduled Tribes: Enrolments among SC/ST groups, although much poorer than the average in several states, appeared to be no worse (and indeed somewhat better in some areas) than other educationally deprived groups (depressed backward classes in some areas and Muslim minorities in others).

The NSSO 52nd round (Table 1) broadly confirms these results. There is an overall deficit of 18 per cent in female-male enrolments for 6-10 year old children, which rises to 24 per cent for older children (11-13 years). Female enrolments are only 55 per cent and 49 per cent of male enrolment in the age groups 6-10 years and 11-13 years in rural Rajasthan, which has the largest gender differential. Bihar, Uttar Pradesh, Orissa and Madhya Pradesh have large differentials in female-male enrolment. Kerala and Assam are the two states where the percentage of girls enrolled is actually higher than boys. Among the educationally poor states, West Bengal has a relatively better record of gender parity.

The analysis of the household data from the NCAER/HDI Survey (NCAER, 1999) also shows similar results, but there is some change in the ranking of states with respect to female-male enrolment ratios, with West Bengal performing much better and Haryana and Gujarat significantly worse than their rankings in term of overall enrolment. But, by and large, states with high enrolment rates also have lower gender disparity. This squares up with analysis of secondary data in nine states in the UNDP-GOI study which shows that at the aggregate level, there is a high level of correlation between total and female literacy and that gender disparities in literacy and enrolment tend to decline at higher levels of educational performance. But the NCAER/HDI survey again confirms that gender disparities in access to enrolment are the highest in the four BIMARU states, and Orissa and these disparities are compounded by exceptionally low levels of educational access among low caste and (especially in the case of Rajasthan and Haryana) Muslim women.

Fortunately, gender disparity in enrolment tends to decline in these states as household incomes increase or as the village development level increases while this relationship is weaker for educationally well performing states (Shariff, 1999, Appendix Table A.6.6). But while gender is undoubtedly an independent source of vulnerability, what is of particular concerns is, the way class, social and gender relationships reinforce one another in order to increase the insecurity and vulnerability of poor, low caste women. This is shown in Table 5, which is based on the results of the UP-Bihar Survey of 2,250 households during 1997-98.

Overall in the study regions of Uttar Pradesh and Bihar, just over half the girls (53.7 per cent) in the 6-13 year age group were in school in 1998 compared to 74.6 per cent of boys. Among each of the social groups — except upper caste Muslims — where also the educational profile of women appears to be different because of Madarsa education, and within each consumption quintile, enrolment among girls is lower than that among boys, indicating the importance of cultural (gender related) factors in determining access to education.

However, enrolment rates are higher both for girls and for boys in the higher quintiles compared to the lower quintiles. In the lowest quintile, nearly two-third of the girls were out of school, with this proportion declining to about one-fifth in the highest quintile. But it is the girls from poor low caste households who have the least access to education. About 70 per cent of SC/ST girls, 75 per cent girls from agricultural OBC households, and 64 per cent girls from non-agricultural OBC households in the poorest category were out of school. Compared to SC/ST girls, 61 per cent of whom were out of school, only about 12 per cent girls from upper-caste households are out of school. The largest

Table 5
Enrolment Rates of 6-13 Year Olds by Gender across Social Groups and Consumption Quintiles

		Per capita consumption quintile					
Caste code		1 (Low)	2	3	4	5 (High)	Total
Upper caste	M	86.72	94.43	95.17	93.73	96.76	95.34
	F	82.10	89.65	69.82	91.89	89.54	87.68
Middle caste	M	42.71	86.56	82.65	100.00	100.00	83.33
	F	64.97	55.58	17.98	57.84	69.10	49.54
Backward agricultural	M	75.44	76.51	76.58	74.18	91.74	79.83
	F	24.65	38.78	75.10	57.13	80.11	57.25
Backward other	M	64.67	74.55	79.42	90.27	85.83	76.92
	F	36.46	50.38	50.84	58.80	66.71	48.40
Muslim upper	M	54.12	45.61	69.60	62.54	100.00	59.67
	F	55.13	46.78	82.18	44.24	100.00	60.50
Muslim backward	M	51.86	57.01	70.69	75.48	85.65	64.22
	F	44.45	30.80	47.49	48.00	57.60	44.03
SC/ST	M	50.44	63.04	64.67	75.08	74.66	60.96
	F	30.57	39.78	41.61	55.74	50.56	38.63
Total	M	58.97	70.22	75.59	80.75	91.57	74.57
	F	35.29	44.27	56.11	63.17	79.48	53.74

Source: UP-Bihar Survey (1997-98).

educational differential is between poor low-caste girls and rich upper-caste males in these areas showing how social, economic and cultural (gender) relations reinforce each other to the detriment of this group of girls.

V. CASTE, CLASS, GENDER AND TYPE OF SCHOOLING

While enrolment and attendance in schools are the first crude indicators that we have of educational access, it is the quality of education which ultimately matters. It is quite possible that expansion in enrolments is accompanied by a significant deterioration in educational quality, nullifying the potential gains from keeping children in school, as recent concerns in Bangladesh demonstrate. In the Indian case, the emergence and growth of a dual system of education (public and private) even in the rural areas has allowed the rich and the powerful to access relatively better quality education in private schools, while the quality of public schooling has steadily deteriorated. Nambissan (1996) appropriately calls this the 'privatisation of quality'.

Overall, between the 32nd, 42nd and 52nd rounds, there has been an increase in the percentage of students enrolled in private schools. According to the NSS 52nd round, 13.7 per cent and 21.3 per cent students were enrolled in private schools at the primary and middle levels. At the primary level, 14.3 per cent male students and 12.9 per cent female students were enrolled nationally in private schools, both aided and unaided; while at the middle level, 22.9 per cent and 21.3 per cent boys and girls respectively were enrolled in private schools. Of late, with greater state reluctance to finance private schools, there has been an increase in private unaided schools, especially in a few states spread over all regions—Jammu & Kashmir, Punjab, Haryana, Uttar Pradesh, Andhra Pradesh and Kerala. The NCAER/HDI Survey shows that private school enrolments tend to be inversely related to the development level of the village at the all India level—suggesting that these schools may have sprung up in poorer areas to overcome supply shortages. Private schools account for 12 per cent of the enrolment in 'low development' villages, compared to 9.1 per cent in 'medium development' villages and 8.1 per cent in 'high' development villages. However, within states the relationship is weak and unsystematic.

It is now well established that despite the Constitution's intent, even government schooling is not free for students at the primary and middle levels, but at the same time private schooling, on average costs several time more when compared to government schools (Tilak, 1996; Srivastava, 1997; NCAER, 1999). According to the NSS 52nd round, at the primary level, annual expenditure per student was Rs. 219 in government schools, Rs. 529 in private aided schools and Rs. 925 in private unaided schools. At the middle level, annual expenditure per student was Rs. 555 for education in government schools, but rose to Rs. 868 in private aided schools and Rs. 868 in private unaided schools. Not surprisingly, the NCAER/HDI Survey finds a systematic relationship between household incomes and private (unaided) school enrolment. The latter rises from 7.2 per cent for the lowest income group to 16.5 per cent in the highest income group. Moreover, the survey finds large differences between social groups in their accessing private school enrolments. Country-wide, private school enrolments were only 5 per cent of total enrolments for SC/STs, but 9.3 per cent for 'Hindus' and 13.3 per cent for Muslims.

Results of the UP-Bihar Survey also confirm significant duality in the access to private schooling (Table 6).

Table 6
Per Cent Enrolled in Private Schools at Primary Level

Adult equivalent quintile	Upper caste	Backward agricultural	Backward other	ST/SC	Muslim	Total
1. (Low)	10.53	15.38	16.67	7.69	22.50	13.40
2.	20.83	16.42	25.81	7.92	17.65	17.20
3.	24.49	23.20	25.30	13.41	21.62	21.54
4,	28.57	21.70	24.00	9.09	10.00	20.36
5. (High)	29.46	27.78	26.92	14.29	39.29	27.90
Total	25.97	22.47	23.38	9.74	21.89	20.34

Source: UP-Bihar Survey (1997-98).

Enrolment in private schools increases in the higher quintiles. Compared to 13.4 per cent enrolment in private schools in the lowest quintile, enrolment in the highest quintile is more than twice as high (27.9 per cent). Only 9.7 per cent SC/ST students are in private schools compared to nearly 26 per cent upper caste students and more than a fifth from each of the other groups. While only 8 per cent SC/ST students in the lowest two quintiles were in private schools, nearly 30 per cent upper-caste students and 40 per cent Muslim students in the highest quintile were enrolled in private schools. Compared to 21.5 per cent boys, only 18.9 per cent girls were in private schools in these two states.

Thus, even with the surge in private schooling, a majority of children at the elementary school level in the rural areas find themselves in schools managed by government. Yet, duality in schooling is an important emerging feature of basic education even in the rural areas in many states. Evidence from two large and educationally poor states (Uttar Pradesh and Bihar) shows that well-off, upper caste, and male students are more likely to acquire private education compared to low caste, poor and female students.

VI. WHY DO CERTAIN STATES AND REGIONS LAG BEHIND IN PROVIDING EDUCATIONAL SECURITY?

The attempt so far in this paper has been to demonstrate that the poor record of certain regions in providing security through education (relative to other regions within the country) was linked to, and indeed reinforced by, persistent caste, class and gender inequalities which were reflected in differentials in educational access. Dominant social groups in these regions enjoy nearly universal access to education but are keen to undervalue the need for educational security to the subaltern groups.

It is not surprising, to note that most of the educationally backward regions have had oppressive systems of land tenure in the past, which (with the exception of West Bengal) did not undergo radical changes in the post-Independence period. With the exception of the tribal areas, the hill regions, and to some extent the eastern states, women's agency in most parts of the educationally poor states has been circumscribed by restrictions on movement, rigid patriarchal norms and values, and a high degree of insecurity. It is not that these states have not seen a measure of social, political and economic change which has loosened the congruence between class and caste, but, instead of championing broad-based change, the emerging socio-political elite has also built itself up on the rubric of the extant inequity.

In an insightful study of the contrasting experiences of Kerala and Uttar Pradesh, Ramchandran (1997) and Dreze and Gazdar (1997) outline the key differences. Kerala's achievements, according to Ramchandran, 'were made possible because of mass literacy and because traditional patterns of gender, class and caste dominance were transformed radically" (Ramchandran, ibid., p. 328). On the other hand, in Uttar Pradesh, "the high concentration of power and privileges deriving from the combined effects of inequalities based on class, caste, and gender has made for an environment that is extremely hostile to social change and broad-based political participation" (Dreze and Gazdar, 1997, p. 107). Dreze and Gazdar contrast the specific areas of change (land reforms, gender relations, basic education, local democracy) which underpinned Kerala's social achievements compared to the inertia witnessed in these areas in Uttar Pradesh.

The case of Kerala is perhaps unique in the broad canvas of social, religious, political cultural and mass movements; the direct concern displayed by governments—ranging from the ruler of Travancore to the post-Independence left government which broadly set the tone of the public agenda; and a social structure which relatively favoured women's agency (Ramchandran, 1997; Thomas, 1997). But the social and agrarian structure may have been less inimical and subsequent social reform movements have perhaps provided greater space for the expansion of social opportunity in Himachal, Tamil Nadu, Karnataka or the other states—though the expansion in many of the states appears favourable only in comparison to the poor record of the Bihar, Uttar Pradesh, Madhya Pradesh and Rajasthan, and the other poor performers (notably Orissa, Andhra Pradesh and West Bengal). In contrast, in the poor performing states (with the exception of West Bengal, which we shall discuss separately), the impact of successful political and social movements on economic and social inequality has been very limited. Radical left movements in a few states such as Bihar and Andhra Pradesh have no doubt challenged existing economic inequities and have had an emancipatory impact on sections of the poorer classes, while also succeeding in bringing issues of social dignity to the forefront. But these movements have so far focussed on redistributive and economic issues. Dreze and Sen (1997) are therefore right in lamenting the absence of broad-based public action in these states which seeks to expand social opportunity—linked to a restructuring of the pervasive caste, class and gender inequalities.

The case of West Bengal appears to be quite different—the state has a strong record of pro-poor political mobilisation and has made a dent in the agrarian structure through limited but important interventions in land reform. The left front government has made the panchayats and grass-root mobilisation the linchpin of its rural development strategy. But apart from a limited spurt of mobilisation in the Total Literacy Campaign, the expansion of basic education (and health) has been a neglected area, at least till recently. The outcome has been low achievements in providing education security to poorer groups, although the social and gender disparity in accessing education is not so significant in West Bengal. Sadly, the recent concern with expanding access to education is occurring at a time when the panchayat movement in West Bengal has reached a plateau and there are no other significant moves to restructure the delivery of basic education (Srivastava, 1999).

VII. CONSEQUENCES OF INEQUALITY

The fact that educational access generally mirrors the prevailing social inequality is hardly surprising since broad-based access to education is implicitly seen by the dominant classes as undermining the existing social order. Fieldwork, which generally evokes 'socially correct' answers from respondents on educational participation of socially deprived groups or women, will, at times, also evoke irate reactions: "do you want them to sit on our heads?", or "a woman's place is in the home" (Lieten and Srivastava, 1999). The point worth emphasising is that the context and the content of education are such that they reinforce social inequalities both through those who opt out of the system and those who stay in it. The dynamics of these processes have been well documented in several studies such as the PROBE Report and Nambissan (1996) and we briefly reiterate some of the features.

First, since the primary school is directly a part of the political arena (polling booths are set up in schools), the siting of primary schools is directly influenced by the locally dominant groups, reducing the chance that the school will be in an area where lower castes, especially girls will feel socially comfortable.

Second, the school environment and the class-room become an extension of the social environment, reproducing the same hierarchies, with the class teacher (generally male and belonging to the dominant caste) at the apex of the hierarchy and low caste students at the bottom. Formal efforts to breach this hierarchy by changing recruitment rules, PTAs and VECs have only been marginally successful.

Third, for reasons discussed earlier, the interest of the local elite in the regular functioning of the schools is low. This, combined with the fact that the teachers themselves are most often drawn from this elite and easily tend to develop a collusive relationship with the educational bureaucracy, lends itself easily to a situation where teacher absenteeism and lack of punctuality is endemic. This has an impact on sending children, particularly girl children, to school, since they may remain unsupervised for an unspecified period of time.

Fourth, the contents and methods of teaching/learning are alienating and divorced from the practical lives of working people. They reinforce the social norms and histories of the dominant elite and are more in line with the learning methods adopted in the past by sections of the elite to acquire a knowledge of scriptures than being attuned to an acquisition of providing a critical understanding of the child's physical and social environment.

Fifth, the timings and the annual school calendar is adopted mainly keeping in view the requirements of an elite divorced from the production process, without taking into account the local production cycle and peak season requirements. For instance, in Uttar Pradesh, school admissions take place during the paddy transplanting season while school examinations take place during the wheat harvesting season. Examination fees have to be deposited in the lean season.

Sixth, educational policy decisions at the state level and their implementation at all levels by the educational bureaucracy, manned generally by members of the social elite, fails to adequately reflect the urgent need to provide educational security to the deprived.

Seventh, physical infrastructure of the school is often culturally inappropriate and very few schools have separate facilities for girls. Formal decisions which are taken ostensibly to improve the cultural context (such as the decision to employ women teachers, or introduce Urdu in schools) often prove to be ineffective because they are not locally contextualised.

Finally, the inhospitable physical surroundings of the school (most schools cannot cope with inclement weather during the monsoons, and have insufficient seating space), shortage of teachers and teaching material, and the distance of schools from the poorer habitations—lead to partial or complete dysfunctionality of the public school system in the educationally poor states.

Yet, shortages apart—which are undoubtedly very important—the structure and the content of primary education in the educationally poor states militates against the inclusion of children, especially girls, from poor, low caste or minority households.

VIII. ARE HOUSEHOLD POVERTY CHARACTERISTICS RESPONSIBLE FOR DIFFERENTIAL PARTICIPATION IN EDUCATION?

The main thrust of this paper so far has been that the structural features of inequality based on caste, class and gender in the educationally poor states explains the differential levels of educational security available to different groups. We have not focussed on poverty per se, because the data show very clearly that poor households behave very differently in accessing education across different regions of the country. There are, however, a number of explanations which focus on individual or household characteristics, or on demand and supply side factors in interpreting differential participation in education. What this section attempts briefly is a partial reconciliation of this evidence with the emphasis on structural features in this paper.

First, logit/probit models which explore participation in schooling often find a number of factors such as gender or social identity of the child, birth order of the child, parental education, number of siblings/dependants—and in a fewer number of cases, the asset/income/occupation status of the household as being important explanatory variables.[5] Most of these factors are related to features of prevailing social relations discussed earlier, while a few relate to economic constraints and household motivation.

Second, a number of empirical studies which explore participation/non-participation (enrolment/non-enrolment/drop-out) relate these decisions to a number of reasons cited by households which are then interpreted as being 'demand' or 'supply' related. Many of these studies then find 'demand' related factors (arising out of economic constraints or involvement in paid/unpaid work) as being significantly more important than 'supply related' factors, implying that non-participation in education has its genesis in household level factors—mainly poverty, but also extending to traditional values—which restrict demand for education, while the supply of schooling (implicitly including its quality) is considerably less important. On the other hand, certain other studies (PROBE, 1999; Dreze and Gazdar, 1997—the former using a sub-sample of the NCAER Sample) point to substantial unmet demand for education among educationally deprived groups in the BIMARU states and pinpoint the supply of education (including its quality) as the villain of the piece.

For instance, NCAER (1999) categorises factors responsible for non-enrolment of children into 'supply related', 'demand related', 'lack of interest', and 'customary factors'. Supply-related factors include 'school too far' and 'dysfunctional school'. Demand factors include 'financial constraints', 'domestic work', 'participation in household economic activity' and 'participation in paid economic activity outside the household'. Lack of interest factors are 'parents did not feel it important' and 'child unwilling'. "Customary" factors are generally cited in the case of female children. The multiple responses add up to over 100. The study found that about 75 per cent of the children were not enrolled because of the lack of interest of customary factors. About 50 per cent of the factors were demand related and only 8 per cent were supply related. "Supply" factors were relatively high in Orissa, Haryana, Uttar Pradesh, Punjab and Madhya Pradesh and were cited by the better-off, medium and large farmers, STs, and the least developed villages. "Demand" factors were predominant among the very poor, landless wage earners and households in which neither males nor females were literate. "Lack of interest" and "customary" factors were dominant in the states of Uttar Pradesh, Bihar, Rajasthan, Madhya Pradesh, and Orissa.

The NSS 50th round also classifies reasons for non-attendance in schools for 5-14 year olds. In rural areas, in the case of boys, 13.7 per cent cited paid/unpaid work as a reason while in the case of girls, these reasons were cited in 15.4 per cent cases. 'Cannot afford' was cited as a reason for 14.9 per cent boys and 16.2 per cent girls, while 'not interested' was given as a reason in the case of 27.5 per cent boys and 29.7 per cent girls. Direct school-related factors are not even mentioned in the survey results.

Compared to this framework, focus group discussion, probing questions and participatory appraisal in the educationally poor states invariably uncover a number of issues relating to the supply of education which have influenced the decision of the household (not) to send a child to school. This conundrum is not very easy to resolve. A review of the fieldwork literature by Bhatty (1998) led her to conclude that "the relationship between poverty, child labour and schooling are more complex than has been acknowledged in the literature so far" (ibid., p. 1735) and that the involvement of non-enrolled children in work—which was not very high—could be both an *ex ante* as well as an *ex post* decision on the part of households. However, Bhatty does find that the opportunity cost of sending children to school may be higher in the case of girls and, moreover, that the direct costs of schooling were a greater deterrent in sending children to school.

Some of the problems with the earlier analytical framework are that demand and supply factors are difficult to disentangle, that respondents may have limited knowledge of the schooling circumstances and may tend to give greater weight to household or individual circumstances in explaining schooling outcomes which are invariably made by the individual child or household on balance.

The UNDP-GOI studies in the seven states, like the PROBE study, found considerable demand for education for both boys and girls among the educationally deprived groups. Nevertheless, the extent of motivation and demand did vary, along with the ability of poor households to overcome potential opportunity cost—considered to be greater for girls—and to translate their demand into effective educational participation. In fact, the UNDP studies concluded that increasing the motivation of parents towards educating their children, especially girl children, and lowering their opportunity cost through availability of regular good quality education and well designed incentives had to become necessary components of a strategy to provide educational coverage to all.

IX. CURRENT INITIATIVES AND FUTURE SCENARIO

Despite some uneven progress, and several official proclamations, the task of providing even minimum educational security to all in the near future is daunting. According to the estimates presented by the UNDP (1999), at the current rates of progress achieved in literacy, states like Rajasthan and Bihar will take more than a century to achieve universal literacy for their female population. The major task is to overcome the social, economic and political constraints in the educationally backward states to provide basic minimum education security to the deprived sections of people. At each level, the challenges are huge. In purely fiscal terms, the educationally poor states will require investments which are several times their current level in order to bring the out-of-school children to school. Estimates by Ramchandran et al. (1997) show that, on the basis of admittedly preliminary estimates, the additional investment requirements in order to achieve universal enrolments for 6-11 year olds were 5.7 per cent of SDP in Bihar, 4.7 per cent of SDP in Uttar Pradesh, 3.9 per cent of SDP in Orissa, 3.6 per cent in Madhya Pradesh, and 3.5 per cent each in Rajasthan and West Bengal. These figures do not take into account the increasing order of difficulty in bringing marginal populations into school. Since 1985-86, in any case, with declining real per capita expenditure on primary education in the poorer states being disproportionately more than the richer ones (UNDP, 1997), these goals are farther away than ever before.

After 1991, the states, led by the centre, have come forward with a number of new initiatives, which are the outcome of a new ideological stance towards development and the expansion of educational opportunity, the orientation of external aid agencies in the social sector, and their own economic imperatives.

First, declining real per capita expenditures in primary education in the first phase after 1991 has brought in large volumes of external resources in primary education in the states in the form of primary/elementary education projects. Some of these externally aided projects, such as Lok Jumbish in Rajasthan enjoyed a considerable degree of autonomy. Other projects (such as the District Primary Education Programmes) also enjoy some degree of autonomy from the state education management structures. There has been some degree of cross-learning and learning from NGO experiences and scope has been provided for community involvement through micro-level planning, village education committees and school construction committees. A number of small but important innovations have been incorporated into the projects which include limited financial decentralisation, improvement in teaching-learning methods and training, and experimentation with alternative learning pedagogies. The major concerns regarding these projects relate to their long term fiscal sustainability and imbalances between the project and non-project areas. Moreover, despite the enormous investment in these projects and their elaborate monitoring, little is known about their impact on enrolments, retention and learning.

Second, the current national and international ideological stance towards development has led to the involvement of a large number of NGOs in all aspects of elementary education beginning from the design of teaching/learning material, to training, MIS and delivery of primary/middle education through schools. In several cases, the flow of talent to the NGO sector and the multifarious presence of this sector has allowed the state to harness new models and technologies and has provided a greater degree of flexibility to otherwise rigid state models. In other cases, the growth of NGOs has been demand driven and there is little check of the quality or cost-effectiveness of their interventions.

Third, in a limited number of cases, the state governments have come forward with new schemes which foster expansion in education while attempting to side-step their own financial and administrative constraints. Examples of these are the *Shiksha Karmi* Schemes in Madhya Pradesh and Rajasthan and the Education Guarantee Scheme in Madhya Pradesh (now promoted as a centrally sponsored scheme). While both schemes seem to have addressed certain problems in the short run, some others may have been exacerbated (such as issues of quality, and the relations between locally recruited and government teachers). Further, it is not clear how incentive issues and transition problems will be dealt with over the medium and long-term. Some of the issues which are now surfacing appear to be the result of transplanting models from one institutional form (NGO) to another (government).

While each of these initiatives appear to have been incrementally and partly successful in some ways they have also raised wider and long-term concerns. In fact, while wider forms of public action are lacking to the extent that non-governmental action has been piggy-riding on government initiatives, it's own future remains uncertain.

Finally, the most major institutional initiative which has begun to unfold itself is the empowerment of panchayats and the transfer of primary and secondary education functions to the PRIs. This transfer of functions and powers, first effected in Madhya Pradesh, has also taken place in Rajasthan and the Uttar Pradesh government has announced its intent to devolve primary education to the panchayats in the very near future. Surprisingly, these states have taken bigger steps towards the devolution of primary education compared to states such as West Bengal, which were early leaders in decentralisation initiative. In principle, the devolution of primary education could increase the accountability of teachers, improve efficiency, and relate decisions on school infrastructure to local needs. The involvement of the local community could lead to a greater alignment of the supply of education to its demand. But this is contingent on assumptions relating to community behaviour and decision-making and the latter may not necessarily be able to represent the needs of the weaker sections. This is especially because of the dominance of the local elite over the representative institutions—directly or by proxy. These factors have been analysed by us elsewhere (Lieten and Srivastava, 1999; Srivastava, 1998; 1999). While the moves towards devolution are too recent—and in many cases too limited—to say anything definitive—we have been arguing that the devolution of power has come at a time when there is a substantial churning from below in many of these states. Consequently, with devolution there is greater leeway for the weaker sections to exercise a say-in decision-making.

However, the basic issue is whether the new bodies will have the resources to devote to primary education or whether devolution as well as the other initiatives outlined above are primarily devices to cut back on the state's own commitment to universal elementary education.

Notes

1. These surveys include the National Family Health Survey of 1992-93; the National Council of Applied Economic Research/HDI Survey of 1994 and the National Sample Survey, 52nd round of 1995-96.
2. The 'UP-Bihar Survey' was designed to study living conditions in the four NSS regions of Uttar Pradesh and Bihar carried out between December 1997 and April 1998 based on a representative sample of 2,250 households in 120 villages in these two states. The survey was sponsored by the World Bank and coordinated by the author.

3. Actually, the NCAER results show a smaller shortfall in ever-enrolment rates. But due to higher discontinuation rates among SC/ST, the gap in current enrolment rates is higher.
4. These studies carried out under the auspices of a research programme of human development sponsored by the UNDP and the Government of India included fieldwork in seven states (Uttar Pradesh, Bihar, Orissa, Rajasthan, Andhra Pradesh, Tamil Nadu and Kerala) during 1995-96. A summary of findings can be found in Srivastava (1997b) and Vaidyanathan (1997).
5. For a summary of results from the UNDP-GOI studies, see Srivastava (1997) and Vaidyanathan (1997).

References

Beteille, Andre (1965), *Caste, Class and Power: The Changing Pattern of Social Stratification in a Tanjore Village*, California University Press, Berkeley.

Bhatty, Kiran (1998), "Educational Deprivation in India: A Survey of Field Investigations", *Economic and Political Weekly*, July 4 and July 11.

Chakrabarty, G. and S.P. Pal (1995), *Human Development Profile of the Indian States*, Working Paper No. 52, NCAER, New Delhi.

Chambers, Robert (1995), *'Poverty and Livelihoods: Whose Reality Counts*, UNDP (mimeo).

Dev, Mahendra (1996), "Social Security for Indian Workers: Performance and Issues", *The Indian Journal of Labour Economics*, Vol. 39, No. 4, October-December.

Dreze, Jean and Amartya Sen (eds.) (1995), *India: Economic Development and Social Opportunity*, Oxford University Press, Delhi and Oxford.

—— (eds.) (1997), *Indian Development: Selected Regional Perspectives*, Oxford University Press, Delhi.

Dreze, Jean and Harris Gazdar (1997), "Uttar Pradesh: The Burden of Inertia", in Dreze and Sen (eds.).

Filmer, D. and L. Prichett (1998), *What Educational Production Functions Really Show*, Policy Research Working Paper 1795, World Bank, Washington D.C.

International Institute for Population Studies (IIPS) (1994), *National Family Health Survey, 1992-93*, Mumbai.

Jabbi, M.K. and K.R. Rajyalakshmi (1997), *Access to Education of the SCs and STs in Bihar*, UNDP-GOI Project on Strategies and Financing of Human Development, Thiruvananthapuram.

Kingdon, Geeta G. (1996), "Private Schooling in India: Size, Nature and Equity Effects", *Economic and Political Weekly*, December 21.

Kishor, Sunita (1994), "Gender Differentials in Child Mortality: A Review of the Evidence", in Dasgupta, Monica, T.N. Krishnan and Lincoln Chen (eds.), *Women's Health in India: Risk and Vulnerability*, Oxford University Press.

Krishnan, T.N. (1996), *Poverty, Gender and Schooling*, UNDP-GOI Project on Strategies and Financing of Human Development, Thiruvananthapuram.

—— (1996a), "Health, Poverty and Labour", *The Indian Journal of Labour Economics*, Vol. 39 No 1, January-March.

Lieten, G.K. and Ravi Srivastava (1999), *Unequal Partners: Power Relations, Devolution and Development in Uttar Pradesh*, Sage, New Delhi.

Nambissan, Geetha B. (1996), *Equity in Education: The Schooling of Dalit Children in India*, Discussion Paper No. 15, Studies on Human Development in India, Project of UNDP.

National Council of Applied Economic Research (NCAER) (1999), *The India Human Development Report: A Profile of Indian States in the 1990s*, New Delhi.

National Sample Survey Organisation (1997), *Economic Activities and School Attendance by*

Children of India, Fifth Quinquennial Survey, NSS 50th round, 1993-94. Report No. 412, Department of Statistics, Government of India.

—— (1998), *Attending an Educational Institutional Institution in India: Its Level, Nature and Cost*, NSS 52nd round 1993-94, July 1995-June 1996, Report No. 439.

PROBE Report (1999), *Public Report on Basic Education in India*, Oxford Univesity Press, New Delhi.

Ramchandran, V.K. (1997), "On Kerala's Development Achievements", in Dreze and Sen (eds.).

—— Vikas Rawal and Madhura Swaminathan (1997), "Investment Gaps in Primary Education: A State-wise Study", *Economic and Political Weekly*, January 4-11.

Sengupta, Sunil and Haris Gazdar (1997), "Agrarian Politics and Rural Development in West Bengal", in Dreze and Sen (eds.).

Shariff, Abusaleh (1996), "Elementary Education in India: Trends and Determinants", Paper presented to the *Second Applied Economic Workshop*, Delhi School of Economics, January.

Srinivas, M. N. (1959),."The Dominant Caste in Rampura", *American Anthropologist*, Vol. 61, pp 1-16.

Srivastava, Ravi (1996),"Agricultural Reforms and the Rural Poor in Eastern Uttar Pradesh", *Background Paper, India Country Economic Memorandum 1996*, World Bank, Washington D.C

—— (1997a), "Access to Basic Education in Uttar Pradesh: Results of Field Study", *Studies on Human Development in India*, Discussion Paper Series, Project of the United Nations Development Programme.

—— (1997b), "Towards Accelerated Human Development: Policy Options and Strategies for Rapid Human Development in India", Background Paper to *India: The Road to Human Development*, UNDP, New Delhi.

—— (1998), *Devolution in India Since the 73rd Amendment: Impact on Safety Nets and the Social Sector*, Background Paper for the World Bank (Reducing Poverty in India: Options for More Effective Public Services, Report No. 17881-IN, Poverty Reduction and Economic Management Unit, South Asia Region, The World Bank, Washington D.C.)

—— (1999), "Two Steps Forward, One Step Back", India 1998: A Symposium on the Year That Was, No. 473, *Seminar*, January, pp. 71-77.

Tilak, J.B.G. (1989), "Education and Its Relation to Economic Growth, Poverty, and Income Distribution", World Bank Comparative Studies, Research Paper No. 3, The World Bank.

—— (1994), "Schooling Levels of the Population of India", *The Indian Journal of Labour Economics*, Vol. 37, pp. 243-253.

—— (1996), "How Free is 'Free' Primary Education in India", *Economic and Political Weekly*, February 3 and 10.

UNDP (1997), *India: The Road to Human Development*, United Nations Development Programme, New Delhi.

—— (1999), *Diversity and Disparities in Human Development: Key Challenges for India*, New Delhi.

Vaidyanathan, A. (1997), *Studies in Elementary Education: An Overview of Findings*, Project on Strategies and Financing of Human Development, UNDP, Delhi (Mimeo).

Vyasji (1999), *Children Standing on the Margins and their Education*, Bihar Education Project (Mimeo, in Hindi).

World Bank (1991), *Gender and Poverty in India*, Washington D.C.

—— (1997), *Primary Education in India*, Washington D.C.

—— (1998), *Reducing Poverty in India: Options for More Effective Public Services*, Report No. 17881-IN, Poverty Reduction and Economic Management Unit, South Asia Region, The World Bank.

11

Education Security for Children: Some Insights from the PROBE Survey

Anuradha De, Claire Noronha and Meera Samson

I. INTRODUCTION

Education is a vital component of social security as seen in a wider framework: a framework which includes capacity building as a primary focus, rather than being limited to a framework of protective safeguard against very low standards of living caused by temporary or chronic deprivation. Much of the literature which deals with the problem of such deprivation or adversity, concentrates on income, and income shortage is, indeed, crucially associated with a low standard of living. But income analysis may not always tell the whole story.

As Dreze and Sen (1999) argue, the ultimate concern of poverty analysis has to be with 'the failure to have the capability to achieve certain minimum levels of basic functioning e.g., the capability to be adequately nourished, to be comfortably clothed, to avoid preventable morbidity, to escape premature mortality,' and so on. They see the income view of poverty as being derivative, since it is the effects of income on people's basic capabilities to lead minimally acceptable lives which is crucial. Social security, then, should also ensure that people have these capabilities.

Viewed in this light, education is a crucial input into the social security safety net being intrinsically concerned with the building of capabilities that enable one to lead a life of 'minimally acceptable' quality i.e., with adequate nourishment, health, etc. This 'enabling' factor has much to do with tangibles like the precious income-earning capacity, but it also has less tangible benefits like, say, enabling one to interact with others with confidence, an ability to act on reflection and so on. Apart from this, education has a range of benefits for society since a confident and educated populace will access opportunities for self-development which will impinge on the society at large.

The building of capability is developed primarily in the vulnerable years of childhood and early adolescence and thus becomes the responsibility of both parents and the state. The importance of education, as well as the dual responsibility of the state and of parents, is well understood by those who framed our Constitution. The Constitution directs that children should be given free and compulsory education till the age of 14, thus advising the state to remove the cost constraint from the education system, 'compelling' parents to send children to school and specifying the number of years for which the state, in tandem with the parent, has to be responsible for the education of each child in the country. Education was seen as a prime instrument for moving towards a more democratic and just society, especially important for a country ridden with class, caste and gender discrimination and oppression, and important for preventing the exploitation of the vulnerable years of childhood in child labour. It is so important that it is only in this case that the Constitution specifies the number of years by which this objective of universal elementary education was to be achieved. It is, of course, debatable whether education till the age of 14 can indeed be enough to enable one to lead a minimally acceptable quality of life. In this paper, however, we are not pursuing this interesting line of argument and instead taking for granted that the eight years of schooling will prove to be sufficient for achieving the required capabilities.

Unfortunately, this basic level of education security is not yet the privilege of the children of India. There is still a massive problem of illiteracy even in the younger age-groups, particularly for females: 45 per cent of girls in the 15-19 age-group are illiterate according to the 1991 Census. Only a small minority (less than 30 per cent) of all adults have completed eight years of schooling (NFHS, 1992-93). The figures not only indicate that the problem will be with us for a long time to come but also that our record in this regard is poorer than that of many other developing countries.[1]

The problem is most acute in certain states, notably the states of Bihar, Rajasthan, Madhya Pradesh and Uttar Pradesh. The absence of education security for children in the rural areas of these states was abundantly clear during the PROBE (Public Report on Basic Education) survey. This paper takes a look at the issue from the evidence gathered during the survey. Section II deals with parents' awareness of the benefits of education and their aspirations for their children. Section III takes a look at the difficulties that parents face in accessing schooling, particularly due to the cost constraint. Section IV looks at facilities provided by the state as seen in the villages visited during the PROBE survey. Section V talks of the repercussions of the situation described in sections III and IV on the stakeholders of the system—the parents, teachers and children; and focuses particularly on the way the system exacerbates gender, class and caste biases in reducing access to education. The concluding remarks, summary in nature, reiterate the need for the state to show greater commitment to the schooling system. Otherwise, education will remain an instrument which works only for the benefit of the advantaged contrary to what was intended by the framers of the Constitution.

II. INCREASED AWARENESS OF PARENTS

When confronted with the dismal statistics of massive levels of illiteracy in the country, a commonly-held myth among more privileged groups is that disadvantaged parents are just not interested in education. "They are only interested in *kheti*," "they'll send the children to school if you give them a little money," "they cannot think beyond the present," were some of the remarks we heard about such parents' lack of motivation. On the contrary, we found (during the PROBE survey conducted in 1996) that parents, even in these educationally-deprived states, perceived both the instrumental and non-instrumental benefits that education could provide. They understood clearly that education was a tool of self-defence and indispensable in modern society. With education they could fill a form, travel where they wished, and prevent others from cheating them. Most of all, they felt that education would open up employment opportunities, and a chance for their children to escape the grinding poverty which surrounded them.

Parents today are far more positive about education than before. This becomes obvious after looking at the figures for the proportion of never-enrolled children in rural areas in the four low-literacy states surveyed. From 55 per cent in 1986-87 (NSSO), it has dropped to just 19 per cent in 1996 (PROBE, 1999). In other words, most parents, even in these low-literacy states, are giving schooling a chance.

Parents were asked as to whether they felt it important for a boy/girl to be educated. Their attitudes to the education of their sons were overwhelmingly positive. Whether we look at responses in different states, or for different castes, or across occupations, or even a breakdown by gender or literacy status of the parents, not less than 99 per cent of the respondents thought it was important for a boy to be educated. However, only 89 per cent felt it was important to educate girls. Although the majority of parents do feel that female education is important, note that there were a sizeable number who were resistant to educating their girls. The resistance was greater in the more disadvantaged groups: those who were illiterate, those working as casual labour and those from historically disadvantaged castes.

One reason for the lower motivation for female education is that parents had greatly differentiated perceptions of the benefits of education for their sons and daughters. Attitudes were related to the way parents saw the future roles of boys and girls in society and the extent to which education would help to safeguard them (Table 1).

Table 1
Motivation for Education

	Percentage of respondents
Why parents think it is important for a boy to be educated?	
improves employment and income opportunities	87
improves social status	29
improves self-confidence or self-esteem	24
Why parents think it is important for a girl to be educated?	
helps to write letters and keep accounts	50
improves employment and income opportunities	40
improves marriage prospects	35

Note: The percentages do not add to hundred since they are not mutually exclusive.
Source: PROBE (1999), Table 3.2.

Although education leading to improved income and employment opportunities was an important consideration for the education of girls, it was the predominant motivation behind the education of boys, and partly explains why parents were far more willing to invest in their son's education. For the girl, marriage considerations were more important, whether it was to find a bridegroom more easily or to write letters and keep household accounts. For a majority of the respondents, educated girls were seen as an asset, better able to run the house and teach the children.

A few parents said that educating girls could lead to problems in getting them married since there were not so many educated boys in their community. In addition, educated boys and their families demanded higher dowries, an additional burden.

Unfortunately, even though parents were keen to educate their daughters, their aspirations remain low. Nearly one-fifth of the parents didn't want their daughters to study beyond class 5 (Table 2). In many cases, this was because there was no upper-primary school in the village itself. Other factors for the lower aspirations for girls education include the fact that there are far fewer employment avenues open for girls; also that, since girls get married and leave their homes to become part of their husband's family, parents are more indifferent to their future employment possibilities; and even that, girls working outside the home is still unheard of in many rural communities. These relatively low aspirations for girls were in sharp contrast to parents' high aspirations for boys (about 85 per cent of parents wanted them to study well beyond class 10). As mentioned earlier these are connected to the differing perceptions of parents about the economic returns from their investment in their daughter's vis-a-vis their son's education.

Table 2
Educational Aspirations

How far would you like your son/ daughter to study? (percentage of responses)	Son	Daughter
Upto grade 5	2	19
Upto grade 8	2	18
Upto grade 10	11	20
Beyond grade 10	28	15
As far as possible	57	28

Source: PROBE (1999), Table 3.4.

In the next section, we shall look at factors which come into play within the environment of the home and which help explain why, in spite of the high motivation for education, there are still so many children out of school.

III. CONSTRAINTS ON PARENTS

Two factors were most commonly cited by parents as constraints to sending their children to school regularly, or even sending them at all: one, that schooling is expensive; and two, that the child is needed at home. Notice that both factors relate to the costs of schooling, whether direct or indirect, and reflect on the 'free' provision of schooling.

1. Direct Costs

Although Tilak (1996) had established that private costs of schooling were high enough to call in question the government's claim of providing free schooling, the myth maintained a fairly stronghold on general perceptions. Just how far cost was a constraint became clear to us only through our survey of the villages in our sample in the four states.

Parents and teachers were asked about their estimates of the private expenditure involved in sending a child to primary school. Parents put this at an average of Rs. 318 per child per year, which is quite close to the teachers' average estimate of Rs. 272. Although the government provides the teachers and the school building, the users, i.e. the parents and children, have to bear the other costs (the two major components of which were the cost of clothing/uniforms and the cost of textbooks).

This does seem to be a fairly significant constraint when one considers the low and uncertain income of a daily-wage agricultural labourer, that he/she may be paying for several school-age children, and that education is not only a long-term investment but it also requires liquidity at short notice, whether it be for books, stationery or clothing. Note that the parents' estimate is not based on what is needed to send the child to school in adequate clothes and with books required by him/her; instead most children in these villages go to school in rags and with a highly depleted school bag and it is these costs that we are looking at: few children possessed the full complement of books for their class.

2. Indirect Costs

Parents also mentioned that the child being needed at home was also a reason for keeping him/her out of school. Childcare was a great problem, particularly for eldest daughters but sometimes for eldest sons as well especially when there was no daughter old enough to bear this burden. Parents were also more reluctant to bear the opportunity cost of forfeiting the girl-child's help with household chores. Again, very poor families were often constrained by sudden illness or death of a household member and had to call on the child to give up school, or not to enrol her at all. Girls were usually the victims, but boys were also called to take up income-earning responsibilities when disaster struck. The absence of even a basic form of protective social security in times of crisis renders the family incapable of fulfilling its responsibility towards the child—for such families the cost of government schooling is itself very high.

However, the situation is more complex than this analysis suggests. The PROBE survey looked at the work patterns of out-of-school children and found that, the great majority of children in the 6-12 years age-group were not engaged in wage labour, but in family chores, whether in the house or in the fields (95 per cent); out-of-school children did only approximately two hours more work than those children who are currently enrolled in school;

For the vast majority of children then, the work that they are required to do is not incompatible with attending school, which on average was for only four hours per day.[2] In fact, our interviews with parents and children indicated that some children are out of school not because they have to work but that they are working because they are out of school. In other words, economic constraints are not the only problem.

3. Other Constraints

There were numerous other constraints which often discouraged parents from continuing the struggle to send their children to school. Access to school was one such problem, particularly in areas where the terrain was difficult, as for example, when the children have to cross a river or go through a forested area. On the whole, the basic provision for eight years of schooling is far from complete.

The deprived section of the population have some constraints special to themselves: ill-health, hunger and malnutrition were also difficulties among deprived families which made regular attendance almost impossible and pointed to the vulnerability of both child and parent without access to different forms of social security. These constraints are caused/aggravated by constraints peculiar to our economy, like access to schools and the employment situation. More privileged families can resort to private schooling at great costs if there is an access problem. Again, unemployment or underemployment was a major problem for many families. But perhaps most important was a number of school-related factors. The system is quite insensitive in the sense that it makes no adjustment in school-timing and school curriculum to suit the needs of rural parents and children. School was an alien—or even hostile—place for many children, an especially important factor where schooling was not a norm for the community. Again, one must remember that the average child in a PROBE village was not equipped even with the right textbooks. A problem which had immense repercussions was the poor quality of the schooling system itself, an issue which we shall deal with in the next section.

4. Government's Incentive Schemes to Offset Schooling Costs

So far we have mainly discussed factors which make the schooling process very fragile from the demand side. The government has made a number of attempts to reduce the costs of schooling by offering a variety of incentives: scholarships, free textbooks, free uniforms, mid-day meals and dry rations. Indirectly, the incentive schemes are themselves an acknowledgment of the fact that the cost of education, whether direct or indirect, is a big deterrent for parents. Some of the schemes are directly targeted at girls and disadvantaged castes. Teachers felt that incentive schemes, on the whole, played a useful role in bringing children into the school. These children were often from the poorest families and the dry rations of 3 kg of wheat, for example, had a tremendous impact on increasing enrolment. Some of the schemes could also have a positive influence on learning outcomes: free textbooks, for example, greatly help the parent and a good mid-day meal scheme would ensure regular attendance as well as provide nutrition.

However, the coverage of government's incentive schemes remains extremely limited. During the PROBE household survey, it was found that of all the SC/ST children enrolled in government schools, only one-fifth had received scholarships, two-fifth had received free textbooks and about half had received dry rations. Except for scholarships, the coverage was very similar to that received by all government school children covered in the survey.

Moreover, the erratic and whimsical implementation of these schemes meant that a lot of the potential gains are frittered away. In some places, textbooks arrived long after the academic year had started, which meant that they had limited usefulness, especially if there were less books than the number required. The scholarship money had not arrived in half the schools where the scheme was operational even after many months of the academic year had passed. The dry ration scheme also brought in its fair share of complaints by parents against teachers for giving them less than their due.

There are two other points: several teachers pointed out that the amount given as scholarship was scarcely enough to make a real dent in compensating for schooling costs. Secondly, little notice is taken of the added responsibilities for the teacher: additional paperwork and the duty of organising the distribution of the money or books or the ration. In the case of the dry ration scheme it sometimes meant losing a whole school-day escorting children to the nearest ration shop. All this results in further reduction of teaching time.

Certainly government schemes to reduce private costs of schooling have made a difference. But there will be real long-term gains in enrolment and retention only if the incentive schemes are devised carefully and implemented systematically and with due consideration of the impact on the schooling environment. Free textbooks which arrive midway through the school year or a cumbersome mid-day meal scheme which becomes the only activity in school (examples of both were found in the course of the survey) are counter-productive. It is a good teaching-learning process which is at the core of an effective schooling system as we shall see in the next section.

IV. EDUCATION SYSTEM IN PROBE VILLAGES

In this section, we look at the child's (and the parent's) experiences of the school environment. How will it serve to attract and retain the child, particularly the first-generation learner? We also look at the support structures for the schooling system which are crucial to disadvantaged parents and their children.

Micro studies suggest that factors which determine learning outcomes can be broadly divided into three groups: household-related, school-related and individual-related. For a large majority of the children, very little support comes from the household. So school-related factors play the key role in their learning achievements, or lack of them.

1. Early Years

What happens to the children in their early years is vital to the success in school at a later date. Provision of education security must begin by providing a sufficient number of *anganwadis*, which can absorb children from all castes and communities, which, by functioning on a regular basis can provide the child with appropriate care. To begin with, only one-third of PROBE villages had a functioning *anganwadi*. To the extent that they functioned, they were food distribution centres. The crucial role that *anganwadis* can play in ensuring care for pregnant and lactating mothers and for very young children, and in preparing them for entry into school is completely overlooked. Here too, first-generation learners are handicapped in the sense that no effort towards learning-preparedness can be made at home, unlike for the children of educated parents.

The location of the *anganwadi* itself is crucial if it is to release the elder children in the family to go to school while the little ones are being looked after.

We are reminded of the fact that education is a subset of society, and that education security is massively dependent on support systems like a good *anganwadi* system if for making it a success.

2. Access to School System

As has been mentioned earlier even the basics of education security is not available: provision for eight years of schooling is simply not available. But on the whole, access to primary schooling is not a major problem in the sense that almost all villages have a primary school. In the few villages without a primary school, clusters of never-enrolled children were common. Upper primary school has major problems: provision by the state, is as yet, simply not adequate according to the PROBE survey. Nearly 71 per cent of the villages did not have an upper primary school. This means an automatic end to the education of girls who are not usually sent out of the village in these parts as we mentioned before, and also an end to the education of many boys from poor families. A further complication relating to upper primary schooling relates to the quality of lower primary schooling: this was simply not good enough for most of the children from disadvantaged families to benefit adequately from the facility.

3. School Environment

Parents and teachers told us about enrolment drives which were undertaken under government orders. But no preparation seems to have been made to improve the school environment into which these small children were being invited. Nor were they given any special attention. The emphasis is only on enrolment. Little thought is paid to retention or achievement or so it seems, as we looked at the schools functioning within the PROBE villages.

(i) Dilapidated School Buildings

The school buildings are uninviting to say the least: broken-down buildings or occasionally none at all. Only 58 per cent have at least two *pucca* classrooms (which was a minimum specified by Operation Blackboard). Several schools do not have a building of their own and have to share it with *dharmshalas/panchayatghars*, and this becomes problematic because teaching often clashed with other uses of the premises. About 60 per cent of the school-buildings surveyed have a leaking roof, which meant that there was sometimes no teaching activity for weeks at a time. Most school-buildings were in need of major repair. In addition, a majority of them do not even have a boundary wall.

(ii) Inadequate School Facilities

While nearly three-fourths of the schools had a blackboard, less than half had a playground. Drinking water was available only in 41 per cent of the schools, while toilet facilities existed only in 11 per cent of the schools. Overall, there was a drastic shortage of teaching aids. Under Operation Blackboard, some schools had received some teaching aids, but they were hardly ever in a usable state, and even more rarely were they being used. Investigators often found them locked up in the school or even in the teacher's house.

The problem of inadequate facilities was further aggravated by poor maintenance and utilisation of the facilities that did exist. Children were seen huddling into one or two classrooms while others were used for storage, residence or non-teaching purposes.

(iii) Scarcity of Teachers

The average pupil-teacher ratio (defined as the ratio of children enrolled to the number of primary teachers appointed) was, as high as 50:1. The problem was acute for children in remote areas because the distribution of teachers was quite uneven. The bigger, accessible schools had more teachers and lower pupil-teacher ratios; many of the remote schools had single teachers looking after upto 172 pupils at one time. Out of the sample of 162 government primary schools, 26 had a pupil-teacher ratio above 75.

Operation Blackboard's promise of at least two teachers in every school, with one of them being a woman, has certainly not been kept. One-third of the schools were functioning as single-teacher schools at the time of the survey. However, multigrade teaching was common even in schools where there was more than one teacher. Female teachers constituted only 21 per cent of the total and were concentrated in the bigger schools and in schools which were more accessible.[3]

(iv) Scarcity of Teaching Time

The problem of teacher shortage was magnified by short hours of work. Our survey led us to believe that at best the schools functioned for about 150 days in the year and that the average teacher spent only about four hours per day at school.

To gain some idea of what the average teacher is doing in those four hours, we looked at what the teacher was doing at the time of the investigators' unannounced visits to the school (Table 3). Shockingly, in around 50 per cent of the schools, there was no teaching activity going on at all at the time the investigators visited the school.

Table 3
Activity Patterns of Teachers

Proportion of schools in which the teachers were engaged in the following activities when the investigators arrived	Percentage
Teaching	53
Minding the class	21
Sitting/standing outside the class	11
In the head-teachers room	7
Talking to the other teachers	18
Other non-teaching activity	23

Note: The options are not mutually exclusive as different teachers were engaged in different activities.

Source: PROBE (1999), Table 4.6.

(v) Stultifying Teaching Methods

Teachers reported that the most commonly used method of teaching was giving written exercises, reading from the blackboard, and writing on the blackboard. However, children's books usually showed that they had copied without much comprehension either from textbooks or guidebooks.

Whatever teaching activity did take place was most often concentrated on classes IV and V. One explanation is that some states had a Board examination at the end of class V.

Class I was not only systematically neglected, but was also typically overcrowded. Under-age children may be enrolled in the hope of incentives. The size varied from five to 152 in the PROBE villages. First-generation learners who come in with no learning-preparedness would need special care. Unfortunately, more than 70 per cent of class I teachers reported that they had to do multigrade teaching.

(vi) Limited Inclusion of Co-curricular Activities

Teachers in general seemed to have no systematic organisation of the day to include sports or other co-curricular activities.

(vii) Atmosphere of Chaos and Discrimination

The general atmosphere allowed for violence both within the classroom and outside. Teachers were used to beating and humiliating the children. Children also dropped out due to being beaten and teased by other children in the playground. Parents complained of lower-caste children being generally neglected, even picked on to do manual chores.

4. Alternative Structures

A network of non-formal schools could be an important transit instrument for a society which has an inadequate protective social security net and an ill-equipped schooling system. It could take care of all those who did not enter school/stay in school for a variety of reasons, ranging from lack of sufficient money for books to the illness of an income earning member and even poor school quality. However, although there was a network of non-formal centres, of which some vague evidence was available in the villages, they were non-functional in most of the PROBE villages. The household survey came up with only two children who were enrolled in an NFE and none who had moved from the non-formal system to the formal system (a major objective of the system). A disturbing tendency which came to light was the setting up of low-cost alternatives with poorly qualified teachers as a permanent solution to the inadequacies of the already ill-equipped formal school system.

V. REPERCUSSIONS

1. Demotivation and Discouragement

Although the government is committed to providing "Education for All" and has taken up several new initiatives in this direction, the reality experienced by many of the stakeholders is exactly the opposite.

First, let us look at the impact on the child. Dilapidated buildings mean that going to school is neither attractive nor stimulating for the child. Overcrowded classrooms and general neglect mean that children are frequently left to play and fight among themselves. The schools where one teacher was responsible for all five classes could organise only minimal teaching-learning activity with children of varying ages and abilities to be looked after at the same time.

With teachers arriving late and leaving early, and not necessarily teaching even when present, children received the message that schooling was not for them. Rather than building up self-confidence and self-esteem, such an environment served to destroy their chances of success, especially for the first-generation learners.

Teaching aids were hardly used; most children did not have even the right textbooks. Lack of sensitivity in the choice of curriculum and medium of instruction also made the school an oppressive place to be in. With copying being the most frequently used teaching method, children experienced a great burden of non-comprehension and with it a sense of failure.

The impact of the relative absence of female teachers in schools in remote villages is not clear, but certainly beatings and humiliation were always associated with male teachers.

In such a system, the teachers themselves felt demotivated. They had problems with the remote locations; the poor infrastructure; the necessity to do multigrade teaching without an adequate supply of textbooks or teaching aids; a curriculum which was not sensitive to the students in their schools; and most of all with their pupils. They blamed the children's parents who did not/could not send the children regularly, or provide a learning environment at home or even pay for private tuitions.

The demotivating environment seemed to accompany the teachers' own lack of accountability to their task. Apart from their shortening of the school-day, and their distraction from the task of teaching even when present in school, there were also glaring inaccuracies in records. Attendance registers were frequently filled up the next day.

The most common complaint from parents was that the teachers did not teach. The teachers on the other hand, blamed the lack of achievement on the home environment. Whatever the reason, achievements of children in these schools were very low. Many children could not read two or three letter words after several years of schooling. In the course of the survey, investigators also looked at children's notebooks and found that even children with several years of schooling had books filled with meaningless scribbles (e.g., see Maya's notebook, p. 48, PROBE, 1999). A parent from Uttar Pradesh expressed the views of other parents when he said bitterly that even if the child sat in the same class for four years he would learn absolutely nothing.

The net result of the burdensome costs of schooling (discussed in Section II) and the poor quality of schooling (discussed in Section III) is that parents and children are massively discouraged from continuing the struggle of sending their children to school on a sustained and regular basis. Tejubai, a *Gujjar* mother from Ujjain expressed this well. She had not enrolled her daughter Rukmini in school. "If I send her to school, I have to pay a labourer to replace her and she learns nothing. See my son Jaswant in class 5. He knows nothing."

Tejubai's story is a classic example of an illiterate, rural family's tentative steps into the world of schooling. Tejubai's two sons were both currently-enrolled in the village school. Both could not read, even after five years of schooling. Tejubai had little reason to continue their education. Her daughter, Rukmini, had not been sent to school at all. Tejubai found even the indirect costs associated with sending Rukmini to school a little too much to afford, particularly in the light of her sons' low achievements flowing out of the dismal quality of the village school.

Under such circumstances it seems a cruel irony to compel disadvantaged parents to send their children to school, a provision which is actually important to break the resistance of that minority of parents who see no need to educate their children, particularly their girl children.

2. Biases of Caste, Class and Gender Aggravated

The PROBE survey brought out clearly that the lack of education security in rural areas works towards aggravating the caste, class and gender biases that already exist. It becomes starkly obvious when we look at firstly, the social background of children who are in school and out of school; and secondly, the social background of children enrolled in private schools vis-a-vis government schools. As we shall see, high aspirations for education seem to have been frustrated by the vagaries of the schooling system. It is the disadvantaged who are more likely to be pushed out of the schooling system. Those who are more advantaged simply opt for private schooling.

3. Out-of-School Children

When we look at Table 4, we see that, across the board, there are many more children out of school than we might expect from the very positive attitudes that parents had towards educating their children: 35 per cent of all SC/ST children, 29 per cent of all OBC children and even 20 per cent of all children of other castes were out of school at the time of the PROBE survey in 1996.

As one might expect, it is the girl child who is much more likely to be out of school. The strong gender bias is in keeping with the much lower aspirations that parents had for girls and strongly interfered with their reasons for wanting to educate them. We found that 71 per cent of the children in our random sub-sample of 333 non-enrolled children were girls. And that, even those who were enrolled, were taken out of school when the expenditure or effort involved in sending them crossed a minimum threshold.

Finally, let us look at the figures for children of parents who are casual labour and compare them with their motivation for education. All but one parent from this group felt it was important to educate their sons; unfortunately there are still 40 per cent of the boys in this group who are out of school. For girls there was some resistance: nearly 20 per cent of parents did not think it important to educate their daughters. The additional impact of the problems associated with schooling resulted in nearly 70 per cent of girls from these families being out of school.

Scarcity of resources meant that families sometimes concentrated on investing in certain children in the family. As suggested in section II of this paper, it is more likely that these would be boys. In 74 families with never-enrolled girls in the 6-12 age-group, there were currently-enrolled boys. But only in two families with never-enrolled boys in the primary-level age-group were there currently-enrolled girls.

The government seems to pay only lip service to the cause of the girl-child with regard to increasing their access to education. A robust school system is more likely to draw in and retain girls.

Table 4 throws some light on the background of parents who are most likely to give up the schooling struggle and for which children. In order to draw in the vast number of out-of-school children and to retain the ones who are currently enrolled, the government must take more cognizance of the needs of first-generation learners, and of social groups who are marginalised by the system. The child must feel that education is an achievable goal for him/her.

Table 4
Out-of-school Children (Aged 6-12) and Their Social Background

(per cent)

Caste	Male	Female	All
SCs/STs	20	52	35
OBCs	16	43	29
Other castes	5	36	20
Casual labour	40	69	53

Source: PROBE (1999).

4. Characteristics of Children in Private Schools vis-a-vis Government Schools

Parents who are discouraged by the quality of teaching in government schools were seen to be taking them out and putting them into private schools. Several teachers from government schools seemed to agree with them. Their own children were in private schools. "No parent who was serious would send their child to a single-teacher school like this one," said a teacher in Madhya Pradesh.

When we looked at the details comparing the clientele of government and private schools (Table 5), we found that government schools have

— a higher proportion of female pupils
— a higher proportion of SC/ST pupils
— a higher proportion of pupils with parents who work as casual labour.

Table 5
Characteristics of Government/Private School Pupils

(per cent)

	Government schools	Private schools
Proportion of female pupils	34	27
Proportion of SC/ST pupils	32	14
Proportion of pupils coming from households with the following as one of its main occupations:		
Farming	73	79
Casual labour	33	19
Wage employment	16	23
Self-employment	14	24

Source: PROBE (1999).

However, it is also worth noting that it is not only those who can afford it to put their children into private schools. The motivation for education is so high and the discouragement with the government schooling system so great that there are disadvantaged parents who are putting one child (most commonly a boy) into a private school while the rest may be enrolled in a government school or even never enrolled at all.

The caste, class and gender biases inherent in this situation are obvious. The costs of schooling are already hard to bear for disadvantaged parents even in the case of government schools where fees are exempt. They are in no position therefore, to send all their children to private schools. Parents who can press for improvements in the schooling quality simply opt out of the system. Their children do better, but the vast majority are left with aspirations but without the wherewithal to fulfill them. The government, by not making schooling of decent quality available to all its citizens, is making education into a privilege of only those who can afford it.

VI. CONCLUDING REMARKS

Even disadvantaged parents are well aware of the importance of education according to the PROBE survey in the four large low-literacy states of north India. Unfortunately, they and their children still face the spectre of an absence of education security for children. Several decades have elapsed since the 'deadline' for achieving this.

Considerable provisions have been made by the state but major hurdles remain: (i) Access—particularly at the upper primary stage; (ii) Cost—both direct and indirect costs of schooling remain a problem for disadvantaged parents; incentive schemes of government have not been able to address the problem adequately; (iii) Support systems like *anganwadis* are lacking, and (iv) Poor quality of schooling is a major issue and creates a massive discouragement effect for all stakeholders.

The net result is that disadvantaged parents, particularly those plagued by survival issues, often tend to give up the struggle to obtain schooling for their children. Biases of class, caste and gender are accentuated by the very medium which sought to remove or at least lessen them: the disadvantaged cannot easily escape by paying for private schooling.

Although parents also have an obligation towards their children's schooling, it seems unreasonable to force them to do so in the present scenario without, at first, improving and strengthening schooling facilities. School facilities have to be considerably improved and strengthened.

The state shows lack of real commitment towards enhancing the quality of education facilities. Several factors show this:

(i) The bill making education a fundamental right has been hanging fire for years. If passed, it would make the right to education justiciable.
(ii) Instead, there is a parallel track of low-cost schooling alternatives being developed which are claiming to address the needs of the people for education security.
(iii) Most damning of all, the budgetary allocation for elementary education in the nineties has remained below 4 per cent, well below official promises to raise this share to 6 per cent.

(This paper is based on the PROBE survey of education facilities in rural areas in the four north Indian states of Bihar, Rajasthan, Madhya Pradesh and Uttar Pradesh. Much of the discussion has been taken from the Public Report on Basic Education, Oxford University Press, 1999. The authors were part of the team which undertook the PROBE survey).

Notes

1. See PROBE, p. 9, where India is compared unfavourably with Sub-Sahara Africa.
2. This is particularly true for the age-group which the survey covered in detail (i.e. 6-12 years). However, the situation could well be more grim of the upper end of the elementary education age spectrum of the focus i.e., 11-14 years.
3. In fact, only 26 per cent of schools covered in the PROBE survey met even a modified version of OB norms: at least two all weather rooms, at least two teachers, and a minimum of teaching aids.

References

PROBE (1999), *Public Report on Basic Education,* Oxford University Press, Delhi.

Dreze, Jean and Amartya Sen (1999), "Public Action for Social Security: Foundation and Strategy", in E. Ahmed, J. Dreze, J. Hills and A. Sen (eds.), *Social Security in Developing Countries,* Oxford University Press, Delhi.

Tilak, J.B.G (1996), "How Free is 'Free' Primary Education in India", *Economic and Political Weekly,* February 3.

PART IV

EMPLOYMENT AND INCOME SECURITY

12

Employment Generation and the Question of Employment Security

Alakh N. Sharma and R.P. Mamgain

I. INTRODUCTION

The concept of employment security in a developing country like India is markedly different from the developed countries. In developed countries where unemployment is largely open/frictional, it is easy to relate employment security with the rate of unemployment, as the former is inversely related to the latter. As such, unemployment insurance is generally introduced in those countries to guarantee a specified minimum income to the unemployed. However, the employment security model of the developed countries cannot be adopted in the developing countries. This is mainly because of the complex and intractable nature of the target group as well as the fact that unemployment can be a cause of heavy loss or interruption of income. Cyclical, open and frictional unemployment, which is normally prevalent in developed countries, is typically low in developing countries. Due to widespread poverty and deprivation, unemployment is, in a sense, a luxury for the poor in developing countries — they are poor not because they are unemployed as such but because they are employed irregularly at low wages and derive low incomes from self-employment based on low assets. Further, the disadvantaged groups are very spatially scattered and occupationally diffuse, as is reflected in the high occupational diversity and instability in employment, in both rural and urban informal sectors (Guhan, 1995).

In such a complex employment scenario, it is difficult to explicitly devise a comprehensive employment security system for the population as a whole in the developing countries. However, notwithstanding the competing demands on budgetary resources in these countries, given the enormity of the problem, there is an urgent need to develop a system of employment security which can target the most needy.

After briefly reviewing the approach adopted in the Indian Plans towards employment generation, this paper (i) examines the growth and structural change in employment and labour market in recent years; (ii) evaluates the mechanisms and measures adopted towards employment security both in the organised and unorganised sectors, and evaluates their effectiveness; and finally (iii) provides the conclusion with an outline of a framework for employment security.

II. EMPLOYMENT POLICY IN RETROSPECT

Removal of unemployment has been one of the main objectives of the development planning in India. The overall approach adopted in the early years of planning emphasised utilisation of labour for development rather than tackling the problem of unemployment as such. Unemployment was not perceived as a major problem warranting independent treatment either in plan modelling or in plan programmes (Papola, 1992, p. 300). The First Five Year Plan (1951-56) followed a strategy based on a long-term perspective with a focus on acceleration in the growth rate of the economy. The plan showed some concern about the problem of underemployment and made some proposals for employment generation in agriculture and allied occupations, irrigation, villages and small industries, and services in the urban area. The Second Five Year Plan (1956-61) recognised the poor performance on the employment front, reflected in an increase in the backlog of unemployment and underemployment (Planning Commission, 1956, p. 27). The plan accorded a relatively higher priority to the capital goods sector along with the objective of increasing the role of cottage and small industries for augmenting the supply of consumer goods. However, the concern for employment continued to be dominated by factors like the critical role of investment, labour productivity, importance of the use of machinery and new techniques for higher productivity. The plan's approach to the sectoral pattern of employment became crystallised around the position that a shift of workforce from agriculture towards mining, modern small and large industries, and transport, construction and communication is inherent in the very process of development. The Third Plan (1961-66) showed very little change in the basic strategy towards employment generation. The plan emphasised the area approach in order to respond to the needs of the specific occupational and skill groups (Planning Commission, 1962, p. 160).

The backlog of unemployment in the beginning of the Second Plan and the net addition to labour force during the period, 1956-61, were estimated at five million and eight million, respectively, which could be taken care of over a period of 10 years with the envisaged growth rate of GDP at 5 per cent per annum. Employment creation was thus treated as a corrolary of the development process in the early plans.

During the 1960s and 1970s the Indian economy experienced an average growth rate of around 3.5 per cent per annum. Employment growth was around 2 per cent per annum during the period, 1961-83, as against the rate of growth of labour force at 2.5 per cent during the sixties and seventies leading to a rise in the backlog of unemployment from five million in 1956 to 11 million in 1977-78. The shift in the structure of employment during this period was also very small compared to changes in the structure of output. The share of agriculture and allied sectors in GDP declined from 54 per cent in 1960-61 to about 39 per cent in 1983-84, while the share of agriculture in employment declined from

73 per cent in 1961 to only 69 per cent in 1983, implying thereby a relative deterioration in average productivity and income levels in agriculture. Estimates of poverty based on levels of consumption expenditure derived from large scale sample surveys initiated in the early seventies also showed that about 54 per cent of the rural population was below the poverty line, defined in terms of the average total consumption expenditure of the households for meeting the per capita norm of 2,400 calories in rural areas and 2,100 calories in urban areas. These trends in the incidence of unemployment and levels of poverty raised doubts about the efficacy of growth in tackling these problems. Although the Fourth Plan (1969-74) stressed greater investment in industry and infrastructure by the public sector in the wake of prolonged recession, some target group-oriented programmes along with some ad hoc self- and wage employment programmes were initiated, which provided only some relief. By the mid-seventies employment was regarded as the most important challenge to be met in the Fifth Plan (1974-79) and a solution was sought primarily in changing the pattern of growth. A view that growth alone could not take care of these problems soon emerged leading to the introduction of a number of special employment programmes in the late seventies.

Acceleration of growth rate, while attempting to deal with the problem of unemployment and poverty through special employment programmes, thus, became a central element of the strategy of the Sixth and Seventh Five Year Plans. Accordingly, many special programmes for poorer groups including women, tribals, unorganised urban poor, etc., were launched. Groups of people like bonded labour, child labour, educated unemployed, etc., also attracted specific attention. While the economy experienced a relatively higher growth of about 5.5 per cent per annum during these plans (sixth and seventh), employment growth was estimated to be only 1.8 per cent during 1978-88 and unemployment to have risen to about 14.5 million by that year and further to 17 million by the end of 1991-92 (Planning Commission, 1992). And this was so in spite of the implementation of special employment programmes on a large scale during the eighties. Thus, arguments that neither a higher growth rate nor special employment programmes *per se* could provide an effective solution to the problem of unemployment began to be advanced in the early nineties and the need for an employment-oriented growth strategy was emphasised. The Eighth Plan sought to adopt a strategy which combined a high level of growth with an emphasis on employment generation, which would ensure faster growth of employment-intensive sectors, sub-sectors and activities. The plan, the launching of which coincided with the initiation of economic reforms in India, aimed at bringing employment into a sharper focus in a medium-term perspective with the goal of reducing unemployment to a negligible level within the next 10 years. Towards this objective, the plan emphasised a structure of growth with a larger contribution of sectors having high employment contents in output and use of production techniques favouring the use of labour to enhance the employment generation potential of growth. Recognising that adoption of such employment strategy would enable attainment of near full employment only over a period of time, the Eighth Plan advocated continuation of special employment programmes to protect the interests of the poor and vulnerable groups.

The Ninth Plan (1997-2002) recognised the importance of productive work and considered it as an end in itself apart from a means to achieve the ultimate end of economic well-being. The primary objective of the plan is to generate greater productive employment in the growth process itself by concentrating on sectors, sub-sectors and technologies which are more labour-intensive in regions characterised by higher rates of unemployment and underemployment. It also lays stress on the quality of employment, regional dimensions of employment, tackling the problem of educated unemployment, and the need for increasing agricultural productivity for ensuring the productive absorption of labour force. The plan says: "in addition to the total number of employment opportunities created, it is equally important to examine both the consistency of the work opportunities with the skill attributes of the labour force and the quality of employment in terms of providing an adequate level of income for the workers." The plan also focuses on special employment programmes, particularly those relating to wage employment.

The essential ingredient of social policy concerning labour and employment, particularly during the first three decades of planning, has been to treat labour not merely as a resource for development, but as a partner in and beneficiary of social and economic development. This philosophy of labour has its roots in the national movement. In fact, many of the legislative provisions for protecting labour were enacted before Independence which were further strengthened later on. Accordingly, comprehensive legislations relating to conditions of work in various sectors, which already existed, were strengthened and provisions of social security were made comprehensive and expanded to include various kinds of risks. Further, detailed laws governing industrial relations and industrial disputes were enacted, and a mechanism for fixing and implementing minimum wages was developed. The basic philosophy behind all these measures was to ensure that labour is not exploited by being employed in sub-human conditions; or subjected to unfair practices in respect of payment of wages, dismissals and retrenchments. While payment of wages is reasonable and fair, minimum security is provided against risks (such as injuries and accidents at work), sickness, maternity and old age. Industrial relations have provided a measure of job security by specifying procedures for settlement of industrial disputes and also stipulating restrictions on employers in laying off and retrenching workers. The basic idea behind all these comprehensive and well meaning protective measures adopted for the benefit of labour was that a section of the workforce was a relatively weaker partner vis-a-vis capital in the production process and that in a poor country like India it was desirable to safeguard their interests not only on considerations of social justice, but also for promoting an appropriate industrial and productive climate.

III. TREND AND PATTERN OF EMPLOYMENT GROWTH IN RECENT YEARS

It would be useful to take a look at the trend and pattern of growth of employment along with important changes in the labour market which have been witnessed during the last two decades or so. This will provide us the necessary backdrop to understand the various nuances and complexities necessary for outlining a framework of employment security in the country.

1. Growth of Employment and GDP

Employment in India has grown at an average annual rate of around 2 per cent over the past four and half decades or so (Table 1). The growth rate varied in different sub-periods— it grew by less than 1 per cent during the 1950s, but by over 2 per cent during the 1960s. The 1970s saw an employment growth of slightly lower than 2 per cent per annum, which decelerated to about 1.8 per cent during the 1980s. During the early 1990s it further decelerated but rose to a little over 2 per cent after 1992.

Table 1
Growth Rate of GDP and Employment

Plans	Annual average growth rates	
	GDP	Employment
1951-56 (First Five Year Plan)	3.6	0.39
1956-61 (Second Year Plan)	4.2	0.85
1961-66 (Third Five Year Plan)	2.8	2.03
1967-69 (Annual Plans)	3.9	2.21
1969-74 (Fourth Five Year Plan)	3.3	1.99
1974-79 (Fifth Five Year Plan)	4.8	1.84
1980-85 (Sixth Five Year Plan)	5.7	1.73
1985-90 (Seventh Five Year Plan)	5.8	1.89
1990-92 (Annual Plans)	3.4	1.50
1992-97 (Eighth Five Year Plan)	6.5	2.44

Source: Planning Commission, Government of India, Five Year Plan Documents.

The growth of employment needs to be seen in relation to the demand for and supply of labour. Labour demand is basically determined by the rate and pattern of growth, particularly the former. The economy registered an annual average growth rate of around 3.5 per cent in gross domestic product (GDP) from 1950s to 1970s and over 5.5 per cent during the 1980s. The growth rate decelerated to below 4 per cent in the early 1990s, but again accelerated to over 6 per cent during 1992-97. The growth rates, of course, fluctuated over different sub-periods, as can be seen from the estimates of GDP growth in different five year plans and during the intervening annual plan periods (Table 1).

One of the reasons for the slow growth of employment during the 1950s, apart from the slower rate of GDP growth, was the large investments made in infrastructure industries which had a low potential for direct employment generation and relatively long gestation periods. As a result, employment during this period grew at a slower pace even in relation to the low GDP. Compared to the secondary effects of heavy investments made earlier, in 1960s the growth of employment was faster even with low GDP. Although the growth in GDP picked up since the mid-1970s and accelerated during the 1980s, the growth in employment did not pick up correspondingly. This was largely because a significant component of the GDP growth came from productivity growth. Further, the industries which grew faster were not employment-intensive.

2. Sectoral Employment Trends

The sector-wise distribution of employment growth shows that the long-term growth rate of employment in agriculture has been only about 1.5 per cent per annum during the 21 year-period, 1973-94, while that of employment in the non-agricultural sector and sub-sectors have been over 3 per cent (Table 2). GDP from the non-agricultural sector expanded at about 5.53 per cent per annum during this period while that from agriculture increased only at 3.01 per cent per annum, implying a faster growth of labour productivity in the non-agricultural sector. The non-agricultural sector with sizeable shares in total employment have in particular registered high employment growth rates: manufacturing employment (weight 9 per cent in 1973) has grown at 3.1 per cent per annum, trade (weight 5 per cent) at 4 per cent and services (weight 8 per cent) at 3.5 per cent per annum. Other sectors have registered even higher long-term growth rates of employment thereby improving their employment shares over the 21 year-period (Table 2).

Table 2
Employment Growth in Different Sectors, 1973 to 1994

(Per cent per annum)

Year	1973-78	1978-83	1983-88	1988-94	1973-94
Agriculture	1.88	1.42	0.40	2.01	1.54
Mining and quarrying	4.87	5.65	6.16	2.29	4.98
Manufacturing	5.83	2.92	2.62	1.70	3.06
Electricity, gas & water supply	12.48	4.27	6.60	3.08	5.66
Construction	1.96	6.85	13.84	-0.25	4.79
Trade	7.15	2.72	4.52	3.13	4.04
Transport, storage, etc.	6.31	5.02	2.99	4.07	4.39
Financial services	1.69	5.89	5.93	8.85	5.56
Other services	3.27	3.41	2.65	4.58	3.48
Non-agricultural sector	5.00	3.78	4.02	2.80	3.69
All sectors	2.73	2.13	1.58	2.29	2.19

Source: NSSO, Reports of the 27th, 32nd, 43rd and 50th round surveys on Employment and Unemployment.

Trends in the growth profile of employment in different sectors show that the period, 1988-94, has witnessed an acceleration of employment growth in the agricultural and non-agricultural sectors excluding construction. Employment growth rates declined during 1988-94 in the non-agricultural sector as a whole (including construction) and within this sector, in manufacturing and trade. The decline in the employment growth rate in the manufacturing sector and the non-agricultural sectors, as a whole, is part of a declining trend observed in the seventies and eighties. The reason why the level of construction employment in 1993-94 was more or less the same as in 1987-88, despite an accelerating GDP growth in this sector during 1988-94, is probably because of the temporary boost given to construction employment in 1987-88 due to drought relief works.

The long-term shift in the composition of the workforce in general away from agriculture has been far less than the shift in the structure of GDP. While the share of agriculture in employment declined from 74 per cent to only 65 per cent during the period, 1972-73 to 1993-94, the share of agriculture in GDP fell from 41 per cent to 30 per cent during the same period. In rural areas, the share of agriculture has declined from 85.6 per cent to 78.2 per cent— a decline of about 7 percentage points— during 1973-94. Overall, employment shares of the secondary and tertiary sectors have risen from 11 per cent and 15 per cent, respectively in 1972-73 to 14 per cent and 21 per cent, respectively in 1993-94. The employment share of the secondary sector has, however, increased only in rural areas (from 7 per cent to 10 per cent) and the share in urban areas has more or less been stagnant with the share of manufacturing in urban areas declining from 26 per cent in 1972-73 to 24 per cent in 1993-94. The share of rural non-farm employment has risen from 14 per cent in 1972-73 to about 22 per cent in 1993-94. The sector's share in female employment in rural areas has increased from 10 per cent to 14 per cent during the same period. The structure of rural non-farm employment has also shifted slightly in favour of the tertiary sector with sizeable improvements in the share of trade and transport within this sector.

3. Changes in Employment Status

There has been a distinct long-term shift in the structure of employment by employment status in favour of casual wage employment. In the rural areas the shift in the structure has been away from self-employment and to some extent from regular wage/salaried employment towards casual wage employment. On the other hand, the shift in the structure of urban employment has been away from regular wage/salaried employment towards casual wage employment. The shift in the structure of male employment has mostly been away from self-employment and regular wage employment towards casual wage employment and in the case of females from self-employment to casual wage employment and regular wage employment (Table 3).

The structural shifts are clearer if they are considered separately for rural and urban areas. In urban areas the shift in the structure of male employment has been away from regular wage employment towards casual wage employment. In rural areas this has been mostly away from regular wage employment towards casual wage employment. The overall structure of female employment has shifted away from self-employment largely towards casual wage employment and to a sizeable extent also towards regular wage employment. Most of the shift away from self-employment in urban areas has been towards regular wage employment while in rural areas it has been towards casual wage employment. The rise in the share of casual wage employment during 1988-94 has been larger in the case of females and in rural areas. Since casual wage employment as the usual principal status employment is certainly inferior in quality to regular wage employment from the point of view of employment security, income security and certain other benefits, it can be said that there has been a long-term deterioration in the quality of employment during 1978-94 among females and in rural areas. Likewise, there has been a very slight improvement in the quality of female employment in urban areas, although the share of regular wage employment in total female employment is still relatively very low (Table 3).

Table 3
Percentage Distribution of Workers (UPS) by Status of Employment

Status/year	Rural			Urban			Total		
	M	F	P	M	F	P	M	F	P
Self-employed									
1993-94	56.9	51.3	55.1	41.1	36.4	40.3	52.9	48.8	51.9
1987-88	57.5	54.9	56.7	41.0	39.3	40.5	53.8	53.1	53.6
1983	59.5	54.1	57.8	40.2	37.2	39.7	55.0	52.0	54.1
1977-78	62.2	56.3	60.4	39.9	42.2	40.3	57.9	54.8	57.0
Regular wage/salaried									
1993-94	8.5	3.4	7.2	42.7	35.5	41.5	17.0	8.3	14.7
1987-88	10.4	4.9	8.6	44.4	34.2	42.7	18.0	8.3	15.2
1983	10.6	3.7	8.5	44.5	31.8	42.2	18.5	7.3	15.3
1977-78	10.8	3.7	8.6	47.2	30.8	44.2	17.9	6.6	14.6
Casual employment									
1993-94	34.6	45.3	37.7	16.2	28.1	18.2	30.1	42.9	33.5
1987-88	32.1	40.2	34.7	14.6	26.5	16.8	28.2	38.6	31.2
1983	29.9	42.2	33.7	15.3	30.9	18.1	26.5	40.7	30.6
1977-78	27.0	40.0	31.0	12.9	27.0	15.5	24.2	38.6	28.4

Note: M-Male; F-Female; P-Persons.
Source: NSSO (1997).

4. Growth of Educated Employment

The rate of growth of employment of the educated, which had risen from 5.60 per cent per annum during 1978-83 to 7.13 per cent per annum during 1983-88, rose further to 7.20 per cent during 1988-94. The rate of growth of regular wage/ salaried educated employment, however, continued to stagnate at around 5 per cent during the periods, 1978-83, 1983-88 and 1988-94, while the rate of growth of educated self-employed and educated casual wage workers rose from period to period. As a result, the composition of educated employment has changed over the years. During 1988-94, the shift in the structure of employment has been from regular employment to self-employment and casual employment. Judging from the structure of educated employment and shifts therein the growth of educated employment seems more from the supply side than induced by demand. The sudden jump in the share of casual employment during 1988-94 at the expense of regular wage employment is a cause for concern (Table 4).

Table 4
Structure (by Employment Status) and Growth of UPS Educated Employment (15 Years+), 1978-94

	Structure (%)				Growth (% per annum)			
	1978	1983	1988	1994	1978-1983	1983-1988	1988-1994	1978-1994
Self-employed	38.4	38.9	42.5	46.2	5.87	9.29	8.71	7.88
Regular wage/ salaried employee	58.8	52.6	2.6	46.7	5.13	5.10	5.04	5.08
Casual wage labour	2.8	3.6	4.9	7.1	11.10	13.83	14.48	13.13
All educated employed	100.0	100.0	100.0	100.0	5.60	7.13	7.20	6.70

Source: As in Table 2.

5. Employment in Organised and Unorganised Sectors

The rate of employment expansion in the organised sector has declined in successive periods. The upturn seen in the rate of growth of overall employment during 1988-94 is not observed in organised sector employment. The growth rate of public sector employment has also declined with the decline being sharper during 1988-94 than during 1983-88. However, private sector employment, which recorded an absolute decline during 1983-88, made a modest recovery during 1988-94. Employment growth rates in all the non-agricultural sub-sectors of the organised sector, except mining and quarrying, manufacturing and trade, have declined in successive five-year periods. In the case of construction, the absolute level of employment fell during 1988-94. Organised manufacturing employment, which had recorded a decrease during the period, 1983-88 registered a modest rise during 1988-94. In the case of mining and quarrying, and trade the declining trend in employment growth has been halted during 1988-94 (Table 5).

Table 5
Growth in Organised Sector Employment, 1973-94

Sector	1973-78	1978-83	1983-88	1988-94
Agriculture	2.22	1.30	1.11	0.35
Mining and quarrying	5.20	2.56	0.88	1.04
Manufacturing	2.30	2.08	-0.09	0.40
Electricity, gas & water supply	3.27	3.67	3.26	1.58
Construction	-1.95	1.91	1.25	-0.62
Trade	-13.26	1.94	1.43	1.56
Transport, storage, etc.	1.62	2.25	1.20	0.42
Services	4.31	2.96	2.25	1.76
Total organised sector	2.45	2.48	1.38	1.05
Public sector	X	2.99	2.17t	1.00
Private sector	X	1.41	-0.43t	1.18

Source: DGET, Successive Annual and Quarterly Employment Review, Ministry of Labour, New Delhi.

Employment growth in the unorganised sector during 1988-94 was not only well above that during 1983-88, but was also such as to reverse the declining trend observed during the three quinquennia spanning the period 1973-88. Employment growth rate in the unorganised sector outside agriculture exhibited a declining trend over the years with the decline during 1973-78 and 1988-94 being very sharp. Within the non-agricultural sector, employment growth rate in transport, financial services and other services registered steep increase during 1988-94, while the rate of growth declined sharply in mining and quarrying, manufacturing and trade. The precipitous decline in the growth rate of construction employment during 1988-94 is largely due to the temporary boost to construction activity in 1987-88 due to drought relief works (Table 6).

6. Trends in Unemployment

Although since the early 1970s, there has been a long-term reduction in unemployment rate as a whole, albeit with fluctuations in different periods, the overall magnitude of unemployment, taking into account both open

Table 6
Growth of Employment (UPSS) in Unorganised Sector Outside Agriculture

Sector	1973-78	1978-83	1983-88	1988-94	1973-94
Mining & quarrying	3.38	11.30	9.64	3.30	7.23
Manufacturing	6.83	3.18	3.25	1.96	3.66
Construction	3.37	8.14	15.96	-0.21	6.17
Trade	8.06	2.74	4.58	3.16	4.46
Transport, storage, etc.	11.22	7.25	4.00	5.89	7.03
Financial services	NA	NA	7.81	16.06	NA
Other services	2.36	5.34	2.91	6.05	4.32
Non-agricultural sector	6.04	4.27	4.69	3.23	4.46
Non-ag. sector excl. construction	6.12	3.98	3.54	3.59	4.26
All sectors	2.74	2.12	1.59	2.40	2.22

Note: Derived from Tables 2 and 5.

unemployment and underemployment, has been rising since 1950s. This has been mainly because of a rise in the labour force.

Labour force increased from 162 million in 1951 to 319 million in 1992, that is, by about 97 per cent over the period, 1951-52, or at an annual average rate of 2.36 per cent per annum. The growth of the labour force has been higher than that of employment. As a result, the magnitude of unemployment has been steadily rising— it was estimated at 0.34 million in 1951, rose to 6.48 million by 1961, and further to 10.11 million by 1974. In 1992, it was estimated to be around 17 million. It showed a decline during 1960s only, as during 1961-69, employment growth was higher than the growth in labour force. The Ninth Plan (1997-2002) (Planning Commission, 1999) has estimated that the total magnitude of unemployment (unemployment plus underemployment) would be around 37 million in 1994. Though open unemployment and underemployment was only 2 per cent in 1993-94, the incidence of unemployment and underemployment taken together was over 10 per cent during that year. Thus, in 1997 the total magnitude (using the same rate of unemployment as in 1994) of unemployment would be around 40 million.

The structure of chronic open unemployment has changed significantly in favour of the educated. The share of the educated (15 years and above) unemployed in total unemployment has increased from 28.8 per cent in 1977-78 to 62 per cent in 1993-94. The increase has been steeper in the case of females—from 40 per cent in 1972-73 to 73 per cent in 1993-94 in urban areas and from 11 per cent to 59 per cent in rural areas during the same period. The gap between the "educated component" of rural male and rural female unemployment has considerably narrowed during the 20 year-period. In urban areas, the "educated component" of female unemployment has exceeded that of male unemployment.

7. The Problem of "Working Poor"

In India,, unemployment *per se* is not the main problem. The fact that the rate of unemployment, even taking into account both open unemployment and underemployment, is only about 10 per cent, whereas the percentage of people below poverty line is about 3.5 times higher, clearly shows that more than unemployment *per se,* the real problem is that of working poor. Although the percentage of poor has significantly declined over the years— from about 55 per cent in 1973-74 to about 35 per cent during 1993-94— the level is still extremely high. In fact, the percentage of people below the poverty line among the unemployed is much smaller than among the employed—in 1993-94 it was 18.5 per cent in case of unemployed compared to 34.3 per cent among the employed. There are more educated among the unemployed. They are unemployed because they have not been able to find work of a minimum income. On the other hand, the poor is willing to take up any work even at very low incomes or under extremely unhealthy conditions. Hence, the poor is less unemployed. Many people continue to work in the unorganised sector which is characterised by low earnings, poor working conditions and lack of social security protection. Figures given in Table 7 reveal that the incidence of poverty is the highest among agricultural labourers in rural areas and casual labourers in urban areas. Agricultural labourers in rural areas are also largely casual labouerers. It is among this category of workers that non-availability of work from time to time would be a major cause of low income and high incidence of poverty. As expected, in urban areas the regular wage/salary earners have the lowest incidence of poverty.

Table 7
Incidence of Poverty by Nature of Employment in 1993-94

Nature of work	Rural poverty (%)	Nature of work	Urban poverty (%)
Self-employed in agri.	29.05	Self-employed	34.68
Self-employed in non-agri.	31.95	Casual labour	61.80
Agricultural labour	56.78	Regular wage/salary earner	20.35
Other labour	39.60	Other households	27.85
Other households	22.48		

Thus, the above discussions show that in recent years some important changes have taken place in the structure of employment and labour market in India. While the growth of employment as a whole had declined during 1980s, it has shown some recovery in the early 1990s. However, employment has grown mostly in the unorganised sector of the economy and that in the organised sector has decelerated. Even the growth of educated employment has been mostly in the unorganised sector. All these point towards an overall decline in the quality of employment generated.

IV. JOB SECURITY FOR ORGANISED SECTOR WORKERS

As has been mentioned earlier, many of the provisions of social security for the workers were enacted even before Independence. During the post-Independence period these provisions were further strengthened and made more comprehensive through various legislative measures. These legislations are of mainly four types (Mathur, 1999):

(i) Labour welfare legislation: These legislations aim to provide basic decent working conditions, adequate safeguards against disease/affliction and some support beyond the working life span. They include a large number of legislative measures in areas covering compensation to workers in case of disability or death of a worker; provision of provident fund/pension to employees; maternity benefit in case of women workers; health insurance and medical benefits; regulation of working conditions like hours of work and minimum age of workers, etc.

(ii) Minimum wage legislation: In view of the extremely low levels of wages in many occupations, the Minimum Wage Act was enacted in 1948 and is applicable to a large number of occupations in addition to that for agricultural workers. Minimum wages fall within the jurisdiction of state governments and some of the progressive ones have extended its application beyond these scheduled types of employment enumerated in the Act. The stipulated level of minimum wage is fixed on the basis of subsistence level requirements and as such does not ensure anything beyond a bare minimum.

(iii) Job security legislation: The objective of these legislations is to provide not only avenues of employment but also some degree of stability to those already in employment. The 1976 legislation made it mandatory for enterprises employing 300 or more workers to seek government's permission before any enterprise could be closed. In addition, in the event of a closure being permitted, the enactment provides for compensation to retrenched workers at a specified rate. An amendment in 1987 further widened the scope of the Act by making it applicable to firms employing 100 or more workers.

(iv) Industrial relations legislation: These legislations pertain to various legislative and other measures governing trade union activity and the machinery for improving the state of industrial relations. They safeguard the rights of trade unions and provide a framework for maintaining industrial peace through detailed procedures of settlement of industrial disputes.

All the above legislative measures apply to the enterprises in the organised sector only, except the minimum wages which also covers the unorganised sector.

The legislative measures enacted in India have often been described as excessive and have been held responsible for slowing down the growth of employment by discouraging investment and growth. It has also been argued by many that as such protection is provided to only a small section of the workforce (nearly 8 per cent), the generation of employment will take place mostly in the unprotected unorganised sector with deplorable conditions of work and as a result, the proportion of protected workers would decline. In the process, the very objective of providing social protection to a large majority of workers, gets defeated.

In the earlier years of planning when the expectations of economic growth were higher and unemployment was thought to be not a serious problem, the issue did not draw much attention. However, with the significantly slow growth rate of employment in the organised sector during 1980s and also not so encouraging trends in 1990s the debate has intensified in recent years, more so after the introduction of economic reforms in early 1990s. It has been argued that overprotection to a small section of workers is not only inimical to growth of employment, but also goes against social justice as the number of workers with deplorable conditions of work is increasing. Of late, restrictive provisions in this regard have come under attack, as they are supposed to negate an 'exit policy' considered necessary for industrial restructuring and attracting foreign investment. In the wake of liberalisation, this problem has been brought into centerstage and there have been frequent demands by the industry and foreign investors to have some kind of 'exit policy'—the right of hiring and firing. In this respect the provisions of the Industrial Disputes Act which lay down conditions and procedures for retrenchment of workers have been widely criticised. It is contended that the provisions are so restrictive that reduction in workforce or closures is extremely difficult even if the employer agrees to pay the required compensation to retrenched workers, and to effect closures in the case of enterprises employing more than 100 workers are not generally granted the permission by the government (mostly state governments).

The issue has generated a considerable debate in the wake of declining manufacturing sector employment, particularly after 1980s. Scholars like Fallon and Lucas (1991) and Ahluwalia (1992) attributed the decline in manufacturing employment to the faster growth of industrial wages relative to consumer prices for industrial workers, abetted by union militancy and job security provisions, resulting in a significant long-term reduction of employment. Papola (1994), taking into account pros and cons of the employment generation vis-a-vis rigidities in the Indian labour market, has examined the issue in detail. Citing recent trends at disaggregated levels and findings of some studies, he has concluded that the real wage increase during 1980s does not seem to be important in promoting employers to opt for capital-intensive technologies which led to stagnation in employment in the Indian manufacturing industries. According to him, the real wage increase did not necessarily lead to higher unit labour cost that should have discouraged employers from expanding employment and resorting to labour-intensive techniques as high increases in real wages were generally closely associated with high increase in labour productivity across industry-groups. Although, the stringent job security regulation may be one of the reasons for the slower growth of employment, this may not be the sole or even major factor in restricting growth in employment in the organised manufacturing sector. An important reason for the decline in the growth of employment seems to be structural and technological characteristics of the industrial growth induced primarily by demand and efficiency considerations (Papola, 1994). That is why, manufacturing growth during the 1980s has been contributed mainly by capital-intensive sectors like chemicals, fertilisers, petroleum products and electrical machinery or by industries, though labour-intensive, having experienced rapid rate of technological change, such as food products. As a matter of fact, during the 1980s the economy as a whole including agriculture, became less and less employment-intensive as reflected in the declining employment elasticities in all the major sectors.

From the above discussions, one should not hasten to conclude that there is no rigidity in the Indian labour market. Irrespective of its impact on employment, a degree of protection to labour may lead to inflexibility in labour adjustment required for restructuring of enterprises in the interest of competitive efficiency. Although in spite of these obstacles, many enterprises were able to adjust their workforce by rationalisation and technological changes, the process has been tardy. Several routes have been found out—illegal closures by not paying electricity bills, etc. All these have only added to the problem of labour—they are neither paid their wages nor their due compensation. This has also resulted into significant industrial sickness as well as prevalence of redudancies leading to their uncompetitiveness. According to an estimate, the extent of redundant labour would be around 4.4 million in the organised sector as a whole (16.5 per cent of total employment in the sector) (ILO, 1996). Although unions have generally resisted to any legislature or executive move to make closure and retrenchment easier, in recent years, unions at enterprise level have generally found to be accepting the inevitability of adjustments in workforce in the face of globalisation and industrial restructuring.

Labour Redundancies and National Renewal Fund

The government has set up a mechanism in the form of an organisation called Board of Industrial and Financial Reconstruction (BIFR) to examine and decide whether the sick private and public sector enterprises could be revived with restructuring or have to close down. In the case of public sector enterprises, the pronounced policy of the government is to effect closures or retrenchments only as a last resort, after all avenues of reviving the unit and maintaining employment are exhausted. And where these measures are inevitable, a National Renewal Fund (NRF) has been constituted to enable enterprises to pay reasonable separation benefits, and assist the workers rendered redundant by their retraining and redeployment. The NRF has three parts: (a) an Employment Generation Fund (EGF) to provide resources for approved employment schemes, to regenerate employment opportunities for employees affected by industrial restructuring in the unorganised sector; (b) the National Renewal Fund (NRF) to deal with the immediate requirements of labour in sick units arising from revival or closure of such units; (c) an Insurance Fund for Employees (IFE) to deal with the future changes in employment structure in the context of changes in technology and modernisation.

While the main objective of NRF was to help in retraining, counselling and redeployment of affected workers, and also employment generation, both in organised and unorganised sectors of the economy, a major part of the NRF expenditure was utilised for compensation payments under Voluntary Retirement Scheme (VRS). The total expenditure on VRS so far has been Rs. 2391.94 crores. A very small amount has been used for retraining. Up to October 31, 1998, about 91,288 workers were surveyed, of which 46,994 were counselled, 33,242 retrained and only 10,215 redeployed (Government of India, 1999,). It is worth noting that only a quarter of the VRS availees were retrained and merely 8 per cent could be redeployed.

Displacement of a large number of workforce through the mechanism of VRS without equipping them with adequate skill and training to re-enter in the job market, has resulted in a huge loss of productive manpower. Though, no major study has been undertaken to follow up the post VRS vocation of the labour, a few studies have pointed out that a majority of these redundant workers have joined the unorganised sector as 'new poor' (Roy Choudhary, 1996). Roy Choudhary finds that 25 per cent of the displaced workers who are working as casual labourers, are not employed even for a full week. Displaced workers also face income loss—the average income of those re-employed dropped by about 44 per cent (Noronha, 1999). This is a social waste of human potential and raises question about the "training" objective of the NRF.

All these point out that retraining for redeployment of displaced workers should be seen as a social safety net and be assessed in terms of its efficacy in reducing the period of unemployment, enhancing or maintaining the income level of displaced workers and equipping them for sustainable employment in industrial environments which may increasingly require different and higher levels of skills. Thus, it is necessary to provide retraining well before the workers are out of work. In effect, retraining should be considered to be an extension of placement efforts.

Unfortunately, the overall performance of retraining for redeployment under NRF has also been less than desirable. A small proportion of VRS availees (25 per cent) opted for training. This is a matter of concern because it shows that retraining is not perceived as a skill improvement strategy for redeployment. Counselling may also act as an important factor in popularising retraining, though in some cases it has been restricted only to giving advice regarding optimum utilisation of VRS funds received. An important factor responsible for the limited interest in training can be the time that elapsed between displacement and availability of counselling. Counselling should, therefore, begin early—ideally, right from the time when those potentially affected by retrenchment have been identified.

All this makes it extremely desirable to strengthen the retraining activities as a measure of social safety net. At the outset, the focus of retraining should not be "just some other skills for employment but enhancing core skills and intellectual skills of the workers which make them more flexible, adaptable and useful to the changing pattern of production." As more and more industrial firms undertake restructuring and start operating in leading edge technologies, the requirement of enhancing the core skills and higher order cognitive skills would become more important. This is a basic requirement not only for retraining but, even more importantly, for the initial training system. Sustainability of employment will depend on this focus (Chandra, 1999).

V. SECURITY PROVISIONS FOR THE WORKERS IN THE UNORGANISED SECTOR

As has been pointed out earlier, the unorganised sector workers are largely insecure and unprotected. Although the government has attempted to provide protection and promotional measures they are only very few. The important measures are as follows:

1. Minimum Wage Legislation

The most important protective measure is the introduction of the minimum wages legislation. Under the Minimum Wage Act, 1948, both the central and state governments have set minimum wages for agriculture as well as for a range of occupations in unorganised industries, which are thought to be particularly vulnerable to "exploitation". There are a fairly large number of occupations for which minimum wages are currently fixed. Though the different state governments have revised the minimum wages from time to time, the wages fixed are still very low. In most of the cases the government while fixing statutory minimum wages have apparently not taken into consideration the minimum requirements of a worker's family to rise above the poverty line (Bhagat, 1997). Worse still, even these bare subsistence level wages, in overwhelmingly large number of occupations across various regions of the country, have not been enforced. Nor has adequate attention been paid to treat minimum wages as an important instrument of employment security and poverty alleviation. On the contrary, it has been argued that higher and stricter enforcement of minimum wages may lead to a rise in prices which may erode the real gains of higher wages; and further that it may reduce the demand for labour consequent to rise in real wages. Ghoshe (1997), while examining the issue in depth, strongly refutes these arguments and finds that they are not really relevant in the context of India. In fact, the minimum wages, even at very low levels and poor reinforcements, have served some useful purpose. First, in many regions they have set the floor level wages. They have a role in pushing wages upwards in slack seasons and in depressed areas including the wages of women. They have also contributed to the strengthening of the bargaining power of labour (Parathasarthy, 1997).

There have been strong and persistent demands from several quarters for wider coverage of minimum wage legislation, higher levels of revisions and stricter enforcement of minimum wages so that they serve the objective of poverty alleviation for the large number of casual workers in agriculture, unorganised industries and services in the country who belong to the poorest segment of the population—they are poor in an absolute sense and low wages is the principal cause of their poverty. Organisations like National Centre for Labour are campaigning for the enactment of a national level legislation on minimum wages which takes into account the minimum wages equivalent to the norms for the poverty line. While it is true that there are problems in the enforcement of this legislation, this should not be cited as an excuse for the non-implementation of the Act. The revised rates and provisions of the Act could be widely publicised throughout the country through media, and village panchyats may be activated towards their implementation. Their wide publicity can become a rallying point for organising the unorganised workers. Further, determined efforts should be made to use the existing labour inspection machinery of the government to enforce the provisions of the Minimum Wages Act. And, of course, the government must ensure that the officially announced minimum wages are paid in all government-sponsored activities like special employment programmes, public works, etc. (Ghoshe, 1997).

2. Welfare Funds

In order to extend a measure of social assistance to the workers in the unorganised sector, several legislations have been enacted by the Government of India to set up five welfare funds in the Ministry of Labour to provide housing, medical care, educational and recreational facilities to workers employed in *beedi* industry, certain non-coal mines and cine workers. Alongside, efforts have been made towards substantially expanding the application of welfare fund approach to cover categories and sub-categories of workers in the unorganised sector.

The scheme of welfare funds is outside the framework of specific employer-employee relationship in as much as the resources are raised by the government on a non-contributory basis and delivery of services is effected without relating to individual worker's contribution. Apart from the welfare funds set up by the central government, various state governments have also formulated welfare programmes and are implementing these through funds created by them for certain categories of unorganised labour.

In India, the ideal example of social security benefits in the unorganised sector that is often quoted is the welfare fund for *beedi* workers. *Beedi* making is a well-regulated trade because it is a very old activity and a specific Act, i.e., the Beedi and Cigar Workers Act, exists for regulating it. This welfare fund is regulated by a tripartite body consisting of the representatives of government, employers and workers. Identity cards (ID) are provided to the workers, who receive minimum wages. Education of children is supported through scholarships and money is provided for the purchase of uniforms for their children. Charges of hospitalisation, insurance in case of sudden death, travel facilities for recreation of the worker are some of the benefits extended to the workers. However, provident fund/pension is not included in the benefits provided and this issue has been taken up for consideration by the government (Unni, undated).

Very often it is asked: how can such social security benefits be funded? The *beedi* worker's welfare fund has been a success because it is funded through a cess of tax on the commodity. Similar options for the benefits for other workers have to be devised. Here again a mix of public and private sector responsibility may be most appropriate—the government, industry (employers) and workers, contributing to a social security fund. The modus operandi for such a fund and its disbursement is of course, crucial if the benefits are to accrue to the most insecure groups in the labour market (Unni, ibid).

Although the welfare funds have played an important role in minimising risks associated with the occupations of such workers, their coverage is very small in comparison to the vast number of workers in the unorganised sector, particularly those involved in home-based work. Obviously, similar funds for other trades and for contract workers should be devised. Moreover, these measures are far from adequate for providing some minimum income to such workers in the unorganised sector. As such, there is no alternative to implement the appropriate support system in the form of training, credit, appropriate technology, etc., for the large number of home-based workers and micro enterprises both in rural and urban areas. There are many examples of proper support system along with organisation of workers that have contributed to the growth of income of such workers/enterprises in several parts of the country. SEWA is one telling example of such an initiative but there are others as well.

3. Major Anti-poverty and Employment Programmes

A number of poverty alleviation and employment programmes have been operational in India, particularly since the beginning of the 1980s. Some basic features of each of these major programmes and an overview of their performance are attempted below, as a backdrop to an assessment of their adequacy in the present-day context .

(i) Self-employment Programmes

(a) Integrated Rural Development Programme

The programme was formally started in the year 1980-81, though it was initiated in 1977-78 in a limited form. From April 1999, it has been restructured and merged with Swarn Jayanti Gram Swarojgar Yojana (SGSY). It provides support to the rural households below the poverty line, with a package of assistance consisting of a subsidy and a bank loan to enable them to acquire productive assets like livestock, manufacturing and processing equipment and business space. Its also stipulates a minimum coverage of disadvantaged groups and women. In order to provide training support for self-employment under the programme and to provide special focus on women and children, two sub-programmes allied to IRDP, namely, Training of Rural Youth for Self-employment (TRYSEM) and Development of Women and Children in Rural Areas (DWCRA) were also put in the operation.

Since the initiation of the programme till 1998-99, a total sum of Rs. 137 billion has been spent as subsidy by union and state governments under IRDP. Around 54 million households have been provided assistance so far. The average level of investment per beneficiary household was about Rs. 3,000 during 1980-85, about Rs. 9,000 during 1992-95 and about Rs. 18,377 during 1998-99, which was about 40 per cent in the form of government subsidy. The average investment per family in real terms did not increase much particularly after the reforms.

The programme, as envisaged in its design, has succeeded to some extent in reaching the poor and amongst them the more disadvantaged groups like the Scheduled Castes (SC) and Scheduled Tribes (ST). According to the concurrent evaluation of the programme, about 88 per cent of the assisted families belonged to the destitute and very poor groups as per official records of their pre-assistance income, but the percentage of assisted families in these two groups was about 47 according to the assessment at the time of the evaluation (Government of India, 1990). The evaluation revealed that 15.96 per cent of the old beneficiaries families could cross the revised poverty line of Rs. 11,000 while 54.4 per cent of the families were able to cross the old poverty line of Rs. 6,400. But the analysis by income-group of families revealed that in case of those within initial income of Rs. 8,501-11,000, 48.2 per cent of beneficiary families could cross the poverty line of Rs. 11,000, which is quite encouraging. The concurrent evaluation also shows that a poor individual beneficiary under IRDP without any skill or experience could not improve his income, and those who did succeed, possessed better skill. The rate of success is higher where individual beneficiaries have formed a group. It is easier to organise a better training for such group. The experience of DWACRA in Andhra Pradesh has been widely thought to be a successful one. IRDP has been more successful in those regions where both infrastructure and markets were well developed. The evaluation shows that indebtedness has increased among the IRDP beneficiaries which raises doubts about the viability of the projects in generating adequate employment and income.

The programme also suffered from certain serious limitations as an effective instrument to raise the income levels of assisted households substantially and permanently to lift them above the poverty line. First, though the programme is termed as integrated, it is, in fact, not at all integrated with other development programmes of the area and thus tends to ignore input and market linkages and infrastructure requirements of assisted activities. For instance, only 3 per cent of IRDP beneficiaries received training under TRYSEM and only 23 per cent of those trained under TRYSEM were assisted under IRDP in 1992-93 as per the evaluation of the Ministry of Rural Development. Second, in relation to the requirements of meeting a quantitative target in terms of the number of families covered, the identification of activities and projects often tends to be arbitrary, and viability and sustainablity aspects are often neglected. Third, the provision of outright cash subsidy often leads to misappropriation of benefits due to lack of a stake and interest from the beneficiaries. Fourth, there was an implicit assumption that the prospective beneficiaries possessed information and skills to be able to choose viable options, had access to raw materials and were aware of markets. These are the disabilities from which the poor suffer which the IRDP did not take into account, particularly those relating to the community decision making. Fifth, there are bureaucratic red-tapism and delays at several levels of implementation of the programme.

(b) Swarna Jayanti Gram Swarozgar Yojana

With the addition of several programmes, viz., TRYSEM, DWACRA, Supply of Improved Toolkits to Rural Artisan (SITRA) and Ganga Kalyan Yojana (GKY) in IRDP over the years, there has been a complete lack of sectoral integration in their implementation as each one started operating as an individual programme and focussed entirely on achieving its own goals. With a view to ensuring sectoral integration and making poverty alleviation programmes more meaningful, these are merged into a simple Programme—the Swarna Jayanti Gram Swarozgar Yojana (SGSY), with effect from 1st April, 1999.

The SGSY aims at establishing a large number of micro enterprises in the rural areas with an emphasis on the 'cluster' approach. In each of the block four to five key activities are to be identified based on their resource endowments, occupational skills and the availability of markets. The results of evaluation of the scheme are yet to be known. However, since SGSY is still a credit-cum-subsidy programme, it is feared that the scheme may face similar difficulties as in the case of IRDP unless the old loopholes and shortcomings are removed effectively.

(ii) Wage Employment Programmes

Short-term wage employment on public works has been an old and conventional device used by governments to provide relief to the poor households from the hardships caused by drought, flood and other natural calamities. The first major programme called "Food for Work" was initiated in India during the 1970s. Subsequently, National Rural Employment Programmes (NREP) and Rural Landless Employment Guarantee Programme (RLEGP) were started with the objectives of providing gainful employment to unemployed and underemployed and building community assets and rural infrastructure.

(a) Jawahar Rozgar Yojana and Employment Assurance Scheme

The experience of implementation of NREP and RLEGP showed that the large investments made in generating employment did not yield commensurate returns in terms of creation of durable and useful assets. Even on the employment generation front, the administrative procedures were not cost-effective and thus a sizeable part of the funds got utilised in overheads. With a view to remove some of these shortcomings a new programme, Jawahar Rozgar Yojana (JRY), was launched on April 1, 1989 by merging NREP and RLEGP. Some basic changes in the *modus operandi* of the implementation were also introduced. The basic objectives of the programme, however, remained the same, except that the creation of additional employment opportunities for the unemployed and underemployed was emphasised as a *primary objective*, and creation of sustained employment by strengthening rural economic infrastructure and also that of assets in favour of the rural poor and improvements in the quality of life in rural areas as a *secondary objective*. A major change introduced in JRY in 1993-94 in comparison with the earlier programmes, was that funds based on pre-determined criteria would be provided to every village panchayat for utilisation towards employment generation in various works within the village to be decided by the village panchayat itself based on the overall guidelines provided by the central and state governments. Since the inception of JRY, 7596.16 million man-days of employment have been generated up to March 1998. The total expenditure during the same period was about Rs. 309 billion.

The Employment Assurance Scheme (EAS) was launched on 2nd October, 1993 in identified backward blocks situated in the drought-prone areas, desert areas, tribal areas and hill areas. Initially it covered 1,772 blocks in the country. The scheme provides for assured employment of up to 100 days during the lean agricultural season to those seeking work, and the work would be of an unskilled manual type. The secondary objective is the creation of economic infrastructure and community assets for sustained employment and development. Since April, 1997, the scheme is being implemented in all the 5,448 rural blocks of the country. Persons above 18 years and below 60 years of age who need and seek employment under the EAS are required to register themselves in the village panchayats where they are residing. They have to be provided work within the area of the block where they are residing, if employment is not available within that panchayat area itself. The wages paid to the workers under the EAS are the minimum agricultural wages for unskilled labourers fixed by the state government concerned.

EAS has been restructured in 1999-2000. It is now an allocation based scheme under which the funds are shared by the centre and state in the ratio of

75:25. The allocation of funds to the state is made on the basis of incidence of poverty and district-wise allocation within a state on the basis of the index of backwardness.

According to a concurrent evaluation by the Ministry of Rural Development during 1993-94, per person about 11 days of employment were generated by JRY during the reference period of 30 days preceding the date of survey. In some poorer states like Madhya Pradesh and Orissa, JRY workers got work for less than 10 days per month. Since the average employment per participant is low at about 11 days in a month and at wage rates of Rs. 33.36 per day, it would mean a supplementary monthly income of Rs. 369 to the household—earning about 40 per cent of the poverty line threshold. Thus, JRY seems to have contributed substantially to the family income of the poor. The concurrent evaluation also shows that the selection of beneficiaries was largely as per the criteria 82 per cent of the JRY workers were poor. However, there are large variations across the states. The percentage of non-poor beneficiaries was quite high in Punjab (56 per cent), Andhra Pradesh (51.7 per cent), Bihar (22 per cent), Karnataka (34 per cent), Kerala (32 per cent) and Uttar Pradeh (30.2 per cent). Among the major weaknesses of the programme as pointed by the concurrent evaluation of Ministry of Rural Development (1993-94) are the delay in the completion of works owing to lack of funds (47 per cent works), non-adherence to the guidelines for providing 30 per cent employment to women (women's share in employment generated was 16.6 per cent) , etc.

The conflict between the employment generation and asset creation objectives, common to all wage employment programmes, has assumed greater significance in the case of JRY, particularly in view of its large outlays. It is, therefore, argued that while the provision of additional gainful employment to the rural poor is the primary objective of the programme and is being met to a significant extent, it is desirable to ensure that such large outlays help simultaneously create useful community and productive assets for sustaining development and employment generation in rural areas.

With an objective to develop village infrastructure, JRY has been strengthened and restructured as Jawahar Gram Samridhi Yojna (JGSY) with effect from 1st April, 1999. The primary objective of JGSY is creation of village infrastructure including durable assets at the village level and assets to enable the rural poor to increase the opportunities of sustainable employment. Another objective is to generate supplementary employment for the unemployed rural poor. Though there is no sectoral earmarking of resources under JGSY, 22.5 per cent of allocation must be spent on schemes for SC/ST families living below poverty line and 3 per cent for creation of barrier-free infrastructure for the disabled. Nearly 30 per cent of employment opportunities are to be reserved for women. Under the programme, each village panchayat has to prepare an annual plan, which shall be approved by the *Gram Sabha*. Priority will be given to the completion of incomplete works. The village panchayats are empowered to execute work schemes up to Rs. 50,000 without seeking any technical approval.

As regards EAS, its success in providing employment has been rather limited. According to Controller and Auditor General's Third Report of 1995, the EAS provided 18 days and 16 days of employment during 1994-95 and 1995-

96, respectively. The evaluation of EAS by PEO of the Planning Commission shows that the scheme provided about 31 days of employment and benefited about one-fourth of the job-seekers under it. The scheme also suffered from several limitations, e.g., bogus reporting, providing employment without assets entailing the risk of again falling below poverty line, etc. It has been suggested by many that in order to improve efficacy of the programme and ensure that the poor and unemployed get up to 100 days of employment in lean agricultural season, the programme should be restricted to backward areas characterised by poor agriculture, chronic poverty and hunger.

(b) Employment Guarantee Scheme (Maharashtra)

Besides the major rural employment and poverty alleviation programmes sponsored by the Government of India, described above, a unique initiative for guaranteeing gainful employment was taken up in the state of Maharashtra in the early seventies and is in operation since then. Aimed at providing gainful and productive employment to the people in the rural areas and small towns who are prepared to do manual work but cannot find it on their own, the Employment Guarantee Scheme (EGS) guarantees work to any person above the age of 18 years normally residing in the villages requiring work. The work can be provided anywhere within the district of the applicant's residence though it is normally provided within eight kms of the residence of the job-seeker. The guarantee is restricted to only the unskilled manual work. Failure to provide work creates a liability on the state to pay an unemployment allowance. The scheme is self-targeting in nature and is totally financed by the state government through a special levy. The wages are paid on a piece-rate basis, but are so fixed for different items of work that an average person working diligently for seven hours a day will earn an amount equal to the minimum wages prescribed for agricultural labour in that area under the Minimum Wages Act.

The total expenditure on EGS has also increased over the years. It dipped marginally in the late eighties and hovered around Rs. 250 crores, but in the nineties it has been in the range of Rs. 350 to 400 crore reaching a peak of Rs. 452 crore in 1992-93. During 1996-97 it was Rs. 366.75 crore. However, in real terms (deflated by SDP deflator) the EGS expenditure has been almost stagnant or slightly decreasing (Ranade, 1998). The wage component of expenditure remained high in the earlier years and declined to as low as 50 per cent in 1988-89, but rose to a level of 75.98 per cent in 1995-96. The main reason for this trend is that capital costs are increasing much faster than wage rates.

Employment generated was the highest at 205 million person-days in 1979-80, remained in the range of 130 to 190 million person-days during 1980-1988 and has been between 80 and 95 million during 1989-97, except 148 million in 1992-93. Thus, the magnitude of employment generated has, of course, not increased correspondingly on account of the rise in cost per person-day of employment generated. The real cost per person-day increased during the 1980s. However, it did not increase in the 1990s (Ranade, 1998).

The EGS, it is generally agreed, has made a somewhat significant impact on the current employment and unemployment situation in rural Maharashtra. A rough estimate for 1991 suggests that without about 90 million person-days of employment generated under EGS, unemployment in rural Maharashtra would have been around 254 million person-days, and thus EGS reduced the magnitude of unemployment by 3.5 per cent and daily status unemployment rate by 1.69 per cent—from 4.82 per cent to 3.13 per cent of labour force. Various evaluation studies show that EGS by itself may not have enabled the participating households to cross the poverty line, but it has raised income levels of the participating households to a significant extent. Thus, the programme should be assessed on the basis of the criterion of reducing the severity of poverty rather than the head count incidence of poverty, and on that score, it has contributed significantly as is indicated by a substantial supplementation made by it to the incomes of the poor households (Datt and Ravallion, 1991; Mahendra Dev, 1992). In addition, it has brought several indirect benefits. These include: (a) the creation of rural assets; (b) an upward pressure on agricultural wages; (c) an insurance for the rural workers; (d) expansion of the right to work for the rural women, and (e) making employment an entitlement enabling collective political action by the poor, and facilitating political mobilisation (Mahendra Dev and Ranade, 1996). Thus, the EGS has benefited the poor in terms of employment and income, notwithstanding its defects like leakages to non-poor and prevalence of corruption among officials and contractors.

(iii) Urban Employment and Anti-poverty Programmes

Special programmes for employment generation and poverty alleviation in India have concentrated mostly in rural areas as the major problem of the poverty exists in these areas. Over the years, it has been realised that poverty in urban areas is as persistent as in rural areas even though its magnitude is smaller. The unemployment rates as revealed by NSSO surveys has always been higher in urban areas than in rural areas. Studies also show that urban poverty is relatively high among self-employed households which account for about two-fifths of urban population. It was, therefore, decided to initiate some anti-poverty and employment generation programmes in urban areas as well. The first initiative in this direction was taken in 1986 with the introduction of the Self Employment Programme for Urban Poor (SEPUP). It provided assistance to the urban households living below the poverty line for starting self-employment ventures on the basis of a bank loan up to Rs. 5,000 of which 25 per cent was to be a government subsidy. During the four years, 1986-90, as many as 9 lakh persons were assisted under the programme, with a total capital subsidy of Rs. 1.2 billion from the government and Rs. 3.7 billion of bank loans. The programme was scaled down as the banks through which it was implemented showed scant interest in it.

(a) Nehru Rozgar Yojana

A major initiative in promoting urban employment was taken in 1989 with the introduction of the Nehru Rozgar Yojana (NRY). It aims at providing employment to the urban unemployed and underemployed poor, through wage work and self-employment ventures as well as upgradation of housing of the poor. The earlier scheme (SEPUP) was merged into NRY, with effect from 1992-93. The NRY consists of the following three schemes:

(i) Scheme of Urban Micro Enterprises (SUME): Under this scheme, the unemployed and underemployed persons belonging to poor families are encouraged to set up small enterprises in service, petty business and manufacturing. The assistance is given on a bank loan-cum-subsidy basis. The scheme is applicable in all urban settlements.

(ii) Scheme of Urban Wage Employment (SUWE): Under this scheme, wage employment is sought to be provided to the unemployed and underemployed persons from poor families in public works in urban settlements with less than 1 lakh population. The works to be undertaken are to be decided by urban local bodies and could be in the nature of construction of public utilities.

(iii) Scheme of Employment through Housing and Shelter Upgradation (SHASU): This scheme aims at improving the shelters of the urban poor through repair, construction and additions to their existing housing units. The assistance consists of government subsidy of 25 per cent of the cost subject to a ceiling of Rs. 1,000 and loan from the Housing and Urban Development Corporation (HUDCO), at a concessional rate of interest and with a repayment period of 10 years. The scheme is applicable to urban settlements with a population of lakh to two million.

It may be noted that even if the envisaged targets fulfilled and the programmes were effectively implemented, the coverage of the programme would still be too meagre in relation to the magnitude of the problem in urban areas. The total wage employment generation in terms of person-days under NRY accounted for only about 2 per cent of the estimated 1,492 million person-days of unemployment in urban areas in 1990. It may, however, be noted that all urban unemployment cannot be sought to be tackled through wage employment in public works. A large part of the urban unemployed are educated and openly unemployed looking for regular full-time work. The need and scope for wage employment programmes like the rural JRY are limited in urban areas, but self-employment offers a substantial scope in urban settlements, particularly in the informal sector. The SUME scheme under NRY seems to be a very limited attempt in this regard in relation to the magnitude of unemployment.

(b) Swarna Jayanti Shahri Rozgar Yojana

Swarna Jayanti Shahri Rozgar Yojana (SJSRY) was launched in April, 1999 subsumming the earlier urban poverty alleviation programmes, viz., Nehru Rozgar Yojana (NRY), Urban Basic Services for the Poor (UBSP) and Prime Minister's Integrated Urban Poverty Eradication Programme (PMIUPEP). The objective of the scheme is to provide gainful employment to the urban unemployed or underemployed poor through encouraging them to set up self-employment ventures or provision of wage employment. There are two schemes under SJSRY—the Urban Self-Employment Programme (USEP) and the Urban Wage Employment Programme (UWEP).

USEP has three distinct components: (i) assistance to individual urban poor for setting up of gainful self-employment ventures; (ii) assistance to group of urban poor women for self-employment—the scheme is called Development of Women and Children in the Urban Areas (DWCUA); and

(iii) training of beneficiaries, and other persons associated with the urban employment programme for upgradation and acquisition of vocational and entrepreneurial skills.

(c) Prime Minister's Rozgar Yojana

Prime Minister's Rozgar Yojana (PMRY) was launched in urban areas during 1993-94, and the most important national level scheme for promotion of self-employment launched earlier, i.e., Self-Employment for the Educated Unemployed Youth (SEEUY), has been subsumed in it since then. PMRY is now extended to rural areas from 1994-95. The objective of the scheme is to provide self-employment opportunities in industry, business and services to one million educated unemployed youth. The scheme is applicable to youth in the age-group of 18 to 35 years, who have passed or failed in matriculation examination or qualified from ITI or who have undergone a government-sponsored technical course for a minimum duration of six months, and have a family income not exceeding Rs. 24,000 per annum from all sources. The entrepreneur is required to contribute 5 per cent of the project cost as margin money and the balance of 95 per cent would be sanctioned as composite loan by banks without any collateral guarantee. The central government would provide subsidy at the rate of 15 per cent of the project cost subject to a ceiling of Rs. 7,500 per individual. During the first year of its implementation (1993-94), 32,000 cases were sanctioned against a target of 40,000. The target for 1994-95 was 2.20 lakh against which, about 1.77 lakh cases were sanctioned. For the year 1997-98, the target was 2.20 lakh and 2.61 lakh cases were sanctioned and 1.57 lakh cases were disbursed. The target for 1998-99 is 2.20 lakh beneficiaries.

An evaluation of PMRY (IAMR, 2000) revealed that PMRY generates employment for about 2.4 persons per unit. Though many more youth are seeking assistance under PMRY, almost half of the total applications are rejected by the taskforce committees of the district industries centres, mainly due to inadequate technical skills. Also, there is a lack of public campaigns focussing on various aspects of PMRY like eligibility, funds availability, skill requirement, market, etc.

4. Adequacy of Existing Programmes in the Context of Economic Reforms

The approach of the government in providing a safety net to the poor against the possible adverse effects of the structural adjustment programme has generally been that of treating it as an integral part of the overall poverty alleviation strategy. Poverty, in any case, is a widespread phenomenon, and the objective of minimising the hardships of the poor during the period of structural adjustment would best be met by ensuring that the overall strategy and programmes for poverty alleviation are suitably revamped and expanded. Given the vast magnitude of poverty, unemployment and underemployment, it would not be feasible to remove them through direct government expenditure. Such expenditure should be enhanced to the extent that resources permit and the coverage of existing programmes should be substantially expanded. But the extent to which poverty could generally be alleviated and adverse effects of structural adjustment on the poor could be mitigated would primarily depend on the pace at which the generation of productive employment opportunities is accelerated. And that, in turn, would depend on how quickly the economy can attain a high and sustainable growth rate. Fortunately, India has been able to quickly absorb the shock of adjustment and the growth rate of the economy has been over 6 per cent during the last few years. However, there are certain developments in the labour market like rise in casualisation and informalisation of the economy which are disquieting. Although poverty levels have not risen in India during reforms, it continues to be high and hence there is need for the continuation of direct measures for poverty alleviation and employment generation.

The strategy adopted for tackling the issues of poverty and unemployment is a two-track one in which the benefits of normal growth process are supplemented by social safety nets. This seems inescapable at least as long as the present high levels of poverty persist. As Bhagwati (1988) points out, the optimal strategy for poverty alleviation is bound to be a mixed strategy involving some consideration of the direct and indirect approaches. A question that is sometimes raised in this context relates to the relative efficacy of the two tracks in this strategy. Special employment programmes like JRY claim investible resources which could otherwise have contributed to the growth process. A study on costs and benefits of the rural works programme in India has indicated that the benefits accruing from such employment programmes contribute directly to the growth process, thereby reducing the force of the "growth foregone" argument.

The importance of these programmes also lies in their contribution in holding the wage rate and in creating some infrastructure in the rural areas thereby adding to the existing stock of infrastructure every year. In wage employment programmes, the emphasis has been more on employment creation than on the building up of infrastructure of a durable or productive type. Although in recent years there has been some changes in the approach to infrastructure building, emphasis on creation of durable infrastructure is still rather weak. The creation of infrastructure particularly minor irrigation, watershed development and roads will enhance agricultural productivity and thereby increase employment in agriculture on a more sustainable basis. In the face of persistence of high levels of poverty along with increasing casualisation of labour market, this kind of safety-net mechanism seems to be desirable, but its linkage with the growth process is also essential.

However, an all-out effort is needed to streamline and strengthen the delivery mechanism of these anti-poverty and employment programmes so as to improve their better targeting and effectiveness. Often the absence of proper coordination among different programmes has been pointed out as an important reason behind the poor performance of these programmes. The government's recent efforts in merging the several programmes may be an attempy to remove this lacuna to some extent.

Another important reason behind the unsatisfactory performance of these anti-poverty and special employment programmes has been lack of people's participation. It has often been said that the approach in implementing these programmes seems to be more technocratic and top-down with poor delivery systems. However, an important landmark in the 1990s is the 73rd and 74th amendments to the Constitution bringing about significant decentralisation by providing for a system of local government based on mandatory elections. This provides an opportunity to strengthen the panchayats to effectively implement the various anti-poverty employment schemes. The panchayats must serve as the principal agencies of programme implementation. The experiences of implementing such schemes in West Bengal and Karnataka have shown that there is enormous potential in this regard. However, the success achieved through decentralisation will depend to a large extent on whether acute inequalities in endowments have been eliminated. In such a setting, the panchayats would be free from the domination of rich and powerful landlords and would be more responsive to the needs of the rural poor. Further, careful consideration should be given to concentrate these programmes in the more depressed regions and states where poverty is endemic rather than spread them thinly in all areas of the country. Some agriculturally developed states and districts have very little utility of rural works programmes. They have, though, a low incidence of poverty, and relatively high unemployment rates in these areas are mainly accounted for by the openly educated unemployed, who are unlikely to opt for work in a wage employment programme.

VII. SUMMING UP: TOWARDS A COMPREHENSIVE EMPLOYMENT SECURITY

On the basis of the foregoing discussion we may provide some elements of a system of employment security in India. Based on the analysis of trends and patterns of employment and labour market, a few broad characteristics of the Indian labour market may be noted, which are relevant in the context of providing employment security. First, in India, most people are employed, as per the time-disposition criterion---the rate of open unemployment on usual status basis is only around 2 per cent (even if we add the underemployed, another 8.4 per cent, the total proportion of unemployed/underemployed adds up to only a little over 10 per cent). However, though most people are employed, the incomes of a large proportion of them are extremely low. Obviously, much of the employment is not adequately productive or remunerative. Second, employment is largely concentrated in the unorganised sector, which accounts for about 92 per cent of the total workforce in the country. The workers in the organised sector (about 8 per cent), are mostly covered by the various social security provisions. On the other hand, the unorganised sector is largely insecured. An overwhelming proportion of workers are self-employed, which comprises a large number of home-based workers also. As such, there is no clear-cut employer-employee relationship in this form of employment. Third, insecurity of income is a characteristic feature of many types of employment. For example, for a casual labourer although the daily wage rate tends to be institutionally fixed, the number of days of employment in a year is uncertain, and consequently, the level of earnings also remains uncertain. In varying degrees, this kind of uncertainty also affects others such as the self-employed with a slender asset-base, regular employees in the informal sector, etc. Fourth, there is wide discrimination in the labour market. Access to employment as well as income from employment tend to depend on the social background of the labour market participant. Though the level of education and skills largely determine employment and earnings, they, in turn, are largely determined by their social background. Further, even where the education and skill levels are similar, factors such as gender, caste/tribe, religion, etc., become important determinants of access to employment and the level of remuneration. This is clearly evident from the case of gender-based discrimination—women clearly have a lower probability of finding employment and of earning the same remuneration from a specific employment than men with equal educational and skill levels. Fifth, there are some socially unacceptable forms of employment like child labour and bonded labour. Although their incidence has declined in recent years, India still has the dubious distinction of having the highest number of child workers in the world. Finally, there is a large section of people, constituting probably the most vulnerable group, who are not integrated or very loosely connected with the mainstream of development. They comprise mostly independent producers/service providers, both in rural and urban areas, such as pavement-dwellers and rag-pickers in the urban areas, landless and very small peasants in the rural areas, forest-dwellers, etc. Such people have limited market contacts and face a high degree of uncertainty in their production conditions, thus threatening their livelihood base.

The above characteristics of the workforce and labour market call for different strategies of employment security for various target groups. The four main types may be identified as:

1. First relates to the job security of the regular salary/wage earners who are largely in the organised sector, either in the public/government or private sectors. Although most of the workers enjoy some kind of security provisions, even among the organised workers the less poor may be identified. Recent years have witnessed the employment of a large number of contract and temporary workers in the organised sector. Although these workers are technically in the organised sector, they may be only marginally better-off than such workers in the unorganised sector. The government enforcement machinery and trade unions have the responsibilities to safeguard the interests of such vulnerable workers. As the process of reforms in the economy gets intensified (and the indications are that it would be) the issue of labour market reforms would have an important place on the agenda. The employers, of course, need some kind of flexibility in adjusting the workforce in the face of global competition. This will be the real test as to how efficiently Indian industrial relations system combines efficiency with safeguarding the genuine interests of labour, particularly the less paid and more vulnerable ones. In a poor country like India, adequate separation benefits to workers should be assured. Utmost care is to be taken while undertaking labour market reforms so that labour is not put to disadvantage. While selective relaxation in case of job security regulations may be given, there is need to make minimum wages even more comprehensive for the organised sector workers. The NRF has not so far been able to properly address the problem of labour redundancy and retrenchment. Retraining and redeployment along with counselling should form an equally important agenda of the

NRF. The training and other government institutions, particularly the almost defunct employment exchanges, should be activated to take care of the redundant and retrenchment workers in the organised sector and offer them appropriate counselling and training for redeployment in other sectors, including unorganised.

From Eighth Plan itself there have been greater emphasis on skill development and vocationalisation of education, but so far not much has happened in these areas. While private training institutions (i.e., computer centres, management training institutes, etc.) have expanded at a phenomenal rate, they have been mostly of inferior quality. Appropriate skill development and training institutions which can cater to the emerging needs of the labour market are desperately lacking and unfortunately the efforts by the government have only been disappointing in this regard. Needless to say, training and skill development needs to be given topmost priority so as to increase the employability of the unemployed and under-employed in the fast changing labour market.

2. The second category concerns the security of the irregular wage workers—casual, contract, etc.—who are largely unprotected, and suffer from high level of uncertainty in their income and employment. Although a large proportion of them are covered by the minimum wage regulations and provisions like welfare funds constituted for certain categories of workers, their implementation is very poor and besides there is no assurance of any specified minimum income. Obviously, for such workers employment security implies some kind of assurance of minimum income and employment through labour market and other interventions. We have discussed earlier the need for making the minimum wages more comprehensive and the need of their periodic upward revisions so that they become an effective instrument of poverty alleviation. Of course, better enforcement through innovative methods are necessary. There have been suggestions for evolving some kind of national minimum wage in the country, but because of opposition from several quarters this idea has not taken off. There are some valid arguments in favour of formulating a national minimum wage and it should not be rejected outright on the plea that this would increase the rigidities in the labour market.

   At the same time the measures for generating supplementary employment and incomes for them are equally important. In this context, the role of direct poverty alleviation and employment generation programmes, even with their limitations, becomes important. These programmes need to be widened and strengthened in order to generate supplementary employment and incomes. Accordingly, a proper mix of self-employment and wage employment need to be devised and properly implemented.

3. The third category is the provision of security for a large number of self-employed people, particularly of those engaged in household and micro-enterprise activities who produce goods and provide services for the market (including home-based workers, street venders, etc.). These workers face uncertainties of the market and should be given adequate access to inputs, services and marketing facilities. In addition, a large

number of workers in this category need security of the work premises as well as legal recognition of their activity. Employment security for such workers essentially implies income security through various interventions—fiscal, labour market, organisational, etc.

Strengthening this sector is extremely important as with the regular wage employment shrinking, the educated unemployed have to find job opportunities as self-employed and these are mostly in the informal sector or outside the organised sector. This points to the need for pursuing strategies that help the informal sector expand, particularly in the high income growth locations, where the income levels in the unorganised sector can be expected to be fairly reasonable and where bulk of the first generation migrants look for work. There is a need for creating more supportive environment for self-employment, both in rural and urban areas. Increasing earnings of such workers is crucial for securing a minimum level of income. Earnings depend on productivity of the worker, the important determinants of which are technologies, infrastructure, capital formation and skills. Since the levels of skills acquired are related to a basic level of education, considerable efforts have to be made to increase literacy and school enrolment at an accelerated pace. A strategy of maxmimising the earnings of the existing workforce will necessarily have to rely on increasing the earnings of workers in the agricultural sector— both cultivators and labour— which accounts for about 55 per cent of the workforce, and the operations require more of the field level skills rather than educational one. Any increase in productivity in the agricultural and allied sector will directly benefit the incomes of labour engaged in them. But in the medium term the prospects of increasing the quality of employment for an average worker, through improvements in productivity, are indeed circumscribed by what is feasible in the agricultural sector, and the improved earnings of the younger, better educated and trained workers, realised through their contribution to growth of output in other sectors. Infusion of new technology in agriculture and improvement in rural infrastructure would be important factors in raising the average levels of rural earnings. Similarly, support to informal sectors in urban areas through access to credit and technology and a more supportive environment will be vital for raising productivity of the urban self-employed and casual workers.

4. Effective policies are needed to abolish the discrimination in the labour market, particularly the gender discrimination. In recent years this has been one of the important policy thrusts, and there have been substantial gains in this area but much remains to be done. There still exists substantial wage disparities between males and females. Further, as the "educated component" of female unemployment has exceeded that of male unemployment in urban areas, and unemployment rates for urban females, educated or otherwise, have not come down since 1983, strategies for employment creation have also to devote increasing attention to improving access of women to education and skills which are relevant and responsive to the needs of the economy. Gender differentials in skill and expertise levels and gender biases operating in the labour market have to be

removed to enhance levels of utilisation of the female labour force. Most importantly, we should outrightly abolish the socially unacceptable forms of labour such as child labour and bonded labour. Their incidence has declined, but we need to pursue our efforts vigorously to eliminate this through legal and various social measures. Of course, employment security to adult will facilitate reduction of child labour to a great extent.

5. An important dimension pertaining to the issue of employment security is the security for workers, comprising independent producers/service providers, who are among the most vulnerable groups and face acute uncertainties in respect of their production. For them, employment security essentially amounts to their livelihood security itself—they are frequently faced with uncertainties of nature like drought, flood, crop loss, etc., as well as damage done by the market forces. Marginal farmers, forest-dwellers, pavement-dwellers in the urban slums, etc., are some examples of such workers who are still not integrated with the market. Thus, their livelihood security need to be provided with a proper mix of insurance scheme, measures to provide them some capital, effective steps towards lessening the uncertainties of frequent loss of income, and measures towards providing supplementary sources of incomes and employment.

All the above mentioned dimensions and issues are important towards formulating an employment strategy for India. However, the efficacy of such a system will largely depend upon the pace and pattern of employment generation in the economy. And hence, employment generation with adequate earnings and productivity should be viewed as the principal objective of development planning. Those sectors and occupations should be identified which are employment-friendly and all efforts should be made to strengthen them. Agriculture will continue to play a dominant role in the creation of employment. As the average income of a worker in the agricultural sector is extremely low, the emphasis should be on creating productive employment and not treating it as a residual sector for the surplus labour. Development of agriculture in backward regions has a very high potential for creating employment and reducing poverty. In agriculture, the potential for indirect employment in the form of agro-industries like food processing seems to be higher than that of direct employment. Allied activities like dairy sector have also high potentials for employment. Agro-processing in general and food processing in particular are going to be important sectors for value addition and have a large employment potential. These opportunities exist in oilseeds, cotton, marine products, poultry, cashew, vegetables, fruits, mushroom and floriculture, apart from the traditional plantation industries of tea and coffee. All these have a large export potential as well an expanding domestic market which can create significant employment. But a concerted policy and action plan is needed to develop them by adequate investment, suitable technological upgradation and proper marketing.

Although manufacturing employment has shown deceleration in employment growth, it seems that there has been some recovery recently. Textile products, chemicals, leather products, transport equipment, etc., have shown relatively good performance on employment front and efforts should be taken to consolidate this trend.

Above all, it is the informal sector---either in rural or urban areas but mostly in the latter—where most of the employment is going to be created. This will be both in manufacturing and services, but the trend shows that services sector have a much higher employment potential than manufacturing. This sector has so far been neglected by planners which is why it is characterised by low productivity. The sector has both self-employed and wage workers, but most of them work under deplorable working conditions with low earnings. A well-planned support system should be provided for the growth of this sector considering all key inputs such as marketing, credit, training, upgradation of technology, etc. For enhancing the capabilities of vulnerable workers in the informal sector a proper blend of education and training is extremely desirable. The experiences across world show that skill development and training are the most important factors in increasing the employability of the workforce in the wake of on-going globalisation. India is taking steps in this regard, but efforts have so far been limited to the organised sector only. There is no escape from taking vigorous measures in this direction if the daunting challenges of poverty and unemployment are to be met.

(This paper draws substantially from Sharma, 2000. Thanks are to T.S. Papola for his advice in formulating ideas for this paper.)

References

Ahluwalia, Ishar J. (1992), *Productivity and Growth in Indian Manufacturing,* Oxford University Press, Delhi.

Bhagat, Manju (1997), "Poverty and Minimum Wages", *The Indian Journal of Labour Economics,* Vol 40, No.4.

Bhagwati, Jagdish (1988), "Poverty and Public Policy", *World Development*, Vol. 16, No. 5.

Chandra, Ashoka (1999), "The Role of Training in Productivity: The Objectives of NRF", in M.L. Nandrajog (ed.), *National Renewal Fund: A Look Ahead,* International Labour Organisation, New Delhi.

Datt, Gaurav and Martin Ravallion (1991), *Impact on Time Allocation and Poverty of Public Works in Two Maharashtra Villages,* Welfare and Human Resources Division, World Bank, Washington, D.C.

Fallon, P. R. and R.E.B. Lucas (1991), "The Impact of Changes in Job Security Regulations in India and Zsimbawe", *World Bank Economic* Review Vol. 5, No. 3.

Ghoshe, A.K. (1997), "Should There be a National Minimum Wage in India", *The Indian Journal of Labour Economics,* Vol 40, No.4.

Government of India (1999), *Annual Report 1998-99,* Ministry of Industry, New Delhi.

—— (1990), *Concurrent Evaluation of Integrated Rural Development Programme: The Main Findings,* Department of Rural Development New Delhi.

Guhan, S. (1995), "Social Security Options for Developing Countries", in Figueiredo, Jose B. and Zafar Shaheed (eds.), *New Approaches to Poverty Analysis and Policy - II,* International Institute for Labour Studies, Geneva.

ILO (1996), *India: Economic Reforms and Labour Policies,* International Labour Organisation, New Delhi.

IAMR (2000), *Evaluation of Prime Minister Rozgar Yojana,* Institute of Applied Manpower Research, New Delhi.

Mahendra Dev, S. (1992), *Poverty Alleviation Programme: A Case Study of Maharashtra with Emphasis on Employment Guarantee Scheme,* Discussion Paper No.77, Indira Gandhi

Institute of Development Research, Mumbai.

—— and Ajit Ranade (1996), *Background Paper for World Bank Country Memorandum for India, World Bank,* New Delhi.

Mathur, Ashok (1999), "Economic Reforms, Employment and Non-Employment: Theory, Evidences and Policy", *Conference Volume of the Indian Economic Association,* 80th IEA Conference, Chandigarh.

National Sample Survey Orgsanisation (NSSO) (1996), *Key Results of the 50th Round Survey on Employment and Unemployment,* Revised Report No. 406, Department of Statistics, Government of India, New Delhi.

Noronha, Ernesto (1999), "Duration of Unemployment and Re-employment", *Management and Labour Studies,* Vol. 24, Nos. 2 and 3, April.

Papola, T.S. (1992), "The Question of Unemployment", in Bimal Jalan (ed.), *The Indian Economy,* Viking, New Delhi.

—— (1994), "Structural Adjustment : Labour Market Flexibility and Employment", *The Indian Journal of labour Economics,* Vol. 37, No.1, New Delhi.

Parthasarthy, G. (1997), "Minimum Wages within Agriculture", *The Indian Journal of Labour Economics,* Vol. 40, No.4

Planning Commission (1956), *Second Five Year Plan,* New Delhi.

—— (1962), *Third Five Year Plan,* New Delhi.

—— (1992), *Eighth Five Year Plan,* New Delhi.

—— (1999), *Ninth Five Year Plan, Vol. 1,* New Delhi.

Ranade, Ajit (1998), "Maharashtra's Employment Gurantee Scheme: Regional Patterns, Scope for Reforms and Replication", *The Indian Journal of Labour Economics,* Vol. 41, No.2.

Roy Choudhary (1996), "Industrial Restructuring, Unions and the State: Flexible Mill Workers in Ahmedabad", *Economic and Political Weekly,* Vol. 31, No. 8.

Sharma, Alakh N. (2000), *Employment Generation Policy in India and Social Safety Needs,* Working Paper, Institute for Human Development, New Delhi.

Unni, Jeemol (undated), *Security in the Labour Market : Self-employed Workers and Employment in South Asia,* Gujarat Institute of Development Research, Ahmedabad (mimeo).

13

Employment Guarantee Scheme and Employment Security

S. Mahendra Dev and Ajit K. Ranade

I. INTRODUCTION

Public works programmes have long been recognised as effective policy instruments of poverty alleviation, especially in rural areas. The case for RWPs (rural works programmes) lies in the self-targeting nature of the schemes. There is a growing theoretical and empirical literature on the impact of public works programmes (or 'workfare') on poverty alleviation (Dreze and Sen, 1989; Ravallion, 1991; Besley and Coate, 1992; Sen, 1995). 'Workfare' is supposed to enable the social planner to separate the non-poor from the poor by connecting income transfers to participation in public works. The public works also fit into the ideas of Nurkse (1957) who regards surplus labour in low-income countries a potential saving useful for capital formation. The objectives of RWPs are to provide employment and to generate 'public goods' such as physical infrastructure. Their policy attractiveness lies in their self-selection characteristics since they can screen out the non-poor better, and also provide wage incomes to the poor. Furthermore, they are useful in the creation and maintenance of rural infrastructure which, in turn, provides positive externalities due to the public good.

A unique feature of the Employment Guarantee Scheme (EGS) of Maharashtra is that it provides employment on public works projects *on demand*. And this guarantee was created through legislation. Such a labour-market intervention in terms of providing employment to the unemployed, on demand, has an impact on the *employment security* of the rural poor. In developed countries, such security is offered by the state through unemployment insurance which is financed by a payroll tax on the working population. A programme such as the EGS acts as a proxy unemployment insurance and indeed, is financed by a payroll tax at the state level in Maharashtra.

The main objective of this paper is to analyse the experience of EGS in Maharashtra in order to learn about employment security. The problems encountered and the lessons learnt in the functioning of these schemes would be useful for suggesting reforms in India's wage-employment programmes.

The paper is organised as follows: Section II provides costs and benefits of EGS, while section III deals with regional dimensions and section IV examines lessons, reforms and the replicability of EGS. The last section provides conclusion.

II. EMPLOYMENT GUARANTEE SCHEME: COSTS AND BENEFITS

The EGS introduced in Maharashtra in the early 1970s is an innovative anti-poverty intervention. It provides a guarantee of employment to all adults above 18 years of age who are willing to do unskilled manual work on a piece-rate basis. The scheme is self-targeting by nature and is totally financed by the state government. The main objectives of the EGS are to improve household welfare in the short run (through the provision of employment) and to contribute to the development of the rural economy in the long run by strengthening rural infrastructure.[1] Here, we examine the costs and benefits of EGS.

1. Costs of the EGS

From a modest beginning of only Rs. 1.9 crore in 1972-73, the scheme expanded to an expenditure of Rs. 443.8 crore in 1995-96 (Table 1). During the 1970s and 80s, the EGS has consistently claimed 10 to 14 per cent of the total plan expenditure of Maharashtra state. During the Eighth Plan period, however, the EGS share in the plan expenditure declined to around 8 per cent.

The cost per person-day (at current prices) increased from about Rs. 4 in the first year to around Rs. 31 in 1989. The real cost per person-day rose in the 1980s and was particularly high in 1989-90. The real cost has not risen in the 1990s. The average real wage per person-day (at 1971 prices) rose from Rs. 1.7 in 1977 to Rs. 3.3 in 1983, then fluctuated until 1988. Since 1988, real wages have been about Rs. 4 because of the rise in minimum wages (Table 1).

If we consider EGS expenditure in real terms (deflated by SDP deflator) it has been almost flat or slightly decreasing. Real agriculture SDP growth in Maharashtra during 1980's was almost stagnant, i.e., showed an almost zero trend growth rate.

From 1977 to 1984, the share of EGS expenditure on wages ranged from 74 to 82 per cent. There has been a significant decline in this share since 1985. The main reason is that the capital costs are rising much faster than wage rates. As a result, the share of wages in total expenditure has declined over time. Based on recent data on share of wage costs, we can say that around Rs.1.66 are needed to transfer Re. 1 to EGS employees. Further, if we assume that 90 per cent of them are poor, Rs.1.84 are needed to transfer Re. 1 to the poor EGS workers.

EGS is completely financed at the state level, although it is approved as a plan scheme by the Planning Commission. Basically the state government levies a special tax on (mainly) the urban sector, as a profession tax, an additional sales tax and so on, and then makes an additional matching grant. The state's EGS expenditure is roughly 10 per cent of plan budget expenditure. This EGS fund is statutorily exclusively earmarked for EGS, and if unspent during a year, is carried forward. It is mainly a redistribution from the urban sector to the rural sector, rather than rural rich to rural poor. Until the mid-1980's the receipts under the EGS tax were greater than EGS expenditures and except for a few

Table 1
Quantitative Dimensions of the EGS, 1972-73 to 1995-96

Year	Total exp. (Rs.crore)	% of wage exp.	Employ-ment gene. (person-days in crore)	Nominal cost per day (Rs.)	Nominal wage per day (Rs.)	Real cost per day (Rs.)	Real wage per day (Rs.)
1973	1.88	N.A.	0.45	4.18	N.A.	3.64	N.A.
1974	1.89	N.A.	0.51	3.71	N.A.	2.73	N.A.
1975	13.72	N.A.	4.81	2.85	N.A.	1.73	N.A.
1976	34.61	90.95	10.95	3.16	N.A.	2.00	N.A.
1977	51.10	75.04	13.65	3.74	2.81	2.23	1.75
1978	51.54	73.98	11.73	4.39	3.25	2.53	1.95
1979	74.17	79.58	16.35	4.49	3.61	2.50	2.19
1980	109.23	81.89	20.54	5.32	4.36	2.63	2.31
1981	122.12	75.90	17.15	7.12	5.40	3.04	2.56
1982	126.17	77.74	15.60	8.09	6.28	3.23	2.63
1983	130.93	76.20	12.80	10.23	7.80	3.90	3.29
1984	184.98	75.34	16.45	11.24	8.41	3.88	3.17
1985	232.04	63.68	17.80	13.04	8.30	4.15	3.06
1986	272.24	66.85	18.95	14.37	9.60	4.23	3.39
1987	243.43	63.47	18.76	12.98	8.23	3.56	2.72
1988	288.31	53.19	13.32	19.06	9.11	4.92	2.76
1989	254.23	50.00	8.13	31.27	15.02	7.52	4.09
1990	239.28	53.30	7.80	30.68	15.53	6.93	3.97
1991	238.92	57.37	8.98	26.16	15.02	5.28	3.77
1992	308.54	65.79	11.94	25.84	16.91	4.51	3.28
1993	421.00	60.30	14.80	30.59	18.45	4.92	3.01
1994	310.00	–	9.74	–	–	–	–
1995	413.15	–	9.41	–	–	–	–
1996	443.75	–	9.70	–	–	–	–
1997	366.75	–	9.01	–	–	–	–

Note: 1. In col. 1, year 1973 refers to 1972-73 and so on. 2. Consumer price indices for agricultural labourers are used for obtaining real wages. 3. Implicit price deflators for SDP of Maharashtra are used to obtain real cost per day.

Source: 1. Cols. 1 to 8, Planning Department, Government of Maharashtra; 2. Col. 9, calculated by the author.

years of shortfall, has shown a surplus. It is claimed that as of March 1996 the accumulated EGS fund was of about Rs. 2,189 crore.[2]

2. Benefits due to EGS

(i) EGS and Targeting

There has been a debate about the effectiveness of the EGS in covering the target group. Using landless labourers as the criterion for target group, the PEO study (1980) shows that only 40 per cent belonged to the target group under the EGS. Ravallion (1991) questions this criterion and rightly says that "it is the poor whom we are trying to reach, not the landless per se"(p. 159). According to him, a better test would be to compare the income distribution among participants with that for the rural population as a whole. Using the results of micro studies, he showed that EGS was well targeted to the poor. For example, Dandekar's study (1983) shows that almost 90 per cent of the EGS workers belongs to poorer sections.

Using ICRISAT Village Level Studies' data, a number of studies have examined targeting performance of the EGS. Most of these studies have concentrated on Shirapur and Kanzara villages of Maharashtra. Walker and Ryan (1990) showed that wealth in the form of total assets was strongly and inversely related to participation in the EGS. Their results also reveal that the size of that relationship was larger for women as compared to men in both the villages. Between the two villages, the inverse relationship was much stronger in Kanzara, where the opportunity cost was higher because of abundant availability of agricultural employment opportunities.

Deolalikar and Gaiha (1993) also examine targeting performance in these two villages. On female participation, this study indicates that the scheme is well targeted to young agricultural labour, females with low levels of schooling who are household heads and who come from low-income and low-asset households. A study by Datt and Ravallion (1992) on these two villages show that, in general, low-wealth people participate in the programme. However, according to this study, there are signs that social stigma and work disabilities dilute targeting performance somewhat. In other words, the possibility of participation of high caste people and people with physical disabilities is less.

However, recent studies by Gaiha (1996a; 1996b) reveal that the EGS was mistargeted contrary to the conclusions of the former researchers. According to these studies, a little over 48 per cent of the EGS participants in 1979 were poor. In 1989, the share of the poor among EGS participants was a little over 27 per cent. Thus, the proportion of non-poor rose more than moderately. Gaiha's conclusions are based on data sets for the same two villages in Maharashtra (viz., Shirapur and Kanzara). However, it has to be mentioned that this evidence may not be true for the entire Maharashtra and the poverty lines used by the author appear to be much lower than official poverty lines. Further, most of the other evidences show that EGS is well targeted to the poor.

(ii) Mitigation of Underemployment and Unemployment at the Aggregate Level

Based on the estimates at the aggregate level it can be concluded that the contribution of the EGS to the total employment/underemployment in the state varies from around less than 10 per cent to one-third. However, the equivalent of 10 to 30 per cent of full-time employment has an impact on a much larger part of that group because the EGS employment is considered only as supplementary or part-time employment.

The average labour attendance under the EGS was approximately 0.50 million in the year 1993-94. In the same year the NSS 50th round data reveal that there were 23.2 million workers (self-employed as well as wage employed) above 15 years. Thus, the share of EGS workers in the total rural workers was only 2.2 per cent in the state. In the absence of EGS, at least theoretically, unemployment among rural workers would have been up by 2.2 per cent.

This is reflected in the trends in unemployment rates for Maharashtra in Table 2. The incidence of unemployment declined much faster in Maharashtra as compared to all-India. The decline was particularly significant between 1983 and 1987-88. This is true for female unemployment also. However, the unemployment for both males and females increased in Maharashtra between

1987-88 and 1993-94. During the same period the female unemployment for all-India declined. The reasons for increasing person-day unemployment in Maharashtra are yet to be explored.

Table 2
Incidence of Person-day Unemployment in Rural Maharashtra and Rural India
(In percentages)

Year	Maharashtra		All-India	
	Male	Female	Male	Female
1972-73	7.7	11.7	6.8	11.2
1977-78	5.9	9.3	7.1	9.2
1983	6.3	7.2	7.5	9.0
1987-88	2.9	3.5	4.6	6.7
1993-94	4.6	4.0	5.6	5.6

Note: Incidence of person-day unemployment is defined as a ratio of unemployment days to labour force person-days.

Source: Various rounds of NSS surveys on employment and unemployment.

(iii) Transfer Benefits under EGS

At the aggregate level we can estimate transfer benefits to the workers under EGS. Assume that the available funds are Rs.100. The gross transfer benefit to the unskilled workers is Rs. 60 (i.e., share of wage costs). Assuming 30 per cent of wages as foregone income and targeting efficiency of 90 per cent, the net transfer benefit would be Rs. 35 to Rs. 40 out of Rs. 100. If we assume Gaiha's finding of 27 per cent of transfer efficiency, only Rs. 11 out of Rs. 100 reach the poor. However, Ravallion and Datt's study (1995) on two villages from Maharashtra (Shirapur and Kanzara) shows that half of the gross budget disbursement directly reaches the participants most of whom are poor. This study found that the foregone income from employment on the public works schemes is quite low—around one quarter of gross wage earnings: most of the time displaced was in domestic labour, leisure and unemployment. It shows that workers are not losing much by participating in the EGS at least in the study villages.

(iv) Impact on Poverty

One criticism of the EGS is that, despite the scheme's existence, poverty in Maharashtra has not declined more rapidly than average. It may be noted that the EGS alone cannot lead to poverty alleviation. As some calculations can show, even if workers work full time on EGS, they can not earn enough to cross the poverty line. The problem of poverty is much wider than the coverage of EGS. The importance of EGS lies in both direct and indirect benefits. Although EGS may not have significant impact on poverty in terms of head count ratio, it has impact on intensity of poverty. It has helped the ultra-poor. Table 3 shows that the gap between the ultra-poor and the poor has been narrowing in recent times. This picture could even be better for districts where EGS is concentrated. The anti-poverty record of EGS is better understood by looking at district or region level data. The macro-level poverty ratios do not fully capture the impact of EGS on the poor because

EGS is concentrated in a few districts. Almost two-thirds of all EGS employment is concentrated in one-third of the districts.

Table 3
Poor and Ultra-poor for Rural Maharashtra, 1977-78 to 1993-94

Year	HCR 1	HCR 2	(HCR2/HCR1) *100
1977-78	63.97	54.10	84.60
1983	45.23	34.70	76.70
1987-88	40.78	28.10	68.90
1993-94	37.93	24.60	64.86

Note: HCR=Head Count Ratio.
Source: 1. HCR 1 from GOI (1993); 2. HCR 2 estimated by the author.

(v) Wage Debate

The dilemma to be resolved is whether it should be below or equal to market wage rate or legally fixed minimum wages (generally market wages are below minimum level). Initially the EGS wages were below the market agricultural wages. In 1988, with the doubling of the statutory minimum wage rate, the EGS piece rates were also doubled. Ravallion et al. (1993) reveal that higher wages led to rationing in the guarantee of employment. They argue that lower wages should be maintained in order to have wider coverage which would help the poor better as compared to the rationing due to higher wages. This issue should be resolved before replicating the EGS to other states. There is some merit in the low wage argument if one wants to concentrate on reducing the intensity of poverty. However, if the aim is to take the poor up to the so-called poverty line, obviously higher wages are needed. In recent years, the workers seem to have been shifting from EGS to JRY in Maharashtra because of the higher wages (Prabhu, 1996). Therefore, one has to verify whether reduction in EGS employment has been due to increase in wage rates or shifting of workers to JRY.

(vi) Indirect or Secondary Benefits

The case for EGS relies more heavily on secondary (or indirect) and stabilisation benefits, rather than on direct benefits. One of the second round effect of EGS is its contribution to the creation of rural assets. The EGS projects mainly relate to soil conservation, land development, percolation tanks and roads. They can have substantial impact on agricultural growth (Sathe, 1991). The EGS has been criticised for neglecting the creation of durable assets and paying more attention to employment generation. There is some merit in this argument but it may not be true for all EGS assets. The related criticism is that the agricultural growth in Maharashtra was very low in the 1980s in spite of EGS.[3] Here too one has to look at the disaggregate data, i.e., trends in agricultural growth at the district level.

Secondly, EGS puts an upward pressure on agricultural wages.[4] The guarantee part of the EGS increases unskilled labourers' bargaining strength in negotiations with an employer or landlord. There are evidences that the EGS wage rate has influenced the agricultural wage rate in Maharashtra (Acharya, 1990). Thirdly, one of the important aspects of the EGS is its insurance function.

In the absence of unemployment insurance in India, EGS can act as an insurance for the rural workers. The existence of a form of income/employment insurance could be quite significant although the increase in employment and income is not very large as compared with the aggregate needs. The EGS also have stabilisation benefit in the sense that the employment under the scheme is high in the lean season (April to July) and low in the peak season (October to January) (Table 4). Fourthly, it is worth noting that in rural Maharashtra, the EGS is known as a "programme of women". Various micro studies have shown that women constitute 40 to 50 per cent of the EGS workers. These large percentages could be due to the predominance of female labour in casual unskilled work in rural areas. Fifthly, by making employment entitlement, the EGS facilitates collective political action by the poor, and promotes the realisation of their common interest. The scheme also makes rural politicians more responsive to the demands of the poor. It provided the poor with opportunities for effective action and encouraged the mobilisation of their political resources and also improved the bargaining position of the rural poor. Noteworthy in this regard is the number of organisations that have emerged to organise the EGS workers.[5]

Table 4
Average Monthly Attendance on EGS Sites

(in 000's)

Month	85-86	86-87	87-88	88-89	89-90	90-91	91-92	92-93	93-94	94-95	95-96	96-97
April	731	686	957	535	534	331	270	696	335	186	292	186
May	820	765	940	532	532	347	282	773	385	223	318	182
June	748	740	769	333	332	297	244	902	391	203	350	165
July	515	621	523	174	173	148	164	502	298	123	283	132
August	475	523	411	129	129	114	110	277	222	104	172	86
September	587	482	357	80	110	90	104	181	196	106	148	63
October	549	420	227	85	97	84	129	142	132	135	109	49
November	505	374	266	90	96	75	161	124	101	147	89	49
December	696	494	361	151	123	104	232	174	106	206	110	52
January	649	601	446	182	186	190	360	226	134	259	117	NA
February	639	739	472	238	246	247	511	270	150	285	131	NA
March	668	1061	493	309	307	253	535	294	175	293	162	NA

Source: Computed from the data from Planning Department, Government of Maharashtra.

(vii) Opportunity Cost to the Workers and to the Society

Participation in EGS involves some costs to the workers. However, since most of the employment under EGS is created during lean season, the opportunity cost of the workers may be low. The social costs could be very low because EGS employment is a net addition to the society.

(viii) Targeting Errors: EGS as Compared to Other Anti-poverty Programmes

The success of the EGS needs to be judged against alternate anti-poverty programmes or policies. Many evaluation studies have shown that the performance of EGS is much better as compared to programmes like IRDP. None of the other programmes have sustained large-scale operations for a lengthy period or dealt with corruption and other administrative problems as effectively as the EGS.

In recent years, there are comparisons between EGS and Public Distribution System (PDS). However, actual information is not readily available for comparing the EGS and PDS. For illustrative purposes, we give here the comparison given by Guhan (1994) in Table 5. It shows that although transfer efficiency is higher under PDS than in EGS, the cost-benefit-ratio in the PDS may be only half of that of the employment programmes. This is because of better targeting in employment programmes. However, it should be noted at the outset that the coverage is much wider for PDS (for more on this, see Mahendra Dev, 1996a).

Table 5
Comparison of Cost-effectiveness in the EGS and PDS in India

	EGS	PDS
1. Budgetary cost	100[1]	100[2]
2. Overheads	50[3]	37[4]
3. Leakage	10[5]	35[6]
4. Gross benefit (1-2-3)	40	28
5. Participation cost	16[7]	Neg[8]
6. Net benefit (4-5) i.e., transfer efficiency	24	28
7. Targeting efficiency (coverage of poor)	0.9	0.4
8. Final transfer to poor (6 * 7) (benefit-cost ratio)	21.6	11.2

Note: 1. Aggregate cost for creating one person-day of employment. 2. Cost of food subsidy. 3. Administrative overheads and non-labour expenditures. 4. Distribution overheads such as freight, storage, costs, interest, etc. being 57 per cent of 65 per cent reaching consumers. 5. Underpayment of wages. 6. In transit and at point of sale. 7. Foregone earnings. 8. Negligible, assuming that foregone earnings due to waiting time and transport costs to retail shops are not significant.

Source: Computed from the data from Planning Department, Government of Maharashtra.

Cornia and Stewart (1995) divide the errors of 'targeted' government expenditures on poor people into two: 'E' mistakes in which benefits are provided to the non-poor as well as the poor, and 'F' mistakes in which some of the poor fall outside the scope of the programme. In employment programmes which are generally self-targeted, the 'E' mistakes would be lower than 'F' mistakes. In the untargeted programme like PDS, the 'E' mistakes (coverage of non-poor) are expected to be larger than in targeted programmes.

Reiterating in the case of EGS, 'E' mistakes are expected to be less and 'F' mistakes are expected to be higher as compared to those of PDS. For example, 90 per cent of the workers working under EGS were poor according to some estimates (Dandekar, 1983). In this case, 'E' mistakes are very low. However, 'F' mistakes are high under employment programmes because many of the poor are not generally covered. Another point is that EGS is considered superior to the PDS even if it does not create any assets (Parikh, 1994). EGS scores much more over other poverty alleviation programmes if secondary benefits such as asset creation, increase in agricultural wages, insurance benefits, etc., are considered. If these benefits are considered, the impact of EGS on poor could be much higher than that of PDS.

To sum up, given some of the limitations in the EGS design and implementation, many studies, particularly at the micro level, have shown that the EGS has made positive impact on the levels of living of poor in Maharashtra. The unemployment rate has declined considerably and incomes of the poor have increased over time.

III. REGIONAL DIMENSION OF EGS

It is worth looking at the regional dimension for better understanding of EGS in Maharashtra. Ranade (1998) contains a detailed study of correlating the employment created under EGS with various parameters such as rainfall, irrigation, productivity, literacy and so on. The following are the findings of the study:

1. Apart from a region-specific variation, there is also a time-specific variation of EGS employment. In other words there is great variation of employment across month, the peak being usually during March to June. Thus, an approach to reforming EGS could be to concentrate EGS efforts only during the lean season of the year.
2. Almost two-thirds of all EGS employment is concentrated in one-third of the districts. Among the districts which consistently figure in the "top ten" list of districts sorted by employment generated since 1979, are Ahmednagar, Aurangabad, Beed, Bhandara, Dhule, Nanded, Nasik Osmanabad, Pune and Solapur. The ranking for cumulative person-days since 1979 is as shown in Table 6 which also reports the average annual

Table 6
Districts Ranked by Average EGS Employment Created from 1979-1997

Rank	Avg. annual person-days*	District	Rank	Avg. annual person-days*	District
1	141.06	Ahmednagar	15	43.03	Parbhani
2	103.95	Bhandara	16	32.84	Nagpur
3	102.76	Solapur	17	31.02	Amaravati
4	97.92	Nashik	18	30.51	Thane
5	76.56	Dhule	19	28.16	Jalna
6	71.37	Aurangabad	20	27.19	Buldhana
7	70.80	Beed	21	26.63	Akola
8	62.83	Osmanabad	22	23.15	Sangli
9	56.89	Nanded	23	22.53	Gadchiroli
10	55.39	Pune	24	20.93	Jalgaon
11	50.58	Latur	25	15.42	Ratnagiri
12	50.30	Chandrapur	26	12.38	Wardha
13	47.20	Yavatmal	27	8.72	Indhudurg
14	43.47	Satara	28	7.03	Kolhapur
			29	4.29	Raigad

Note: * Person-days in lakhs; Average computed using 1979-80 to 1996-97 data.,
Source: Computed from the data from Planning Department, Government of Maharashtra.

employment on EGS. Of these, Ahmednagar has been in the top two districts in six of the past 10 years in terms of EGS employment.

3. The percentage share of top 11 districts' EGS employment is given in Table 7 which shows that this is almost always above 70 per cent. It is fair to say that one-third of Maharashtra's districts account for three-fourth of EGS employment. Although the proper perspective would be to look at the population and in this respect EGS employment may not appear as skewed as when looked at in terms of districts. There is, however, a definite bias toward western Maharashtra, even though the number of agricultural workers is higher in the Vidarbha region of eastern Maharashtra.

Table 7
EGS Employment Share of Top 11 Districts

Year	Per cent	Year	Per cent
1984-85	73.33	1991-92	64.82
1985-86	75.88	1992-93	70.27
1986-87	76.01	1993-94	71.37
1987-88	72.94	1994-95	73.09
1988-89	72.80	1995-96	74.86
1989-90	65.07	1996-97	70.37
1990-91	61.51		

Source: Computed from the data from Planning Department, Government of Maharashtra.

4. Some of the features common to districts with high EGS employment are: (a) that they all have predominantly dryland agriculture; (b) the average size of operational landholding is somewhat higher than the state average of 2.65 hectare; (c) they together account for more than 70 per cent of land under sugarcane in the state (the most prominent district being Ahmednagar, followed by Nashik and Solapur), and a fairly high percentage of area devoted to fruits and vegetables (prominent being Nashik). The major crop in Beed, Nanded and Osmanabad is *jowar*. For Ahmednagar, Nasik, and Solapur it is sugarcane, although in terms of area *jowar* is prominent in Ahmednagar and Solapur (Table 8); (d) the percentage of the population reporting as workers is high for these districts, and so also the percentage of women workers as a proportion of total workers.

5. EGS data suggests a strong negative correlation between rainfall and EGS employment. All the rank correlations are significant at 5 per cent level, and most are also at 1 per cent level. Since high demand districts are predominantly rain fed, and produce mostly a single crop, this correlation is as expected. Moreover this also suggests a strong complementarity with labour demand for sugarcane, which is very seasonal, and peaks during harvesting season. This complementarity has also been indicated in Herring and Edwards (1983) and in a micro study conducted by Development Group (Sathe, 1991). It is worth noting, that in some other tests that we conducted to measure the correlation between normal rainfall for a district and EGS employment, for years upto 1987 the (negative) correlation was strong, but thereafter in the early 1990's the correlation

Table 8
Size Holdings, Sugarcane and *Jowar* in Dominant EGS Districts

District	Avg. size of operational landholding	Area under sugarcane as % of district	Value of sugarcane as % of district	Area under *jowar* as % of district	Value of *jowar* as % of district
Ahmednagar	2.78	3.2	40.9	48.6	19.5
Aurangabad	2.73	1.3	18.5	38.2	22.7
Beed	2.96	0.9	12.1	45.2	29.0
Bhandara	1.49	0.2	1.1	5.9	1.3
Dhule	2.71	1.7	13.4	24.8	16.4
Nanded	3.02	0.8	5.3	41.0	25.9
Nashik	2.98	3.1	29.7	10.9	4.8
Osmanabad	3.83	1.0	11.0	38.6	23.4
Pune	2.68	2.5	24.5	51.1	18.3
Solapur	3.7	2.5	30.2	68.9	25.3
State	2.65	-	-	-	-

Source: *Profile of Districts*, CMIE, 1993.

though still negative is not as strong. This indicates that EGS employment is not merely determined by a region's normal or average rainfall pattern, but in fact is strongly affected by a particular year's actual rainfall. This reinforces the notion of region and time-specific pattern of EGS demand for work. It is thus more meaningful to look at the annual impact of rainfall on EGS demand, and not just a correlation between a region's average rainfall and EGS employment.

6. Demand for EGS employment is high in low productivity districts. However, the correlations with three year averages are not significant in some cases. But the 1986-89 average employment is correlated negatively with per hectare productivity data as reported in CMIE (1993), and is significant at 5 per cent level. Interestingly the correlation with respect to individual year data of 1981-82 is significant.
7. The gross irrigated area as a percentage of gross cropped area for the whole state is 11.85 per cent. Given that EGS employment is concentrated more in the arid districts with a substantial area under *jowar* (rain fed) it is to be expected that EGS employment is negatively correlated with irrigation related variables. As has been commented by Echeverri-Gent (1993) this correlation probably points to an underlying political dynamic, which has made EGS very prominent in western Maharashtra (where there a greater cropped area is under irrigation), as against eastern Maharashtra, which has managed to get comparatively lesser EGS employment. Our opinion is that apart from the political clout of western Maharashtra (including sugarcane intense districts such as Ahmednagar), this correlation points out the connection of EGS with cultivators rather than landless labourers.
8. Since EGS is a demand-driven scheme it would be expected that it would be concentrated in areas with a higher proportion of agricultural workers. As Echeverri-Gent (1993), Dandekar and Sathe (1990) and Sathe (1991) have commented, the correlation of EGS employment with proportion of

agricultural workers in the district is negative. This is so for various reasons: (a) In Maharashtra 74 per cent of those below poverty line are cultivators, not landless workers. This is because traditional dryland agriculture is able to keep them occupied for only five months of the year. So in the remaining part of the year they have to depend on EGS. Landless workers have a greater mobility and do not have to depend on EGS as much. Sathe (1991) reports that 58 per cent of his sample EGS households were cultivators. (b) The design of EGS takes into account that it does not interfere with "normal" agricultural operations like sugarcane harvesting. Hence wages under EGS may not be as attractive to agricultural workers, especially in peak season. Additionally since they are not paid daily, and tied to the group productivity, they are not as attractive as farm work wages. (c) Cultivators being more "tied to the land" have fewer seasonal migration options. Also to the extent EGS provides supplementary income as secondary wage earning, it results in greater cultivator households being represented in EGS. (d) Agricultural workers are more predominant in eastern Maharashtra (Vidarbha region) which seems to have a smaller political pull as far as attracting EGS employment is concerned.

Geographic and Seasonal Targeting

From the above findings and from the past 25 years' of data it is clear that demand for EGS employment is region specific. Stark examples are provided by the districts of Thane and Sangli. Thane, being adjacent to Mumbai is a highly industrialised district, and resultantly there is not much demand for EGS from the district as a whole. However, all of EGS employment is concentrated in two blocks (*talukas*) of the district (Jawhar and Mokhada), which have a very high proportion of tribal population. This is testimony to EGS's targeting efficiency.[6] Thus, this can be used to explore the idea that EGS can be focused more on regions which have historically shown to be vulnerable. Such geographic targeting along with other criteria can prove more effective in reaching the needy. In Sangli district six out of eight talukas are drought prone, but total EGS demand is relatively small. In this district too the case of geographic targeting can be explored.

The case for seasonal targeting is similar. EGS employment peaks during the slack season of April to July. Thus, instead of guaranteeing employment throughout the year, it may be concentrated more effectively to the slack season of the year. This is consistent with EGS's original intent of not interfering with 'normal' agricultural operations and production. To the extent that it is a labour market intervention, choosing appropriate time and place can make it more effective and less disruptive.

IV. LESSONS, REFORMS AND REPLICABILITY

1. Lessons from EGS

One of the important lessons that the EGS has taught is that rural public works can be designed and administered on a large scale. Further, taxing the urban middle class and rich for the EGS funds indicates that it is also a means for urban-rural transfers of resources. Another important lesson one can learn from the EGS is regarding the wage rate to be followed in rural public works programmes.

Initially the EGS wages were below the market agricultural wages. In 1988, with the doubling of the statutory minimum wage rate, the EGS piece rates were doubled. The EGS is now required to pay wages at the statutory minimum rates, which are higher than market rates. 'This requirement implies substantial budgetary outlays and potentially high social costs in lost output from alternative employment' (World Bank, 1990). As mentioned above, Ravallion et. al (1993) argue that lower wages should be maintained in order to have wider coverage which would help the poor better as compared to the rationing due to higher wages. They also show that after the increase in 1988, the EGS wages did not have impact on agricultural wages. Rationing of the EGS also dampened the expected second round income effects arising through agricultural labour market and the insurance effect. Recent experience, however, suggests that there is a need for increase in EGS wages because these wages are less compared to programmes like JRY. Half the resources for the EGS budget are provided by the urban population. Government officials say that finance has not been a problem. There is widespread support for the EGS because it offers something for everybody and is one of the state's most popular programmes. It has the support of all groups for varying reasons. These factors are responsible for sustainability of the programme. Maintenance and utilisation of assets created under EGS are observed to be far from satisfactory. Some evaluation reports on this aspect have been summarised by Acharya (1990). The evaluation shows that the utilisation of assets has not been uniformly satisfactory in all the districts. In some other areas, however, the assets created under the EGS in the surveyed areas has led to positive developments on agriculture and rural non-agriculture activities. Other RWPs can learn lessons from the EGS regarding its success and failures in maintenance and utilisation of assets. There are many lessons to be learnt from the role of voluntary organisations which help in delivering the EGS benefits to the workers. For example, Lal Nishan Party is active in helping the poor in Pune, Dhule and Ahmednagar districts. A study on Jawahar Taluka of Thane district (Deshpande, 1988) shows that the existence of a receiving mechanism in the form of a labour organisation namely, Bhoomi Sena helped in improving the delivery of the EGS benefits.

As shown by Dreze (1990) the public works programmes helped in preventing the famine during the drought of 1970-73 in Maharashtra in spite of the low and declining per capita availability of foodgrains in the state. African countries can learn a lot from the experiences of Maharashtra in the prevention of famines. In addition, EGS offers lessons on how to reach the poor in an effective manner, reducing gender inequities, responsiveness to crisis, responsiveness to seasonal fluctuations and spatial differences in poverty and, generating many indirect benefits.

2. Reforms under EGS

The EGS has been in existence for a long period—25 years so far. There is a need for some changes which would be more effective in helping the poor without altering the basic structure of EGS. Some of them are the following:

(i) Wage Rate

The workers under EGS in Maharashtra seems to be shifting from EGS to JRY because of the higher wage rates in the latter. The data for 1995-96 shows that around 9.12 crores person-days were created under JRY. This number is almost equal to that created under EGS. There is a need to have some parity between these two schemes. The wage rate must be raised in such a way that a person working 300 days a year can lift himself or herself and dependents above the poverty line.

(ii) Resources under EGS

The government may resort to employment rationing if the hike in EGS wages is not accompanied by a matching increasing in the outlay. This seems to have happened in the late 1980s. In real terms, there has not been much increase in the outlay under EGS in recent years. The resources have to be increased if the government is serious about increasing wage rates under the scheme. Apparently, there is accumulated surplus of nearly Rs. 2,000 crores in the Employment Guarantee Fund. These funds can be utilised for paying higher wage rates and better infrastructure.

(iii) Asset Creation and Organisational Aspects

Some organisational aspects have to be sorted out in EGS. Improper planning, inadequate project selection and design, lack of technical and organisational supervision, and finally long delays in implementation have affected the productive quality of capital constructed. The EGS has been criticised for neglecting the creation of durable assets by paying more attention to employment generation. The initial emphasis on creation of durable assets got watered down due to public pressures for starting road works. One major weakness of the EGS is the lack of adequate planning for assets. It may be noted that volatile demands from the workers also creates problems for the projects. Droughts, natural calamities or even seasonal changes cause dramatic shifts in demand. Because of sudden increase in demand, new projects have to be undertaken which may be of little productive value (Dantwala, 1978).

(iv) Maintenance of Assets

Maintenance and utilisation of assets are observed to be far from satisfactory. The problems in ensuring adequate maintenance are two-fold. First, there has been a considerable delay in handing over completed works to the *zilla parishads* for maintenance. Second, even where the works have been handed over, the local bodies did not allocate resources for the maintenance of the EGS assets. Consequently, the maintenance of assets has been neglected. There is a need to allocate some part of the EGS funds for maintenance of the assets.

(v) People's Participation

Some evaluations have shown that the EGS plans and implementation is dominated by bureaucracy without people's participation. People's participation in selection and management would improve the productivity and sustainability of the assets.

(vi) More Importance to Watershed Development

Water management is crucial for increasing agricultural production and productivity in Maharashtra. It may be noted that even after utilising the ultimate irrigation potential, over 60 per cent of the cultivated area may have to depend on uncertain rainfall. Therefore, EGS projects should concentrate more on water conservation. Similarly, emphasis has to be given to the promotion of horticulture.[7] There are already models like *Pani Panchayats*, *Ralegaon Shindi*, etc.

(vii) Involvement of Voluntary Organisations for Effective Implementation of EGS

Along with local people's participation, involvement of voluntary organisations would improve the working of EGS. Corruption and leakages in the EGS has been a point of major concern. A number of cases of corruption have been cited in the reports of the legislature committee on the EGS from time to time.[8] Involvement of NGOs and local people can reduce the corruption.

3. On Replicability of EGS

The EGS model has inspired the nation-wide programmes of EAS (Employment Assurance Scheme) and JRY (Jawahar Rojgar Yojana). Furthermore, similar programmes have been tried out at the state level in states like Andhra Pradesh. There are, however, important differences between EGS and some of these schemes. In this sub-section we discuss some limitations and the extent to which the EGS model of Maharashtra is replicable elsewhere.

(i) Drought Legacy

EGS took shape in the extended droughts of 1971-73 and the massive relief programmes undertaken by the state. These relief programmes were supervised by the State Revenue Department (whose representative is the Collector of each district), and implemented by the technical departments. The drought period provided the state administration with a lot of experience in planning and supervision of projects on a large scale. The elaborate planning process does include inputs from the *taluka* level EGS committees, and also sometimes village level panchayats. But the authority rests with the revenue department and the technical departments. This substantial experience database has shaped the way EGS has been implemented in subsequent years. The concentration of drought relief and related activities under EGS is seen in the fact that the Konkan region of western Maharashtra, which gets relatively high rainfall, has generated much less EGS employment. The drought legacy and the earlier experience, in some sense limits the replicability of EGS in other parts.

(ii) Tax Base

The financing of EGS is through taxes raised from the urban areas, mainly the Mumbai metropolitan region. This tax is a profession tax on all wage earners and specially earmarked for EGS. The state government makes a matching grant from its plan funds. As mentioned above, the tax base for running EGS is the industrial/urban workers. Also Maharashtra has the third highest per capita SDP, and thus the programme is funded by Mumbai's dynamic industrial and services sector. It is also supposed to be a deterrent to migration of rural labour into an already overcrowded metropolis. There is some evidence that the percentage of within state migration into Mumbai has been limited as compared to from out of state migration (Godbole, 1990).

The peculiar nature of this well-endowed tax base also makes the EGS experience unique to Maharashtra. The passage of the EGS Act of 1977, came in the wake of the severe droughts of the early 1970's and hence there was a considerable consensus among various political parties and other vested interests in its passage. The tax support has continued without much agitation, although lately there is some evidence of some misgivings about the usage of EGS funds and the propriety of taxing the urban worker for rural schemes.[9]

(iii) Political Economy and Cropping Complementarity

Herring and Edwards (1983) pointed out that EGS was supported by *"kulak* power" since it took care of surplus labour during the lean season. This has also been hinted at in Sathe (1991). It has also been argued that contrary to initial appearances, EGS actually benefits cultivators, both small and large. It frees them from the obligation to support workers in the lean season, and it gives them access to public goods and assets created on EGS projects.[10] EGS provides a source of immense patronage to local as well as state level politicians since they are seen as beneficiaries of workers and cultivators.

EGS employment is designed to be nicely complementary to the one-crop (*rabi jowar*) and the sugarcane harvesting season. This has made it possible to implement a massive labour marker intervention programme such as the EGS without upsetting the normal agricultural operations, or even earning the ire of the bigger farmers. In fact, it is claimed that the EGS non-participants have often benefited from EGS (Sathe, 1991) in terms of (a) irrigation related public goods and other asset creation, and (b) an alternative arrangement to take care of surplus labour during slack season, without affecting their availability during peak seasons. For these reasons the success of EGS type schemes in other states depends on how relevant are the political economy factors in those states.

V. CONCLUSION

This paper shows that the EGS provided employment security to some sections of unskilled workers in Maharashtra. It shows that India needs public works as one of the mechanisms for poverty alleviation. The public works are often criticised, with some justification, for creating unproductive (low productive) assets. It is also argued that these programmes provide only short-term relief and supplementary income (current benefits) and are not useful for long-term benefits.[11] As Dantwala (1978) mentions, "the public works approach to unemployment would make sense if it is so organised that there will be progressively less and less reliance on it, so that ultimately it becomes redundant." It may be noted that they are not meant to function as a permanent escape route from poverty. One has to recognise the insurance or stabilisation function of these schemes. Also, the primary objective of most of these schemes is guaranteeing employment and poverty alleviation. Moreover, as mentioned above, the success of a public works programme needs to be judged against alternative poverty alleviations programmes. In other words, one has to examine whether there are any other programmes which can reach the poor cost effectively as compared to public works.

However, a case can be made for creating productive assets under wage employment programmes without diluting the primary objective of poverty alleviation. Effective involvement of panchayats, planning of projects at local level using local priorities, involvement of voluntary organisations, right to information at panchayat level and, social mobilisation, etc., can contribute for creation of high productive assets and better maintenance of the created assets. Also, for the effectiveness of the programmes it is important that projects of these schemes are identified in the framework of planned development of an area.

Finally, special wage employment programme is not a substitute for a sustained and broad based growth process. However, in a country like India, which has surplus labour and poor infrastructure, public works can be a useful component of poverty alleviation strategies.

Notes

1. For more details on EGS, see Mahendra Dev (1995; 1996).
2. For details, see Mhatre (1997).
3. Suresh Tendulkar, Delhi School of Economics (personal communication).
4. There is also casual evidence of a labour shortage in Maharashtra, along with significant seasonal unemployment.
5. Also see Echeverri-Gent (1988), Subba Rao (1992), Hirway and Terhal (1994) on the benefits of EGS.
6. Details of EGS in Thane district can be found in a comprehensive study by Deshpande (1988).
7. There is already one scheme on horticulture under EGS.
8. It may be noted, however, that compared to other anti-poverty programmes in India, corruption may be lower in the EGS. The decisions of the officers responsible for planning and implementing the EGS are more open to outside scrutiny.
9. See Mhatre (1997).
10. There is evidence of rising water tables in some prominent EGS districts caused by percolation tanks and *nallah* bunding undertaken in EGS.
11. Another valid criticism of public works is that they do not increase the skills of workers. Also, in future, skill based workers are going to get much higher wages and the wage employed people continue to get lower wages (Dantwala, 1996). The gap between unskilled and skilled would widen further particularly after the introduction of economic reforms in the country.

References

Acharya, S.(1990), *Maharashtra Employment Guarantee Scheme: A Study of Labour Market Intervention* , ILO-ARTEP, Delhi.

Besley, T. and S. Coate (1992) "Workfare vs. Welfare: Incentive Arguments for Work Requirements in Poverty Alleviation Programmes", *American Economic Review,* Vol. 82, pp. 249-261.

Cornia, G.A. and F. Stewart (1995), "Two Errors of Targeting", in van de Walle and K. Nead (eds.).

Dandekar, K. (1983), *Employment Guarantee Scheme—An Employment Opportunity for Women,*

Gokhale Institute of Politics and Economics, Pune.

Dantwala, M.L (1978), "Some Neglected Issues in Employment Planning", *Economic and Political Weekly*, Vol. 23, No. 6&7, pp. 291-294.

—— (1996), "Employment Guarantee Scheme", *Economic and Political Weekly*, March 2.

Datt, Gaurav and Martin Ravallion (1992), *Impacts on Time Allocation and Poverty of Public Works in Two Maharashtra Villages*, Welfare and Human Resources Division, World Bank, Washington, D.C.

Deolalikar, A. and Raghav Gaiha (1993), *Targeting of Rural Public Works: Are Women Less Likely to Participate*?, Discussion Paper Series #93-05, Institute for Economic Research, University of Washington, Seattle.

Deshpande, S.K. (1988), *Local Level Management of a Rural Anti-poverty Programme: A Case Study of the Employment Guarantee Scheme of Maharashtra*, A Dissertation submitted in partial fulfillment of the requirements of the Fellow Programme in Management, Indian Institute of Management, Bangalore.

Dreze, Jean (1990), "Famine Prevention in India", in Dreze, Jean and A. Sen (eds), *The Political Economy of Hunger*, Clarendon Press, Oxford.

—— and Amartya Sen (1989), *Hunger and Public Action*, Clrendon Press, Oxford.

Echeverri-Gent, John (1988), "Guaranteed Employment in an Indian State: The Maharashtra Experience", *Asian Survey*, Vol.28, pp.1294-1310

Gaiha, R. (1996a), "Do Rural Public Works Influence Agricultural Wages? The Case of the Employment Guarantee Scheme in India", *Oxford Development Studies*, Vol. 25, No.3.

—— (1996b), "The Employment Guarantee Scheme in India: Is it Mistargeted?, *Asian Survey*, Vol. 36, No. 12.

Godbole, Madhav (1990), *Rural Employment Strategy: A Quest in the Wilderness*, Himalaya Publishing House, Bombay.

Guhan, S. (1994), "Social Security Options for Developing Countries", *International Labour Review*, Vol. 133, No.1

Herring, R.J. and R. M. Edwards (1983), "Guaranteeing Employment to the Rural Poor: Social Functions and Class Interests in Employment Guarantee Scheme in Western India", *World Development*, Vol. 11, pp 575-592.

Hirway, I. and P. Terhal (1994), *Towards Employment Guarantee in India*, Sage Publications, New Delhi.

Mahendra Dev, S. (1995), "Alleviating Poverty and Maharashtra Employment Guarantee Scheme", *Economic and Political Weekly*, Vol. 30, No. 41 and 42.

—— (1996), "Experience of India's (Maharashtra) Employment Guarantee Scheme: Lessons for Development Policy", *Development Policy Review*, Vol. 14, No. 3.

—— (1996a) "Food Security: PDS vs. EGS—A Tale of Two States", *Economic and Political Weekly*, Vol. 31, No. 27.

Mhatre, Anil (1997), *25 Years of EGS: Strengths and Weaknesses* (in Marathi), Y. B. Chavan Pratishthan Publication, Mumbai.

Nurkse, Ragnar (1957), *Problems of Capital Formation in Underdeveloped Countries*, Basil Blackwell, Oxford, first published in 1953.

Parikh, K.S. (1994), "Who Gets How Much from PDS: How Effectively Does It Reach the Poor?, *Sarvekshana*, Vol. 17, No. 3 Jan-March.

PEO (1980), *Joint Evaluation Report on Employment Guarantee Scheme in Maharashtra*, Programme Evaluation Organisation (PEO), Planning Commission, New Delhi.

Ranade, Ajit (1998), "Maharashtra's EGS: Regional Dimensions, Scope for Reforms and Replication", *Indian Journal of Labour Economics*, Vol. 41, No. 2.

Ravallion, Martin (1991), "Reaching the Rural Poor through Public Employment: Arguments, Evidence, and Lessons from South Asia", *The World Bank Research Observer*, Vol. 6, No. 2.

—— and Garav Datt (1995), "Is Targeting through a Work Requirement Efficient? Some Evidence for Rural India", Chapter 15 in van de Walle and K. Nead (eds.).

—— and S.Chaudhuri (1993), "Does Maharashtra's Employment Guarantee Scheme Guarantee Employment? Effects of the 1988 Wage Increase", *Economic Development and Cultural Change*, Vol. 42, No. 2.

Sathe, M.D. (1991), *Rural Employment and Employment Guarantee Scheme in Maharashtra*, Development Group, Vijayanagar, Pune, Maharashtra.

Sen, A. (1995), "The Political Economy of Targeting", Chapter 2 in van de Walle and K. Nead (eds.)

Seetha Prabhu, K. (1996), "Promotional and Protective Social Security during Economic Reform: A Study of Two Indian States", *Review of Development and Change*, Vol. 2, No. 1.

Subba Rao, K. (1992), "Interventions to Fill Nutrition Gaps at the Household Level: A Review of India's Experience", in Harriss, B., S. Guhan, R.H. Cassen (eds.), *Poverty in India: Research and Policy*, Oxford University Press, Delhi.

Van de Walle, D. and K. Nead (eds.) (1995), *Public Spending and the Poor: Theory and Evidence*, Johns Hopkins University Press and World Bank, Baltimore.

Walker, T.S. and James G. Ryan (1990), *Village and Household Economies in India's Semiarid Tropics*, Johns Hopkins University Press, Baltimore.

World Bank (1990), *World Development Report*, Oxford University Press, New York.

PART V

VULNERABLE GROUPS

14

Social Security for Women Workers

V. Gayathri

I. INTRODUCTION

In the recent decades, social security policies have fed a large volume of academic scholarship but the core of its scholarship has been on the state and its regulatory relationship with the market (Dreze, 1991; Pascal, 1986). This is evident from the dominant western models of security regimes as their basic premise is that the state has the moral responsibility to ensure the security of its citizens against any market externalities and other economic contingencies. As a corollary, it alludes that the state's protective measures are primarily for those who participate in the market economy. This also assumes that there is equitable access to the market which functions on the principles of equity. This has invariably led to the exclusion of those who cannot access or fall out of the market. The implications of this for the developing countries are much larger than for the richer economies for the obvious reason that there is a wide variation between the former countries in the proportion of those who are out of the market. Nevertheless, across these countries, irrespective of the levels of economic growth, the largest group of potential fall-outs of the market is that of women.

By analysing the existing social security measures that are meted out to women workers, this paper tries to throw light on the nuances of policies that benignly as well as visibly perpetuate the prevailing gender ideologies. The paper is arranged as follows: Section II discusses the various issues related to the women in the formal workforce and the entry of women into the arena of social policies in general. It also analyses the data on women in the workforce in India to bring out major trends in the employment pattern while the section II deals with the social security mechanisms that are made accessible to women workers. This section provides an explanatory framework to understand the relationship between the disparities in the market economy as well as in the social policies and the other forms of disparities imposed on women by the existing gender ideology. It then summarises the discussion with potential strategies to revamp the social security system that is sensitive to the specific problems of women workers.

II. WOMEN IN THE WORKFORCE

Since the growth model of post-industrial societies does not hold true for many of the third world countries, women's participation in the workforce in these countries has to be understood within the framework of the specific growth patterns that emerged following their political freedom. In India, economic policy has been based on the concept of 'mixed economy' and the post-independent development policies have determined the categories of labour employed for various forms of production. The consideration of categories of labour into which workers can be drawn leads to questions of how workers, particularly women, gain access to various types of employment and the mechanisms by which this occurs (Baud, 1992). In the context of India, only a very small group of women gain access to the formal sector. A large majority of women work either in the agricultural sector or tend to be concentrated in 'informal' employment ranging from household work to traditional productive tasks.

Many believe that the question of women's greater involvement in certain categories of work is a natural fall out of rational choice. They posit that men and women have equal information about the labour market and equal power in making choices that are designed to maximise utility and profit. In other words, the household is seen as a unit of consumption and not a place of work, where women weigh the advantages of 'leisure' within the household against further economic gain while making choices about the sector and categories of work in which they would like to involve themselves. The problem in understanding the household as a unit of consumption is that inequality is taken for granted. There is no attempt to explain why only women need to make the choice between opting for better 'quality' jobs and taking on greater responsibility within the home.

The second set of explanatory theories were largely descriptive in that they begin by describing the labour market. Work in the primary sector is characterised by good wages and security, while jobs in the large secondary sector have low wages, no social security and are 'dead-end' in nature. Further, these sectors draw their labour from different sources. Given that in the Indian context, the secondary sector has the overwhelming majority of working population, this explanatory theory was adapted to explain the different categories of work within the large informal or secondary sector. However, here too, men dominate in better 'quality' jobs, while women cluster around poor quality jobs. A natural corollary of the above is that movement from the 'worse' categories is rather difficult because promotion to better quality work requires, on the one hand, re-skilling and on the other, a demand side pressure. The obvious flaws in this argument lie in that it does not explain why the categories of work in which women dominate are amongst the least valued. It merely assumes that the role differentiation between men and women imposes certain types of work for women and others for men. Discrimination against women workers in the labour market is merely seen as a result of the norms on which they are selected (Armstrong and Armstrong, 1990).

Similarly, the bringing of women into the realm of social policies can be traced to the post-independence period. Social security policy was explicitly grounded in the notion of the family. At this point, it must be mentioned that social policies (health, housing, education, etc.) seem to be overtly egalitarian and unconcerned with the individual to whom they relate. However, a closer scrutiny of the policy as well as its practice reveal that these policies have in explicit ways constructed the family by delineating workers, breadwinners and dependents. Certain assumptions underlie the choices that have been made in social policy; the first is that women are available to do housework and for the caring of children and the aged, and the second relates to their income, whereby it was presumed that women work only when the family income needed augmentation. Therefore, there was neither any attempt to value women's work nor was interruption in work seen as a serious problem.

A change in social policies can be discerned in the seventies and eighties, when women's economic contribution was formally recognised. Based on equity considerations, women were included in almost all the income generation programmes. However, it seems that their inclusion was more of an afterthought, as these concerns have not percolated to other social policies. For instance, the family's male breadwinner was still targeted in programmes providing for rights to housing. In fact, social security provisions were only made for those women who had no support from the male breadwinner. Thus, social security was grounded in the supporter-dependent relationship that men and women share. The nineties have seen a slight shift in approach in that social policy now recognises that the exclusion of women from its realm amounts to dis-empowering them in that the most vulnerable section of the population has been left insecure. However, there are still problems in the practice of this policy as the state has been unable to disentangle men and women from their supporter-dependent identities.

This is also evident in the case of India. Schematically, the dominant development notions that have influenced the way in which social security programmes for women have been conceptualised in India can be divided into three phases, marked by the features as shown in Table 1.

Table 1
Dominant Development Models and Social Security

Period	Dominant notions	Main features of social security programmes
1950-1970	Welfare	Community development programmes, welfare institutions for most vulnerable
1970-1990	Equality and equity	IRDP, JRY, welfare institutions for most vulnerable
Post-1990	Empowerment	IRDP, JRY, welfare institutions for most vulnerable, reservation to political bodies, special financial assistance to vulnerable women like widows, supplementary nutrition programme, TRYSEM, DWACRA

With the consolidation of Constitution in 1950, the government formally guaranteed rights to basic needs to all and, as is well known, has reiterated the same commitment in successive planning periods. However, the issue of social security for women workers was not directly addressed mainly because implicitly and sometimes explicitly, the state (as evidenced in public policies and programmes) assumed that the family is an altruistic unit (Banerjee, 1996).

Also, women's entry and presence in the workforce were assumed to be a result of large-scale familial poverty. For instance, a large body of the government programmes directed resources and employment mainly to men based on the implicit assumption that the associated benefits will be shared equitably with women and children.[1] Thus, there was a lack of a macro perspective about creation of jobs for women. As a consequence, women's role in the fast modernising economy was largely static. A quick review of the available data on women's workforce participation shows that women's roles in the economy have been either static or steadily eroding as the economy began to modernise[2] (e.g., textile industry; fishing since the introduction of trawlers). This is evident from the fact that there was little change in women's experience of industrial employment in spite of the policies promoting rapid industrialisation through state intervention in India (Banerjee, 1989).

The seventies and eighties saw a change in the state's approach to women's employment. The government of India repeatedly professed its commitment to women's empowerment through their participation in economic activities and, therefore, launched many schemes for promoting women's employment. However, this has made little difference to the relative or absolute position of women workers in India (Banerjee, 1996 ; Hirway, 1999).

Thus, as can be inferred from Table 1, women's employment has often been linked to other programmes or larger development agendas. A direct consequence of this has been the denigration of women's work as secondary or marginal. Further, it has contributed to the conceptualisation of women as reserve labour force, secondary workers and in the recent years as 'numerically flexible' workers. These concepts get crystallised as women are found mostly in the secondary and less skilled part of labour force.

The growth of employment rate ostensibly casts doubt on the argument that women's employment occupies a secondary and marginal status in India (Table 2). One has to look beyond these numbers not only for substantiation but also to establish its far-reaching implications for state policies concerning women workers. To begin a closer analysis to this effect, a sector-wise composition of women's employment is considered.

The results of the recent surveys of the NSS (50th and 52nd rounds present useful information on the impact of structural adjustment programme (SAP) on the employment scene of women in India. Conducted after the initial phase of stabilisation, it refers to the rising phase of the economy under the SAP. The data on the growth of employment during the last two decades (Table 3) show that there has been acceleration in the rate of growth of total employment in the country during 1987-94. The annual rate of growth of employment in the Indian economy during 1983-88 increased from 1.77 per cent to 2.23 per cent during 1987-94. In terms of long run growth of employment also, there is acceleration in the rate of growth from 1.95 per cent per annum during 1977-78 to 2.05 per cent during 1993-94. The overall picture is, thus, one of acceleration in the growth of employment in the post-reform period.

Ironically, this period (1987-94) reports the lowest of all growth rates for female employment in rural areas. The rate has been as low as 0.87 per cent during this period. However, this has to be seen against the relatively low growth rate of agricultural production (3.85 per cent) and of the non-farm sector

Table 2
Work Participation Rates by Sex, 1951-1994

	Rural areas			Urban areas			India		
Year/source	T	M	F	T	M	F	T	M	F
1951 Census	39.1	53.9	23.4	39.5	53.5	25	37.1	56.4	14.7
1955 NSS (9)	-	-	*	43.2	59.2	26.6	32.4	51.4	11.6
1961 Census	43	57.1	28	45.1	58.2	31.4	33.5	52.4	11.1
1971 Census	34	52.7	13.9	36.1	53.6	15.5	29.6	48.9	7.1
1972-73 NSS (27)	40.7	52.7	27.8	42.8	53.6	31.4	32.6	49.4	13.2
1977-78 NSS (32)	41.6	53.4	28.9	43.8	54.4	32.6	33.9	50	15.3
1981 Census@	36.8	52.6	19.8	38.9	53.8	23.2	30	49.1	8.3
1983 NSS (38)	41.8	53.5	29.3	44.2	54.3	33.7	34	50.9	14.9
1987-88 NSS (43)	40.9	53	28	43.3	53.9	32.3	34	50.6	15.2
1989-90 NSS (45)	41.5	53.9	27.9	43.7	54.8	31.9	33.7	51.2	14.6
1990-91 NSS (46)	40.4	54.2	25.4	42.7	55.3	29.2	33.8	51.3	14.3
1991 Census*	37.5	51.6	22.3	10	52.5	26.7	30.2	48.9	9.2
1993-94 NSS (50)	42	54.5	28.6	44.4	55.3	32.8	34.7	52	15.4

Notes: * Excludes Jammu & Kashmir; @ Assam is excluded; T=Total; M=Male; F=Female; the ratios based on the 27th, 32nd and 38th rounds of the NSS have been obtained by weighting the WPRs for broad age-groups by interpolated population figures from the smoothed age distributions of the population enumerated in 1971 and in 1981 and the projected population for 1986. The estimates for 1987-88 take account of the projected population on January 1998 but not age-specific WPRs.

Source: Visaria (1999).

for the same period. Further, the overall long-run growth rate of women's employment in the country has also been fairly low (1.27 per cent per annum). In fact, this is much lower than the earlier growth rates of female employment (Table 3). It is to be noted that the gap between the growth rates of male and female employment has gradually increased over the years, while there were 389 women workers for every 1000 male workers in 1987-88, there were only 359 women workers for every 1000 male workers in 1993-94.

Table 3
Growth of Employment, 1977-78 to 1993-94

	Rural			Urban			Total		
	M	F	T	M	F	T	M	F	T
Employment (in millions)									
1993-94	180.24	74.32	254.56	63.68	13.56	77.44	244.12	87.88	332.00
1987-88	157.69	70.55	228.24	51.75	10.94	62.69	209.44	81.49	290.93
1983	147.94	65.92	213.86	45.37	9.60	54.96	193.31	75.51	268.82
1977-78	136.20	59.86	196.06	36.11	7.66	43.78	172.32	67.52	239.84
Annual rate of growth (%)									
1977-78 to 1983	1.51	1.77	1.59	4.23	4.18	4.22	2.11	2.06	2.10
1983 to 1987-88	1.43	1.52	1.46	2.97	2.95	2.97	1.80	1.71	1.77
1977-78 to 1987-88	1.48	1.66	1.53	3.66	3.62	3.66	1.97	1.90	1.95
1987-88 to 1993-94	2.25	0.87	1.84	3.57	3.64	3.59	2.59	1.27	2.23

Note: 1. NSSO 32nd, 38th, 43rd and 50th round rates applied to the estimates of population based on 1971, 1981, and 1991 Censuses; 2. M=Male; F=Female; T=Toal.

Source: Hirway (1999).

A sectoral analysis of female employment growth rates (Table 4) shows that the increase in female employment during 1987-88 and 1993-94 has been largely in respect of casual labour. There is a big jump in the percentage share of casual women workers between 1987-88 and 1993-94, the percentage going up from 38.6 per cent in the former period to 42.9 per cent in the latter. This trend is alarming especially for the reasons that the share of casual employment for women was more or less stable during the previous two NSS rounds and, a number of schemes and programmes were launched for promoting women's employment.

The increase in the share of women's participation in casual labour may be attributed to the decline in the self-employment of women (from 53.1 per cent to 48.8 per cent). The share of regular employment has remained constant at 8.3 per cent. There are, however, some differences between rural and urban female workers, while the former shows a clear decline in the share of regular employment, the latter shows a clear increase in it.

Table 4
Percentage Distribution of Workers (UPS) by Category of Employment

Years	Rural			Urban			Total		
	M	F	P	M	F	P	M	F	P
Self-employment									
1993-94	56.9	51.3	55.1	41.1	36.4	40.3	52.9	48.8	51.9
1987-88	57.5	54.9	56.7	41.0	39.3	40.5	53.8	53.1	53.6
1983	59.5	54.1	57.8	40.2	37.2	39.7	55.0	52.0	54.1
1977-78	62.2	56.3	60.4	39.9	42.2	40.3	57.9	54.8	57.0
Regular wage/salaried									
1993-94	8.5	3.4	7.2	42.7	35.5	41.5	17.0	8.3	14.7
1987-88	10.4	4.9	8.6	44.4	34.2	42.7	18.0	8.3	15.2
1983	10.6	3.7	8.6	47.2	30.8	44.2	17.9	6.6	14.6
1977-78	10.8	3.7	8.6	47.2	30.8	44.2	17.9	6.6	14.6
Casual wage									
1993-94	34.6	45.3	37.7	16.2	28.1	18.2	30.1	42.9	33.5
1987-88	32.1	40.2	34.7	14.6	26.5	16.8	28.2	38.6	31.2
1983	29.9	42.2	33.7	15.3	30.9	18.1	26.5	40.7	30.6
1977-78	27.0	40.0	31.0	12.9	27.0	15.5	24.2	38.6	28.4

Note: M=Male; F=Female; P=Person.
Source: Sharma (1997).

The rural employment scenario for women workers is, thus, very worrying considering that their shares in regular as well as self-employment declined, while the proportion of women in casual employment has considerably increased (from 40.2 per cent in 1983-84 to 45.3 per cent in 1993-94). A similar trend is noticed in the case of the urban female workers too. In contrast to the decline in the proportion of causal labour amongst the female workforce, the present is witnessing an increase in women's participation in casual labour.

The net outcome of the above trend is that presently more than 45 per cent of the rural female workforce work only as casual labour with low wages and 43 per cent of the total female workforce in India work under conditions of uncertain and intermittent employment with no benefits. If employment generation is an important macro condition for providing security, it is necessary that economic growth is not only more broad-based but also more employment-intensive. This primary requirement for providing social security to women workers, i.e., removal of deprivation and vulnerability, has not only been left unfulfilled, but by all indications relegated as a lower issue in the list of priorities.

III. ROLE OF CARE ECONOMY

A cursory glance at the available literature in India reveals a lower pace of events compared to the paradigmatic shifts in the global discourse on social security. That the terms of discourse are Euro-centric can be one of the reasons for this behooved status. Moreover, the affordability argument put forward by the third world countries prevents the osmosis of newer frameworks of security systems and allows only sporadic semi-permeation. This is especially evident in our understanding of the relationship between women and social security.

The burgeoning literature on social security since the eighties in the western countries has generated varying analytical constructs with which security regimes can be studied. Amongst these, gender has emerged as the category that gained maximum attention. At the core of all these is the interrelationship between state, the care economy and the market economy or in other words, differential positioning of women in relation to the trio of state, family and market. Based on the specific configuration of this trio, typologies of welfare regimes are formed, viz., social democratic, liberal and conservative (Esping-Anderson, 1989). Yet irrespective of the classification employed, it is the dominance of either the market or the state over the family that determines the nature of a social security system.

The family may not play any significant role in the social policies of a market driven or of an interventionist state as the citizenship bearing individual forms the subject of protectionism. Nevertheless, in states with a quasi-welfare status, that is, regimes that neither rely on the market nor depend on a highly interventionist state, social policy assumes significance when the family fails. If citizenship rights are taken as the referral point to analyse the relation between the state, market and family, it brings out certain consequential insights. Citizenship not only holds the key to rights and duties in the domain of economic activity and in the democratic politics, but also in the private sphere of the family. The reference here is specifically to the tasks of providing care undertaken exclusively by women. When care giving is delegated to women as part of their duties, corresponding rights are missing in the family sphere as well as from the market and the state. Besides, the fact that this care work is unpaid, restricts the access to the market, and devalues the paid work that women undertake in the market. Many studies that focus on the relation between gender, care and citizenship deal with this critical question. Does the involvement of women in the tasks of care in families as dutiful citizens exclude them from the market? Does the primary identity of the care-giver provide them with a different kind of social citizenship or identity that is determined by their familial identity? Such queries have enabled the incorporation of family as a relevant category in gender analysis of social security systems.

The perspective that emerged from many such alternative analytical scrutinies of social policies has formulated the concept of 'care economy'

(O'Connor, 1996; Pascal, 1986). In the conventional sense of the term, any economy involves production, distribution and consumption. And, in tune with this definition, family becomes the arena of the production (through social norms and sanctions, and when new members are socialised to continue the production), distribution (to individuals who need care at various points of time like children, sick, aged, etc.) and consumption (made available by the breadwinner). To reiterate, how does the full-time participation of women in the care economy affect their relation to the market?

One obvious and established consequence of this perception is the invisibility of women's unpaid work and hence, their exclusion from the protective arm of the welfare state. As a corollary, the unpaid status makes them economic dependents on the breadwinner or in a more general sense, they have to completely depend on the altruism of the family. Any failure in this arrangement—absence of or lack of support by the male breadwinner or non-altruistic values and practices of the family—lacks protection since the concept of vulnerability is intrinsically related to market failure and the consequent fall in income.

A contrasting scenario can exist only in liberal, social democratic welfare states. These welfare systems make provisions for the care economy and also protect women from the failure of the family (widows, single parents, aged, unemployed). This model of welfarism that includes the vulnerability of the care economy, popularly known as the Scandinavian model, is therefore, referred to as the prototype of a women-friendly security system. These countries ensure that the women are not dependent on the family by activating female labour market participation through the provision of public child care and parental leave. The emancipatory potential of such a welfarism is questioned; for it seems to have merely replaced women's earlier dependency on the patriarchal family by dependency on the patriarchal state. For any real emancipation, women need to be independent of the state as well as the family. Hence, for these critiques, the litmus test for a women-friendly welfare state is whether the security measures recognise and relate to women solely as wives and mothers or as workers. Nevertheless, there is widespread consensus that women's social citizenship is realised better when the state takes on the responsibility of caring and thus, imputing upon it a value.

Insights from the above discussion, posited against the Indian social security system, provide a backdrop to analyse it from the perspective of women workers. At the outset, the Indian social security system has to be qualified for its almost absolute lack of any provision for direct social security for women workers. It is restricted to setting up of a few welfare institutions and providing some minimal financial assistance or social relief to destitute women such as widows. The state has, however, attempted since the fifties to provide security to families by concentrating on designing and implementing policies which relate to land, self-employment, wage employment and basic needs like food, health, housing, etc. The thrust of all of these programmes being the family, the immediate beneficiary is the head of the household. This has two implicit assumptions: the head of the household is a male and he is the main breadwinner. The woman worker is rarely targeted for any specific social security, excluding those that trickle down to her as mothers, wives, etc. In fact, it is only since the late eighties that attempts were made to provide her with employment through programmes of skill upgradation such as TRYSEM, STEP, etc.

Since the seventies the Indian women's movement has been raising objections to the lack of a gender sensitive policy mainly on the ground that it is mythical to assume that the existence of traditional social-security mechanisms recognises social rights and ensures minimum subsistence to all. Further, they have effectively demonstrated that the family rarely functions as an altruistic unit. Many village studies have ample evidences, which demolish the patriarchal conception of an altruistic family and the so-called traditional social security system. These criticisms, besides highlighting the exclusion of women workers in social security, and relegating them to the status of subsidiary earner, emphasise this as a serious omission on the part of the state.

As far as workplace security is concerned, agriculture related patron-client relationship as another form of traditional social security system has been widely discussed. However, as has been repeatedly shown, these relationships were essentially between the landowners and men who worked as permanent farm servants. Poor women have always been working as casual labour, thus, being completely left untouched by this system of social security.

The majority of the women workforce is involved in the informal sector (Table 4). This concentration of women workers in the informal sector needs explanation from two angles. From the perspective of women, is it a preferred or a forced choice? And, what are the characteristics of the sector that enable it to absorb a large number of women workers? Along the same lines, we need to ask: why is that formal sector employment is not preferred by women or is there an inherent bias in the sector against women workers?

It is a well established fact that irrespective of the criterion, or mix of criteria chosen to characterise the informal sector, a majority of men and women in India will be found in this sector. The informal sector is further characterised by the overwhelming concentration of women in the lower rungs—in low-paid and insecure jobs. While analysing the structures and practices, which restrict women's access to employment in the formal sector, many micro studies have found poor literacy as well as lack of skills. Along with this, women face the additional burden of choosing 'flexible' jobs even within the boundaries of the informal sector as they need to strike a balance between their full-time involvement in the care economy and paid work. Even the small proportion of women who find themselves in secure formal sector jobs also need to work out a balance of working hours vis-a-vis the care economy and the market economy. Thus, there is a dynamic equilibrium, or balance, between women's involvement in the housework on the one hand, and employment on the other (Walby, 1997).

Given the minimal social security that the formal sector offers and the absolute lack of the same in the informal sector, women workers can continue employment in both the sectors depending on the extent to which they can sustain this dynamic equilibrium. Any contingency in it, mainly in terms of increased demand for time by the care economy, leads to a difficult choice of either quitting the work or coping with the increased burden. This choice is seldom an individual one. It is determined by the wider social and economic factors. This is amply illustrated by studies that have utilised time use data.

The genesis of time use data as a category and tool for analysis has to be understood in the context of the following: (i) the mounting criticism on the census definition of work, which undermined the contribution of women's unpaid labour to the economy; (ii) the emergence of feminist methodology and gender as an analytical category, which in turn, aimed at highlighting the strategic choices women make in care economy and production economy, and to value in monetary terms the contribution of women's household work.

Many empirical studies help in highlighting the fact that women invariably are full-time employees of the care economy and their involvement in the market economy as full-time or part-time employees is decided by a multitude of economic and social pressures. However, the state, while formulating the social security system has not taken cognisance of women's full-time involvement in the care economy. This is evidenced in the type of social security mechanisms that the Indian state offers to women workers.

IV. SOCIAL SECURITY PROGRAMMES FOR WOMEN

There are three basic programmes that concern women workers and can be broadly defined as social security measures. They are employment promoting programmes, social relief and public provisions like health care, public distribution system etc.

Unemployment is a problem, which will be solved with greater job creation. However, in recent years there is an incipient understanding that job creation may lead to disguised unemployment. But, this has not yet been translated into policy. In fact, the important point about the Indian social security system, especially when applied to women workers is that it operates in an economic environment in which the following belief system still predominates: (i) India is a developing country and, therefore, income support of the kind given through the western social security system is unfeasible; (ii) Given the structure of its economy and thereof, employment (self-employed, casual labor, etc.), conventional social security measures will be difficult to operationalise; and (iii) India has a large traditional social security network and therefore, it only requires to be complemented and strengthened through the efforts of the state.

Such a belief system has led the state to largely focus its efforts on total employment generation, which it still hopes will result in the 'leap frogging' of the Indian economy, thus, enabling women also to benefit. Additionally, as mentioned earlier, the state has initiated a few programmes designed specifically to augment the nature and type of women's work. However, the failure of the state-backed employment promotion measures can be deduced not only from the dismal growth rates in women's employment across the board but also the increased casualisation of the women's labor in the post-reform period (Table 4). As we have shown, SAP has had a negative impact on the status of women's employment—the only major source of social security which is available to poor rural women workers in India.

Social relief covers assistance to widows and measures like old-age pension. There is no specific labour insurance or any other direct programme which targets the women worker specifically. The largest social security programme for the poor still comes under the umbrella of direct public provision of health, housing, food, etc. However, as in the case of macro policies, which largely aim at job creation, these too are male head of the household-centric and do not specifically target the woman worker.

It must be noted that some definite changes in social policies are being introduced as there is a clear need felt by policy makers to protect vulnerable sections such as women. However, these have not yet been translated into the provision of a full-fledged programme targeting women workers. From amongst the various public provision programmes, the most popular set of official programmes are still the ones which aim to create employment—those which are designed to (a) create self-employment in non-farm activities and (b) provide wage employment through public works. This is a consequence of seeing women workers, social security as independent from the macro growth process of the economy. They seem to believe that social security is a micro-level instrument without having anything to do with the distortions of the growth process. Consequently, while designing policy, the impact of structural adjustment on women workers was not considered. This also resulted in the state adopting piece-meal and ad-hoc measures and naturally, measures whose coverage is so small that it is inconsequential in the larger scheme of protecting women workers from vulnerability and deprivation.

In the final analysis, there is a need to first recognise the massive contribution of women workers both to the family and to the economy. Further, before designing any social security measures for women workers, it is necessary to identify their major sources of vulnerability and then alleviate these in a comprehensive manner. As is evident, operationalising social security for a poor country like India, especially for poor women, is not an easy task. In order that the social security measures adopted by the state achieve any degree of success, it is necessary that there is a clear-cut targeting of women workers as a separate group which needs to be protected from the insecurities associated with intermittent and low wage employment as well as their commitment to undivided responsibilities in the care economy. Unless the time consumed in the unpaid tasks of the care economy is accounted for by the state, the effectiveness of the existing employment generation programmes will also be limited. Further, the reach of the programmes will be restricted to those women who are privileged to sub-contract the care economy tasks to paid or unpaid women workers.

Lessons can be drawn from the long-standing experience of the Scandinavian model of social security for women workers as discussed earlier. However, it should be noted that the task of care economy in these countries is more or less limited to the task of social reproduction, i.e., bearing and raising children. But in India, social reproduction is merely one of the many care tasks that women devote themselves to. Along with caring for the aged and children in the family, as many time use studies reveal, maximum of women's time is consumed in accessing basic provisions such as water, fuel, food, etc. Given that the care economy is much wider, the state has the responsibility to intervene in provisioning all the major tasks that are being imposed upon women.

V. CONCLUSION

Clearly, the impact of economic growth on women has neither been in terms of increased opportunities nor in increased workforce participation. In fact, as has been demonstrated, the SAP regime has exposed women to greater vulnerability by relegating them to the sphere of casual labour. Further, the compartmentalised provisioning of basic social security has had a negligible impact on women in that it has not been able to even relieve women of their burden involved, especially in terms of time spent, in accessing the basic necessities. Women face the sole responsibility of dealing with the care economy and, therefore, their involvement in the market economy is limited and from time to time curtailed. The involvement of women in the market economy as full-time or part-time workers, or to be completely out of it, mainly depends on their options vis-a-vis the care economy. The obvious and the most common option is to bear the burden of both responsibilities which has other ramifications in personal as well as professional life. The second option of provisioning alternate care system—unpaid and paid—either by the extended family or by paid labour. This option, though for different reasons, is increasingly becoming unviable for the poor women as well as for those who can afford it. Given such a scenario, the state's social security policy cannot be oblivious to the intrinsic relationship of a women's life to care economy and has to recognise interventions in this as a necessary step towards enhancing women's participation in labour force.

Therefore, any attempt to increase women's WPRs, bereft of this crucial attention to the provisioning for the care economy, is bound to have only partial effect. Further, it has been well established that mere economic growth cannot take care of women's interests. Given this, one can draw upon the experiences of other countries to develop a suitable model for India, wherein the women workers' social security concerns are adequately addressed.

(The author is grateful to Professors Alakh N. Sharma and Indira Hirway for their encouragement and comments. Thanks are also due to Piush Antony for her repeated inputs on the paper.)

Notes

1. In the 1950s, it was assumed that through community development programmes, the family would benefit and, therefore, women. At the same time, women were targeted in 'care' related programmes such as providing nutrition to the children, etc. In the 1970s and 80s, when the gains from women's employment was recognised as significant to supplement the family income, their entry into the workforce was advocated. But no attempt was made to provide for the time she spent on her unpaid work. It was again assumed that the family would find a solution to the problem. It has now been established that women have, in fact, been suffering from the triple burden of taking care of the family, earning an income and making provisions for basic needs.
2. See Baud (1992) for a detailed analysis of women's work in the textile industry in India.

References

Armstrong, J. and P. Armstrong (1990), *Theorising Women's Work*, Garamond Press, Toronto.

Banerjee, Nirmala (ed.) (1989), *Indian Women in a Changing Industrial Scenario*, Sage Publications, New Delhi.

—— (1996), "The Structural Adjustment Programme and Women's Economic Empowerment", in Rao, Nitya, *et al.* (eds.), *Sites of Change: The Structural Context for Empowering Women in India*, Friedrich Ebert Stiftung and United Nations Development Programme, New Delhi.

Baud, I.S (1992), *Forms of Production and Women is Labour: Gender Aspects of Industrialisation in India and Mexico*, Sage Publication, New Delhi.

Breman, J. (1985), *Of Peasants, Migrants and Paupers*, Oxford University Press, New Delhi.

Dreze, Jean (1991), "Publica Action for Social Security: Foundations and Strategy", in Ahmed F., et al. (eds.) (1991), *Social Security in Developing Countries*, Oxford University Press, Oxford.

Esping Anderson, G. (1989), "The Three Political Economies of the Welfare State", *Canadian Review of Sociology and Anthropology*, Vol. 26, No. 1.

Hirway, Indira (1999), "Economic Reforms and Women's Work", in Papola and Sharma (eds.).

O'Connor (1996), "From Women in the Welfare State to Gendering Welfare State Regimes", *Journal of the International Sociological Association*, Vol. 44, No. 2.

Papola, T.S. and Alakh N. Sharma (eds.) (1999), *Gender and Employment in India*, Indian Society of Labour Economics and Vikas Publication Pvt. Ltd., New Delhi.

Pascal, G. (1986), *Social Policy*, Routldge, London.

Sharma, Alakh N. (1997), *Trends in the Structure and Pattern of Employment and Unemployment in India*, Working Paper Series, No. E/188/97, Institute of Economic Growth, Delhi.

Visaria, Pravin (1999), "Level and Pattern of Female Employment, 1911-1994", in Papola and Sharma (eds.).

Walby, Sylvia (1997), *Gender Transformations*, Routledge, London.

15

Crime, Gender and Society in India: Insights from Homicide Data

Jean Dreze and Reetika Khera

I. INTRODUCTION

Freedom from violence, as an aspect of the quality of life, is a neglected issue in development studies. Most people would rather avoid being mugged, beaten, wounded, or tortured, and it is also nice to live without fear of these traumatic experiences. Thus, protection from violence may be thought of as one of the "capabilities" that contribute to the quality of life (Sen, 1985). Violence also affects human well-being in indirect ways, as when armed conflicts undermine economic growth or the functioning of public services. If development is about improving the quality of life, the issue of violence should be a major concern of the discipline. Yet, it tends to receive little attention outside specialised circles.

There is another reason why protection from violence is a "capability" of much interest: it does not necessarily improve as income levels rise. Many other basic capabilities, such as nutrition, longevity, and literacy, are positively related to per-capita income, and tend to improve with economic growth even in the absence of direct intervention. Protection from violence, however, is not a convenient by-product of economic growth, and indeed there are spectacular cases of violence rising against a background of rapid improvement in per-capita income and other development indicators. Dealing with violence in the society is, therefore, intrinsically a matter of public action. The latter, in turn, calls for careful investigation of the causes of violence.

One possible reason (among others) why violence is an under-researched issue in development studies is the paucity of relevant data. War-torn zones are not the best site for a household survey, and even basic data on criminal violence in developing countries are seldom available in a convenient and reliable form. The Indian government, however, publishes a good deal of information on murders; this paper is a preliminary attempt to analyse these data.

Our main concern is to explore the links between murder rates at the district level and various socio-economic variables such as poverty, urbanisation, literacy, and the demographic and social composition of the population.[1] Regression analysis points to a robust negative correlation between murder rates and the female-male ratio in the population. This particular pattern receives special attention in this paper.

II. DATA AND ISSUES

Crime in India, an annual publication of the Government of India (Ministry of Home Affairs), presents district-wise data on a range of "crimes" such as murder, rape, kidnapping, theft, burglary and arson. These statistics are compiled from police records. One suspects a good deal of under-reporting for most of these crimes, but murder data are likely to be fairly accurate.[2] Accordingly, we shall restrict our attention to murders.[3] Before doing so, it is worth noting that crime rates are not well correlated across different types of crime. For instance, the ranking of Indian states by level of crime varies a great deal depending on which crime one is looking at (one interesting exception is Kerala, which has low levels of crime across the board). Similarly, trends over time often diverge between different types of crime.[4] Thus, the findings of this paper may not apply to crimes other than murder.

Figure 1 plots the all-India murder rate (murders per million persons) from 1953 to 1995. A significant upward trend can be seen from the mid-70s onwards. In 1995, the murder rate was 41 per million. This is a relatively low murder rate for a country in the "medium human development" category.[5] Interestingly, the Crime in India data suggest that murder rates are not markedly higher (on average) in urban areas than in rural areas.[6] In urban areas, a striking pattern is the wide variation between major cities, where murder rates in 1995 ranged from 7 per million in Calcutta to 164 per million in Patna.

Figure 1
Murder Rate in India, 1953-95
(Murders per million)

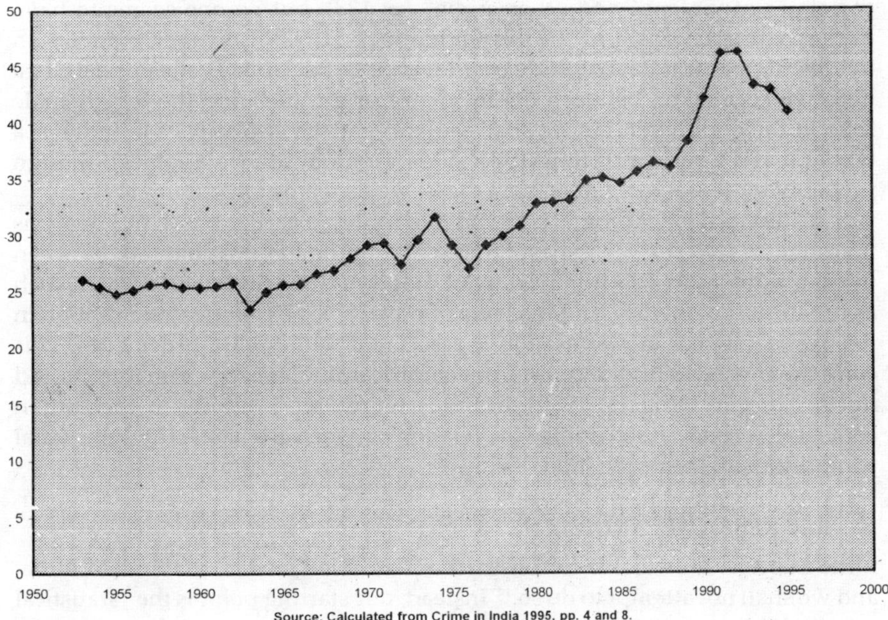

Source: Calculated from Crime in India 1995, pp. 4 and 8.

Some basic features of homicide in India can be tentatively gleaned from case studies, police reports and related sources.[7] Offenders are mainly young men. Murders by women are extremely rare, and are usually committed in response to provocations such as harassment or infidelity (infanticide is another significant pattern, largely unrecorded). In the case of murders committed by men, folkore has it that the main motives are "*zan, zar,* and *zamin*" (women, gold, and land).[8] There is an element of stereotype here, but the general notion that disputes relating to property and women account for a substantial proportion of murders is consistent with the evidence (such as it is) from police records and court proceedings.[9] Altercations and vendettas are other common antecedents. Scattered evidence suggests that perpetrator and victim often belong to the same family, caste, community or peer group. In a striking case study of 144 convictions for murder in central India, Driver (1961) found that victim and offender belonged to the same caste in 84 per cent of the cases.[10] The main motives were disputes over property, living arrangements, sexual matters and transgressions of social norms.

Earlier statistical analyses of Indian crime data are few and far between. An important contribution is Baldev Raj Nayar's *Violence and Crime in India* (Nayar, 1975).[11] The author focuses on temporal and regional patterns in crime rates, and how these might be explained. Unfortunately, his statistical analysis of the determinants of "murder and kidnapping" (pp. 121-22) produced little result, partly because it was based on 18 observations only (one for each state). Interestingly, "police strength" had a positive coefficient in this regression, but this finding has to be taken with a pinch of salt, given the possibility of reverse causation.[12]

In the concluding pages of his book, Nayar pointed out that "district level data may provide more satisfactory results in respect of the social and economic correlates of violence and other crime" (p. 128), but no-one seems to have pursued this useful hint. Philip Oldenburg (1992), however, noticed an interesting pattern based on district-level data for Uttar Pradesh: there is a negative correlation between the incidence of murders and the female-male ratio in the population. As we shall see, this pattern also applies in India as a whole (even after controlling for a wide range of other variables), though probably for reasons different from those suggested by Oldenburg (1992).

Aside from extending Nayar and Oldenburg's earlier work, our analysis investigates two further issues. First, we examine the possible link between murder rates and various indicators of modernisation and development such as urbanisation, literacy, and the level of poverty. One common assumption in this respect is that modernisation is associated with high murder rates. This conjecture receives little support from empirical studies of crime in Europe and north America (Rogers, 1989), but it is worth reexamining in the Indian context.[13] Second, we scrutinize the relation between crime rates and the social composition of the population.

III. REGRESSION VARIABLES

Little material is available to construct a plausible "model" of crime in India, and we shall not attempt to do so.[14] Instead, our starting point is the "statistical approach" to regression analysis (Deaton, 1997, p. 63), where the regression function is simply interpreted as a conditional expectation: in this case, the expectation of the murder rate conditional on various socio-economic variables of interest.

The regression variables and their means are listed in Table 1. The unit of analysis is the district, and the reference year is 1981.[15] The relevant data are available for 319 districts, accounting for about 90 per cent of India's total population.

Table 1
List of Regression Variables

Variable name	Definition	Variable mean
MURDER	Murders per million persons, 1980-82 (unweighted average of 1980, 1981, 1982 annual figures)	33.4
LITERACY	Crude literacy rate, 1981 (%)	34.1
URBAN	Proportion of the population living in urban areas, 1981 (%)	20.5
POVERTY	Sen index of rural poverty for the region where the district is situated, 1972-3	0.18
SC	Proportion of scheduled-caste persons in the population, 1981 (%)	16.0
ST	Proportion of scheduled-tribe persons in the population, 1981 (%)	9.2
FMR	Female-male ratio: females per 1,000 males, 1981	933
Q5RATIO	Ratio of male q_5 to female q_5 (q_5 is the probability of dying before age 5), 1981	0.91

Source: *Crime in India* (Government of India, annual), for murder rates; Government of India (1988), for Q5RATIO; Jain et al. (1988), for POVERTY; Census of India 1981 for other variables. The "variable means" are unweighted averages of district values.

The district is a useful unit of analysis in this context. It is, indeed, natural to focus on the murder rate as a characteristic of the society, rather than on the propensity of particular individuals or households to commit murders. A higher level of aggregation than the district, on the other hand, would miss important local variations in murder rates and their social context. A state-level analysis, in particular, would be too coarse, as there are wide inter-district variations in murder rates within states. In Uttar Pradesh, for instance, the annual murder rate varies from 2.9 per million persons in Garhwal to 106 per million in Pilibhit.

Our dependent variable is the murder rate (MURDER), defined as the annual number of murders per million persons. For this variable, we have taken an unweighted average of the annual values for 1980, 1981 and 1982. This helps to even out transient variations in murder rates, which are unlikely to have much to do with the right-hand side variables. State-level means of the murder rate for India's "major states" are given in Table 2. These range between 25 and 35 per million in most states, with much higher murder rates in Madhya Pradesh and Uttar Pradesh, and much lower rates in Kerala.[16]

Table 2 also gives state-level means of the independent variables. The latter require little elaboration, except for the poverty indicator. In the absence of district-level poverty estimates, our poverty indicator is the "Sen index" for the region where the relevant district is situated. The "region" is an

Table 2
State-level Means of the Regression Variables

	Murder	Literacy	Urban	Poverty	SC	ST	FMR	Q5ratio
Kerala	15	70.4	15.4	20.9	10	1.0	1032	1.12
Orissa	21	34.2	13.1	32.1	13	24.9	981	1.03
Maharashtra	25	44.3	26.0	23.6	7	10.1	961	1.01
Karnataka	25	38.5	24.5	14.5	15	4.9	963	1.02
Gujarat	26	43.7	26.4	15.5	7	14.2	938	0.92
Andhra Pradesh	26	29.9	23.3	15.8	15	5.9	975	1.06
Haryana	27	35.4	21.9	3.7	19	0.0	871	0.82
Rajasthan	27	24.4	19.3	14.8	17	13.8	923	0.89
West Bengal	27	38.8	23.2	28.4	22	7.2	916	0.98
Tamil Nadu	31	46.8	33.0	17.6	18	1.1	977	1.02
Bihar	32	26.2	12.5	24.8	15	8.3	946	0.86
Punjab	36	39.1	27.7	3.8	27	0.0	880	0.88
Uttar Pradesh	50	28.2	18.0	13.0	21	0.5	892	0.84
Madhya Pradesh	51	27.9	19.6	19.3	14	21.1	933	0.96

Note: States are arranged in ascending order of the murder rate (first column). For Assam (where the 1981 Census did not take place), the relevant data are not available. All entries are unweighted averages of the relevant district values.

intermediate unit between the district and the state. Most states have three to five regions, each made up of a collection of contiguous districts. The implicit assumption here is that poverty levels do not vary a great deal between districts within a specific region.[17] Another qualification is that the reference year for our poverty indicator is not 1981 but 1972-3, the closest year for which region-level poverty estimates are available. For further discussion of these qualifications, see Murthi, Guio and Drèze (1995).

Aside from those listed in Table 2, we tried a number of other independent variables, including population density, the proportion of agricultural labourers in the population, and the Gini coefficient of per-capita expenditure.[18] However, these variables had unstable coefficients, and were not statistically significant. To reduce multicollinearity problems, we dropped them from the regressions reported in the next section.

We begin with ordinary least squares (OLS) estimation. The possibility of a feedback effect from murder rates to female-male ratios will be addressed through instrumental-variable (IV) estimation.

IV. EMPIRICAL FINDINGS

The main results are presented in Table 3. Our "baseline" regression appears in the first column. Among the development-related variables (literacy, urbanization and poverty), only literacy has a significant coefficient, with a negative sign. This lends support to the hypothesis that education exercises a moderating influence on criminal violence.[19] In this connection, it is worth recalling that Kerala has some of the lowest crime rates in the country, not only in terms of murders but also in terms of other crimes.

The finding that urbanisation bears no significant association with murder rates goes against the popular notion that criminal violence is relatively high

Table 3
Regression Results

Independent variable	Murder	Murder	Murder-PM[a]	Murder	Murder
Estimation method	OLS	OLS	OLS	IV	OLS
Constant	173.09	43.07	198.86	141.46	169.70
Literacy rate	-.28**	-.50**	-.28**	-.33**	-.20*
(LITERACY)	(-2.65)	(-4.65)	(-2.56)	(-2.62)	(-1.82)
Level of urbanisation	-0.10	.21**	-0.12	-0.02	-0.06
(URBAN)	(-1.07)	(2.46)	(-1.23)	(-0.17)	(-.59)
Sen index of poverty	-12.84	-36.42**	-12.78	-18.58	-7.84
(POVERTY)	(-.85)	(-2.32)	(-.81)	(-1.08)	(-.52)
Scheduled castes'	.20	.51**	0.20	.27	.24
population share (SC)	(1.06)	(2.68)	(1.04)	(1.27)	(1.31)
Scheduled tribes'	.26**	.26**	.26**	.26**	.33**
population share (ST)	(2.92)	(2.72)	(2.70)	(2.74)	(3.53)
Female-male ratio	-.14**	-	-0.16**	-.11**	-.11**
(FMR)	(-6.88)		(-7.74)	(-2.42)	(-4.51)
Ratio of male to female	-	-	-	-	-31.69**
child mortality (Q5RATIO)					(-2.21)
R^2	0.27	0.16	0.30	0.17	0.28
Number of observations	319	319	319	319	319

Note: *Significant at 10% level (t-ratio in brackets); **Significant at 1% level; [a] Murders per million males (multiplied by two, to facilitate comparison with other columns).

in cities. As noted earlier, however, this notion is not supported by available crime data. Also, bearing in mind that the main causal antecedents of murder in India appear to be disputes about property, family and related matters, and that the disputes in question usually involve closely-related persons, we would not expect particularly high murder rates in urban areas, with their more anonymous environment and formalised property rights.[20] What does seem to be a matter of concern is the emergence of a culture of high violence in certain cities, such as Patna and Lucknow.

Poverty, like urbanisation, bears no significant association with murder rates; to the extent that there is any association, it is negative (i.e. higher poverty levels are associated with lower murder rates). This goes against another common cliche, namely that murder rates are particularly high among the poor. This view was quite influential among colonial administrators during the pre-independence period.[21] It is also a standard prediction of Becker's model of crime, with its focus on the opportunity cost of time (Glaeser, 1999). The poor, so goes the argument, have lower returns to legal activity, and a lower opportunity cost of jail time, both of which raise the incentive to commit crimes. It is not difficult to see that this argument, on its own, is far from convincing in the Indian context. For one thing, poverty is associated not only with low wages but also with high levels of risk aversion. For another, the risk of being caught and convicted in the event of committing a murder tends to be much higher among the poor than among the rich. Indeed, the Indian judicial system is anything but impartial between different classes. While it is not uncommon for a privileged and influential person to "get away with murder", the poor live in terror of the police and the courts.

These findings pertaining to development-related variables are broadly consistent with those of Bhatnagar (1990). Among the various socio-economic variables and development indicators examined by the author (pp. 59-67), none showed a statistically significant correlation with murder rates at the state level. The author also found a negative (though not statistically significant) relationship between literacy and all types of crime, with the notable exception of "cheating".

The baseline regression also indicates that districts with a higher proportion of scheduled-caste or scheduled-tribe persons in the population have higher murder rates (in the case of scheduled tribes, this association is statistically significant). It is tempting to jump to the conclusion that these sections of society have a higher propensity to kill their fellow human beings, but this does not follow. Indeed, at least two alternative explanations are possible. First, members of these social groups may be special targets of criminal violence. Indeed, they are "soft" targets, with a limited ability to retaliate or take legal action. Second, it is possible that a significant proportion of murders arise from caste or communal conflicts, and that of such conflicts are particularly likely in areas where disadvantaged groups account for a larger share of the population. While these explanations may seem unconvincing in light of the fact that the social distance between offender and victim appears to be quite small in many cases, available evidence on the social background of offenders and victims is too scant to rule them out.

The strongest pattern emerging from the baseline regression pertains to the female-male ratio, which is *negatively* correlated with the murder rate (i.e. murder rates are higher in districts with low female-male ratios). This correlation is very robust, as can be guessed from this variable's large t-ratio: no matter which other variables are included or excluded from the regression, we found that the female-male ratio remained highly significant, always with a negative sign.[22] Further, the size of the coefficient of the female-male ratio is quite large: it implies, for instance, that the "predicted" murder rate for a district with Kerala's female-male ratio (holding other independent variables at the mean) is only about half as large as the predicted murder rate for a district with, say, Uttar Pradesh's female-male ratio.

The second column of Table 3 shows what happens if the female-male ratio is dropped from the regression. The main difference with the baseline regression is that urbanisation is statistically significant, with a positive sign (i.e. more urbanised districts have higher murder rates). However, this regression equation is misspecified, since it omits a variable of crucial importance, namely the female-male ratio. Thus, while urbanisation appears to have a positive effect on murder rates (Table 3, column 2), this effect is entirely "accounted for" by the higher masculinity of the population in the more urbanised districts (Table 3, column 1). The more general lesson is that analyses of crime in India are likely to be seriously incomplete, perhaps even distorted, if they fail to take into account the gender dimension of the problem.

V. GENDER AND CRIME

Let us now consider some possible explanations for the negative coefficient of the female-male ratio in the baseline regression.

1. Demographic Weights

The first explanation that comes to mind is a plain "arithmetic" one: since men are far more violent than women, populations with a higher proportion of men naturally have higher murder rates.[23] Closer scrutiny of the results, however, indicates that the observed association between female-male ratios and murder rates is mediated principally by variations in sex-specific murder rates, rather than by variations in the demographic weights (i.e. male and female population shares) used to aggregate these sex-specific murder rates to obtain the overall murder rate. Formally, the murder rate (say *k* for short) may be written as

$$k \equiv m.k_m + (1-m).k_f \qquad \text{...... (1)}$$

where m is the proportion of men in the population, k_m is the "male murder rate" (i.e. number of murders committed by men divided by male population) and k_f is the female murder rate, similarly defined. Equation (1) substantiates the demographic explanation: if sex-specific murder rates do not vary across districts, the overall murder rate is bound to be negatively correlated with the female-male ratio as long k_m is larger than k_f. If sex-specific murder rates vary across districts, a regression of *k* on the female-male ratio would still produce a negative coefficient as long as inter-district variations in sex-specific murder rates are uncorrelated with the female-male ratio. However, equation (1) also suggests an elasticity of *k* with respect to *m* of *at most 1* in absolute value.[24] By contrast, using the baseline regression (Table 3, first column) and the identity:

$$m \equiv 1/(1+\text{fmr})$$

where fmr is the female-male ratio, we find that the implicit elasticity of *k* with respect to *m* is larger than 8 in absolute value. In other words, the estimated effect of the female-male ratio on the murder rate is much larger than we would expect from the arithmetic explanation alone.

To illustrate the point, consider the afore mentioned contrast between Garhwal and Pilibhit in Uttar Pradesh. Since the proportion of males in the population is about 13 per cent higher in Pilibhit than in Garhwal, we would expect the murder rate itself to be up to 13 per cent higher in Pilibhit than in Garhwal, based on the arithmetic explanation alone (i.e. assuming identical sex-specific murder rates in the two districts). In fact, the murder rate is about 35 times as high in Pilibhit (106 per million) as in Garhwal (2.9 per million); further, the baseline regression suggests that about one third of this gap is accounted for by the contrast in female-male ratios (0.85 in Pilibhit versus 1.08 in Garhwal).

To look at this issue from another angle, we can shift the focus from the murder rate to the number of murders per male, i.e. the number of murders divided by the male population (MURDER-PM in Table 3). Note that when k_f is close to zero, which is the case in India, MURDER-PM is essentially the same as k_m. As the third column of Table 3 shows, the regression results are much the same when MURDER is replaced with MURDER-PM on the left-hand side, reinforcing the notion that the results are driven by variations in sex-specific murder rates (specifically, k_m) rather than variations in the demographic weights used in aggregating these sex-specific murder rates to obtain *k*. In fact, if sex-specific murder rates were independent of the female-male ratio, we would expect the latter to have a positive coefficient in this regression, bearing in mind the identity:

$$\frac{\text{murders}}{\text{male population}} \equiv k_m + k_f \frac{f}{m} \qquad (2)$$

(the latter follows from dividing both sides of (1) by *m*). Contrary to this prediction, the co-efficient of female-male ratio in the third regression presented in Table 3 is negative.

2. Violence-Induced by Preference for Male Child

Next, we turn to Oldenburg's (1992) explanation for the negative bivariate correlation between murder rates and the female-male ratio in Uttar Pradesh. Oldenburg advanced the hypothesis that, in areas with high levels of violence, preference for male children is particularly strong, because sons are valued as a protection against violence as well as for the exercise of power: "my hypothesis [is] that families in west central UP want (or need) more sons than families elsewhere because additional sons enhance their capacity to literally defend themselves or to exercise their power" (ibid., p. 2659). In this line of explanation, the direction of causation runs from violence to low female-male ratios, rather than the other way round.

Oldenburg's hypothesis prompted an incisive rejoinder from Mitra (1993), who argued that this hypothesis gives too much weight to the "physical security" factor in fertility decisions: "protection from violence such as disputes with neighbours (leading to murders) is just one single component of the huge spectrum of social security the parents expect to derive from having more sons" (p. 67). This statement, however, merely challenges the idea that regional variations in female-male ratios might be primarily due to variations in levels of violence. Even if that it is not the case, Oldenburg's hypothesis may still have some merit in explaining the observed correlation between female-male ratios and murder rates.

To test this hypothesis, we move from OLS estimation to a standard two-stage procedure, where the female labour-force participation rate is used as an "instrumental variable" for the female-male ratio. More precisely, in the first stage the female-male ratio is regressed on the female labour-force participation rate and the other independent variables listed in Table 3. In the second stage, we rerun the baseline regression (Table 3, first column), with the female-male ratio in each district being replaced by the predicted female-male ratio derived from the first-stage regression. Roughly speaking, this procedure essentially amounts to using female labour-force participation as an exogenous proxy for the female-male ratio.[25] If Oldenburg's hypothesis were correct, and provided that the murder rate does not influence (and is not influenced by) the level of female labour-force participation, we would expect the coefficient of FMR in the second-stage regression to be devoid of significance.[26] Instead, as the fourth column of Table 3 shows, the coefficient of FMR in this two-stage regression remains negative and statistically significant. The size of the coefficient is now smaller, as one would expect, but the reduction is not large. This suggests that the reverse causation effect, such as it may be, is not the driving force behind the observed association between the murder rate and the female-male ratio.[27]

This leaves two possibilities. First, there may be a direct causal link running from the female-male ratio to the murder rate. Second, it is possible that both variables are jointly influenced by some other feature of the society, not captured by any of the variables included in the regression.[28]

The notion of a direct causal influence of the female-male ratio on the murder rate (leading the latter to rise where there is a shortage of women) has some intuitive appeal, but is difficult to formalise. Various ideas can be invoked here: male competition for women; social stress associated with a shortage of women; the taming effect of female companionship on men; the violent tendencies of unmarried men; and so on. Effects of this type have indeed been plausibly invoked in specific contexts, such as the high incidence of criminal violence among Indian migrant labourers in the British Caribbean colonies.[29] In this particular case, however, a large proportion of murders (notably those described as "wife murders" by the colonial administration) were directly related to sexual matters. In general, it is not easy to specify how and why a shortage of women should translate into a large number of murders, many of which have no direct connection with sexual matters.

3. Violence and Patriarchy

Turning to the second possibility, one line of argument is that low female-male ratios and high murder rates are simply two manifestations of a patriarchal environment: patriarchal values and practices manifest themselves both in high levels of violence and in a strong preference for male children (leading, in turn, to low female-male ratios). In fact, it can be argued that patriarchy, in the broad sense of the subjugation of women, is intrinsically based on violence or at least the threat of it. From this perspective, it is not surprising that areas of high violence are associated with sharp gender inequalities, of which low female-male ratio is one manifestation.

This reasoning would have particular force if regional variations in murder rates are largely driven by variations in the propensity to kill women. In this case, low female-male ratios (reflecting parental neglect of female children) and high murder rates (reflecting large numbers of murders of women) would simply be two manifestations of one phenomenon–violence against females. In the absence of information on the gender of murder victims, it is difficult to probe this hypothesis.

A related version of the argument focuses on the historical role of violence in the emergence of patriarchal norms and institutions. Marvin Harris (1993), among others, has stressed "the importance of warfare in shaping gender hierarchies"; specifically, the author notes that "wherever conditions favored the development of warfare among bands and villages, the political and domestic subordination of women increased" (p. 61).[30] It is possible that the history of warfare in specific parts of India, such as the Gangetic plain, has left a legacy both of continuing violence of gender inequality and male preference. That the so-called "martial castes" of North India, in particular, are notorious for their fiercely patriarchal culture and low female-male ratios.[31] There is also some evidence (and not just from Hindi films) that they have high murder rates.[32] While these communities represent a small section of the population, the fact that they are often seen as role models by large sections of the society (Srinivas, 1989) gives them much social influence in some areas.

Another possible aspect of the nexus between violence and patriarchy relates to land ownership. In India, both regional contrasts and comparisons between different communities suggest a close relation between gender inequality and land property. For instance, female-male ratios tend to be particularly low among the property-owning castes (Miller 1981). Similarly, areas of densely-populated fertile land, with a long history of settled agriculture and private land ownership (e.g. the western Gangetic plain), tend to be associated with low levels of female labour force participation, an emphasis on the joint family, patrilocal post-marital residence, the practice of dowry, and related patriarchal norms.[33] All these, in turn, lead to a devaluation of female children relative to male children, and low female-male ratios. These particular communities and regions are also likely to be prone to property-related conflicts and violence. Given that a substantial proportion of all murders are property-related, we might expect a negative association between female-male ratios and murder rates, mediated by property relations.

4. Sex-specific Migration

Inter-district variations in female-male ratios have two main sources: (i) variations in the relative survival rates of boys and girls, and (ii) sex-specific migration. Thus, a district with a low female-male ratio may be characterised either by a sharp anti-female bias in child survival, or by high levels of net male in-migration.[34] While the former may be seen as a symptom of patriarchy, the latter is an entirely different phenomenon. To distinguish between the two, the last column of Table 3 presents one more variant of the baseline regression, where the ratio of male to female child mortality (Q5RATIO) is included as an additional right-hand-side variable. The results are much the same as before, and, interestingly, both FMR and Q5RATIO are highly significant, with a negative sign. This suggests that a strong connection between female-male ratios and murder rates remains even after controlling for the "patriarchy effect" (captured by Q5RATIO). One possible reason for this is that male in-migration, like patriarchy, simultaneously reduces the female-male ratio and enhances the murder rate. The underlying causes of the latter effect remain speculative.

VI. CONCLUDING REMARKS

Three significant patterns emerge from the tentative analysis presented in this paper. First, murder rates in India bear no significant relation with urbanisation or poverty. Second, education appears to exercise a moderating influence on criminal violence. Third, the strongest correlate of the murder rate is the female-male ratio: districts with higher female-male ratios have lower murder rates.

The causal relationships underlying this connection between female-male ratios and murder rates call for further investigation. What seems clear is that there is a strong link of some kind between gender relations and criminal violence (not just violence against women, but violence in the society as a whole). Earlier studies of crime in India seem to have missed this essential link. Similarly, standard criminology textbooks pay little attention to the relation between gender and crime (except through the specific prism of "crime against women"). Yet, this issue may be crucial in understanding criminal violence in different societies.

We end with an important qualification, which also points to possibilities of further research. This paper has taken a "static" view of crime, which relates murder rates to various district characteristics at a single point of time. The sociology of crime, however, suggests that the *changes* that are taking place in society may also have much influence on crime rates.[35] For instance, while there may be little relation between the level of urbanisation and the murder rate, a high *rate of growth* of cities may be associated with a high murder rate in urban areas (and perhaps even in rural areas). Similarly, the absence of a significant correlation between poverty and the murder rate in cross-section data does not preclude the possibility that economic *recessions* are associated with high levels of violent crime.[36] Given the ready availability of annual data on crime in India, there is much scope for further investigation of these dynamic effects.

(This paper, which was originally presented at the seminar on which this book is based is reprinted herewith the kind permission of Population and Development Review. The authors are grateful to Pranab Bardhan, André Béteille, Robin Burgess, Robert Cassen, Arvind Das, Angus Deaton, Anne-Marie Goetz, Madhu Kishwar, Prabhu Mohapatra, Mamta Murthi and Amartya Sen for helpful comments and suggestions).

Notes

1. This approach is similar to that of the "cartographic school" of criminology, pioneered by Adolphe Quetelet and others in the 19th century; on the history and contribution of the cartographic school, see Gibbons (1977), pp. 131-3, and the literature cited there.
2. The main qualification is that most cases of female infanticide are likely to be unrecorded. The findings of this paper should be read in that light.
3. What counts as a murder is, of course, partly a matter of interpretation and social construction. In this paper, which relies on official data, we are constrained to rely on the definition given by the Indian Penal Code. The latter states that murder is "an act of commission or omission by a person who has the knowledge and the intent that his act will cause death or such bodily injury as will result in the death of another" (Driver, 1961, p. 154).
4. According to Jean-Claude Chesnais (1981), the combination of declining homicide rates with *rising* overall crime rates is a typical feature of economic development (p. 443).
5. *Human Development Report 1999* presents some international data on "intentional homicides" (Table 23, pp. 221-4). Among 47 "medium human development" countries for which data are available, India ranks 30th in descending order of murder rate. In "high human development" countries, murder rates tend to be comparatively low. On these and related patterns, see also Fajnzylber *et al* (1998).
6. See e.g. *Crime in India 1995*, p. 51. For crimes *other* than murder, urban crime rates seem to be higher than rural crime rates in many cases (e.g. burglary and theft), even after generous adjustments for under-reporting in rural areas; on this, see also Clinard and Abbott (1973), p. 17.
7. Useful studies include Kerawalla (1959), Driver (1961), Bayley (1963), Ahuja (1969), Unnathan and Ahuja (1988), Das and Chattopadhyay (1991), Dube (19996a, 1996b). There is also something to learn from studies pertaining to the pre-independence period, despite major changes in the social context of crime in India; see e.g. Edwardes (1924), Somerville (1931), Walsh (1929, 1930), Haikerwal (1934).
8. According to Edwardes (1924), "most of the murders committed in districts as widely separated as the Panjab, Bombay, and Burma" relate to these "three powerful stimuli" (p. 18). The source of this information, however, is not clear from the text.

9. See e.g. Driver (1961), Table 4, and Unnathan and Ahuja (1988), p. 65. *Crime in India 1995* includes a table on "motives of murder" (pp. 290-1). The percentage distribution, based on 37,464 murders committed in 1995 all over India, is as follows: "personal vendetta or enmity", 15.2 per cent; "property dispute", 10.6 per cent; "love affairs and sexual causes", 6.7 per cent; "gain", 4.7 per cent; "dowry", 2.2 per cent; "class conflict", 0.6 per cent; "lunacy", 0.3 per cent; "casteism", 0.3 per cent; "communalism", 0.3 per cent; "other motives", 59.1 per cent. Obviously, the large share of the residual category "other motives" (which presumably includes all cases where no specific motive was identified) makes it difficult to interpret these figures.

10. In the case of murders committed by women, the association between offender and victim is even closer. In a study of 77 murders in Rajasthan and Punjab, Ahuja (1969) found that "in 61 cases, the victim was a member of the offender's family" (p. 123); the victim was the offender's husband in as many as 42 cases.

11. See also Rao (1981, 1988a, 1988b), Bhatnagar (1990), Subramanian (1992), for related discussions of violent crime in India.

12. In a similar vein, Glaeser (1999) notes that in the US "there is a very high positive correlation between the number of police per capita and the amount of crime per capita" (p. 11), most likely because the latter affects the former.

13. Bhatnagar (1990, p. 69) argues that in India "increasing level of socio-economic development... is inversely related to the volume of crimes". However, this conclusion receives only weak support from his own statistical analysis. The latter, like Nayar's, is based on cross-section regressions at the state level, with only 20 observations.

14. There have been few attempts to develop formal analyses of the causes of crime in developing countries; for a useful introduction, see Glaeser (1999).

15. The motivation for this choice of reference year is the availability of a wide range of district-level data from the 1981 census. A similar analysis based on 1991 census data (combined with the 1981 data) is in progress.

16. Another area of exceptionally low murder rates is the hill region of northern India, consisting of Jammu and Kashmir, Himachal Pradesh, and Uttarakhand (the hill districts of Uttar Pradesh). The states of Jammu and Kashmir and Himachal Pradesh are not included in our analysis, for lack of relevant data. In Jammu and Kashmir, there is some evidence of a sharp increase in murder rates in the 1990s, possibly associated with rising political violence in the state; see e.g. *Crime in India 1995*, p. 51.

17. Strictly speaking, unbiased estimation only requires intra-regional variations in poverty levels to be uncorrelated with the right-hand side variables in the regression equations.

18. The Gini coefficient, like the poverty index, was a region-level variable for 1972-3. This is likely to be a poor indicator of "trend" levels of economic inequality around 1981, as the Gini coefficient varies a great deal from year to year (see Drèze and Srinivasan, 1996). It is possible that a better index of economic inequality would have more explanatory power. Fajnzylber et al (1998) find a strong positive association between inequality and violent crime in international data; on this issue, see also Hsieh and Pugh (1993) and Kennedy et al (1998), and the literature cited there.

19. In Chesnais' (1981) assessment, the progress of elementary education has been the major force behind the secular decline of criminal violence in Europe during the 19th and 20th centuries. As the author eloquently puts it: "Echec du dialogue, la violence commence là où s'arrête le pouvoir du verbe" (violence is a failure of dialogue, which begins where the power of the word ends). Also relevant here are recent surveys in the United Kingdom and the United States indicating exceptionally high rates of dyslexia among offenders: around 50 per cent, compared with 4 to 20 per cent in the general population (Klein, 1998). Fajnzylber et al. (1998), however, find no significant association between criminal violence and literacy in international cross-section data. This "crime-education puzzle", as the authors call it, may be due to higher reporting rates in countries with higher education levels.

20. Urbanisation presumably enhances the incidence of greed-motivated murders (e.g., those linked with burglary); as things stand, however, such murders appear to be quite rare in India.
21. On this point, see Kerawalla (1959), pp. 19-20. It is possible, of course, that this view had greater credibility at that time than it has today.
22. Preliminary analysis of 1991 data generates the same pattern (and also supports our 1981 results in other respects).
23. There is ample evidence that most murders in India are committed by men; see e.g. *Crime in India 1995,* p. 147. This is, in fact, a world-wide pattern; see Chesnais (1981) and Spierenburg (1998).
24. To see this, note first that for given k_m, the elasticity of k with respect to m is largest when k_f is zero. In that case, $k\,^{\circ}\,m.k_m$ and the elasticity in question is one.
25. The two variables are highly correlated, mainly because female labourforce participation has a strong (positive) influence on the female-male ratio. This influence seems to work mainly through differential survival rates of boys and girls: boy preference is particularly strong in areas with low rates of female labour-force participation. See Rosenzweig and Schultz (1982), Kishor (1993), Murthi, Guio and Drèze (1995), among others.
26. The possibility of a direct interaction between female labour force participation and the murder rate cannot be ruled out. In particular, high levels of violence may deter women from working outside the household. As an alternative, we also tried using the 1901 female-male ratio as an instrumental variable; the results are very similar.
27. A Hausman-Wu test rejects the hypothesis of exogeneity of the female-male ratio.
28. Strictly speaking, female labour force participation also has to be influenced by the unobserved variable, otherwise this hypothesis would fail to explain why the coefficient of FMR remains significant in the IV regression.
29. For an extensive discussion and critique of the arguments, see Mohapatra (1995). One referee suggests that this line of analysis also applies to the 19th century "wild west" in America, and adds that "young males in the absence of female companions are apt to get into a very bad mood".
30. Harris (1993) makes an important distinction between internal and distant warfare. The latter "enhances rather than worsens the status of women since it results in avunculocal or matrilocal domestic organizations" (p. 66). The author gives the example of the matrilineal Iroquois, but the observation is also relevant to the Nairs of Kerala (who, like the Iroquois, have a tradition of distant warfare as well as of matriliny).
31. See Drèze and Gazdar (1997), pp. 105-7, and the literature cited there.
32. In a study of village Palanpur (western Uttar Pradesh) spanning five decades, Drèze and Sharma (1998) note that most murders over this period were committed by Thakurs. The authors also mention various other indicators of the continuing influence of militaristic values among the Thakurs: they have the monopoly of guns in the village, spend time in body-building, strive to get jobs in the army and the police, etc.
33. These associations need not apply if land inheritance is matrilineal; this is one possible reason why they have limited relevance in Kerala, which has a tradition of matrilineal inheritance for a substantial section of the population.
34. Female migration can be plausibly overlooked here. Women do "migrate" at the time of marriage (from their natal home village to their husband's village), but this is unlikely to have a major effect on district-specific female-male ratios; the same applies to post-marital female migration, since married women in India rarely migrate without their families. Similarly, the female-male ratio at birth is unlikely to vary significantly between different regions, though this may have changed in recent years with the spread of sex-specific abortion.
35. See, e.g., Robert Merton's (1938, 1957) "strain" theory of crime, which builds on Emile Durkheim's (1951) notion of *anomie* (normlessness), most likely to prevail at times of

rapid social change. Various other sociological theories of crime also involve an explicit or implicit focus on the pace of social change.

36. A strong argument in this direction (for the pre-independence period) is presented in Haikerwal (1934).

References

Ahuja, Ram (1969), *Female Offenders in India*, Meenakshi Prakashan, Meerut.

Bayley, David H. (1963), "Violent Public Protest in India: 1900-1960", *The Indian Journal of Political Science*, Vol. 24.

—— (1969) *The Police and Political Development in India*, Princeton University Press, Princeton.

Bhatnagar, R.R. (1990), *Crimes in India: Problems and Policy*, Ashish Publishing House, New Delhi.

Chesnais, Jean-Claude (1981), *Histoire de la Violence en Occident de 1800 à nos Jours*, Laffont, Paris.

Clinard, M.B. and Abbott, D.J. (1973), *Crime in Developing Countries: A Comparative Perspective*, Wiley & Sons, New York.

Das, S. and B. Chattopadhyay (1991), "Rural Crime in Police Perception: A Study of Village Crime Notebooks", *Economic and Political Weekly*, 19 January, pp. 129-35.

Deaton, Angus (1997), *The Analysis of Household Surveys*, Johns Hopkins, Baltimore.

Drèze, Jean and P.V. Srinivasan (1996), "Poverty in India: Regional Estimates, 1987-88", Discussion Paper No. 70, Development Economics Research Programme, London School of Economics (forthcoming in *Journal of Quantitative Economics)*.

—— and Haris Gazdar (1997), "Uttar Pradesh: The Burden of Inertia", in Drèze, J.P., and A.K. Sen (eds.), *Indian Development: Selected Regional Perspectives*, Oxford University Press, Oxford and New Delhi.

—— and Naresh Sharma (1998), "Palanpur: Population, Society, Economy", in Lanjouw, P. and N.H. Stern (eds.), *Economic Development in Palanpur Over Five Decades*, Oxford University Press, Oxford and New Delhi.

Driver, Edwin D. (1961), "Interaction and Criminal Homicide in India", *Social Forces*, Vol. 40.

Dube, Saurabh (1996a), "Telling Tales and Trying Truths: Transgressions, Entitlements and Legalities in Village Disputes, Late Colonial Central India", *Studies in History*, Vol. 12, No. 2, pp. 171-201.

—— (1996b), "Village Disputes and Colonial Law: Two Cases from Chattisgarh", in Jayaram, N. and S. Saberwal (eds.), *Social Conflict*, Oxford University Press, Delhi.

Durkheim, Emile (1951), *Suicide: A Study in Sociology*, translated by J. Spaulding and G. Simpson, Free Press, Glencoe Ill.

Edwardes, S.M. (1924), *Crime in India*, reprinted 1988, Printwell Publishers, Jaipur.

Fajnzylber, P., D. Lederman and N. Loayza (1998), "What Causes Violent Crime?", World Bank, Washington, D.C. (*mimeo*).

Gibbons, Don C. (1977), *Society, Crime, and Criminal Careers*, Prentice-Hall, Englewood Cliffs, NJ.

Glaeser, Edward L. (1999), *An Overview of Crime and Punishment*, National Bureau of Economic Research, Cambridge, MA (mimeo).

Government of India (Annual), *Crime in India*, Ministry of Home Affairs, New Delhi.

—— (1988), "Child Mortality Estimates of India", *Occasional Papers, No. 5 of 1988*, Demography Division, Office of the Registrar General, New Delhi.

Haikerwal, Bejoy Shanker (1934), *Economic and Social Aspects of Crime in India*, Allen & Unwin, London.

Harris, Marvin (1980), *Cultural Materialism: The Struggle for a Science of Culture*, Random House, New York.

—— (1993), "The Evolution of Human Gender Hierarchies: A Trial Formulation", in Miller, B. (ed.), *Sex and Gender Hierarchies,* Cambridge University Press, Cambridge.

Hsieh, C. and M.D. Pugh (1993), "Poverty, Income Inequality, and Violent Crime: A Meta-analysis of Recent Aggregate Data Studies", *Criminal Justice Review*, Vol. 18.

Jain, L.R., K. Sundaram and S.D. Tendulkar (1988), "Dimensions of Rural Poverty: An Inter-Regional Profile", *Economic and Political Weekly*, November, Vol. 43-45, pp. 2395-2408.

Kennedy, B.P., I. Kawachi, D. Prothrow-Stith, K. Lochner and B. Gibbs (1998), "Social Capital, Income Inequality, and Firearm Violent Crime", *Social Science and Medicine,* Vol. 47, pp. 7-17.

Kerawalla, Perin C. (1959), *A Study in Indian Crime*, Popular Book Depot, Bombay.

Kishor, Sunita (1993), "'May God Give Sons to All': Gender and Child Mortality in India", *American Sociological Review,* Vol. 58, pp. 247-65.

Klein, Cynthia (1998), *Dyslexia and Offending: Intervention for Change*, Dyspel Project, London.

Merton, Robert K. (1938), "Social Structure and Anomie", *American Sociological Review,* Vol. 3.

—— (1957), *Social Theory and Social Structure,* Free Press, New York.

Miller, Barbara (1981), *The Endangered Sex,* Cornell University Press, Ithaca.

Mitra, Arup (1993), "Sex Ratio and Violence: Spurious Results", *Economic and Political Weekly*, January 2-9, p. 67.

Mohapatra, Prabhu (1995), "'Restoring the Family: Wife Murders and the Making of a Sexual Contract for Indian Immigrant Labour in the British Caribbean Colonies, 1860-1920", *Studies in History,* Vol. 11, No. 2, pp. 227-60.

Murthi, M., A.C. Guio and J.P. Drèze (1995), "Mortality, Fertility and Gender Bias in India: A District Level Analysis", *Population and Development Review,* Vol. 21, pp. 745-82.

Nayar, Baldev Raj (1975), *Violence and Crime in India: A Quantitative Study,* Macmillan, Delhi.

Oldenburg, Philip (1992), "Sex Ratio, Son Preference and Violence in India: A Research Note", *Economic and Political Weekly*, December, 5-12, pp. 2657-62.

Rao, S. Venugopal (1981), *Dynamics of Crime,* Indian Institute of Public Administration, New Delhi.

—— (ed.) (1988a), *Perspectives in Criminology,* Vikas, New Delhi.

—— (1988b), "Contemporary Trends of Crime", in Rao (1988a).

Rogers, John D. (1989), "Theories of Crime and Development: An Historical Perspective", *Journal of Development Studies,* Vol. 25, pp. 314-28.

Rosenzweig, M.R. and T.P. Schultz (1982), "Market Opportunities, Genetic Endowments, and Intrafamily Resource Distribution: Child Survival in Rural India", *American Economic Review,* Vol. 72, pp. 803-15.

Sen, Amartya (1985), *Commodities and Capabilities,* North-Holland, Amsterdam.

Somerville, Augustus (1931), *Crime and Religious Beliefs in India,* The Criminologist, Calcutta.

Spierenburg, Pieter (1998), *Men and Violence: Gender, Honor, and Rituals in Modern Europe and America,* Ohio State University Press, Ohio.

Srinivas, M.N. (1989), *The Cohesive Role of Sanskritization and Other Essays,* Oxford University Press, Delhi.

Subramanian, K.S. (1992), "Political Violence, Social Movements and the State in India", *Discussion Paper 308,* Institute of Development Studies, University of Sussex.

Unnathan, T.K.N. and Ram Ahuja (1988), "Sub-culture of Violence: The Indian Context", in Rao (1988a).

The PROBE Team (1999), *Public Report on Basic Education in India,* Oxford University Press, New Delhi.

Walsh, Cecil (1929), *Indian Village Crimes,* Ernest Benn, London.

—— (1930), *Crime in India,* Ernest Benn, London.

16

Social Security for the Aged

Moneer Alam and Piush Antony

I. INTRODUCTION

Social security refers to the various mechanisms by which society protects its members from economic contingencies and other exigencies encountered by individuals or groups due to certain disadvantages faced by them. In traditional societies these mechanisms were embedded in the economic organisation or social relations determined by the specific spatio-temporal context. However, the growth of markets and the rise of modern nation states, especially the welfare state regimes, have eventually redefined social security largely in terms of the provisions made available by the state to its citizens against market failures and other vulnerabilities.

Amongst various other ambivalent areas emerging from such an understanding of social security, defining vulnerability and identifying vulnerable groups have been a major area of contention. While focus on market-related vulnerabilities preclude a large section of population who cannot access the market or priced out of the market, vulnerability defined in terms of deprivations of specific social groups or individuals involves issues of reach and coverage and also tend to be limited to certain kinds of vulnerabilities. Groups of individuals identified on the basis of vulnerability are mainly the differently abled, the elderly, the women, etc. This paper, focussing on the social security measures provided for the elderly in India, discusses their vulnerability in the context of the trends in population growth skewed towards the aged and changing family values disfavouring the older generation. It also attempts an exploratory analysis of health status of the aged and brings out the need to incorporate health insurance for the aged as an integral part of the social security system in India.

Followed by this introduction, section II of the paper, reviews the issues related to the aged and their vulnerability, which are yet to gain space in the centre stage of discussions on social security in India. This is followed by a discussion on the ageing pattern of population in the country in Section III. Section IV deals with the trends in dependency burden. Though it is not increasing alarmingly, the analysis indicates that the severity of the dependency burden may go up with changes in the country's economic environment with growing privatisation, imposition of user charges, and informalisation of labour market etc. Some of the macro economic implications of ageing are analysed in section V. Considering positivity in age-morbidity relationship, section VI is largely devoted to health problems of the aged population. A part of this discussion is also towards suggesting a strategy that aims to provide some insurance cover against the risks of failing health and disability in older age. While this strategy has not been fully conceived at the policy level, we posit that such a scheme is almost imperative because of the growing dissatisfaction among people with the public health care facilities, and the rising cost of private medical services options for financing a social health insurance cover are provided in section VII. The important findings of the paper are summarised in the last section.

II. SOCIAL SECURITY FOR THE AGED: SOME ISSUES

Two issues have been at the centre of the current debate on the ageing population.[1] One is the outcome of the growing realisation that ageing results in certain inequalities—both within and between the households. Another emanates from the rising concern among analysts about social security requirements of the aged people to ensure their mental and physical well-being. Before discussing the specific issues, a brief review of the relevant studies is attempted.[2]

Pivotal to the on-going debate on ageing in India has been its socio-demographic implications including emotional insecurities, loneliness, lack of familial care, financial hardships and the livelihood requirements of the aged. This is clearly evident from studies by Soodan (1975); Sharma and Dak (1987); Mahadevan and Audinarayana, (1992); Mahajan (1992); Devi (1992); Rajan, et al. (1999), etc. More recently, however, some literature is available on the health problems of the ageing population, in particular the nature of various geriatric diseases and the difficulties faced by the older people in coping with them. Some authors have argued for evolving an extended system of old age support with health security as an important component. This is more explicitly observed in recent studies by Reddy (1996); Rao and Townsend (1998); etc. Their studies provide an exhaustive account of the worsening health condition of the ageing population, both sex-wise and in rural and urban areas.

Dandekar (1996) has come out recently with a comprehensive analysis of ageing and its multifaceted problems. The study, drawing heavily on Maharashtra experience, has examined the difficulties faced by the elderly due to poor health, adverse socio-economic conditions, non-working status, lack of independence, widening inter-generation gaps, etc. The gender dimensions of these problems have also been discussed in the study at various levels. One of the findings of the study brings out the precarious health condition of the older population. It also provides evidence to show that even a meagre financial help to them (especially to the rural poor) would result in a considerable reduction of their hardships. The study, however, makes no mention of the possibility of certain health insurance options for the aged. Further, the study also seems to assume that the benefits of old-age pension would reach the intended beneficiaries without the risk of being shared by others.[3] Dandekar, and most of the other studies mentioned above, has also missed the macro-economic implications of ageing.

Another dimension of the discussion on old age dependencies and its burden emanates from studies using 'levels of living' as a criterion for viewing poverty and its outcome for low-income rural households and other vulnerable segments of the population. A study by Visaria (1980) deals with some of these issues. One of the core issues of this comprehensive research on income distribution in selected Asian countries, including two western states in India, was an examination of the relationship between the living standard of households, its size and age profile—particularly the age of the head of the household. This relationship was examined in the study to ascertain the life cycle effects on inequalities at the household level. A similar relationship was studied by Deaton and Paxon (1993) on the basis of annual household surveys from Taipei, China (1976-90), Great Britain (1969-90), and United States (1980-90). The study clearly suggests an increase in inequalities over the later stages of the life cycle for all the three countries.

A comprehensive study by Agarwal (1990) on the problems of inequalities in sharing inter and intra-household resources and its implications for coping up with livelihood insecurities—especially by women and the aged—provides some useful insights on the debate on poverty and the need for empowering the poor through institutional reforms. Citing examples of women, small and landless agricultural households and other rural poor, she argued that the entitlement which ensures the relative bargaining strength of individuals is determined by some personal traits and capabilities, ownership endowments, exchange entitlements, access to communal (like village commons, forests or other common property resources) or social (friendship or kinship) resources, etc. As the weaker segments (women, landless labourers or those in older age - groups) are invariably endowed with lesser bargaining strength, they are liable to suffer far greater poverty risks, especially at the time of contingencies. The study makes out a strong case for seriously considering these limitations and inequalities while framing public support policies for the poor.

Cain (1981; 1985a; 1985b) has made several important contributions to confirm Leibenstein's old-age security hypothesis, which suggests that parents in poor countries are motivated to reproduce in anticipation that children would support them at the time of their old age or some other forms of disability. This link between children and economic security, as argued by Cain, provides a floor to the fertility decline, especially in poor areas of rural south Asia, and an insurance against the risks of income losses due to ageing, debilitating illness or any other threatening events. It also helps to avert distress sales of the arable land in rural areas. This argument is however strongly denied by the advocates of micro-economic theory of fertility who focus on the "value of money" or "positive rates of time preference", with higher values attached to the present than future consumption (Lindert, 1983). Some of the observations by Rajan, et al. (1999) however support the logic behind the old age security viewpoint. Nevertheless, this logic is increasingly becoming less relevant among educated urban households. And, Dreze and Sen (1989; 1991) have been consistently arguing for strong social security measures to ensure protection against decline in basic standards of living, and promotional efforts for enhancing the normal living conditions of those deprived and faced with precarious conditions.

Public Policies for the Aged

As in the case of many other developing countries, the social security system in India largely caters to those in the formal sector workforce. This inherent bias limits old age security schemes to retirement benefits. Other old age provisions (mainly those related to the needy, destitute, widowed and rural poor) are few and extremely limited in its coverage. Moreover, some of these provisions exist largely on paper and have been hardly ever analysed regarding their effectiveness. They also suffer from anomalies like cumbersome application procedures, difficult eligibility criteria, irregular and delayed payments, etc. (Kumar, 1998). Moreover, hardly any of the available social security plans cover health care requirements of the elderly, barring those who worked in the organised public or private establishments.

Studies on social security provisioning in India suggest many other lapses, particularly at the implementation level. Dreze and Sen (1991) point out that much of this provisioning has been directed towards reducing socio-economic disparities through direct measures of poverty alleviation. Consequently, some important indirect measures like health care, literacy (particularly, female literacy), gender empowerment, improvement in living conditions, etc., have lagged behind, along with the omission of old age care and social security for the elderly.

The aged are more likely to be exposed to the cold winds of social security as they are seen as dependents of the younger ones. As the social security practice in India centres around employment, the less previliged ones in the unorganised sector or those who are out of the labour market like the elderly, women and disabled, fall out of the old age security provided by the government mainly in terms of pensions. The plight of the elderly is worse-off when perceived from both these view points. Moreover, many of the social security policies are designed around a conventional ideal family model and protects that model in practice. However, notwithstanding the fact that the family is not an altruistic unit, any failure in the existing family model can adversly effect the elderly. It has been established by many studies that increasingly there is neglect of the domiciliary care for the elderly (Rajan, et al. 1999). In any case as pension system covers a meager percentage of the elderly and they belong mostly to the middle and upper strata, the elderly from the poorer households are susceptible to more vulnerability. Hence this remains —the reach and coverage of old age benefits—as one of the daunting challenges for India's social security policies.

Social security for the aged in India consists of both the schemes: contributory as well as non-contributory. The former is based on contributions from workers and their employers—supplemented by the government contributions. These, *inter alia,* include Employees' State Insurance Scheme (ESIS), Provident Fund, Pension and Deposit Linked Insurance schemes, etc. Some important non-contributory schemes include Workmen's Compensation Act (1923), the Maternity Benefit Act (1962), National Social Assistance Programme (1995), and the Payment of Gratuity Act (1972).[4] In addition, there are some other protection plans by the government to prevent destitution caused by disabilities, old age or other calamities. Old age homes, mobile geriatric services, adoption of elderly, marginal subsidies on purchase of plane and train tickets are also available to persons of 65 years and more. A National Policy on Older Persons is also in the offing. Major employment assistance programmes have also been launched to help the landless and rural poor. Many of them have, however, suffered from serious limitations (Kumar, 1998). Further, they have hardly been able to meet the growing problem of old age poverty in the country.

III. TRENDS IN AGEING: A CLOSER SCRUTINY

Demographically, India has achieved a substantial reduction in fertility and mortality, which is likely to accelerate further, and has made improvements in life expectancy at all stages of the life span. While a plethora of literature can be found on these, it may be noted that it often remains confined to their demographic outcomes. For example, changes in the age structure of the population have mostly been discussed in the limited context of human power formation and labour market issues. Some of the recent studies with an implicit or explicit concern for some of these issues, include a work by Visaria (1998) on youth unemployment where he attempts to compute additional labour force in the coming few years and match them with likely additions in the job market. The old-age dependency and its attendant health and social security problems have hardly been a matter of serious analytical concern[5]. This is particularly true for India, but most other countries of the region are no exceptions. This lack of interest may also be noticed from the limited concern among planners and policy makers to examine the macro or micro economic implications of ageing for savings, consumption, investments, labour supply, public transfers, government expenditure, medical care, inter or intra-household inequalities, family system, etc. In contrast, most of these issues have received much more serious attention in countries of East and South-east Asia including Korea, Thailand, Malaysia, and Singapore.

Though India is yet to join the group of countries where longevity, high share of non-working greying population or weak family system become a matter of serious concern, a closer scrutiny of trends in the population growth do send warning signals. The warnings emerge from the large population of those in the 60 and higher age-groups (i.e., more than 56 million in 1991, accounting for over 6.7 per cent of the total population). This is likely to further grow and at a much faster pace overtime, due to a growing probability of living to the age of 60, and life expectancy at 60. This becomes even more serious as the country lacks a proper social security system[6] for the ageing population, which becomes important with growing changes in the reproductive behaviour of people, and growing adherence to small family norm. Together, these changes might affect the traditional family system in India, and leave a very large fraction of the elderly population to fend for themselves. Particularly, the health care requirements of elderly persons may be an issue of much greater concern. More so, because the government delivery of health care in the country is grossly inadequate. This is true with respect to any measure, whether it be quality or availability. Conversely, health care delivered in the private sector is prohibitively costly. Therefore, a very large fraction of the elderly population may not be able to consume these services in the absence of a well-conceived health care security system.

Besides, there are numerous issues regarding the overall economic behaviour of the older people, for example, the nature of goods and services required by the growing number of persons in higher ages. Evidence drawn from many other countries have revealed obvious differences between the elders and the non-elders in their pattern of consumption requirements (Deaton, 1995). Similarly, old age persons tend to dissave. Thus, a rising share of older population is expected to have a lower savings rate, affecting the overall investment in the economy. In addition, a large body of this literature has also recognised the labour market implications of an ageing population (Hurd, 1997) though in the Indian context it remains a moot issue for next few decades.

Going by these realities, this section explores the socio-economic implications of changes in the age profile of population in India. Two issues are at the core of this analysis: one is the ageing pattern of the country's population which is expected to become more and more skewed in favour of the aged.[7] The other is to examine certain socio-economic implications of ageing including the question of health care requirements of those in later stages of their life cycle.

Shifts in the age composition of India's population (Table 1) underlie two possibilities. One, the declining fertility-mortality behaviour of people may soon place India in the group of countries with a substantial aged (60+) population (Bhat, 1992). Two, the problems of old age dependencies in the country may grow at a much faster pace due to the growing size of 60+ population. Both of these possibilities are fraught with an increasing burden of several degenerative diseases and injuries with considerable strain on the already overburdened public health care system. In addition, income needs and emotional instability of the aged and the lack of old age support facilities further compound the issue. Table 1 helps to draw out some of these points clearly.

Despite shifts in the age structure of the population and the growing size of the elderly, figures in Table 1 in no way suggest any shortage of working age population in India over the coming years. The share of population in the 15-59 age-groups is shown to be increasing (mainly because of the demographic momentum) overtime—from 56.2 per cent of the total population in 1901 to about 64 per cent in 2020.[8] This is unlike the greying economies of Europe and North America, which are faced with the serious problem of an ageing labour force. Yet another point apparent from Table 1 relates to the share of female dependencies. This Table shows that the share of females in the 60+ age-groups has consistently been higher than their male counterparts.

This pattern is substantiated by Table 2, which represents the old age dependencies for males and females separately since 1901. Table 2 also reveals higher female survivorship—share of 60+ women in the population is always higher than the men in similar ages (see also chart 1)—which leaves them with greater risks of widowhood in their older ages. This trend is significant as it has many ramifications for the government and as well as for the society at large. An important issue, for example, may be the health care and the livelihood requirements of the destitute elderly women, either facing the problems of widowhood or at the risk of widowhood due to higher longevity and survivorship chances.[9]

Table 1
Age Structure of Population in India, 1901-2001

(Percentage)

Census	Males			Females		
years	0-14	15-59	60+	0-14	10-59	60+
1901	39.2	56.2	4.6	38.0	56.5	5.5
1911	38.8	56.4	4.8	38.1	56.4	5.5
1921	39.4	55.6	5.0	39.0	55.6	5.5
1931	40.0	56.1	3.9	40.0	55.8	4.2
1941	38.1	57.1	4.9	38.4	56.7	4.9
1951	37.1	57.4	5.5	37.9	56.3	5.8
1961	40.9	53.6	5.5	41.2	53.0	5.8
1971	42.0	52.3	5.7	42.2	51.8	6.0
1981	39.8	54.1	6.1	39.6	53.8	6.6
1991	37.7	55.6	6.7	37.8	55.5	6.7
2001*	34.0	59.0	7.0	34.5	58.4	7.1
2011*	28.4	63.5	8.1	28.5	63.2	8.3
2020**	25.1	64.0	10.9	-	-	-

Notes: * Figures based on Technical Group Projection on Population (1996); ** UN projections for combined male & female population.
Source: Decennial Population Censuses.

Table 2
Trends in Old Age Dependency by Sex, 1901-2011

Years	Males (60+)	Females (60+)
1901	8.19	9.73
1911	8.51	9.75
1921	8.99	9.89
1931	6.95	7.53
1941	8.58	8.64
1951	9.58	10.30
1961	10.26	10.94
1971	10.90	11.58
1981	11.28	12.27
1991	12.05	12.07
2001	11.86	12.16
2011	12.76	13.13

Source: Based on Table 1.

In addition, Tables 1 and 2 together highlight the need to strengthen the family support system for the elderly, which is slowly losing ground in India, especially in the urban nuclear families. This change has been noted by Dandekar (1996, p. 38) in her study.[10] This study cites examples from a survey on the living arrangements of the aged in Madras city to show the existence of a good number of elderly persons who lived either all alone or with spouses without any family support. Although the fraction of loners in Dandekar's study (only 8 per cent) and in other earlier studies are not very large, it may not be totally implausible to expect an increase in the size of such populations by now. Similar details about the living arrangements of the rural elderly suggests that the share of persons living alone or with non-family members is

Chart 1
Projections of the Aged

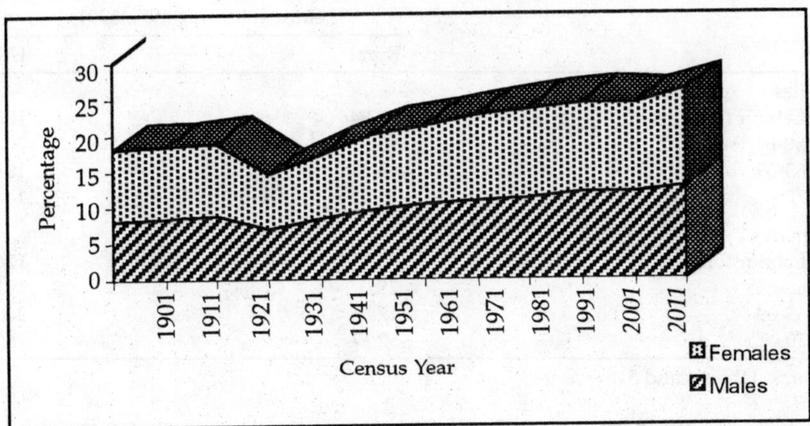

Source: Table 2.

6 per cent (Cain, 1985a, p. 15). But this information is equally dated and must have lost much of its significance in the context of the present study. The study by Rajan, et al. (1999, pp. 39-43) reconfirms a decline in co-residence of elderly with children, particularly if they are newly married.

Growth of the Elderly Population and Labour Force

Few observations can be made on the growth pattern of the labour force and the elderly population. The first one relates to our estimates of the labour force obtained on an annual basis from 1971 to 1991. We notice that these estimates match closely with the NSS, especially for the later years.[11] It however differs for the earlier years—more so around 1972-73 and 1977-78. This is possibly due to differences in estimates of population used to derive the labour force (see the details given in Appendix).

The second observation stems from the slower growth of the labour force in relation to the elderly population during the years between 1971 and 1991. This is evident from Table 3 and Chart 2. They also suggest a much faster expansion of the urban labour force over these years for both males and females.

Another interesting point to be learnt from Table 3 (and its attendant chart) is the growth pattern of the older population[12] that has outpaced the growth of the labour force. We notice that the size of the elderly population (especially those in the 65-69 age bracket) has increased much faster during these years than the labour force, especially in the urban areas. A similar trend may also be noted for the rural areas, but the pace turns out to be slower. Table 3 further suggests that the rural elders grew less rapidly compared to their urban counterparts. It suggests the problems of large-scale impoverishment, poor health conditions and shortage of necessary medical facilities for the rural elders in most villages. This table also supports the findings in most other studies regarding the survivorship and growth of female population in higher ages (Sharma and Xenos, 1992). We notice a

Table 3
Differentials in Growth of Ageing Population and Labour Force, 1971-1991

Sex	% Growth (during 1971-1991)	
	Rural	Urban
Males		
Labour force	46.84	102.96
60-64	20.97	100.00
65-69	93.33	183.33
70+	35.42	144.44
Females		
Labour force	32.15	126.47
60-64	28.07	91.67
65-69	117.86	240.00
70+	52.17	166.67

Source: Tables 4 and 5.

higher growth of urban females in 65+ ages and urban males for those in 60-64 age-group. However, it is evident from Table 3 that the males have outnumbered the females (Chart 2).

IV. LABOUR FORCE AND LEVELS OF DEPENDENCIES

Based on the estimates of population and the labour force, trends in dependencies are computed. These trends are derived from the population in the 15-59 age-groups, and those in the labour force. Table 4 provides dependencies obtained for rural and urban areas separately, and for dependants in the younger and older age-groups (see Appendix for methodology and computations).

Chart 2
Growth of Elderly Population and Labour Force

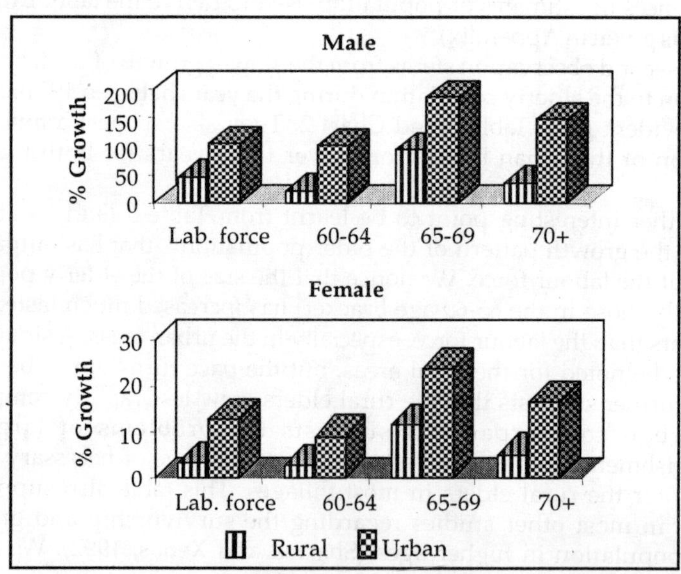

Often, dependencies are computed in relation to the size of population in the 15-59 or 15-64 age-groups (Srinivasan, 1998). We, however, departed from this and computed dependencies in relation to the labour force. Two reasons account for this shift. One, the nature of this study that is more concerned with economic implications of ageing. Another reason arises from the major questions that the study addresses such as—who really bears the burden of dependency? Is it the labour force or whosoever in the age-group 15-59? As a good fraction of those in the 15+ age-groups are themselves dependent on others (e.g., students, sick and mentally infirm or voluntarily unemployed), we felt that the burden of dependency falls more on the former. We, therefore, present below the dependencies—young[13] and old—based on our estimates of labour force. Population based dependencies are also provided to compare the two definitions.

The dependency burden of the labour force i. e., average numbers of dependencies per individual in the labour force is shown in Table 4. This Table presents the young and old age dependencies for the rural and the urban population separately and after combining them together.[14]

Several interesting points can be discerned from this Table. The first is of course obvious, i.e., the burden of old age dependencies has generally increased, often at a faster pace in urban areas (Chart 3). Moreover,

Table 4
Dependency Burden on Labour Force, 1971-91 (Male and Female Combined)

(Ratios)

Year	Rural dependencies		Urban dependencies		Aggregate dep. (R+U+O+Y)
	Younger dep.	Older dep.	Younger dep.	Older dep.	
1971	0.983	0.143	1.148	0.146	1.153
1972	0.969	0.143	1.104	0.145	1.135
1973	0.955	0.143	1.079	0.144	1.120
1974	0.942	0.143	1.054	0.142	1.104
1975	0.930	0.144	1.029	0.141	1.091
1976	0.917	0.144	1.005	0.140	1.076
1977	0.904	0.144	0.984	0.139	1.062
1978	0.902	0.146	0.983	0.141	1.062
1979	0.898	0.147	0.982	0.142	1.060
1980	0.895	0.149	0.981	0.144	1.060
1981	0.892	0.151	0.980	0.146	1.059
1982	0.885	0.150	0.979	0.148	1.053
1983	0.881	0.149	0.979	0.151	1.051
1984	0.876	0.149	0.969	0.152	1.044
1985	0.871	0.148	0.959	0.153	1.038
1986	0.866	0.148	0.949	0.154	1.032
1987	0.861	0.147	0.939	0.156	1.027
1988	0.856	0.147	0.937	0.158	1.022
1989	0.847	0.146	0.928	0.160	1.013
1990	0.842	0.146	0.935	0.164	1.011
1991	0.856	0.149	0.920	0.165	1.022

Source: Based on Appendix, Tables 2 and 5.

definitional changes introduce substantial variations in the burden of dependencies. For example, a change from the concept of working age (15-59) population to labour force significantly increases the levels of rural and urban dependencies.[15]

Another interesting point is the low rural-urban differentials in the burden of old age dependencies. This is despite some declining trend in the rural dependencies over the eighties (Chart 3). This trend may also be discernible at the aggregate level. These are, perhaps, the outcome of intermittent changes in the LFPR; and may not therefore be considered significant from the policy viewpoint. Nevertheless, given the inadequate earnings and lower bargaining strength of a majority of the rural poor, a marginal decline in dependency ratios may not mean much to many of them.

Chart 3
Dependencies/Labour Force Ratios

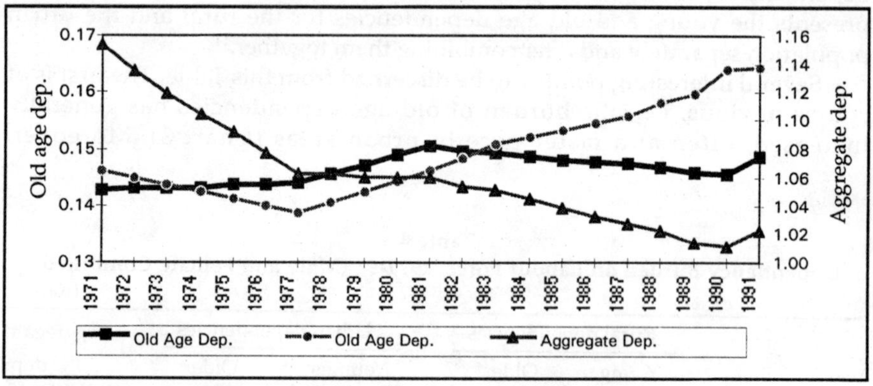

Source: Same as in Table 4.

V. MACRO ECONOMIC IMPLICATIONS OF AGEING

The analyses in the earlier sections do not ostensibly suggest old age dependencies or its macro-level shifts as an issue of serious consequences. Table 4, for example, suggests a very marginal increase in the level of rural dependencies and its burden , i.e., from 6.99 in 1971 to 6.71 in 1991 (in other words, seven persons in the labour force to support each elderly in 1971 to 6.7 persons two decades later). That too, with a parallel decline in the young age dependencies. The situation in urban areas may however, look a little more serious with 6.85 to an elderly in 1971, down to 6.06 in 1991. Again, this is accompanied by a simultaneous decline in young age dependencies.

If viewed in terms of its average effects, perhaps no grave concerns can emerge from such indications. But a macro perspective—mainly in terms of large scale poverty, unemployment, increased privatisation under the liberalised economic regime, informalisation of labour market and, above all, the growing rate of increase in elderly population over the coming years—do predict certain unhealthy trends. There is ample evidence to suggest that the quality of employment in the country has suffered due to growing casualisation of employment (Alam and Mishra, 1998). This not only adds to social unevenness but also enhances the severity of any dependence, whether young or old. Hence, to expect that poor families may really be able to maintain their elderly dependants with all their poor health conditions and many other problems is a doubtful proposition.

This issue, as already noted, is further compounded by debilitating poverty in large segments of rural and urban population. There are evidences to show that about a one third of the country's total population is still below the poverty line (*Sarvekshana*, 1998, p. 17-18).[16] Even those who are immediately above the poverty level are no less vulnerable. While the age structure of persons in abject poverty is not readily available, one may safely surmise that a substantial proportion of them must be the elderly people. If one accepts this proposition, a set of related questions invariably emerges. How do these elderly lot survive and what would be their quality of life? Who bears the burden of old age dependency and how? What would happen to the poor elderly during the second and third generation reforms? What are the basic needs of the elderly and how much would it cost (comprising food, shelter and health care) in a liberalised regime? How can old age poverty be defined, and does or doesn't it differ from general poverty? These and many other related issues in our view makes old age security problems, which also includes the severity of old age dependencies on the poor households, a subject for serious concern.

The rapid population ageing in most developed countries has several macro economic implications, particularly for the size of the working age population and labour force. Besides, it also affects the overall savings and consumption behaviour in the economy. Some of the studies conducted to examine these implications of ageing clearly suggest a decline in the savings rate, which affects the functioning of the capital markets as well.[17] However, this paper restricts itself to the health-related issues of ageing to highlight the macro implications of an ageing population.

Health and Ageing

Of late, evidences have been mounting to suggest the Indian scenario of a population with poor health status showing improvements in longevity and survival chances. Emphasised along with this is the complementarity between ageing (old age) and sickness incidence and the growing cost of health services. In addition, a significant amount of the literature has also been devoted towards showing the inadequacy of the public health care.[18] Following is an analysis into these issues using the available data referring to the health situation of the ageing population.

Health status and its quantification underlie many conceptual and empirical issues. While we do not intend to go into those details, it ought to be noted that the health status measurements require identification of sickness related losses both in terms of: (i) premature deaths (defined as the differences between actual age at the time of death and life expectancy at that age), and (ii) days of healthy life lost due to indisposition, disability and changes in psychological and social functions of individuals. Recently, this concept was applied by the World Bank in its World Development Report (1993) to derive the global burden of diseases (GBD). The report—which provides the GBD both for India and China separately—clearly indicates a very high burden of communicable and non-communicable diseases suffered by large fractions of the old and young in India (Table 5). It may be noticed that older persons suffer very heavily due to various non-communicable diseases—as many as 42 per cent of them suffer from these conditions. Those carrying the communicable diseases are however fewer, about a tenth of the former.

Table 5
Burden of Communicable and Non-communicable Diseases by Age-group, 1990 (All-India)

	Communicable, maternal & perinatal			Non-communicable diseases		
Age-group	DALYs* (in millions)	Percentages	Rate/1000 population	DALYs* (in millions)	Percentages	Rate/1000 population
0 - 4	97.9	66.3	840.7	33.4	28.3	286.6
5 - 14	15.4	10.4	78.3	9.8	8.3	49.6
15 - 44	27.1	18.3	70.5	27.3	23.1	71.1
45 - 59	4.7	3.2	50.2	22.6	19.2	242.0
60 +	2.6	1.8	44.8	25.0	21.1	425.2
(All ages)	147.7	100.0	173.9	118.1	100.0	138.9

Note: * DALYs refer to the loss of healthy life years resulting from disease related disabilities.
Source: *World Development Report*, World Bank, 1993 (Table B.4, p. 220).

Greater risks of sickness in older population can also be noted from the health surveys conducted by the National Sample Survey Organisation (NSSO) and the National Council of Applied Economic Research (NCAER).[19] Based on the 42nd round NSS, a study by Reddy (1996) has cited a considerably high fraction of ageing population in the country that suffers from severe physical or mental disorders.[20] This study has also attempted to look into the nature of assistance provided by the states to such persons. Further, it reconfirmed our earlier contention that there is absolute lack of, or negligible, support from the state for the aged.

While these analyses are illustrative of the health problems of the ageing population in India, further substantiation needs analysis of two related issues viz., the size of the ailing elderly population by type of disease with its growth pattern, and the escalation in the cost of medical services, particularly the diagnostics and drug prices. It is the latter which makes the health insurance system almost imperative, especially for the old-age population which suffers from multiple risks of life including failing health conditions, livelihood difficulties, etc.

Disease-wise estimates of ailing population are a useful device by which the planning process can be geared towards disease prevention and proper resource allocation in the health sector. In India, such attempts could not be made effectively due to serious conceptual and data limitations. Nevertheless, based on a very simplistic method, we have tried to estimate the population suffering five specific diseases—namely, partial and complete blindness, tuberculosis, leprosy, malaria and limbs impairment. The prevalence rate of these diseases were obtained from the all-India National Family Health Survey, 1992-93. We applied this information on the estimated 1992[21] population. Table 6 (see also Appendix, Table 6) provides the details.

Table 6
Prevalence of Specific Diseases among 60-69 and 70+ Population (Combined Males and Females)

(Percentage)

Age-groups	Estimated pop. (1992)* (M+F)	Blindness Part-ial	Blindness Comp-lete	Tuber-culosis	Leprosy	Phy. Impair. of limbs	Malaria
Rural							
60-69	29,158,564	15.096	1.244	1.812	0.371	1.183	5.005
70+	13,552,888	21.222	3.252	1.731	0.297	1.721	4.546
All ages	640,634,834	2.686	0.430	0.512	0.130	0.667	3.896
Urban							
60-69	8,988,611	12.747	0.877	0.998	0.150	0.900	1.800
70+	4,730,824	17.772	2.035	1.033	0.072	2.141	1.817
All ages	224,786,696	2.306	0.375	0.344	0.092	0.559	1.729
All-India(R+U)							
60-69	38,147,175	13.685	1.024	1.323	0.238	1.013	3.080
70+	18,283,712	20.329	2.937	1.550	0.239	1.830	3.840
All ages	865,421,530	2.587	0.416	0.468	0.120	0.639	3.333

Source: Based on estimated population for 1992 and the NFHS (1992-93, All India, Table 8.1, p. 202).

Two points need to be mentioned here. One is the rise in the prevalence of diseases at higher ages. We notice that the share of older population that suffers from various ailments is far greater than others. Moreover, it increases substantially with age. Two, among the major health problems of the aged, the worst perhaps is the vision impairment. This is evident in Table 6. It also suggests that this problem is much higher among the rural elders. This is followed by the problem of tuberculosis, which is far more dangerous from the public health viewpoint. Moreover, this disease has strong social dimensions with illiteracy and poverty as the two basic determinants. Some other health problems with considerable damage to the quality of life can also be noted from Table 6.

Added to the growing disease prevalence among the aged are the escalation in charges (or tariff) for diagnostic and medical care. Specially, prices of many essential and commonly used medicines have risen steeply since recent amendments in the drug policy.[22] A study by Rane (1995) has documented some of these issues—particularly the increase in drug prices over a brief period of less than two years, i.e., December 1993 to September 1995. We reproduce these figures in Table 7 to illustrate the point in argument. We notice that the medicines used in treatment of diseases such as tuberculosis or anaemia have risen twice or even more over a short span of two years. As both the conditions—anaemia and tuberculosis—are poverty driven, even a small increase in the treatment cost of these ailments would severely affect the low-income households. Table 7 highlights a number of other commonly used medicines which have also registered a high increase in their selling prices over the past few years. Obviously, this and similar hikes in cost of other curative and diagnostic services—are likely to pose serious issues for the future health management strategies in the country.

Table 7
Comparison of Drug Prices: Pre and Post Drug Policy Change

Medicines	Group	Price before NDP (Rs.) (Dec. 1993)	Price after NDP (Rs.) (Sept. 1995)	Percentage rise
Alludrox Gel	antacid	13.49	28.93	114.50
Myambutoe	anti T.B.	5.92	12.64	113.50
Corex	cough syrup	9.39	19.55	108.20
Lanoxin	cardiac	1.95	4.00	105.10
Dilantin	anti-epilepsy	21.65	44.41	105.10
Thromycin	antibiotic	9.68	19.25	98.90
Calmod	tranquilliser	3.35	6.65	98.50
Neosporin	skin ointment	11.86	22.94	93.40
Incidal	anti-allergic	2.91	5.50	89.00
Gardinal	anti-epilepsy	6.8	12.69	86.60
Bronkotab 4	anti-asthma	2.93	5.18	76.80
Banocide	anti-helminth.	11.18	20.10	75.40
Diabinese	anti-diabetic	2.66	4.60	72.90
Paraxin	antibiotic	11.67	20.00	71.40
Terramycin	antibiotic	3.82	6.11	60.00
Calpol	anti-pyretic	7.49	11.67	55.80
Subamycin	antibiotic	7.6	11.69	53.80
PZA	anti T.B.	17.12	23.10	52.50

Source: Rane (1995), pp. 2977-78.

Opinion also began to converge among planners and health officials to rationalise public health expenditure with larger allocations on primary and preventive health care services. Following externalities and private benefit arguments, this process ultimately favours: privatisation of most hospital services or imposition of user charges. Without questioning its rationality, we submit that such a strategy should be proceeded by some institutional arrangements like old age social security and health insurance.

VI. OLD-AGE HEALTH/MEDICAL CARE REQUIREMENTS: NEED FOR HEALTH INSURANCE

Two major components of old age security requirements are livelihood—including food and shelter—and health/medical or disability care. Perhaps, the latter involves far more serious constraints mainly due to growing longevity associated with serious risks of sickness, disability and widowhood, and, high treatment cost due to inflation in the medical sector. Moreover, the quality of care has declined sharply, despite an increase in the number of paid services in public hospitals. The emerging consensus to privatise health care without significant externalities, and no access to the ESIS or the CGHS health services by almost 90 per cent of the country's population, pose a serious challenge to the government with regard to the health care requirements of the elderly. Some of the recent suggestions to encourage family ties through legislation and fiscal incentives or self-help sermons to older persons may not be more than a partial solution—if a solution at all.[23]

Currently, the health care system in India suffers a serious paradox—a very high expenditure (around 6 per cent of GDP, over three-fourth of which comprises private out-of-pocket expenses by individuals) without a matching outcome.[24] Often, low quality services, difficulties in accessing health care by the poor and underprivileged, misplaced subsidies, etc., are considered responsible for this mismatch. Yet another causal factor is the inadequate finances to run public facilities. Health insurance is therefore, considered as the only solution to ensure access and quality. This may however, require strong regulations and a strict monitoring of both the provider and the insurer agencies (Ellis, et al., 2000).

In India, health insurance facilities are available in many forms. These include the more formal insurance cover comprising mediclaim,[25] personal accident protection plan,[26] Jeevan Arogya Beema[27] of the General Insurance Corporation (GIC), Jeevan Suraksha or other speciality insurance plans of the Life Insurance Corporation (LIC). Besides, there are health benefits provided by the centre and state governments through Employees State Insurance Scheme (ESIS) and the Central Government Health Scheme (CGHS). In addition, there is employer's compensation of health expenses as well. These programmes, however, cover a handful of higher-income people or those employed in the organised public or private sectors. A very large majority of the population—almost 90 per cent of the total—is not covered under any such scheme. They are forced to rely either on private health care providers or on inefficient public health care delivery system. Both are difficult options that hardly suit the elders and other low-income people.[28]

The solution to some of these problems lies in serious efforts to evolve a social health insurance system[29] for the older persons with universal coverage against selected conditions based on careful analyses and profiling of major geriatric diseases, risk factors, premium per elderly person and a viable financing mechanism.

VII. FINANCING OF SOCIAL HEALTH INSURANCE : LIKELY OPTIONS

Constitutional references notwithstanding, growing fiscal constraints in India may not allow governments in the centre and state to shoulder any major financial commitment. Rather, some of the existing commitments may be down- sized to conform with the emerging wisdom to rationalise government expenditure and allocation of public resources. Hence, to expect that the government would on its own be able to create a sustainable health care system for the elders is futile. Attempts may however, be made to generate a fund under the public corpus that helps to meet the health insurance premium of the elderly persons with a package of benefits, which covers the risks of a few selected and most commonly occurring conditions.[30] Singapore has adopted similar strategies to meet the cost of medical care of its population. A Medisave scheme, for example, was designed by the Singapore government in the early eighties to meet the medical costs of the elderly. This was shortly followed by another scheme (Medishield scheme) to provide a low cost catastrophic illness insurance cover to its population. A public endowment fund was also created by the government to ensure that the basic medical care is not denied to citizens for non-payment (Phua and Teng, 1998).

Creation of such a fund to finance a social security system in India may, however, require serious attempts towards reviewing and understanding the country's own requirements, and the social (and health) security system in other countries—particularly in Singapore, Malaysia, Japan or certain other East Asian economies. India may adopt a pay roll tax system (on the lines of the provident fund) to create a health/medical or disability fund with a matching contribution from the employer. To be more precise, employees in the organised sector may be mandated to contribute a proportion of their salary/wages with contributions from employers as well. The system may run on the lines of the provident fund with the difference that the money so deducted may remain with the government even after retirement, which will then be used to pay the health insurance premium for the individual and spouse over the life time.

What was suggested above is however, not the real issue. It is the coverage of poor and informal sector people which poses the real problem. While an analysis of this issue is beyond the purview of this study, any such attempt would have to consider the following—a morbidity profile of the elderly population to find the most prevalent conditions, size of the risk bearing population, treatment cost, and age- adjusted premium. To finance such a mandatory social insurance plan, government may, *inter alia*, consider devising a suitable "cess", especially on health hazardous industries comprising, for example, tobacco and tobacco products, makers of *pan masaala*, snuff and alcoholic beverages, transporters, automobile manufacturers, industries engaged in production of certain chemicals and dye, and similar other polluting units which cause major sickness. Government may also consider sharing part of the burden to meet its Constitutional obligations. User charges may also be imposed on several non-essential items. Such a plan may initially be considered for the elderly and other vulnerable groups including the widows. Public health insurance agencies, particularly the General Insurance Corporation and its subsidiaries may be entrusted with this responsibility.

Admittedly, it may not be easy to accomplish the task of universal insurance for a variety of administrative and financial difficulties. However, given the seriousness of the problem, an attempt in this direction cannot be postponed for any longer.

It may also be noted that the country has many such schemes in operation, though most of them were drawn up to serve different objectives. The LIC, for example, is currently running a group insurance policy at a premium of Rs. 10 for every Rs. 1000 benefit. Coverage up to Rs. 5000 under this plan is subsidised with a capital grant from the government. The SEWA Bank's scheme of integrated insurance and voluntary health services may also serve to point towards some useful lessons. A review of many such schemes by Jhabvala (1998) provides a good starting point.

VIII. SUMMARY AND CONCLUSION

Demographically, India has registered a number of significant changes over the past 50 years. Prominent amongst these are: a persistent reduction in the fertility of a large segment of the Indian population which may accelerate, and improvement in life expectancy at all stages of the life span. Simultaneously, it has been observed that demographic ageing, a global phenomenon may hit India in the coming decades. However, much of the recent literature on demographic transition in India has not given sufficient attention to the implications of these changes for old age dependency and social security. In particular, the implications of these changes at the macro and/or micro-economic levels for consumption, savings, investment, health care requirements, labour market, social security transfers, family system, inter and intra-household inequalities etc., have not been properly investigated.

These issues are of prime importance in the Indian context as the 1991 Census shows a considerably large proportion of population in the 60 and above age-groups (more than 56 million, or a little over 6.7 per cent of the total population), which would grow larger over time. Along-side, social security and health care support for a large segment of this population is extremely weak, if not absent altogether. Besides, not just on equity considerations but also from a macro economic perspective of growth, the overall economic behaviour of the elderly, especially their consumption pattern, saving propensity warrants a detailed analysis.

Considering these facts, this study looked into shifts in ageing and dependency burden over time based on our estimates of population in the younger and older age-groups during 1971-91 and health problems of the elderly population, which remain almost completely unaddressed despite large scale poverty, frequent and complex nature of old age diseases, inadequate health care provided by the government, rising drug prices, and unaffordable tariffs of private medical facilities.

The results clearly indicate a rising trend in old age dependencies that might increase further, especially in urban areas. These results also indicate the greater survivorship chances of elderly women, particularly for those aged 65 and over. This may as well lead to a growing number of elderly widows in society with a larger burden to meet their subsistence and health care needs. This study, therefore, strongly favours including these issues in the current debate on poverty and need for arranging age based security.

Another interesting result relates to the faster growth of the elderly population in relation to labour force. Our results indicate that the size of elderly population has grown faster than the labour force during the period between 1971 and 1991. This is particularly true for the urban areas. However, in view of the existing trend of demographic momentum, labour market implication of the ageing is viewed to remain a moot issue in the country for next few decades, though it ought not to be considered as sufficient to ensure old age security. A large majority of low income households would require formal security cover to survive the growing role of the market.

A considerable part of the study has been devoted to the morbidity issues of the aged population. The major issues identified being low health standards of elderly population due to serious disabilities and a high rate of disease prevalence, rising drug prices, inadequate health/medical facilities in the government sector, complete lack of facilities for geriatric diseases, growing pressure from fiscal reformists to restructure public health expenditure with a greater emphasis on primary and preventive care suggest that the problem of the elderly defies an easy solution.

While the need for health sector reforms may not be denied, it may however, be argued that a change in the system needs to be preceded by certain institutional arrangements. One such arrangement in this particular case involves an expansion of health insurance mechanisms in the country, to cover the low-income elderly households. The study emphasises the need for raising a public fund by taxing industries which cause health hazard or act as a pollutant. The corpus, supplemented by government funds may be used to finance the health/medical insurance cover provided to entire aged (60+) population against selected and more degenerative diseases. For the organised sector, the same may be arranged by devising a payroll tax with contribution from employers to meet the post-retirement health and disability insurance premium. Certain successful experiences of providing health security for the informal sector workers or for the elderly, implemented by NGOs within the country, provide valuable insights for addressing the issues related to the aged population who are not covered by the pension system. Along with this, lessons from other countries including Malaysia, Singapore and Japan can also be a starting point for reviewing the security mechanisms available to the elderly in our country.

(Part of the results presented in the paper are taken from an earlier study by Moneer Alam and R.N. Agarwal, 1999)

Appendix

ESTIMATION OF DEPENDENCY BURDEN: METHODOLOGY

Three intermediate calculations were made to obtain a time series of the dependents labour force rations. We began with the calculation of the annual population by sex and age-groups. The base line information for these calculations were obtained from the last three Censuses (i.e., 1971-91), which provide data on rural-urban population by sex and age groups. As the age structure of the 1991 population was not available at the time of this exercise, we relied on Bose (1996, p. 81) for this information. Moreover, population for Assam in 1981 and Jammu & Kashmir in 1991 are the Central Statistical Organisation's (CSO) estimates and used in absence of the actual Census data.[31] These estimates helped us make the total (all-India) population comparable for all the three-Censal years (1971-91) under consideration.

App. Table 1 presents the age-wise break-up of population for each census year. This Table has served as the basis for all subsequent calculations, namely population in different age -groups (from 0-4 to 70+), size of dependant population (defined as those in 0-14 and 60+ age-groups), total labour force and dependencies. All these calculations have been derived for the period 1971-1991. Based on information in App. Table 1, the average annual growth of population was computed for each age-group during 1971-81, and 1981-91. This formed our step two. These rates were later applied to compute the population in each age-group over the required time period. Finally, for the ease of presentation, these age-groups were combined into six broad categories (i.e., 0-9, 10-14, 15-59, 60-64, 65-69 and 70+). App. Table 2 gives the estimates of population for selected years.

Step three required measuring the aggregate labour force at the all-India level to work out shifts in the dependency burden. We derived these estimates based on the sex-wise labour force participation rates (LFPR) provided by the National Sample Survey (NSS) for the rural and urban population at different points of time (App. Table 3). Because the LFPRs are mostly quinquennial, certain prorate adjustments have been made[32] to compute the size of the annual labour force (App. Table 4). Sex-wise and rural-urban estimates of labour force are presented in App. Table 5—again for the selected years.

App. Table 1
Rural, Urban and Sex-wise Age Structure of Population, 1971–1991 (%)

	Age-groups						
	0-9	10-14	15-19	20-24	25-29	30-34	35-39
1971 Population							
Rural males	29.979	13.021	8.549	7.034	6.889	6.264	5.950
Rural females	30.435	12.100	8.079	7.862	7.649	6.764	5.907
Urban males	25.345	12.192	10.156	9.756	8.208	7.169	6.527
Urban females	28.016	12.760	9.892	9.386	8.214	6.770	6.042
Total population	29.480	12.549	8.661	7.865	7.448	6.602	6.004
1981 Population							
Rural males	27.324	13.496	9.619	7.817	7.087	5.985	5.611
Rural females	27.509	12.682	9.018	8.426	7.479	6.402	5.870
Urban males	23.235	12.152	10.767	10.358	8.750	7.187	6.341
Urban females	25.256	12.559	10.569	10.151	8.763	6.722	6.012
Total population	26.659	12.923	9.641	8.615	7.623	6.370	5.842
1991 Population							
Rural males	25.800	11.300	11.000	9.600	7.700	6.700	5.800
Rural females	25.400	11.100	10.200	9.700	7.800	6.800	5.900
Urban males	22.300	10.600	10.300	9.900	9.100	8.200	6.900
Urban females	22.500	10.600	10.200	10.700	9.200	7.900	6.500
Total population	24.780	11.048	10.520	9.810	8.108	7.085	6.070

	Age-groups						
	40-44	45-49	50-54	55-59	60-64	65-69	70+
1971 Population							
Rural males	5.218	4.370	3.970	2.500	2.766	1.349	2.141
Rural females	5.052	4.019	3.644	2.323	2.685	1.311	2.171
Urban males	5.628	4.466	3.696	2.123	2.132	1.022	1.579
Urban females	4.830	3.637	3.231	1.965	2.294	1.097	1.866
Total population	5.162	4.176	3.745	2.342	2.623	1.276	2.067
1981 Population							
Rural males	5.143	4.459	4.107	2.518	2.907	1.481	2.446
Rural females	5.110	4.390	3.708	2.558	2.858	1.528	2.462
Urban males	5.568	4.512	3.722	2.326	2.183	1.125	1.772
Urban females	4.759	4.071	3.291	2.155	2.318	1.274	2.100
Total population	5.141	4.398	3.821	2.469	2.734	1.432	2.331
1991 Population							
Rural males	4.900	4.300	3.600	3.200	2.300	1.800	2.000
Rural females	5.000	4.500	3.700	3.200	2.400	2.000	2.300
Urban males	5.700	4.700	3.900	2.900	2.100	1.500	1.900
Urban females	5.400	4.400	3.500	2.900	2.200	1.700	2.300
Total population	5.105	4.438	3.665	3.123	2.297	1.819	2.131

Source: Census of India 1971, 1981 and 1991.

App. Table 2
Estimates of Population by Broad Age-group, 1971–1991

(Selected years)

Year	0-14	15-59	60-64	65-69	70+	All ages
Rural males						
1971	96,866,997	114,312,461	6,231,597	3,039,905	4,823,706	225,274,666
1975	101,730,873	124,103,513	6,819,056	3,385,077	5,457,465	241,495,984
1980	108,242,364	137,653,057	7,631,858	3,872,169	6,368,009	263,767,458
1981	109,605,750	140,552,367	7,805,694	3,977,695	6,567,593	268,509,099
1985	113,718,458	156,400,572	7,664,483	4,636,953	6,534,322	288,954,788
1990	119,161,197	179,171,535	7,491,556	5,616,739	6,492,971	317,933,998
1991	120,291,780	184,166,391	7,457,442	5,836,259	6,484,732	324,236,603
Rural females						
1971	90,884,355	109,610,902	5,736,749	2,801,670	4,638,401	213,672,077
1975	95,327,187	119,133,283	6,314,342	3,197,330	5,236,785	229,208,927
1980	101,291,857	132,305,173	7,118,787	3,771,381	6,094,461	250,581,659
1981	102,543,236	135,122,653	7,291,578	3,898,011	6,282,1[illegible]7	255,137,645
1885	105,865,637	149,029,231	7,296,306	4,658,471	6,559,676	273,409,321
1990	110,185,618	168,609,503	7,302,219	5,820,950	6,923,865	298,842,155
1991	111,072,571	172,847,179	7,303,402	6,086,168	6,999,094	304,308,414
Urban males						
1971	22,041,520	33,897,734	1,251,818	599,937	927,362	58,718,371
1975	24,933,485	39,748,097	1,463,991	722,370	1,125,026	67,992,969
1980	29,097,900	48,514,959	1,780,471	911,122	1,432,367	81,736,820
1981	30,012,199	50,489,892	1,851,545	954,421	1,503,255	84,811,313
1885	32,916,121	57,775,681	2,059,045	1,209,311	1,745,736	95,705,894
1990	36,961,192	68,457,559	2,351,420	1,625,682	2,104,558	111,500,410
1991	37,830,289	70,831,179	2,414,699	1,724,785	2,184,728	114,985,679
Urban females						
1971	20,541,950	27,187,738	1,155,527	552,844	940,215	50,378,274
1975	23,319,904	32,396,694	1,357,899	686,853	1,153,507	58,914,857
1980	27,336,782	40,348,407	1,661,410	900,929	1,489,400	71,736,928
1981	28,221,081	42,161,262	1,729,812	951,166	1,567,507	74,630,828
1885	30,408,281	49,281,137	1,925,388	1,213,062	1,847,425	84,675,293
1990	33,386,997	59,970,470	2,201,241	1,644,057	2,268,628	99,471,393
1991	34,017,529	62,382,598	2,260,984	1,747,124	2,363,756	102,771,990

Source: Estimates based on the growth rates of population in different age brackets given in Appendix, Table 1.

App. Table 3
Labour Force Participation Rate, 1972-73 to 1992

Year**	Rural males	Rural females	Urban males	Rural females
1972-73	0.551	0.321	0.521	0.142
1977-78	0.565	0.345	0.543	0.183
1983	0.555	0.342	0.540	0.159
1987-88	0.549	0.331	0.534	0.162
1989-90*	0.555	0.321	0.533	0.150
1990-91*	0.559	0.293	0.537	0.150

Note: *Information based on thin sample used by the National Sample Survey Organisation (NSSO); Figures relate to the usual status of individuals; LFPR represents the size of labour force as percent of population;** LFPRs for the years between 1972-73 and 1977-78 are the interpolated values. This has been followed for the subsequent periods as well.

Source: Based on various rounds of the NSS results as reported in the *IAMR's Manpower Profile (India)*, 1996, pp.98-99.

App. Table 4
Prorate Adjusted LFPRs, 1971-91

Year	Rural		Urban	
	Males	Females	Males	Females
1971	0.548	0.316	0.517	0.134
1972	0.551	0.321	0.521	0.142
1973	0.554	0.326	0.525	0.150
1974	0.557	0.331	0.530	0.158
1975	0.559	0.335	0.534	0.167
1976	0.562	0.340	0.539	0.175
1977	0.565	0.345	0.543	0.183
1978	0.563	0.345	0.543	0.179
1979	0.562	0.345	0.543	0.175
1980	0.560	0.345	0.543	0.171
1981	0.558	0.345	0.543	0.167
1982	0.557	0.345	0.543	0.163
1983	0.555	0.342	0.540	0.159
1984	0.555	0.339	0.540	0.160
1985	0.554	0.337	0.540	0.160
1986	0.553	0.334	0.540	0.161
1987	0.552	0.331	0.540	0.161
1988	0.549	0.331	0.534	0.162
1989	0.549	0.331	0.534	0.162
1990	0.555	0.321	0.533	0.150
1991	0.559	0.293	0.537	0.150

Source: Appendix, Table 3.

App. Table 5
Estimates of Labour Force, 1971-91 (Rural-urban & Male-female)

(Numbers)

Year	Rural labour force (M)	Rural labour force (F)	Total rural labour force	Urban labour force (M)	Urban labour force (F)	Total urban labour force	Aggregate labour force
1971	123,450,517	67,520,376	190,970,893	30,357,398	6,750,689	37,108,087	228,078,980
1975	134,996,255	76,784,990	211,781,245	36,308,246	9,838,781	46,147,027	257,928,272
1980	147,709,777	86,450,672	234,160,449	44,383,093	12,267,015	56,650,108	290,810,557
1981	149,828,077	88,022,488	237,850,565	46,052,543	12,463,348	58,515,891	296,366,456
1985	160,080,953	92,138,941	252,219,894	51,681,183	13,548,047	65,229,229	317,449,123
1990	176,453,369	95,928,332	272,381,700	59,429,719	14,920,709	74,350,427	346,732,128
1991	181,248,261	89,162,365	270,410,626	61,747,310	15,415,799	77,163,108	347,573,735

Note: Estimates based on the time series of population in Appendix, Table 2 and adjusted LFPRs presented in Appendix, Table 4.

App. Table 6
Estimates of Elderly (60-69 and 70+) and Total Population Suffering from Specific Diseases, 1992 (Males + Females)

(in million)

Age-groups	Estimated pop. (1992)* (M+F)	Blindness		TB	Leprosy	Phy. impair. of limbs
		Partial	Complete			
Rural						
60-69	29,158,564	4.402	0.363	0.528	0.108	0.345
70+	13,552,888	2.877	0.441	0.235	0.040	0.233
All ages	640,634,834	17.207	2.755	3.280	0.833	4.273
Urban						
60-69	8,988,611	1.146	0.079	0.090	0.013	0.081
70+	4,730,824	0.841	0.096	0.049	0.003	0.101
All ages	224,786,696	5.184	0.843	0.773	0.207	1.257
60-69	38,147,175	5.220	0.391	0.505	0.091	0.386
70+	18,283,712	3.717	0.537	0.283	0.044	0.335
All ages	865,421,530	22.388	3.600	4.050	1.039	5.530

Source: Based on estimated population for 1992 and the NFHS (1992-93, All India, Table 8.1, p. 202).

Notes

1. A third and more recent concern of this debate relates to the effects of old age support on economic behaviour of the recipients. An issue to be examined, for example, may be the disincentive effects of transfers on savings or labour supply behaviour of the recipients. These issues have at length been described, among others, by Atkinson (1995).
2. It ought to be clarified that the review of studies presented here is very limited and confined to only a few selected readings on this otherwise a very vast subject. Therefore, this study should by no means be treated as an attempt to provide an exhaustive review of literature on ageing or its related problems.
3. The redistributive consequences of transfers have been examined by Case and Deaton (1998) in their recent paper which looks into the behaviour of social pensioners in South Africa. The study suggests that the pension is an effective mechanism in reaching to the poorest households and their children. The study agrees with the possibility that some of the benefits may be accruing to the younger and presumably better-off person.
4. For a comparison of various social security instruments in India and other countries, see Singh (1997).
5. A few notable exceptions included the studies by Mead Cain which have examined the material consequences of reproductive failures (which also serves as a basis for Leibenstein's old age security proposition) for countries like India and Bangladesh. Some of these works have been cited very briefly in Section 2 of this paper.
6. Another drawback with the social security system in India is its limited coverage - to only a small fraction of working population employed in organised public or private sector establishments. In addition, social security benefits are also provided to poor households by the government as part of its anti-poverty measures. One such illustration may be the centrally operated National Social Assistance Programme (NSAP), which became functional since August 1995. An important component of this programme includes the old age pension scheme for the destitute men or women who completed 65 years of age, and do not receive any financial support from the family. The amount payable under this programme is Rs. 75 a month. The other two schemes under the NSAP are the national maternity benefit scheme and the national family

benefit scheme. Most of these schemes (including the NSAP) are directed to help the households which are below poverty level, and without any regular means of subsistence.

7. Old age, aged, older population, elders, etc., are used here interchangeably, and imply the age-groups including 60 years and above.

8. This might in due course open up some interesting possibilities for countries like India to seek advantage of the current trade regime (WTO) and enhance agressively their human power export to the greying economies. It may however need to formulate skill formation strategies that meet the labour market requirements of the recipient countries.

9. For further discussion, see Dandekar (1996); Rao and Townsend (1998); Rajan, et al., (1999).

10. A front-page report in *The Times of India* (Sunday, April 5, 1998) reconfirms the growing menace of this problem. There are also indications that the Government of India (Ministry of Welfare) is currently in the process of formulating a national policy on old age population to safeguard the interest of the elders.

11. The NSS estimates of total labour force for 1990-91 (cited by the Institute of Applied Manpower Research in its *Year Book on Manpower Profile*: India, 1996, pp. 98-99), for example, was 347.6 million. This figure fully corresponds with our own in App. Table 5.

12. The Rajan, et al. study (1999) provides an interesting comparison of the rates at which the elderly and the non-elderly will grow over the coming years. The study suggests that the rate of elderly growth will be much faster than the non-elderly. By 2021, for example, the "... growth rate of elderly will be one-and-half times higher than the growth rate of the general population" (pp. 24-25).

13. Though we are not directly concerned with the young age dependencies, these are suggestive in the sense that they represent an inverse pattern with those of the old age dependencies. To be more precise, while the old age dependency is on the rise, an opposite is true for the younger dependants.

14. Though the main thrust of this exercise is not so much on the young age dependencies, we presented them in these Tables to see how do they compare with the old age dependencies and its trends. These details further serve to argue that some of the advantages drawn from the declining fertility may eventually be used to subsidise the services required for the old age care.

15. A further shift in concept from the labour force to the workforce may raise the dependency levels even more.

16. The details provided in the above cited issue of *Sarvekshana* suggest a total of 30 per cent rural population with monthly per capita consumption expenditure (MPCE) below RS. 190, and 28 per cent urban population below RS. 265. A further break-up of this population by type of households suggests the rural agricultural labour with maximum poverty (49% of them are below RS. 190), followed by other types of labour (31%), self-employed in non-agriculture (25%) and self-employment in agriculture (22%). Similarly, in urban areas as high as 57 per cent of the casual workers are below RS. 265 MPCE. Almost 31 per cent of the self-employed and 17 per cent of the wage/salary earners also suffer a similar fate.

17. For an analysis on the effects of ageing on savings-consumption behaviour in the Indian economy See, Alam and Agarwal (2000).

18. For a review of literature on the quality of health care provided by the government, see Ellis, Alam and Gupta (1997).

19. A detailed description of information provided by the NSS since its first morbidity survey conducted during October 1953 March 1954 (i.e., 7th round) is provided by Gumber and Berman (1995). An analysis by Shariff (1995) provides several useful details about the two health surveys conducted by the NCAER in 1990 and 1993. This analysis reconfirms the growing prevalence of morbidity with age (see Table 3, pp. 36).

20. Reddy (1996) distributes elderly into 60-64,65-69 and 70+ age groups. The study shows that of those "10 per cent over 60 years of age, suffer from impaired physical mobility, and another 10 per cent are hospitalised at any given time, both proportions rising with increasing age. Of the population aged 70 years or over, more than 50 per cent suffer from one or more chronic conditions."
21. It ought to be clarified that this exercise is purely illustrative and is confined only to diseases covered by the NFHS (1992-93). Moreover, the data limitations of the NFHS due to the known problems of subjectivity and reporting biases may as well have vitiated some of our estimates.
22. It refers to the New Drug Policy (1994), and the Drug Policy Control Order. For a further discussions on them, (see Rane, 1995).
23. For a more recent information on disease prevalence among the aged, see the 52 round of the NSS for 1995-96.
24. These suggestions were made by participants in a recent conference "21st Century: A New Environment or the Elderly—Making the Transition", organised jointly by the Ministry of Welfare (Government of India) and the Helpage India, at Vigyan Bhavan, New Delhi on March 18-19, 1998. These are also contained in the proposed National Policy on Elderly Persons.
25. For a discussion on these issues, see Burman (1995, 1996); Ellis, et al. (1997), etc.
26. It helps to reimburse hospitalisation and other medical expenses including consultation fee, investigations, various surgical interventions, medicine, blood, oxygen, hospital room charges, nursing/intensive room care and domiciliary hospital care.
27. Covers the risks of accidental injuries resulting in loss of life or disablement for persons in age-group 5 to 70 years.
28. This is also a medical reimbursement scheme being offered to people on individual basis. The premium for the youngest age-group is only 70 rupees, as against a coverage limit of Rs. 5000 annually. Higher premiums are charged for older persons or those with spouse or dependants.
29. A point to be noticed here is the exclusion of the "old old" from insurance covers to minimise the insurer's risk. For example, persons exceeding 70 years of age are not covered under the personal accident policy of the GIC. Similarly, those over 75 years of age are excluded from the Mediclaim policies. Also, there are many other exclusions being used to minimise the burden of claims. A well-conceived regulatory mechanism with provisions for its effective implementation is therefore essential. Also, those who are denied insurance cover due to certain age bar should exclusively be considered as the state responsibility. Recent projections suggest that more than 2 per cent of the total population was in 1996 in 70+ age-group, and may therefore depend more heavily on public facilities.
30. Initially, this insurance cover may only be for the older persons, and can subsequently be extended to all other social groups. This is nevertheless a complex issue, and is raised simply to initiate a discussion.
31. Census enumeration in these states could not be held in the respective years due to the law and order problems.
32. The prorate adjustment factor was derived as: LFPR77-78-LFPR72-73/5. Adjusted LFPRs are shown in Appendix, Table 4.

References

Agarwal, Bina (1990), "Social Security and the Family: Coping with Seasonality and Calamity in Rural India", *The Journal of Peasant Studies*, Vol. 17, No. 3, pp. 341-412.

Alam, Moneer and Mishra S.N. (1998), "Structural Reforms and Employment Issues in India: A Case of Industrial Labour", *The Indian Journal of Labour Economics*, Vol. 41, No. 2, pp. 271-292.

Alam, Moneer and R.N. Agarwal, (1999): "Ageing, Macroeconmic implications and Health Insurance Requirements in India", *The Indian Journal of Labour Economics*, Vol. 42, No. 3, pp.471-499.

Atkinson, Anthony B. (1995), "On Targeting Social Security—Theory and Western Experience with Family Benefits", in Dominique van de Walle and Kimberly Nead (eds.), *Public Spending and the Poor: Theory and Evidence*, The John Hopkins University Press, pp. 25-68.

Bhat, P.N. Mari (1992), "Changing Demography of Elderly in India", *Current Science* (Special Issue on Demography and Epidemiology), Vol. 63, No. 8, 25 October, pp. 440-448.

Bose, Ashish (1996), *India's Basic Demographic Statistics*, B.R. Publishing Corporation, New Delhi.

Burman, P. (1996), "Health Care Expenditure In India", in Monica Dasgupta, et al. (eds.), *Health, Poverty, and Development in India*, Oxford University Press, New Delhi.

—— (1995), "Financing of Rural Health Care in India: Estimates of the Resources Available and Their Distribution", Paper prepared for an *International Workshop on Health Insurance in India*, Banglore, September 20-22.

Cain, Mead (1985a), *The Fate of the Elderly in South Asia: Implication for Fertility*, Population Council, Centre for Policy Studies, Working Paper No. 116, November.

—— (1985b), *Consequences of Reproductive Failures: Dependence, Mobility, and Mortality among the Elderly in Rural South Asia*, Population Council, Centre for Policy Studies, Working Paper No. 119, November.

—— (1981), " Risk and Insurance: Perspectives on Fertility and Agrarian Change in India and Bangladesh", *Population and Development Review*, Vol. 7, No. 3, pp. 435-474.

Case, Anne and Deaton, Angus (1998), "Large Cash Transfers to the Elderly in South Africa", *The Economic Journal*, Vol. 108 (September), pp. 1330-1361.

Census of India (1971 and 1981), *Social and Cultural Tables*, Part IV A, Series-1, India.

Dandekar, Kumudini (1996), *The Elderly in India*, Sage Publications, India.

Deaton, A.S. (1995), "Inequality Within and Between Households in Growing and Ageing Economies", in M. Quibria (ed.), *Critical Issues in Asian Development*, Oxford University Press, pp. 18-38.

——and C. H. Paxson (1993), *Inequality and Aging: An East Asian Perspective*, Research Programme in Development Studies, Princeton University (mimeo).

Devi, D. Radha (1992), "Work Participation of the Aged in India", in P. Krishnan and K. Mahadevan (eds.).

Dreze, Jean and A.K. Sen (1991), "Public Action for Social Security: Foundation and Strategy", in Ehtisham Ahmad, Jean Dreze, et al. (eds.), *Social Security in Developing Countries*, Clarendon Press, pp. 3-40.

—— (1989), *Hunger and Public Action*, Clarendon Press.

Ellis, Randall P., Moneer Alam and I. Gupta (2000), "Health Insurance In India: Problems and Prognosis", *Economic and Political Weekly*, Vol. 35, No. 4, pp. 207-217, January.

Gumber, Anil and Peter Berman (1995), *Measurement and Pattern of Morbidity and Utilisation of Health Services—A Review of Recent Health Interview Surveys in India*, Gujarat Institute of Development Research, Working Paper Series, No. 65, March.

Hurd, M. (1997), "The Effects of Demographic Trends on Consumption, Saving, and Government Expenditure in the United States", in Michael D. Hurd and Naohiro Yashiro (eds.), *The Economic Effects of Aging in the United States and Japan* (A National Bureau of Economic Research Conference Report), University of Chicago Press, pp. 39-57.

Jhabvala, Renana (1998), "Social Security for Unorganised Sector", *Economic and Political Weekly*, May 30, pp. L-7 - L-11.

Krishnan, P. and K Mahadevan (eds.) (1992), *The Elderly Population in Developed and Developing Economies*, B.R. Publishing Corporation, New Delhi.

Kumar, Vijaya, S. (1998), "Responses to the Issues of Ageing: The Indian Scenario", *BOLD*, Vol. 8, No. 3, pp. 7-26.

Lindert, P.H. (1983), "The Changing Economic Costs and Benefits of Having Children", in R. A. Bulatao, and R. D. Lee et al. (eds.), *Determinants of Fertility in Developing Countries*, Vol. 1, Academic Press.

Mahadevan, K. and N. Audinarayana (1992), "Demographic and Social Implications of the Elderly in India", in Krishnan and Mahadevan (eds.).

Mahajan, A. (1992), "Social Dependency and Abuse of the Elderly", in Krishnan and Mahadevan (eds.).

Phua, K. H. and Yap Mui Teng (1997), "Financing Health Care in Old Age: A Case Study of Singapore", in Nicholas Prescott (ed.), *Choices in Health Care and Old Age Security*, Proceedings of a Conference Sponsored by the Institute of Policy Studies, Singapore, and the World Bank, Nov. 8, pp. 33-42.

Rajan, S. Irudaya, U.S. Mishra and P. Sankara Sarma (1999), *India's Elderly: Burden or Challenge?*, Sage Publications, New Delhi.

Rane, Wishvas (1995), "Drug Prices: Sharp Rise after Decontrol", *Economic and Political Weekly*, Vol. 30, No. 47, November 25, 1995, pp. 2977-2980.

Rao, Saumya Rama and John W. Townsend (1998), "Health Needs of Elderly Indian Women: An Emerging Issue", in M. Krishnaraj, Ratna M. Sudarshan and A. Shariff (eds.), *Gender, Population and Development*, Oxford University Press, Delhi.

Reddy, P.H. (1996), "The Health of the Aged In India", *Health Transition Review*, Supplement to Vol. 6, pp. 233-243.

Sarvekshana (1998), Journal of The National Sample Survey Organisation, Vol. 21, No. 3, pp. 17-18, 74th Issue, January-March.

Sen, A.K. (1981), *Poverty and Famines: An Essay on Entitlement and Deprivation*, Oxford University Press, Delhi.

Shariff, Abusaleh (1995), *Health Transition in India*, National Council of Applied Economic Research, Working Paper, No. 57, October.

Sharma, M.L. and T.M. Dak (1987), *Ageing in India—Challenge for the Society*, Ajanta Publications.

Sharma, S.P and Peter Zenos (1992), *Ageing in India: Demographic Background and Analysis based on Census Materials*, Occasional Paper No. 2 of 1992, Office of the Registrar General and Census Commissioner, New Delhi.

Singh, Parduman (1997), *Social Security System in Developing Countries: Asia, Africa and South America*, Friedrich Ebert Stiftung, New Delhi.

Soodan, K.S. (1975), *Aging in India*, Minerva Associates, Calcutta.

Srinivasan, K. (1998), *Basic Demographic Techniques and Applications*, Sage, New Delhi.

Visaria, P. (1980), "Poverty and Living Standards in Asia", *Population and Development Review*, Vol. 6, No. 2, pp. 189-223, June 1980.

—— (1998), *Unemployment among Youth in India: Level, Nature and Policy Implications*, ILO, Employment and Training Paper No. 36, ILO, Geneva.

World Bank (1993), *World Development Report: Investing in Health*, Published for the World Bank by the Oxford University Press, p. 220.

Yashiro, N and A. Sato Oishi (1997), "Population Aging and the Saving-Investment Balance in Japan", in Michael D. Hurd and Naohiro Yashiro (eds.), *The Economic Effects of Aging in the United States and Japan* (A National Bureau of Economic Research Conference Report), University of Chicago Press, pp. 59-87, Chicago.

17

Social Security for Scheduled Castes in Unorganised Sector

Sukhadeo Thorat

I. INTRODUCTION

In a developing country like India, the concern for social security should be with the direct role that public policy can play in reducing deprivation and eliminating vulnerability. In this context, Dreze and Sen (1991) observed that the basic idea of social security should be to use social means to prevent deprivation and vulnerability to deprivation. Deprivation and vulnerability are integral to the lives of the majority of the population in poor countries like India. For many, deprivation is a chronic state arising from the absence of assets that can ensure adequate livelihood. A crucial policy issue is, therefore, how lives and livelihoods can be made more secure against adversity and deprivation. Accordingly, social security needs to be treated as being the provision by social means of certain basic amenities during periods of very low standard of living, irrespective of whether the same are the results of chronic deprivation or temporary diversity. It also requires that society should either offer work to the needy persons or provide them with means of subsistence, which implies that the right to work in some form and the right to social security are complementary to each other.

In this context social security can be seen to have two aspects, namely, protection and promotion. While the former is concerned with preventing a decline in the basic condition of living, the latter aims at enhancing the normal living conditions and dealing with regular and persistent deprivation (Sankaran et al., 1994). The first one goes by the name of income maintenance and the second by the name of income support. The traditional concept limits the scope of social security to income maintenance. For obvious reasons, there can be no maintenance of income unless there is already an income. And if there is some income, its maintenance would have no meaning unless it guarantees a minimum standard of living. Considering the fact that large numbers of people in India are either unemployed or underemployed, the primary objective of social security should be to ensure that everyone has a minimum income and that this is adequate for the maintenance of a reasonable standard of living. Assurance of an income in the case of persons who are able to work can be operationalised by providing them with work. Right to work, therefore, needs to be viewed as a necessary concomitant of the right to social security.

In India, protective social security measures have been extended to the organised sector. In the unorganised sector, however, reliance has mainly been on promotional measures.

The main purpose of this paper is to examine the effectiveness of social security measures with respect to one of the most deprived and vulnerable sections of Indian society, viz., the Scheduled Castes (or untouchables). The Scheduled Castes (SCs) who constitute about one-fifth of India's population, are mostly employed in the unorganised sector of the economy, i.e. agriculture and the urban informal sector. Social security in the unorganised sector is mainly of a promotional nature. It includes measures to improve income earning capabilities and also protective measures such as minimum employment guarantee programmes for wage labour.

Given the limited availability of data, this paper takes a macro-level view of social security in rural and urban areas mainly by evaluating the current situation of SCs with respect to: (a) occupational status, with a purpose to understand the improvement, if any, in access to agricultural land and other capital assets in rural and urban areas; (b) employment situation in rural and urban areas; and (c) the level of poverty among the various occupational groups in rural and urban areas. The paper concludes by throwing up some pertinent issues for wider consideration.

II. SCHEDULED CASTES AND SOCIAL SECURITY

The SCs, who constitute nearly one-fifth of India's population in 1991, present a somewhat different and complex case from that of other deprived groups in the country. The discrimination and deprivation arising out of the caste system and untouchability have affected them far more adversely than any other group in Indian society. Their problems differ from those of other deprived groups primarily in two respects. Firstly, for historical reasons the incidence and nature of social and economic deprivation measured by any indicators of human development is far more intense in their case (Thorat, 1996). They are far too behind other identical groups of Indian society with respect to access to agricultural land and capital assets, but also in terms of employment and social capabilities. Secondly, and more importantly, caste and untouchability-based discrimination in social and economic spheres still continue and as a result they have to face far more hostile and antagonistic situations. Economic and social discrimination against SCs prevail in significant degree in rural and urban areas, both inside and outside the market, i.e. regarding access to sources of income such as agricultural land, capital, property, employment, and social services, etc. (Banerjee and Knight, 1991). Given the significantly higher degree of socio-economic deprivation among SCs, a set of highly targeted programmes have been developed to meet the challenges under the Five Year Plans as also through the non-plan channel.

In so far as these measures intend not only to provide some source of income but also to maintain a minimum level of income, they are in the nature of social security measures. They can be categorised in the following manner: (a) measures to provide minimum wage employment support both in rural and urban areas, with special emphasis on rural areas, where there is a lack of employment opportunities around the year due to drought or agricultural activities not being in operation. The main purpose of these programmes is to provide minimum wage employment and income on an yearly basis particularly in drought-prone and agriculturally less developed areas; (b) measures to provide access to public services such as housing, health care and education; and finally (c) protection against discrimination in access to land, capital, social services, employment, etc., through the reservation policy and preferential treatment.

The programmes which assure minimum income include the employment programmes like the Jawahar Rozgar Yoajana (JRY) and the Employment Assurance Scheme (EAS). The objective of JRY is to provide supplementary employment to unemployed and underemployed persons in rural areas. These programmes also aim at strengthening assets in favour of poor people. Persons below the poverty line constitute the target group and preference is given to SCs and STs, in proportion to their population.

Under the JRY, housing construction is also undertaken through the Indira Awas Yojana in which preference is given to SC households who are victims of atrocities, households below the poverty line, households headed by widowed or unmarried women, SC/STs affected by flood, fire, earthquakes and similar natural calamities. Similarly development of private agricultural land under the Land Development Scheme and irrigation under the Millions Wells Scheme of marginal and small farmers is also undertaken free of cost. In both the schemes, the small and marginal farmers, particularly SC/STs and freed bonded labourers, are given priority.

In addition to the JRY, a new scheme known as Employment Assurance Scheme (EAS) was launched in 1993, which now covers 2,446 blocks in over 261 districts situated in drought-prone, desert, tribal and hill areas. The scheme aims at providing assured employment of 100 days of unskilled work to rural poor in the age-group of 18-60 years. The Nehru Rozgar Yojana which was introduced in 1992 also initiated a wage-employment programme for urban poor. An additional scheme for urban employment has also been introduced for the urban poor for creation of income earning assets.

From the priority of target group it is clear that the focus is really on deprived and vulnerable sections of the rural society and, therefore, these programmes are in the nature of social security measures in so far as they intend to provide sources of income and to maintain the current income at a certain minimum level.

The IRDP also falls in this category. The IRDP was launched as a credit linked programme of self-employment for poverty alleviation. The objective is to enable the identified rural poor families to augment their income in order to cross the poverty line through acquisition of credit-based productive assets. While the target groups consist of small and marginal farmers and artisans below the poverty line, 50 per cent of assisted families are from the SC/ST category. A similar scheme of self-employment has been introduced for the urban poor under the Nehru Rozgar Yojana as also the separate Scheme for Urban Micro Enterprise. In addition, the Training of Rural Youth for Self Employment (TRYSEM) has been started with the aim of providing basic technical and managerial skills to rural youth from families below poverty line and thus enable them to take self-employment or wage employment. A similar programme has also been introduced for women.

III. IMPACT OF PROMOTIONAL MEASURES: MACRO ANALYSIS

The anti-poverty programmes, and wage employment programmes of various kinds, are in the nature of social security measures, in so far as their main focus is promotional and income maintenance of persons below the poverty line and of free bonded labourers (SCs), widows, single women, artisans, etc. Various schemes for the self-employed are intended to provide income earning assets (such as land and capital) and to improve the efficiency of already existing productive assets on the marginal farmer's land (i.e. land improvement and irrigation) so as to make them economically viable self-employed units and help them cross the poverty line, presumably forever. Wage employment programmes, on the other hand, have been developed to provide supplementary employment to those who are critically in need of such employment.

In this section we try to assess the impact of these programmes on the levels of living of the SCs. In the absence of direct indicators of level of living we take alternative indicators such as occupational status, employment, consumption expenditure and poverty. What kind of changes in occupational status, employment, and poverty situation of SC persons are likely to emerge? The way the self-employment, wage employment and other programmes have been designed, we expect the following changes to occur: (a) The proportion of land owning self-employed cultivators should increase. Priority in the distribution of surplus land under the ceiling, government land and other land should bring a shift in the occupational status of a substantial proportion of the SC population from wage labour to self-employed households. Further, the improvement in private agricultural land (through levelling, drainage, etc.) and irrigation should also transform marginal and small farmers into viable cultivators; (b) Similarly, the proportion of self-employed households/persons in the rural non-farm sector and in urban area should increase due to self-employment programmes under IRDP; (c) The expected increase in the proportion of self-employed, should lead to a corresponding decline in the proportion of wage labour households; (d) The wage employment programmes should reduce the unemployment among the SC wage labourers in rural areas; (e) With an increase in self-employed activities and wage employment, the incidence of poverty, both in rural and urban areas, among the SC household persons should decrease, and finally, in relative terms, the gap between the SC and Others (i.e. non-SC/ST) should reduce.

1. Access to Agricultural Land

About three-fourths of the SCs live in rural areas where the main source of income is either cultivation of agricultural land (as self-employed farmer), wage labour or some type of non-farm wage or self employment. The surplus land made available through land ceiling, government land and other lands are distributed to landless SC persons, with the aim of providing a minimum source of income. As on September 30, 1996, about 52.13 lakh acres had been distributed at the all-India level. Of these, about 18.08 lakh acres were distributed to SCs, and 26.74 lakh acres to non-SC/ST persons. A total of 51.21 lakh beneficiaries have been so far covered, of which 18.49 lakh were SCs and 25.53 lakh non-SC/STs (Tabel 1). The land distributed per beneficiary in the SC category households comes to 0.977 acre which was less than the corresponding 1.047 acres for non-SC/ST households. Of the total land distributed to SC households, however, West Bengal alone accounted for about 20 per cent, followed by Uttar Pradesh. In terms of the share in beneficiaries also West Bengal alone accounted for nearly 43 per cent, followed by Uttar Pradesh (13 per cent), Andhra Pradesh (12 per cent) and Bihar (12.4 per cent).

Table 1
Distribution of Surplus Land to SCs as on September 1996

	Total area and beneficiaries		Area distributed and no. of SC beneficiaries						
State	Area distributed	Total no. benef.	Area distributed	No. of benef.	% share in area	% share in no. of benef.	% share in all-India area	% share in all-India no. of benef.	Average area distributed
A.P.	594352	521563	226890	216537	38.17	41.51	12.55	11.71	10.4
Asssam	479878	441804	45746	43406	9.53	9.82	2.53	2.34	1.05
Bihar	303217	372529	179161	229832	59.08	61.69	9.91	12.43	0.779
Gujarat	133999	31376	83247	14584	62.12	46.48	4.60	0.78	5.20
Haryana	87259	27392	37623	11753	43.11	42.90	2.08	0.63	3.20
H.P.	3340	4400	2305	2934	69.01	66.68	0.12	0.15	0.785
J & K	45000	450000	0	0	0	0	0	0	0
Karnataka	117147	31415	71133	18953	60.72	60.33	3.93	1.02	3.75
Kerala	64283	145106	25197	62174	39.01	42.84	1.39	3.36	0.40
M.P.	185313	72131	49433	21528	26.67	29.84	2.73	1.16	2.29
Maharashtra	554870	14580	161715	41945	29.14	29.83	8.94	2.26	3.85
Orissa	154298	135219	49075	45561	31.80	33.69	2.71	2.46	1.077
Punjab	103487	28287	44015	11301	42.53	39.95	2.43	0.61	3.89
Rajasthan	452176	77899	145317	28453	32.13	36.52	8.03	1.53	5.10
Tamil Nadu	162369	135269	62096	59729	38.24	44.15	3.43	3.23	1.03
U.P.	390501	346209	263815	236599	67.55	68.33	14.59	12.79	1.11
W.Bengal	965293	2151632	359519	800870	37.24	37.22	19.88	43.31	0.44
Total	5213328	5120859	1807575	1848833	34.67	36.10	100.00	100.00	0.97

Source: Report of the Commission for SC/ST, 1995-1996, Delhi.

Table 2 presents the situation of SCs with respect to ownership of agricultural land in rural areas for 1982 and 1992 (landownership data is not available for earlier rounds, i.e. 1953, 1961, 1971 landholding surveys for SCs). In 1992 about 13.34 per cent of SC households in India were landless. The ratio was higher as compared to the corresponding figure of 10.54 per cent for non-SC/ST households. At the state level, 13 out of 17 states show higher incidence of landlessness among SCs in 1992. The percentage of landless households among the SCs was relatively higher in Maharashtra (24.31 per cent), Madhya

Pradesh (20. 53 per cent for SCs and 6.0 per cent for other), Haryana (9.0 per cent SCs and 1.81 per cent for others), Kerala (14.33 per cent SC and 7.67 per cent for others), and Madhya Pradesh (20.53 per cent SCs and 12.57 per cent for others).

Despite the distribution of ceiling-surplus land to about 18.5 lakh beneficiaries, the percentage of landless households among SCs has increased from 12.62 per cent in 1982 to 13.34 per cent in 1992, while the corresponding rate has remained constant at around 10 per cent for the non-SC/ST group. This increase in the percentage of landlessness has come from the states of Himachal Pradesh, Madhya Pradesh, Jammu & Kashmir, Punjab, Kerala, Orissa and Tamil Nadu (Table 2). In rest of the states the percentage of landless households among the SCs had declined during the 1982-92 period .

Table 2
Percentage of Landless and Near Landless Households among SCs
(Percentage to total rural households)

State	1982					1992				
	Land-less	Less than half acre	Bet-ween half & one acre	Upto one acre	Land-less & upto one acre	Land-less	Less than half acre	Bet-ween half & one acre	Upto one acre	Land-less & upto one acre
A.P.	13.58	44.34	7.95	52.29	65.87	12.49	49.95	9.91	59.86	72.35
Assam	5.02	36.98	17.27	54.25	59.27	5.52	37.10	7.94	45.04	50.56
Bihar	35.58	69.78	9.76	79.54	89.24	19.73	62.62	6.15	68.77	88.50
Gujarat	23.86	44.69	6.38	51.22	75.06	18.09	34.11	4.22	38.88	56.42
Haryana	10.09	87.52	0.97	88.49	98.58	7.95	73.10	3.63	76.73	84.68
H.P.	6.01	34.71	9.96	44.67	50.73	7.09	22.67	5.37	28.04	35.13
J & K	0.66	41.56	3.58	45.14	45.80	4.00	34.37	7.91	42.28	46.28
Karnataka	14.52	38.41	8.51	46.92	61.44	10.69	32.60	2.67	35.27	45.96
Kerala	16.56	77.33	5.35	82.68	99.24	14.33	79.32	–	79.32	93.65
M.P.	18.11	24.21	2.55	26.76	44.87	20.53	19.04	3.17	22.21	42.74
Maharashtra	26.39	33.42	3.38	36.80	63.19	24.31	32.13	2.99	35.12	59.43
Orissa	7.2	47.78	6.70	54.18	61.38	11.19	49.82	9.78	59.60	70.79
Punjab	6.01	56.84	2.96	89.50	95.81	6.7	85.57	1.43	87.00	93.78
Rajasthan	12.91	18.10	2.40	20.50	33.41	76.11	29.10	6.18	35.28	43.04
Tamil Nadu	14.5	61.66	7.48	69.14	83.64	19.21	57.4	9.82	67.03	86.24
U.P.	7.18	40.88	18.33	59.21	66.39	6.15	45.98	16.08	62.06	68.21
W.Bengal	19.13	42.74	11.05	53.79	72.92	12.02	47.66	11.64	59.30	71.32
India	12.62	47.97	9.53	57.50	70.12	13.34	47.50	8.89	56.39	69.73

Source: NSS Landholding Survey, 1982 and 1992.

Conversely, at the all-India level, nearly 87 per cent of the SC households owned some land in 1992. However, of these nearly 72 per cent were marginal holdings owning less than five acres of land. This ratio was much higher compared to the corresponding figures of 55 per cent for others (non SC/STs). Between 1982 and 1992, the ratio of marginal farmers has remained constant at around 72 per cent, but there has been some improvement in the area owned by them from 22.62 per cent in 1982 to around 30 per cent in 1992.

Table 2 presents more detailed information consisting of the percentage of households owning no land (i.e. landless), those owning less than 0.50 acre and those lying between 0.50 and one acre. At the all-India level in 1992, nearly 56 per cent of SC households owned less than one acre and of them nearly 47.5 per cent owned less than half acre. The landless and near landless (i.e. those owning less than one acre) put together accounted for nearly 70 per cent of the total SC households. The proportion of landless and near landless households among SCs was astonishingly high at 93 per cent in Punjab and Kerala, followed by 88 per cent in Bihar, 86 per cent in Tamil Nadu, 84 per cent in Haryana and around 70 per cent in West Bengal, Orissa, Andhra Pradesh and Uttar Pradesh. The incidence was relatively low in low rainfall or dry farming states of the country.

Between 1982 and 1992, the proportion of landless households increased marginally at the all-India level and this was mainly due to the increase registered in Himachal Pradesh, Jammu & Kashmir, Madhya Pradesh, Orissa and Tamil Nadu. The increase was quite prominent in Orissa. The remaining states showed a decline in the various magnitudes.

The proportion of those owning less than half acre remained constant at around 48 per cent between 1982 and 1992. But it has increased in Andhra Pradesh, Rajasthan, Uttar Pradesh and West Bengal and declined in the other states. Taking the ratio of landless and near landless into consideration, while the rates remained relatively stable at the all-India level, the ratio increased in Andhra Pradesh, Orissa, Rajasthan, Tamil Nadu and Uttar Pradesh and declined in nine other states.

2. Trends in Self-employment in Farm and Non-farm (Rural) Sectors

Even though nearly 87 per cent of SC households own some land, since most of them are marginal owners, their capacity to eventually pursue cultivation as an independent and viable economic activity is extremely limited. It is precisely because of this vulnerable character of marginal holdings that attempts have been made under IRDP and JRY to improve the productive capacity of marginal and small farmers particularly SC through improvement of land (under private land development programme) and irrigation facilities (under Million Wells Scheme). Along with supply of inputs at subsidised rate, the improvement in land and irrigation is expected to improve land productivity and make the marginal and small farmers economically viable and hence self-employed cultivators.

Table 3a shows the percentage of self-employed households for 1987-88 and 1993-94. At the all-India level, in 1991, the percentage of land-owning households among the SC households was about 87 per cent. But NSS data for the same period shows that only 19.12 per cent of this were self-employed cultivating households. This ratio was about the same as that obtained during 1987-88. The percentage of self-employed cultivating households among non-SC/STs on the other hand was more than double, both during 1987-88 (43.3 per cent) and 1993-94 (42.22 per cent).

It is important to note that the proportion of SC self-employed cultivating households in rural areas was the lowest in Punjab (4.31 per cent), closely followed by Kerala (5.97 per cent), Tamil Nadu (6.99 per cent), Haryana (8.64

Table 3a

Percentage of Self-employed among Schedule Castes and Others

(Percentage to total rural households)

State	SEA® 1987-88		SENA® 1987-88		SEA® 1993-94		SENA® 1993-94		SE (U) 1993-94		SE (U) 1987-88	
	SC	OT	SC	OT	SC	OT	SC	OT	SC	OT	SC	OT
A.P.	8.8	31.2	7.1	15.6	8.4	27.79	4.98	15.43	. 15.2	35.0	17.06	31.62
Assam	44.47	44.5	17.1	12.2	32.49	39.88	19.47	11.84	30.7	37.7	37.82	35.4
Bihar	9.9	39.8	7.2	14.4	10.68	45.45	6.83	13.11	24.4	38.1	31.71	36.83
Gujarat	10.1	38.2	4.3	10.0	7.43	34.16	7.77	10.17	14.3	35.0	31.71	36.83
Haryana	5.88	56.0	17.4	14.50	8.64	50.90	15.20	17.09	31.1	42.0	14.20	30.16
H.P.	50.6	70.5	15.5	6.3	48.3	65.07	14.59	8.32	33.9	26.7	13.79	20.25
J & K	39.5	54.0	9.5	12.8	40.19	62.77	10.62	9.85	28.4	33.40	36.23	34.81
Karnataka	12.4	41.0	6.9	11.6	15.94	44.81	9.27	13.78	14.33	33.0	18.75	33.95
Kerala	4.8	27.0	8.6	16.8	5.97	23.0	4.87	14.72	11.7	33.6	10.17	33.00
M.P.	30.5	55.5	11.4	9.9	31.92	54.47	5.89	7.9	29.2	35.2	21.76	35.39
Maharashtra	11.3	40.2	13.8	8.8	8.37	31.07	7.90	8.03	16.3	27.4	13.55	30.95
Orissa	8.9	NA	4.4	NA	20.93	39.42	17.7	15.98	36.7	36.6	38.68	28.0
Punjab	4.9	51.7	11.9	19.1	4.31	54.64	16.70	15.42	34.2	47.9	31.61	45.89
Rajasthan	27.4	53.5	15.0	14.3	32.97	64.46	12.92	11.26	30.8	41.3	40.17	40.82
Tamil Nadu	6.9	27.7	5.9	16.0	6.99	25.08	4.07	16.20	17.4	30.4	17.03	29.89
U.P.	30.9	62.5	11.3	13.2	31.67	61.29	11.26	13.90	44.9	46.0	33.87	48.55
W.Bengal	23.2	32.1	15.4	17.8	22.92	30.96	17.77	23.55	32.9	29.7	26.87	32.09
India	18.9	43.3	11.0	13.8	19.12	42.42	13.89	10.32	13.89	26.0	35.2	24.08
	18.8		5.5									

Note: SEA®=Self-employed in (rural) agri; SENA® =Self-employed in (rural) non-agri; SEU= Self-employed in urban sector; SC = Scheduled Caste; OT = Non-SC/ST (other).

per cent), Maharastra (8.37 per cent), Gujarat (7.43 per cent), Andhra Pradesh (8.4 per cent) and Bihar (10.08 per cent). The situation in Punjab and Haryana is obviously quite disturbing because it was expected that the new agricultural technology would make the SC marginal and small farmers viable. However, the reasons for the contrary results are quite obvious. In Punjab and Haryana, the proportion of SCs who owned less than half acre of land is astonishingly high, i.e. 86.84 per cent in Punjab and 87.52 per cent in Haryana in 1982, and 85.57 per cent in Punjab, and 73.1 per cent in Haryana in 1992. Even high yielding technology with support from the government could not have converted such mini-holdings into economically viable units. Same is the case with Kerala: the proportion of SCs owning less than half acre was 77 in 1982 and 79.72 in 1992. The ratio of self-employed households was, however, relatively higher in Himachal Pradesh, Assam, Rajasthan, Uttar Pradesh and West Bengal. In these states the ratio ranged between 31.07 per cent in Uttar Pradesh to 48.3 per cent in Himachal Pradesh.

Coming to the rural non-farm sector, at the all-India level, the proportion of self-employed non-farm households was 10.32 per cent for SCs in 1992, which is lower compared to the corresponding figure of 14 per cent for others. This ratio was relatively high and more than the national average for Orissa, Punjab, Assam, Haryana and Himachal Pradesh. The proportion was quite low in Kerala, Madhya Pradesh, Karnataka, Maharashtra, Tamil Nadu, Himachal Pradesh, Bihar and Gujarat. In these states the ratio ranged between 4 and 7 per cent.

In about eight states, the proportion of SC households in the rural non-farm sector was lower than non-SC/ST households. On the other hand, in a few states like Assam, Himachal Pradesh, and Orissa, the ratio for SC was higher than other households. In the remaining states, the ratio for both SC and other households was more or less the same. The lower proportion of self-employed in the rural non-farm sector in several states, despite self-employment programmes under IRDP in rural areas, reveals the weakness of the schemes with respect to the SCs.

3. Self-employment in Urban Areas

Disparities in access to capital are far more glaring in urban areas. In 1993-94, the proportion of SC households depending on self-employment was 24 per cent, which was lower by 11 percentage points as compared to the other households (35.05 per cent). With the exception of Assam, Jammu & Kashmir, Orissa and Punjab the percentage of SC self-employed households in urban areas was quite low as compared to other households. Orissa is the only state where the ratio of self-employed SC households was higher than other households by a substantial margin.

4. Incidence of Wage Labour in Rural Areas

High incidence of landless and near landless households among the SCs has obviously created an enormously high level of wage labour among them. The statistics generated on a regular basis by the Population Censuses, National Sample Surveys and Rural Labour Enquiries related to magnitude of rural labour bring out this fact quite clearly (Table 3b).

According to the Population Census of 1991, the percentage of agricultural labour among the Scheduled Castes was 55.37, which was more than double the ratio for non-SC households (25 per cent). In fact, SC agricultural labour alone account for 35 per cent of the total agricultural labour in the country although their share in total rural population is only 17 per cent. Over time the proportion of agricultural labour among the SCs has also increased from 53.37 per cent in 1981 to 55.12 per cent in 1991.

The disparities in the incidence of agricultural labour between SC and non-SC/ST population were fairly widespread across states. For instance, the proportion of agricultural labour among the SCs was 77.48 per cent in Andhra Pradesh, 75.64 per cent in Bihar, 75 per cent in Tamil Nadu, 63.18 per cent in Haryana, 69.71 per cent in Punjab, and 62 per cent in Karnataka. The disparity indeed was quite large in Punjab, Haryana, Andhra Pradesh, Tamil Nadu and Rajasthan. In the "green revolution states" of Punjab and Haryana the ratio of wage labour among the SCs was more than five times the corresponding ratio for other households.

Table 3b presents the percentage of wage labour households among the SCs and other households during 1974-75, 1983-84 and 1987-88 and 1993-94 in rural areas. In 1993-94, of the total rural households, 61 per cent were wage labour households. This ratio was much higher compared to 36.26 per cent for the other households. Similar differences prevailed during 1987-88 and earlier years (i.e. 1974-75, 1983-84 and 1987-88). For example, the ratio of rural labour households for Scheduled Castes stood at 57.41 in 1974-75, 63.18 in 1977-78,

Table 3b
Magnitude of Wage Labour among Schedule Castes, Rural

(Percentage to total rural households)

State	1974-75		1983-84		1987-88		1993-94		1981 *AL		1991 *AL	
	SC	OT	SC	OT	SC	OT	SC	OT	SC	OT	SC	OT
A.P	72.87	32.56	79.29	39.2	75.90	42.34	66.6	37.0	72.68	33.72	77.40	39.17
Assam	37.08	21.57	25.97	31.98	29.29	31.55	38.16	38.16				
Bihar	78.73	27.06	75.65	29.69	77.35	32.69	76.82	30.20	76.51	31.06	75.64	33.39
Gujarat	74.67	20.73	57.05	30.18	73.33	38.82	59.19	31.52	58.95	23.26	57.88	24.64
Haryana	58.41	7.77	72.84	15.65	67.50	10.36	64.64	16.57	5.72	9.21	63.18	12.40
H.P.	11.45	1.73	17.24	3.65	27.16	9.79	27.98	10.82	NA	2.05	5.65	2.72
J & K	13.16	3.89	27.59	16.04	36.04	16.83	29.87	8.25	NA	NA	NA	NA
Karnataka	69.24	30.04	75.27	35.25	74.78	38.29	68.62	31.92	51.72	26.70	56.70	29.81
Kerala	84.59	36.86	81.48	44.75	78.08	42.74	73.04	38.8	60.95	26.82	57.80	25.25
M.P.	39.20	16.72	48.94	25.74	52.35	26.23	57.7	29.90	43.03	20.55	43.57	20.72
Maharashtra	68.18	32.03	64.10	40.08	66.90	39.03	59.3	33.85	58.30	30.47	62.30	29.79
Orissa	60.77	16.51	54.58	31.03	60.17	31.25	53.61	30.28	50.28	20.27	49.45	21.20
Punjab	67.96	6.52	69.71	13.34	72.83	14.17	64.01	14.52	69.49	10.96	69.71	12.62
Rajasthan	18.99	2.78	42.28	9.79	53.23	22.55	46.18	14.39	19.25	4.96	24.33	7.43
T. Nadu	77.36	34.31	82.58	42.93	80.57	44.07	82.62	44.04	68.88	30.75	71.77	35.52
U.P.	45.51	10.42	48.78	13.62	51.86	15.65	51.76	15.92	37.09	11.58	41.34	14.83
W. Bengal	49.66	59.74	59.33	37.59	53.96	36.33	52.92	33.25	46.94	24.64	46.06	22.48

Note: SC= Scheduled Caste ; OT= non SC/ST; *= Population Census; AL= Agricultural Labour

Source: 1. Rural Labour Enquiry Reports 1974-75, 1983, 1987-88, 1993-94, Simla; 2. Population of India, 1981 and 1991.

62.55 in 1983, and 63.10 per cent in 1987-88. In all these years the level of wage labour among the SCs was two times higher than the corresponding level for other households.

At the state level, in 1993-94 the percentage of rural labour households among the SCs was 82.76 per cent in Tamil Nadu, 76 per cent in Bihar, 73 per cent in Kerala, 68 per cent in Karnataka, 66.6 per cent in Andhra Pradesh and 64 per cent each in Punjab and Haryana. These ratios were far higher than the level obtained for other households, i.e. 44.04 per cent in Tamil Nadu, 30.20 per cent in Bihar, 38.8 per cent in Kerala, 31.92 in Karnataka, 37 per cent in Andhra Pradesh and around 15 per cent in Punjab and Haryana.

A comparison of the proportion of wage labour households across states for the earlier years indicates that in 1974- 75, 1983-84, 1987-88 and 1993, with the exception of Assam, the incidence of wage labour among SCs was higher than in other groups. In 1987-88 in most of the states, the level of wage labour household among SCs was twice the corresponding level for other households. The disparity across social groups was quite high in Haryana, Punjab, Uttar Pradesh and Himachal Pradesh. In fact, in Punjab and Haryana the level was higher by seven and five times, respectively, while it was about three times higher in Uttar Pradesh and Himachal Pradesh. In 1983-84, in all the states the difference between SCs and other households regarding the level of wage labour was more than double. The disparities were much greater, again, in Haryana, Himachal Pradesh, Punjab, Rajasthan and Uttar Pradesh.

Another way to look at the disparities in the incidence of wage labour among the two social groups is to see the gap in the share of wage labour in relation to their share in total rural households. In 1983-84 and 1987-88 the SCs constituted 23 per cent and 20.54 per cent of the total rural households in the country, respectively; however, they comprised 32.64 per cent and 35 per cent of the total labour households in the country. So their share in labour households was more by about 12 percentage points. In all the states, the share of the labour households exceeds the corresponding share in rural households. The difference in the relative share, however, differs considerably across states. The relative share in labour households was indeed quite high in states like Haryana, Himachal Pradesh, Jammu & Kashmir, Punjab, and Tamil Nadu. In fact in Haryana, Himachal Pradesh, Punjab, Tamil Nadu, and Uttar Pradesh, SCs households account for 68.97 per cent, 50 per cent, 74.3 per cent, 79.42 and 52 per cent of labour households respectively, although their share in total rural households stood at 27.42, 17.36, 36.50, 25.30, 26 and 30.80 per cent, respectively. The segregation of the SCs into manual labour was thus quite clear.

It is important to note that not all wage labourers belong to landless households. A substantial portion of them owned some land; but the average size of the land owned by them being very small, many of them have to resort to wage labour. In 1987-88, about 76 per cent of the labour households owned some land. This ratio was very high in Assam (93.55 per cent), Haryana (84 per cent), Himachal Pradesh (84.20 per cent), Jammu & Kashmir (87.37 per cent), Karnataka (86 per cent), Kerala (95 per cent), Orissa (90.33 per cent), Rajasthan (82.37 per cent), and Uttar Pradesh (80 per cent). In case of the other states, the ratio was around the national average. Thus, a substantial portion of the land-owning households among the SCs (as well as among other households) resorted to wage employment due to the small size of their holdings. In fact, in 1987-88, 75 per cent of land-owning wage labour households owned less than 1.50 acres.

The year 1987-88 was a drought year and therefore the proportion of rural labour households with land is relatively high in most of the states. The year 1983 presents a more normal situation. During this year about 38 per cent of the labour households owned some land. The ratio of land-owning wage labour households was higher than the all-India average in a few states, i.e. 77.68 per cent in Himachal Pradesh, 76.22 per cent in Kerala, 52 per cent in Uttar Pradesh and Rajasthan, 47 per cent in Karnataka and 40 per cent in Andhra Pradesh.

In fact, at the all-India level, 66.8 per cent of land-owning households come from the less-than-one-acre size category and another 25.55 per cent from the one to 2.5 acre-size category. It is imporant to note that in a fairly large number of states the proportion of rural labour households belong to the farm size category of less than one acre. In a few states like Jammu & Kashmir, Andhra Pradesh, Kerala, Madhya Pradesh, Rajasthan and Tamil Nadu the proportion of rural labour households was relatively high and it varied between 30 per cent and 45 per cent. In Gujarat, Kerala, Madhya Pradesh, Maharashtra, Punjab, almost one-fifth of the rural labour households owned 2.5 acres and above. A high incidence of rural labour households among the land-owning households indicate both small size of the land possessed and low productivity of land, despite the land and irrigation improvement programmes under IRDP and JRY for SC marginal and small farmers.

5. Casual Wage Labour: Urban Areas

In urban areas the proportion of casual labour among the SC households was, again, much higher than the corresponding figure for the other households (Table 3c). In fact, disparities between SC and other households were of a high order. In 1993-94, the percentage of casual labour among the SCs was 27 per cent, which was two and half times more than that for other households. The ratio was higher by three times in eight states, four to five times in two states, one and a half times in six states and eight times in one state. About 62 per cent of the total SC households in urban Kerala reported casual labour, as against 26.6 per cent for other households. The proportion of casual labour was comparatively higher among the SC households in Kerala (61.74 per cent), Tamil Nadu (42.86 per cent), Haryana (34.64 per cent) and Karnataka (34.49 per cent).

Table 3c
Magnitude of Casual Labour among Scheduled Castes, Urban

(Percentage to total urban households)

	Casual labour				Regular wage/salaried			
	1987-88		1993-94		1987-88		1993-94	
	SC	OT	SC	OT	SC	OT	SC	OT
Andhra Pradesh	33.6	15.6	29.55	15.12	32.5	3.81	43.75	38.37
Assam	10.1	7.3	24.01	6.32	52.8	47.7	35.85	46.15
Bihar	29.8	10.2	23.82	9.63	39.5	39.5	33.82	36.30
Gujarat	32.6	11.9	15.64	10.25	51.3	45.2	48.14	38.73
Haryana	22.1	10.3	34.65	6.88	44.1	39.2	35.39	44.62
Himachal Pradesh	16.4	6.1	16.74	3.98	37.4	47.4	47.78	43.44
Jammu & Kashmir	25.0	4.5	13.04	1.51	35.5	41.7	42.75	53.34
Karnataka	26.9	16.4	34.49	12.66	24.8	38.2	40.00	44.76
Kerala	59.6	18.6	61.74	26.65	24.8	35.1	23.06	30.18
Madhya Pradesh	23.1	7.6	27.17	9.76	41.8	48.9	43.49	47.13
Maharashtra	24.7	9.1	23.18	6.80	50.2	55.1	48.96	52.62
Orissa	27.3	6.4	17.84	6.65	19.8	48.6	38.25	50.55
Punjab	27.4	5.9	22.43	7.23	32.7	39.8	42.77	41.26
Rajasthan	23.8	6.9	17.92	5.29	42.7	46.6	33.39	43.43
Tamil Nadu	37.4	13.7	42.86	11.33	39.4	47.7	26.83	41.06
Uttar Pradesh	20.7	7.4	28.95	7.69	29.3	35.7	30.72	34.04
West Bengal	15.0	8.3	16.08	10.32	46.7	54.3	52.01	49.79

Note: SC = Scheduled Caste; OT= Non-SC/ST

Source: National Sample Survey, Quinquennial Survey on Employment and Unemployment, 1987-88 and 1993-94, Delhi.

In case of regular wage and salaried persons, the proportion among SC households was less than that of other households; however, the differences were not as large as in the case of casual labour. In about 12 states, the share of SC regular wage or salaried households was less than that for others. In Andhra Pradesh, Gujarat, Himachal Pradesh, Punjab and West Bengal, however, their share was more than the corresponding figures for other households.

6. Disparities in Unemployment Rates

Since more than 60 per cent of the SC workers in rural areas and more than 30 per cent in urban areas depend mainly on wage employment, their earnings are obviously determined by the level of employment and wage rates. The SC workers seem to suffer from possible discriminations in the employment market. Table 4 shows the unemployment rates of the SC vis-a-vis the other worker for 1977- 78, 1983, 1987-88 and 1993-94. In case of usual status there are no significant differences in the unemployment rate of the SCs and others, either in rural or urban areas. This is not surprising, for a person is considered to be usually employed if he or she has worked for more than 180 days in a year. Since the SC workers have limited alternative sources of income, other than wage employment, their participation in work throughout the year is likely to be higher than that of others. However, as soon as we move on to the unemployment rate based on Current Weekly Status (CWS) and Current Daily Status (CDS) the picture changes dramatically, in so far as the unemployment rate of SCs turns out to be higher than that of other workers. In 1993-94, the unemployment rate based on CDS was 4.30 per cent for SC (male), which was higher than the 2.7 per cent figure for others. Similarly, in 1977-78 and 1983, the unemployment rates based on CDS for SC male workers were 6.73 per cent and 7.16 per cent, respectively, significantly higher than the 3.90 per cent and 4.03 per cent figures for others, respectively. A similar gap exists for female labour too. The unemployment rate for SC females on CDS basis was 2 per cent in 1993-94, 4.09 in 1977-78 and 4.23 per cent in 1983, which was again higher than 1.11 per cent, 0.97 per cent and 0.91 per cent, respectively for other females. The higher unemployment rate based on CWS and CDS clearly shows that underemployment among SC workers was of a much higher order as compared to other workers.

Table 4
Unemployment Rate (Aged 5 Years and above) in Rural Areas

Category/year	Male				Female			
	UPS	US	CWS	CDS	UPS	US	CWS	CDS
			Scheduled Castes					
1993-94	0.90	0.60	1.90	4.30	0.30	-	1.10	2.00
1987-88	1.30	0.90	-	-	1.40	1.10	-	-
1983	1.10	0.76	3.22	7.16	0.40	0.23	2.16	2.23
1977-78	1.10	0.00	2.93	6.73	2.20	0.00	1.90	4.00
			Others					
1993-94	1.20	0.90	1.60	2.70	0.44		0.80	1.11
1987-88	1.70	1.10	-	-	0.48	0.70	-	-
1983	1.30	1.90	2.15	4.03	0.43	0.29	0.91	1.72
1977-78	1.57	0.00	2.15	3.90	1.53	0.00	0.97	0.97

Source: Same as in Table 3c.

The disparities in the unemployment rates based on CDS and CWS observed at the all-India level emerged quite clearly in a majority of the states. In 1993-94, in all the 17 states the unemployment rate based on CDS was higher among the SC households. Similarly in 1977-78 and 1983, in 14 out of the 17 states, unemployment rates for male workers were higher for SCs as compared to the other households. The unemployment rates were higher for female SCs in 14 to 15 states in 1977-78 and 1983-84.

7. Urban Areas

In case of urban areas too, a more or less identical picture is observed (Table 5). In all the four years, i.e. 1977-78, 1983, 1987-88, and 1993-94, the unemployment rates based on US and CWS for male and female SC households tend to be slightly higher than others. Thus, the difference between the unemployment rates of SC households and other households based on CWS and US, is marginal. But as we move on to CDS, the gap between SCs and others emerged quite clearly both for male and female categories. For example, the unemployment rates based on CDS were 4.9 per cent, 7.3 per cent, and 7.2 per cent in 1993-94, 1987-98 and 1983-84, respectively for SC males. For others the rates were 3.3 per cent, 5.35 per cent, and 5.28 per cent, respectively during these same years.

Table 5
Unemployment Rate in Urban Areas

	US				CWS			CDS		
Category	1977-78	1983-84	1987-88	1993-94	1977-78	1983-84	1993-94	1977-78	1983-84	1993-94
SC										
Male	3.4	3.20	3.50	2.6	4.50	4.4	3.30	7.37	7.20	4.90
Female	3.40	0.80	1.10	0.00	1.1	1.20	0.00	4.20	1.7	1.7
OT										
Male	3.33	3.1	3.20	2.40	4.24	4.0	2.70	5.35	5.35	5.28
Female	2.60	0.90	1.20	1.10	0.00	1.0	1.30	0.000	1.42	1.4

Note: SC= Scheduled Caste; OT= Non-SC/ST.
Source: NSS Employment/Unemployment Reports 32nd, 38th and 43rd, and 50th round.

At the state level, in 1993-94, 11 out of 17 states, in 1977-78, 14 out of 17 states, and in 1983-84, 12 out of 17 states show higher unemployment rates for SC males. In case of SC females the unemployment rates based on CDS were higher for all states in 1977-78, 1983-84 and in 12 states in 1993-94. It may be mentioned that even in the case of principal and subsidiary status, in nine out of 17 states, unemployment rates for SC males were higher than that for other households.

8. High Incidence of Poverty

With higher incidence of wage labour along with higher unemployment/underemployment rates, the SCs are likely to suffer from low income and low consumption and hence also a higher level of poverty. Table 6 presents the poverty ratio for SCs and others for the years 1987-88 and 1993-94 at the all-India level, totalled as also separately for self-employed and wage labour households both in rural and urban areas. The poor households among these two occupational groups have been the target of self-employment and wage-employment programmes for quite sometime now.

In 1993-94, about 48 per cent of SC households were below the poverty line in rural areas as compared to 31.29 per cent for the general population. The poverty level among the SCs was thus higher by as much as 17 percentage points in comparison to the other households.

Table 6
Percentage of Persons below Poverty Line by Household Type for each Social Group

Category	SE in agriculture		SE in non-agriculture		Agriculture labour		Non-agriculture		Other		All	
	87-88	93-94	87-88	93-94	87-88	93-94	87-88	93-94	87-88	93-94	87-88	93-94
Rural												
SC	41.21	37.70	41.6	38.19	59.77	60.00	46.49	41.44	29.98	29.00	50.07	48.14
Others	25.57	25.57	31.42	29.49	53.30	52.34	34.45	35.59	19.26	20.19	34.37	31.29

Category	SE		Regular salary wage earner		Casual labour		Other		All	
Urban										
	87-88	93-94	87-88	93-94	87-88	93-94	87-88	93-94	87-88	93-94
SC	61.48	54.60	43.69	35.28	73.45	69.48	56.84	45.00	56.84	49.90
Others	33.60	33.64	25.26	19.04	70.1	60.60	32.21	26.06	37.21	29.66

Source: Based on Consumption Expenditure Survey, NSSO, 1987-88 and 1993-94.

What is striking in all this is the magnitude of poverty disaggregated among the various household types. In 1993-94, the incidence of poverty was about 60 per cent among agricultural labour households, followed by 41.44 per cent among non-agricultural labour households. Even 38 per cent of households engaged in self-employed activities in agriculture and an equal proportion in (rural) non-agricultural sector (38.19 per cent) were below the poverty line. In each of these household categories, however, the proportion of SC households was much higher than that of their counterparts among the non-SC/ST groups.

In urban areas, about 50 per cent of the SCs were below the poverty line in 1993-94, as compared to 29.66 per cent among the others. Further, the incidence was astonishingly high among the casual labour households (69.48 per cent). Even among the self-employed persons, the level of poverty was about 52 per cent among the SC households; the corresponding figure was about 34 per cent for the others. The incidence of poverty was also to the tune of 35.28 per cent among regular SC/ST wage/salaried persons which was much higher compared to others (19 per cent). Whereas the disparities in the level of urban poverty between the two social groups were relatively high in the case of self-employed and regular wage earner/salaried workers, it was much less in the case of casual labour.

Table 7 presents the state-wise poverty ratio for SC and all households (inclusive of SC/ST households, in which case the overall ratio of poverty will be slightly lower as compared to figures for non-SC/ST households alone) for the years 1983, 1987-88 and 1993-94. Significant inter-state and inter-social group disparities in the level of rural and urban poverty are evident. The poverty ratio in rural areas for the SC varied between 18 per cent in Himachal Pradesh and 70.56 per cent in Bihar. The incidence was particularly high in Bihar (70.56 per cent), and Uttar Pradesh (59 per cent), and low in Punjab and Andhra Pradesh. In urban areas the poverty ratio varied between 14.34 in

Assam to 62 per cent in Tamil Nadu, the level being higher than the national average in Uttar Pradesh (50 per cent), Karnataka (61 per cent) and Bihar. The ratio was relatively low in Himachal Pradesh, Haryana, Kerala and Punjab.

Table 7
Percentage of Poor: Head Count Ratio

	Rural						Urban					
	1983		1987-88		1993-94		1983		1987-88		1993-94	
State	SC	All	SC	All	SC	All	SC	All	SC	All	SC	All
A.P.	37.41	26.50.	51.36	40.13	29.58	29.92	54.70	44.63	26.00	15.92	43.82	41.51
Assam	43.05	42.60	48.74	26.38	36.76	39.35	30.09	17.39	45.39	45.01	14.34	13.15
Bihar	80.89	64.30	52.82	50.42	65.90	52.63	69.14	57.71	70.66	58.21	55.16	45334
Gujrat	39.21	29.80	47.61	40.63	39.63	28.67	52.43	39.63	32.26	22.18	44.99	27.07
Haryana	36.44	20.56	44.45	23.48	27.88	16.22	33.88	17.79	46.56	28.03	23.58	13.09
H.P.	27.35	17.00	14.11	9.23	20.13	16.28	15.40	6.18	38.39	30.34	18.52	8.58
J&K	41045	26.04	0.00	17.14	37.70	25.70	36.60	14.82	NA	NA	NA	NA
Karnataka	52.68	36.33	54.38	43.37	52.30	32.87	64.93	49.06	46.36	29.88	61.59	40.21
Kerala	62.24	39.03	62.06	48.65	38.28	29.10	62.00	43.63	36.43s	25.76	31.59	29.57
M.P.	58.42	48.90	70.24	54.69	51.72	41.52	68.85	48.17	45.83	40.64	65.00	49.70
Maharashtra	59.32	45.23	64.96	40.57	53.80	40.78	69.00	38.99	51.64	37.93	52.56	34.03
Orrisa	75.84	67.58	65.95	50.61	67.60	57.64	62.68	44.11	48.95	49.72	47.45	40.59
Punjab	25.30	13.20	36.59	23.86	27.93	12.60	26.60	12.91	22.08	14.95	27.96	9.08
Rajasthan	40.47	33.50	51.79	40.37	37.87	33.22	55.36	38.99	38.38	26.26	48.63	31.63
T.N.	67.46	53.99	72.28	49.22	64.05	45.80	63.37	43.88	44.05	32.48	61.00	44.34
U.P.	57.20	46.45	56.63	50.27	56.49	41.10	57.28	45.22	58.99	42.28	58.02	36.06
W.B.	72.53	63.05	47.77	32.21	53.59	48.30	45.60	32.84	45.29	40.28	37.73	22.51
All-India	57.77	45.61	56.41	42.15	50.58	39.06	36.48	40.12	48.11	37.27	49.48	33.66

Source: NSS Consumption Expenditure Surveys, 1983, 1987-88 and 1993-94.

This comparative account of the economic position of SCs does provide a convincing evidence on the continuing economic inequalities associated with caste. The proportion of self-employed persons among the SCs is extremely low, and as a result, the level of manual wage labour is astonishingly high. High incidence of wage labour among the SCs, however, is not matched by a favourable employment rate and wage earning. The unemployment rate among them is more than double as compared to that among others. Given the high level of wage labour coupled with higher unemployment rates, the poverty level is high among the SCs as compared to the rest of the population in the country. This is particularly true in the case for wage labourers, who constitute the bulk of the workers among the SCs. It is thus beyond doubt that the historical impact of traditional caste-based restrictions on the ownership of property, employment and occupation still adversely affect the SC groups to a very significant extent.

IV. ECONOMIC DISCRIMINATION IN PRIVATE SECTOR AND IMPLICATION FOR SOCIAL SECURITY

To what extent the economic inequalities are the result of historical factors, and to what extent are they due to a continuation of economic discrimination in the market is a complex question. While we do know in some measure about the first, little is known about the second, i.e. market discrimination.

The issue of market and pre-market discrimination acquires urgency in the present context of the massive move towards privatisation and channelisation of jobs, capital inputs and social services through the market. At present, the SCs are partially protected against economic discrimination, particularly in the job market, by the reservation policy in government and public sector jobs and services and preferential treatment in various state-run programmes, which are in the nature of social security measures. But with a declining role of government and public sector, they would now increasingly depend on market which suffers from various kinds of imperfections, including the one based on caste-based market discrimination. This has serious implications for social security measures in both the organised and unorganised sectors.

The macro and some micro-level evidence, however, indicate the presence of substantial discrimination against the SCs, in both rural and urban markets. The macro-level evidence presented in the preceeding section revealed a very high incidence of landlessness and near-landlessness among the SCs. The lack of access to agricultural land could be due to a weak resource position of SCs. But a few studies also point towards the imperfect workings of the land markets where access to land among the SCs is severely limited (Nanchariah, 1988; Thorat and Deshpande, 1998). Similarly, the NSS data shows that the unemployment rate (based on CWS and CDS) are much higher for the SCs. The Rural Labour Enquiries also show that wage rates received by the SCs rural labourers in rural farm and non-farm activities tend to be on the lower side, particularly in rural non-farm activities. To what extent the differences in the unemployment rate and wage rate of manual and semi-manual labour are due to differences in productivity, and to what extent they are due to job and wage discrimination is an issue which needs detailed examination.

Some micro-level studies, however, bring out the presence of discrimination against untouchables in various markets. Banerjee and Knight (1991), and Deshi and Singh (1995) have brought out the significant presence of caste and untouchability-based economic discrimination. Even if discrimination is no longer practised, the effects of past discrimination could carry over to the present, for instance, in the choice of occupation. This may help explain why discrimination is greatest in case of operative jobs, where contracts are more important for recruitment, and not in white-collar jobs in which recruitment involves formal methods. The economic function which the system performs for favoured castes suggests that discrimination is based, consciously, or unconsciously on economic interest, making prejudice more difficult to eradicate. The studies on Andhra Pradesh (Venketeswarlu, 1990) and Karnataka (Khan, 1995) also provided evidence on economic discrimination in occupation, employment, wages and loan and in other economic spheres. The Orissa study of 1987-88 (Tripathy, 1994) observed discrimination in land, credit and labour markets in rural areas. In the light of this evidence on market discrimination (through which the access to job, capital, product and even services generated in private sector are channelised) it would not be improper to suggest that there is a need to provide protection to the workers belonging to SC/SC households so that they get the necessary access. At present, it must be noted, there is no such protection to the SC workers in the private organised or unorganised sectors against the market failure associated with economic discrimination based on caste and untouchability.

V. SUMMARY AND CONCLUSION

It has been seen that a very large proportion of SC persons are engaged in the rural and urban informal or unorganised sectors. About three-fourth of them live in rural areas. Among the total rural households nearly 63 per cent earn their living as wage labour and the remaining are engaged in self-employed economic activities of various kinds. Despite the operation of the wage employment programmes targeted at poor and vulnerable sections for the past several years, they have not been able to provide a minimum standard of living to a large number of SC households, as nearly 60 per cent of agricultural labour households and a little more than 40 per cent of wage labour households in the rural non-farm sector are below the poverty line; they have consequently failed to achieve a minimum level of income and consumption.

In case of self-employed persons, at the micro level, promotional measures have also helped only to a very limited degree. The land reform measures have failed to provide surplus land to SC/ST households in any substantial measure. The land and irrigation improvement measures under IRDP, JRY and other related measures, could not transform more than 19 per cent of them into viable producers. Even among self-employed households in agriculture, about 38 per cent were below the poverty line, while another 38 per cent of the self-employed in rural non-farm activities were also below the poverty line. It is quite clear that the SCs are engaged in petty and low-productivity self-employed activities. The IRDP and wage employment programmes have helped some improve their income level but they are inadequate in magnitude and coverage as the vast majority of SCs, particularly wage labourers who constitute more than 60 per cent of the SC workers, lack adequate social security support.

In urban areas the situation is equally alarming as social security programmes of promotional nature such as credit and training support for self-employment and wage employment started much later in comparison to rural areas. The marginal impact of these measures is quite evident.

This implies the necessity of having a closer and critical look at the working of anti-poverty programmes in terms of their level and coverage. If the purpose of these programmes (i.e. IRDP and EP) is to provide minimum capacity and income support, then these programmes fall short of the intended objectives. Hence, there is a need to increase the level and coverage of self-employment and wage-employment programmes and also improve their implementation. Moreover, in case of SCs, the issue of economic discrimination in factor and product markets, particularly in job, wage and capital markets also needs to be seriously addressed. The security cover that they receive under government and public sector against possible discrimination is nearly absent in the private organised and unorganised sectors. In view of the growing thrust towards privatisation, and increasing dependence on the market for jobs, capital and social services, the extension of protection and social security cover through reservation or other related measures in agriculture and the urban industrial sector is necessary.

References

Banerjee, Biswajit and J.B. Knight (1991), "Caste Discrimination in Indian Urban Labour Market", *Journal of Developing Economies*, Vol. 7, pp. 277-307.

Deshi, A.K. and H. Singh (1995), "Education, Labour Market Distortions and Relative Earning of Different Religious Caste Categories in India", *Canadian Journal of Development Studies*, December 21.

Dreze, Jean and A.K. Sen (1991), "Public Action for Social Security Foundation and Strategy", in Ahmed et al. (eds.), *Social Security in Developing Countries*, Clarendon Press, Oxford.

Khan, Mumtaz Ali (1995), *Human Rights and the Dalits*, Uppal Publishers, Delhi.

Nanchariah, G. (1988), *Land and Caste*, Himalaya, Delhi.

Sankaran, T.S. et al. (eds.)(1994), *Development of Social Security Programmes in Developing Countries*, Har-Anand Pub., Delhi.

Thorat, S.K. (1996) "Ambedkar on Economics of Hindu Social Order: Understanding its Orthodoxy and Legacy", in Fernandes, Walter (ed.), *The Emerging Dalit Identity*, Indian Social Institute, New Delhi.

—— and Ram Deshpande (1998), "Caste System and Economic Inequality: Economic Theory and Evidence", in Saha, G. (ed.), *Status of Dalits*, Sage Publications, Delhi.

Tripathy, R.B. (1994), *Dalits: A Sub-human Society*, Ashish Publishing, Delhi.

Venkateswarlu, D. (1990), *Harijan-Upper Class Conflict*, Discovery Publishing, Delhi.

18

Social and Economic Security for the Scheduled Tribes

Harishwar Dayal and Anup K. Karan

I. INTRODUCTION

The Scheduled Tribes (STs) constituting approximately 8 per cent of population form the most marginalised group in the Indian society. Though several historical reasons account for their social and economic marginalisation, it is indeed intriguing to find that more than half a century of developmental efforts of independent India has not yet been able to make any dent into their insecure livelihoods. Any analysis to understand this persisting phenomenon invariably leads to the 'territorial marginality' of these groups (D'Souza, 1990). Most of these tribal communities still live in inaccessible terrains and the efforts to develop the infrastructure in the rural areas are yet to make any inroads to their habitations. Therefore, the territorial marginality continues to be a convenient excuse to justify their social and economic vulnerability. While their traditional systems provided them with social and economic securities to the extent that a primitive culture could afford (Vidyarthi, 1974), the development interventions in the latter half of the 20th century have exposed them to a series of insecurities. These include displacement from their natural habitat, loss of traditional modes of livelihood mainly because of the modern conservation rules of forests and finally, a social system that devalues their skills. Further, even the developmental policies formulated exclusively for them could not result in building their capabilities to enable them to participate in the mainstream of the development processes. Such a reading that the processes of development have been detrimental to the tribal communities gained momentum in the 1980s and also formed a powerful critique of the dominant development model. This is manifested in several works in the following decade providing vivid details of the displacement of tribals in the wake of many development projects, describing them as 'refugees of development and victims of internal colonisation' (Devalle, 1992; Fernandes, 1992; Singh, 1995).

Against this background this paper attempts to profile the social and economic (in) securities of tribal communities vis-a-vis other communities. The paper is based on the qualitative and quantitative information collected from the randomly (stratified) selected twelve villages in the three districts of the state of Jharkhand[1]. The quantitative information was collected through household interview schedules, while that on the qualitative aspects was gathered through Participatory Rural Appraisal (PRA) methods[2]. Secondary data from Census, National Sample Survey Organisation (NSSO), and National Family Health Survey (NFHS) have been referred to for comparing and/or substantiating the observations.

II. A GENERAL PROFILE

The percentage of ST population below the poverty line has been significantly higher than that of the general population or even the Scheduled Castes (SCs) and other underprivileged groups. As per NSSO, in 1987-88, 52.6 per cent of the ST population was below poverty line as against 33.4 per cent of general population and 44.7 per cent of SCs. The sex ratio among the tribal groups, though higher than that of the total population, has declined since 1981 (from 981 to 972). The level of literacy among the tribals is not only very low but also continues to show a considerable gap between males and females. Besides, food and nutritional deficiency and poor access to health care have led to a high morbidity rate among these groups. It has been found that the incidence of deficiency and infection-related diseases is very high among them while diseases related to cardo-vascular and nervous system is very low (Burmon, 1999). Weiner (1978) finds that in Chhotanagpur (now the state of Jharkhand) the main cause of backwardness among the *adivasis*, as expressed by themselves, are the problems of land alienation, exploitation by *dikus* (earlier moneylenders and Zamindars and now white-collar workers, politicians and traders and businessmen), and unemployment.

Jharkhand, recently carved out from Bihar, comprises of 18 districts and 203 blocks. The tribal population constitutes 27.67 per cent of the total population of this area and is predominant in eleven of its districts. In 112 of its blocks, which constitute the fifth schedule area[3] and are covered by the tribal sub-plan[4] the tribal groups account for 50 per cent of the total population. This area is inhabited by 30 notified scheduled tribe groups, out of which eight are primitive tribal groups (PTG). The agro-physical, soil and climatic condition of the state is such that besides agricultural productivity being low, it is unevenly distributed throughout the region, and varies widely during the year. The soil, though rich in micro-nutrients, is poor in macro-nutrients; the terrain is undulated and suffers from soil erosion. A large part (91.63 per cent) of the area under cultivation is rainfed. The total cultivable land in this area is also very low—only 22.54 per cent of the total geographical area of this region is under cultivation, of which 40 per cent is of good quality, low-lying paddy land (*Don*). As much as 87 per cent of cultivated area is mono-cropped. All this results in very low productivity of land.

The high incidence of poverty among the tribals of this region reflects their poor access to food. Apart from the high incidence, the inter regional and inter community variations in the levels of poverty are significant. While tribal communities in rural areas are more poverty-ridden than the urban communities, within the rural areas, certain tribal communities have higher levels of poverty than others. For example, 58 per cent of the tribals are below the poverty line and in the rural areas it is even worse with as much as 63.2

per cent. The condition of 'Ho' is the worst among all the tribal groups of this area—72 per cent of them live below the poverty line. They are followed by 'Santhals' (68.8 per cent), 'Oraon' (57.6 per cent) and 'Munda' (50.5 per cent). The level of food deprivation, measured in terms of number of meals skipped, however, is the highest among 'Santhals' (12.5 per cent), and lowest among 'Ho' (3.4 per cent), while the 'Oraon' (4.5 per cent), 'Munda' (7.7 per cent) and other tribes (8.9 per cent) fall in between the two groups (Sarvekshana, 1994). According to another survey only, 12.6 per cent of 'Sauria Paharia' (a PTG) people do not get two square meals a day throughout the year (Urmilesh, 1999). Due to the presence of Christian missionary and their philanthropic efforts within the region, particularly in fields of education, health, credit market, etc. the Christian tribals have been able to maintain a comparatively better socio-economic status in terms of education, female literacy, and labour market participation.

In view of the non-homogeneity among the tribal groups[5], three categories can be identified particularly in terms of levels of education, and their interactions with non-tribal population in the region. These are: i) primitive tribal groups (PTG), ii) non-Christian tribal, and iii) Christian tribal. The incidence of poverty and deprivation is the highest among the PTGs, who have a poor resource base and live in remote and relatively inaccessible areas. The Christian tribal group of the region have a better level of education and employment status in comparison to their non-Christian counterparts.

The present paper attempts to profile the status of surveyed households *vis-à-vis* their education, employment, food security, and health with a stock-taking exercise of various social and economic security mechanisms prevalent among the tribal groups of the newly formed state of Jharkhand. It provides an overview of the nature and extent of insecurities faced by these groups against the traditional mechanisms followed by them and the security measures that the state has formulated for them. The social security benefits provided by the state are analysed in detail to bring out accessibility and hence the effectiveness of the specific need of the tribal population in the state. While analysing the primary database, Christian tribal households have been treated separately owing to their different socio-economic status and exposure in comparison to that of the non-Christian tribal and non-tribal households. Taking into consideration the inter-community differences, social security measures and delivery system need to be formulated.

III. EDUCATIONAL STATUS AND SECURITY ISSUES

1. Level of Literacy

According to the 1991 Census, only 27.52 per cent of the tribal population of this region is literate. Female literacy is as low as 15.41 per cent. Regional variations and inter-group differences in literacy levels are also worth noting. In eight of the 13 districts of Jharkhand, the literacy level of certain groups is even worse than the average figure. In three of them, namely Sahibgunj, Dumka and Giridh, it is even less than 20 per cent. Among the PTGs it is less than 10 per cent, and only 5.74 per cent of the Birhor are literate. Comparatively, literacy among the Christian tribal group has been not only higher., but also there has been less gender discrimination in terms of access to basic education.

Although in recent years there have been some improvements in the literacy levels, our primary data shows that nearly half of the population above the five years of age is still illiterate, as level of literacy is only 50.74 per cent in the region (Table 1). The level of literacy among non-Christian group is 41.02 while among the Christian it is 68.54 per cent.

Table 1
Level of Literacy in Different Population Groups by Sex

Sex	Population groups			
	ST	ST (Ch)	Non-ST	Total
Male	54.68	77.27	75.22	64.17
Female	26.41	60.00	44.48	36.93
Total	41.02	68.54	59.71	50.74
Index of discrimination	2.07	1.29	1.69	1.74

Note: Index of discrimination has been calculated as the ratio of male to female literacy.

The male-female break up of the level of literacy within the region shows a high level of gender disparity in terms of access to education. The level of literacy among non-Christian tribal women is only 26 per cent, which is less than half of their male counterparts. The index of discrimination calculated in terms of ratio of male to female literacy was more than two in case of non-Christian tribals. Apart from higher level of literacy among the Christian tribals the discrimination index is also the lowest (only 1.29).

The level of literacy at more disaggregated levels for different age groups, occupational status of the households, and land holding groups are presented in Table 2. The literacy rate among the Christian tribals in all the occupations has been better than that of the non-Christian tribals. Except for the agriculture labour class, they are in fact more literate than even the non-tribal people. It is interesting to note that among the Christian tribals the literacy is more than 90 per cent in the 15-24 age group, and closer to 90 per cent in the 25-29 and 10-14 age groups. Among the non-Christian tribals the literacy is the highest among the 10-14 age group (71 per cent). In fact, the literacy rate in the lowest age group (5-9) is higher than in the higher age group (10-14) for all the three population groups (Table 2).

The households were classified on the basis of the occupation of the head of the households, and it is found that those belonging to the agricultural labourer households have the lowest literacy, while that of people belonging to the regular employed households, have the highest. Therefore, it can be inferred that, any kind of employment security leads to better access to education resulting in higher levels of literacy. The level of literacy among the households, in which the head of the households are non-workers, is also very low (except in case of Christian households). There is also a direct relation between size of landholding of the tribals and literacy. The levels of literacy are higher among the households with bigger landsize, both for tribal and non-tribal households. The literacy among the landless is the lowest—it is only 31 per cent in case of landless tribal households. Interestingly, among the Christian landless tribals the literacy is the highest. Most of the landless from this community are employed in some kind of regular works or some better paid

Table 2
Percentage of Literates among Tribal and Non-tribal Population by Age-group, Occupation and Landholding Size

	Population groups			
	ST	ST (Ch)	Non-ST	All
Age group (in years)				
5-9	62.59	79.31	78.41	69.70
10-14	71.35	89.74	87.88	78.96
15-19	55.20	91.30	70.37	64.19
20-24	44.86	92.00	65.22	57.71
25-29	33.66	88.00	61.19	50.26
30-59	23.59	53.47	43.03	33.99
60 & above	6.41	20.00	24.44	14.19
Occupation of head of HH				
Non-workers	34.42	64.71	45.65	39.20
Self-employed in agriculture & allied activities	39.97	66.83	66.57	51.48
Self-employed in other activities	48.33	71.43	52.83	52.21
Agricultural labour	31.03	33.33	43.18	38.16
Non-agricultural labour	40.00	75.00	62.50	53.64
Regularly employed	71.01	90.00	88.00	78.07
Land size (in acres)				
Nil	30.91	78.57	47.42	44.58
Up to 1	37.87	61.40	57.72	48.93
1 to 3	41.37	68.93	63.41	49.80
3 to 5	45.61	66.67	65.28	52.49
Above 5	45.95	72.00	71.01	60.39
All	41.02	68.54	59.71	50.74

jobs, and they seem to be more conscious of the benefits of education in the job market (Table 2).

2. Enrolment and Drop-outs

Among the three social groups taken into consideration, the rate of enrolment is the highest for the Christian tribal children. However, 16 per cent of the children, even among them, is 'never enrolled' and an additional (approximately) 3 per cent are 'dropouts'. The highest dropout rate as well as percentage of 'never enrolled' children are found among the non-Christian tribals. In all approximately 50 per cent of the children are out of school either because they are 'never enrolled' or because of dropouts (Table 3). One of the most important reasons for non-attendance of schools by children was the abject poverty among the tribals. Other reasons include the location of the schools, at distant places and in high caste/non-tribal settlements low quality of education in government schools, frequent and even prolonged absence of teachers, and irregular and in many cases non-supply of mid-day meals or grains.

In an effort to provide educational security to tribal children, the government has initiated three important measures in the region. These are (i) opening up of *anganwadi* centres, (ii) provision of primary schools in each and every village, and (iii) opening up of residential schools in the region of tribal concentration. Apart from these, the government also has introduced schemes for the free distribution of textbooks and stationary, book bank, and awarding scholarships for the tribal students. However, all these schemes have shown very little impact because of various institutional and structural constraints.

Table 3
Percentage Distribution of Children (5-14) by Their Educational and School Status

Population group	Never enrolled	Drop-out	Enrolled	Among enrolled		
				Attend NFE	Govt. school	Private school
ST	35.69	14.17	50.14	7.07	85.33	7.61
ST (Ch)	16.00	2.67	81.33	6.56	36.07	57.38
Non-ST	18.14	12.56	69.30	8.05	87.25	4.70

It can be seen from Table 3 that out of the total enrolled children approximately 6 per cent are enrolled in government run non-formal education (NFE) centres. Although *anganwadi* centres were found in most of the villages, and also the enrolment register in these centres were impressive, the attendance was very low. This is also evident from the high percentage of 'out of school children'. In a few villages, the location of these centres also worked as a disincentive as these centres are located in the non-tribal *tola* (hamlet). The *anganwadi* centres are run under the Integrated Child Development Scheme (ICDS) and are supposed to provide regular health check-up to the children. But it was found that no doctor or nurse visited most of the centres. The only activity, which is carried out frequently, relates to registering the weights of the attending children. Though the highest percentage of children are enrolled in government primary schools, in the case of Christian community more than 50 per cent of the enrolled children are attending private schools. Most of the private schools in the region are run by Christian missionaries and the non-Christian tribals have little access to them mainly because of differential fees charged by these schools for Christian and non-Christian communities.

The low educational status of tribal groups in this region can be explained in terms of three types of problems, namely, economic, infrastructural and institutional. A large number of tribal children, as we have seen above, do not go to school because of economic reasons. Most of them are child workers or help their parents in their domestic chores or out-migrate with their parents in the lean season. However, the prospect of getting foodgrains in the school improves the prospects of enrolments. Enrolment is low also because of the deficiency of infrastructure—three of the 12 surveyed villages did not have even primary schools; in two of them it was located at a distance of two to five k.m. Half the number of schools were single-teacher schools and in two of them teachers were absent for a long time; eight of them were without desks and three of them without a blackboard. The *Adivasi Awasiya Vidyalay* (Tribal Residential School) set up by the Welfare Department of the Government of India serves very little purpose as very few children are able to get admission in this school. All of them use the traditional teaching methods and no effort has been made to introduce the concept of joyful learning and improve teaching-learning process. All these factors have contributed in making education unattractive, and in lowering the enrolment and increasing the dropout rate.

Institutional degradation is reflected in the poor attendance of teachers, intensity of teaching, management of school, and teacher-parent relationships, etc. also contribute to low enrolment, high dropout rates and poor educational attainments of the tribal students.

IV. INSECURITIES OF EMPLOYMENT AND INCOME

Employment and income security are essential for attaining reasonable levels of purchasing power and food security (Mahendra Dev, 1999). However, in a poor economy, low rate of unemployment is not a measure of employment security. Such economies are characterised by high worker participation rates (WPR). In a region or population group, with high intensity of poverty, a larger proportion of youth and old people participate in the labour markets at a wage rate, which is even below the subsistence wage, in order to supplement their family income.

1. Workforce Participation and Occupational Structure

The WPR among the surveyed tribal households is as high as approximately 97 per cent, both for male and female (taking both primary and secondary occupations into consideration). It is much higher in comparison to the non-tribals as well as their Christian counterparts. Nevertheless, the WPR in primary occupation for the male is approximately 90 per cent while for the females only 20 per cent (Table 4).

Table 4
Work Participation Rates among Tribals and Non-tribals as Per Their Primary and Primary+Secondary Occupations

Caste	Sex	Occupation	
		Primary	Primary +secondary
ST	Male	90.18	97.48
	Female	20.41	96.50
ST (Ch)	Male	86.52	94.38
	Female	41.18	80.00
Non ST	Male	85.66	92.62
	Female	12.50	79.46
All		56.22	92.19

The low female participation rate on the basis of their primary occupation reflects the high level of gender discrimination in the labour markets of the region. This is in addition to the fact that there is less recognition of females' work as an economic activity. Most of their works are taken as merely providing assistance to their male counterparts and are treated as secondary works. Among the Christian tribals, the WPR, for females is substantially higher than that among the non-Christian tribals. The overall participation rates for the Christian workers is lower in comparison to that for the non-Christian tribals on account of a higher proportion of youth from the former category pursuing education and the fact that a large proportion of them are better placed in the labour market.

The tribals of the region are primarily agriculturists. They cleared the forest and practised settled and/or shifting cultivation. The increased population pressure, eviction from forest, reduced access to forest and alienation of land due to non-tribal incursions in the cleared forest areas compelled them to participate in the wage labour market and other occupations. The occupational structure of the workers on the basis of primary as well as secondary occupations is given in Table 5. More than 65 per cent of the tribal workers are primarily involved in agriculture and allied activities as self-employed, while approximately 15 per cent of them are primarily wage labourers. Less than 5 per cent of the workers reported themselves working as agricultural labourers on the basis of primary occupation. However, most of the small and marginal tribal cultivators used to work in others' fields under the *madaiti*[6] (shared labour) system. Among the Christian community more than 20 per cent are involved in regular service, of which only 6 per cent of the tribal and approximately 10 per cent of the non-tribal workers are engaged in this occupation.

Table 5
Occupational Structure of the Tribals and Non-tribals as Per Their Primary and Secondary Occupations

	Primary occupation				Secondary occupation			
Occupations	ST	ST (ch)	Non ST	Total	ST	ST (ch)	Non ST	Total
Agriculture and allied	66.82	65.18	50.63	61.65	49.40	38.14	50.00	48.42
Agricultural labour	4.67	2.68	5.91	4.76	29.00	16.95	23.06	25.88
Non-agricultural labour	14.49	8.93	8.02	11.71	10.57	18.64	7.22	10.35
Service	6.31	21.43	9.70	9.52	0.15	2.54	0.28	0.44
Trades	4.44	1.79	20.25	8.88	2.42	3.39	10.83	5.18
Other occupations	3.27	0.00	5.49	3.47	8.46	20.34	8.61	9.74
All	100.00	100.00	100.00	100.00	100.00	100.00	100.00	100.00

Employment security is also understood in terms of maintaining the same or improving the social status because of any change in the employment status of the workers. The occupational structure presented in Table 4 also gives an idea of change in the employment status of the workers within a short time period. The secondary occupation of the workers is the alternative occupation available to them. Although agriculture is the dominant occupation in the region, the percentage of casual wage earners (agricultural as well as non-agricultural) in case of tribals, becomes more than double if secondary occupation is taken into consideration. It is important to note here that very few workers in this region report themselves as agriculture labour on the basis of their primary occupation. However, the proportion of agricultural labour increases by more than 20 per cent on the basis of secondary occupation (highest increase being in case of tribal workers). This indicates that most of the cultivators resort to casual wage employment and other occupations (collection of minor forest products, woods, fodder, etc.) during lean seasons. Change in the social status of the workers on account of frequent change in employment status from cultivators to casual wage labour is mainly the result of very low employment opportunities in agriculture of this region. Trade also provides very little employment opportunities to the tribals of this region as this activity is dominated by non-tribals.

A substantial number of tribal workers are working in illegal mines, in transportation of minerals and other low paid/less remunerative vocations or otherwise migrate. Many illegal mines continue to function in this area; either vacated by the respective departments as safe extraction was not possible or because they were created without proper planning. Presently they function with the help of unscrupulous persons in connivance with the local officials. We observed that many small illegal coal mines at Palasthali, Bara Rampur, Kasta, Jarkundi, Mohit Nagar, and Kanthikur in Dumka district, in the absence of proper safety measures are accident-prone exposing tribal workers to considerable risks both to their life and health.The coal thus extracted is transported by the tribals through their cycles to the actual users or middlemen. And they have to carry heavy load of coal on undulated terrain over long distances, they are prone to several chronic ailments, which in turn affect their life expectancy.

The economic deprivation of the surveyed tribal groups needs to be understood against the low wages and the minimal employment opportunities. Across the types of employment that they engage in, irrespective of the skills required or hardships involved, the wages remain the same. In non-skilled work, in both agriculture and non-agriculture sectors, the males are paid a wage between Rs. 25 to 35, while the females get between Rs. 15 to 25. Lack of employment opportunities within the region has also increased the intensity of migration. It was found that approximately 30 per cent of the households had at least one migrant member in the family. Migration from the region has been both seasonal (of temporary nature) and permanent. Among the workers, the percentage of migrants varied from 20 to 30 per cent from region to region. Most of the workers (except Christian tribal community) are seasonal migrants particularly during agricultural off seasons. The seasonal migrants usually migrate in groups through some middlemen. The middlemen also provide advances to the migrants, which is deducted from the wages or collected after they return to the native village.

Being original settlers of this region, they have a more even land distribution pattern in comparison to that of many of the non-tribal regions. Landlessness among them was found to be less than 10 per cent, while most of them have an average size of land between 1 to 3 acres. It can be seen that even within the tribal region tribals have better land distribution in comparison to the non-tribals (Table 6).

Table 6
Percentage Distribution of Tribal and Non-Tribal Households by Size of Land

Caste	Land size (in acres)				
	Nil	Up to 1	1 to 3	3 to 5	above 5
ST	5.65	31.30	41.74	13.91	7.39
ST (Ch)	9.26	25.93	40.74	7.41	16.67
Non ST	15.54	47.97	20.27	9.46	6.76
All	9.49	36.34	34.26	11.57	8.33

In an agricultural economy, land is the primary asset from a subsistence point of view. Apart from enabling utilisation of family labour, it provides food security, and reduces vulnerability to the fluctuations in the labour and food markets. Access to land is, in fact, important not only for providing the rural poor with a primary asset but also from the point of view of "deconcentrating the economic and political power of large landlords, which enables them to reduce wages, increase rents, operate in interlocked credit markets, and exercise diverse forms of extra-economic oppression over the poor" (Guhan, 1995). In Jarkhand, even after a comparatively better distribution of land among the tribals, interlocking of labour and credit market is prevalent. Landlords often resort to various types of exploitative labour arrangements, to extract a large surplus from stagnant agriculture. The prevalence of *Kamiauti* (a type of attached labour system) and extent of exploitation caused by it in Palamau district has been very well documented by Mundle (1979). However, in view of the increasing presence of ultra political parties such as Moist Communist Centre (MCC), Peoples' War Group (PWG), etc. in recent years, particularly in Palamau and Gumla districts, the system of *Kamiauti* is increasingly on decline[7].

2. Land Alienation

Land being the only productive asset, guarantees tribals employment and income security. Therefore, possession of land was the main issue behind most of the tribal uprisings—the Kol rebellion (1831-32) or Birsa Ulgulan (1895-1900) or the Sibu Soreng Hul (1970-76). Several legislative provisions have been made to restrict the alienation of tribal land and to ensure restoration of the land already alienated from them. These include Chotanagpur Tenancy Act (CNTA) 1908, Santhal Pargana Tenancy Act (SPTA) 1949, Scheduled Area Regulation (SAR) 1969 and the provisions of fifth schedule. Also, as money lending is the main tool of tribal land alienation Bihar Money Lenders (Regulation of Transaction) Act, 1939, have been suitably amended. These Acts, however, allow acquisition of land for public purposes—Section 49 of CNTA and Section 53 of SPTA allows acquisition/transfer of tribal land for public purposes (reasonable and sufficient purposes). Consequently, often good quality cultivable lands (*Don*) is acquired for such purposes. Moreover, land requirements in all such cases are not properly assessed and usually lands in excess of requirements are acquired for public projects. The tribals who were thus alienated from their lands are given neither proper compensation for their land nor any benefit from the projects for which their lands have been acquired.

Apart from the government, individuals (mainly non-tribals), have also contributed to alienation of tribal land through manipulation of the existing laws. This has happened because of various factors such as the loopholes in the tenancy legislation, slackness in the implementation of restrictive provisions in the forest Acts and certain other socio-economic factors (Bhatia, 2000). Several methods have been adopted by individuals for alienating tribal land such as collusive title suits, getting the land declared *chapparbandi*, mortgage, outright sale, encroachment, transfer of land in false names or by marrying tribal girls (Sinha, 1968). According to another study, there has been massive alienation of tribal land in this area though there is evidence of a substantial decline in its incidence since 1970. Nevertheless this trend has enhanced the extent of employment insecurity among the tribals. Initiation of a number of SAR cases after 1970 and an increase in general awareness among both the tribals and non- tribals about provisions of SAR, have proved to be a deterrent to the non-tribals in buying lands (Sharan et al, 1999).

Regarding restoration of land to the tribals and the right to have access to land and forest, the government has initiated several measures to prevent land alienation, restore the alienated land and distribute the surplus land among the landless. While introducing measures to improve the access to forest, the government has attempted to balance environmental concern with the forest dependency of the tribals. At the outset, in pursuance of the objective of rehabilitating and resettling tribals displaced by public projects, Section 71A of Chhotanagpur Tenancy Act (CNTA) has been amended by including elaborate provisions to restore to the tribals the possession of the land unlawfully transferred.

Consequent to the government's legislative action, small pieces of cultivable lands (slightly less than an acre to two acres) have been distributed among the landless tribals or among those having small land holdings. Table 7 shows that 8 per cent of the tribal households have received land under the scheme of land distribution. The scheme appears to be well targeted as mostly those having less than two acres of lands have been its beneficiaries.

Table 7
Distribution of Land among Tribal Households by Their Land Size

Land size (in acres)	% of households benefited
Nil	16.67
Up to 0.5	12.50
0.5 to 1	13.04
1 to 2	6.67
2 to 5	5.06
Total	8.09

Besides this, there have been other efforts to restore land of the tribals. In the year 1986-87 slightly more than seven thousand (7278.76) acres of lands were restored to the tribals by the courts. According to the twenty-eighth report of the Commissioner for Scheduled Castes and Scheduled Tribes, by 1987, more than twelve thousand (12,740) cases of tribal land alienation were pending in the courts of this area, out of which 65 per cent (8,292) cases were disposed off in 1987. A study conducted by IAS probationers in four districts of Jharkhand (Dumka, Hazaribag, Giridih and Gumla) found out that only 50 per cent of cases of tribal land alienation filed in the designated courts of this area were admitted and the rest were rejected mostly on flimsy grounds (LBSN, 1991).

Redistribution of land among the tribal households is grossly insufficient, in view of the large scale land alienation of the tribals. All incidents of tribal land alienation are not reported to the courts (see Box 1) because the affected tribals are either ignorant, or have fear of retaliation by the usurper or do not want to face the agony and distress caused to them while the case is pending. A large number of the cases filed are not registered (50 per cent as per LBSN study). Regrettably, some of the cases are disposed off in favour of the transferee using the loopholes of the legislation. In some others, even where the judgement has been delivered in favour of the tribals, they have failed to get possession either because the other party goes on appeal so that the case is kept pending for long or in collaboration with concerned officials manage to delay the restoration process.

Box 1
Usurpation of Land by Landlord

Two acres of land of Rama Oraon, an educated (eleventh pass) tribal youth of Baradih village of Gumla block, has been usurped by the powerful Rajput landlord of the same village. His father, who is no more, had mortgaged this piece of land for a loan of Rs. 500 on a *bhugat bandha* contract some 15 years back for his education and for the treatment of his mother and it was not restored back to him. Rama Oraon realised that his problem of poverty could be solved only if his land is restored to him. He, however, has not filed any case for the restoration of his land because of the fear of retaliation by the landlord for whom he works as a labourer.

The villagers at some places have set their lands free from the control of the land grabbers (Box 2). During *Sibu Soreng Hul* (1974–76) the villagers at many places helped their friends to regain possession of their land, which was illegally occupied by others. Tribals in thousands forcibly harvested the crops

Box 2
Restoration of Land through Community Support

Joseph Murmu of Karmatand village of Shikaripara block in Dumka district, informed us that a large part of their land had been usurped by the *Sahus* and *Surhi* of Barmasia Panchayat. Their parents were addicted to alcohol for which they used to take a loan from the latter by mortgaging their land. The land, once mortgaged, was never returned to them. During the 'Hul' period, on the call of Sibu Soren, the villagers in a united manner drove out the usurpers and restored the land to the original owners.

In Andhradih village also the tribals of the village on the initiative of the educated village youth, got united in the early nineties against the *Sahus* (moneylenders) of the same village. The *Shaus* had usurped a large area of their land using the same method--mortgaging their land for petty loans. Through their movement the tribals set their land free from the control of the *Sahus*, who out of fear released their control over such land.

from the alienated tribal lands. The district administration, latter on, restored large pieces of land to the original tribal owners. In Giridih and Dhanbad, 2378.42 and 2066.84 acres of alienated lands respectively were restored to the original owners by the district administration (Iyer and Maharaj, 1982).

Of late, the local opposition has, however, succeeded in preventing the displacement in some cases and ensuring proper settlement in other cases. Netarhat field firing range and Koel-Karo Projects are examples of this, though the threat of displacement of the people has not totally disappeared from here. There are also cases of rehabilitation of people displaced from Maithon, Surhichua and Mayurakshi[8].

Rights of Tribals in Reserved Forests

Over the years, the tribals of this region have been able to gain some concessions and facilities for using forest resources. The government has accepted in principle that the needs of the local tribal have to be met from the forest. Accordingly, even in reserved forests (which are generally free of rights), the tribals living in the vicinity have been allowed to collect fruits, flowers, twigs leaves (barring *kendu* leaves), roots, etc. for their requirements. Some of the traditional rights of the tribals in protected forests have been legalised by including them in forest settlements. They are now entitled to collect minor forest products (MFP), take a head load of dry and fallen fire woods, collect timber for agriculture and household purposes and send their animals for grazing free of cost or on payment of nominal fees. The state government of undivided Bihar had taken steps to ensure a fair share for the tribals in MFP as well as a fair price for it. It has formalised *kendu* leaves, *sal* seeds and many other minor forest products and set up government organisations and tribal co-operatives for procurement of the same. However, though the government had formally acceded the ownership right over minor forest products to the tribal groups in January 1990, the decision has not yet been implemented.

The forest department, in some areas, has successfully introduced joint Forest Management (JFM) practices in which the tribals have jointly shared the responsibility of protecting the forest and the right to use its products[9].

3. Employment Generation and Poverty Alleviation Programmes

With a view to assure employment and income security to the tribals, the government has initiated several programmes such as IRDP, TRYSEM, DWACRA, PMRY, and ITDP aimed essentially at creating avenues for self-employment. Under these schemes, income-generating assets have been distributed among poor tribals. The Integrated Tribal Development Project (ITDP) has provided such assets to the tribals on 100 per cent subsidy, while under IRDP, TRYSEM, DWACRA and PMRY, subsidised loans have been given to them for buying these assets. EAS (Employment Assurance Scheme) and JRY (Jawahar Rojgar Yojna) with its components, Indira Aawas Yojna (IAY) and Million Well Scheme (MWS), have been introduced for creating wage employment. Most of these programmes are carried out during the agricultural lean season and are intended to reduce unemployment and migration among the tribal people. The wage employment programmes also have the objective of creating community assets, which can support the tribals in their economic endeavours.

Table 8
Percentage of Tribal Households Who Benefited from Government Programmes

Land size (in acres)	JRY	IRDP
Nil	11.11	11.11
Up to 0.5	15.00	22.50
0.5 to 1	17.39	36.96
1 to 2	12.00	29.33
2 to 5	8.86	40.50
5 & above	11.54	30.77
Total	12.32	31.69

The coverage of the two most important government programmes, i.e. JRY and IRDP, in the state has been very poor. It was found that only 12 and 32 per cent of the households benefited under the JRY and IRDP programmes respectively (Table 8). The coverage of IRDP, in terms of the percentage of households that benefited under this programme, is higher in comparison to that of the JRY. In the surveyed villages more than 31 per cent of the households have benefited under IRDP, while the beneficiary households under JRY have been only 12 per cent. However, JRY is slightly better targeted in comparison to IRDP in terms of coverage of the poor households. The coverage under these two programmes have been evaluated on the basis of their land holdings and it has been found that the landless households were the group that benefited the least (except two to five acres of holdings in case of JRY) from these two programmes. For the distribution of IRDP loans the lending institutions always looked for some kind of security and hence, preferred the households with bigger landholding sizes.

A wage employment programme like JRY is basically a self- targeting programme, as it involves the participation of the poor who directly benefit from it. But some of the tribals owning even five or slightly more than five acres of land are also found participating in this programme—11.54 per cent of tribals owning five and more acres of land were among the beneficiaries of the programme. Such programmes assume particular significance since monocroping and the low productivity of land limits their prospects of securing full time employment. Not surprisingly the tribals are inclined to readily accept this type of wage employment, which gives them more wages than what is prevalent in the village.

The presence of these government programmes in the villages, however, has helped in disseminating the knowledge about Minimum Wages Act in the villages, particularly in terms of minimum wage rates and wages for males and females. However, in many of the villages the wages paid under JRY works are reported to be lower than the prescribed norm and gender discriminatory. Moreover, the employment opportunities created under JRY varied between 200 to 260 labour days per village during one year of reference. This means that, on an average, the programme could generate 8 to 10 days of employment for a group of 25 workers in a village. The government has thus failed to create adequate employment opportunities of the type required, which could have taken care of employment-related deprivation of the tribals, i.e. of inadequate employment opportunity and low wage.

V. FOOD SECURITY

Besides the communal ownership of land, tribal communities traditionally maintained *pancha system* (a community-based food storage system) in this area. According to this system, everyone has to contribute food items to this common store during times of surplus so that these could be made available to all in times of food scarcity. Over the years, however, due to various exogenous and endogenous factors this system disappeared and today these communities are faced with the problem of variability and instability in the supply of food items.

Livestock and forest products are other sources, which supplement the stable availability and supply of food reasonably. Goats and poultry are sold in times of need. Nevertheless, under the present living conditions they are unable to maintain a large livestock as they have (a) a low resource base to feed them, (b) to out-migrate and (c) a less developed local market for the animal-products. Some of the tribals have reduced the number of their animals because their children, who earlier used to take care of their animals, now attend schools. The change in the composition of forest in terms of a decline in the species and restrictions on their access over forest resources have adversely affected the food security of the tribals.

The food calendar exercise in the sample villages also revealed the prevalence of an acute food crisis for at least four months in a year, when many of the villagers have to skip a few meals or have to be content with inferior grains like *gora, gondli, khesari, madua, sawa,* etc. Based on the food calendar, prepared by some tribal women in different villages, the months of shortages and starvation have been identified (Chart 1).

From Chart 1 it is evident that a substantial percentage of the households in the Jharkhand region face starvation for at least three to four months. In addition they face food shortage for three to five months, thus, leaving only three months when the people have a reasonable amount of food. Even during this period, the poor are often unable to afford pulses and wheat because of their low income levels. There is also inter-village variation in the periods of starvation. In Palamau and Gumla districts, the starvation periods are the summer and monsoon months between April and August, while in Dumka, this period begins in June-July and ends in September-October. Dumka and Palamu also differ from Gumla in that even maize is unavailable during periods of starvation, thus forcing the people in Gumla to consume *madua* and *gondli*. In addition to the months of starvation, the region is also characterised by shortage periods. Except for about five winter months, from October to February-March, all the other months seem to be either periods of shortage or periods of starvation.

This food problem has been further compounded by the recent shift in the cropping pattern. The only source of sustenance during the food deficit months—the ingredients for *saag*, and cereals such as *goda* and *gondli*--- are being fast depleted by the cultivation of wheat and maize. This implies that

Chart 1
Months of Food Shortages and Starvation in Study Villages

District/ village	Months of availability	Months of shortage	Months of starvation	Food items consumed during starvation
Gumla district				
Andhradih	Kartik to Magh	Bhado, Ashwin, Falgun, Chaitra	Baisakh to Sawan	saag,khesari,madua, goda, gondli, mahua
Baradih	Aghan to Falgun	Chaitra, Baisakh, Bhado, Ashwin, Kartik	Jayestha, Asarh, Sawan	saag, gondli, madua
Sarapmunda	Ashwin to Baisakh	Sawan, Bhado	Jayestha, Asarh	local vegetables and saag, goda, gondli, madua
Gujharia	Kartik to Magh	Falgun to Jyestha	Asarh to Ashwin	bodi, local sagg, madua, sem, khesari
Palamau district				
Udaipura	Aghan to Baishak	Bhado, Ashwin, Kartik	Jaystha Asarh, Sawan	mahua, maize, local saag, and vegetables
Ghutwa	Chaitra to Asarh, Aghan to Push	Magh, Falgun, Kartik	Sawan, Bhado, Ashwin	local saag, and vegetables, sattu, bodi dal.
Bahera Kalan	Kartik to Falgun	Ashwin Chaitra, Baishakh	Jayestha to Bhado	sawa, kodo, maize saag, and vegetables
Karma	Aghan to Falgun	Chaitra, Baisakh, Bhado, Ashwin, Kartik	Jayestha, Asarh, Sawan	maize, sattu, jinora, mahua, madua local vegetables and saag.
Dumka district				
Rampur	Aghan to Baishakh	Jyestha, Ashwin, Kartik	Asarh, Sawan, Bhado	fish, local saag and vegetables, mahua, maize
Maheshpur	Aghan to Chaitra	Baisakh, Jaystha Kartik	Asarh, Sawan, Bhado, Ashwin	local saag and vegetables, mahua , maize
Karma Tand	Kartik to Magh, Baisakh to Asarh	Falgun, chaitra	Sawan, Bhado, Ashwin	fish, maize, local saag and vegetables
Indravani	Aghan to Falgun	Chaitra, Baisakh, Jayestha, Ashwin, Kartik	Asarh, Sawan, Bhado	local saag and vegetables, fish , maize

Note: Months are as per Hindi calendar. See note 10, for corresponding seasons.

the tribals now have to increasingly buy their food in the open market. Given their low economic status, they have no option but to resort to eating even less nutritious food during this period.

There are large differences in the quality of food taken by different sections of the population due to the wide difference in the kind of food items consumed by them during the deficit months. Though the rich and very rich manage to eat well throughout the year, the intake of food among middle income households tend to vary between various months. In the case of the poor and very poor communities, consumption of rice and wheat is restricted to the

Box 3
Anomalies in PDS

Karma is a remote village in Chainpur block of Palamau district. The PDS shop is not located within the village. It is located four km. away in a neighbouring village. The villagers complain that though they sometimes get kerosene and sugar, they seldom get foodgrains from there. Many a times because of the distance they do not get information about the availability of the provisions. In other villages also the tribals complain that they do not get food items. Though all the twelve villages, we surveyed, were covered by PDS facility except one, in all other villages the inhabitants were getting only kerosene and sugar (in Baherakalan the villagers get food items also). The inhabitants of all the villages however, complained of insufficient supply. In Baradih and Andhradih (both in Ghaghra block of Gumla district) the villagers complained that the shopkeepers sell off the provisions in black market and do not give them their due. The PDS shopkeepers had a different story. They complained that they neither get the supply on time, nor in sufficient quantity. Worse still, they also reported to pay bribe to the personnel of the supply department, which they compensate by selling part of the supply in the open market.

months when employment opportunities are better and hence there is an improvement in food availability. During the remaining period, they are forced to consume inferior cereals such as *goda, gondli* and *mahua*. Further, though the 'rich' and 'very rich' (households categorised by the villagers during 'wealth ranking exercise' in the villages) consume vegetables and other nutritious food items such as milk, egg, etc., the poor are very often unable to afford these items. However, due to their proximity to the forests, the poor in the region are able to eat wild fruits and herbs, which are relatively more nutritious. But as mentioned earlier, the depletion of forest and hurdles involved in accessing forest, make the collection of wild fruits and herbs problematic.

The public distribution system (PDS) has an important role in meeting the food deficiency of people in several parts of India. However, access of the tribals to PDS facility is very low—very few of them (3 to 4 per cent) get foodgrains or *janta* cloth. The tribals living in the remote areas do not have easy access to the PDS facility, while those who live in villages where PDS shops are located, do not get all the items in sufficient quantity and at the right time (see Box 3).

Recently the government has introduced the *"lal Card"* for the poor under the targeted public distribution system (TDPS) to enable them to receive food grains from PDS shops at a lower price. However, the coverage of the programme so far has been limited. As per the data collected from different blocks under survey, only 50 to 60 per cent of the people below poverty line were provided this facility. Moreover, there are also instances of wrong identification of beneficiaries, leading to dissatisfaction among the villagers over the distribution of *lal cards*.

The panchayati raj institutions have been given powers (a) for social auditing of PDS in order to ensure higher accountability and proper targetting of food supplies, (b) to invoke Essential Commodities Act to eliminate shortages, (c) to use NIC network for effective monitoring of PDS, (d) to institute a grievance cell for redressal of complaints, and (e) to conduct surprise inspections. These measures, if properly implemented, will undoubtedly make PDS effective in assuring food security to the tribals of this area.

In view of the grim food scenario, efforts have also been made to increase productivity of agriculture in this region. Birsa Agriculture University, Ranchi, has developed high-yielding seeds of local variety crops (Birsa 101 and 103 for example), which are suitable for local agro-climatic conditions. It has also taken steps to make the cultivators aware of these seeds through its extension works. Since the *kharif* season of last year, the New Agricultural Technology Project (NATP) has been launched in three districts of the state on a pilot basis. A co-ordinated effort has also been made at the district, block and village levels to introduce new and better technology based on agro-climatic conditions and the capability of the farmers in the area.

A major step has also been initiated to improve the irrigation facility in this area. The World Bank supported 'Bihar Plateau Development Project (BPDP)' has provided irrigation to 67 blocks of Jharkhand leading to an improvement in production and productivity of agriculture in this region. *Jaldhara* and Rural Infrastructure Development Fund (RIDF) of NABARD have also helped in the creation of irrigation facilities. Work on 261 medium irrigation projects is underway and these will provide irrigation to 26,460 hectares of land in this area. Out of these, 184 projects have been taken up by BPDP and 77 by RIDF. Besides, work on 210 lift irrigation projects is also in progress and these are expected to provide irrigation to an additional 20,509 hectares of land.

VI. HEALTH SECURITY

The tribals in Jharkhand have a very poor health status. As many as 59 per thousand tribals reported sickness in the last 30 days in the 44th round of NSS. The incidence of sickness among tribal groups as reported by NSS shows that it was highest among the Ho (96 per thousand) and lowest among Santhal and Oraon (47 and 46 per thousand respectively) (Sarvekshana, 1994). The National Family Health Survey, 1993 (NFHS) also reported their poor health status. According to it, (i) the infant mortality rate among the tribals of this area is 97.2 per thousand, (ii) 78.8 per cent of their children do not receive antenatal care, (iii) 57 per cent are not immunised, (iv) 81.8 per cent of their women do not get tetanus toxoid injection during pregnancy, and (v) more than 60 per cent of their children suffer from malnutrition (<2SD %weight for age). Our survey also confirmed the high incidence of skin disease, leprosy, T.B., malaria and diarrhoea. In Shikaripara block, some cases of encephalitis were also reported. The poor health status of the tribals is attributed to various factors such as high degree of nutritional deficiency, high level of pollution, occupational hazards, lack of awareness, superstition, poverty, lack of safe drinking water, poor hygiene and inadequate medical facilities.

Traditionally, the tribals used to depend on herbal medicines and magico-religious treatments provided by their *ojhas* (spiritual person authorised for this purpose). Today, dependence on herbal medicines is gradually waning due to lack of knowledge about the benefits of such medicines as well as due to sharp decline in their availability. Thus, though some tribals continue to prefer the magico-religious treatment, they are gradually loosing faith in it. As a result their dependence on modern medical facilities has increased. Yet, before opting for modern methods of treatment the tribals prefer to go to *ojhas* and quacks for treatment even though this can adversely affect their health. This tendency among the tribals is revealed by our group discussions with the local villagers, indicating the strong influence of traditional beliefs on the tribals.

The government has taken certain steps to activate the existing medical facilities and set up additional facilities for providing medical assistance to the tribals. Specifically, intensive malaria eradication/control programmes are being carried out in rural areas and T.B., leprosy and filaria centres have been established in all the district of the state. Furthermore, WHO-sponsored Modified Leprosy Elimination Campaign (MLEC), started from April 1998, which is doing some good work in identifying and treating leprosy cases in this area. Immunisation and health awareness programmes have been launched for the benefit of the tribals with *Sakcharta Samities* and *Anganwadis*. These efforts have shown good results in some areas.[11] *Sakcharta Samities* are, however, found operating in only two of the twelve villages, while seven out of ten *Anganwadi* centres are involved in providing health support to the children and mothers of the villages. They monitor the growth of the children, perform health check ups, help in their immunisation and provide maternal health care and hygiene-related services and information.

Some of the NGOs are also involved in providing health and hygiene-related facilities. AROUSE, for example, is providing health and hygiene-related education to the inhabitants of Gujharia village of Kurdeg block. A Christian mission was also found to be providing health facilities to the inhabitants of the villagers of Kurdeg and Shikaripara blocks. However, the reach of the missionaries in providing health care has always been limited both in terms of coverage and intensity.

The government has also introduced a medical aid programme for the tribals under which patients belonging to Scheduled Tribes suffering from acute and chronic diseases are reimbursed partially the cost of medical treatment incurred by them. Additionally, separate health programmes have been introduced for Paharia, one of the primitive tribal groups. Many of the Paharia boys and girls have been trained on basic health care and Paharia health centres have been set up in hilly region near Paharia habitat. The government has adopted some good hospitals/nursing homes of the area for the treatment of sick people of the Paharia community.

Limitations of Health Programmes

The success of all the government programmes, however, depends essentially on the extent to which the tribals have easy access to health centres and other facilities. Our survey revealed some glaring shortcomings, in this regard. The malaria inspector visits the village only when malaria spreads, and therefore, preventive measures are rarely initiated before the diseases break out resulting in a sharp increase in the incidence of deaths. Primary health centres and sub-centres are present in only three and four villages respectively. In another two villages they are located at a distance of two to five kms. and in the rest more than 5 k.m. Not surprisingly, the surveyed households across the villages complained about poor health facilities---not only in terms of the unavailability of doctors but also the high cost of private medical facilities[12]. Thus, there is an urgent need to improve the existing health facilities of both the preventive and curative types and create additional facilities for the tribals of this region. The preventive health measures that are needed include steps to control pollution, provision to provide safe drinking water and introduce universal immunisation, spraying of insecticides, introduction of education and awareness programme for the tribals about aspects relating to health and hygiene, distribution of mosquito nets to the needy and the creation of additional well equipped health centres.

VII. CONCLUSION

The above analyses show that the insecurities that the tribal communities face in the state of Jharkhand are varied and many. The gravity of the situation has to be viewed against the almost complete disappearance of their traditional social security mechanisms along with the reactive, un-integrated and often limited reach and coverage of state-sponsored security measures. The social and economic deprivation of the tribals, as is evident from the discussion, can be attributed essentially to the low productivity of their land, low literacy, and alienation of resources, mainly due to the mass influx of non-tribals into the region. Earlier, they had a traditional support system, which helped to prevent them from being exposed to the risk of deprivation and vulnerability. With the increase in population pressure on land and other resources and the alienation and displacement of the tribals from such resources, the need for providing social security to the tribals has become imperative.

Government agencies have been in the process of evolving an organisational structure and formulating result-oriented development programmes in such key areas as education, health, nutrition, agriculture, marketing, forestry, communication, etc. Some progress has, no doubt, been made in providing these services, but, as the Ministry of Home Affairs admits, 'the actual benefit trickling down to the tribals have not been consistent with the promises made, the expenditure has not resulted in the benefit that should have accrued to them .....the developmental programmes for the tribal area did not yield desired result' (Bhowmick, 1993). A few non-government agencies (NGOs) have also initiated steps to introduce social security measures for the tribals. Apart from their limited reach, full benefits of their programmes would depend on the capability, motivation, and commitment of their personnel, intensity of their efforts and the resources at their disposal. Though these organisations have provided both promotional and protective social security to a large number of tribals, a large proportion still remain uncovered, suggesting that their efforts are inadequate and need to be strengthened. They should also look into the basic sources of deprivation and vulnerability—the low level of agricultural production and productivity, low value for their labour and production, the alienation of their land, fall in their access to forest and exploitation by others. The technique of intervention should be participatory and should aim at developing their own mechanism for tackling the problems.

(The paper draws from the study, Poverty and Livelihood in a Tribal Region, done by the present authors under the auspices of the Institute for Human development. Details can be seen in Dayal and Karan, 2000. The authors are thankful to Alakh N. Sharma, V. Gayatri and Piyush Antony for their detailed comments and suggestions on an earlier draft of the paper.)

Notes

1. The state of Jharkhand was recently created by bifurcating the state of Bihar. The southern plateau part of Bihar consisting of 18 districts was named as Jharkahand.
2. The data were collected from twelve villages covering three districts of the state of Jharkhand, for the larger study entitled *Poverty and Livelihood in a Tribal Region*, under the auspices of the Institute for Human Development, New Delhi. The districts were Gumla, Palamau, and Dumka. For details of the survey design and methodology, see Dayal and Karan, 2000.
3. Jharkhand lies in the fifth schedule area of the country, which comprises of the tribal states of south, central and western regions of India. The social security cover available to the tribals living in this area is considerably less than that enjoyed by those living in the sixth schedule areas.
4. These blocks are grouped into 14 integrated tribal developments projects (ITDP), also called meso projects.
5. The non-homogeneity of tribal community has been widely discussed in literature. See for example, Beteille (1974), Vidyarthi (1974), Burman (1984), Singh (1985), Badagaiyan (1986), Doshi (1990), Sachchidanand (1990), etc. For a detailed review of literature on the issue, see also Sharma (1997).
6. System of shared labour among small tribal farmers of the region, particularly for sowing and harvesting purposes is known as *madaiti*. Since agriculture of this region is mainly mono-cropped, the demand for wage labour in agriculture is very low, in order to meet some intensive labour works, such as sowing and harvesting, the tribal farmers cooperate with one another by extending their labour without any wage.
7. We found *Kamiauti* in its exploitative form at Karma (Palamau) and Baradih (Gumla but adjacent to Palamau). The workers as *kamia* of the landlord are paid lower than the prevalent wage, though they have to work very hard, are assaulted very frequently by their masters and enjoy little freedom.
8. Nutan Para tola of Rampur village, Kundhit block and Dumka District is inhabited by displaced people of Maithon Project. They told us that earlier the officers of the project wanted to give them only monetary compensation. But when they refused to move from their village without alternative land then they were shown a few alternative sites. They selected the present one and so they were settled here.
9. 'Van Prabandhan Evam Sanrakshan Samitee' (forest management and conservation committee) was functioning successfully at Udaipura village of Latehar block (Palamau district). It includes five neighbouring villages as its members. Every village has its own village committee, which functions under the supervision of the central committee having two members from every village. They make the villagers aware of the benefits of forest and works for its protection and also distributes the forest products equitably among the villagers. The villagers appeared to be happy with this committee, as it has ensured them uninterrupted access to forest products.
10 The months of Asadh, Sawan, Bhado and Aswin correspond to the rainy season ranging over the months of the latter half of June to the end of October; Kartik, Agahan, Push, and Magh are the months of winter corresponding to the months from beginning of November to the end of February; Falgun, Chaitra, Baisakh, and Jyestha are the months of summer corresponding to the months from March to June.
11. *Sakcharta Samities* of Rampur and Maheshpur villages (both in Kundhit block of Dumka district) are commendable examples of NGOs engaged in the task of educating the villagers about aspects of health and hygiene.
12. The villagers of Rampur told us that they prefer to take their patients to Siwari in West Bengal, which is located at a distance of 45 k.m. from their village because of the availability of better facilities there, besides being free of cost. Though there is a referral hospital in the neighbourhood but, strangely enough it has no doctors.

References

Badagaiyan, S.D. (1986), "Class and Ethnicity: Chhotanagpur in the 19th Century", in K.L. Sharma (ed.) *Social Stratification in India*, Manohar Publications, Delhi.

Beteille, Andre (1974), *Six Essays in Comparative Sociology*, Oxford University Press, Delhi.

Bhatia, Mukhmeet (2000), "Chotanagpur Tenancy Act: Plugging the Loopholes", *Bulletin of Bihar Tribal Welfare Research Institute*, January 2000.

Bhowmick, Pradip Kumar (1993), *Dynamics of Tribal Development*, Inter India Publications, New Delhi.

Burman, B.K. Roy (1982), *Report of Committee on Forest and Tribal in India*, Ministry of Home Affairs, Tribal Development Division, New Delhi.

—— (1999), *Draft Executive Report of the Tribal Studies Committee*, Indian Council of Social science Research, New Delhi

D'Souza, Victor (1990), *Development Planning and Structural Inequality: The Response of Underprivileged*, Sage publication, New Delhi.

Dayal, H. and A.K. Karan (2000), *Poverty and Livelihood in a Tribal Region*, Institute for Human Development, New Delhi (mimeo).

Deogharia, P.C. (1992), *TRYSEM : An Evaluation (A Case Study of Ranchi District)*, Unpublished Ph. D. Thesis, Department of Economics, Ranchi University, Ranchi.

Dev, S. Mahendra (1999), "An Overview of Social Security in India", *The Indian Journal of Labour Economics*, Vol. 42, No. 3.

Devalle, S.B.S. (1992), *Discourses on Ethnicity: Culture and Protest in Jharkhand*, Sage Publications, New Delhi.

Doshi, S.L. (1990), "Ethnicity and Class among Bhils of Rajasthan", in K.L. Sharma (ed.)

Fernandes, W. (1992), *National Development and Tribal Deprivation*, Indian Social Institute, New Delhi.

Guhan, S. (1995), "Social Security Options for Developing Countries", in Figueiredo, Jose B. and Zafar Shaheed (eds.), *New Approaches to Poverty Analysis and Policy - II*, International Institute for Labour Studies, Geneva.

Iyer, K. Gopal and R.N. Maharaj (1982), in Nirmal Sengupta (ed.), *Fourth World Dynamics: Jharkhand*, Authors' Guild, Delhi.

LBSNAA (1991), *Report on Tribal and Forest Question in Bihar*, Land Reforms Unit, Lal Bahadur Shastri National Academy of Administration, Mussoorie.

Mundle, Sudipto (1979), *Backwardness and Bondage: Agrarian Relation in a South Bihar District*, Indian Institute of Public Administration, New Delhi.

Sachchidanand (1990), "Patterns of Politico-Economic Change among Tribals in Middle India", in Frankel Francine R. and M.S.A. Rao (eds.), *Dominance and State Power in Modern India: Decline of a Social Order*, Oxford University Press, Delhi.

Sarvekshana (1994), *Report on Living Condition of Some Major Tribes in India*, NSSO, 44th round, National Sample Survey Organisation, Government of India, New Delhi.

Sharma, K.L. (1997), "Social Stratification Among Tribes in India", in K.L. Sharma (ed.), *Social Stratification and Mobility*, Rawat Publications, New Delhi.

Sharan, R. et al. (1999), "Land Alienation of Tribals in the Jharkhand Region of Bihar: Process and Pattern", *Social Change*, Vol. 29. Nos. 3 and 4.

Singh, A.K. (1995), "Endangered Tribes of India: Boobytrap of Development", Paper presented in *seminar on Agriculture Growth, Employment, and Rural Poverty in India: Emerging Issues in the Context of Structural Adjustment Programme;* Organised by the Indian Society of Labour Economics, Patna, Dec. 8-10.

Singh, K.S. (1985), *Tribal Society in India: An Anthropo-Historical Perspective*, Manohar Publications, Delhi.

Sinha, A.K. (1993), *A Critical Evaluation of the Work of Various Development Scheme in Ranchi, with Special Reference to Ormanjhi Block.*, Unpublished Ph.D. Thesis, Department of Economics, Ranchi University, Ranchi.

Sinha, B.K. (2000), "Educational Prospects for Jharkhand: A Need for Cautious Optimism", Paper presented in a *Seminar on Sustainable Development in Jharkhand*, Organised by CSDJ Ranchi, October 12-13.

Sinha, S.P. (1968), *The Problem of Tribal Land Alienation of the Tribals in and Around Ranchi*, Bihar Tribal Welfare Research Institute, Ranchi.

Urmilesh (1999), *Jharkhand : Jaduee Jameen Ka Andhera* (in Hindi), Prakashan Sansthan, New Delhi.

Vidyarthi, L.P. (1974), "Tribal Ethnography in India", *A Survey of Research in Sociology and Social Anthropology*, Vol. III, ICSSR, Popular Prakashan, Bombay.

Weiner, Myron (1978), *Sons of the Soil: Migration and Ethinic Conflict in India*, Princeton University Press, Princeton.

PART VI

Micro and State-Level Experiences

19

State-assisted Social Security for Poverty Alleviation and Human Development: Kerala's Record and Its Lessons

K.P. Kannan and Shaji K. Francis

I. INTRODUCTION

In recent times social security has come to mean a wide variety of schemes and programmes usually taken up by the state for the benefit of the public at large or the poorer sections in particular, whose basic entitlements would not otherwise be satisfied due to such reasons as unemployment, illness, old age, or death or a combination of these. In this sense, social security serves the function of protection from adversity. In such situations which are characteristic of a large number of developing countries, there is another dimension of social security arising out of structural embedments and manifested in terms of persistent poverty of significant sections of the population due to inadequacy of entitlements (such as food) and basic capabilities (such as education and health). In this sense, social security arrangements need to take care of the problem of deficiency in human capabilities. Such dimensions of social security require to be addressed by institutional arrangements, referred to as promotional social security in the sense of promoting human capabilities that could lead to a higher standard of living. In the contemporary context, therefore, a distinction is often made between the protective and promotional aspects of social security. These two are also equated with what is called 'support-led social security' and 'growth-mediated social security', respectively (Dreze and Sen, 1989, p. 183). The relative merits and demerits of either approach is a controversial one as there is no conclusive evidence to show that the former always results in a trade-off between growth and equity and the latter always involves equitable growth. There is, in our view, an intersection where supported and growth-mediated social security meet that could take care of both the adversity and deficiency aspects.

A generic definition of social security as given by de Swan (1988), is: "Social security arrangements are collective remedies against adversity and deficiency" (p. 153). At a conceptual level, this may be seen as consisting of 'protective' and 'promotional' types of social security from the point of intention that spheres of protection and promotion can be more meaningfully delineated and the importance of targeting more clearly highlighted. That this division is not so clear will be evident from many examples where both the elements of protection and promotion are simultaneously present. Take the case of supplementary nutrition provided to children from poor families, while it certainly protects those children from the adverse effects of family poverty, it also helps them grow into healthy adults thus establishing a higher level of basic human capability for work and other pursuits than otherwise. Keeping such overlapping in view we have attempted a conceptual framework to develop a typology of social security arrangements in Kerala, by now so well-known for its widespread and state-assisted social security arrangements. The elements crucial in developing a typology in the Indian context are discussed below:

II. KEY ELEMENTS OF SOCIAL SECURITY SYSTEM IN INDIA

1. Source

This relates to the arena of public action that normally divides into state and non-state action. The latter could be quite important but depicting it in a negative way (non-state, non-government) is not saying much. These could be arising out of public interest concerns of citizens' organisations (political parties, charitable organisations, etc.) or by organisations and institutions based on affiliations of community or religion or class (e.g. trade unions). We recognise that, at a conceptual level, we need to come to terms with the nature of public action arising out of non-state intervention that can be characterised as social security. This should, in our view, lead to a better appreciation of the need for collective care in a society where a majority of the population are vulnerable to situations of adversity and deficiency. In this paper, however, we confine ourselves to only state-assisted social security arrangements. But some of these arrangements in Kerala are clearly related to the initiatives and participation of non-state organisations, as we shall see later.

2. Coverage

This could be either universal (as for example, in the case of primary health care for all citizens in many countries) or targeted. In the latter case, a common practice is to identify sections of population based on their innate vulnerabilities such as childhood, old age, and gender. There is also the widely prevalent approach based on the organisation of production. Thus, in what is called the formal or organised sector, those who are hired for work by an employer become entitled to certain social security entitlements that often enjoy legal guarantee. On the other hand, for those who work in the so called informal or unorganised sector, work seldom carries any social security entitlements. And when it does, it hardly ever enjoys legal support. In the case of the developing countries, to make matters worse it is this latter segment that employs an overwhelming section of the workers.

3. Intention

First of all, this refers to the motivational aspect, in order to identify whether or not an action or a programme is intended to provide social security. Further, it helps in the separation between those that are intended as promotional and those that are intended as protective. In the Indian context, it would appear that a large number of social security arrangements, especially for the poor, are intended as promotional. In fact, the existence of protective social security arrangements are so few that the aspect of immediate adversity and deficiency seems to have been grossly neglected. This is especially so when some of the basic vulnerabilities, such as hunger and illness, constrain the ability to participate effectively in the promotional programmes.

4. Impact

There could be situations where a certain public action is not intended as social security but it impacts on its beneficiaries in a way that a social security action would do.

Based on the above factors, we have worked out in Table 1, a typology of social security arrangements that are basically state assisted. The type of programmes included in this typology are those that are in vogue in Kerala at present. By consciously broadening the definition of social security to protective as well as promotional programmes, our typology encompasses a large number of programmes that are not classified as "social security" in government documents. But most of them come under the broad budgetary classification of "social services expenditure."

There are two popular myths that one has to counter when making out a case for state-assisted social security in a developing agrarian society. One is that in such societies there are traditional mechanisms (in the form of family, kinship and community) that address the need for social security. At any rate the entry of the state in the realm of social security is thought to be a modern phenomenon. This perhaps underlines why a number of states in their modern incarnation in many developing countries do not still address the issue of social security, especially the protective forms, adequately. The second myth is that societies which are still poor (in per capita income terms) and dominantly agrarian in character can ill-afford to address the issue of social security from the point of state assistance because there is still not enough accumulation. This is closely linked to the first one except that the social security system that goes along with formal sector employment is taken for granted. A more recent version of this argument has come from those who advocate economic liberalisation through such programmes as structural adjustment. In an attempt to reduce the fiscal deficit of the state, resources allocated to social services in general and social security in particular get a declining share of the total budgetary resources. This is closely linked to the argument that programmes that are growth-promoting should get precedence over those that merely seek to support people.

These two popular myths, it would appear, enjoy very little historical support. Social security systems were part of public administration even in early agrarian societies. This is true not only with respect to Europe (see, e.g., de Swan, 1988) which witnessed a steady development of the bourgeois class as well as the establishment of the nation-state, but also in such Asiatic systems as India. Social security systems were part of the responsibilities of the state even when traditional systems were existent. And secondly, the state did not

Table 1
A Typology of Social Security System in Kerala

Category	Promotional	Protective/Preventive
	A. Universal	
1. All population	1. Free school education up to the secondary level (10 years)	1. Primary health care 2. Public distribution system
	B. Target-oriented	
2. Youth (means-tested)		1. Unemployment assistance
3. For the poor (means-tested)	1. Distribution of land 2. Housing schemes 3. Special assistance	1. Targeted public distribution system 2. Secondary and tertiary health care
4. Most vulnerable among the poor	1. Welfare schemes for the disabled	1. Care homes for orphaned children (limited coverage) 2. Pension for the old aged destitutes 3. Pension for the disabled
5. Formal sector workers/employees	1. Financial assistance for housing 2. Various loan facilities	1. Retirement benefits (e.g., pension, gratuity) 2. Provident fund 3. Medical benefits 4. Social insurance
6. Informal sector workers/labourers (including the 'sel- employed' such as small farmers & artisans)	1. Special assistance through welfare funds (children's education) 2. Special programmes for selected groups (fish workers) 3. Asset and income generating programmes like Integrated Rural Development Programme (sponsored by the central government) 4. Employment creation programmes (sponsored by the central government)	1. Labour cooperatives to protect employment (limited coverage) 2. Social insurance through welfare fund 3. Old-age pension through state budget or welfare funds 4. Special relief programmes
7. For poor women only	1. Supplementary nutrition and health care schemes 2. Welfare programmes (assitance for marriage, skill development)	1. Care homes for the most vulnerable 2. Special assistance (legal assistance through Women's Commission)

wait for a sufficiently high level of accumulation, that which is historically associated with the industrial revolution to initiate social security programmes. Early state systems scarcely made such fine distinctions as between the formal and informal sectors, although it could be argued that those employed in the administrative apparatus of the state might have enjoyed a higher level of social protection. This argument is crucial to our paper because we deal with the experience of Kerala where the state-system has been consistently attempting to provide a modicum of social security for workers irrespective of their employment status in the formal or informal sector. In other words, the social security system that the workers in the formal sector enjoy in India by virtue of its legal backing is sought to be extended to workers in the informal sector by creating innovative institutional arrangements and backing it, wherever feasible, with legal support. This is in addition to the creation and expansion of a social security system for the citizens, especially the poorer sections, beyond their work-status. This has largely been in the form of what we have argued earlier (Kannan, 1995), and sought to be reinforced from the perspective of social security, 'poor relief' programmes for a large number of citizens facing adversity and deficiency due to certain vulnerabilities (such as age) or deprivation (such as destitution). Therefore a very brief recounting of some selected historical experiences in social security may be in order. This we do with respect to Europe as well as India.

III. SOCIAL SECURITY IN AGRARIAN SOCIETIES: SOME HISTORICAL SUPPORT

Abram de Swan's *magnum opus* (de Swan, 1988) captures the spirit of the times in tracing the evolution of social security programmes in European societies. To begin with, it was the Church, beginning with the ninth century, which sought donations from the settled farmers and general public to feed and maintain the vagrants, beggars and the sick, i.e. those who could not work and earn a livelihood. Compulsory levies for the upkeep of the poor was not common in those times. When the modern period began, rights to private property and use were well established in Europe and those who did not own land, worked on other people's property to eke out a living. By the 16th century, long before the beginning of the industrial revolution, large cities in Europe had well established 'poor houses' where thousands of poor were looked after so that the local communities could live peacefully. It was the Elizabethan poor laws which, for the first time in 1601, stipulated the standards for looking after the poor; and the Church levied sufficient 'poor rates' on the land owners in order to finance the whole set up. Around that period the responsibility of looking after the poor was shifted from the Church to the locally elected 'overseers of poor'. As time went by, these societies were gradually getting more and more involved into a system of direct administration of the poor. In those times—as it indeed is in our own times in India among large sections of the rich and the middle class—the general notion was that the poor are so, because they are lazy. Within the framework of this logic in the 17th century 'work houses' were established to provide work and shelter to all able-bodied unemployed, vagrants and other poor. Severe punishments, including death sentences, were imposed for repeated begging and vagrancy.

The industrial revolution, unlike many other revolutions, shook the very foundations of the agrarian system in rural areas and the commercial/mercantile system in the urban centres in Europe. However, even during the dawn of the industrial revolution, orphanages, old age asylums, insanity wards and maternity houses were run by local governments and a system of social security supported by the state was gaining more and more importance in Europe. Collective action was the spontaneous answer by the elite sections of European society to the threat posed by crime, cholera, anarchy and squalor resulting from large numbers of unemployed, vagrants and the sick. The shift from individual action to collective action (as represented by the state) occurred not out of any philanthropic motive, but due to the threat that these posed to the established social order as thousands migrated into the cities each day in search of work and a better living during the period of the industrial revolution. By the last decade of the 19th century, the social security system, as we know it now, was well embedded in the social fabric and governments were having well established systems for the care of the destitute and the poor.

In India, social security seems to have been a concern of the state from a very long time in the past. Kautilya, the political advisor of and a minister to the ruler Chandragupta Maurya in the fourth century BC, in his treatise on Economics, *Arthasastra,* that dealt with public administration and public finance, recorded many dictums on the state's duties to the subjects and vice versa. Kautilya refers to various types of pensions, provisions made for those who died in harness, and public poor relief. Public poor relief, in this view, was one of the major duties of kings. The king was entrusted with the responsibility of maintaining the orphans and the indigent. The king had to remain alert against natural calamities and pestilence. In times of famine or epidemics it was he who had to rescue the public. It is also recorded that kings used to keep as reserve half the produce from royal farms or the taxes paid in kind for relieving the unforeseeable distress of his subjects. Though Kautilya made provisions for pensions and maintenance allowances, giving doles was strongly discouraged. For instance, it was the duty of the state to maintain the widows, the virgins, the convicts, the old prostitutes, and the Devadasis. But he pleaded that in return for the state's benevolence they must work in the state-run spinning factories (Bhattacharya, 1970, p. 16).

There are records to suggest that during the eighth century also social security provisions were common in India. The great Sanskrit scholar Sukracharya had described in his treatise on justice, *Sukraniti*, the various measures taken by the rulers in this regard. There were special provisions for sickness benefits, pensions, old age benefits, and maintenance allowances. It was stipulated that in cases of servants falling ill, those who had put in more than five years of service were entitled to three-fourths of their usual wages though such benefits cannot continue for more than six months. There was also a provision for premature death of a servant wherein the master would have to pay allowance at the rate of half the salary to his family (Bhattacharya, 1970, p. 17).

Waves of invasions seem to have led to, among many other things, a decline in social security provided by the state. Although no systematic account of social security during the rule of the Moghuls is available, giving alms was a part of charitable and religious duties. Perhaps there was a decline in state-assisted social security programmes during this period. Social security, as a result, increasingly became the concern of religious institutions, trusts and popular saints. The decline of state-assisted social security might perhaps explain the role of traditional institutions of family, caste and village communities in catering to social security requirements of the members.

The colonial state had not bothered much about social security for the people at large except in the form of temporary relief measures when acute calamities like famines or floods brought in large scale deaths and destruction of crops. The emergence of factories led to the emergence of trade unions and collective pressures were exerted for certain types of social security for workers in case of accidents. Gradually, the organised sector came to enjoy a number of social security measures as a result of a combination of factors such as pressures from trade unions, resolutions of the International Labour Organisation (which was established in 1920) and upon examples from Britain. However, the overwhelming majority of workers and people dependent on the unorganised sector for their livelihood were outside the reach of any state-assisted social security system.

This legacy, without major modifications, seems to have been carried over even after independence. It was only during the sixties that the problem of poverty received the state's attention in a direct form. Increasing food shortage and droughts and other natural calamities during the sixties and early seventies led to the design of poverty alleviation programmes in the form of emergency employment, distribution of foodgrains at subsidised prices, etc. These were the initial target-oriented social security programmes for those in the informal sector. Provision of basic education and primary health care, although highlighted as a laudable objective, were quite limited in their outreach and its spread has so far been so abysmally slow that these two still remain as basic challenges to India's attempt in eliminating poverty and enhancing basic human capabilities. The protective aspect of social security seems to have received much less attention in independent India when compared to the promotional aspect. It is only in the last few years that some attention has been given to this at the national level, by recognising the need to protect the poor and the aged as well as strengthen the food security cover to the poor.

It is in such a national scenario, where social security has not been all that high on the policy agenda, that we examine the record of Kerala, which has treaded a different path, and attempt to draw lessons for the rest of India. The only other state that comes close to the record of Kerala is perhaps its neighbouring state of Tamil Nadu.

IV. SOCIAL SECURITY SYSTEM IN KERALA

We shall follow the basic framework for categorising the various social security schemes given in Panel I. Given the broad definition to social security, inclusive of both protective and promotional programmes, one finds that there exists a very large number of schemes, programmes and projects for social security in Kerala. We have done a head count of these various schemes and programmes and find that there are 141 of them as on 1993, including the major ones upon which we would like to focus in this study.[1] This is not, in our opinion, a positive development as it hardly reflects a genuine concern for the specificities of problems and/or beneficiaries. Rather they have arisen in the context of the functioning of the state system in India with various departments initiating a large number of programmes at different points of time, both in the context of development planning and outside. We shall later argue that such a plethora of programmes is best taken care of by its reduction within a system of more meaningful reorganisation.

The major social security programmes in Kerala are the following and may be classified as per our typology.

We provide below the details of these major programmes.

Panel I
Social Security in Kerala

Protective	Promotional
1. Primary health care through government health care centres (for all)	1. Free school education upto 10 years (for all)
2. Public distribution system (for all except self-sufficient farmers producing foodgrains)	2. Distribution of house sites (for the landless) and housing schemes (for the poor)
3. Free noon meal for school children	3. Income and employment oriented programmes (for the poor)
4. Supplementary nutrition schemes (for the poor by self-selection)	4. Special programmes for creation of entitlements and basic capacities for depressed castes (SC/ST)
5. Old age pension (for destitute, widows, physically disabled and informal sector workers)	5. Affirmative action for depressed castes (SC/ST) in govt. jobs and higher educational institutions
6. Social insurance and other benefits through the institution of welfare funds (for workers in the informal sector)	6. Affirmative action for intermediate castes (in government jobs and public higher educational institutions)

1. Protective Social Security

(i) Primary and Preventive Health Care System

Both the aspects of protection and promotion are involved in the health-care system. The curative institutions at the village level are the primary health-care centres established by the government. This clearly caters to the protective needs of the people. The directly promotive aspect is taken care of in the preventive health care programmes such as provision of safe drinking water, immunisation, eradication campaigns for malaria, TB, etc. From the point of social security, two important features of the health-care system needs emphasis. One is the early recognition of the state's responsibility to provide health care services to the people and the other is the spatial spread of, at least, the primary health care services both in rural and urban areas.

It is now well known in the literature that Kerala had the benefit of an enlightened and liberal policy towards medical and public health systems even before independence. The rulers of the State of Travancore (which now forms the southern half of Kerala) had initiated policies relating to public health as early as the 1860s which, in the years to come, paved the way for an active state policy with regard to health care (UN/CDS, 1975, p. 116).

The government's health sector expenditure formed 9 per cent of the total budget expenditure in 1980-81 and six per cent in 1995-96 as against 7 and 5 per cent for all states in India. The share of expenditure for the health sector cannot be considered high any more as a fairly higher share is being realised in many other states of India. In fact, the per capita expenditure on health in Kerala is found to be below that of some other states such as Rajasthan and Gujarat.

A rough indicator of availability is the number of beds. If we add to the beds available in both the government and non-government sectors, the number of beds per 100,000 population works out to 380 in 1997. This was 263 in 1991 compared to 76 for the country as a whole. Kerala, therefore, established a considerable lead, for quite some time, in the matter of availability of health care services.

The impact of such a health care system cannot be viewed from the supply side only. It is now well known that a combination of factors, which prominently includes the literacy and education of women and their consequent awareness about health care, had contributed considerably to making use of the available facilities. This should also be viewed in the context of the high level of achievement in matters relating to preventive health care programmes such as immunisation.

The impact of all these is too well known to need any repetition here. But the impact in terms of the demographic transition characterised by low levels of infant and child mortality, maternal mortality, general mortality and consequent increase in life expectancy that was ten years higher than the national average in 1991 (70 years as against 60 years for all India) needs to be noted. Despite these achievements, the government health care system has run into several second generation problems which we shall deal with separately.

(ii) Food Security

Perhaps the most important protective social security measure in Kerala is the food security system. This has four important components: (a) the PDS for all households; (b) free noon meal scheme for school children; (c) the supplementary nutrition programme for children in the age groups of 0-4, and 5-12; and (d) old-age pension for the poorer sections.

(a) Public distribution system

Although the PDS in Kerala does not have the advantage of such a long period of positive public policy, as in the case of health care, its origins also go back to the pre-independence days when food rationing was introduced in India at the start of the second World War. It took almost a quarter of a century to establish a public distribution system in India as part of the public policy on food security (see, e.g., Mooij, 1999, pp. 65-73). In Kerala the system was expanded during 1964 at a time when the state was undergoing an acute food shortage. This shortage is structural to the Kerala economy in that a major share of value added in the agricultural sector is effected through the production of cash crops such as coconut, rubber, tea, coffee, spices, etc., earning or saving considerable foreign exchange for the national economy. Even at the best of times, Kerala could not produce more than 40 per cent of its foodgrain requirements. This has been recognised by the central government which agreed to supply the foodgrains (mainly rice and wheat) to meet the requirements of the PDS. Therefore, the introduction of PDS in Kerala is part of the overall concern of the state to take care of its food security. As such, almost all the households (except a small percentage of households—around 2-3 per cent—with self-sufficiency in foodgrains through own production) have been brought under the PDS. This resulted in the establishment of a large network of ration shops throughout the state. The relevant details are given in Table 2.

Table 2
Public Distribution System in Kerala

Year	Household ration cards (lakhs)	Ration permits to institutions (nos.)	Distribution of			
			Rice ('000 M.Ts)	Wheat ('000 M.Ts)	Sugar* ('000 M.Ts)	Kerosene* ('000 KL)
1975	36.16	7634	531	490	97	107
1985	43.73	7922	1412	110	142	235
1995	56.54	13173	1130	423	150	360
1996	57.75	13553	1401	492	148	380
1997	59.52	–	1608	353	154	372

Note: * allotment only.

By establishing a PDS covering almost the entire population, Kerala has become the only state in India with complete coverage offering a modicum of food security to the entire population for the last three-and-a-half decades. In addition to rice and wheat, the PDS also distributes sugar, kerosene and cooking oil. It also used to distribute coarse clothes, the demand for which has now dwindled. This is perhaps a sign of the declining nature of the chronic forms of poverty in Kerala.

By all accounts, the poor are the strongest beneficiaries of the PDS in Kerala. Two-thirds of their requirement of foodgrains are covered by the PDS and this proportion has remained remarkably stable over the years, from the early seventies to the nineties (UN/CDS, 1975, pp. 48; Dev, 1994). Almost the entire requirements of sugar, kerosene and cooking oil of the poor are met by the PDS. Since the introduction of the Targeted PDS by the central government, Kerala has been following a dual pricing system. Although the central government has accepted the share of the poor in Kerala's population as 25 per cent (as per the poverty line calculations followed by the Planning Commission), the Kerala Government has extended the benefits of TPDS to 42 per cent of the population since there are those who are just marginally above the officially determined poverty line. This is expressed, in the context of Kerala by a strong political pressure from all parties in favour of the poor.

In addition to the PDS, the state government has a network of fair price shops run through a corporate entity called the Kerala State Civil Supplies Corporation. The prices in these shops are marginally lower than the open market prices. In addition, by their strong market intervention in selling essential items during festival seasons such as Onam, Christmas and Ramzan, the state is able to provide a measure of stability to the prices of essential commodities. Here again the system is not without its problems. The problem of leakages have been already noted (Mooij, 1999, pp. 149-55). An additional problem is the quality of the distributed items. People generally complain about the quality of the foodgrain distributed; the state government in turn blames the central government for supplying low quality foodgrains. The ration shop dealers complain about their very small profit margins and are always seeking ways to increase profits. Despite all these drawbacks, the PDS has come to stay in Kerala as an integral part of public policy on social security.

(b) Free noon-meal scheme for school children

While the PDS in Kerala is the most important component of the food security system for the people in general and poorer sections in particular, provision of cooked food to the vulnerable among the poor (by self-selection) has come to assume a crucial role in the larger scheme of social security (Table 3). Coverage ratio is well above 50 per cent, almost double the incidence of head-count poverty estimates for Kerala in 1993-94. While the latter provides a clear cut-off mark for poverty, the coverage ratio could be interpreted as a sign of a substantial number of families being at the margin of the poverty line, even if marginally above it, and considering the free noon-meal for their children a source of relief.

Table 3
Free Noon-Meal for School Children

(in lakhs)

Year	No. of students in primary level	No. of students in upper primary level	Total eligible students	Students enroled in the scheme	Col. (5)as % of col. (4)
1978-79	25.70	–		18.27	71
1988-89	26.37	18.06	44.43	32.00	72
1989-90	25.96	18.48	44.44	20.56	46
1990-91	25.27	19.00	44.27	20.57	46
1991-92	24.72	19.30	44.02	24.10	55
1992-93	24.21	19.33	43.54	23.42	54
1993-94	23.72	19.08	42.80	24.00	56
1994-95	23.25	18.67	41.92	21.21	51
1995-96	22.51	18.39	40.90	20.86	51
1996-97	21.98	18.13	40.11	23.75	59

Source: Government of Kerala, *Economic Review*, Annual Series.

(c) Supplementary nutrition for pre-school children and nursing mothers

A third and equally important component in the food security system is the various schemes for providing supplementary, but free, nutrition to pre-school children and expectant or nursing mothers. This scheme is of relatively recent origin (compared to the above two) and is modest in terms of its coverage. The CDS study, while noting the existence of such a programme, stated that "in terms of the quantity involved, this programme is not significant" (UN/CDS, 1975, p. 41). However, by the late seventies, the programme widened its reach to cover more than a million pre-school children. This programme in fact was a combination of a number of earlier schemes such as Special Nutrition Programme, Applied Nutrition Programme, Composite

Programme for Women and Children, the World Food Programme supported feeding scheme, One-Meal-a-Day Scheme, Health and Nutrition Programme and the by now well known national programme called Integrated Child Development Scheme (ICDS). Through a series of reorganisations, the ICDS has now emerged as the most important scheme followed by ANP/CPWP and the SNP.

The ICDS was started in the mid-seventies and was intended to provide 300 calories and 8.15 grams of protein per child. For women, the provision is 500 calories and 15 grams of protein per day per person. These rates are roughly equivalent to one-fourth of the requirements of the beneficiary groups. The schemes stipulates that this has to be provided for 300 days in a year. In Kerala approximately 84 per cent of the beneficiaries are children and the rest expectant/nursing mothers. Table 4 shows that close to a million beneficiaries are now covered by the scheme. About 80 per cent of the financial requirements of the scheme is covered by assistance from the central government. The Applied Nutrition and Composite Programme for Women and Children though slightly different in orientation, are also sponsored by the central government. The Special Nutrition Programme, started by the state through commodity aid from various agencies, has been progressively integrated into the ICDS. Its aims are the same as that of ICDS. Currently, SNP is in existence in areas which are not covered by the ICDS.

Table 4
Number of Beneficiaries in Nutritional Programme for Children and Women

('000s)

Year	ICDS	SNP	ANP/ CPWP	WFP	OMD	HNP	Total
1977-78	57	200		200	–	–	457
1981-82	199	518	574	230	370	136	2027
1991-92	855	47	200	–	–	99*	1201
1995-96	960	–	123	–	–	–	1083

Note: * Refers to beneficiaries under the Feeding Centre Programme; ** Closed in April 1985 as part of the effort to streamline the nutrition programmes.
Source: Government of Kerala, *Economic Review*, Various Issues.

The supplementary nutrition programmes are implemented with the help of a large number of women's welfare organisations called *Mahila Samajams* and other organisations in the state. *Anganawadis* and *Balawadis* have been set up with the help of these organisations. Young, educated women in rural areas, who face the highest incidence of unemployment in Kerala, are recruited as volunteers and receive only a monthly honorarium. The current rate of honorarium is around Rs. 600, which is equivalent to nine days of the wages of female agricultural labourers. For all these programmes there are about 18,500 centres including 11,268 centres under the ICDS.

(d) Old-age pensions to destitutes and rural labourers

Unlike the primary health care system and the Public Distribution System, this one is targeted only towards the poor, based on their social or physical vulnerability or their status as labourers in the unorganised sector. The system of giving old-age pension has to come to occupy an important place in the social security provisioning in Kerala because its coverage, progressively being extended to most rural labourers, was around 60 per cent of the aged-poor in Kerala in 1991 under the two major pension programmes viz, destitutes and agricultural labourers (Table 5). The four most prominent schemes of old-age pension for the poor are: (1) Pension to the Destitutes and Widows; (2) Pension for the Handicapped; (3) Pension for old-aged agricultural labourers; and (4) Pension for the old-aged fishworkers. All these have been in existence for more than ten years now, with the first one being in effect for 40 years. The number of pension schemes now in vogue in Kerala is around 17.

Table 5
Beneficiaries and Amount of Benefit under Major Pension Schemes

	1979-80	1989-90	1992-93	1993-94	1995-96	1996-97
Old-age disputes						
No.	134500	124355	187310	187310	132450	142500
Rs. lakhs	546.37	1178.63	1401.32	1630.00	1727.33	NA
Rs. per capita per month	34.00	78.98	62.34	72.52	108.68	NA
Physically handicapped, etc.						
No.		72835	90306	90906	91700	94800
Rs. lakhs		698.59	895.23	915.00	1085.05	NA
Rs. per capita per month		79.93	82.61	83.88	98.60	NA
Agriculture workers						
No.		299758	340776	345650	312944	312944
Rs. lakhs		2144.16	1451.46	2000.00	3457.28	3457.28
Rs. per capita per month		59.61	35.49	48.22	92.06	92.06
Fish workers						
No.			25780	25780	30756	26967
Rs. lakhs			220.21	220.21	279.32	279.32
Rs. per capita per month			71.18	71.18	75.68	86.32

Source: Government of Kerala, *Economic Review*, Various Issues.

The pension schemes can be divided into two broad categories: those that are directly borne by the state out of its budgetary resources and those that are introduced through the creation of social insurance mechanisms such as the setting up of welfare funds. The four prominent ones mentioned above are directly funded by the state. The schemes introduced through the welfare funds are yet to find a firm footing. There are serious problems of collection of contributions from the employers and employees. Although these schemes, such as the ones for old-aged coir, cashew and handloom workers, have been in existence for the last ten years or so, there is no evidence to show that pensions are disbursed on any regular basis. The pension schemes in Kerala are notable for their coverage of those sections which do not have much political clout. Thus a number of smaller groups have also come to enjoy the old-aged pensions. These are sportsmen, journalists and cine artists in indigent conditions, leprosy and cancer patients and freedom fighters. The last one, of course, is not means-tested and hence the disbursement under this head is not based on their economic condition but is instead a social recognition of their services during the freedom movement. More than ten thousand persons received 'freedom fighters' pension' in 1996-97.

Taking the coverage of these pensions in 1991 as an illustration we find that it is indeed an impressive achievement. If the pension schemes under the welfare funds are included, the coverage would rise considerably. However, it is only during the last three to four years, that these pensions are being paid on a regular basis.

(iii) Social Insurance and Welfare for Informal Sector Workers

This is perhaps an innovative form of social security for workers in the informal/unorganised sector. While employment in the formal/organised sector carries with it certain social security benefits, no such legally enforced social security system exists in the informal sector. In the context of Kerala, workers in the informal/unorganised sector are as strongly organised (if not more) as workers in the formal/organised sector in the form of trade unions or associations of self-employed (see, e.g., Kannan, 1992). Over time they have come to acquire a certain level of political clout and their demands can hardly be sidelined by the political system in Kerala. Some of them, such as workers in coir processing, agricultural labourers, toddy tappers, have been in the forefront of earlier political struggles of radical political parties such as the Communist Parties in the thirties, forties and fifties.

In order to meet their demands for some kind of social insurance and other non-wage benefits, a new institutional innovation was introduced in the form of welfare funds. The government took the initiative, with active support from trade unions, to set up funds through contributions from workers, employers and the government. The task of identifying and fixing the employers' share was usually taken up by the government through a variety of mechanisms. These funds were then given statutory backing with the governing body consisting of the representatives of the government, trade unions and the employers. The secretarial functions were entrusted to the Department of Labour.

These funds usually addressed three or four major social security concerns of the workers. These are: (i) social insurance for accidents, disability and death, (ii) financial assistance for illness and maternity, (iii) financial assistance for children's education, marriage of daughters, and (iv) house construction. A number of welfare funds have also introduced monthly pension payments on retirement or on completion of a certain age subject to some minimum years of service.

A detailed study of these social insurance schemes is not attempted here. Currently there are 19 welfare funds in Kerala with 14 of them having statutory status. The workers covered are :(1) *Toddy* Workers, (2) Head Load Workers, (3) Motor Transport Workers, (4) Cashew Workers, (5) Khadi Workers, (6) Coir Workers, (7) Fish Vendors, (8) Handloom Workers, (9) *Abkari* Workers, (10) Construction Workers, (11) Agricultural Workers, (12) Auto Rickshaw Workers, (13) Tailors, and (14) Other selected workers. Available information does point to the fact that the coverage of these welfare funds is quite impressive although in some non-statutory welfare funds, workers have not been enthusiastic enough to enrol themselves because of what they consider to be too small benefits. Some of the welfare funds are financially quite sound and have been a source of help for the state government in times of financial crisis.

Despite the importance of these innovative forms of social insurance for the workers in the informal sector, there are a number of problems that demand attention of the concerned parties. We shall take them up later on.

2. Promotional Social Security

(i) Free School Education

This universal programme of social security has a fairly long history in Kerala. Open access to formal school education was initially limited to the upper castes in Hindu society till about the second half of the last century, although a small minority of lower caste members had their own arrangements to acquire formal education. Non-Hindu communities enjoyed greater access to public schools although it was also limited. Social reform movements, beginning in the last quarter of the century had made access to schools and right to education a major agenda of their struggles and this prepared the ground for the subsequent evolution of an enlightened public policy aimed at gradually universalising school education (see, e.g. Nair, 1981). Since independence the growth in the spread of schools in Kerala has been truly remarkable and by the time of the formation of the state lower primary schools were in place in almost all villages of Kerala. The growth in the number of schools show that whereas the total number of primary schools has remained the same from the early sixties to the late nineties, the increase in the total number of schools has been around 25 per cent. Given the fact that the enrolment ratio for Class I to X is close to hundred per cent, there is hardly any problem of coverage except in the case of a few tribal settlements in the hilly areas. During 1991-92 the total school enrolment was around 5.9 million which works out to more than 98 per cent of children in the age group of 6 to 15 or more than 90 per cent of children in the age group of 6 to 16 years.

Until the early sixties only primary schooling was free. A nominal fee had to be paid for classes VI to XI. This was abolished in 1960 and since then the first ten years of schooling has been free for both girls and boys. Children of Scheduled Castes have also been able to take advantage of the state-supported schooling system by attaining a share in enrolment that was somewhat above their share in population by the mid-eighties.

What the school system in Kerala now faces is a number of second generation problems. Given the declining birth rate, there has been a fall in the absolute number of children born and hence enrolment in the primary stage. The highest ever recorded enrolment in the school system was in 1991 and 1992 with a total student strength of 5.9 million; this has declined to 5.4 in 1998. As a result a number of primary schools were closed down because of falling student-teacher ratio (a class strength of below 25 is classified as 'uneconomic'). Around 1,730 schools are now classified as uneconomic but have not been closed down due to local level pressures as well as organised pressure exerted by teachers. Teachers who have thus become 'surplus' are now categorised as 'protected teachers' because they are allowed to continue in service . The number of such protected teachers increased from around 1,500 in 1994 to around 2,300 in 1998, of which nearly 58 per cent were in the primary division. There is also the problem of inadequacy of infrastructural facilities.

(ii) Housing

(a) One lakh housing

At the level of the promotional social security system, we have already noted the system of free school education upto the secondary level. Most other programmes are of a poverty alleviation type. Here a major programme that kicked off a series of subsequent schemes for the poor is that of housing. The concern for housing for the poor became a matter of public policy in 1971 when the Land Reform legislation was finally passed in Kerala. The original intention to distribute surplus land to the landless did not materialise for a number of reasons (see, e.g., Raj and Tharakan, 1983). As a second best solution, landless agricultural labourers were given the right to retain and own 10 per cent of the land belonging to the land owner households for whom they worked, and set up their own houses on that 'surplus' land. Those who could not get such land and were homeless were subsequently brought under a massive programme called One Lakh Housing financed by mobilising resources from the state budget, public institutions and voluntary labour. Although the target achieved was only around 56 per cent, it was a remarkable achievement in itself in such a short period of time (see for details UN/CDS, 1975). Subsequently, a number of housing schemes were implemented, some under the central government schemes.

(b) Other housing programmes

Our estimate of the poor housing condition in Kerala, based on the data from a 1987 survey (see Kannan et al., 1991), was 18 per cent of the households. This is in spite of the various housing programmes since the early seventies. We have identified that, as in many other cases, there is a proliferation of schemes and they numbered around 22 since the late eighties. Of these we could identify 11 schemes as those meant for the poor. Under these schemes the number of houses built come to around 341 thousand until 1996-97.

A recent survey (conducted in 1998) on migration in Kerala (Zachariah, et al., 1999, p. 196) estimates 'poor housing' (thatched roof and mud walls) at 10.5 per cent. If this is an indication of the decline in the share of poor housing it is the result of highly publicised public policy followed by an action programme initiated in 1971 and subsequently implemented through a number of schemes. Even then it is important to emphasise the fact that the acceleration in the programme since 1987 has been quite remarkable. The total number of houses built for the poorer sections up to 1986 was 1.88 lakhs compared to 3.41 between 1986 and 1996.

(iii) Income and Employment Generation Programmes

Despite the fact that there are a large number of social security programmes emphasising both protection and promotion, a notable weakness in the whole framework is the inadequacy of a meaningful income and/or employment generation programme designed by the state. The programmes that are now in vogue are the three centrally-sponsored programmes: (i) Integrated Rural Development Programme (IRDP); (ii) Jawahar Rozgar Yojana for rural employment generation; and (iii) Training of Youth for Self Employment. In terms of coverage these programmes have impressive statistics, but they hardly added up to anything of significance. For example, the IRDP has assisted, on an average, 89,600 families annually between 1980 and 1992. One-third of these families belong to the SC and ST category. But the per capita investment of around three thousand rupees (in real terms) per family hardly works out to the cost of even buying a cow, let alone a cross-bred high-yielding one. Leakages in implementation are well known but hardly ever investigated in any systematic manner. Pilot studies indicate that a quarter of the funds can be reckoned as leakage. The story is the same with regard to the employment generation programmes.

(iv) Constitutional Protection to Socially Disadvantaged

In the discourse on social security in India, the working of the constitutionally guaranteed protective measures to the socially most depressed sections of society, the Scheduled Castes and Scheduled Tribes, is not usually recognised as a legitimate realm of enquiry. We think that this is a major drawback of the discourse because the Scheduled Castes and Scheduled Tribes not only constitute the most socially disadvantaged sections but also economically the weakest, with a higher incidence of poverty than any other social group (see, e.g., Chelliah and Sudarshan, 1999, ch. 2). While the constitutional protection is for reservation of a share of jobs in the government sector as well as admissions to educational institutions, both the central government as well as the state governments in India have a number of other protective and promotional programmes aimed at the SC/ST group.

In the context of Kerala the Scheduled Castes form around nine per cent while the Scheduled Tribes form only around 1.5 per cent of the total population. The latter group is concentrated in two districts (Wayanad in the north and Trivandrum in the south), mostly in the hill areas. The achievements of this group is hardly commensurate with the expenditure and organisation through various schemes; there is in fact a strong criticism that these programmes have done more harm than good to the tribal population. Land alienation is a major issue which has eluded a satisfactory solution so far. Some progress has however been made in the area ot school education.

In contrast to this, the group of Scheduled Castes seems to have made some modest progress in a number of areas compared to their earlier socially and economically dependant position at the time of independence. The most striking feature of this change is in the social sphere that has given them a measure of independence from the land owner households to which they were traditionally attached. Various social reform movements and the radical political mobilisation has bestowed in them a measure of social dignity with its attendant consequences in political awareness, participation in labour markets, etc. The most notable progress is in the area of literacy and school education. The literacy rate among Scheduled Castes in Kerala is considerably higher than the literacy rate of males belonging to all castes and religious communities in India. Access to school education is now marginally higher than their share in total population. What is more impressive is the share of girls who receive formal education; this goes to show the positive impact of affording social opportunity to those who were denied of it hitherto. In higher education also, the share of the SC group is close to their share in total population (Table 6). This shows further, that the younger generation has an entirely different set of social opportunities, and consequently a different social profile, than their parents and earlier generations. The impact of such a change is being felt slowly but surely.

Table 6
Share of SC and ST Children in School Enrolment

Year	Total enrolment (Lakhs)	Percentage of SC	Percentage of ST
Lower primary			
1980	25.95	11.87	0.94
1985	25.95	11.55	1.20
1991	24.20	11.59	1.41
1996	21.41	10.54	1.37
Upper primary			
1980	16.94	11.21	0.56
1985	17.77	11.43	0.78
1991	19.33	11.28	0.99
1996	17.90	11.06	1.06
High school			
1980	13.14	9.94	0.42
1985	13.43	10.72	0.48
1991	15.50	10.68	0.73
1996	16.04	10.62	0.84
Technical education (1996)			
Tech. high School	6155	10.15	0.34
Polytechnic	6660	20.16	1.62
Engg. college	2683	20.10	1.60

Source: Government of Kerala, *Economic Review*, 1981,1985,1991,1997.

The policy of affirmative action has also ensured a proportionate share of political power to the SC population especially at the lower levels of the government. Available evidence (Table 7) indicates that the share varies between 8 to 10 per cent (for middle level and higher positions) and between 12 to 15 per cent for lower level positions as against their population share of nine per cent. But it should be underlined here that the policy of affirmative action is confined to jobs in the government sector only. In the labour market as a whole such a commensurate share is unlikely to have been achieved given the relative differences in both inherited and acquired endowments as well as the stratified and segmented nature of the labour market. At the lower end of the labour market, like casual unskilled jobs in the agricultural occupations, there is definitely a change in expectations of the younger generation of Scheduled Castes as they are increasingly opting out of such jobs which were traditionally looked down upon as of 'demeaning' or 'low status' (see, e.g., Francis, 1990; Kannan, 1999). But a large share of employment opportunities for Scheduled Castes is still confined to the primary sector.

Table 7
Share of SC and ST in State Government Employment

Year	Total enrolment	Percentage of	
		SC	ST
Gazetted officer			
1986	20274	8.63*	–
1990	23070	8.48	0.35
1994	23477	10.84	0.50
Non-gazetted officer			
1986	242637	10.22*	–
1990	255273	9.02	0.50
1994	245611	10.01	0.80
Last grade			
1986	45821	13.63*	–
1990	41754	12.39	4.14
1994	39787	14.93	1.30

Note: * for both SC and ST
Source: Government of Kerala, *Economic Review*, 1987, 1991,1995.

A large number of promotional and protective programmes are exclusively designed and implemented for SC/ST groups. While there is a strong case for an indepth evaluation of the effectiveness of these programmes and their impact on the SC/ST groups, we are inclined to hypothesise, based on our general understanding of the working of the various programmes, that the Scheduled Castes have made some significant gains in the areas of literacy and school education, health status, food security, housing conditions, and share in government jobs. These are due to a combination of universal programmes as well as special efforts to incorporate these socially disadvantaged groups into the mainstream. The case of Scheduled Tribes is a debatable one, especially if their experience of large scale land alienation and transformation into casual agricultural labourers with very little achievement in human capabilities is kept in mind.

V. A QUICK ASSESSMENT

It is well known that social security programmes in Kerala are part of the state government's public policy on economic development in general and poverty alleviation, in particular. The emphasis on the latter has led not only to protective measures but also promotional measures thus implicitly recognising the importance of what is now called advancing 'entitlement' and 'capabilities'. Such divisions are more conceptual than practical in that those programmes intended as protective measures often have strong promotional implications also. Programmes such as health care and supplementary nutrition are cases in point.

Two basic programmes viz., primary health care and school education have by now become universal in their coverage in Kerala. In fact, substantial progress in terms of coverage (both spatial and population) was achieved by the middle of the seventies (see, e.g., UN/CDS, 1975). In school education, the coverage for primary schooling had been completed by then. This has placed Kerala on the forefront in terms of universal literacy (especially of the younger generation), school enrolment and average years of schooling. What is striking, from an all- India perspective, is the achievement in terms of gender. Not only is the enrolment rate for girl children as high as that for boys, they even seem to be performing better at the higher levels of schooling especially at the high school level. Drop-out rates for girls is lower than that for boys at the secondary level. This is in sharp contrast to the all-India situation. The fact that the state has been providing free education upto the secondary level to all children, by ensuring adequate spatial coverage, has perhaps been instrumental towards such an achievement.

The second generation problems with regard to school education have more to do with quality than quantity. In fact, the pressure of quantitative expansion has practically ceased at all levels, more so at the primary level. Given the fact that the state bears the entire expenses on school education (both government schools and private schools with the exception of a small percentage of unaided private schools), very little resources are available for improving infrastructure and the curriculum. Such improvements are now sought to be introduced by borrowed funds. The dissatisfaction with quality gets articulated as parents, including those who are poor, expect much better results. The percentage of students who pass the school-leaving examination has not been more than 50 per cent.

In the case of health care, primary level facilities now cover all the villages. While health care, at all levels, are free for the poor, there are a number of problems associated with utilisation. Patients have to incur expenditure on medicines that are not available in the health care centres and have to take recourse to private facilities for tests, etc. Given the phenomenal expansion in the private health care facilities, a large proportion of the people, including the poorer ones, prefer to use such facilities because of the inadequate facilities and services at the state health care centres. A survey conducted in 1987 reported that 48 per cent of the households prefer not to visit the nearest primary health centre even if it is physically accessible (see Kannan et al., 1991, p. 129). A repeat survey of a sub-sample in 1996 revealed that this percentage has remained the same. In Kerala, the problem of restoring the credibility of primary health care facilities has now become a major challenge, thought it has not been sufficiently appreciated at the policy level.

The strength of the health care system in Kerala lies perhaps in its preventive aspects in some selected spheres. Immunisation programmes are successfully organised with almost 100 per cent coverage, especially those involving young children and pregnant mothers. However, environmental sanitation, especially the disposal and processing of wastes is largely a neglected area, especially in urban centres. Eradication of mosquitos also poses a major challenge. The coverage of households with safe drinking water and toilets is relatively high.

An important component of the social security programme in Kerala is that of food security. We would argue that there are three major components to the food security system in Kerala. One is the public distribution system which covers 92 per cent of the population. The needs of the poor are taken into account in this universal system by giving a higher level of subsidy. Apart from food, the system also meets almost the entire requirement of kerosene, which is a basic need for cooking and/or lighting in poorer households. The second is the supplementary nutrition programme targeted towards children: one, pre-school children with some health care elements, and the other, noon meal for school-going children upto 12 years of age. The third is the old age and other disability pension for the poor. This started with destitutes and was subsequently extended to physically handicapped, widows and rural labourers. This could be treated as food security as they are targeted only towards the poor. We have attempted an estimation of the coverage of these food security schemes for 1991 and presented the result in Table 8. It is interesting to note that the major programmes such as PDS, supplementary nutrition and pension for agricultural workers cover more than the estimated poor below the poverty line. In fact, 92 per cent of the population are covered under PDS, 44 per cent of pre-school children are covered under the supplementary nutrition programme, 70 per cent of the children between five and 12 years are covered by the free noon-meal scheme and more than the main agricultural labourers above 60 years are covered by the old-age pension scheme. In the case of agricultural labourers, the much higher coverage is perhaps due to the fact many of them are only marginal agricultural labourers and have to do a variety of jobs in the casual labour market because of declining employment opportunities in agriculture.

A valid question that could be raised here is: why should there be people below the poverty line in Kerala (the head count ratio varied from 25 per cent to 33 per cent in 1991) when more than the estimated poor are covered by one or more of the social security schemes? The answer to this lies in the fact that the benefits are still too meagre to pull them out of even the officially determined poverty line. For instance, the PDS is able to cover only two-thirds of the requirements of rice of the poorer households, the calories provided for children cover only one-fourth of their daily requirements and the real value of old age and other pensions has steadily declined over the years to cover hardly one meal a day. In 1980, the agricultural labourers pension was Rs. 45 per month; in 1991 the real (deflating it with the CPI-AL) value was only Rs. 25.

Within the scheme of social security, the most innovative of all schemes is perhaps the institution of social insurance through the formation of welfare funds for workers in the informal sector. Here again the coverage has been steadily increasing over the years, most of the important occupations having been covered by the second half of the nineties.

However, these welfare funds are now facing a number of problems. Out of the 19 welfare funds, only about half are working effectively in terms of enrolment of workers and financial management. A number of welfare funds have not been able to fulfil the intended mobilisation of funds. At the same time, a large bureaucratic set up has been built around these funds and in some cases the establishment charges have taken up a disproportionate share of the funds. These problems are related to the coalition political process in Kerala

Table 8

Selected Food Security Cover for Poor in Kerala: Some Estimates for 1991

(Nos. in 000s)

Total population			Estimated poor[a]	Beneficiaries	Col. (5) as % of col. (4)	Col. (5) as % of col. (3)
Male	Female	Total			Public distribution	
14289	14810	29099	9602	26696	278	92
Children (0-4)					Supplementary nutrition	
Boys	Girls	Total				
1410	1349	2759	911	1201	132	44
Children (5-12)					Free noon-meals	
Boys	Girls	Total				
1760	1701	3461	1142	2410	211	70
Old aged (60+)					Old age pensions	
Male	Female	Total				
1689	1371	2560	845	505.3	60	20
Widows					Widows pension	
Male	Female	Total				
137	1298	1435	474	129.3	27	9
Total agricultural labourers (60+)			Pension for agricultural labourers			
Main workers						
Male	Female	Total				
108	40	148	87	344.3	396	233
(298)	(55)	(353)	(151)		(228)	(96)
Divorced/deserted/widowed					Pension	
Male	Female	Total	3			
167	1461	1628	537	51.76	10	3
Physically disabled					Pension	
Male	Female	Total				
		145	48	8.35	17	6

Notes: 1. Except for 'physically disabled', columns 1, 2 and 3 are from the 1991 Population Census Reports. For physically disabled, the source is the *Report of the National Family and Health Survey: Kerala, 1992-93*. The information pertains to, on a per 1000 population basis, 11.0 for partial blindness, 3.0 for complete blindness and 6.6 for physical impairment. The number of estimated poor is based on an incidence of 33.3 per cent as the head count ratio for 1991; 2. The number of estimated poor for 1991 is based on the highest estimate of the available figures. The Planning Commission's Expert Committee estimated the percentage of population below the poverty line in Kerala as 25.43 for 1993-94 while the World Bank estimated it at 33.8 for 1990-91 and 31.07 for 1993-94. We have taken the 1990-91 estimate and estimated the number of poor by taking the HCR at one-third of the population (33.33 per cent). For agricultural labourers, it is well known that the HCR is much higher than that for the general population. For 1993-94, this has been estimated as 58.8 per cent for India. We have applied this figure to Kerala. The HCR for self-employed in agriculture was 31.1 per cent in 1993-94; 3. The estimate of the number of physically disabled is from the National Family Health Survey for Kerala, 1992-93; 4. The beneficiaries under the head 'children (0-4)' refer to the various nutritional care programmes such as the Integrated Child Development Service, Special Nutrition Programme, etc. The number of beneficiaries may include women (as mothers), but this is likely to form only a small proportion of the total; 5. The beneficiaries under the head 'children (5-12)' years refer to the number of children availing of the Free Noon-Meal in Schools; 6. The old-aged (60+) beneficiaries refer to those receiving old-age pension from the state. The categories included here are destitute and agricultural labourers; 7. All other beneficiaries refer to those receiving old-age or special (as in the case of widows) pension.

and its attendant rent-seeking behaviour by political interest groups. But the success of a number of welfare funds should ensure the reform of others now facing problems.

The impact of various housing programmes discussed above can be measured by examining the quality of housing. Given that 'poor housing' now constitutes only around 10 per cent of the total housing, this may, indeed be reckoned as a significant achievement in the all-India context.

There are few income/employment generating programmes in Kerala that could come under social security. Those that are implemented are centrally sponsored poverty alleviation programmes such as the IRDP and the JRY, etc. The per capita benefit of these programmes is too meagre to make any perceptible dent on poverty. In terms of employment generation, they hardly give employment for more than a few days per labourer. Here again, funds have been spread too thinly without being able to make significant reductions in poverty on their own.

VI. LESSONS FROM KERALA'S EXPERIENCE

Kerala has demonstrated the possibility of extending social security in the context of a low income agrarian society to a significant proportion of the population who are outside the formal sector of employment and face innumerable hurdles in overcoming poverty. The provision of social security, as defined here in the broad sense of the term, has been achieved in a variety of ways which needs to be noted. These are: (i) programmes that are financed and implemented by the state government (such as school education and health care); (ii) programmes that are primarily designed and implemented by the State but funded by both the state and central governments (such as public distribution system and supplementary nutrition); (iii) programmes that are designed and funded by the central government but implemented by the state (such as IRDP, rural employment programme, JRY); (iv) programmes that are designed and funded by both central and state governments such as housing for the poor; (v) programmes that are jointly designed, implemented, and in some cases funded by the state government and non-state organisations such as the welfare funds. Such a diversified nature of funding possibilities point to the fact that financial constraints need not necessarily be the main hurdle in establishing a broad-based social security system in a low income agrarian economy.

It has often been cited that Kerala spends a larger share of its budgetary resources for state-assisted social security and related activities. Though this is still the case, the difference between Kerala and all other states is gradually narrowing. At the all-India level, 29 per cent of the total expenditure of all states was for the social sector in 1980-81; this was 47 per cent for Kerala. In 1998-99, these shares were 36 per cent for all states as well as for Kerala. However, expenditure on the social sector on a per capita basis is still higher for Kerala than the all-India figure. We have examined the data on revenue expenditure and found that by the end of the eighties the share of budgetary expenditure for 'social services' in Kerala and at the all-India level had converged (Table 9). In fact, such a convergence has come at a time when the social security system has been sought to be extended in Kerala for more and more sections of the

Table 9
Total Budgetary Expenditure and Social Service Expenditure for all States and Kerala

(in Rs. crores)

		1980-81 (R.E)	1985-86 (R.E)	1995-96 (Accounts)	1996-97 (Accounts)
1. Total revenue expenditure	AS	14930.65	33058.86	145003.93	168949.89
	KE	6742.42	1441.90	5026.37	6788.11
2. Total capital expenditure	AS	6984.37	12695.75	32579.84	33818.88
	KE	185.54	533.44	1095.50	1154.42
3. Grand total expenditure	AS	21915.02	45754.61	177583.77	202768.77
	KE	857.96	1975.34	6921.87	7942.53
4. Total exp. on social services	AS	6268.85	14139.30	56227.80	63836.77
	KE	372.07	814.90	2379.53	2779.10
5. % of total social services exp. to grand total exp.	AS	28.61	30.90	31.66	31.48
	KE	43.37	41.25	34.38	34.99

Note: AS = All states, KE = Kerala, RE = Revised estimates.
Source: RBI Bulletins, Various Issues.

population (such as free noon-meals for children in the upper primary level, old-age pensions for rural labourers other than agricultural labourers, additional subsidy involved in the PDS for the poorer sections, etc.). At the same time, it should also be noted that Kerala's higher share for social service expenditure has been mainly due to expenditure for education and that too for school education. In other sub-sectors of the social service sector the share has not been different from the all-India picture. In fact, certain items of expenditure such as housing has received a lower share in Kerala compared to the corresponding all-India figures (Table 10). Therefore, what do we understand from the point of allocation of budgetary resources?

It is, however, important to note that the per capita expenditure on social services in general and its components in particular has been consistently high in Kerala viz-a-viz all-India (Table 9). This can be seen as the result of two developments. One is the declining rate of growth in population particularly since the early eighties and, second, an increase in the resource mobilisation by the state. Here again there is a tendency for narrowing of the gap between Kerala and the country as a whole.

Certain inadequacies of the social security arrangements in Kerala need to be highlighted especially in the context of continuing poverty. One is the quantum of benefits with regard to certain crucial programmes such as food security and employment security. These are basically in the nature of poor-relief only and they are unable to address the problem of the shortfall in food consumption to enable the poor to meet the calorie requirement to cross the poverty line. Rather than expanding the coverage of these programmes, there is need for strengthening the existing ones (such as the supplementary nutrition and free noon-meal programmes). The payment of monthly pensions in money terms is perhaps a case of declining value because there is no periodic compensation to protect the real value of the money. This was, in fact, pointed out by a committee appointed by the State Planning Board in 1993 but its

Table 10
Per Capita Expenditure on Social Services, All States

(Rs. in current prices)

Item		1980 -81	1985 -86	1994 -95	1995 -96	1996 -97
Social services expenditure (Items 1 to 11)	AS	90.84	188.30	527.45	613.86	679.45
	KE	146.50	300.49	714.52	767.66	884.64
1. Education, arts , sports & culture	AS	45.60	92.72	282.21	320.59	356.78
	KE	86.15	155.06	453.38	470.24	523.85
2. Health, medical & family welfare	AS	22.80	39.81	86.66	96.59	105.31
	KE	29.78	58.17	129.61	134.60	144.16
3. Water supply & sanitation	AS	–	10.35	42.60	44.07	51.87
	KE	–	0.54	27.65	32.92	32.82
4. Housing	AS	2.12	2.48	9.50	11.58	13.60
	KE	2.03	1.92	11.25	14.20	13.66
5. Urban development	AS	–	3.06	13.83	16.40	21.10
	KE	–	–	3.32	4.37	27.31
6. Welfare of SC/ST & other backward classes	AS	–	11.34	36.18	39.66	46.23
	KE	–	–	24.36	2.22	67.71
7. Labour & labour welfare	AS	3.03	3.4	7.50	8.11	8.69
	KE	8.36	7.07	18.47	16.90	17.32
8. Social security and welfare	AS	10.25	10.87	24.43	26.75	29.81
	KE	16.47	28.19	29.84	31.36	38.10
9. Nutrition	AS	–	2.2	9.48	23.55	19.95
	KE	–	–	3.37	3.46	3.69
10. Relief on account of natural calamities	AS	–	9.91	10.00	21.05	20.91
	KE		46.76	10.13	26.93	9.10
11. Others	AS	3.02	2.20	4.99	5.69	5.20
	KE	1.90	2.78	3.12	6.09	4.36

Note: AS = All states ; KE = Kerala.

recommendations have not been followed through by the government (Government of Kerala, 1996).

This brings us to the question of whether or not food security programmes involving direct transfer of commodities is a more effective mechanism than money transfer in alleviating poverty. If the commodity transfer is also time and location specific (as for example, noon meal at schools), then there is a greater degree of effectiveness in delivery. The case of pensioners is again an example here since they do not receive the pension amount on a regular basis but are given once or twice a year.

The issue of employment security has not received adequate attention in the context of Kerala context although unemployment and underemployment are the most pressing problems in Kerala today. Employment and income generated through such centrally-sponsored programmes as the Integrated Rural Development Programme and rural employment programme (JRY) is hardly commensurate with the magnitude of the problem of unemployment. Unlike other social security programme, the organised pressure for employment-generating programmes has also not been sufficient to force the state to respond to it in some meaningful manner. In contrast, those who are employed have come to exercise, through trade unions, a greater pressure on policy making and this has been responded to in a variety of ways including minimum wage regulations, welfare funds for social insurance and state-assisted old-age pensions.

Although we have not examined the social security arrangements through a gender lens, we think it is necessary to do so at a later point in time. Two comments may be made at this stage in order to initiate a discussion. One is that gender discrimination is hardly discernible when it comes to the creation and protection of basic entitlements and capabilities. Thus school enrolment for girls is as impressive as that for boys; in fact the drop-out rate for girls is somewhat lower than that for boys. Health care also does not discriminate on the basis of gender. This is manifested in the low infant mortality and a sex ratio in favour of females. Given the universal nature of PDS and its benefits, it is the women members of the households, especially from the poorer sections, who stand to benefit most by that system. Supplementary nutrition programmes are run by women and there is no reason to believe that female children are under-represented in these programmes. Second, gender discrimination is quite entrenched when it comes to employment, labour markets and related spheres of activity. Women's work participation rate in Kerala is one of the lowest in the country. Their options are limited mostly to the primary sector. Wage disparity between men and women in casual employment is not less than that for other parts of India. All these have resulted in high unemployment rates among women, particularly among educated rural women, low earnings and a greater degree of insecurity than among men. Social insurance via welfare funds were initially started for occupations where men were predominant, minimum wage enforcement is less effective in female employment and even unions do not consider women eligible for time-wages even when they work in factories such as cashew processing units (Kannan, 1983).

It is equally important to examine the effectiveness of social security arrangements from the point of the socially depressed sections (earlier socially excluded) of the population such as Scheduled Castes and Scheduled Tribes. Here again the story would be similar to that of women in society. These sections of the population, especially the Scheduled Castes, are now in a position to take advantage of programmes that seek to create and protect basic entitlements and capabilities but face discrimination in other crucial domains of life such as employment and labour markets. All these raise a number of issues concerning the further strengthening and effectiveness of social security arrangements in a way that may help eradicate poverty and help human development among sections of the population experiencing relatively greater deprivation.

An oft-repeated question, given Kerala's record in economic growth, is the supposed trade-off between equity (as represented by the share of expenditure for social services) and growth. The assumption here is that expenditure on social services represent only considerations of equity (i.e. protection) and not growth (promotion). Such a clear-cut bias is not visible in the case of Kerala, since both protective and promotional programmes form part of its social security system. There is also the problem of overlapping since what is directly perceived as protective (e.g. supplementary nutrition) can have a strong promotional content. The question of growth versus equity in terms of the relative emphasis on social security and other items of expenditure cannot be meaningfully answered without bringing in a number of other factors that determine economic growth. After more than a decade of low growth, the economy of Kerala has been growing at a rate of more than 6 per cent per annum since the late eighties (Kannan, 1998). However, such high growth has largely, if not only, been contributed by the growth in the services sector. Employment growth is strikingly low; similar is the case of such subsectors as food grains production and manufacturing.

(This paper is based on the author's ongoing study on Collective Care Arrangements for Workers and Non-Workers in the Informal Sector funded by the Indo-Dutch Programme of Alternatives in Development (IDPAD). We are thankful to Jan Breman for his support and encouragement).

Note

1. According to the State Planning Board's publication on *Social Welfare Programmes in Kerala* (1993), there were 55 social security schemes administered by Social Welfare Department (15), Social Welfare Advisory Board (8), Labour Welfare Funds (17), Rural Development Department (6), Labour Department (2), Revenue Department (3), Fisheries Department (4). In addition, the Departments of Scheduled Castes and Scheduled Tribes is reported to have 61 schemes. Also there are 25 schemes administered by various other departments and agencies (see Government of Kerala, 1993).

References

Abram De Swan (1998), *In Care of the State*, Polity Press, Cambridge.

Bhattacharya, Vivek (1970), *Social Security Measures in India*, Metropolitan Book Co. Pvt. Ltd, Delhi.

Chelliah, R.J. and R. Sudarshan (eds.) (1999), *Income Poverty and Beyond: Human Development in India*, Social Science Press, New Delhi.

Dreze, Jean and Amartya Sen (1989), *Hunger and Public Action*, Oxford University Press, Delhi.

Francis, Shaji (1990), *Dynamics of Rural Labour Markets: An Analysis of Emerging Agricultural Labour Shortage in a Kerala Region*, M.Phil Thesis submitted to the Jawaharlal Nehru Univesity, Centre for Development Studies, Thiruvananthapuram.

Kannan, K. P. (1983), "Evolution of Unionisation and Changes in Labour Processes under Lower Forms of Capitalist Production : A Case Study of the Cashew Industry of Kerala", in Das, A.N. et al. (eds.), *The Worker and the Working Class: A Labour Studies Anthology*, Public Enterprise Centre for Continuing Education, New Delhi.

—— (1991), *Health and Development in Rural Kerala: A Study of Linkages between Socio-economic Status and Health Status*, Kerala Sasthra Sahitya Parishad, Thiruvanthapuram.

—— (1992), "Labour Institutions and the Development Process in Kerala", in Papola, T.S. and Gerry Rodgers (eds.), *Labour Institutions and Economic Development in India*, International Institute for Labour Studies, Geneva.

—— (1995), "Public Intervention and Poverty Alleviation : A Study of the Declining Incidence of Rural Poverty in Kerala, India", *Development and Change*, Vol. 26, No. 4, October.

—— (1998), "Political Economy of Labour and Development in Kerala", *Economic and Political Weekly*, December 26.

—— (1999), "Rural Labour Relations and Development Dilemmas in Kerala : Reflections on the Dilemmas of a Socially Transforming Labour Force in a Slowly Growing Economy", *Journal of Peasant Studies*, January-March.

Mahendra Dev, S. (1994), "Social Security in the Unorganised Sector: Lessons from the Experiences of Kerala and Tamil Nadu", *The Indian Journal of Labour Economics*, Vol. 37, No. 4.

Mooij, Jos (1999), *Food Policy and the Indian State: The Public Distribution System in Karnataka and Kerala*, Oxford University Press, Delhi.

Nair, Gopinathan P.R. (1981), *Primary Education, Population Growth and Socio-economic Change: A Comparative Study with Particular Reference to Kerala*, Allied Publishers, New Delhi.

Raj, K.N. and P.K.M. Tharakan (1983), "Agrarian Reforms in Kerala and its Impact on the Rural Economy: A Preliminary Assessment", in Ghose, Ajit Kumar (ed.), *Agrarian Reforms in Contemporary Developing Countries*, Croom Helm, London.

U.N./C.D.S. (1975), *Poverty, Unemployment and Development Policy: A Case Study of Selected Issues with Special Reference to Kerala*, Department of Economic and Social Affairs, New York.

Zacharia, K.C. et al. (1999), *Migration in Kerala State, India: Dimensions, Determinants and Consequences*, Centre for Development Studies, Thiruvananthapuram (mimeo).

20

Social Security in Uttar Pradesh: Moving beyond Policy to Governance

Nisha Srivastava

I. INTRODUCTION

The concept of social security, as defined by the ILO, refers to the "protection which society provides to its members, through a series of public measures, against the economic and social distress that otherwise would be caused by the stoppage or substantial reduction of earnings resulting from sickness, maternity, employment injury, unemployment, invalidity, old age and death; the provision of medical care; and the provision of subsidies for families with children" (quoted in ESCAP, 1992). Thus defined, the concept of social security relates to public action encompassing three main forms of provisions: contingency-related income transfers, medical care and family assistance, and income transfers conditioned by interruption in earnings (Dev, 1996).

This concept of social security has been questioned in the context of developing countries which have a large unorganised sector, and where much of the population is subject to chronic deprivation. A broader view links the concept of social security to the use of social means to prevent deprivation, and vulnerability to deprivation (Dreze and Sen, 1991). Two different aspects of social security can be distinguished, protective and promotional. The former is concerned with preventing a decline in living standards due to contingencies. The latter is concerned with the entitlement of general living standards and the expansion of basic capabilities of the population, and is seen as a long-term challenge (Dreze and Sen, 1989; 1995). The two-way link between growth and social security is quite clear, but it is generally useful to restrict the scope of social security to measures that lead to creation of entitlements, and help prevent deprivation or vulnerability to deprivation.

There are a large group of promotional and protective measures that contribute to social security and the line separating these measures is not always easy to draw. Promotional measures, or income-support measures, include providing access to basic health and education, land distribution, anti-poverty programmes directed at asset creation and employment, minimum wages and programmes to improve food and nutrition security. Protective security covers contingencies such as old age, widowhood, maternity, disability and employment injury and can be covered under a programme of social assistance (Guhan, 1994).

It is a travesty of our development paradigm that while legislations governing the social security needs of organised workers are relatively comprehensive and efficient, the vast majority of the ill-paid and insecure unorganised workers are given no succour. Social security protection is needed by both, the poor and the non-poor. The commitment to a socialistic pattern enshrined in our Constitution led to the enactment of legislations such as The Factory Act, 1948, The Maternity Benefit Act, 1941, Employees State Insurance Act, 1948, Employees Provident Fund Act (1979), Payment of Bonus Act, 1965 and so on. However, these benefited only a small percentage of workers in the organised sector, while the vast majority in the informal, unorganised sector remained beyond the pale of such legislation.

This paper looks at some issues of social security in Uttar Pradesh, one of the poorest and most backward states of the country. Section II profiles the trends and magnitude of poverty in the state. Section III assesses the performance of the state in providing security to the poor. The analysis is restricted to the rural areas where the vast majority of the poor live. Section IV looks specifically at employment security and food security, and raises what should be the most elemental of all social security concerns: the right to a secure life. While quantitative macro data is important in assessing performance, qualitative participatory studies provide rich insights because they are based on people's own perceptions of their security needs and how best they are, or can be, served. We look at the evidence from both sources.[1] Section V of the paper looks at institutional structures and issues of governance. Faith is now being pinned on panchayats to deliver where top-down delivery systems failed earlier. Will panchayats be able to meet the social security needs of the community? We examine some of these issues in the light of evidence from Uttar Pradesh.

II. TRENDS AND MAGNITUDE OF POVERTY IN UTTAR PRADESH

Estimates of poverty in 1993-94 show that Uttar Pradesh has the highest number of people below the poverty line. With 17.9 per cent of India's rural population, the state has 20.3 per cent of the country's poor. Not only does the state have a large absolute burden of income poverty, it also ranks low among Indian states with regard to other indicators of deprivation. Table 1 gives the rank of Indian states on the basis of alternative indicators of well being.

Between 1957-58 and 1993-94, the state's achievements in the direction of poverty reduction has lagged behind the rest of the country by about 6 per cent. Most of the slow down in the state's comparative performance can be attributed to the most recent period. Between 1957-58 and 1987-88, Uttar Pradesh achieved a reduction in poverty by 13.6 per cent (from 55 per cent to 41.6 per cent). In comparison, the rest of the country achieved a reduction in poverty by 16.6 per cent. Between 1987-88 and 1993-94, the rest of the country achieved a further reduction in poverty by 3.2 per cent. During the same period, poverty in Uttar Pradesh rose slightly by 0.2 per cent.

From the point of view of social security provisioning it is useful to think of the poor as belonging to three groups (Subba Rao et al., 1997). Firstly, those

Table 1
State Rankings by Alternative Indicators of Well Being

State	Head count index[a]			Life expectancy[b]		Infant mortality[c]	Literacy rates[a]	
	Total	Rural	Urban	Male	Female	Male	Female	
Punjab	16	16	16	13	12	14	8	11
Andhra Pradesh	15	15	14	7	5	8	2	5
Gujarat	14	14	15	6	6	10	11	9
Kerala	13	11	10	14	13	15	16	16
Haryana	12	13	12	11	10	7	9	8
Rajasthan	11	10	11	4	4	4	4	1
Himachal Pradesh	10	12	13	-	-	-	14	14
Karnataka	9	7	7	10	7	9	7	7
Tamil Nadu	8	6	6	9	9	12	12	12
Maharashtra	7	5	4	12	11	13	15	13
West Bengal	6	9	8	8	8	11	10	10
Assam	5	8	9	-	-	5	13	15
Uttar Pradesh	4	4	5	2	3	3	3	3
Madhya Pradesh	3	3	3	1	1	2	5	4
Orissa	2	2	1	3	2	1	6	6
Bihar	1	1	1	5	-	6	1	2

Note: (a) 1993-94; (b) early 90s; (c) 1995. The ranking is from highest (16) to lowest (1).
Source: World Bank (1998).

who are able to work but have low incomes arising from low productivity. Second, those who are unable to work (the elderly and handicapped) and in the third category we can place those people who are forced into temporary poverty by unforeseen events such as drought, recession or structural adjustment policies. The security needs of each group would be met by different kinds of measures. For instance, while food for work schemes may meet the income needs of the first group, they would be irrelevant for the second group whose security needs can only be met by transfers in cash or kind. The persistence of poverty underscores the need for effective social security measures, but at the same time, the sluggish growth trends suggest that these measures should also be growth enhancing.

III. SOCIAL SECURITY TO THE POOR

1. Employment Security

The case for employment security in Uttar Pradesh rests on the following facts: Firstly, the majority of workers in the state are still dependent on agriculture, which provides little or no work for much of the year. Secondly, 70 per cent of all landholdings are below one hectare and landlessness has grown so much so that workers have little to fall back on during lean seasons. Thirdly, absorption of labour in agriculture and availability of agricultural employment have been low and appear to be declining in the poor regions (Lieten and Srivastava, 1999; Sharma, 1997). The Jawahar Rozgar Yojana (JRY) was started in 1989, to cater to the income and employment security needs of the rural poor. The JRY was refashioned and rechristened as the Jawahar Gram Samridhi Yojana (JGSY) in April 1999. It is as yet too early to assess the impact—at the village level—of the modified scheme, although one may hazard an opinion on possible outcomes on the basis of the design of the scheme. In this section, therefore, we first evaluate how far the earlier version of the scheme, the JRY has benefited the poor and thereafter, discuss the changes in the format of the scheme and its implications.

The JRY began by amalgamating two earlier programmes, the NREP and the RLEGP. Under the JRY, central allocations to the states were decided on the basis of the proportion of poor in the state. Inter-district allocations within a state were determined on the basis of a weighting scheme which gave equal weights to the proportion of SC/ST population in each district and the inverse of agricultural productivity per worker. Allocation to blocks and *Gram Panchayats* were made on the basis of (equal) weights given to the SC/ST population and the total population. Seventy per cent of the JRY funds were allocated directly to *gram panchayats* while 15 per cent each were allocated to the block and *zilla panchayats*/DRDA.

The JRY was conceived of as a community-based programme. Schemes implemented under the programme were to be decided upon in village assemblies according to guidelines laid down by the government of India. The labour component in the works was specified at a minimum of 60 per cent and the use of mechanical equipment and tractors was prohibited. JRY accounts were to be jointly held by the *pradhan* and a panchayat member or panchayat secretary.

The second employment scheme, the Employment Assurance Scheme (EAS) was launched in 1993-94 with the objective of providing assured employment in unskilled manual work to the rural poor, upto 100 days under the public works programmes. The scheme was extended to cover all the blocks in the state in 1997-98. The EAS is a 'demand-driven' scheme and requires that those who need employment under the scheme register themselves with the village panchayats where they reside. Employment is supposed to be provided whenever 20 or more workers demand work, but even if 10 or more workers demand work they may be provided employment for a period of up to 30 days. The expenditure under EAS is shared between the centre and the states on an 80:20 basis.

In contrast to the JRY, the District Collector is in-charge of the scheme under EAS and is responsible for allocating the work among the implementing agencies (the line departments or the block). Works started under the EAS are expected to be labour intensive and the wage component (on unskilled labour) connot be less than 60 per cent, unless the excess cost on materials is provided from other sectoral programmes.

A specific feature of the employment generation programmes in the state is the emphasis on dovetailing the programmes with other departments working towards the building of social and physical infrastructure. Dovetailing of JRY with sector department projects was started in 1993-94. The labour: material cost in the JRY/EAS component is meant to be kept within the norms prescribed (60:40) and the additional expenditure on material inputs are provided by the line departments. In the EAS, as a result of dovetailing and allocations to *gram panchayats*, the utilisation of available funds had gone up to 70 per cent in 1997-98 from about 52 per cent in the previous year.

In the EAS, the employment guarantee objective of the scheme has been diluted by its universal extension to all areas, while it's demand-driven nature is compromised by the top-down nature of the schemes. While these are national design features of the scheme, in the state "demand drivenness" is interpreted as a demand for funds, linked to the capacity of the block/district to spend the funds already allocated and place a demand for more. The important corrective, that the demand for employment should come from the unemployed workers, with the state responding by activating off-the-shelf schemes, does not appear to have occurred and the registration of workers, itself incomplete in many places, has virtually no link with the programme. This accentuates the top-down character of the scheme. Even at the present scale, JRY and EAS resources have only a limited potential for employment generation if they are thinly spread. Hence the dilution of geographical targeting in the EAS is worrying. The distinguishing feature of the EAS today is its potential to integrate with departmental plans and not its employment-generating potential *per se*. However, the national design does not prevent the state from implementing a coherent strategy of geographical targeting at the block and the district level, and integrating this strategy with a demand-led pattern of employment generation.

Available evaluations and field assessments highlight the inadequate employment security provided by the government programmes. Further, efficiency of the programmes also vary across states. Table 2 gives average rates of participation of different groups of the population in the employment generation programmes at the all-India level and for Uttar Pradesh. The average odds of participation for the poorest quintile is lower in Uttar Pradesh than for the country as a whole.

Table 2
Average Participation Rates in the Public Works Programmes by Quintile Groups of Per Capita Expenditure: India and Uttar Pradesh

Quintile of expenditure per capita		Public works	
		Participation rate (%)	Average odds of participation
Poorest	India	5.0	1.23
	U.P.	4.0	1.05
2nd	India	4.6	1.13
	U.P.	4.1	1.08
3nd	India	4.2	1.04
	U.P.	4.2	1.11
4th	India	3.5	0.86
	U.P.	3.6	0.95
5th	India	3.4	0.83
	U.P.	2.9	0.76
All	India	4.1	
	U.P.	3.8	

Note: The table gives the average participation rates and the odds of participation, defined as the ratio of the quintile specific participation rate to the mean participation rate for each programme. Calculations are based on the National Sample Survey, 1993-94 .

Source: Lanjouw and Ravallion, cited in World Bank (1998).

Subba Rao (1998) finds that flows of programme funds from the centre to the states and from the states to the districts are generally well targeted. Relatively poorer regions and districts received resources commensurate with the incidence of poverty. However, actual expenditures fell short of allocations.

The concurrent evaluations of JRY carried out by the Ministry of Rural Areas and Employment suggest that the state's performance is poorer in some respects compared to the country as a whole. For example, the January-December 1992 evaluation found that JRY had generated 3.24 person-days of employment per family in Uttar Pradesh in a reference period of 30 days compared to 5.17 days nationally. Wages had a share of 45.5 per cent of expenditures in Uttar Pradesh, compared to the national share of 53 per cent and the norm of 60 per cent. The share of female employment was a dismal—8.3 per cent all over the country. In Uttar Pradesh it was even lower at 6.3 per cent (Table 3).

Table 3
Employment Schemes in Uttar Pradesh: Physical and Financial Progress up to March 2000

	Progress of JRY/JGSY			Progress of EAS		
Financial progress (Rs. in lakhs)	1999-2000	1998-99	1997-98	1999-2000	1998-99	1997-98
Outlay	44797.55	52742.93	47301.56	49456.55	49575	45050
Funds available						
i. Misc. rec.		1191.3			3428.16	
ii. Opening balance of the year	5471.85	8494.04	11942.77	5581.5	17089.02	17888.57
iii. Total release	44680.34	51293.71	44673.38	51946.17	43881.04	39866
Total funds available	50152.19	60979.05	56616.15	57527.67	64398.22	57754.57
Exp. against total availability	35804.8	55507.2	48122.11	40846.19	58816.72	40665.55
% Expenditure against outlay	79.90	105.20	101.70	82.60	118.60	90.30
% Expenditure against total funds	71.40	91.00	85.00	71.00	91.30	70.40
Balance at the end of month	14347.39	5471.85	8494.04	16681.48	5581.5	17089.02
Physical progress (Employment generated in lakh man-days)						
Target	Not fixed	626.28	561.71	624.66	770.17	456.39
Achievement	438.89	691.39	599.49	485.73	754.31	522.76
% Achievement		110.40	106.70	77.80	97.90	92.10

Source: *Annual Progress Report* of Programmes implemented by the Department of Rural Development, Government of Uttar Pradesh.

The Second Concurrent Evaluation (1993-94) indicated that nearly 41,000 below poverty line households were employed in 630 study panchayats and 464,000 person-days of employment were created in JRY and other public works programmes. Thus, not more than 12 person-days of employment were created for each below-poverty-line (BPL) family employed in the scheme. This compares to a figure of about 16 person-days nationally. Uttar Pradesh had only

4 per cent of women beneficiaries and compared unfavourably with the national average of 17 per cent. These figures were way below the norm of 30 per cent. Against the norm of a 60:40 ratio between the wage and non-wage components of total expenditures, the ratio in Uttar Pradesh was 46:54, which also compared unfavourably against the national average of 53:47.

The Second Concurrent Evaluation found that the wages paid under JRY were Rs. 23.7 for males and Rs. 23.3 for females, compared to the prescribed minimum wage of Rs. 25. The prevailing lean season market wages for unskilled labourers were Rs. 29.4 and Rs. 26.3 for males and females, respectively. Thus, on average, JRY wages were lower compared to the lean-season wages. Other studies have reported wide regional and local variations; with market wages being considerably higher in some regions, and somewhat lower than the legal minimum wages in other regions (Lieten and Srivastava, 1999). As a result, workers are unwilling to work at the stipulated JRY wage in developed regions, whereas in poorer regions, people wanted more of work than was available.

Other micro studies reveal high leakages, much lower wage labour component than stipulated, and negligible role of the village assembly and village councils in project planning and supervision. In a careful study of 39 village panchayats spread over five blocks in two districts of Uttar Pradesh, the leakage in wage and material costs was estimated at around 40 per cent and the wage component of total cost was estimated at 29 per cent as against a norm of 60 per cent (Shankar, 1994). The study also found that the employment generated in the JRY was only 16 days per employed worker.

There are few evaluations available of the impact of EAS. An early study of EAS carried out in 1996 (Srivastava, 1996) in three blocks of Allahabad and Gorakhpur districts reported that problems of recruitment of non-local labourers, low wages, arrears in wage disbursals were quite endemic to the schemes studied. Family cards had been distributed in the villages but the labourers employed in the EAS schemes were often non-local and were not registered.

Field studies also suggest that the amount of employment generated under the two schemes is low. In the study cited earlier (Srivastava, 1996), less than five per cent labourers, predominantly male, had been employed in JRY-funded public works for an average period of 13 days. Fewer labourers had worked in EAS for an average of 17 days. Taken together, about 8 per cent labourers received employment for 15 days on average. Wages in JRY were about 33 per cent lower than the stipulated minimum, and those in EAS were about 10 per cent lower than the JRY wages.

Subba Rao's (1998) study finds that even the government's own figures show that the objective of the EAS of providing 100 days of employment to everyone who is registered for employment is far from being realised. He computes the number of person-days of employment created per registered person in each district of the state for the year 1997-98. This varied from a low of 2.6 days in Bijnor to a high of 85.6 days in Ghazipur. This suggests that the variation in the number of person-days of employment created across districts is very large (Table 4). On an average 20 person-days of employment per registered person were recorded under EAS.

Table 4
EAS/JRY Employment

Programme	Total no. of districts	Distribution of districts by number of days of employment created per registered person					
		Less than 10 days	10-19 days	20-29 days	30-39 days	40-49 days	50 or more days
EAS	62	5	22	14	9	6	6
JRY	62	4	19	16	8	6	9

Source: Subba Rao (1998).

Those seeking employment under JRY were not required to register themselves, but we may assume that the records of those registered for EAS also reflect the demand for employment under JRY, since both programmes basically serve the same purpose. On this assumption, Subba Rao (1998) finds that the number of person-days of employment generated per registered person under JRY was only 23. Table 4 gives the variation in employment generated across districts.

Qualitative, village-level studies show up the employment security measures in a worse light (Srivastava, 1998; Kozel and Parker, 1998). Focus group discussions reveal that most people have a hazy awareness of the schemes and know little of the norms governing them. Even though, till 1999, the creation of public and social infrastructure was treated as a secondary objective in the employment generation programmes, it was this aspect of the programme, rather than the potential to create jobs, that was widely recognised and had greater popularity.

Very few men or women reported getting work under the schemes. The few who had secured work said that it was only for 10-12 days in a year and related other grievances. Employment was given only to those who were close to the *pradhan*. Preference was given to those who were willing to work for lower wages but sign for higher amounts. Some workers complained that their wages for work done a year ago had not been paid to them and when they went to ask for their dues they had been humiliated. Low caste informants said that the *gram sabha* meetings were not well publicised and initial enthusiasm about these meetings waned away when it was realised that they would not be heard and that the proceedings would have little bearing on the final decisions taken. Some informants also said that the funds available through these programmes would have to be increased before expecting them to provide any meaningful level of employment opportunities.

In the qualitative PRA studies, informants were asked to suggest improvements in the employment programmes. Many of their suggestions focused on improving transparency. In the view of these informants, the intended beneficiaries of these schemes should be informed of the programme's objectives, rules of operation, the amount of funds available and other relevant details in each village. Increased public awareness, elimination of corruption and misuse of funds were also mentioned as a critical requirement for improving the effectiveness of the employment assurance programmes.

2. Gender Dimensions

It is important to acknowledge the gender dimension in income and employment security. Providing women with jobs does not radically alter a women's status, circumscribed as it is by centuries of economic deprivation and discriminatory social norms, but it may increase her entitlements and her ability to deal with her situation. That is why it is essential to monitor how far government interventions in employment security have benefited women.

Table 5 shows that even in a government programme which stipulates that 30 per cent of those employed should be women, the number of women that in fact secured work was far below the norm. Moreover, men are able to migrate to nearby cities and towns to increase their earnings and employment. Women, on the other hand, are constrained in their mobility—they can go in search of work only if accompanied by male members. The provision of employment in the lean season is therefore especially critical for them.

Table 5
Percentage Distribution of JRY Workers by Sex

State	Total workers	Male (%)	Female (%)	State	Total workers	Male %	Female (%)
Andhra Pradesh	1100	80.36	19.64	Madhya Pradesh	2245	79.78	20.22
Assam	1145	95.11	4.89	Maharashtra	1450	69.1	30.9
Bihar	2449	96.73	3.27	Punjab	600	99.33	0.67
Gujarat	925	68.97	31.03	Rajasthan	1500	63.8	36.2
Haryana	800	90.25	9.75	Tamil Nadu	1040	70.19	29.81
Himachal Pradesh	600	89.67	10.33	Uttar Pradesh	3150	96	4
Karnataka	1000	73.6	26.4	West Bengal	1820	89.02	10.98
Kerala	695	71.51	28.49	All-India	23174	83.23	16.77

Source: GOI (1997).

Table 6 shows the average wages paid to male and female workers in the JRY. Women are discriminated in two ways. Not only are women paid less than the official norm but their wages are also lower than the corresponding male wages. Another discrimination that women face is that while men graduate quickly to the status of a skilled worker and correspondingly higher wages, women cannot aspire to that status even after years of work.

Table 6
Average Wages per Person-day under JRY and Prevalent Local Wage Rates during Lean Seasons

(Rs.)

State	Unskilled workers (JRY)		Minimum wage	Wages of skilled workers	Local wage rate in lean season	
	Male	Female			Male	Female
Uttar Pradesh	23.66	23.25	24	45.64	29.38	26.32
All-India	26.08	24.51		46.21	28.75	25.04

Source: GOI (1997).

3. Shift in Focus: A Farewell to Employment Security

Lastly, we conclude by noting the modifications to the erstwhile JRY in the revised JGSY scheme. The most significant change is that the focus has shifted from employment generation to infrastructure development. Employment generation is now officially the secondary objective. The changed focus is also reflected in the relaxation of other norms. The earlier wage: material ratio of 60:40 has been made flexible and "may be suitably relaxed to enable the build-up of demand-driven infrastructure" (GOI, 1999). Translated on the field, this means practically a farewell to the norm. The other stated objective of the JRY of ensuring that 30 per cent of the beneficiaries are women has also been done away with.

At the conceptual level, the complete reversal in focus from employment generation to infrastructure development may be seen as a severe blow to employment security. The scheme, for all its shortcomings, was well targeted towards the poor who would now be denied whatever minimal security the earlier scheme provided. At another level, it may be argued that the revisions are a pragmatic and level-headed acceptance of ground realities. The JRY was widely seen by the poor as an infrastructure-building programme in any case, and the employment provided per person was minimal. The waiver—or what practically amounts to one—of the wage: material norm and the female employment norms also appear to be a realistic acknowledgement of what most studies had shown—that they were simply not being implemented. Be that as it may, in the changed scenario, the prospect of providing employment security appears to have receded further.

IV. FOOD SECURITY

The need for food security in Uttar Pradesh, a state which is not food deficient, is not obvious. Nor should it have been necessary. The state produced 41.8 million tonnes of foodgrains, which is 22 per cent of the total foodgrain production in the country. The state is the largest producer of wheat in the county, producing 35 per cent of the national output. At 247 kg per year per capita, it is also the third highest among major states in per capita foodgrain production. Despite this, however, the steep inequalities in income and purchasing power and the poor record in food management by the state have made provisioning of food security an imperative. Food hunger, measured by the proportion of households not able to get two square meals a day, was reported by 3.4 per cent households in the state in 1993-94 (NSSO, 1996). In the Survey of Living Conditions (SLC) Study[1] (1998), carried out in the poor Eastern and Bundelkhand regions of the state, food hunger measured by the same yardstick, was reported by 6.2 per cent households. In the same study, the share of food in total consumption expenditure in rural areas was estimated at 61. 5 per cent, while in urban areas this was 55.9 per cent (Srivastava, 2000).

The gargantuan structure of the public distribution system (PDS) was set up in the country to meet the food needs of the poor. Criticisms with regard to leakage, poor targeting, and low accountability to the community led to the streamlining and renaming of the scheme in 1997. It came to be known as the Targeted Public Distribution Scheme (TPDS). How well has the state been able to provide food security to the poor? We look at the evidence from some recent studies to provide answers.

The three major reforms introduced in the TPDS were, firstly, a change in norms governing allocation to the states so that states with a higher incidence of poverty receive a proportionately higher allocation of foodgrains; secondly, targeting the programme more narrowly so that only households below the poverty line would be eligible; and thirdly, giving the state and local level bodies a greater role in monitoring and supervising the operations.

The old-styled PDS was streamlined for better targeting and efforts were made to increase the participation of stakeholders. A state-wide survey was launched to identify afresh households which were below the poverty line, the criteria being defined by a mix of factors, including income, land and asset ownership. The *gram sabha* or village assembly had an important role to play in identifying the households which were below the poverty line, including and excluding names by consensus. It was thought that this would bring about transparency in the process. In Uttar Pradesh 95.5 lakh households were identified as living below the poverty line. These constituted 41 per cent of all households (Table 7). This was well above the national average of 36 per cent.

Table 7
Number of Below Poverty Line (BPL) Households by State

State	BPL households as percentage of all households	No. of BPL households (lakhs)	State	BPL households as percentage of all households	No. of BPL households (lakhs)
Uttar Pradesh	41	95.48	Rajasthan	27	21.66
Bihar	55	85.90	Gujarat	24	19.95
Maharashtra	37	60.45	Assam	41	19.05
Madhya Pradesh	46	57.10	Kerala	25	15.35
West Bengal	36	46.59	Haryana	25	7.33
Tamil Nadu	35	45.76	Punjab	12	4.3
Andhra Pradesh	22	32.65	J&K	25	3.8
Orissa	49	31.82	Himachal Pradesh	28	2.96
Karnataka	33	28.76	Total	36	590.44

Source: GOI (1997a).

The high percentage of poor households in Uttar Pradesh, reflects on the critical importance of food security. Despite pervasive poverty, earlier studies had shown small number of households in Uttar Pradesh, relative to other states, that made use of the PDS (Mahendra Dev, 1996) (Table 8). Some of the explanations for the low utilisation of the PDS emerged vividly in the qualitative studies, which were able to capture the social and perception-related dimensions of the problem. Apart from the well-known shortcomings of leakages and insufficient rations, participants stated that one of the main reasons they did not go to the ration shops was that, more often than not, these were situated in the upper caste hamlets. Typically, shop owners either belonged to the upper castes or were operating it on their behalf. In the Allahabad study (Srivastava, 1998), one Scheduled Caste youth said, he was so incensed by the abusive behaviour of the shopkeeper that he threw the kerosene he had purchased right in front of the shop and vowed never to come back. The location and ownership of PDS shops also have other implications for its use by intended beneficiaries. Deliveries do not confirm to a fixed schedule so people do not come to know when the supplies arrive. The quantum is restricted and demand is high. Moreover, even though the guidelines say the shop should be open for several days in a month, in practice it opens only for one day, so that intentionally or otherwise, the principle of 'first-come, first-served' operates. Households, which live in the proximity of the PDS shop, first come to know when supplies arrive and draw benefit from it.

Table 8
Percentage of Rural Households Using PDS, 1994

State	Percentage using PDS	State	Percentage using PDS
Andhra Pradesh	69	Orissa	6
Bihar	5	Punjab	6
Gujarat	50	Rajasthan	25
Haryana	9	Tamil Nadu	83
Himachal Pradesh	76	Uttar Pradesh	7
Karnataka	78	West Bengal	11
Kerala	80	North-Eastern Region	24
Madhya Pradesh	37		
Maharashtra	55	All- India	36

Source: NCAER/HDI Survey, as quoted in Mahendra Dev (1996).

Informants also stated that PDS shopkeepers charge prices higher than the officially stipulated ones. The other problem is that the poor do not have enough money to buy their full quota in one go. If on the particular day that the shop is opened and rations are sold, a poor household does not posses enough cash to buy their quota, they have to forgo their rations for the entire month. The quality of foodgrains was often seen to be inferior to that available in the market, though some felt the quality varied from month to month, "sometimes it is good, sometimes it is bad—it is *sarkari* service after all: this is the way the *sarkar* works."[2]

Subba Rao (1998) found that the pricing policy under the reformed TPDS had benefited the poor. When the difference between PDS prices and the market prices used to be small, the poor, or for that matter the rich, had no interest in the PDS. With the introduction of the TPDS, the poor were assured a price which was half that of the issue price for 10 kg of grain per month. These changes appear to have had a favourable impact and improved delivery. This was reflected in increased lifting of foodgrain allocations by the state government. In 1995 before the TPDS was introduced, only 41 per cent of the total cereal allocations were 'lifted'. In 1997, following the introduction of TPDS, off-take had improved to 86 per cent for wheat and 67 per cent for rice (Table 9).

With the budget of 2000 and subsequently, there have been further changes. These were: (a) the issue price of rice and wheat has been increased, while simultaneously increasing the entitlement of eligible poor households to 20 kilos of cereals; (b) subsidies on cereal purchase to above poverty line (APL)

Table 9
Off-take of Foodgrains for PDS as Percentage of Allocation in Uttar Pradesh

	Wheat			Rice			Total cereal		
	Allocation	Off-take	%	Allocation	Off-take	%	Allocation	Off-take	%
1993-94	972.6	391.60	40	535.60	232.50	43	1508.20	624.10	41
1994-95	1185.60	203.20	17	549.60	197.30	36	1735.20	400.50	23
1995-96	1185.60	225.90	19	549.60	209.50	38	1735.20	435.40	25
1996-97	1037.98	893.60	86	532.20	356.80	67	1570.18	1250.40	80
1997-98	1214.82	867.2	71	526.09	320.98	61	1740.91	1188.18	68
1998-99	940.53	500.23	53	459.3	259.36	56	1399.83	759.59	54

Note: (1) Allocation and off-take are in '000 tonnes; (2) % refers to off-take as a percentage of allocation; (3) Figures for 1998-99 relate only to December 1998.
Source: Department of Civil Supplies, Government of Uttar Pradesh.

households has been completely removed; (c) sugar has been removed from the list of subsidised commodities; and (d) there has been a hefty rise in the price of kerosene distributed through the PDS.

An argument is sometimes advanced that poor agrarian households either grow their own requirements of foodgrains or receive it in kind as wages and therefore the utility of PDS is not critical. This does not appear to be the case. Firstly, the PDS assumes special significance for poor families during the lean season. Figure 1 shows the monthly variation in the purchase of foodgrains by the lowest two quintiles. It also tells us the periods when the need for effective provisioning is highest.

Secondly, the PDS provides a cushion when market prices rise. Moreover, prices in village markets are often higher than those in cities. The rich can afford to buy at lower prices from the cities, but for the poor that is not an option. The SLC study shows that a much higher percentage of households in the lowest consumption quintile purchase from the PDS as compared to households in the higher quintiles (Table 10).

Figure 1
Seasonal Variations in Purchase of Wheat by Poor

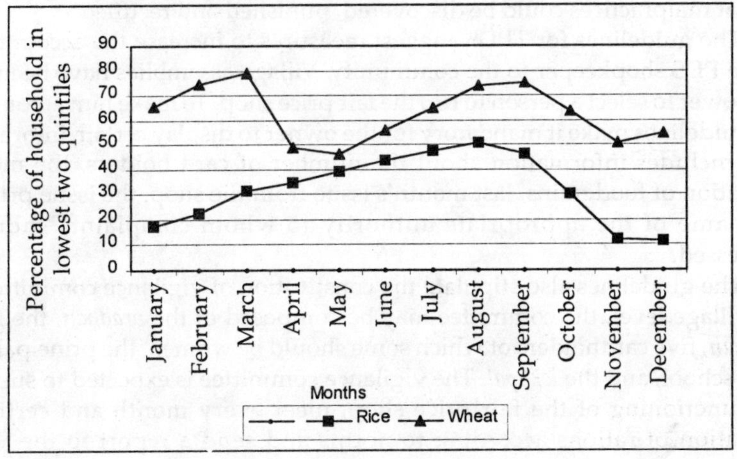

Table 10
Percentage of Households by Quintile Group Purchasing Wheat/Rice from PDS in Uttar Pradesh, 1998

Percentage of households who have made purchase in	Per capita consumption quintile					
	1 (lowest)	2	3	4	5 (highest)	Total
Last 30 days	21.0	14.9	15.0	11.6	7.1	13.9
Last 60 days	26.8	18.0	18.1	15.7	7.9	17.3

Source: Survey of Living Conditions Study, 1998.

Table 11 shows that roughly half the quantity of rice and a little less than half of wheat consumed per month by the poorest 40 per cent households is purchased either from the market or from the PDS shops. Therefore, the importance of subsidised grains for the poor should not be underestimated. Instead, emphasis should be given on improving the system.

Table 11
Average Consumption per Household of Rice and Wheat by Source (Households belonging to lowest two quintiles only)

Food item	Amount consumed		
(Kg)	Purchased	Home grown/ Wages in kind	Total
Rice	23.78	27.88	51.66
Wheat	25.63	35.07	60.70
Total	49.41	62.95	112.36

Source: Survey of Living Conditions Study, 1998.

A number of suggestions were offered in this direction. Poor informants said that the shops should be located in poor/Scheduled Caste hamlets and the educated-unemployed among these communities should be entrusted with the responsibility of operating them. The problems of accessing supplies were fewer when the ration shopkeeper was local and belonged to the lower castes. People also felt that there should be greater supervision by higher-level officials so that malpractices could be discovered, punished and rectified.

The guidelines for TPDS suggest measures to increase the accountability of the PDS shopkeeper to the community. Village assemblies have been given the power to select a person to run the fair price shop. To make him accountable, the guidelines make it mandatory for the owner to display certain information. This includes information about the number of card holders, the monthly allocation of foodgrains, last month's issue from the shop, the issue price and the name of the appropriate authority to whom complaints should be addressed.

The guidelines also stipulate the constitution of vigilance committees. At the village level, the committee may be composed of the *pradhan*, the former *pradhan*, five cardholders of which some should be women, the principal of the local school, and the *lekhpal*. The vigilance committee is expected to supervise the functioning of the fair price shop, meet every month and certify the allocation of rations according to norms and send a report to the Supply

Inspector. Further, the license of the owner may be withdrawn if his operation is not satisfactory. This, however, does not always translate into practice.

Informants in the village surveys (Srivastava, 1998) gave specific instances when complaints had been made against errant shopkeepers to the *pradhan* and block officials. Nevertheless, no action was taken against them. In one case, in a village in Allahabad district, the license of the shopkeeper was withdrawn after several complaints. However, instead of giving the license to someone else in the same village, people were told to make their purchases from the fair price shop in an adjoining village. The drudge involved and the cost in terms of forgone wages proved too high. The solution offered was worse than the problem and the former corrupt shopkeeper was reinstated.

Despite all these limitations, and the fact that the PDS supplies only a fraction of the household's foodgrain needs, informants did not want the PDS discontinued. The argument was simple. In the words of one of the poor labourers, "It may save us only one rupee, but it is a rupee saved. If it is closed, the money will be diverted to the rich. Even this will not come to us" (Srivastava, 1998).

1. Integrated Child Development Scheme (ICDS)

The scheme caters to the nutrition and health needs of young children, and pregnant and lactating mothers. Take-home rations are provided on a weekly basis to pregnant and lactating mothers and 0-3 year-children. The Auxiliary Nurse and Midwife (ANM) is supposed to visit the ICDS centre and carry out medical check ups for women and young children. *Anganwadi* workers are appointed on the recommendation of a village development committee with eligible women from the following categories being recruited according to priority: widows, deserted women and women below the poverty line.

Visits to ICDS facilities in 35 villages spread over 13 districts (SLC, 1998) and Participatory Rural Appraisal Studies in three districts of eastern and southern Uttar Pradesh (Kozel and Parker, 1998) bring out a number of weaknesses in the functioning of the *Anganwadi* centres: (i) The centres are often located in well-off localities and the *Anganwadi* workers belong to the upper castes. This lowered the possibility of participation by the poor and the malnourished belonging to the lower castes; (ii) Most of the centres did not function on a regular basis. Both early learning and the distribution of nutritional supplements were taking place very sporadically and on a very small scale; (iii) Contrary to what was commonly believed, there was a ready market for diversion of the nutritional supplements; (iv) The bane of the programme was the large number of posts that were lying vacant, both at the supervisory level and at the level of the anganwadi worker.

The Mid-day Meal Programme was introduced as a central government scheme in Uttar Pradesh in 1995-96. The programme aims at providing a nutritional supplement through a mid-day meal that will also provide an incentive for school participation and attendance by school-going children. The state government has opted for providing a monthly ration of three kg of foodgrain to school-going children whose monthly attendance is certified as being a minimum of 80 per cent. The distribution of the grain is handled by the ration shop and is certified and monitored by the school teacher.

An early assessment of the scheme in two districts of eastern Uttar Pradesh (Srivastava, 1996) showed a positive impact on enrolments: teachers and local community members reported that effective enrolment rates had gone up by 20 to 25 per cent in areas where the school rations had been regularly received and distributed. But teachers were concerned that the quantity of rations once decided could not easily be varied during the school year. Community pressure on the enrolment of under-age children was another factor mentioned by them. Discussions with community members and elected panchayat leaders also confirmed a positive impact on enrolments. Nonetheless, officials expressed a number of concerns, in particular the pressure on teachers to enrol under-age children and certify the attendance of students.

2. Freedom from Fear of Violence and Social Security

In Uttar Pradesh, the concern for social security should begin with the concern for the most fundamental right of any human being: the right to life. If development is about improving the quality of life, the issue of violence should be a major concern of social security.

Yet it is, unfortunately, what Dreze and Khera (1999) call, 'something of a blind spot in development studies'. They view protection from violence in the framework of the 'capabilities approach': a perception of security and freedom from fear enhances a person's efficiency. Viewed from this perspective, crime statistics reflect the widespread insecurity in Uttar Pradesh. After Madhya Pradesh, the state reported the largest number of crimes among all states in 1998. At the all-India level, crimes went up by 3.4 per cent between 1997-98, in Uttar Pradesh the increase was recorded at 20.7 per cent (Table 12).

The threat to women's security takes many forms: foeticide, female infanticide, molestation, rape, kidnappings, dowry harassment and murders and other forms of domestic violence. Women are very often the first targets in caste and communal violence (Srivastava, 1999). Crimes and the consequent insecurity have particularly adverse implications for women and girl children. Their mobility and access to education and health get severely restricted. Opportunities for political participation shrink even further.

As Table 13 reveals, the cases of violence against women have been increasing. The National Crime Records Bureau in its report for 1994 stated, in what is a damning indictment of our judicial system, that "There is a low level of conviction and very high level of acquittal. Out of total cases in which trials were completed, 41.5 per cent ended in conviction in 1990, 34.2 per cent in 1991, 33.8 per cent in 1992, 30.3 per cent in 1993, and 30 per cent in 1994. Acquittal is showing an increasing trend over the years. The rate of disposal of cases in court was 23.9 per cent in 1992, 16.8 per cent in 1993, and 17.7 per cent in 1994. On an average, 80 per cent of cases remain pending for trial. This is a disquieting situation."

V. SOCIAL SECURITY AND ISSUES OF GOVERNANCE

The success of social security measures depends, *inter alia*, on three parameters: correct formulation of schemes, adequate finances and strong governance. They are not mutually exclusive in so far as they are all rooted in the political economy of the state and influence and impact on each other. Nonetheless, it is

Table 12
Incidence and Rate of Cognisable Crimes (IPC) under Different Crime Heads and Percentage Variation during 1997-98

	Incidence	Rate	Percentage variation	Incidence	Rate	Percentage variation
	Murder			Attempt to commit murder		
UP	8303	5.1	7.1	8497	5.2	21.6
All-India		4	3	30707	3.2	4.7
	Kidnapping			Dacoity		
UP	4369	2.7	17.6	1207	0.7	19.5
All-India	23504	2.4	7.3	8064	0.8	2.5
	Preparation & assembly for dacoity			Robbery		
UP	111	0.1	-15.3	5342	3.3	19.8
All-India	1263	0.1	20.4	23565	2.4	6.4
	Burglary			Theft		
UP	12072	7.4	22.9	33290	20.3	19.6
All-India	119130	12.3	5.1	287792	29.2	3.9
	Riots			Criminal breach of trust		
UP	7851	4.8	41.8	3867	2.4	25.1
Total	91201	9.4	-0.7	16186	1.7	7.4
	Cheating			Counterfeiting		
UP	4641	2.8	28.7	71	0	24.6
All-India	38173	3.9	8.4	1353	0.1	-39.3
	Arson			Hurt		
UP	1220	0.7	-1.2	14269	8.7	-10.8
All-India	13083	1.3	5.8	235513	24.3	3.1
Other	IPC crimes			Total cognisable crimes under IPC		
UP	64088	39.1	25	284461	112.4	20.7
All-India	744769	76.7	2.6	1779111	183.3	3.4

Source: Crime in India, 1998, National Crime Records Bureau, Ministry of Home Affairs, Government of India, New Delhi.

Table 13
Incidence and Rate of Cognizable Crimes (IPC) against Women and Percentage Variation during 1997-98

	Incidence	Rate	Percentage variation	Incidence	Rate	Percentage variation
	Rape			Kidnapping & abduction of women		
UP	1605	1	10.2	2882	1.8	17.2
All-India	15031	1.5	-2	16381	1.7	4.9
	Molestation			Sexual harassment		
UP	2423	1.5	19.8	2571	1.62	348.6
All-India	31046	3.2	0.9	8122	0.8	40.1
	Dowry deaths			Cruelty by husbands and relatives		
UP	2229	1.4	24.8	5113	3.1	50.7
All-India	6917	0.7	15.2	41317	4.3	12.9

Source: Crime in India, 1998, National Crime Records Bureau, Ministry of Home Affairs, Government of India, New Delhi.

analytically useful to draw a distinction between them. In this section we argue that while there are many ways in which the design of social security schemes can be faulted, and finance in a resource-starved economy will always be a constraint, it is really a crises in governance that has perpetuated poverty and stagnation and has made social security cover for the poor an elusive dream.

1. Changing Approach to Development

The more things change, the more they remain the same. Nowhere is this more strikingly true than in the state of Uttar Pradesh. It is not that there has not been any change; in fact, the last decade has seen tumultuous and dramatic changes in the social and political spheres. The rhetoric of poverty alleviation has resulted in a battery of schemes for the poor. Nonetheless, as far as the lives of the poor are concerned there has been no significant change.

There has been a paradigm shift in our approach to development over the years. Growth and the trickle down that it promised to the poor failed in the initial years of our planning. The realisation that growth must be tempered with redistributive concerns and that a single-minded pursuit of growth would not banish poverty resulted in the appreciation of the basic needs-approach to development, which aimed at the achievement of a certain specific minimum standard of living. The approach changed, new policies were worked out, but poverty stubbornly refused to go away. With the persistence of poverty came the awareness that unless a direct attack was made on poverty it was not going to loosen its stranglehold. With this thinking as its basis an armoury of poverty alleviation programmes was inaugurated.

The changing terms of this discourse on development, and the changes in policies and programmes show that if nothing else, policy making in this country has not been rigid and inflexible. Moreover, the design of the programmes and the changes made in them from time to time reflect some sensitivity, at least on paper, to ground-level social realities.

The expenditure on social security measures in rural areas, though nowhere near what is required in terms of needs, has been high (Table 14). Moreover, as the Table shows, even the allocated expenditure has not been fully utilised. Dreze and Gazdar (1997) have demonstrated that proportions of government expenditure allocated to health and education, for instance, are similar in Uttar Pradesh and south India. In absolute terms as well, differences in per capita expenditure on social services is not high but the outcomes are markedly skewed, with Uttar Pradesh trailing far behind.

It is striking that programmes to ensure social security to the poor appear to have been flexible and responsive, at least in concept, to needs and criticisms. What is equally striking is that they have hopelessly floundered in the field. Why is it that policies that look so perfect on paper, work so imperfectly in the field? While it is true that the design of the schemes may leave much to be desired and funds in a resource-constrained state will never match the needs, the real problem lies elsewhere. It is located in a crisis of governance.

2. Failure of Governance

Governance is a catch-all word that implies existence of appropriate and just policies, rules, regulations, legislation, transparency, accountability and a respect for the rule of law. In its essence, the key components of governance would be a long-term vision, a commitment to the vision and capacity to implement it. Vision in a democratic polity refers to a shared vision that is

Table 14
Expenditure on Safety Net Programmes in Uttar Pradesh

(Rs. million)

Programme	1995-96			1996-97			1997-98		
	Release	Funds available	Expenditure	Release	Funds available	Expenditure	Release	Funds available	Expenditure
1. Employment									
(a)JRY	4730.1	5661.6	4812.2	4115.7	5391.6	4212.3	8722.8	9716.1	7716.8
(b) EAS	4505.0	5775.4	4066.5	2656.2	3772.2	1983.3	2139.0	3432.6	2316.7
2. Housing	2732.8	3330.5	2884.1	2510.8	3579.8	2767.5	2550.0	2582.9	2328.3
3. IRDP	2098.8	2460.7	2126.6	1840.2	2810.6	2145.6	1759.5	2840.1	1926.6
4. Social assistance									
(a) Old-age pension		1390.0	772.6		1110.8	5884.9		572.6	354.6
(b) Family benefit		332.0	151.1		341.1	154.3		314.7	190.5
(c) Maternity benefit		234.1	898.5		289.5	155.9		177.7	127.0
5. Food and nutrition (ICDS)		1418.1	1122.9		1044.4	921.3		1540.9	838.8

Source: Departments of Rural Development, Social Welfare and ICDS, Uttar Pradesh.

evolved "through formal and informal processes of discussion/negotiations with various classes and social groups, e.g. political leaders, bureaucrats, private entrepreneurs, donors, NGO's, mass organisations, other pressure groups, etc. " (Shobhan, 1998). Good governance also means commitment by the authorities to take hard decisions to concretise the vision. The third feature of good governance is the capacity of the authorities to implement the vision, where capacity would hinge on, among others, factors such as inherited institutions, or cultural values.

In Uttar Pradesh, the failure of governance has been a comprehensive failure in all the three components. There has been no visionary leadership. Successive governments have lacked an overarching vision and commitment to reduce poverty or ensure the rights of the poor. The biggest failure has been in capacity building. In fact, the capacities of most existing institutions are being systematically eroded. The law and order situation is in a state of near collapse. Financially the state is in a mess. There are no systems of accountability or transparency. Mechanisms of accountability exist only on paper, where neither merit rewarded nor malfeasance penalised.

In the wake of pervasive disillusionment with the past record of governance in the state, does the devolution of power to panchayats offer any hope for improved social security for the poor?

The question is not rhetorical. Top-down approaches of development failed because they did not involve the people in decision making. Devolution is an important means of involving people as active agents of change. It allows people to influence and control the decisions that affect their lives by increasing local participation in decision making. It is in the area of decentralisation that the state has moved forward fastest and where these moves have generated most controversy. The Uttar Pradesh government declared 1999-2000 the 'Year of Decentralisation' and transferred the functions of 31 departments to the panchayats, strengthening their control over schools, health care centres, *anganwadis*, village infrastructure development and so on. If panchayats become genuine institutions of democracy whereby the poor get a voice, and if they can improve the delivery of services like primary education and health, if they can make surplus land available to the vulnerable, they can indeed go a long way in not only providing a social security blanket but genuinely empowering the poor.

There is no doubt that decentralisation must be encouraged and extended. At the same time, the experience of the past few years has sounded warning bells which must be heeded if decentralised units are not to become miniaturised photocopies of the same elite-dominated, saturated-to-the-gills-with-corruption model existing at the top. There are many indications that this may in fact be the trend in many parts of the state.

Firstly, field reports from an ongoing research programme sponsored by the Planning Commission in eight districts of Uttar Pradesh suggest that in many villages, *gram sabha* meetings are rarely held. When they are, there is little participation and the planning, selection of sites and implementation of development works is done arbitrarily by the dominant groups.

Secondly, systems of audit are weak and have still not been put in place in the PRI structure to effectively handle the workload that has increased dramatically with decentralisation. While the handling of accounts at the district level is weak and ineffective, at the village level it is 'virtually non-existent'. This is fast leading to a 'decentralisation of corruption'. Corruption and power have intimate links with violence. As enhanced resources flow into panchayats without adequate audits and checks, the opportunity grows for the elected functionaries to make quick money and wield power. Stakes in elections rise. Elections to be fought not contested, as the large scale violence in the panchayat elections in Uttar Pradesh, held in June 2000, testify. Some people, including candidates and policepersons, were killed and several others wounded. There was police firing and reports of abduction of candidates. In one village in Allahabad district where intimidation did not stop the lower castes from fielding their candidates, there was violence and almost all the lower caste families had to flee the village in terror. Country liquor, money and other enticements were distributed to win votes. There were reports of deaths and blindness caused by consumption of spurious liquor distributed by contestants.

The portents are ominous. "Panchayati Raj", notes the editorial in the July 2000 issue of *Panchayati Raj Update*, "has failed to produce a different political culture." Further it observes: "...What kind of panchayats will such large scale violence produce? Despotic rule of the *pradhan* is one sure outcome. Panchayats will not function democratically. Corruption will rise. The *gram sabha* will be reduced to a farce. In sum, Panchayati Raj will become an instrument of oppression and exploitation. This is not self-rule but self-denial—for the silent majority."[3]

Finally, it may be said that there are limits to what can be achieved through 'state sponsored' solutions. Measures such as this, which do not alter the basic power equations and leave control of resources by the rich unaltered, suffer from inherent constraints. So long as the poor continue to be assetless, economically marginalised and heavily dependent on their exploiters, there is little hope of any real transfer of power to the poor—least of all poor women. Other measures to improve the economic condition of the poor—distribution of land, enhancement of non-farm employment opportunities, land improvement programmes and so on—are needed to enable them to exercise power more effectively.

These concerns need to be addressed if panchayats are to play their legitimate role as truly democratic institutions of governance.

Notes

1. The evidence comes from qualitative studies conducted in some of the poorest districts of Uttar Pradesh and Bihar in 1997-98. The districts are Allahabad and Gorakhpur in eastern Uttar Pradesh and Banda in the Bundelkhand region (Kozel and Parker, 1998; Srivastava, 1998). This qualitative study in the first phase was followed by an expanded quantitative study in the second phase, which covered 2250 households in 120 villages in 25 districts of Uttar Pradesh and Bihar. This study was called the UP-Bihar Household Survey of Living Conditions (referred to in this paper as SLC, 1998). For this paper, only the data canvassed from Uttar Pradesh (not Bihar) has been used for the analysis. Both the studies were sponsored by the World Bank.
2. A landless labourer's comment in the Allahabad study (Srivastava, 1998).
3. "Editorial", in *Panchayati Raj Update*, Vol. 7, No. 7, July 2000, Institute of Social Sciences, New Delhi.

References

Dreze, Jean and Amartya Sen (1989), *Hunger and Public Action*, Clarendon Press, Oxford.

—— (1991), "Public Action for Social Security", in Ahmad et al., *Social Security in Developing Countries*, Oxford University Press.

—— (eds.) (1995), *India: Economic Development and Social Opportunity*, Oxford University Press, Delhi and Oxford.

—— (eds.) (1997), *Indian Development: Selected Regional Perspectives*, Oxford University Press, Delhi.

—— and Harris Gazdar (1997), "Uttar Pradesh: The Burden of Inertia" in Dreze and Sen (eds.).

—— and Reetika Khera (1999), *Crime, Gender and Society in India: Some Clues from Homicide Data*, Working Paper No 66, Centre for Development Economics, Delhi School of Economics, Delhi.

ESCAP (1992), *Social Development Newsletter*, No. 29.

GOI (1997a), *Focus on the Poor: Guidelines for the Implementation of the Targeted Public Distribution System*, Ministry of Food and Civil Supplies, Government of India, New Delhi.

—— (1997), *A Report on Concurrent Evaluation of Jawahar Rozgar Yojana* (June 93-May 94), Ministry of Rural Areas and Employment, Government of India, New Delhi.

—— (1999), *Swarnjayanti Gram Swarozgar Yojana: Guidelines*, Ministry of Rural Development, Government of India, New Delhi.

Guhan, S. (1994), "Social Security Options for Developing Countries", *International Labour Review*, Vol. 133, No. 1.

Kozel V. and B. Parker (1998), *Poverty in Rural India: The Contribution of Qualitative Research in Poverty Analysis*, World Bank, Washington D.C. *(mimeo)*.

Lieten, G. K. and Ravi Srivastava (1999), *Unequal Partners: Power Relations, Devolution and Development in Uttar Pradesh*, Sage Publications, New Delhi.

Mahendra Dev, S. (1996), "Social Security for Indian Workers: Performance and Issues", *The Indian Journal of Labour Economics*, Vol. 39, No.4, October-December.

NSSO (1996), *Level and Pattern of Consumer Expenditure*, Fifth Quinquennial Survey, NSS 50th Round, 1993-94 , Department of Statistics, Government of India, Delhi.

Shankar, Kripa (1994), "Jawahar Rozgar Yojana: An Assessment in UP", *Economic and Political Weekly*, Vol. 29, No. 29.

Sharma, Alakh N. (1997), *Trends in the Structure and Pattern f Employment and Unemployment in Indian*, Working Paper series No. E/188/97, Institute of Economic Growth, Delhi.

Shobhan, Rahman (1998), *Crisis in Governance: A Review of Bangladesh's Development 1997*, Centre for Policy Dialogue. University Press, Dhaka.

Srivastava, Nisha (1998), *"Only God Can Save Them: Understanding the Multiple Dimensions of Poverty"*, Project on Qualitative Dimensions of Poverty in UP and Bihar, World Bank, Washington D.C. (mimeo).

—— (1999), " Exposing Violence Against Women: A Campaign Against Domestic Violence in Uttar Pradesh", *Economic and Political Weekly*, February 20.

Srivastava, Ravi (1996), *Agricultural Reforms and the Rural Poor in Eastern Uttar Pradesh*, Background Paper, India Country Economic Memorandum, World Bank, Washington, D.C.

—— (2000), *Food Security and the Targeted Public Distribution System in Uttar Pradesh*, Paper presented at Seminar on *Food Security in India: The Emerging Challenges in the Context of Economic Liberalisation*, Organised by the Institute for Human Development, New Delhi.

Subba Rao, K. *et al.* (1997), *Safety Net Programs and Poverty Reduction: Lessons from Cross-Country Experience*, World Bank, Washington, D.C.

Subba Rao, K. (1998), *Anti Poverty Programmes in Uttar Pradesh: An Assessment and Reform Options*, The World Bank, Washington D. C. (mimeo).

World Bank (1998), *Reducing Poverty in India: Options for More Effective Public Services*, World Bank, Washington, D. C.

21

Social Security in Andhra Pradesh

S. Indrakant and M.C. Swaminathan

I. INTRODUCTION

In the developing world, large proportions of people lead lives of such deprivation, not transient but chronic, as to provide proof of the Hobbesian description of life as being 'short, brutish and nasty.' Social security in such a context has to have a wider canvass than of merely insuring against risks to the existing standard of life as in the case of the developed world.

The proportion of people working in the organised sector with a clear employee-employer relationship is very small in the developing world unlike in the developed world. A large proportion is incapable of protecting themselves through participation in the insurance or capital markets due to not only their poverty, but also their illiteracy and ignorance. Besides, sheer numbers make the task of providing them with any assistance a daunting task. Over one third of the population of India fall in the category of chronic poor. There is an equal proportion that fall into poverty in the years of low agricultural output, decline in employment or inflation.

Social security, as a legally enforceable right, exists only against transient risks to existing standards of life and that too only for the small proportion of people employed in the organised sector. To the very large proportion of people engaged in agriculture and other unorganised sectors of economic activity, there is only one such statutorily protective right, that of minimum wages under the Minimum Wages Act. For them, the rest is based on government programmes, which are subject to budget and other constraints, such as the honesty of implementing agencies, and are not legal rights that can be enforced.

Some measures are designed to protect existing entitlements of the vulnerable; these include the enforceable rights as well as some schemes for those in the unorganised sector like famine relief measures. The others are designed to enhance the entitlement baskets of those suffering chronic deprivation. These latter measures can be further categorised into those that aim to add to the entitlement basket straightaway and those that attempt to do so through measures of capacity building so as to make the enhancement sustainable. These various typologies are not mutually exclusive. Many schemes combine both types of efforts, but nevertheless it is useful to note these points.

In this paper an attempt is made to present a picture of the status of social security in Andhra Pradesh in the broader sense applicable to developing economies. Section II describes the social security provided to the workers in the organised sector. Section III presents an account of the working of the Minimum Wages Act, with respect to agriculture and other scheduled rural employments in the state. Section IV delineates the attempts to protect the entitlements of the vulnerable. Section V reports the findings of macro-and micro-level surveys on the Rice Subsidy Scheme. Section VI deals with the efforts to build capacities of the needy sections of society. Section VII describes efforts to enlarge the entitlements of the vulnerable. And, Section VIII concludes the discussion.

II. SOCIAL SECURITY IN ORGANISED SECTOR

The usual status employment (principal and subsidiary) in Andhra Pradesh was estimated at 29.56 million in the 45th round of the National Sample Survey Organisation (NSSO). The 1991 Census placed the number of workers at 28.45 million. Employment in the state public sector in 1991 was reported to be 1.2 million and that in the registered factory sector at about 0.7 million. Total employment in the organised sector was thus about 2 million or 7.5 per cent of total employment. Traditional social security measures thus cover less than one-tenth of the workers in the state.

Social security measures in the developed world cover against the following nine risks: unemployment, injury at work, sickness, maternity, medical expenditure, invalidation, old age, death of bread winner and the largeness of the family. The Indian labour laws cover eight of these; the exception being the last. The Industrial Disputes Act provides for compensation to workers retrenched due to closure of establishment or reduction of workforce. Reduction of workforce is often made difficult under provisions of this and other laws (Sick Industries Act, for instance). The Workmen's Compensation Act, 1923 and the Fatal Accidents Act, 1985 enjoin payment of compensation to a worker or his survivors in case of injury to or death of the worker. The Employees' State Insurance Act provides against sickness, maternity, injury in employment and for medical care and funeral expenses. The Maternity Benefit Act requires the granting of maternity leave with pay and assistance towards expenditure on child birth. The Employees' Provident Fund and Miscellaneous Provisions Act makes it compulsory for specified industries and classes of establishments to set up a Provident Fund. There are three components: the Provident Fund to which the employees and employers contribute, the Employees' Family Pension Scheme and the Deposit Linked Insurance Scheme. The Provident Fund accumulations with interest thereon are refunded on retirement or at death while in service; withdrawals therefrom are also permitted for specific purposes. Under the Employees' Family Pension scheme, the family is paid pension in case of death of the employee while in service. The Deposit Linked Insurance Scheme provides for insurance. The Gratuity Act makes it mandatory, in certain industries and classes of establishments, the payment of gratuity on termination of employment after a qualifying service.

Apart from these measures, there are programmes for enhancing the capabilities of workers, such as programmes for workers, education and upgradation of skill. There are many general criticisms of these provisions. The first is that these are piecemeal and do not provide for a comprehensive social security net under an integrated legislation. The second is that these cover only a small fraction of the needy population. There is also criticism from an entirely opposite point of view: there is so much of security of employment in these sectors that it has inhibited the growth of the sector and employment therein prolonging the misery of those who can not enter into it. The pressure for adopting an exit policy is growing on the ground that the most radical social security network provides job security for a minority at the cost of majority.

III. PROTECTION IN UNORGANISED SECTOR

The Minimum Wages Act, 1948 was enacted with a view to fixing minimum wages and regulating the conditions of work of those employed in the unorganised and sweated industries, i.e. industries in which labour is by and large unorganised or too inefficiently organised to bargain for itself. The Act requires the appropriate government, union or state, to fix minimum rates of wages payable to employees (defined as persons employed for hire or for reward to do any work, skilled or unskilled, manual or clerical, etc.) in an employment specified in part I or part II of the Schedule to the Act. The government may refrain from fixing rates of minimum wages in respect of any scheduled employment in which there are less than 1000 workers in the entire state. The scheduled employments number 52 in part I and 2 in part II, of which agriculture is one. The other employment in part II is employment in forestry and timbering operations. Among those in part I are grain and oil milling, weaving, carpentry, toddy tapping, tobacco processing including *beedi* rolling, shops and commercial establishments, eateries and restaurants, brick kilns, etc.

Section 4 of the Act lays down that the minimum wages fixed in scheduled employments may consist of: (a) a basic rate and a special allowance to neutralise variations in the consumer price index numbers applicable to such workers; (b) a basic rate of wages with or without neutralisation for cost of living and the cash value of supplies of essential commodities at concessional rates; and (c) an all inclusive rate allowing for the basic rate, the cost of living allowance and the cash value of concessions.

Minimum wages are prescribed on the basis of recommendations made by committees set for the purpose from time to time. The committees usually adopt a judicious balance of factors like the basic needs of workers, average number of earning members in a household, the general conditions prevailing in the industry, the prevailing wage rates and prices and the capacity of the industry to pay. The basic needs of workers are sought to be defined in terms of a minimum standard of living or minimum consumption levels such as calorie requirement of food, clothing and housing. Two general principles have been adopted in the last decade. These are: (a) minimum wages be adjusted for variations in the cost of living indices so as to maintain them at a constant level in real terms; and (b) workers be given a share in the fruits of development, the latter being defined as a part of the increase in GNP after allowing for further capital accumulation.

Agricultural labour is the largest proportion of workers covered under this Act. In Andhra Pradesh, wage rates in agriculture are fixed once in every two years. Wages are prescribed for different activities like ploughing, transplanting and harvesting. These rates vary between different zones, identified on the basis of the level of agricultural activities and the existing levels of wages. Labour Inspectors of the Labour Department monitor observance of the law. Based on the complaints received from the labourers offending landlords are to be prosecuted in labour courts.

The findings of an evaluation conducted in mid-1980s shows that more than 51 per cent of casual labour received less than the prescribed minimum wage (Government of Andhra Pradesh, 1987). A far higher proportion of women than men were short-changed in this respect. The reasons for a large proportion of workers receiving less than the legal minimum wages are lack of employment opportunities in the slack season, the low returns from agriculture, illiteracy and ignorance among workers about the provisions of the Act, and the remedial measures available therein. The basic issue was identified as one of raising demand for labour rather than that of enforcement of minimum wages. This requires carefully planned location and timing of works under the employment generation programmes which need to be taken up in the slack season and in areas where wage rates are depressed.

IV. SCHEMES TO PROTECT ENTITLEMENTS OF THE VULNERABLE

There are a number of schemes to protect the vulnerable against down side risks. Some of these can be further subdivided into ones that seek to reach those that cannot participate in the labour market and ones that protect entitlements of those who can participate in the labour force. The categories are however, not mutually exclusive, since some schemes cover both types, such as those under drought and other natural calamities. Public works in years of adverse seasonal conditions have been used in this part of the country for nearly two centuries as a self-targeting mechanism to ensure minimum entitlements for survival of the poor. In recent years these are not distinguishable from employment programmes undertaken to raise the level of demand for labour and thus provide employment for a larger number of days in all years irrespective of the behaviour of the monsoons. These are covered under a later section. The rice subsidy falls in the category of schemes aimed at protecting the entitlements of the vulnerable in all years primarily as a protection against loss of consumption due to rise in the prices of foodgrains.

There are schemes to protect the entitlements of those employed in the urnorganised sector in the state, though with a number of limitations. These cover downside risks arising out of (a) famine, floods and other natural calamities; (b) household factors such as destitution, old age, maternity; and (c) a persistent shortage of nutrition/income. Under the first category of natural calamities, assistance is provided for immediate consumption, for restoration of housing in case of floods, etc., and for employment in public works until the next monsoon in case of drought. Public works taken up to provide employment in years of failure of monsoon have sustained large number of people in the chronically drought affected areas of Rayalaseema and southern Telangana. The expenditure on relief (drought and other natural calamities) was

Rs. 350.16 crores during the Seventh Five Year Plan, with Rs. 141 crores in 1986-87 and Rs. 104 crores in 1989-90 being the peak outlays. In the five years ending 1999-2000, this outlay was Rs. 1047.5 crores.

There are a number of schemes to protect the entitlements of the poorest of the poor against household factors. The scheme for rehabilitation of beggars under the Andhra Pradesh Prevention of Beggary Act, 1979 maintains several beggar homes. There are 50 orphanages in the state to accommodate, in all, 5000 orphans. The 1991 Census count of orphans in the state is 93,000 in the 0-4 age-group, 90,000 in the 5-9 age-group, and 80,000 in the 10-14 age-group, making a total of 270,000. The accommodation in the orphanages in the state is, thus, far short of requirements. A part of the balance of this need is met by voluntary action, which is supported by the Social Welfare Fund to which the government proposes to contribute Rs. 81.75 lakhs during the Ninth Plan. Physically handicapped destitutes with no means of livelihood and indigent agricultural labour of 60 years and above are given a monthly pension of Rs. 30 a month and indigent widows a pension of Rs. 50 a month. These pension schemes have been integrated with the Government of India scheme of pensions introduced as part of the National Social Assistance Programme under which a pension of Rs. 75 a month is payable to poor persons above 65 years of age. The state government has planned to cover 8.96 lakh persons under this scheme against the GOI provision for 6.44 lakh persons. The 1991 Census age distribution for the state places 6.78 per cent of population in the 60+ age-group. The 1991 Census population of the state being 660 lakhs, and given the poverty levels, it is amply clear that the proposed coverage is far short of the number of people in need of such support. Another pension scheme introduced recently is one which pays Rs. 100 to all ex-servicemen and this does not have any means test. There is a special insurance scheme for rickshaw pullers under which the state government pays a premium of Rs. 5 per person for 1.40 lakh rickshaw pullers to provide them two types of cover viz., medical expenses upto Rs. 1,000 in case of occupational hazards and ailments, and Rs. 6,000 in case of incapacitation/death. Between 1995-96 and 1999-2000 this outlay has amounted to Rs. 586 crores.

There are a number of schemes aimed at poor women and children. The state government supports voluntary action to rehabilitate women in distress and children in need of care and protection to the extent of 45 per cent to supplement the union government's contribution of 45 per cent (with the balance 10 per cent to be met by the voluntary agency). There are 82 children's homes to look after orphan children each with a capacity to house 60 children. To rehabilitate *jogins* (women dedicated to temples as child brides), one home has been built. Of the 16,300 *jogins* nearly 7,500 have been covered under a variety of schemes such as old-age pensions, schooling, admission into welfare hostels, provisions of house sites and weaker section housing, assignment of land, TRYSEM and IRDP. An amount of Rs. 121 lakhs was spent during the Seventh Plan and Rs. 30 lakhs in 1996-97 on such schemes for the rehabilitation of *jogins*. Following the National Perspective Plan for Women, an integrated approach has been adopted to help poor women. Telugu Balala Mahila Kendrams (residential-cum-training complexs) have been built and set up in all the districts, each with a capacity to house 100 poor, destitute women and

30 children where they are provided boarding and lodging, trained in functional literacy, non-formal education, cooking, gardening, and other skills for an independent living. These *Pranganams* also run diploma and certificate courses for 100 unemployed women day-scholars in skills that are in demand such as mid-wifery, auxiliary nursing, secretarial practice, etc.

Women agricultural labourers are provided Rs. 900 in four monthly instalments during the high risk of the first and second pregnancies to make up for loss of wages in the two months preceding and two months following child birth for nutrition and medical expenditure. During this period they are also provided free medical examination, immunisation for themselves and the offspring, etc. This scheme has also been integrated with a similar scheme under the National Social Assistance Programme and proposes to cover four lakh women which, given the demographic features of the state (crude birth rate of 25, sex ratio of 972 and poverty ratio of less than one fifth among the major states) may cover the needy. A new scheme for the protection of the girl child has been introduced in the Budget for 1996-97 by which it is proposed to endow Rs. 5000 to every newborn girl child to be paid to her when she attains the age of marriage, i.e. 18 years (later enhanced to 20 years). The scheme is expected not only to protect the girl child during her growth but also to ensure that she is not married off before the legal age for marriage. The mean age at marriage being lower than the legal prescription as well as the mean in other states, this provision has been found to be significant. The amount provided in the budget is Rs. 25 crores which will cover 50,000 girl children born during the year.

The Integrated Child Development Services (ICDS) is an important scheme for protection of the entitlements of poor and undernourished children. It is an ambitious scheme for enhancing the health, nutrition and learning opportunities for pre-school children and their mothers by simultaneously providing all the required services at the village level. The scheme provides children below the age of six and pregnant and nursing mothers with (a) supplementary nutrition; (b) immunisation; (c) health check-ups; (d) referral service; (e) treatment of minor illnesses; (f) nutrition and health education; (g) pre-school education for children in the 3-6 age-groups; and (h) convergence of other supportive services such as potable drinking water, sanitation, etc. The critical impact objectives are (i) reduction in severe malnutrition among children of 6-36 months of age by 50 per cent, (ii) increase in the proportion of children of 6-36 months of age in normal and grade 1 status by 25 per cent, (iii) contribute to the reduction of infant mortality rate from the current level to 60, and (iv) contribute to reduction of incidence of low birth weight by 30 per cent. There are important supplementary components such as the scheme of Women's Integrated Learning for Life (WILL) in which literacy skills and knowledge of good health, hygiene, nutrition, family planning, home management and child care are provided; the IGA through which income generating activities are initiated and the Adolescent Girl's Programme under which three adolescent girls are provided supplementary nutrition on the scale of the pregnant/nursing mothers and are trained to be an intermediate agent between the ANM and the target group. The scheme has been described as India's gift to her deprived and underprivileged children for survival and development. Field visits to some of the *anganwadi* centres in Andhra Pradesh and Orissa reveal that, with some modifications, ICDS can play a key role in reaching targeted groups (Radhakrishna, et al., 1998). The cost of transferring one rupee income to the target group through ICDS scheme to the government is Rs. 1.76. The corresponding figure in case of PDS is over Rs. 4.

An analysis of the state government outlays on the four important components of entitlement protection schemes for the years 1995-96 to 2000-01 shows that the proportion of these outlays to the total outlays of the state government have declined sharply in the last few years (Table 1). They formed 10.9 per cent in 1995-96 and have been declining since then and have become 5.9 per cent in the budget for 2000-01.

Table 1

Budget Allocations for Protection of Entitlements of Vulnerable Sections

(Rs. in lakhs)

Sl. no.	Item	1995-96	1996-97	1997-98	1998-99	1999-00	2000-01
1.	Women and childwelfare	5348	8261	11350	14890	39286	21548
2.	Other social security and welfare	6036	9936	12442	13889	16281	17836
3.	Natural calamities	15395	31495	17509	25706	14646	20100
4.	Nutrition and PDS	115820	82009	68763	81460	109086	107981
5.	Total	142599	131701	110064	135945	179299	167465
6.	Total state outlays	1303588	1452374	1563030	1832879	2259391	2829926
7.	Per cent of item 5 to item 6	10.9	9.1	7.0	7.4	7.9	5.9

Source: Government of Andhra Pradesh, *Budget in Brief, 2000-01.*

V. RICE SUBSIDY SCHEME

The government of Andhra Pradesh introduced the subsidised rice scheme in the early 1980s to improve the consumption levels of the weaker sections of society. Households with annual income of less than Rs. 6000 were regarded as poor and were issued green cards. Other households were issued yellow cards. A household with a green card was entitled to 5 kg of rice per person per month subject to a ceiling of 25 kg at Rs. 2 per kg. Besides rice, they were entitled to sugar and kerosene also. A household with a yellow card, in the initial years, was permitted to purchase rice from fair price shops but at a higher price of Rs. 3.50 per kg. Later on, this facility was withdrawn. However, the yellow card holders were entitled to a higher quota of sugar and kerosene. Occasionally, edible oil is also supplied to the card holders through fair-price shops.

The scheme was modified by the Congress government in 1991. The green cards were replaced by white cards and yellow cards by pink cards. The ceiling on the rice for white-card holder was initially reduced to 16 kg. But later on it was again increased to 20 kg. On account of the increase in issue price by the

FCI, the state government increased the ration price to Rs. 3.50 per kg. After its victory in 1994 election, the Telugu Desam government restored the ceiling on rice to white-card holders to 25 kg. Further, the ration price was reduced to Rs. 2 per kg Again in August 1996, ration price was raised to 3.50 per kg and the ceiling was reduced to 20 kg per card. On account of the hike in CIP the ration price was further raised to Rs. 5.50 per kg.

Presently, there are 113 lakh white-card holders and 52 lakh pink-card holders in the state. The subsidised rice scheme covers nearly 70 per cent of the population while only 30 per cent of the population are estimated to be poor. Thus, the benefits of the scheme is enjoyed by non-poor households as well. At the same time, micro-level studies reveal that a large number of poor households do not have ration cards.

Over 40,000 fair price shops (FPS) are functioning in the state. Unlike in many other states, the network of FPS in rural Andhra Pradesh is fairly good. About 33,000 FPSs are catering to 27,000 villages in the state. In Andhra Pradesh, on an average, there is one fair price shop for every 1,750 persons as compared to the national average of one fair price shop for every 2000 persons. Each fair price shop, on an average, caters to 400 card holders. However, in the twin cities of Hyderabad and Secunderabad each fair price shop caters to over 700 card holders.

1. Central and State Subsidies

The subsidised rice scheme involves the provision of subsidy by both the state and the central government. The central subsidy per tonne increased from Rs. 534 in 1982-83 to Rs. 4,748 in 1998-99 (Table 2). This increase was partly due to regular enhancement in procurement price and partly due to rise in the administrative cost of FCI. The mounting buffer-stock is responsible for increase in the storage cost. During the same period, the state subsidy per tonne increased from Rs. 29 to Rs. 2512. It may be noted that in 1983-84, the state subsidy per tonne jumped by about Rs. 500 i.e. from a low level Rs. 29 to Rs. 523. This jump is on account of introduction of the subsidised rice scheme. Inspite of hikes in Central Issue Price, the Government of Andhra Pradesh kept the Retail Issue Price at Rs. 2 per kg. In 1991 it was raised Rs. 3.50 per kg but in January 1995 it was again reduced to Rs. 2 per kg. As a result, in 1995-96 subsidy per tone registered a peak level of Rs. 4,133. It declined during the later years as retail issue price was raised Rs. 3.50 per kg in August 1996. On account of the scheme, the government expenditure on subsidy substantially increased during the period under the study. In the year 1995-96 it touched a record level of Rs. 1,124 crores. It declined to Rs. 781 crores in 1998-99. However, in the following year the expenditure on subsidy again increased as Central Issue Price was enhanced from Rs. 7.50 per kg to Rs. 9.05 per kg in February 1999. The introduction of Targeted Public Distribution System (TPDS) in 1997 provided some relief to the state government. Under the scheme, 10 kg of rice per month per family living below the poverty line was released by the central government at half of the Central Issue Price. Consequently, the state government is able to obtain 20 per cent of requirement of rice at a reduced rate. In other words, the introduction of TPDS has merely amounted to a partial transfer of state burden to the centre. In March, 2000 the central government hiked the Central Issue Price of BPL rice from Rs. 3.50 to Rs. 5.89 per kg and of

APL rice from Rs. 9.05 to Rs. 11.78 per kg. This is likely to increase the subsidy expenditure of the state from Rs. 1100 crores to Rs. 1400 crores.

There are some critical studies on the extent of subsidy provided by the state government. For instance, Olsen (1989) has examined the cost involved in the subsidised rice scheme. She points out that in 1987-88 the subsidy on rice scheme was more than the entire state expenditure on public health, and it matched with the entire cost of elementary education in the state. Subba Rao (1987) found that in 1985-86, the cost to the state for providing Re. 1 worth of subsidy was Re. 1.

Table 2
Central and State Subsidy on Rice Scheme

(in Rs./tonne)

Year	Central subsidy	State subsidy	Total subsidy
1980-81	340	–	340
1981-82	429	–	429
1982-83	534	29	563
1983-84	667	524	1191
1984-85	749	725	1474
1985-86	773	613	1386
1986-87	804	818	1622
1987-88	809	994	1803
1988-89	817	809	1626
1989-90	1242	1390	2632
1990-91	1280	1512	2792
1991-92	805	1973	2778
1992-93	869	1206	2075
1993-94	967	1504	2471
1996-97	2371	3106	5477
1997-98	3296	2608	5904
1998-99	4748	2512	7260

Sources: 1. *Economic Survey*, Ministry of Finance, Government of India; 2. Budget Papers of Food Corporation of India; 3. Memorandum of Andhra Pradesh submitted to the 10th Finance Commission and Explanatory Memorandum of Andhra Pradesh Volume IV/2, pp. 240-241.

2. Utilisation of PDS

National Sample Survey Organisation (NSSO) in its 42nd round, i.e. 1986-87, collected information on utilisation of public distribution system. The results of the survey reveal that in case of rice and sugar, nearly 60 per cent of the rural households depend partially or wholly on PDS. In case of kerosene, the percentage is slightly higher (65 per cent) (Table 3). In urban areas, half of the households purchase rice and kerosene from fair price shops. Around 70 per cent of urban households visit FPS to purchase sugar. A rural household with a ration card, on an average, buys slightly over 4 kg of rice, and about half kg of sugar per person per month. If the total population is taken into account, the per capita quantity of rice distributed through the PDS would be only 2.5 kg. This reduction is mainly due to the fact that only white card holders are entitled to get rice. The per capita quantity of sugar distributed through PDS is only

0.33 kg. The difference in per capita quantity distributed through PDS and quantity purchased per user arises because of incomplete coverage of PDS. PDS rice forms only about 18 per cent of cereal consumption per household in Andhra Pradesh.

Table 3
Purchases from PDS

Item	Rural		Urban	
	Per capita quantity (kg/month)	Per user quantity (kg/month)	Per capita quantity (kg/month)	Per user quantity (kg/month)
Rice	2.52	4.24	1.98	4.23
Wheat	0.01	0.76	0.23	1.60
Sugar	0.33	0.56	0.56	0.65
Kerosene	0.38	0.53	0.65	1.26
Edible oil	0.09	0.19	0.14	0.27

Source: NSSO Report No. 362.

About a quarter of the households in rural areas could not buy rice and about 18 per cent could not buy sugar because they had either no entitlement or no ration card. The corresponding figure for kerosene is much higher (over 40 per cent). In urban areas half of the households could not buy from fair price shops either because they had no entitlement or no ration card (Table 4).

Table 4
Percentage of Persons having no Entitlement/Ration Card

Item	Rural	Urban
Rice	24.14	44.83
Sugar	17.53	53.82
Kerosene	41.60	53.42

Source: NSSO Report No. 362 and 355.

3. Leakages in PDS

Due to the policy of delivery of foodgrains at the doorsteps of FPS the leakages at the first level, i.e. at the FCI godown level, is minimal in the existing PDS network. The system of delivering the foodgrains at the doorstep of the fair price shop appears to be working reasonably well in most parts of the state. In Uttar Pradesh and Bihar, the FPS dealers have to lift their allotment from FCI godowns and transport it to their shops at their own expense. Consequently, leakages at the first level is high and often the foodgrains do not reach the villages.

The leakages at the second stage, i.e. village or town level, in Andhra Pradesh is likely to be substantial. The income of FPS dealers is very low. The dealers' gross margin per month varied in the range of Rs. 700-1165 (Indrakant, 1996). The FPS dealers tend to increase income through bogus cards, diversion of quantities not taken by card holders, etc. Venugopal (1992) found that in 1986, the number of ration cards in circulation (139 lakhs) exceeded the estimated number of households (121 lakhs) by about 15 per cent or by 8 lakhs. The leakages at the third level, i.e., household level, is not likely to be much because the price of rice in the fair price shop is much lower than the open-market price of coarse cereals.

4. Targeting of PDS

The extent of exclusion of poor persons and inclusion of non-poor persons in PDS can be gauged from a recent field study (Indrakant, 1996). The study covered two backward villages, viz., Nettampadu and Singtham, two developed villages, viz., Narsayapalam and Machavaram, and a moderately developed village, viz., Jaggasagar spread in the districts of Mahaboobnagar, Medak, Karimnagar and Guntur, respectively.

In the backward villages, nearly half of the poor (i.e., with monthly per capita expenditure below Rs. 182) did not posses white cards (Table 5). On the other hand, in the two developed villages almost all the poor households had white card. A large percentage of non-poor households in the developed villages also managed to obtain white cards.

Table 5

Coverage of Households under Rice Scheme in Selected Villages

	Nettampadu		Singtham		Jaggasagar		Narsayapalem		Machavaram	
Class	A	B	A	B	A	B	A	B	A	B
VP Rs.(0-137)	100.00	17.19	27.38	19.61	73.14	15.97	–	–	100.0	3.16
MP Rs. (137-182)	55.65	42.46	40.94	32.80	77.75	18.49	97.85	19.09	100.00	15.07
MC Rs. (182-228)	56.67	28.09	73.27	25.85	44.01	32.31	63.58	27.60	94.99	38.73
R Rs. (228-273)	38.95	7.24	21.47	10.62	39.68	16.23	2.54	23.86	77.71	15.48
VR Rs. (above 273)	–	5.02	–	11.12	–	17.06	24.82	29.45	38.24	27.56
Total	59.56	100.00	40.02	100.00	46.67	100.00	65.62	100.00	77.59	100.00

Notes: 1. VP=Very Poor, P=Moderately Poor, MC=Middle Class; R = Rich, VR = Very Rich.
2. figures in brackets represent PMCE.
3. A= Percentage of households covered by Rice Scheme, B= Percentage of households in the category.

Source: Indrakant (1996).

Cornia and Stewart (1993) have classified the errors of targeting into two types, viz., 'E' error, i.e., inclusion of non-poor in the scheme and 'F' error, i.e. exclusion of poor from the scheme. Table 6 presents the extent of these two types of errors in targeting in the five selected villages. In the two developed villages almost all the poor households are covered by the scheme. In irrigated areas, households having less than two acres have been issued white cards. There are many non-poor households having less than two acres of land. For the state as a whole, Venugopal (1992) has estimated that in 1983 there were about 30-45 lakh ineligible white card holders. In backward villages, both types of errors in targeting are large. A large percentage of poor households are excluded from the scheme while a sizeable percentage of beneficiaries of the scheme belong to the non-poor category. In developed villages, the scheme has provided access to food to most of the poor. However, a large percentage of beneficiaries are non-poor households (Table 6).

Table 6
Errors in Targeting in Selected Villages

Village	E' error (in %)	F' error (in %)
Nettampadu	39.36	30.48
Singtham	63.08	59.85
Jaggasagar	59.32	20.66
Narsayapalem	71.94	3.41
Machavaram	80.24	0.00

Note: Type E means percentage of non-poor households among the white-card holders. Type F means percentage of poor households not having white card. Households having monthly per capita expenditure less than Rs. 182 are considered as poor households.

Source: Indrakant (1996).

5. Impact of PDS

The subsidised rice income has improved income levels and calorie intake of the people. The magnitude of monthly income gain per person in the selected villages ranged between Rs. 5 and Rs. 14 during the first round (when the ration price of rice was Rs. 3.50 per kg) and between Rs. 8 and Rs. 20 during the second round (when the ration price of rice was Rs. 2 per kg (Indrakant, 1996). It formed about 3 to 6 per cent of per capita expenditure during the first round and 4 to 7 per cent of per capita expenditure during the second round. The extent of benefit is relatively more in the developed villages. Consequent to these income gains, poverty declined by 4 to 13 percentage points in the five selected villages during the first round. The extent of decline was of course larger during the second round. In three villages, the benefits match the cost of implementation of the scheme while in the remaining two villages, the cost of implementation exceeds the benefits derived from the scheme. In short, the impact of the scheme is not uniform across the five selected villages and the developed villages seem to have benefitted more than the backward villages.

Attempts have been made to provide macro-level estimates on gains to the poor from the scheme (see Table 7). The first estimate shows the net-gain after allowing for changes in the open-market prices brought about by reduction of supplies due to procurement as well as the farm income feedback effects on demand. The other estimates do not account for these secondary effects. The effects of the open-market prices become important because, of the bottom 20 per cent households, less than 14 per cent buy all their rice from the PDS, 56 per cent buy only a part of their needs from PDS and the other 30 per cent rely entirely on the open market (Parikh, 1994).

Radhakrishna et al., (1997) have estimated that per capita monthly gain in income due to PDS in 1986-87 was nearly Rs. 6 in rural areas and nearly Rs. 8 in urban areas. Consequently, there was 5 percentage point and 3 percentage point reduction in poverty in rural and urban areas of the state. With better targeting much better results could have been achieved. A more rational policy to provide

Table 7
Estimated Income Gain from Rice Subsidy for Poor

Source	Rural population	Per capita gain/annum (Rs.)
Radhakrishna & Indrakant (1988)	Bottom 40 per cent	23
Parikh (1994)	Bottom 20 per cent	31(1)
Howes and Jha (1992)	Bottom 20 per cent	35(2)
Hanumantha Rao & Jayashree (1994)	Below poverty line	15(3)

Notes: 1. Estimate of subsidy for those buying wholly and partly from PDS averaged out for all (including those not availing PDS) in bottom two deciles.
2. Estimate for separate two bottom deciles averaged.
3. Estimated benefit per household reduced to per capita assuming average household size of 5.

food security would be to issue larger quantities of foodgrains through PDS at a price higher than existing ones instead of issuing a small quantity of foodgrains at a highly subsidised price (Indrakant, 2000).

VI. SCHEMES FOR ENHANCING ENTITLEMENTS OF THE VULNERABLE

These schemes can be broadly divided into those which promote self-employment and those which promote wage employment. Among those intended to do the former are those who attempt to endow the needy with assets. There are schemes for distribution of government wastelands, especially to *dalits*. The Scheduled Castes Finance Corporation also acquires land for assignment to *dalits*. The corporation also funds land improvement ventures and digging of wells and acquisition of pump sets. These activities of the State Scheduled Castes Cooperative Finance Corporation (SSCCFC) are assisted by the National Scheduled Castes Finance Corporation. The state SCCFC also provides margin money for acquisition of assets as well as training for undertaking such income generating activities. The Girijan Corporation undertakes similar activities for tribals. It also assists in the marketing of minor forest produce gathered by them. The Women Finance Corporation and the Minorities Finance Corporation undertake similar activities for their respective clientele. The Integrated Rural Development Programme assists groups of poor women to undertake gainful economic activities by providing them with a revolving fund and helping them market the products. An evaluation of the performance of this scheme found that non-poor had been covered, and that the rate of success was low due to lack of technical knowhow and marketing problems (Parthasarathy, 1995). In recent years, these women's groups are being assisted in building up of the required financial management capacities to enable them to access commercial credit.

The Integrated Rural Development Programme (IRDP) has been in operation for almost 20 years and there are many assessments of its performance. The findings of the Fifth Round of Concurrent Evaluation for Andhra Pradesh (Venkatramiah et al., 1997) shows that: the programme has covered 12 per cent of rural households; three-fifths of the assets of the old beneficiaries (those provided with assets prior to March 1994) are still in use; the average net annual income from these assets is less than two months wage earnings at the prevailing rate for agricultural field labour (man) in the state; the percentage of households with incomes below the poverty line of Rs 11,000 has declined from 75 per cent to 46 per cent; and the proportion of non-poor receiving IRDP assets is 25 per cent.

The NSS survey of participation in the IRDP (50th round, only 1993-94) shows that participation in Andhra Pradesh is less than half that in Maharashtra and only two-thirds of the all-India average. This could be due to the per capita investment being higher. However, there is no rising monthly per capita consumption; therefore, there is no particular preference for the poor (Table 8). The broad conclusion is that while it has contributed to the reduction of poverty in the state it has not been effective enough. As the programmes are top-down and paternalistic in nature, in recent years, attempts to involve the beneficiaries in the choice of schemes and in monitoring them are being made.

Table 8
Participation in IRDP and Public Works

MPCE (Rs.)	Per 1000 number of households: Receiving IRDP assistance			Practicing in public sector		
	Andhra Pradesh	Maharashtra	All India	Andhra Pradesh	Maharashtra	All India
< 120	24	63	60	14	130	75
120-140	33	115	72	25	119	65
140-160	28	65	66	36	86	67
160-190	43	107	69	64	95	65
190-210	40	95	68	46	107	66
210-235	45	66	61	40	105	61
235-265	38	90	67	59	90	61
265-300	57	91	66	55	86	58
300-355	34	63	55	51	61	49
355-455	44	64	62	37	53	52
455-560	32	46	56	27	72	52
560-and above	38	50	50	48	41	49
All 39	77	63	46	85	59	

Source : *Sarvekshana*, Vol. 21, No.4, April-June, 1998.

A new programme has been taken up in this state incorporating these lessons. The state government has set up a Poverty Eradication Mission with the name *Velugu* (light) to implement and monitor two internationally assisted poverty alleviation projects, the one for the urban poor being assisted by the Department for International Development (DFID), Government of United Kingdom and the other for the rural poor by the District Poverty Initiatives Project (DPIP) funded by the World Bank. These propose to innovate participatory methods through capacity building measures for community action by the poor. The Poverty Eradication Mission proposes also to take up research and documentation on participatory poverty alleviation processes and to provide a platform for advocacy in favour of micro and macro-policies benefitting the poor. DPIP is expected to make an impact on over three million families in 180 poor *mandals* in six drought-prone/tribal predominated districts over five years. It is also expected to influence the other programmes and institutions in becoming more receptive to the needs of the poor and thus generate a larger impact than that indicated by its coverage or outlays.

The rural employment programmes have, in general, raised employment levels and contributed to a rise in the wage rates. A large number of man days of employment are claimed to have been created in Andhra Pradesh. In 1995-96, 642 lakh mandays of employment at a cost of Rs. 317 crores was generated under JRY Programme (Table 9). In other words, to generate a day's employment, government spent around Rs. 50. During the same year, 252 lakh man days of employment with an outlay of Rs. 122 crore was created under the EAS programme. However, participation rate in these schemes is less than that for the country as a whole and about half of that in Maharashtra. Parthasarathy et al., (1998) have concluded that in 1989-90 the Jawahar Rozgar Yojana in Andhra Pradesh could cover only 16 per cent of unemployment. The NSS survey shows that there is no inverse relationship between participation in these employment schemes and monthly per capita consumption expenditure. This could be due, *a priori*, to wrong allocation of funds or to the concern for the quality of assets built, resulting in the substitution of manual labour by materials and skilled labour or finally to leakages (Swaminathan, 1999). It is obvious that these schemes, have become works-oriented and therefore contractor-friendly, instead of raising employment levels for unskilled labour. Rural Employment Guarantee Schemes (REGS) introduced in 1981 and again in 1994 enthused the poor into registration under the scheme and attracted approval and preference over the

Table 9
Rural Development in Andhra Pradesh and India

(Rs. in Lakhs)

Programme	Andhra Pradesh		All-India	
	1995-96	1996-97	1995-96	1996-97
IRDP				
Amount utilised	8624	6434	107716	59001
Credit disbursed	9402	7740	170133	99299
Number of beneficiaries	122863	96817	2089600	989639
SC %	35.5	31	33.8	34
ST %	10.4	10.1	14.8	11.4
Women %	25.5	32.7	33.4	33.1
Handicapped %	1.3	0.7	0.6	0.4
JRY				
Total expenditure (Rs. in lakhs)	31706	17488	396608	215693
Emp. generated (lakh mandays)	642	49	7956	3691
EAS				
Total expenditure (Rs. in lakhs)	12250	25510	166085	210221
Emp. generated (Lakh mandays)	252	437	3339	3619

Source: Rural Development Statistics, NIRD, 1998.

other employment schemes from the academic community and non-governmental agencies in the field but were given up soon after introduction. The reason was the preference of the new governments for untargeted rice subsidy scheme over the self-targeting REGS.

VII. CAPACITY BUILDING MEASURES

Capability constraints limit the functionings of a large number of poor and vulnerable. Efforts are being made to enhance their capabilities to enable them to lead a long and healthy life. Most of the public expenditure on social services contribute to this end though all of it is not directed at the most deserving. In this direction an attempt has been made to identify such items that contribute to the building up of the capabilities of the vulnerable. While including all outlays on (a) water supply, sanitation, housing and urban development; (b) family welfare; (c) social welfare (SC, ST, BC), and (d) rural development, outlays on items other than primary education in the education sector and on medical education training and research have been excluded. These exclusions have been made on the ground that the excluded items do not contribute to the building up of the capabilities of the vulnerable. Table 10 shows the outlays and their proportion to the total outlays. The proportions rose from 22.2 per cent in 1995-96 to 26.7 per cent in 1998-99 but have since then come down to the level of a little less than 22 per cent. An analysis for an earlier period, the Seventh Plan, estimated that the benefit to the rural population from these expenditures was Rs 7.75 per month which constituted 9 per cent of the per capita income of rural poor (Parthasarathy et al., 1998).

Table 10

Budget Outlays on Building Capabilities of the Vulnerable in A.P.

(Rs. lakhs)

Item	1995-96	1996-97	1997-98	1998-99	1999-00	2000-01
1. Water supply, sanitation, housing and urban development	31763	51583	62712	99687	65942	110951
2. Medical and public health	56294	69719	79736	98221	122385	137463
3. Family welfare	12907	16830	16576	22074	22282	29520
4. Elementary education	73316	85792	95153	35652	45865	43410
5. Welfare of SC, ST, BC	56498	61638	65918	85758	106176	123917
6. Rural development	58206	72954	98489	148624	150489	116438
7. Total (1 to 6)	288984	358516	418584	490016	513139	561699
8. Total budgetary outlays	1303588	1452374	1563030	1832879	2259391	2829926
9. Per cent of item 7 to item 8	22.2	24.7	26.8	26.7	22.7	19.8

Note: 1. Includes both Revenue and Capital Expenditure; 2. Medical and health excludes outlays on teaching, hospitals, research and training.

Source: Budget in Brief, 2000-01, Government of Andhra Pradesh.

The impact of these expenditures in terms of improvement of the health and education conditions of the poor do not show noticeable results. The infant mortality rate in the state is 75 in rural areas, 38 in urban areas and 66 for rural-urban combined as against 77, 45 and 72, respectively for India and 15, 17 and 16, respectively for Kerala. In respect of IMR the state ranks 8th among the 15 major states in India. The maternal mortality rate is also at a high figure of 159.

The number of persons who are illiterate (per thousand), aged 15 and above is 646 in the rural areas, 284 in the urban areas and 551 for both areas combined. The state has the fourth highest illiteracy rate among all the states of India. The proportion of illiterates among females is 772 in rural areas and 384 in urban areas. The number per thousand persons between age 5 and 14 not currently attending school is 568 in rural areas, 397 in urban areas and 522 for both areas combined. This proportion in the state is the sixth highest among all the states of India. The proportions are higher among females, 630 in rural areas and 430 in urban areas. The proportion of poor is estimated at 29 per cent in rural area and 31 per cent in urban areas (World Bank, 1997).

In terms of the index of health status, taking into account four factors, namely crude birth rate, crude death rate, infant mortality rate and longevity, Andhra Pradesh ranks at 6 in 1990 (Hanumantha Rao, 1993). An index of educational status of rural areas of 17 major states, compiled as a weighted sum of the percentage distribution of the population by education status, ranks this state at 14 in 1991. This rank has declined since 1971.

Many attempts are being made to set right this poor situation. In the last two years the government of Andhra Pradesh has been running summer camps for out-of-school children school to prepare them to get back into school. This has been undertaken in collaboration with a non-governmental organisation, the M.V. Foundation, in its efforts to draw working children back to schools through community action. In the new World Bank aided District Poverty Initiatives Project one component is to bring children-at-work back to school through preparatory schooling and community action. It also has provisions for taking up of individual toilet and sewerage disposal arrangements in the villages covered by it. This project also has in-built provisions for capacity building for the communities in the areas of health and sanitation, and education including child labour. It also provides for training and supporting para-technicians in the areas of health and sanitation, education as well as agriculture and animal husbandry. There are several projects for improving sanitation and drinking water facilities.

The changing feature of poverty level in Andhra Pradesh indicates that while it declined fastest among all the Indian states of the union in the two decades between 1973-74 and 1993-94, the rate of decline slowed down in the second of the two decades over the first. This happened despite a large step-up in the outlays on poverty alleviation programmes and the introduction of the rice subsidy scheme. This could be due to the difficulty of reaching the lower rungs of the poor. Among other reasons could be cited the slackening of the growth rate and the weakening of the inverse relationship between growth and poverty. It has been pointed out that there are two key aspects in which the design of these schemes is defective. Firstly, they are 'soft options'; they seek to distribute renewable resources, subsidies, dual prices, etc., instead of the non-renewable resource of land (Vyas and Bhargava, 1995). Secondly, they do not involve a transfer from the non-poor to the poor; the costs for the benefits distributed are met out of revenues gathered through indirect taxes, mostly from the poor (sales tax and revenues and duties on cheap liquor) or saved from public investment that may have added to growth or to the capacity building of the poor.

VIII. CONCLUSION

In developing countries such as ours, the concept of social security needs to cover a wider set of situations than in the developed countries. Apart from downside risks to existing earnings, the raising of the levels of income and the quality of life need to be taken up. Social security is made available to employees of the organised sector consisting of employees of government, public sector and selected industries in private sector. There is perhaps a case for modifying the existing security of employment so that new enterprises are not disinclined to provide more employment.

In the rural areas there is a need to guarantee employment for the unskilled manual labour. Such a scheme cannot take off unless there is a commitment to pay compensation whenever employment is not provided to a seeker. Such a provision will not only strengthen the entitlement of the poor but also make the administration look actively for employment-oriented development processes. A general increase in the incomes of the poor will raise the demand levels for a number of goods, thus raising the performance of the economy of the state. The rice subsidy scheme can be tied up with this programme so that the subsidy is limited to the poor, since the identification of the poor becomes easy if it is linked to participation in the employment guarantee scheme. In fact, better food security can be ensured by improving the targeting and plugging of the leakages in the existing PDS. A more rational policy would be to supply a larger quantity of foodgrains through the PDS at prices higher than the existing ones, instead of issuing a small quantity of foodgrains at a highly subsidised price. The old, the sick, the handicapped and the destitute have to be covered under the National Social Assistance Programme (NSAP).

There is a need for a far greater effort in respect of the education and health sectors. The present position, with the state ranking among the lowest in these sectors, is a matter of concern. The ICDS programme holds a great promise in fighting malnutrition among children and mothers. The Vision 2020 Document of the state sets ambitious aims in this regard. These call for combined efforts of the state, civil society and the public at large.

References

Cornia G.A. and Frances Stewart (1993), "Two Errors of Targeting", *Journal of International Development*, Vol. 5, No. 5, pp. 459-490.

Government of Andhra Pradesh, (1987), *"Report on Evaluation of Implementation of Minimum Wages in Andhra Pradesh"*, Finance and Planning Dept., Hyderabad.

Hanumantha Rao, K. (1993), *Levels of Living in Rural India*, National Institute of Rural Development, Hyderabad, (mimeo).

—— and Jayashree (1994), "Food Insecurity and Impact of Programmes to Reduce It: Case of Andhra Pradesh", Paper presented at *Seminar on Food Security*, Padmavathi Mahila University, Hyderabad.

Howes, Stephen and S. Jha (1992), "Urban bias in the Public Distribution System", *Economic and Political Weekly*, Vol. 27. pp. 1022-1030.

Indrakant, S. (1996), *Food Security and Public Distribution System in Andhra Pradesh-A Case Study*, CESS, Hyderabad (*mimeo*).

—— (2000), "Food Security and Public Support : A Study of Andhra Pradesh", in Krishnaji, N. and T.N. Krishnan (eds.), *Public Support for Food Security—The Public Distribution System in India*, Sage Publication, Delhi.

Olsen, Wendy K (1989), "Eat Now Pay Later: Impact of Rice Subsidy Scheme", *Economic and Political Weekly*, Vol. 24, No. 28, pp. 1597-1611.

Parikh, K.S. (1994), "Who Gets How Much from PDS: How Effectively Does it Reach the Poor", *Sarvekshana*, Vol. 17, No. 3.

Parthasarathy, G. (1995), "Trends and Dimension in Employment and Unemployment in Andhra Pradesh ", in Sudhakar Reddy, S. and K. Lakshminarayana (eds.), *Review of Employment Trends and Programmes in Andhra Pradesh*, Centre for Economic and Social Studies, Hyderabad.

—— and V.M. Durgaparmeswari (1998), "Perspectives from States—Andhra Pradesh", in Rao, V.M. (ed .), *The Poor in Hostile Society*, Vikas Publishing House, Delhi.

Radhakrishna, R. and S. Indrakant (1988), "Effects of Rice Market Intervention Policies in India; The Case of Andhra Pradesh", in Johnson, J.K. (ed.), *Evaluating Rice Market Intervention Polices—Some Asian Examples*, Asian Development Bank, Manila.

Radhakrishna, R., K. Subba Rao, S. Indrakant and C. Ravi (1997), *India's Public Distribution System—National and International Perspectives*, Discussion Paper No. 380, World Bank, Washington, D.C.

Radhakrishna, R., S. Indrakant and C. Ravi (1998), *India's Integrated Child Development Services Programme—Assessment and Options for Reforms*, Centre for Economic and Social Studies, Hyderabad.

Subba Rao, K. (1987), *Interventions to Fill Nutrition Gaps at the Household Level: A Review of India's Experience*, Institute of Economic Growth, Delhi.

Swaminathan, M.C. (1999), "Poverty and Human Development in Andhra Pradesh", in Balakrishna, S. and S.V. Rangachari (eds.), *Poverty Decline and Human Development Factors in Some States*, National Institute of Rural Development, Hyderabad.

Venkatramaih, P., S. Galab, M. Gopinath Reddy and M.C. Swaminathan (1997), *Evaluation Report on the Fifthth Round Concurrent Evaluation of IRDP in Andhra Pradesh*, Centre for Economic and Social Studies, Hyderabad (mimeo).

Venugopal, K.R. (1992), *Deliverance from Hunger : The Public Distribution System in India*, Sage Publication, New Delhi.

Vyas, V.S. and Pradeep Bhargava (1995), "Public Intervention for Poverty Alleviation: An Overview", *Economic and Political Weekly*, Vol. 30, No. 41-42, pp. 2559-2572.

World Bank (1997), *Poverty in India Fifty Years After Independence*, World Bank, Washington, D.C.

22

Flexibilisation, Informalisation and Social Security for Labour in New Industrial Towns

G. Vijay

I. INTRODUCTION

India has witnessed significant structural changes in its economy over the last decade. The economic liberalisation and the consequent opening up of the market have resulted in the growth of new industries. Deregulation has provided an impetus to the process of change in the technology and business organisation of the firms, which has accelerated the process of what has been termed as flexibilisation and therefore informalisation in the new industries. The new industries have come into existence in neither the classical urban nor the rural pockets but in new townships. Growth of "informalisation" coupled with the phenomenon of increasing rural-new township migration in the post-structural adjustment period have made the conditions of labour highly vulnerable[1] (Ghosh, 1995). It can be observed that there is an inclusion-exclusion complex operating in the labour market, which is a conflicting process of development. It is a combination of inclusion in the opportunity and social security structures in the new townships for the different categories of rural unemployed on the one hand and their exclusion in different forms, on the other.

Flexibilisation is operationalised through casualisation and contractualisation of jobs. The casualisation and contractualisation of jobs has led to informalisation of the labour market, so that the formal institutions of social security such as the state, trade unions and skills have a marginal role to play. It is in the light of this, this paper tries to study the question of social security provided to labour in the organised sector in the context of its informalisation.

The following sections address questions such as: What are the insecurities faced by the labour? How vulnerable are the workers to the pressures of working and living environments in the context of informalisation of the organised sector? How is social security defined in an informalised setting? What are the emerging institutions of social security? What are the factors determining vulnerability of labour and their access to the institutions of social security? What is the structure of inclusion-exclusion complex?

II. METHODOLOGY

For this study, Kothur, a new industrial township located in Mahaboobnagar district, 30 kilometres to the south-west of Hyderabad, is selected. The district of Mahaboobnagar is well known for its *palamoor* labour, and has the dubious distinction of witnessing the highest seasonal migration in the country—over one million annually to different parts of the country. Paradoxically, the industrialised parts of the district witness massive inflow of migrant labour from different parts of the country. This paradox poses a challenge to research. Kothur, with a total population of over ten thousand, is the most industrialised township of Mahaboobnagar district, comprising 14 medium and large scale industries entailing a total investment of Rs. 1,6876 lakhs, and provides employment to 1,329 permanent and casual labour. The town has 27 small scale industries with a total investment of Rs. 528 lakhs, and provides employment to 982 permanent and casual labour. The small scale and medium and large scale industries employ 3,046 and 4,188 labourers, respectively on contractual basis.

The study is based on a sample of one large scale, two medium scale and four small scale enterprises, which have different modes of business organisation, use different technologies, recruit labour through different methods and produce different commodities. As stated above, the area witnesses massive in-migration. The migrant labour may be broadly classified into two categories based on the distance of place of origin into long and short distance migrants. The sample consists of 20 units of short distance, ten units of long distance migrant workers and five units of local workers, and includes two units of casual labour and the rest of contract labour. A study of five permanent labourers has also been carried out.

The data pertaining to the working environment have been collected through structured questionnaire, unstructured interviews, from the workers, the contractors and the managements (owners/managers) of the firms. The data on housing have been collected through the survey of 30 houses by way of a structured schedule, and data pertaining to water have been gathered through scientific tests, respectively. In respect of data on water, samples of water from tank, agricultural field and drinking water have been collected from various places in the specified manner in six bottles of one litre each. The samples have been tested for the presence of various chemicals, metals and radioactive substances through laboratory tests. The possible diseases caused by the presence of these parameters have been correlated with the actual diseases in the town. The data pertaining to disease pattern has been collected from the Employee's State Insurance Corporation ESIC-Med 6 and ESIC- Med 6A forms from the local ESI dispensary. The data relating to consumption expenditure, which also accounts for nutritional status have been collected from six *kirana* (grocery) shops where the labourers make monthly credit purchases called *khathas*. Rest of the data has been collected by the author during his one month stay at the Kothur new-township. Most of the analysis, therefore, is based on participant observation.

III. KEY ISSUES AFFECTING LABOUR

1. Insecurities of Labour

In order to conceptualise social security, the insecurities of the labour need to be comprehended. The labour in the new industries suffer from different types of insecurities. Besides the well-recognised insecurities like inadequate security of job, lack of minimum wage legislation, housing, health facilities, and absence of retirement and old-age benefits, there are several other insecurities to which the casual and contract labour are exposed. For new entrants to the labour market, gaining access to food and shelter is a problem, because to gain employment, an entrant needs information and a certain amount of credibility which is lacking. As a result, their accessibility to food and shelter gets reduced. All these factors make the prospect of staying in the labour market uncertain. Even after gaining employment, because of flexibilisation in the form of casualisation and contractualisation, there is employment insecurity, which implies irregular incomes. With specific reference to contractual jobs, there is no evidence to suggest that a worker has worked for a contractor. Workers often face the prospect of being cheated by not being paid their wage even after they start working. Any contingency which requires money makes the labour insecure. Moreover, since there is a perception that the migrant workers tend to monopolise the opportunities in the new industries, there is an antagonistic relationship between the migrants and the local labour. In such a situation, a migrant worker must have a strong base to be able to survive in a hostile social environment. These different insecurities, in turn, reflect varying degrees of vulnerability. In order to conceptualise the notion of vulnerability, there is a need to analyse the working and living environment of labour.

2. Working Environment of Labour

(i) Size of Organisation and Type of Management

As is evident in Table 1, factors that affect the working environment can be classified into different categories. It has been found that the working environment of labour is better in the large scale industries and worse in medium and small scale industries. It can also be observed that though a higher wage is paid in organisation with *Lala* type of management,[2] long working hours, absence of holidays, drudgery of work and work hazards[3] in these organisations suggest that the working environment here is worse than in smaller establishments. In the case of firms managed by professionals and yet where their owners pay frequent visits, wages are low, working hours are long, holidays are fixed but wages not paid for this period. Further, work here involves less drudgery and relatively less risk, and as such, working environment in such firms is relatively better than that in the firms with *Lala* type of management. In the case of group managed firms, the labour (a) do peripheral jobs like loading and unloading; (b) are paid minimum wages; (c) enjoy the benefits of ESI and PF; and (d) work less harder than in the *Lala* type of management firms and the firms where the owner pays frequent visits. One could, therefore, deduce that as the mode of business organisation becomes less personal, the conditions of the labour improve.

Table 1
Classification for Working Environment

Factor	Classification
1. Scale	Large & medium scale and small scale
2. Business organisation	*Lala* type of management, frequently visited by owner, group managed
3. Technology	Low level skill technology, medium level skill technology, high level skill technology
4. Distance	Long distance migrants, short distance migrants, and locals
5. Gender	Male and female

Source: Field study.

(ii) Technology

In the case of firms that involve low level of skills, which can be acquired in a week's time such as the pharmaceuticals, there is no scope for upward mobility of the workers, while in those with medium level technology, which takes about six months to learn, like in textiles and steel factories, there is a scope to enter *seth's khata*[4] or become a casual labourer with a fixed wage. Further, in case of the higher level technology which takes two years to learn, like in fibre glass industry, the *badli* system is prevalent which is also a type of casual labour but having a far better working environment than the casual labour in the medium range technology. It can therefore be concluded that the more complex the technology adopted by an organisation, or higher the level of skill required, the better is the working environment of labour.

(iii) Distance of Workplace from Place of Origin of Worker

Though the long distant migrant labourers are better paid, given the fact that they have long and compulsory working hours and no holidays, they do work that involves excessive drudgery and are prone to work hazards. The short distance migrant labourers on the other hand, though low paid, engage in work which involves less drudgery, have fewer holidays, and less work hazards than the former, and therefore are better-off than the long distance migrant labourers. Though the local labour is employed in some industries that started before 1990s, their work environment with respect to working hours, social security benefits and work hazards is far better in comparison with the long distant and short distant migrant labour.

(iv) Mode of Recruitment

The permanent employees enjoy better working environment than that of casual and contract labour. When compared to casual workers, the working environment of contract workers is relatively poorer.

(v) Gender

Female contract labour is paid low wages, employed in low skilled jobs, in comparison with the male contract labour, though they often work for 12 hours a day. However, work assigned to women does not involve hard labour and is not prone to work hazards. There is a trend towards feminisation of work

(Deshpande, 1992; Deshpande and Deshpande, 1997; Kundu, 1997; and for a critique see Banerjee, 1997) in a few industries such as the pharmaceuticals, electronics and ceramics.

3. Living Environment of Labour

(i) Poor Housing Condition

The houses of the migrant labour in the new townships are often small and congested. On an average, each house consists of a long living room (10 feet by 7 feet) in which four to five adults stay. Most of them are semi-*pucca* constructions with tiled or tin roofs and in some houses a wall of three feet is raised to provide for a kitchen. Eighty per cent of the houses do not have bathroom or latrine facilities and in some, a corner of a small room is used as a bathroom. In some others, small thatched roof with curtains are erected outside the house, which is used as a bathroom. Worse still, there are no sewage or drainage facilities, resulting in the clogging of drain during rainy season. People have to walk to a distance of up to half kilo metre to attend nature's call. Most of the houses have electricity and the approach roads to the houses are motorable mud roads.

(ii) Lack of Safe Drinking Water

During the early eighties, *Kothur cheruvu* (tank) was the major source of drinking water and there was a well in the midst of the village. However, in the late eighties and early nineties, due to lack of rains, the well dried up. With the rise of industrialisation, especially the textile and chemical industries, tank water is completely polluted. In the recent past, the village has been provided with a common tap, the water to which is supplied by a overhead tank. The water samples of the tank and the drinking water have been tested. The results suggest that the polluted Kothur tank water has percolated to reach the ground water thus making the ground water unfit for consumption. Since there is no other source of drinking water, all the residents of the township, of which those dependent on industries constitute 62.5 per cent, consume unsafe drinking water. This leads to a host of water borne diseases, such as dysentry, other infection, parasitic skin infections, diarrhoea and enteritis, disease of the teeth, and diseases of bones.

(iii) Low Nutritional Status

According to the nutrition experts of the National Institute of Nutrition, in their classification of work as sedentary, moderate and hard, the work of industrial workers falls under moderate work. Based on extensive research, the experts have arrived at a figure of 2875 kilo calories as the energy requirement of the industrial workers who do eight hours of work. The actual energy levels of the short distance and long distance migrants suggests that though both the categories are under-fed, the short distance migrants get 2372 kilo calories and the long distance migrants get 2494 kilo calories of energy. Thus, under-nourishment has to be analysed in the backdrop of the fact that industrial workers in Kothur work for 12 hours a day. Undernourishment over a period could lead to loss of weight in the early stages. Experts suggest that such undernourishment might not get reflected in any disease pattern but it does prevent the workers from performing efficiently due to weakness. However, the disease pattern suggests a vitaminosis and other deficiency status and anaemia as largely prevalent. This is a direct consequence of under-nourishment.

The social context of the long distance migrant labourers is very different from that of the short distance or local labourers. For the former, the first problem they encounter is language. They find it difficult to interact since they cannot communicate. It can be observed that as a result of this, the vegetable vendors and shopkeepers quote higher prices and discriminate the long distance migrant labourers. In addition, when both the long distance and short distance migrants compete with the locals at the common taps or at ration shops, the locals accuse them of coming from a different place and trying to dominate them. However, it can be observed that the short distance migrants have greater interaction with the locals than the long distance migrant labourers. As a result there is a lack of sense of belonging to the place of destination even after long years of stay. A case study, presented in Box 1, substantiates the point.

BOX 1

Social Context of Long Distance Migrant Labourer

Sishupal Singh is a 40 year old who migrated along with his wife and four sons to Kothur to get employed in a small scale tin box manufacturing factory. He has an assistant Mahender Singh who also migrated along with his family. Both stay within the premises of the factory in the small quarters provided to them by the owner. It is sixteen years since they have migrated to Kothur. On the eighth of February, five masked men came to their house early in the morning and after confirming the identity of Sishupal Singh, attacked him brutally with sticks. Hearing the shouts for help, Mahender Singh came out of the next door only to be injured severely on head. When enquired about the plausible cause of the attack, Sishupal Singh came out with an apologetic reply. He stated that the only three sources that could get him attacked were the villagers, the *mafia* or the owner himself. He said that he paid the *mafia* regular *chandas* and was a loyal worker so there was no reason to suspect the *mafia* or the owner. He said that there was a possibility that they initiated the attack, but maintained that generally the reasons for antagonising the villagers were to be found in tussles after consuming alcohol, having illicit relations or misbehaviour. He said that he had none of these qualities. Who attacked Sishupal Singh and Mahender Singh and the motive behind the attack was not clear until the police investigations proved that the villagers were behind the attack. The police stated that the attack was a fallout of a confrontation that Mahender Singh had with the local people six months back. Sishupal Singh owns a small piece of land close to the factory in which he is a contractor. The local villagers were using his open land for attending to nature's call. Mahender Singh had objected to this and there was a tussle. The case went to the police. However, there was a compromise between the two parties arrived at by the intervention of the *mafia*. Six months later the same villagers attacked Sishupal Singh and Mahender Singh. One can, therefore, see why they cannot identify themselves with Kothur village even after sixteen years of stay and still feel vulnerable.

Culturally, the long distance migrant labourers find themselves more alienated. The festivals which are considered important by them are different from those celebrated by the locals. Unlike the short distance migrant labourers, the long distance migrant labourers find the manner in which marriages performed to be very different. The long distance migrant labourers, especially those belonging to the upper caste from Uttar Pradesh and Bihar, complain that they cannot practise the caste system. This implies that some of the migrant labourers, especially the long distance migrants, are unable to reconcile with the changed relationships. The long distance migrants also face culture shocks unlike the short distance migrants since they cannot come to terms with the fact that women come out of their homes and work along with men.

While some workers are included in the mainstream of development assuring them benefits of a better working environment based on a better wage, limited working hours, less drudgery of work, and less work hazards, some workers are excluded from what could be characterised as a better working environment. Similarly, in the living environment as well, while some have the opportunity to enjoy the benefits of a better living environment, which is determined by better housing, water, nutritional, social, and cultural conditions, some are prevented from availing such an opportunity. Thus, the inclusion-exclusion gets expressed in different permutations and combinations of factors in the working and living environments. Based on the variables chosen to determine these environments, a scale of insecurity can be constructed.

IV. CONCEPTUALISING SOCIAL SECURITY

Social security is a very complex concept and connotes different meanings in different contexts. It has been defined in various terms by different scholars and institutions. According to the *Encyclopaedia Americana* 1983, (Vol. 26, No. 186), social security consists of "public programmes intended to protect workers and their families from income losses associated with old age, illness, unemployment or death. The term is sometimes also used to include a broad system of support for all those who, for whatever reasons, are unable to maintain themselves."

It has, however, been argued that "in studies on social security, 'society' is often understood as 'state' and accordingly 'public measures' are considered to be synonymous with state laws" (Leliveld, 1991). It is maintained that "by giving such a limited interpretation of 'society' and 'public measures' in the definitions, a whole range of mechanisms and forms of social security functioning at other levels (household, family, community, etc.) are overlooked". Alternatively, it is suggested that "'society' can easily be understood as a constellation of families, kin-groups, clans, villages and the state;... 'public' can also be interpreted as 'public action' which can be found at all levels of the society" (Leliveld, 1991).

The basic idea of social security is to use social means to prevent deprivation and vulnerability to deprivation. Deprivation and vulnerability are integral to the lives of many in the poor countries. In developed countries unfavourable outcomes in economic activity frequently mean real hardship but in poor countries they often lead to death or destitution. For many, severe deprivation is not merely a matter of an unfortunate fall from a previously more comfortable position but is a chronic state arising, for example, from the absence of any asset or resource that can ensure adequate livelihood. A crucial policy issue therefore is: how can lives and livelihoods be made more secure against adversity and deprivation. Accordingly, we define the objective of social security as to prevent by social means, very low standards of living irrespective of whether these are the result of chronic deprivation or temporary adversity. The term 'social security' may then be viewed as a measure of success in meeting this objective (Ahmad, et al. 1991).

It is also suggested that the term social security be used to indicate, perhaps illuminate, a set of social problems, rather than looking for clear boundaries of the concept. The social problems as understood by Beckmann relate to certain uncertainties that people in developing countries have to face: whether or not they will have enough to eat tomorrow, have a roof above their head, be cared for when they are ill, etc. In the most general sense, then, social security refers to "the efforts of individuals, kin-groups, villages and state institutions to overcome these insecurities".

In the new townships, these insecurities are overcome by resorting to different mechanisms through different institutions. In the organised sector, trade unions have been the only well inquired institutions for gaining access to social security. However, there is a clear shift in the types of institutions, which are classified into (a) collective and individual at one level suggestive of the nature of mobilisation to access resources; (b) formal and informal[5] suggestive of the nature of the hierarchical relation between the provider and the receiver of social security benefits; and (c) internal and external[6] suggestive of the evolutionary path of the institution.

The above classification and the related statistics indicate the emerging patterns of decreasing role for formal institutions and vice versa for collective and individual, internal and external informal institutions (Table 2).

Social security strategies may be classified into survival strategies and innovative strategies. Survival strategies, as the name suggests, is a defensive strategy to use resources with the objective of sustaining life, while the innovative strategy, is aimed at acquiring greater resources to supplement existing resources. All collective institutions with the exception of trade unions—Assistant Labour Commissioner's (ALC) office, caste, gender, and religion based organisations and *Mandala Nirudyoga Sangrama Parishad*—may be classified as those adopting survival strategies and individual institutions with the exception of shopkeepers, houseowners as those adopting innovative strategies.

1. Collective Formal Modes of Social Security

(i) Formal Internal Institutions Based on Political Support: Trade Unions

The trade union movement in the area was started by the local permanent labourers and picked up in a large scale industry. It was observed that this movement had an impact on the working environment of labour. Initiated by local and short distance migrant skilled labourers who were taken on a casual basis with a demand to be made permanent, it was quite active in the late 1980s

Table 2
Classification of Institutions

	Workers benefited	% share in the total
Collective formal external		
ALC office	462	4.62
Collective formal internal		
Trade unions	1541	15.41
Credit societies	90	0.9
Collective informal internal		
Family	2766	27.66
Friends	9300	93.00
Relatives	2280	22.8
MNSP	100	0.1
Caste organisations	NA	
Gender based organisations	56	0.56
Religious organisations	NA	
Individual formal external		
Owners/managers	713	7.13
Sarpanch	NA	
Individual formal internal		
Senior workers	NA	
Contractors	7234	72.34
Individual informal internal		
Shopkeepers	NA	
Local leaders	NA	
Mafia	NA	
Individual informal external		
Houseowners	NA	

Note: From the universe of 10,000 workers.

and early 1990s. It was in the early part of mid-1990s that the trade union movement started becoming weak. Interestingly while the industries which have predominantly local workers co-opted the unions by introducing production incentives, management of industries which employ short distance migrants have weakened the movement through manipulation by splitting the trade unions and by closures. However, it is noteworthy that in those small scale industries that started in the early 90s and where long distance migrant labourers are employed, there are no trade unions. This trend began after an attempt to start a union by long distance migrants led to a physical assault on the workers.

(ii) External Institution Based on State Support

The Assistant Labour Commissioner's (ALC) office is the only formal organisation available for the redressal of grievances of the workers. Stationed at Shadnagar, which is ten kilometres away from Kothur, the ALC is approached by the workers who are not paid minimum wages. The office also carries out inspections of the factories on its own. However, in a recent move, the state government has removed inspection of industries and industry related matters from the jurisdiction of the Assistant Labour Commissioner posted at Shadnagar and transferred these powers to the Assistant Commissioner of Labour (ACL) who is based in the district headquarters. As a result, the institution has become unapproachable to the workers for two reasons: firstly, the distance between Kothur and the district headquarters is about 70 kilometres and secondly, since the ACL is a higher authority in the hierarchy than the ALC, there are greater bureaucratic hassles in approaching him than the latter.

(iii) Internal Institution Based on Social Ties: Family, Friends and Relatives

Social networking is one of the most significant institutions that provides social security. It mainly consists of social groups such as family, friends and relatives. Various identities such as class, caste, region, workplace, place of residence, etc., determine the extent of social networking. As one worker aptly puts it, "if we were to realise that one of us is missing, there must be at least a few individuals willing to come in search of him". The point is clearly brought out by the case study as presented in Box 2.

BOX 2
Social Networking and Social Security

Munna Kumar (25) is an upper caste migrant labourer from Chhapra district of Bihar. He had come to Kothur five years ago on being informed about a vacancy in one of the industries by a friend belonging to the same village. After landing at Kothur, for the first few days before he was actually employed, it was one of his relatives who gave him shelter and food. He joined as a contract labourer in a textile firm. He was initially assigned the role of a helper under a senior printer in printing division. Munna was paid on daily wage basis of Rs. 55 per day. Being a sincere, sharp and a cheerful worker, he became friendly with the senior printer and learnt the technique of printing from him. Three years later, the senior printer left the firm as he was offered a better pay in another firm. Munna Kumar then became the senior printer. He now works on a regular basis as a casual labourer. He has a fixed wage of Rs. 3000.

Once Munna Kumar started getting a fixed wage, he got his mother, father, brother and his sister to Kothur. His father soon secured a job as a watchman and his brother also started working as a contract labourer. His sister goes to school while mother stays at home. He secured jobs for about nine other members belonging to his caste from Bihar all of whom stay in the same neighbourhood. Some of the workers got children, without bringing the complete family along with them. They wanted to get their children educated. However, since the workers work for 12 hours a day, looking after the children became a problem. Munna Kumar's mother performs this important task of feeding the children in the afternoons when the children return home for lunch. She also takes care of them in the evenings till the fathers or uncles return. After returning from the work at 9 p.m., the workers spend some time together. These are the only moments of social life and relaxation.

Social networking serves the important purpose of providing the required information and helps in establishing contacts and eventually gaining of employment. It is through this networking that access to facilities such as housing is gained. It also helps in getting money when in grave need. In the absence of a family, social networks assume this role. Social networking also has the important function of generating social and cultural life.

(iv) Internal Institution Based on Political Support

The unemployed youth association is yet another collective institution based on political support. Known as *Mandala Nirudyoga Sangrama Parishad* (MNSP), it tried to voice the needs and interests of the local educated unemployed. This organisation was set up in 1997. The local youth put forth a demand that 15 members belonging to Kothur and nearby areas be absorbed into one of the firms. It organised a demonstration (*dharna*) before the firms. The local youth feel that both the dominant parties—the Telugu Desam and the Congress—have not taken up the issue of the local educated unemployed youth seriously. In fact, it is stated that the local Telugu Desam MLA intervened and tried to dissuade the youth from struggling to secure jobs. The local youth have approached *Madiga Dandora,* a *dalit*[7] organisation to voice their cause. On January 22, 1999 the local educated unemployed youth under the leadership of *Madiga Dandora* organised a *rasta roko* (road blockade) in protest against the demand of employment opportunities to the local youths. There are, according to an estimate, a hundred educated unemployed youth in Kothur village and three thousand educated unemployed in Kothur *mandal.*[8]

2. Individual Formal External Modes of Social Security

(i) Institution Based on Political Support: Sarpanch

The local governing body referred to as panchayat is one of the institutions which extends political support to the labour in acquiring a better living and working environment. The panchayat and more specifically the *sarpanch* or the president, who is an elected representative, plays a role in securing employment opportunities. The panchayat also attempts to provide amenities such as drinking water, roads, sanitation, electricity, ration cards, etc. Thus, by extending such benefits to the labour and by making the conditions of labour less insecure, the panchayat has come to acquire the status of an institution that provides social security to the local worker.

(ii) Internal Institution Based on Patronage: Owners/Managers

The owners/managers, promote contract workers to the status of casual workers based on loyalty and efficiency of the former, thus decreasing the uncertainty of employment. They also provide the latter with loans to meet contingencies. This facility is, however, restricted to those casual labour who have long period of service to their credit. This institution can help in getting many other benefits, as the case study in Box 3 illustrates this point.

(iii) Internal Institution Based on Patronage: Senior Workers

In both the medium level and high level skill technology industries, there are no formal training programmes for the newcomers, so that whatever a newcomer learns largely depends on his relation with the senior skilled workers. Due to the practice of flexibilisation, there is multi-tasking implying that the workers have to perform different tasks. As a result, there is no stability in the type of work performed, thus, denying the worker an opportunity to specialise which in the long run can improve the working environment of the labour. It is this stability in the type of work performed which is ensured by patronage by senior skilled workers.

BOX 3
Patronage of Owners

Murali (38) is a migrant from Trichur, Kerala. He joined Koya pipes industry in 1984. Though, he has studied only upto second class, he is extremely articulate. He shows immense self-confidence. He knows four languages (Telugu, Hindi, Tamil and Malyalam) and has a capacity to put across his point with great clarity. He has also the capacity to convince others in case of a contentious issue. Prior to his joining the industry, Murali underwent treatment for three years in a government hospital for serious injuries in an accident. He knew the insides of how a hospital functions. It is in this background that Murali's company in-charge, Gopi, preferred to take him along when he had to undergo surgery for hernia. When Gopi got operated, Murali was with him till he recovered and served him with all sincerity. After few weeks when Murali returned to the factory, there was a new relationship between him and Gopi. When Murali returned, his leg injury for which he underwent treatment, revived and he had to undergo surgery. Gopi came to Murali's rescue. He collected Rs. 50-100 from all the employees and he himself contributed Rs. 1000 and gave Murali Rs. 6000 to undergo the operation. He also granted Murali a few weeks' leave. After recovering completely, Murali returned to his work. After a couple of years, Gopi saw to it that Murali's services were regularised. Unlike the other long distance migrants in the company, Murali was made permanent. He had the advantage of belonging to place from where his owner hails from. This did help his case. He now draws a salary of Rs. 2040 per month. He has also been given a family quarter where he stays along with his family.

(iv) Internal Institution Based on Transactional Support: Contractors

The contractor or the middleman is the most important institution in the operationalisation of the system of contract labour. The contractors are mostly the relatives, friends or persons whom those working in these firms take into confidence.[9] In the early seventies when the contract labour system began into the grape gardens in Kothur, the contractor was an informal institution. However, owing to pressures from trade unions, labour inspectors and because of inefficiencies felt by the managements and contractors themselves in managing the labour, the system of contract labour has been formalised. According to the procedure for engaging workers on contract, the contractor has to deposit money with the firm to which he supplies labour and with the labour commissioner in order to acquire a license from the labour office by agreeing to abide by certain rules which include: payment of minimum wages to the labourer as stipulated by the labour act, provision of Employees' Social Insurance (ESI) and Provident Fund (PF) and abiding by the provisions for labour holidays. The contractor has to maintain a roll book in which information relating to attendance, number of hours worked and payments made are to be recorded. These records are occasionally inspected. However, the practice of the system of contract labour depends on the informal agreements between the contractor and the labourers and not by the prescribed rules.

The contractor acts as a nodal point between the firms and the labour market. However, a contractor is not an employee of any of the firms. The contractors operate either individually or on partnership basis, and therefore have two roles to play: one, in relation to the managements of the firms and the other in relation to the labour. Since, there is a stiff competition for labour, what the contractor needs to attract labour is goodwill.[10] It is as a part of this endeavour that in cases of minor accidents or sickness prompt treatment is provided by the contractors (see Box 4). It is to be noted that contractor must be assured of loyalty from the labourers. There are other important functions performed by the contractor that determine the social security provided to the workers—one is to decide whom to retain and whom to retrench during periods of fluctuations in demand and the other is to recommend the names of the labourers to be absorbed as casual labour. For a case study, see Box 4.

BOX 4

Role of Contractors

Yadamma (25) is a female contract worker in a pharmaceutical company. She is a local and belongs to *mangali* (barber) caste. She is an illiterate. She worked as an agricultural labourer before she joined a company. When she joined two years back, she was paid Rs. 45 as daily wage, and now she receives Rs. 52. Though she does not have an ESI card, Rs. 2 of every Rs. 100 she earns is deducted towards medical expenses. She, however, states that because the company manufactures baby oil, the floor is stained with oil and is very slippery. Once she slipped and hurt herself. The contractor paid her Rs. 200 towards her medical expenses. Such informal payments are made only to regular workers.

3. Individual Informal Internal Modes of Social Security

(i) Institution of Coercive Protection: Mafia

The origins of the *mafia* can be traced to the formation of a cricket club by the local youth in the early nineties. The club began as a political institution, with vocal and aggressive youth as its members. It was frequently approached by the contract and casual labour for redressal of their grievances, which resulted in strengthening of its position as an institution aimed at protecting the interests of the workers. The cases for which it was approached include those of *moral hazard* where the contractor might not pay the wage after getting work from the labourer, accident compensation, and also those of reinstatement of labourers who have been suddenly retrenched. The *mafia* has since acquired a political status with its leaders taking the position of presidents of trade unions from outside. This has led to political factionalism in the area.

The leaders of the *mafia* are drawn from the middle and peasant castes and they are involved in agriculture, real estate and other businesses. Their cadre is drawn from the pool of the local unemployed youth. While playing the important role of providing some kind of social security to the labourers, they extort money from the industrialists in the name of festival *chanda* (donations) and other development activities. It is also interesting to observe that, of late, the industries have started funding the *mafia* willingly since the latter helps in preventing the labourers from organising.

(ii) Internal Institution Based on Trust: Shopkeepers

Shopkeepers act as an important source of social security. The workers approach them for credit purchases of consumer goods and some shopkeepers also lend money. To begin with, generally, workers approach the shopkeepers through the contractors, *mafia*, or other workers. However, over a period of time a bond of trust develops between the worker and the shopkeeper which actually sustains the relationship. The case study, as presented in Box 5, brings out this point vividly.

BOX 5

Contractors and Social Security

Devinidhi Eshwar (35) a Brahmin from Begusarai in Bihar was working as a helper in a small scale industry which does printing on rexine cloth. The machinery for the industry was purchased in Faridabad. The then fitter of the machines who came to Kothur to fix the machine brought Eshwar with him. Now Eshwar has fifteen years of experience and draws a salary of Rs. 2898. He migrated along with his wife, who is a reserved person. Having parted with family and friends and relatives, restrictions were imposed on her movements in the township within a few years of stay. Unable to bear the stress of the new atmosphere, Eshwar's wife developed psychological problems. She has bouts of depression and is used to crying uncontrollably. She has to be taken to a psychiatrist during such periods involving additional expenditure on the medical examination and medicines. The neighbourhood knows of Eshwar's problem. Eshwar has a *khata* with a *kirana* shop in the township. During the period when Eswar's wife becomes depressed, the shopkeepers give Eshwar additional time to repay the *khata* money.

(iii) Internal Institution Based on Political Support: Local Leaders

The local leaders are best described as *piravikars*. These are heads of small groups motivated to work for a political party and regularly interact with the local people and do not have any formal position in the party but wield considerable influence on bigger leaders, capable of influencing policies owing to the power they derive from their smaller group. These leaders lobby for some individuals who approach them for help through their political and bureaucratic connections.

It is clear from the above that social security provisioning is undergoing a change from formal to informal institutions. It would not be an exaggeration to state that it is also undergoing a shift from collective to individual modes.

4. Dignity as Part of Social Security

Dignity can be a dividing line between the social security that people try to ensure in order to gain access to various institutions of social security to fight the insecurities of living and working environment, and the respectable social status every human being ought to have. This is a proposition that deserves further probing. To cite a few instances, when the contract labourer approaches the contractor or when the casual labourer approaches the owner for an advance pay, or is absent for a day, or commits a mistake at workplace, the labourers are abused and sometimes manhandled. It can also be observed that in the new-industries, highly qualified workers who seek social security cover are made to do menial jobs—at common taps, shops or in any other social interaction, any slip on the part of the labourers or his family members would invariably provoke the locals, especially the socially well-off, to make adverse remarks.

For example, frequent instances of sexual harassment on the lines of *quid-pro-quo*, have been attributed to the loose character of young female labourers working in some industries. Further, when asked if they would like to save money and spend it on their marriage, they angrily reported that considering the type of reputation that workers in industries enjoy they would rather not get married. The humiliation suffered by female workers is evident from their harassment by the male residents, which goes without protest. The victims are mostly short distance migrant female labourers in both the above instances.

Dignity acts as an important measure of the limit of security in both the working and living environments. In view of the above instances one could define lack of dignity in terms of human beings coerced by circumstances into leading lives of low self-esteem. Dignity can thus be viewed as the limit of social security, the presumption being that where the labourer is ensured of his/her social security, he/she begins to care for dignity.

It can be observed that most of the institutions of social security have an intrinsically undignified relationship vis-a-vis the workers. While the institutions of solidarity, political support and trust have a propensity to enhance dignity, institutions of patronage, coercive support and transactional support have a propensity to perpetuate undignified relationships. While some labourers succeed in gaining access to institutions that also make possible the provision of dignity, some are compelled by circumstances to take refuge in the institutions that perpetuate undignified relations. It is also in this sense that one can look at the process in terms of the inclusion-exclusion complex. More conceptualisation needs to be done in this area.

It can be observed that there is an overlap of functions being performed by the above-mentioned institutions of social security. Not all workers have equal access to all these institutions. Rather, it is mostly a combination of these institutions which actually provides social security to the labour to survive in the working and living environments created by rapid industrialisation. In respect of each set of institutions, there are certain specific attributes that determine the probability of gaining access to them.

5. Variables Determining Access to Social Security Institutions

(i) Class

In terms of class, the labourers mostly belong to the section of small and marginal farmers who have migrated because of lack of water facilities or flood. There are also those farmers who have migrated because of non-viability of agriculture due to sub-division. The labour market also consists of displaced artisans. However, those who own land or other assets in the place of origin enjoy greater security because the probability that they are provided with money in the hour of grave need is high. Labourers drawing a fixed wage of more than Rs. 3000 and who have a stable job tend to bring their families with them which, in turn, increases the need of social security.

(ii) Caste

Though it needs to be probed if there is any pattern in the castes that migrate, it has been observed that some of the upper caste labourers from Bihar and Uttar Pradesh have migrated to work in the new industries, since the caste factor acts as a barrier and does not allow them to work as labourers in the fields. It is also worth mentioning that in the recruitment of labour to the industries, caste is not a significant factor. There are a cross section of castes found in the labour market. It can, however, be observed that the lower castes are not compelled to reveal their identity; they work and stay in the same places as the upper castes and, thus, in a way enjoy a better status than they would have in the rural areas.

Caste acts as an important factor in social networking. Thus, the presence of a particular caste in greater numbers increases the probability of gaining access to institutions of social security.

(iii) Gender

Generally, the local women are excluded from the labour market. But those who succeed in entering the labour market, have a high probability of gaining access to all institutions of social security. There are very few long distance migrant women since generally these women do not go to work in the industries and due to cultural factors are restricted to their homes. Family is the only institution which the women can approach for getting social security benefits. The short distance migrant women, however, form an active part of the labour market—apart from social networking they contact the contractors and shopkeepers. However, unlike the local and long distance migrant women who always have families, the short distance migrant women consist mainly of widows, divorcees, and unmarried women, which constitute one of the most vulnerable sections of the labour market.

(iv) Worker-Dependency Ratio

The worker-dependency ratio has a significant role in determining the probability of gaining access to social security institutions in industrial centres. Most of the migrants come without families and stay with friends or relatives. However, if there is a large number of workers in a family, the probability of being secure increases, especially in the case of contract labour. This can be explained by way of a case study (Box 6).

(v) Distance

The local labourers, as is clear from the explanation of the gender factor, are excluded from this labour market. It is characterised by laziness, incompetence, arrogance, dishonesty and tendencies to unionise. The long distance migrant labourers, on the other hand, are generally considered to be hard working, sincere, docile and unorganised. This image helps in gaining access to relatively stable employment. It is, therefore, the short distance migrant labourers who suffer uncertainty of employment though they have access to a greater number of social security institutions than the long distance migrant labourers. The trade unions prefer to support non-locals rather than the locals, who have a stake in the local politics because they possess immovable

BOX 6
Worker Dependency

Maheshwari (20) stays along with her sister in a small house in Kothur. Both the sisters work as contract labourers in the industries. Both the sisters wake up at 4 a.m. in the morning, cook food and go to the company at 5 a.m. though the company starts at 6 a.m. This is so because they have to get a card from the contractor for the day to get employed in the firm. This card which is actually a kind of an authorisation to get employed for the day is provided on first-come-first-served basis and therefore, getting the card assumes great significance in the lives of a contract worker as there is intense competition for work. Under such conditions, where there are two individuals of the same family who come to work in a firm, the probability of getting the card from the contractor increases. In the firm, they work from 6 a.m. to 11 a.m. At 11 a.m. they have their lunch which they carry in boxes and then work from 12 p.m. to 4 p.m. after which they are provided with tea. They then work up to 6 p.m. and come back to their homes. At home they wash clothes, clean the utensils, clean the house, cook food, eat and sleep at 9:30 p.m. Such a strenuous routine often makes the workers fall sick. Under such conditions, having an additional worker in the family ensures a constant flow of income and consequently greater social security.

assets such as a house and therefore have greater interest in securing a better living environment which is determined by the local government. If the leadership of the local government is given by a different political faction while the trade union is affiliated to another political faction, the loyalties of the local was wavering. The inverse of this logic applies to the local governments which prefer the locals in extending support as an institution of social security.

(vi) Skill

Skill acts as an important factor in determining social networks and patronage of the owner or the trade unions. This is so because the skilled labourers are generally promoted from contract to casual labour. The casual labour system has two practices. One is where the casual labourers act as mini-contractors who themselves hire four or five workmen and do some work assigned to them within a stipulated time. Such practices are there in textile industry. The other type of casual labour is the system of *badli* labour. The *badlis* are semi-skilled labourers who are employed on regular basis and who generally assist the skilled labourers. These labourers do the skilled work in the absence of the skilled workers. The system has evolved to reduce absenteeism among the permanent skilled workers in the large scale firms. The specific status of the casual labour however depends on the experience of the worker.

(vii) Method of Recruitment

The mode of recruitment determines the probability of gaining access to particular institutions of social security. Depending on the mode of business organisation and whether or not there are trade unions in the firm, the probability that casual labourers have access to the owner and the trade unions is relatively high. If workers are recruited through the contractor, the probability of their gaining access to the social security institutions at workplace gets restricted only to the contractor.

(viii) Time

The time factor influences the number of social security institutions one can approach for securing the required benefits. The longer the time of stay in the place of destination, the greater is the number of institutions that can be accessed. For workers, generally, social networks are the institutions through which they enter the labour market. However, in cases where the duration of stay is extended, depending on the combination of attributes, other institutions can also be approached.

V. CONCLUSION

While those possessing certain combination of attributes get access to a combination of social security institutions, it is possible that those with another such combination are excluded from access to many institutions of social security. Thus, even in this sense one could analyse the process in terms of inclusion-exclusion. Once all workers with these attributes are embedded in the scale of insecurity, the factors making the conditions of workers more vulnerable become evident. Simultaneously, the study of attributes in relation to the social security institutions a worker approaches establishes the possibility of inclusion or exclusion into the social and economic structure of new industrialisation. It is however important to note that every worker is identified by a combination of these variables which determine the actual probability of gaining access to a combination of the institutions of social security. Once vulnerability of labour to different forms of insecurities in the working and living environment are assessed and probability of overcoming it are estimated, policy measures can then be initiated either to strengthen the existing social security institutions or generate new institutions. Measures can also be initiated to assist those that are most vulnerable.

Notes

1. Vulnerability is being prone to or susceptible to damage or injury. Vulnerability means the characteristics of a person or a group in terms of their capacity to anticipate, cope with, resist, and recover from the impact of natural disaster. In this context, however, it refers to the capacity to anticipate, cope with, resist and recover from an impact of structural changes. Normally, vulnerability is closely correlated with socio-economic position.
2. *Lala* type of management refers to the proprietor cum manager who runs the business based on traditional knowledge. This system is predominant in firms owned by the *marwaries*.
3. The disease pattern suggests that injury of eye, asthama, bronchitis, other respiratory disorders, skin infections, other diseases of the skin, wounds and burn and scalds represent the work hazards.
4. Seth's *khata* means the account of the owner. It implies that such labour is directly recruited by the owner, who is accountable for his payment and other benefits unlike in the case of the contract labour where the contractor and not the owner is accountable.

5. For definition, see North (1990).
6. For definition, see Kasper and Streut (1998).
7. A political term used to express organisation of oppressed (lower) caste people.
8. *Mandal* is an administrative unit comprising of some number of villages.
9. It is necessary that those who recommend a certain person to be appointed as a contractor, is from the managerial cadre.
10. Goodwill can be defined as consisting of certain characteristics like paying the labour their wages honestly and in time, lending money to the labourer when in grave need, not using coercive methods such as abusive language or physical assault, etc.

References

Ahmad, Ehtisham, Jean Dreze, John Hills and Amartya Sen (eds.) (1991), *Social Security in Developing Countries*, Clerendon Press, Oxford.

Banerjee, Nirmala (1997), "How Real is the Bogey of Feminisation?", *The Indian Journal of Labour Economics*, Vol. 40, No. 3.

Deshpande, Sudha (1992), "Structural Adjustment and Feminisation", *The Indian Journal of Labour Economics*, Vol. 35, No. 4.

——— and Lalit K. Deshpande (1997), "Gender-based Discrimination in the Urban Labour Market in India", *The Indian Journal of Labour Economics*, Vol. 40, No. 3.

Ghosh, Jayati (1995), "Employment and Labour under Structural Adjustment: India since 1991", *The Indian Journal of Labour Economics*, Vol. 38, No. 4.

Kasper, Wolfgang and E. Manfred Streut (1998), *Institutional Economics: Social Order and Public Policy*, Edward Elgar, Cheltenham.

Kundu, Amitabh (1997), "Trends and Pattern of Female Employment in India: A Case of Organised Informalisation", *The Indian Journal of Labour Economics*, Vol. 40, No. 4.

Leliveld, A.H.M. (1991), *Social Security in Developing Countries: Some Theoretical Considerations*, Research Memorandum, University of Amsterdam.

North, Douglass, C. (1990), *Institutions, Institutional Change and Economic Performance*, Cambridge University Press, Cambridge.

23

Public Action, Social Security and Unorganised Sector

Ramesh C. Datta

I. INTRODUCTION

It is now widely recognised that the development model pursued by the developing countries in general has created dual economies, wherein the benefits of growth has accrued only to a small segment of the society. The masses—millions in number—have been socially excluded and are suffering from persistent deprivation associated with generally low standards of living and various kinds of social insecurities. In fact, in the recent years, the non-rivalrous 'pure public goods' of yesteryears are also being increasingly contested—exhaustible common property resources and the poor and the weak alike are being squeezed out. Labour and the markets in India are getting fragmented. Casualisation of the workforce since 1980s has been increasing. More recent data has shown that both self-employment and salaried employment have declined in the 1990s. Furthermore, the vulnerability of labour in the once 'protected and privileged' organised sector continues to fall below the basic standard of living, and that too despite the provisions of the so-called 'safety net' benefits. A visit to the families of the beneficiaries of 'voluntary retirement schemes' under the National Renewal Fund (NRF) is sufficient to drive home this point. In fact, many of the organised sector textile workers, who started as casual workers in the mills and after working for years as *badli* workers became permanent over the years are today losing regular employment under the various voluntary retirement schemes. They have again become casual workers and in the process have lost all the protective social security benefits. As their children, because of the poor socio-economic conditions of the family, have also dropped out of schools, they have also lost the opportunity to avail the benefits of the so-called promotional social security measures. And in the process, the NRF—the human face (or mask?)—has not been able to act as an effective preventive social security measure for these workers.

However, it has also been recognised by scholars in the field of development economics that the neglect of social opportunities due to the lack of adequate progress in social security, has been detrimental to the economic and social development of developing countries, including India. This means that in order to attack the growing social and economic inequalities in the society, it is necessary to expand social security provisions.

Under these circumstances, the Government of India aimed at the enhancement of access to work with 'improved quality of employment' in its Approach Paper to the Ninth Plan. We know that one of the basic indicators of the 'quality of employment' is the working conditions at the workplace and the social security provisions attached therewith. In this regard, scholars over the last one decade, in their research, have advocated for 'public action' as a strategy to achieve 'social security'. According to Dreze and Sen (1995), public action can play a central role in bringing social opportunities within the reach of the masses. Furthermore, the vigilance and the involvement of the public can be quite crucial not only in ensuring an adequate expansion of minimum social security but also in monitoring their functioning.

The concepts of both, public action and social security, have been redefined. The definition of social security has been made more comprehensive and the unorganised working poor, who received very little attention in the writings of scholars, have been brought back to the centre of development research.

II. PUBLIC ACTION

"Public action", according to Dreze and Sen (1991), "is not ....just a question of public delivery and state initiative. It is also.... a matter of participation by the public in the process of social change".... It "includes not merely what is done for the public by the state, but also what is done by the public for itself". But it is also a reality that, "the role of the public in exerting pressure for social security through social, legal, and political processes is hindered by the relative powerlessness of those in need in developing countries" (Burgess and Stern, 1991). "Within the organised sector, public employees are much better placed regarding access to social security and levels of benefit. They are not only highly unionised but also are close to, in fact, a part of the state power structure" (Appasamy *et al.*, 1996). Mackintosh (1992) defines 'public action' as, "purposive collective action, whether for collective private ends or public ends." According to him, "collective, purposeful manipulation of the public environment constitutes public action, whether through legislation, lobbying, self-organisation or rigging the market!" We believe that in a democratic society trade unions are voluntary associations of people, like non-governmental organisations, and that they are engaged in purposive collective actions through legislation or lobbying, seeking to promote the public good or assist the deprived through social, political, and humanitarian institutions, with the aim of protecting and promoting their living conditions. It may be true that excessive wage demands can lead to labour-saving technological investments but that, meaning the former, is only one of the reasons behind the introduction of labour-saving technological changes. Collective action of the 'active pressure groups' is countered by the employers primarily to gain or enhance control over the labour. It is the union of Self Employed Women's Association that lobbied at the International Labour Organisation to pressurise the state for the basic social security benefits of its workers. The trade unions, as labour market institutions, have played a significant role in the achievement of social security benefits for the organised sector. The voluntary non-government groups and the unions associated with the unorganised sector workers are similarly attempting to influence the direction of governmental policy and action as, for example, in the case of social security benefits for the 'domestic workers' in the state of Maharashtra.

III. SOCIAL SECURITY

The concept of social security that emerged in the early decades of the 20th century centred around the protection that society should provide to its members through a series of public measures against the social and economic distress that otherwise would have been caused by a sudden stoppage or substantial reduction in income resulting from specific contingencies like sickness, workplace injury, maternity, invalidity, disability, old age and death. Fundamentally, social security in its conventional form is intended to provide some minimum standard of living to people who are unable to earn their livelihood due to health reason, unemployment and old age. This has been the operational policy-oriented definition of social security. The enactment of social security legislation like the Workmen's Compensation Act, 1923; the Employees' State Insurance Act, 1948; the Employees' Provident Fund and Miscellaneous Provisions Act, 1952; the Maternity Benefit Act, 1961; and the Payment of Gratuity Act, 1971, was the result of the struggle of thousands of workers and their associations to institutionalise the above notion of social security.

In recent years scholars have defined social security in a more comprehensive sense, which refers to the creation of conditions that would enable the poor to satisfy their basic needs in a sustainable manner. This definition of social security, therefore, covers chronic or structural conditions of insecurity arising out of extreme poverty and incapacity to acquire income-earning resources as well as the forms of insecurity of a more contingent type mentioned above. The former refers to the promotional social security programmes mostly of the macro type like employment guarantee scheme, Jawahar Rozgar Yojana, IRDP, public distribution system of foodgrains, health, education and nutritional programmes-Integrated Child Development Services, etc., while the latter, more conventional types of social security measures, have been put under protective categories.

The formal social security system in India has developed in a series of phases. Factors which initiated a move towards the evolution of social security mostly have their origins in the pressure put by labour in its collective struggle against oppression and exploitation, on the 'state' in the late 19th century, and this movement got further impetus with the establishment of the International Labour Organisation. "(T) here were two other forces responsible for progressive labour legislation in this country, viz., the anxiety of influential Manchester men to see that the factory conditions here were not unfavourable factors in their competition with the Indian textile industry, and secondly, the growing power of the trade union and labour movement......It is a characteristic feature of labour legislation in India enacted so far, that the state has largely played the part of a mere legislator and has hardly interested itself in the prosecution of any security or welfare schemes, or financially participated in them" (Adarkar, 1944). However, the fact remains that "social security is a relatively neglected area in terms of both policy and research. Indian Plan documents have been virtually silent on the topic. The implementation of such social security as is available in the country is fragmented between the centre and the states and, at each level, among different ministries, departments and agencies. There is little coherence in policy formulation, programme designing, implementation and monitoring. The data base is particularly poor. The academic literature on the subject is uneven. While formal social security legislation and its implementation have received attention (it is largely in terms of historical and descriptive accounts), there is very little literature on protective social security relating to the non-formal and unorganised sectors. On the other hand, there is considerable research output mostly of an evaluatory kind on promotional aspects: employment generation, IRDP, basic needs....." (Guhan, 1994).

Unfortunately, the social security system in India has taken the form of a dualistic pattern in which a small segment of the workforce has been able to obtain the protective social security benefits while a large segment has remained unprotected, primarily because of not being able to organise themselves, and therefore has been made to rely on promotional social security measures.

IV. UNORGANISED SECTOR

The unorganised sector refers to that part of the economy where earning one's livelihood is extremely precarious. Employment relationships, wages and other working conditions are *de facto* not protected or regulated. In India, this sector employs 91.5 per cent of the total workforce. Workers in this sector are either self-employed or sell their labour as causal workers. There is complete absence of any legal protection with regard to wages, employment, health and safety measures. One of the major reasons for their being denied any legal protection is that they are caught in a labour process where it is virtually impossible to establish any kind of regular employer-employee relationship. As a result, the workers in this sector do not qualify as beneficiaries of any 'protective social security measures'. Further, since the workers in this sector are illiterate, relatively less skilled, and thus have weak social capabilities, they are unable to avail benefits from most of the promotional social security measures.

V. MATHADI LABOUR MARKET

The focus of this paper is the *Mathadi* labour market where selling physical labour is the sole source of livelihood for most of the workers. This labour market has all the characteristics of an unorganised flexible labour market. It has the piece-rate wage system that makes wage-cost flexible and has numerical flexibility along with an easy exit route for the employer. The labour cost varies according to the amount of work done by the worker and work available in a multi-employer situation. In spite of all these constraints the workers here have been able to get 'basic protective social security' mainly through public action.

1. Brief History

Decasualisation schemes for dock labourers in the 1950s (and for the *badli* workers in the textile mills in Mumbai at about the same time) were the first of their kind to evolve a method to secure basic protective social security for unorganised workers by 'regularising' their intermittently available work and developing employer-employee relationships. Under this scheme the tripartite body could get for the workers, as a statutory right, benefits such as an attendance allowance of 50 per cent of daily wages, weekly off, one-day holiday wage and 12 days minimum guaranteed wages. Anna Sahib Patil, who had the experience of working on the docks during the dock worker struggle to decasualise themselves in the early 1950s, initiated the process of organising Mathadis in the late 1950s in Mumbai. Efforts on similar lines were also made in Pune by Baba Adhav and in Dhule by Paranjpe.

A *mathadi* is a worker who carries a load on his head, back, neck and/or shoulders. His work mainly constitutes physical labour and he is expected to be strong and sturdy enough to bear heavy physical weights to be carried to considerable heights for stacking. His work normally consists of loading, unloading, carrying, shifting, weighing, taping, bending and stacking. All this work was performed in a 'gang' or 'tolli'—all the workers in a *tolli* used to belong to the same village and often were related to each other. According to their convenience some of them used to go to their native places, and some others, mostly their relatives, used to come and take their place in the *tolli*. The *tolli* workers used to work under a head-man known as *mukadam*, who actually used to arrange for the work for which he was responsible to the employer, collect the labour charges from the employer, and distribute the wages among the workers. However, there was no fixed employer. In fact each employee had many employers. Many a time, the *mukadam*, by conniving with the employer, used to exploit *tolli* workers. Since the availability of the work was dependent on the arrival, availability and departure of ships, trains, goods, trucks or customers, it was extremely difficult to predict the time and volume of the work. As a result there were no fixed hours of work; rather work used to be spread over the day. Moreover, there was no overtime, and no paid holiday or leave. In addition the location of work was also geographically spread all over greater Mumbai.

Under the Minimum Wages Act (1948), minimum wages were fixed for employees in various industries in Greater Mumbai. However, since *mathadis* did not have any employer as such and because their work did not fall under any "Scheduled Employment", they could not get the benefits of the Act. They also could not get any benefits from the provisions of the Mumbai Shops and Establishments Act, 1948, because they were neither wholly nor principally employed by any one employer and accordingly the benefits of overtime, paid weekly holiday, leave, etc., under the Act were not available to them. But even under other Acts like the Factories Act, 1948, Employers' Provident Funds Act, 1952 or Employees' State Insurance Act, 1948, they could not enjoy the benefits accruing from them as their work was not considered to be continuous or for any consecutive number of days for the same employer. With regard to the question of payment of compensation to the workers for any physical injury or death, which were not very uncommon during the course of the loading and unloading work, the *mathadi* workers could not fall within the purview of the Workmen's Compensation Act, 1923, as the employers argued that their dealings are only with the *mukadam*.

Under these circumstances collective representation was made by the trade unions to the government in, 1962 to conduct an inquiry into the conditions of work and wages of *mathadi* workers in Greater Mumbai. Over a period of about three years reports were submitted to the Government of Maharashtra by three committees: (a) Report of the Mathadi Labour Enquiry Committee, Greater Mumbai, 1965, (b) Report of the Lokhandi Jatha Kamgar Enquiry Committee, 1965, and (c) Report of the Committee for Unprotected Labour, 1967. The recommendations of these committees formed the basis of the enactment of the Maharashtra *Mathadi, Hamal* and other Manual Workers (Regulation of Employment and Welfare) Act of 1969. However, the political economy aspect of this development is also quite significant. Many of the *mathadi* workers had come to Mumbai for work from the western part of Maharashtra—Satara, Kolhapur, Sangli, etc. Most of them were staunch followers of Anna Patil and their sheer numerical strength had made them politically influential. Political leaders during those days like Anna Patil, Y.B. Chawan and Vasandada Patil had also come from the same area and therefore could develop a pressure group for 'public action'. The background of the Act does indicate the role played by institutions. It also shows that the interaction between interest groups is critical in determining the ultimate impact of purposive collective action.

2. Present Scenario

Since 1969, the *Mathadi* labour market has been regulated by the Mathadi Tripartite Boards. Today, there are around 50,000 registered employers with almost one and a half lakh workers registered under 30 different boards in the state of Maharashtra. Each of these boards is headed by a chairman appointed by the Government of Maharashtra. In addition, there is an equal number of representatives from the unions and employers' association. Each board has its own staff including a secretary, personnel officer, chief accountant, inspectors and clerks. All this staff gets paid out of the levy—which is negotiated every 3-4 years—collected from the employers.

The main characteristics of the *Mathadi* labour market before and after the enactment of the *Mathadi* Act in 1969 are given in Table 1. As can be seen from the table, although the Mathadi labour market has quite a few characteristics of an unorganised sector it has managed to retain the still, almost all the protective social security benefits for its workers. We have presented the salient features of three major Mathadi Boards in Mumbai in Table 2. In addition to this various social security benefits, which a typical board provides to its workers out of the levy, are given in Table 3. Interestingly, many of the workers in these three boards are income-tax payees and have paid income-tax amounting to over a crore of rupees to the government.

The main functions of a board are to settle disputes between the union and the employer, arrange meetings for negotiations, get new employers and workers registered and distribute wages and social security benefits. At the workplace site *mukadams* direct *tolli* workers, distribute work and allocate workplace, coordinate between the employers and the board, tally and give 'daily work sheets' to the board, etc. A *mukadam* also has to handle disputes between the workers.

Table 1
Characteristics of Mathadi Labour Market

Before 1969	After the Act in 1969
Physical manual labour	Establishment of tripartite board
Flexible workplace	Registration of employee and employer
No fixed hours of work and spread over the entire day	Bargained minimum piece rate wages (per tonne or per piece) and levy once in three years.
Workers work in *tollis* under a Mukadam	Basic piece rate wages linked to the Consumer Price Index
Wages by piece rate	Overtime and double rate after 9.30 p.m.
No fixed employer	Disappointment pay
Multi-employer	
Volume and the time at which work available uncertain	Since the workers are paid through banks they have developed banking habits and have bought insurance policies
Workers in a *tolli* mostly come from same village—often related to each other. Even replace each other.	A hospital has been set up for medical care and sickness
No regularity in or continuity of work but work`permanent	
No paid weekly off or holiday	Settlement and agreements signed over working conditions between the union and management of many large Indian and multinational companies.
No provident fund, medical benefit, compensation allowance, HRA, LTA, etc.	Social security benefits accident
Average wages earned Rs. 150 to Rs. 200 per month (1962)	Average wages earned Rs. 2,000 to Rs. 10,000 per month (1997)
There were 15000 to 17000 *mathadis* in Mumbai in 1962	Around 75,000 *mathadis* in Mumbai in 1997
Mostly illiterate	Many literate
No retirement age	Still no retirement age
Nature of work – loading, unloading, stacking, taping, bending, weighing, bundling, etc. (all manual)	Nature of work remains the same
Union – present	Presence of strong union(s)
Exploitation by *Mukadam*	*Mukadam* is one of the *mathadis* in a *tolli.*
No direct employer-employee relationship.	Employer-employee relationship is developed and mediated by the Mathadi Board(s). In quite a few cases agreements/settlements are signed between large companies and the workers' unions

The boards also sign long-term 'wage and work description' agreements between some major large companies, including some MNCs, and specific '*tollies* of workers', under the Maharashtra Mathadi, Hamal and Other Manual Workers (Regulation of Employment and Welfare) Act, 1969.

3. Health

One of the major achievements of the *mathadi* workers has been to start their own hospitals. In 1976, Anna Patil started a dispensary under a trust on a part-

Table 2
Main Features of Three Mathadi Boards

	Grocery markets and shop's unprotected workers (1970)	Goods transport unprotected workers (1971)	Railway goods cleaning and forwarding unprotected workers scheme (1976).
Registered employers	4706	3296	1261
Actual workers	14686	13026	7471
Number of *tollies*	1100 (size 1 to 250)	1600 (size 2 to 200)	107
Average monthly wages for all workers (Rs. crores)	4		
Wages + levy (Rs. crores)		4.71	–
Levy for the last month (Rs. crores)	1.48		
Average monthly wages of workers (Rs.)	2723 + 35%	4085 (including levy)	3873 (including levy)
Wage variation	(750 to 10,000)		(733 to 5188)
Total annual turnover (Rs. crores)	64	52	28
LIC policy holders	2800	5000	1200
Income tax-payers	2251 (tax paid 1.52)	1500	1591 (Tax paid Rs. 99,79,056 in 1996-97)
Administrative staff	97	63	47
Administrative expenses	2.5% of levy		
Unions	12		3
Membership fees (Rs. per annum)	11 to 51	101	51
Dearness allowance	CPI linked	CPI linked	CPI linked
P.F. contribution by workers	8.33%	8.33%	8.33%
Hospital contribution by workers (Rs. per month)	20	20	20
Profession tax (Rs. per month)	15-30	15-30	15-30

Table 3
Levy Rate and its Distribution for Social Security

Grocery market and shops board	(Rs.)
Total levy	37.00
Provident fund	8.33
Ex-gratia	13.50
Administrative expenses	2.05
Gratuity	3.00
Paid leave	4.50
Accident compensation	1.00
Paid holiday	1.00
Medical benefits	1.00
L.T.A.	0.62
H.R.A.	2.00

time basis and by 1978 it had started working full-time. Today, there are two hospitals with an annual budget of Rs. two crores, which are run by six *mathadi* boards, and 12 dispensaries. The hospitals have facilities for 75 beds. Each of the six boards contribute two per cent of their levy and each worker contributes Rs. 20 per month. These hospitals provide diagnostic services (radiology, pathology and sonography) for around 40,000 workers and their families. Each hospital has a dental unit and special departments of opthalmology, orthopedics, general surgery, skin, chest and cardiology. There are 35 medical officers, 35 specialists, 60 paramedics, and 30 non-medical staff attached to the hospitals. Everyday, around 2500 workers get treatment and about five surgeries are performed. The hospitals have also been organising educational programmes and exhibitions at workplace sites to bring AIDS-related awareness among workers. Almost 80 to 90 per cent of workers come to the hospitals with fractures, spondylitis, hernia and other similar problems. According to the chief medical officer, most of these workers suffer from osteoarthritis—degeneration of all joints, and PID—prolapsed inter-vertibrate disc. All their diseases are primarily due to physical stress. Although, according to International Labour Organisation, a worker should not be made to carry more than 50 kg. of weight, many Mathadi workers carry upto 100 kg. in their bid to augment their earnings. Unfortunately, osteoarthritis is not recognised as an occupational disease by the International Labour Organisation.

4. Housing

Mathadi workers, with the help of *mathadi* boards, have been able to get housing facilities on ownership basis for about 4000 of them. For this purpose they have taken loans from GIC, HDFC, and also drawn from their provident fund.

5. Education

The boards are also trying to promote formal education among *mathadi* families. Since 1982, they have instituted quite a few scholarships for the children of *mathadi* workers—more than 100 children have been given scholarships in 1997.

In the last few years some of the *mathadi* boards have been able to get the workers insured against accidents, injuries and death. For example, Mathadi Boards in Pune are paying Rs. 152 per annum as premium, out of the Board's administrative account, to cover workers for a benefit of Rs. 25,000 in case of injury and Rs. 2,00,000 in case of death. This scheme has been worked out by the *mathadi* Board with the General Insurance Corporation.

VI. PROBLEMS OF MATHADI WORKERS

Over the last few years, with the introduction of structural adjustment programme, medium and large enterprises in the organised sector have been restructuring their businesses and in the process retrenching thousands of workers under voluntary retirement schemes. Many firms being unable to handle the 'redundancies' have put the redundant workers on to *mathadi* work, reducing the work load on the latter. Since *mathadis* are piece-rated workers whose social security benefits are linked to the wages they earn, their overall living standards are bound to decline.

Many large firms have also been automating their loading and unloading activities, which has reduced the volume of work available to *mathadis*. The introduction of cranes and conveyor belts at Railway Coach Factory, and elimination of small booking of wagons in railways, have not only reduced the wages of *mathadis*, but also generated redundancies in the *mathadi* labour market.

Probably the more important problem that has to be attacked is the prevalence of osteoarthritis, which is a slow degeneration of bones and joints due to physical stress and which cannot be compensated for, as it is not recognised by the ILO as an occupational disease.

VII. CONCLUSION

Notwithstanding the various constraints posed by the salient characteristics of the unorganised sector in India, our study has shown that it is possible to improve the low standard of living of the working poor through collective, purposeful manipulation of the public environment—public action—whether by means of legislation, lobbying or self-organisation. In this regard, one can learn from the experience of SEWA, which organised the home-based workers and has been able to get them social protection. There is no reason why the enormous problems faced by the workers of the powerloom sector in Maharashtra cannot be reduced by enacting a legislation, irrespective of the various constraints referred to as hindrances coming in the way. This is also true for domestic workers. It also indicates that the callousness of the policy makers rationalised on the basis of financial constraints is superficially exaggerated.

However, for purposes of social mobility, it seems that protective social security is not sufficient. Promotional social security measures related to investment in human capital and social capital, which build the 'social capabilities' of the individual, are essential to move out of the secondary labour markets.

(This is a revised version of the article earlier published in Economic and Political Weekly).

References

Adarkar, B.P. (1994), *Planning of Social Security in India*, Kitabistan, Allahabad.

Ahmed, E. et. al. (1991), *Social Security in Developing Countries*, Oxford University Press, New Delhi.

Appasamy, P. et al. (1996), *Social Exclusion from a Welfare Rights Perspective in India*, International Institute for Labour Studies, International Labour Organisation, Geneva.

Burgess, R. and N. Stern (1991), "Social Security in Developing Countries: What, Why, Who, and How?" in Ahmed et al. (eds.).

Dreze, J. and A. Sen (1989), *Hunger and Public Action*, Clarendon Press, Oxford.

—— (1991), "Public Action for Social Security", in Ahmed et al. (eds.).

—— (1995), *India Economic Development and Social Opportunity*, Oxford University Press, Oxford.

Guhan, S. (1994), *Social Security for the Unorganised Poor: A Feasible Blueprint for India*, Discussion Paper, ILO, Geneva.

Mackintosh, Maureen (1992), "Introduction", in Wuyts Marc et al. (eds.), *Development Policy and Public Action*, Oxford University Press, Oxford.

List of Contributors

Moneer Alam : Institute of Economic Growth, Delhi.

Piush Antony : Institute for Human Development, New Delhi.

Harishwar Dayal : St. Xavier's College, Ranchi University, Ranchi.

Anuradha De : Collaborative Research and Dissemination (CORD), New Delhi.

Jean Dreze : Centre for Development Economics, Delhi School of Economics, University of Delhi, Delhi.

R.C. Datta : Tata Institute of Social Sciences, Mumbai.

Shaji K. Francis : Centre for Development Studies, Thiruvananthapuram.

V. Gayathri : Institute for Human Development, New Delhi.

S. Indrakant : Department of Economics, Nizam Collage, Osmania University, Hyderabad.

Sandhya V. Iyer : Department of Economics, University of Mumbai, Mumbai.

K.P. Kannan : Centre for Development Studies, Thiruvananthapuram.

Anup K. Karan : Institute for Human Development, New Delhi.

Reetika Khera : Centre for Development Economics, Delhi School of Economics, University of Delhi, Delhi.

Amitabh Kundu : Centre for the Study of Regional Development, Jawaharlal Nehru University, New Delhi.

S. Mahendra Dev : Center for Economic and Social Studies, Hyderabad.

R.P. Mamgain : Institute of Applied Manpower Research, New Delhi.

Claire Noronha : Collaborative Research and Dissemination (CORD), New Delhi.

K. Seeta Prabhu : Department of Economics, University of Mumbai, Mumbai.

R. Radhakrishna : Vice-Chancellor, Andhra University, Vishakhapatnam.

Anuradha Khati Rajivan : Indian Administrative Service; currently with Tamil Nadu Women's Development Corporation, Chennai.

Ajit Ranade : Economist; currently working in the ABN Amro Bank, Mumbai.

Meera Samson : Collaborative Research and Dissemination (CORD), New Delhi.

Alakh N. Sharma : Institute for Human Development, New Delhi.

A.K. Shiva Kumar : United Nations Children's Fund (UNICEF), New Delhi.

Nisha Srivastava : Department of Economics, Allahabad University, Allahabad.

Ravi S. Srivastava : Centre for the Study of Regional Development, Jawaharlal Nehru University, New Delhi.

M.C. Swaminathan : Formerly with the Department of Finance and Planning, Government of Andhra Pradesh, Hyderabad.

C.P. Thakur : Formerly with the Faculty of Management Studies, University of Delhi, Delhi.

Sukhadeo Thorat : Centre for the Study of Regional Development, Jawaharlal Nehru University, New Delhi.

J.B.G. Tilak : National Institute of Educational Planning and Administration, New Delhi.

C.S. Venkata Ratnam : International Management Institute, New Delhi.

G. Vijay : Research Scholar, Institute of Social Studies, The Hague, The Netherlands.

List of Abbreviations

ANM	Auxiliary Nurse and Midwife
APL	Above Poverty Line
BIFR	Board of Industrial and Financial Reconstruction
BPL	Below Poverty Line
CBO	Community Based Organisation
CED	Chronic Energy Deficiency
CGHS	Central Government Health Scheme
CMNMP	Chief Minister's Nutrition Meal Programme
CDP	Community Development Programme
CPIAL	Consumer Price Index for Agricultural Labour
DPIP	District Poverty Initiatives Project
DGFASLI	Director General Factory Advice Service & Labour Institutes
DRDA	District Rural Development Agency
DWCRA	Development of Women and Children in Rural Areas
EAS	Employment Assurance Scheme
EGF	Employment Generation Fund
EGS	Employment Guarantee Scheme
EIUS	Environment Improvement of Urban Slums
ESCAP	Economic and Social Commission for Asia and Pacific
ESI	Employees State Insurance
ESIS	Employment State Insurance Scheme
FCI	Food Corporation of India
FMR	Female-Male Ratio
GBD	Global Burden of Diseases
GDP	Gross Domestic Product
GIC	General Insurance Corporation
GKY	Ganga Kalyan Yojana
GNP	Gross National Product
GOI	Government of India
HCR	Head Count Ratio
HDFC	Housing Development Finance Corporation
HPIM	Human Poverty Index Modified
HUDCO	Housing and Urban Development Corporation
IAMR	Institute of Applied Manpower Research
ICDS	Integrated Child Development Scheme
ILO	International Labour Organisation

IMF	International Monetary Fund
IPI	Income Poverty Index
IRDP	Integrated Rural Development Programme
ITDP	Integrated Tribal Development Programme
JGSY	Jawahar Gram Samridhi Yojana
JRY	Jawahar Rojgar Yojana
LFPR	Labour Force Participation Rates
LIC	Life Insurance Corporation
MNC	Multinational Corporations
MPCE	Monthly Per Capita Consumption Expenditure
NABARD	National Bank for Agriculture & Rural Development
NCAER	National Council of Applied Economic Research
NFHS	National Family Health Survey
NGO	Non-Governmental Organisation
NIOH	National Institute of Occupational Health Surveys
NIPFP	National Institute of Public Finance & Policy
NNMB	National Nutrition Monitoring Bureau
NREP	National Rural Employment Programme
NRF	National Renewal Fund
NRY	Nehru Rojgar Yojana
NSAP	National Social Assistance Programme
NSDP	National Slum Development Programme
NSS	National Sample Survey
NSSO	National Sample Survey Organisation
OBC	Other Backward Castes
PAP	Poverty Alleviation Programmes
PDS	Public Distribution System
PDS	Public Distribution System
PEO	Programme Evaluation Organisation
PMRY	Prime Minister's Rojgar Yojana
PRA	Participatory Rural Appraisal
PRI	Panchayati Raj Institution
PROBE	Public Report on Basic Education
RLEGP	Rural Landless Employment Guarantee Programme
RPDS	Revamped Public Distribution System
RWP	Rural Works Programme
SAP	Structural Adjustment Programme
SC	Scheduled Caste
SCCFC	Scheduled Castes Cooperative Finance Corporation
SDP	State Domestic Product
SEEUY	Self-Employment for the Educated Unemployed Youth
SEPUP	Self-Employment Programme for Urban Poor
SEWA	Self Employed Women's Association
SJGSY	Swarn Jayanti Gram Swarojgar Yojna
SHASU	Scheme of Employment through Housing and Shelter Upgradation
SITRA	Supply of Imporved Toolkit to Rural Artisans
SJSRY	Swarna Jayanti Shahri Rojgar Yojana

SLC	Survey of Living Conditions
ST	Scheduled Tribe
STEP	Support to Training & Employment Programmes
SUME	Scheme of Urban Micro-Enterprises
SUWE	Scheme of Urban Wage Employment
TISCO	Tata Iron and Steel Company
TNINP	Tamil Nadu Integration Nutrition Project
TPDS	Targeted Public Distribution System
TRYSEM	Training of Rural Youth for Self-Employment
TUPEP	Trade Union Programme for Environmental Protection
UBS	Urban Basic Services
UBSP	Urban Basic Services for the Poor
UN	United Nations
UNDP	United Nations Development Programme
UNICEF	United Nations Children's Fund
USEP	Urban Self Employment Programme
VRS	Voluntary Retirement Scheme
WILL	Women's Integrated Learning for Life
WPR	Work Participation Rate
WTO	World Trade Organisation

Index